My Crown Is A Secret

Volume 1

Garrick David Pattenden

Copyright © 2025 Garrick David Pattenden

All rights reserved.

ISBN: 978-1-83417-003-9

DEDICATION

For the children — and for every adult who still carries the soul of a child within their heart. And especially for Marc MK Kenzie who will turn 10 years old this June 22nd, 2025. May your heart always carry the spark of adventure, wonder, and the endless love of family.

With all my love,

Garrick

CONTENTS

	Acknowledgments	i
1	Before I Knew Who I Was	1
2	The Door Beneath The Ivy	22
3	The Blood That Remembers	44
4	The Puzzle Inside DNA	61
5	Decoding The Truth	85
6	The Crown Beneath the Stones	110
7	The Guardians of the Line	137
8	The Threads We Follow	167
9	Childhood and Research	194
10	The Seasons That Whisper	219
11	The Secret Breached	349
12	Data Records Breach	284
13	A Storm Is Brewing	315
14	Homeward Sovereigns	376

PREFACE

This is not a story about kings and crowns in the way the world expects. Nor is it a tale bound by the strict borders of history, religion, or tradition. This is a story of memory — of how the past whispers through the hearts of children who carry far more than their years suggest. It is about family: not only by blood, but by choice, by love, and by the quiet covenants formed when souls recognize each other.

Some may read this through the narrow lens of adult reason, seeking explanations that fit rules they have long accepted. But children know better. They see with hearts uncluttered by fear. They understand that family is not simply who you descend from, but who holds your hand when the world grows quiet. In these pages live those truths — where adoption is not absence, where love makes room, and where crowns are not always worn upon heads, but carried in the soul.

The world may not always understand such things. That is fine. This book was never written for the world. It was written for those who already know.

— Garrick David Pattenden

CHAPTER 1: BEFORE I KNEW WHO I WAS

Benedict Adrian Harvick, was born in the warm part of the year, when dragonflies hovered low and the trees whispered longer than usual. His mother said he came in on a soft wind — not rushed, not late — just quiet. The nurses swaddled him in blue. His mother wrapped him in stillness. She had the kind of heart that counted every breath, not with panic, but with knowing. She had heard stories about miracles. This wasn't one of them. This was something else — something the doctors didn't say aloud, but felt in the weight of every silence between heartbeats. She didn't blink. Not once.

By the time he was nearly three, Benedict had died three times. Once at eleven months. Again at eighteen months. And a third time at just two years old. Not in poems. Not in stories. His lungs had caved in like paper lanterns after rain, folding in on themselves until even air seemed too heavy. His body stilled. His spirit… floated. He left the world before he knew what a world was. Each time, he felt it — the lifting, the letting go. Not like a dream. Not like sleep. A separation. Light. Endless. White. It was not warm or cold. Not loud or silent. There were no angels. No golden gates. Only whiteness that sang without music.

He never told anyone what he saw. Not really. Not even when he could speak in full sentences or count his fingers without help. Not when they asked him if he believed in heaven. He didn't know how to answer. Because what he saw was not heaven. Not a place. Not a being. It was a presence. Pure. A pull without hands. A whisper without sound. And always — always — it brought him back. Not the machines. Not the wires. Just the voice. A voice he didn't know, but knew. His father wasn't there. Not at the hospital. Not beside the bed. Only his mother, brushing his forehead, waiting for him to breathe again. And somehow… he always did.

He was not a loud child. He watched more than he spoke, and listened even when no one was talking. At night, he would lie awake staring at the ceiling, fingers folded together, waiting for something. He wasn't sure what. Just something. His mother said he used to stare like that when he was a baby — not at lights or toys, but corners. Walls. Spaces where nothing stood. He began to draw early. Crayons first, then pens, then ink. But what he drew didn't look like animals or people. He drew shapes. Lines that circled themselves. Patterns no one had taught him. Symbols no one could name.

There was one drawing that returned again and again. A cross that wasn't a cross. A crown that didn't look like any crown in his picture books. And always beneath it, without realizing, he would scribble the same name: Horváth. His teachers thought it was a made-up place. A castle from a dream. A child's wandering imagination. They laughed about it in the staff room. But he didn't remember dreaming it. It just came. As if it had always been there — tucked behind his ribs. One day, his mother asked him why he kept drawing the same castle over and over. He didn't answer. He didn't know.

But something in him whispered, You do know. The castle was always drawn the same way: four towers, a gate too wide, and a river running beneath the stone. No one taught him how to draw water like that, but he knew how it flowed — fast beneath the bridge, slow beside the hill. He drew it with certainty, like memory. Not story. And in the upper corner of every page, as though his hand had a will of its own, he would always press three dots in a triangle. His teachers thought it was decoration. But deep in his chest, he felt it was something else. A mark. A map. A sign.

At six years old, he began to draw something new. Not shapes. Not dreams. A crest. Over and over. Always the same. A shield split in four — black lions and golden ones, facing inward as if guarding something. A knight's helm above it, eyes forever closed. A ribbon below it, with a single word he did not understand: Constancy. No one taught him that word. No teacher ever wrote it on the board. His mother said he must've heard it on television. But he hadn't. And every time he wrote it, the letters curved as though they'd written themselves. The lions never looked the same — sometimes roaring, sometimes proud — but they were always watching. Silent. Waiting.

He didn't show his classmates. They wouldn't understand. They laughed at him once for drawing castles, so he stopped sharing. But this one he drew in secret — on napkins, in margins, behind cereal boxes. His mother found one under his pillow. "What's this?" she asked. "I don't know," he replied. "It's just always there." She smiled, kissed his forehead, and forgot. But he didn't. That night, he saw it again. In his mind. Burning gold and black behind his eyelids. He thought it was just a dream. But when he woke, the image was already on the page before breakfast. Again.

There was only one adult who didn't dismiss it. A man named Jeff. He wasn't a family friend. Just a man that Benedict knew. Just someone who came by every few days. Quiet, always polite, never asking too much. He worked in records or libraries or something that no one could explain. The boy didn't care. Jeff never laughed at his drawings. In fact, the first time he saw the crest, he didn't say a word. He simply stared, gently picked it up with both hands like it was ancient, then nodded once. "Draw what you remember," he said. "Even if you don't know what it is." He never offered stories, never explained. He simply came and went — always leaving behind old books, maps, and a feeling that the boy would only later name: curiosity.

The house grew quieter after Alan left, that was Benedict's biological father. Not all at once, and not with a bang — just slowly, like a cupboard door that never quite closed again. His mother stopped setting three places at the table. She started humming to herself in the kitchen, not because she was happy, but because the silence needed something. Benedict didn't ask questions. He didn't have to. He'd already learned that grownups rarely gave answers worth keeping. But the air was different now. He came home from school, and no one asked how his day was. He stopped looking at the front door. It stopped opening.

That's when Jeff started coming more often. Not every week. Not even every month. Just… when it mattered. Always with a book in his coat, or a folder under his arm. He never stayed long. Sometimes an hour. Sometimes just long enough for tea. He'd bring things — library cards, old photos, sometimes books no one had checked out in years.

Benedict didn't ask why. One afternoon, Jeff sat at the table reading through pages that looked older than the kitchen itself. Benedict slid into the chair across from him and peeked over the edge. "What're you reading?" he asked. Jeff glanced up, half-smiling. "Old records. Family stuff. Royal families. It's just something I study." Benedict squinted. "Royal?" "Yup," Jeff nodded. "Kings and castles. That sort of thing."

Benedict didn't say much. Just "Huh." But inside, the word echoed like it had been waiting years to be spoken. He looked down at the crest he'd doodled on the corner of his notebook. The same one he'd drawn since he was six. He slid it closer to Jeff without meaning to. "I don't know why I keep drawing this," he muttered. Jeff looked at it for a long time. "You don't need to know," he said. "Just don't stop." Benedict sat quietly for a moment, then leaned closer. "Do you think there's such a thing as a king no one knows about?" Jeff didn't answer. He just turned a page. "That's the most dangerous kind," he whispered.

Jeff didn't always bring books for Benedict. Sometimes he just left them behind — a stack on the table, a pile near the hallway, like breadcrumbs for someone who didn't yet know he was hungry. One afternoon, Benedict found one under the cushion of the couch. An old book. Dull brown cover. No title. No spine markings. The kind of thing most people would forget. But something about the weight of it made him stop. He opened it halfway and ran his fingers down the inner edge where the pages met. That's when he felt it. A crackle. A fold. A sliver of paper so thin it might've been dust. He slid it out carefully, like it might tear just from being looked at.

It was folded in three. Yellowed. The corners curled like old leaves. But the moment he opened it, his heart skipped. At the top of the page, in faded pen — not typed, not printed — was a name. His name. Not Benedict. His real name. The one no one used. The one written on school forms and forgotten birthday cards. Only this wasn't a card. It was a page from something. A record. A note. And the date in the corner was from years before he was born. He blinked. Checked again. The same name. The same spelling. And beneath it, something that looked like a code — or a place. Horváth, March 17.

He stood there for a long time, just staring. His mother was in the kitchen. Jeff had already left. The room felt smaller somehow. Quieter. He folded the page again, slower this time, and tucked it back where he found it. But his fingers were shaking. That night, he didn't draw. He didn't read. He just lay in bed listening to the wind outside and wondering: How can something be written before you exist? The next time Jeff came by Benedict didn't mention it. He just watched him. And Jeff, as always, said nothing.

The next time Jeff stopped by, Benedict didn't come to the door. He stayed in the other room, half-hidden behind the kitchen wall, sketchbook in hand. He wasn't drawing the crest this time. Or the castle. Or even the river. What flowed from his pen looked older. Smoother. Like it had always been there, waiting for his hands to remember it. Jeff said hello to his mother, poured himself a cup of tea, and waited. He didn't ask where Benedict was. Didn't call him out. He just waited in the quiet. Ten minutes passed. Then twenty. Finally, Benedict stepped into the kitchen and set his sketchbook on the table without a word.

Jeff looked at it. A single page. A house, maybe — or a church — with strange latticework carved into the corners. No windows. One large door. At the top, an archway etched with symbols Jeff hadn't seen since before Benedict was born. Below it, written in the smallest script, were the words: Horváth. March 17. Jeff didn't blink. He just studied it for a while, then looked up at the boy, who stood silent, arms folded. Benedict didn't fidget. Didn't speak. He was still — completely still — like someone listening to thunder from inside their chest.

"You found something," Jeff said. It wasn't a question. Benedict nodded. Just once. "In the book," he murmured. "You left it." Jeff's eyes didn't leave the drawing. "No," he said softly. "Not me." He traced the lines on the page with his fingertip, reverent as if it were glass. "Some things leave themselves." He flipped the page slowly, as if afraid of what might come next. But Benedict had already moved on to another sketch. And this one wasn't drawn from memory. It was drawn from a feeling. A gate. A crest. And a shadow that looked very much like a crown — only upside down.

The next morning, Jeff didn't knock. He never did. Benedict's mother always left the door unlocked when she knew he was due to visit. He stepped in with the same slow gait, nodded a soft greeting, and made for the kettle like he belonged there. On the kitchen table, waiting exactly where Benedict had left it, was the new drawing. Jeff didn't call out. Didn't ask. Just turned the sketch around, pulled his glasses from his coat pocket, and sat. The lines were finer this time. Deliberate. The curves of the roof, the etched stone, the door — half-shadowed, half-lit. Vines coiled round the windows like secrets climbing home.

Jeff didn't speak for a long while. Then he tapped the edge of the page twice. "You've seen it." Not asked. Stated. Benedict, standing by the doorway to the hall, nodded. "In a dream," he said. "But not just once." He paused. "Four times now. Same house. Same garden. Always the same light — evening, not morning. And there's… there's a sound. Words. Not English. I think it's real. But I don't know what they mean." Jeff's fingers pressed gently against the edge of the page, as though afraid it might burn. "It's not a dream," he said. "It's a memory. But not yours alone."

Benedict stepped forward. "What do you mean?" Jeff leaned back. "You ever hear something you don't understand, but feel it anyway? As if it's older than understanding?" Benedict frowned. "Like music from another room." Jeff smiled, not with his mouth but his eyes. "Exactly."

He tapped the bottom corner of the page where Benedict had once again — without planning — drawn three tiny dots. Triangle. Same as always. "This is the key," Jeff murmured. "This is what they've left you." Benedict looked down at the page. "Who?" Jeff didn't answer. Not yet. He just reached into his coat and handed him a folded paper. "Look again. But this time, listen."

The paper was older than any Benedict had ever touched. Not like the yellowed pages of library books or the brittle edges of his grandfather's Journal. No. This was different. Its surface felt more like skin than paper — dry, stretched, and soft at the edges. The fold had clearly been undone many times, but it still resisted as though it didn't want to open for just anyone. Jeff said nothing. He only watched. Benedict sat down slowly, spreading the page on the wooden table where the light from the window fell just right. It was faded — almost too faint to read — but the ink had not disappeared. It clung to the fibres like a breath held too long.

The writing wasn't in English. Or anything close. The letters were curled, arched, and strange. Like vines in a storm. Some parts looked like music — not notes, but something that danced the same. Benedict stared at it, brow furrowed. He didn't speak the words, but they spoke to him. Not in the way people talk. In the way trees murmur when no one's around. The way wind wraps itself around your ankles without asking permission. "This is... old," he whispered. Jeff nodded. "Older than anything you've ever read. Older than any king you've been taught about. It's the kind of script they buried in stone so it couldn't be stolen."

Benedict's hand hovered over a word near the middle. A word he hadn't heard, but knew. Benedicere. That's what it looked like. Almost his name, but not quite. "What does this mean?" he asked. Jeff leaned forward, only barely. "To bless. Or to be marked. Or… to remember." Benedict blinked. "Is this a name?" "It could be." Jeff looked down. "Or a title.

Some names are too old to be names. They become something else. A reminder. A crown, maybe." Benedict looked up, heart pounding. "Why would I be marked?" Jeff didn't answer. Instead, he reached into his satchel and placed a single brass key on the table. It didn't shine. It listened. "Because you're the only one who remembers."

Benedict didn't touch the key at first. He just stared at it — as if it might move, or whisper, or vanish if he blinked too slowly. It was smaller than he expected. Not a grand, ornamental thing from fairy tales. Just a simple brass shaft, the teeth worn smooth from age, the bow etched faintly with the same symbol he drew in the margins: three dots, set in a triangle. His breath caught. He didn't remember showing Jeff that part. Not once. Not in any drawing, not aloud. And yet, here it was — the mark, his mark — staring up at him from a real object laid in daylight. A key from a place no one could name. From a time no one remembered but him.

That night, he dreamt of a door. Not in a castle, not in a house. It was set into the earth, round and weathered, hidden beneath vines and a moss-covered stone. He reached for it, key in hand, but the dream shifted. He was no longer standing. He was kneeling. Small hands on damp soil. Something behind the door waited. Not a monster, not a treasure — something stranger. A truth. A truth that hummed like a name in his chest, one he hadn't learned to speak yet. When he woke, the pillow was damp beneath his cheek. But in his hand, clutched so tight his knuckles ached, was the key. Cold. Real. Waiting.

He didn't tell his mother. She would smile and say he'd imagined it. That it was from Jeff, or from a box of old toys in the attic. But Benedict knew. He knew. This wasn't a toy. And it wasn't just a key. It was a beginning. That morning, he sat with his cereal and toast, pretending to read the comic pages, but his eyes flicked constantly to the key, now resting beneath a folded napkin at the corner of the table. Jeff hadn't returned. Not yet. But Benedict was already planning. Not a scheme. Not an adventure. A search. For the lock. For the door. For the thing waiting on the other side of memory. That late afternoon as Jeff popped by to see what Benedict figured out, turned into an evening where Jeff and Benedict went for a walk.

They reached the edge of the path at twilight, where the thickets curled like fingers and the brush whispered beneath their shoes. It had rained earlier, just enough to stir the smell of moss and old bark. Jeff didn't speak. He never did at first. He let the woods do the talking — let the boy's breath steady as the trees closed in around them. Benedict moved carefully, one step at a time, like he'd been here before. But he hadn't. Not really. Just once in a dream. And yet, as the trees thinned and the air opened, there it was — the house. Stone, crooked, and ancient. Half-swallowed by ivy, but not forgotten. Never forgotten.

"It's the place," Benedict said, softly. "From the dream." Jeff stood beside him, arms folded. "It's older than the town," he said. "Older than the roads. People say it was built by no one, for no one." "That doesn't make sense," Benedict said. Jeff smiled, the way he always did when truth didn't need to explain itself. "Try the door." Benedict hesitated.

Then from the little pouch around his neck — the one his mother said he'd always worn, even before he remembered how — he drew out the key. Not a toy. Not brass or silver. It looked like iron carved from memory. Ornate. Worn. Etched with the same triangle of three dots. He didn't remember where he got it. It was just… his.

Jeff stepped back. The door, once swollen with years, seemed to breathe in. Benedict fit the key into the lock. It turned. Not a click. Not a creak. A tone. Low. Like the hum of a cello beneath stone. The door opened just enough for light to spill from inside — not electric, not candlelight. Something in between. Something older.

The doorway gave way with a softness Benedict didn't expect. No groaning hinges, no dust-clouds stirred — just a cool breath of air, as if the house had been holding it for years, waiting to exhale. The light inside wasn't golden or flickering like in old movies. It was quiet. Silver, almost. Like moonlight remembered. It spilled across the floor in long lines, touching the stones and faded rugs with the hush of reverence. Benedict stepped in, Jeff just behind, careful not to touch anything. The room was round. Perfectly so. Wooden beams arched overhead like ribs in a giant's chest. Shelves lined the walls — curved, uneven, handmade. Every one of them packed with books, scrolls, and objects he didn't recognize.

There were maps too. Hanging from nails. Draped over chairs. Rolled and tied in bundles with string that looked as though it would crumble if unknotted. But what caught his eyes first wasn't the books or the maps. It was the tapestry on the far wall — a great cloth hung by iron hooks, dyed deep navy, edged in threadbare gold. In its centre: a crest. His crest. The one he had drawn since he was old enough to grip a pen. The lions. The helm. The word beneath: Constancy. But older. Older than he could've imagined. As if his hand had remembered something the world had forgotten. "I didn't make this up," he whispered. Jeff shook his head. "No," he said. "You remembered it."

Benedict stepped forward, and as he did, the floor beneath his feet whispered — not cracked or shifted, but whispered. As if the house recognised him. Welcomed him. A low chime echoed from the corner of the room, though no clock could be seen. "What is this place?" Benedict asked. Jeff scanned the walls, then the ceiling, then the stone table at the centre of the room, where an unlit lantern stood beside a book wrapped in cloth. "This," he said, "is where the truth begins to speak." Benedict turned. "Whose truth?" Jeff met his eyes. "Yours. And those who left it behind, waiting for you."

The chair beneath the tapestry looked as though no one had sat in it for a hundred years. But the dust on the cushion was broken. Shifted. As though someone had been there recently — or something had. Benedict reached toward it without thinking. Tucked beneath the cloth of the seat, just out of sight, was a book. No title on the spine. Just thick, forest-green leather, weathered at the edges but still warm to the touch. Jeff didn't notice until Benedict had already lifted it. He turned to the table, gently clearing a space between the curled maps without moving them — just sliding his hand beneath, so nothing would tear. The book landed softly on the stone, and Benedict opened it without a word.

There, on the very first page, was his face. Not a sketch. Not a faded portrait. A full image — as if someone had taken a photograph only days ago. His dark hair, his brow slightly creased the way it always was when he was thinking too hard. His eyes wide, searching, serious. A face that didn't belong in an ancient book, but here it was, staring right back at him. And below it, a name. His name. Not scribbled. Not guessed. Written. Lettered in the same looping ink as the ancient script Jeff had shown him. But it wasn't Benedict. Not at first. The name read: Benedicere of Horváth.

Jeff stepped forward, slowly, reverently, as if approaching a grave or a crown. "You found it," he said. His voice was different — rougher, unsteady. Not quiet this time. Not guarded. "You weren't supposed to find this. Not yet." Benedict looked up. "But I did." Jeff's hand brushed over the name, not touching it. Hovering. "You're not going to believe this," he said. "Try me," Benedict replied. Jeff exhaled — not like someone tired, but someone remembering. "That name," he whispered, "is one we were told never to speak again. But it's yours." He turned the page. "Welcome back, Benedicere. It's time you knew the truth."

The book felt heavier once they left the old house. Not because of its size or weight, but because of what it carried. Jeff wrapped it in soft linen before they stepped beyond the vines, like someone cradling an heirloom. Benedict didn't speak much on the walk home. His mind spun too quickly for words — every footstep echoing with questions he didn't yet know how to ask. Jeff didn't press. At the door to Benedict's flat, Jeff paused. "It belongs with you," he said, pressing the bundle into Benedict's arms. "But bring it back. You'll need more than what's written on those pages. And so will I." He held Benedict's shoulder for a moment. "I'm here. You understand? Whatever this is, wherever it leads — you're not alone."

The door creaked open, and Benedict stepped inside. His mother was already asleep, the hallway light left on for him. He padded quietly to the small bookshelf near his bed, slid the wrapped book into the second shelf behind some older paperbacks, then paused. There, on the desk. A folded sheet. Plain white paper. His name scrawled in pen — not "Benedicere," but the name he'd known all his life: Benedict. He opened it. The handwriting was crooked, uneven — not like his mother's. His heart skipped. He recognized the shape of the letters. His father's. Alan. The man who had vanished when he turned seven. No warning. No calls. Nothing. "Benedict," the letter began.

"I know I don't have the right to speak after all this time. But I need to tell you something before someone else does. Before you find it out and think I ran because of it. I didn't. I ran because I didn't know how to carry it." The letter wasn't long, but it was enough. Alan spoke of the family name, once whispered in parishes and townships in Great Britain.

Denmark. Wales. Germanic Europe. Ireland. England. France. On his mother's side — Sweden. Norway. Hungary. He didn't name kings or crowns. But Benedict didn't need him to. The bloodline spoke for itself. And when he folded the letter back and tucked it under his pillow, the book — the one Jeff had helped him find — shifted softly on the shelf. Almost like it breathed. And when Benedict looked again, the ribbon that marked the place he'd left it in… had moved.

That night, the book remained on the shelf — unopened. But something in the room felt different. Benedict lay in bed with the letter from his father folded beneath his pillow and the blankets pulled to his chin. The moonlight filtered through the curtains like the thin, silent fingers of an unseen visitor. Outside, the wind picked up, not howling, not crying — just breathing. He closed his eyes and slipped into sleep with the soft hum of the night in his ears. It was the first dream that came gently — like a memory trying not to wake him. No castles. No voices. Just stone. Cold stone beneath bare feet. Archways covered in ivy. A long corridor with candles flickering, though no one had lit them.

He walked slowly, following the sound of dripping water. No fear, just curiosity. His hand brushed the stones as he moved, and though they were unfamiliar, he knew them. Knew every crack, every corner. He passed a mirror — not a mirror. A pane of something cloudy, warped like old glass. But his reflection was clear. Not his sweater. Not his shorts and t-shirt. A long robe, dark blue, embroidered with gold. His crest on the shoulder. A circle of thorns on the chest. The words Constancy Shall Not Fail carved beneath the rim. His eyes… were still his eyes. But older. Wiser. Tired. He turned, but no one was there. Only the sound of waves against a cliff he could not see.

The second dream came later that night. Deeper. The kind that pulled him from sleep only to drop him back again. This time, he stood in a village — not his, not now. A place of wooden homes, dirt paths, and faces that bowed without knowing why. A bell rang in the distance. People knelt. He looked down at his hands. Older again. A ring on one finger. Heavy. Not silver. Not gold. Something black. Etched.

When he looked up, a tower stood behind the villagers. A banner flew from its top — blue and white. The crest. His. He didn't speak. He didn't move. But he knew — this was once his home. Before. Long before. As the dream began to fade, something stirred at the edge of his vision. A silhouette. A figure in shadow — wearing a crown that shimmered like shadowed sunlight. It turned. And it was him. Just him. Not smiling. Not frowning. Just knowing. And then—He woke.

Benedict peeled the shirt from his back sometime before midnight. It clung to him like a wet rag, and the ceiling fan wasn't doing much. He tossed it to the floor, wiped the sweat from his neck, and slid his feet across the hardwood to the bathroom. He sat down, quiet and sleepy, the way his mum had always taught him. It was better that way — no noise, no mess. Just stillness. He liked that about the night. No one asking questions. No one pretending to know answers. Just him. And that heavy heat that seemed to hold every breath like a secret. When he climbed back into bed, he didn't pull the covers. Too hot. He just lay there. Waiting. Not sure for what.

The dream didn't come quickly. It arrived slow, like smoke curling beneath a door. A sound first — not a voice, not music, just… sound. Language, maybe. But not one he knew. Something older. Like the vowels were made of wind and the consonants came from stone. He stood barefoot in a forest, the kind no one mowed or fenced in.

Branches clawed the moonlight. Beneath his toes, the grass was damp, cool, wild. He walked without knowing why, like something had pulled his name into the trees and he had no choice but to follow. Then he saw it — the house. Or what was left of it. Old. Tilted. Covered in vines. But not ruined. Just waiting.

He approached the steps. They didn't creak. The door opened on its own. Inside, no lights. Just that same voice — not loud, not soft. Just present. And on the wall, something glowed faintly. A tapestry, maybe. Or a banner. It bore the crest — his crest — but with a change. A star now hovered above it. And beside the crest, barely visible, a shape. A face. His face. Worn by time, older than memory, but unmistakable. He reached toward it. And woke. Not with a gasp. Not with panic. Just a slow blink. Morning had come, and the sun fell across his floor like gold from a dream. He sat up, rubbed his face, and whispered only one word:

"Why?"

The sun hadn't risen much when the knock came — three gentle taps on the door, followed by the low creak of it opening before anyone answered. Jeff never waited. He always knocked first, but never hesitated. Benedict was already awake, sitting on the couch in nothing but his underwear, rubbing his eyes and blinking at the light that streamed in like liquid gold. "Morning," Jeff said, lugging something in under one arm. Not a box. A rectangle. Metallic. Vented. Benedict's mother looked up from the kitchen and smiled with relief. "Oh, thank God," she said. "That heat nearly baked us alive." Jeff chuckled and nodded at the unit. "Window opens upward, right?" She nodded. "Fits like a glove."

Benedict followed him to the window, watching with quiet curiosity. Jeff slid the unit into the one spot where the air moved freely, locked the bellows to the sill, tightened the brackets, and plugged it in with a practised hand. The hum was instant. Cold air spilled into the room like a secret shared. "Better?" Jeff asked. Benedict nodded, feeling the sting of sweat vanish from his neck. But his eye caught something else — the familiar canvas bag near Jeff's feet, slumped beneath his coat. Without thinking, Benedict picked it up. "I'll put it on the table." Jeff only nodded. And when the bag landed, the world seemed to hush.

Jeff unzipped it slowly, like unsealing something sacred. Inside: three worn books, and a map — old, folded, edges curled like autumn leaves. Benedict leaned in. One book's spine was stitched, the title nearly vanished. The map didn't show countries but rivers, towers, forests curling around a silhouette. Benedict stared. "That's the place," he whispered. "From the dream." Jeff didn't blink. "I thought I saw something on the tapestry," he said softly. "Didn't trust myself. But if you saw it too... we need to go back. Today." Benedict didn't pause. "Let's go."

Annemarie watched them from the kitchen, one hand on the sink, the other wrapped around a lukewarm mug of tea. She smiled — not joy, but inevitability. The kind that said, I knew this was coming. When Jeff and Benedict leaned over the map in half-whispers, she said nothing. She only nodded when Benedict glanced back. "Go," she said softly. "But be careful. It's not just the woods that remember things." Benedict didn't understand. Yet.

They left before noon, packs light, air cool, hearts loud. The trees greeted them like old friends. Even Jeff, who'd been here before, moved slower than usual. Benedict led. Past the fence line, beyond blackberry bushes, through the rabbit-thin gap in the thicket. There it stood — the house, worn and weathered, its roof slanting like a nod from the past. Inside, the tapestry still draped over the old chair. Jeff entered first. Benedict followed. This time, neither spoke. Something had shifted.

Benedict knelt, brushing aside the tapestry. Beneath, where once was only wood, now sat a small indented mark — round, deliberate, slightly off-centre. Jeff crouched beside him. "That wasn't here before," he whispered. "No," Benedict replied. "But I think it always was." His finger traced the edge. "Look." In the corner, where wood met frame: a triangle of three dots. Jeff's breath caught. "You marked this." "No," Benedict answered. "I remembered it." Then his hand pressed gently under the seat. A soft click gave way — a small hidden compartment opened beneath. Inside: a parchment, folded carefully, and a locket.

Later, back at Benedict's flat, the home was cooler. Another night had come and gone, and with it, more dreams. Benedict sat at the kitchen table, head tilted, fingers resting on a drawing he hadn't yet shared. "Can I tell you something first?" he asked as Jeff leaned forward, his eyes soft but watchful. Benedict hesitated. Not from mistrust, but from the strange way dreams sounded foolish in daylight. "I saw it again. But different. From above, like flying. Then I was inside. There was a voice — not speaking like us. It sounded old. Like stone trying to remember sunlight." He lowered his eyes. "I didn't understand it, but it felt like I should."

Jeff studied the drawing: the house, three dots, the familiar mark pressed into the page. "You didn't see it," Benedict added softly. "But I think it was always there." Jeff sat back. "Do you know what you just described?" Benedict shook his head. "Memory. Not from now. From before." Jeff unzipped the green bag once more — books, papers, a folded map. "When I saw this again last night," Jeff said, placing it beside the drawing, "I thought it was coincidence. But now? I'm not so sure." Benedict leaned closer. "You think we should go back?"

Jeff smiled faintly. "We have to. But first, let's cool off. Kids don't solve mysteries sweating their socks off." He paused then, tapping his fingers lightly on the table, his gaze shifting from the map to Benedict, studying him for a long moment. His voice lowered just slightly, almost like he was letting the thought form aloud as it came to him. "But Benedict," he said softly, "there's something else, too." Benedict looked up. "This—" Jeff gestured to the drawings, the map, the old books, "—it's all pointing to something much older than you and me. Deeper. What we're looking at... it isn't just in stories. It's in you."

He leaned forward, voice even gentler now. "I think... it might be time we get some answers from inside you. Not just memories. Blood." Benedict frowned, curious. Jeff nodded. "DNA, kid. Genetics. I think a test might tell us what the maps can't. It's like a key to the parts of the puzzle we can't see yet." He smiled faintly again. "The rest — we'll leave to the dreams. Let's go get that DNA test taken care of, what do you say Ben?" Benedict looked at Jeff for a moment, then replied "Okay, let's go then, but you're coming in with me."

The clinic didn't smell like lemon wipes. It smelled like iron — faint and sharp, like a whisper from deep inside the earth. Benedict sat on the tall chair, feet dangling, eyes wide but steady as the nurse prepared the vial and needle.

She smiled in that way adults do when they aren't sure if a child understands how serious something really is. He wasn't afraid. Not really. He had questions — but not the kind anyone here could answer. They were older questions, older even than his dreams. "This will be quick," the nurse said gently, tying a blue band around his arm. "Just a little pinch."

Benedict didn't flinch. The needle slipped beneath his skin, and he watched the dark red pull into the tube like a secret being drawn out. He wondered if, somewhere inside that vial, the answers he was looking for were hiding — not just about his family, but about himself. Jeff sat behind him, silent as ever, reading one of his battered old maps. His mother, Annemarie, smiled from the corner, her hand resting on the strap of her purse like she might squeeze it for luck.

The nurse sealed the vial, labelled it with a name — his — and placed it into a padded carrier for the lab. "That's it," she said warmly. "Now it goes to the specialists. Might take a few weeks." A few weeks. To Benedict, it sounded like a lifetime. Jeff ruffled his hair as they stepped into the sun outside. "You did good, kid," he said. Benedict tilted his head back, looking at the sky as if it might answer. "Jeff... what if they find something?" Jeff smiled, but it wasn't the kind of smile that promised easy answers. It was the kind that hid whole histories behind it. "Then," he said quietly, "we'll finally have a few more pieces of the puzzle."

The days after the blood test stretched longer than Benedict expected. Time didn't move like it used to. He still went to school, still read his books, still drew late at night — but now, the drawings had shifted again. The castles were there, yes, and the crests too. But new shapes crept onto the paper. Arched bridges. Forest paths. A great hall with banners he couldn't name but instinctively coloured blue and gold. Jeff came by often, but neither of them spoke much about the test. They didn't need to. The waiting was loud enough.

The summer stretched on, not hurried, not still — just unfolding like an old scroll, inch by inch. The house remained standing in its crooked quiet, but they didn't return. Not yet. The dreams were doing their work. And so was the waiting. Days slipped into weeks. School let out. The air grew thicker with heat that stuck to the windows like breath.

Mornings came earlier; nights grew heavier. Benedict spent hours drawing — always drawing — but now the images deepened. The old house appeared again and again, but layered with things he hadn't seen before. Underground chambers. Winding staircases carved into stone. Symbols woven into doorframes. Faces, blurred but familiar. Each drawing felt less like imagination and more like memory climbing back up through him.

Jeff continued his quiet visits. Some days they spoke at length. Other days, they said almost nothing. He would bring another old book, another brittle map, another theory he wouldn't fully explain. And always, Jeff's gaze returned to Benedict's drawings like someone reading a diary he didn't want to intrude upon.

The dreams thickened too. Sometimes they came two or three in a single night — layers within layers. Benedict saw towers overlooking rivers he could not name. Great halls lit by candlelight. Long corridors of stone arches where echoes whispered in a tongue his waking mind barely recognized but his spirit seemed to cradle. He no longer feared these dreams. They didn't haunt him. They waited for him.

In the afternoons, he and Jeff sometimes sat on the porch while cicadas hummed. Annemarie would watch from the kitchen window, her face a quiet mixture of knowing and worry. She rarely asked questions now. She sensed, as mothers often do, that something ancient was unfolding beneath her roof — something neither she nor Jeff could stop.

At night, the dreams grew stranger. He saw faces now — but never fully. Silhouettes behind heavy stone windows, eyes watching, never blinking. Sometimes there were voices, but only faint echoes — like the language was hiding behind a thin wall. The words weren't clear, but the feeling was. Like belonging to a place he'd never visited but always carried. Every morning he woke more tired than the night before, his hands stiff from gripping the sheets. The key sat beneath his pillow, cold against his fingers.

One evening, Jeff arrived with two mugs of cocoa and no books. They sat on the couch, side by side, saying nothing for a long time. Finally, Benedict whispered, "Do you think I'll even want to know what they find?" Jeff didn't answer right away. He simply took a slow sip.

"That's not the real question," he said at last. "The real question is — will you recognize what you already know?" Benedict stared at the steam curling from his mug. The room exhaled with him.

The days pulled forward like slow waves on a shore that didn't know if it was coming or going. The test was done. The waiting had begun. But the waiting wasn't empty. Every night, the dreams returned — stronger now, like something calling him from further away. Benedict stood on mountains that overlooked rivers he couldn't name, walked through stone halls that echoed his footsteps like whispers, and always — always — the three stars above the crest watched him silently from the banners.

The language returned too. Not clear. Not loud. But closer. Words that slipped through him like water through fingers. Sometimes he woke with a single word on his lips, one he couldn't write. And when he tried to draw, the lines shifted again. Less of castles now — more of roads. Paths leading into thick forests, into old ruins where doors waited beneath the earth, with keyholes shaped like spirals.

Jeff watched him change without pushing questions. He would visit, bring tea, and leave another book behind like a breadcrumb on the trail. "Not all keys open doors," Jeff once said while placing another old map down. "Some open memories first." Benedict only nodded, tracing his finger across the curling rivers drawn in ink centuries ago. "But what if the doors aren't here yet?" Benedict asked softly. Jeff smiled faintly. "Then we're still being invited."

One night, the dream shifted again. Deeper. He stood before a mirror — but not like one he had ever seen. It was wide, framed in black iron, and its glass was clouded like stormy water. The reflection stared back at him, but it was not just his. He was older. Wiser. The robe he wore shimmered dark blue with gold threading, and the crest — his crest — blazed across his shoulder. His eyes looked back at him with knowing.

In the reflection's hand was a scroll — sealed with the same red wax as the one they found under the house. The reflection did not speak. It simply nodded once, and as Benedict reached out toward the glass, the entire mirror pulsed with light. Not warmth. Not cold. Just... presence.

He woke before dawn, this time without sweat slicking his back, heart pounding beneath his ribs. Sitting up, he whispered into the empty room, "Why do I remember things I never lived?" The key beneath his pillow vibrated faintly — as though answering without words. And for the first time, Benedict was afraid not of what he might find, but of what he might already know.

The following morning, Jeff arrived earlier than usual. The sunlight had barely touched the treetops when he knocked — a rare thing for him. Annemarie opened the door while tying her robe, blinking against the early light. "You're up early," she smiled, stepping aside.

Jeff nodded with a strange tension in his shoulders. "I couldn't wait any longer. The results should arrive any day now." He glanced toward Benedict, who sat at the kitchen table tracing the three-dots triangle into the condensation on his glass of orange juice. As Jeff sat down, he slid a small, sealed envelope across the table. Not from the clinic — this one was older. Handwritten.

The paper yellowed at the edges. "I found this tucked inside one of the maps last night. I don't know how I missed it before." Benedict stared at it. His fingers hovered over the seal. "From my father?" he asked quietly. Jeff exhaled. "Yes. From Alan."

The envelope sat between them, heavy as stone. Benedict didn't open it. Not yet. "Jeff..." His voice wavered. "Why do I feel like I'm standing between two worlds?" Jeff's smile was soft but heavy. "Because, Benedict... you are."

The envelope sat untouched on Benedict's desk for two days. He would stare at it before school, after supper, before bed — but never open it. It wasn't fear that stopped him. It was weight. Every dream, every drawing, every silent knowing behind his ribs seemed to swirl inside that thin paper shell.

He almost feared that once the seal broke, something inside him would break too. So instead, he waited. He drew. The drawings grew stranger again — not castles this time, but roots. Roots that tangled like knotted veins beneath towers he couldn't name. The triangle of three dots appeared over and over, like muscle memory slipping past his thoughts.

At night, the dreams pushed harder. Now he could hear the voices clearer — though still not quite enough to understand. They spoke in rhythm, like songs from far-off halls. And sometimes — though only for a breath — he saw flashes of faces in dim candlelight.

Not strangers. Family. He didn't know how, but he knew they belonged to him. Once, he woke with a single word pulsing against his skull: Árpád. The sound of it tasted both sweet and strange, like honey on a foreign tongue. He whispered it into the dark, not even knowing what it meant. But somewhere deep inside, the name fit. Like it was always his.

Jeff came that evening again, sitting quietly beside him without a word. They played a game of chess they never finished. Halfway through, Benedict asked softly, "Do you ever feel like you're remembering things that never happened to you?" Jeff didn't answer right away. He only watched the board, then moved his knight forward, toppling a pawn. "That's the thing about memory," he said gently. "Sometimes it belongs to people we've never met — but who made us who we are." Benedict looked down at the envelope once more. This time, his hand trembled as he reached for it.

The scrolls sat untouched on the table as Benedict finally spoke — not with the excitement of discovery, but with the slow, careful weight of something much older. "Jeff..." His voice cracked. "Can I tell you something strange?" Jeff looked up from the parchment, sensing the shift. "Of course."

Benedict stared at his hands for a moment, then lifted his eyes, almost afraid of how it would sound. "I've died. Not like a feeling. For real. Three times." His words landed heavy, like stones being laid in a quiet pond. "When I was a baby, my lungs... they just stopped. I don't remember much. But I do remember what came after." He paused. "It wasn't like they say in stories. No angels. No people. No streets of gold. Just... white."

Jeff sat back, not speaking, not interrupting. Benedict went on, his voice quieter. "The light — it was so bright, but not warm or cold. It wasn't even scary. Just... there. Like forever lived inside it. But then there was a voice. It wasn't English. It wasn't my mom. It wasn't the doctors. Just... a voice. It said: You're not done yet." Jeff's breath caught slightly, but he stayed silent. "And the weirdest part?" Benedict whispered. "I didn't understand the words. Not back then. But now — I do. A little. It was another language. I think... I think it was Hungarian. Known as Magyar.

Jeff finally broke his silence, his face pale but steady. "Hungarian?" Benedict nodded. "I don't know how I know. I can't speak it. But I understand parts of it when I hear it. Like someone speaking inside me." The scrolls rustled slightly as Jeff exhaled, almost like the room itself was listening. "Benedict," he said softly. "I don't think you're just remembering stories. I think you're remembering who you are."

The letter arrived quietly. No knock. No phone call. Just the soft thump of an envelope sliding through the mail slot and landing face-down on the hardwood floor. Benedict hadn't even noticed it at first. It was Jeff who picked it up when he arrived that afternoon, brushing the dust from its corner as though handling something delicate. "Here it is," Jeff said softly, handing it to him.

Benedict stared at the envelope, his fingers tracing the printed label. His full name. His birthdate. The clinic's return address printed in plain black ink. The paper felt heavier than it should. He sat at the kitchen table, heart steady but slow, as though his whole body had paused in reverence.

Annemarie hovered nearby, not speaking, her hands wringing the corner of her apron unconsciously. Jeff simply sat across from Benedict, waiting. "Do you want me to open it?" Jeff finally asked. Benedict shook his head once. "No. It's mine." His thumb slid under the flap carefully, peeling the adhesive without tearing. Inside: two sheets, clipped together at the corner. The first was ordinary — bold headings, dates, numbers — but the second held the words they had waited for. "Y-chromosome haplogroup: R-S660," Benedict read aloud, his voice barely more than a whisper. "Mitochondrial haplogroup: H5a1."

He paused. His pulse felt louder now, not faster, but louder — as though it were no longer beating inside him but beside him. The words weren't entirely new. Jeff had mentioned them before, in quiet conversations, in old books and scrolls.

But now they were printed. Real. Official. Jeff exhaled like someone setting down a burden. "There it is." "It's the same," Benedict whispered. "Same as on the scroll." Jeff nodded, leaning forward. "Denmark. Norway. France. Ireland. Wales. Hungary. And more. "And Hungary," Benedict echoed.

Jeff tapped his finger gently on the name. "Árpád. Béla. The blood remembers." The air in the room seemed to lean closer, like even the walls were listening. Annemarie crossed her arms, her face pale but calm. "It means what you've seen in your dreams, what you've drawn... it's not your imagination," she said softly.

"It's in your blood." Benedict set the pages down on the table but kept his hand atop them, as though afraid they might float away. "I don't understand how I know any of this." "You don't have to understand it all at once," Jeff said. "Your body already knows. Your spirit's known longer than your mind has."

Benedict swallowed, blinking slowly. "Jeff... who else knows?" Jeff's mouth tightened slightly. He glanced at Annemarie, who only gave the faintest nod. "For now? Just us. But there are others who could know, if they ever looked hard enough." The silence stretched. The test results sat beneath his palm like an ancient relic disguised in modern paper. He could feel the weight pressing through the thin sheets, pressing through the room, pressing through him. Finally, Jeff stood. "This doesn't end anything," he said. "This just starts the next part." Benedict looked up at him, his throat dry but his voice firm. "Then I'm ready." Jeff smiled, though his eyes remained serious. "Good. Because what comes next — you won't find it in blood samples."

The house Never changes. But something inside Benedict had shifted. He walked differently now—not faster, but as though his feet remembered something his mind could not name. The dreams had moved through him like a river under ice. The wind felt familiar. The way the grass leaned. The way the ivy coiled across the stone chimney.

Even the light—soft and slanting—felt like an old song sung quietly for his return. When they reached the iron gate, Benedict paused only briefly, his fingers brushing against the cold bars. "It's here," he said softly, almost to himself. Jeff watched, not speaking, giving the boy space.

There was no need for guidance now. This was Benedict's path. Jeff followed behind as Benedict slipped through, careful not to disturb the wildflowers or the moss-softened stones. The boy walked with a kind of steady reverence, as though listening for instructions only he could hear. Past the old well. Three steps toward the leaning chimney. A pause beneath the crooked beam where ivy had grown thick as ropes. Benedict crouched low and pressed his fingers into the rough edge of stone, searching by touch rather than sight. His hands moved with quiet certainty, as though the stones themselves whispered beneath his fingertips. Then— he found it. A small hollow. The carved keyhole.

Without hesitation, Benedict pulled the key from his pocket. The one wrapped in parchment so many weeks ago. The one that had somehow always belonged to him. Jeff offered a flashlight, but Benedict only shook his head. "I don't need it."

The key slid into place, turning not with a click, but with a breath—a long, exhaling sigh, like a door yielding not from force, but recognition. The stone shifted backward, revealing not stairs or chambers, but a hidden compartment cut neatly into the wall. Inside, sealed in cracked wax, lay a scroll within a leather tube, untouched by dust or time.

Benedict hesitated, his breath shallow. "You do it," he whispered. Jeff shook his head softly. "Not this time, Benedict. This one was always yours." With care, Benedict withdrew the tube, unwrapping the aged leather as if unrolling an ancient secret. The wax seal cracked gently, releasing a faint scent of old parchment and something else — something like rain on stone. The scroll unfurled, its parchment curling slightly as it breathed after its long sleep. At first, the writing meant nothing to him. Strange shapes, curling lines, runes like tiny twisted branches. But slowly, names and words rose from the mystery like islands breaking through fog.

"Denmark... Sjælland... Fyn... Tromsø... Leknes... Harstad... Bodø..." Benedict whispered them aloud as his eyes moved across the script. The names felt oddly familiar, though he could not have said why. They sat on his tongue as though they belonged there, like stories waiting to be retold. Jeff knelt beside him, his voice steady. "Those are places, Benedict. Places tied to your family. Places that carried your ancestors forward." "My ancestors?" Benedict looked up, confusion furrowing his brow. Jeff smiled softly, never breaking his calm. "Long lines of people. Generations who lived before you, but who are still part of you. Every person comes from somewhere, Ben. And sometimes... those places leave marks."

The scroll continued to unfurl, revealing more names — Ireland, Wales, France, England, Norway, Sweden, Hungary. The list was long, wrapping itself like a spiral of time. Benedict's heart beat louder. "But how do I know these names? I've never been to any of these places." "You haven't," Jeff said quietly. "But your blood has." Benedict blinked, staring at the curling script, his small hand running gently across the parchment as though afraid to break it. "But... this is from the test, isn't it? The blood test?" Jeff nodded. "Parts of it, yes. The test tells us where your ancestors walked long ago. Thousands of years back. The science helps us find the trail. But this scroll—this came long before tests. This was written for someone who was meant to remember."

"Me?" Jeff hesitated. "Maybe. Or maybe someone like you who carried it forward." He glanced at the bottom of the scroll. Benedict's eyes followed. There were other symbols now — intricate spirals, triangles of three dots, and strange curling letters that bent like vines. Two names rested at the very bottom. Benedict sounded them out carefully. "Ár...pád... and Béla." The words tasted unfamiliar, yet familiar at once. Like echoes from a dream he couldn't quite place. They sat heavy on his tongue, but his mind offered no meaning.

Jeff's voice remained steady. "Old names. From old stories. Very old." "Who were they?" "Leaders. Kings. People from a far corner of the past." Jeff's gaze held steady, never rushing. "You don't need to know everything yet. What matters now is that your family's path touches those places." Benedict's breath caught. "Kings?

But... I'm not..." "You're you," Jeff interrupted gently. "That's all you need to be right now." Benedict stared at the parchment again. The names, the places, the swirling patterns — it all felt heavy, like a great stone in his chest. Not frightening. Not confusing. Just... heavy.

Jeff placed a calming hand on his shoulder. "Ben, listen to me: you don't need to carry answers tonight. What you've found here — this is just the beginning. You'll learn more. In time. And when you're ready, the rest will come." "But why do I feel like I've seen this before?" Benedict whispered. "Because part of you has," Jeff answered. "You may not remember with your head. But your blood... it remembers." The wind stirred outside the stone walls, brushing leaves across the doorframe. The scroll curled slightly under Benedict's fingers, as though sighing in rhythm with his breath.

"Come on," Jeff said softly after a moment. "Let's wrap this back up for now. There's more to find. But not tonight." Benedict nodded, reluctantly rolling the scroll back into its tube, the parchment creaking softly like old leather stretching. The wax seal no longer held, but the tube closed snug around its secret. As they stepped back into the cool air beneath the trees, Benedict looked up at the sky, its stars beginning to pierce the twilight. "Jeff..." Benedict asked quietly, "how far back does it go? My family." Jeff smiled faintly, watching the boy's young face glow in the softening light. "Further than you can count. Farther than stars."

CHAPTER 2: THE DOOR BENEATH THE IVY

The rain had softened overnight, not heavy, not loud — only steady. A kind of rain that belonged to old places. It whispered against the windows of the house as though gently reminding them both that the world outside would wait. Inside, the air was warm, stirred gently by the hum of the small electric heater Jeff had brought in last autumn. The smell of old paper mixed with the faint scent of rain-dampened wood. The house was breathing with them.

Benedict sat at the table, knees tucked under his chest, sketchbook in his lap. His pen glided carefully across the paper, each line deliberate, each curve a memory his young hands could not quite explain. The drawing was of the house again — the one beneath the ivy, the one that now lived in both his dreams and his waking life. This time, though, the door was different. Wider. More detailed. The carved symbols around the frame came to him without effort, as if his fingertips had carried them across centuries.

Jeff sat nearby, quietly sorting through another bundle of old papers. His glasses perched low on his nose as his eyes scanned the curling edges of scrolls that had long since lost their crispness. He said nothing, as was his way. The silence between them was not empty. It was full — full of patience, full of the unspoken.

Benedict paused his drawing for a moment, glancing up at Jeff. He watched the man's steady hands move with the same quiet reverence they always did when handling old records. Even now, Jeff handled each document as though it contained something fragile, something sacred. Benedict admired that about him. There was a kind of stillness in Jeff that made the world feel less frightening. Less uncertain.

His mother had once told him that some people fill a room with their words, while others fill it with their presence. Jeff was the second kind. His words were few, but his presence... it filled the space like an anchor. The rain tapped softly on the window again. Benedict lowered his legs from the chair and sat upright, watching Jeff longer this time. His heart stirred — not quickly, but with a weight that had been slowly building over many months. Since his father left, the world had changed. It hadn't broken all at once. It had simply emptied, like a room with one chair missing.

Alan's absence was like a doorway that no longer opened. But Jeff had been there. Not filling the gap like a replacement piece, but standing beside it. Steady. Present. Never trying to take his father's place. Never asking for anything. Only there. Always there. When the dreams had confused him. When the tests had frightened him. When the scrolls had whispered names he could not understand. Jeff had listened. Had never mocked. Had never doubted. Just… stayed.

And tonight, as the rain continued to fall like a quiet hymn, Benedict's heart could no longer hold the weight of his silence. He set his sketchbook down slowly and stood. His bare feet touched the cool wood of the floor with only the faintest sound. He walked toward Jeff, his breathing steady but his chest tight. The distance between them was only a few feet, but it felt larger than any map they had studied together.

Jeff glanced up as Benedict approached, lowering the paper slightly. His brow softened, but he did not speak. He simply waited, sensing that the boy was carrying something delicate in his hands — not paper, but words. Benedict stopped directly in front of him. The boy's small hands curled slightly at his sides. His eyes met Jeff's — not with the nervous darting of a child seeking approval, but with the earnest gaze of someone standing at the edge of something vulnerable. His lower lip trembled, but his voice did not.

"Jeff," he whispered, his voice barely above the hush of the rain, "can I… can I say something to you?" Jeff's voice was gentle. "Of course." Benedict swallowed. The tears had already gathered in the corner of his eyes. Not from pain. Not from fear. From something much deeper.

"I know... I know you're not my father," Benedict said, his voice breaking slightly. "But... but you've been here. You stayed. When he left. You always stay." He paused, his throat tightening. The words gathered behind his ribs like waves. "And I don't want to call you Jeff anymore. I mean, I can… if you want. But... but I feel like you're... my dad."

The word hung in the room like a candle's flame, delicate and full of warmth. He wiped at his eyes quickly, embarrassed by the tears but unable to stop them. "I love you like a dad. And I... I just needed you to know." The silence that followed was unlike any they had shared before. It wasn't awkward. It wasn't empty. It was sacred. The kind of silence that filled every corner of the room and wrapped them both inside something ancient and unspoken.

Jeff's throat moved as he swallowed, lowering the paper fully to his lap. His face didn't break into a wide grin. He didn't burst into tears. Instead, his expression softened into something rare — something the boy had not yet seen fully in him before: vulnerability. He slowly removed his glasses and set them on the table. Then, reaching forward, he placed one hand on Benedict's shoulder — firm, steady, warm. His thumb rubbed gently against the boy's sleeve.

"Ben…" Jeff whispered, using the name he so often did, but now it carried a different weight. His voice trembled for the first time since Benedict had known him. "There's no greater thing you could have ever said to me." Benedict blinked, his tears now flowing freely. Jeff leaned forward, pulling him gently into his chest, wrapping his arms around the boy with a kind of fatherly embrace that carried not possession, but belonging.

"And if you let me," Jeff whispered softly, his chin resting lightly atop Benedict's head, "I will be that for you. I will always be here. Always." Benedict pressed his face into Jeff's shirt, his small hands gripping tightly at his side. He didn't sob. He simply breathed — deep, steady breaths that finally felt safe.

Jeff closed his eyes, holding him. The rain continued its song against the windows. And in that moment, beneath the whispers of ancestry, beneath the mysteries of ancient names and scrolls, beneath the shadows of fathers who left and fathers who stayed — a boy found his Dad, and a man found his son.

The rain had passed by morning, leaving the air thick with the scent of wet leaves and stone. Mist still clung in small patches beneath the trees as Jeff and Benedict stepped carefully along the winding path that led away from the house. The light broke softly through the canopy above them, dappling the ground in shifting pools of gold. They walked side by side without speaking at first.

It was not the silence of distance, but of understanding. Words were not always needed between them anymore. They had entered a new place — one neither of them could name but both recognized. Jeff carried the leather tube containing the scroll in one hand, cradled close to his chest, as though carrying something living. Ben walked just slightly ahead, his small hand occasionally brushing the tall grasses at the path's edge.

When they reached a clearing, Jeff paused. His eyes lifted to the sky, watching the thin clouds roll like slow waves. Ben stopped too, turning to face him. There was a quiet expectancy in his eyes — not waiting for instruction, but open to whatever his mentor, his protector, might wish to share. Jeff drew a long breath. "Ben..." He spoke the shortened name for the first time. It slipped easily from his lips, soft, familiar. "May I call you that?"

Ben smiled immediately — wide and unguarded. "I would love that," he said, his voice light but full. Jeff's eyes softened as he nodded. And then Ben's smile faded only slightly, not from fear, but from the weight of what had been stirring inside him since the night before. He stepped forward, closing the small space between them, standing now directly in front of Jeff beneath the high branches that swayed above. "Can I ask something too?" Ben whispered, his voice trembling again — but this time with hope, not nerves. Jeff waited, patient as ever. "Anything."

Ben lifted his chin, his voice barely rising above a breath. "Would it be all right if... if I called you Dad?" The question landed between them like a soft beam of sunlight breaking through fog — not dramatic, but sacred. Jeff's throat caught. His hand gripped the leather tube a little tighter, not from reluctance, but to steady himself against the rush of emotion that climbed inside his chest. His jaw shifted as he swallowed the surge that tried to tighten his throat.

Slowly, with reverence, he lowered himself onto one knee — to meet Ben eye to eye, face to face, without height between them. "Yes," Jeff whispered, his voice rich but steady. "Yes, Ben. It would be more than all right." Ben's breath quivered, his eyes damp. Jeff reached out and placed both hands gently upon the boy's shoulders.

His voice deepened, warm as earth. "And would it be all right, Ben, if I called you, my son?" Ben's answer was simple, immediate, and true. "Anytime." And with that word, the space between them dissolved. Jeff pulled him close once again, holding him not as a teacher, nor as a guide, but as a dad holds a son — with arms that promised not rescue, but belonging.

The wind brushed lightly through the trees, as though the forest itself was bearing witness to what had just been spoken into being. The unseen voices of the past — those ancient names, those long rivers of bloodline and memory — seemed for a moment to grow quiet, honouring the new covenant that now lived between these two souls.

For the first time since Alan had left, Ben no longer carried the hollow emptiness of what had been missing. He had not found a replacement for his father. He had found his Dad. They stood in that clearing for some time, saying nothing else. The rain had washed the path clean, but the road ahead remained long. And yet — now they would walk it together.

The afternoon sun poured gently through the window, streaking soft light across the wooden floor. Ben sat on his bed, his legs pulled up to his chest, the envelope resting on his lap like a sleeping bird that neither stirred nor breathed. Jeff sat nearby, not rushing him, letting the boy hold this moment. The letter had been waiting for weeks. Untouched. Quiet. Alan's handwriting stared back at them both. But today, it was time. Ben finally whispered, "Do you think it'll help, Dad?"

Jeff gave a small, steady nod. "I think it might, son. Maybe not with everything... but enough to show you more of the path." He placed a gentle hand on Ben's back. "Whatever's inside, you're not reading it alone." Ben drew a breath, slid his thumb beneath the old seal, and opened the letter with care. The paper inside was slightly worn but intact. Alan's words were written clear, as if finally spoken after years of waiting. And Ben read aloud:

Ben,

I know this letter comes too late. And for that, I won't make excuses. But what I write now is not about me — it's about you.

You've likely seen more than I ever did. And you've probably already discovered things I barely began to understand. But I want to leave you with something. A truth I never had the courage to follow myself.

Our family doesn't begin where you think. The name you carry holds deeper roots than most ever see. You are part of places older than these towns, older than any single country. Kent is only one small corner.

There is Denmark in your blood. Norway. Ireland. Wales. France. And Hungary — much deeper still. These names have followed us for thousands of years, like rivers joining from faraway springs.

You may hear the names Béla. You may hear Árpád. If you haven't yet, you will. These are not just kings from books. They are part of your story. Part of your blood. Part of your line.

I was told once by an old historian that some families don't wear crowns on their heads, but carry them in their bones. You, my son, carry such a crown.

I don't expect you to understand all of it now. But one day you will. And when you do — I want you to know this: never stop searching. Never stop drawing your map. You are not lost. You are being written.

Your life is far more important than you yet know. Trust those who walk beside you. Listen to your dreams. Listen to the voice inside you that remembers the stories no one else dares to tell.

Where I stumbled, you will walk. Where I turned away, you will continue forward.

Keep going, Ben. The answers wait for you.

—Alan

Ben's voice slowed as he reached the final lines, his throat tightening slightly, but no tears fell. He folded the letter softly and held it in his lap, staring at it for a long moment. Jeff reached over, resting his palm against Ben's shoulder. "How do you feel, son?" Ben breathed deeply, steady. "Stronger." Jeff smiled. "That's exactly what he should've given you." His voice was warm. "Not guilt. Not excuses. But pieces of your path." Ben nodded, gripping the letter one last time before placing it gently inside the drawer of his nightstand. "I'm ready to keep going, Dad." Jeff's voice softened, his eyes warm with pride. "Then we keep walking. Side by side."

The rain whispered against the windowpane as Jeff stepped into the kitchen, carefully balancing a canvas bag on one arm and a small cardboard box tucked under the other. The house smelled of Annemarie's banana bread and the faint aroma of tea still steaming on the table. Ben sat waiting, eyes fixed on the glowing laptop Jeff had set up earlier that morning. The screen displayed a blank family tree — digital, not paper, with little empty boxes waiting to be filled. The emptiness on the screen made Ben's chest feel heavier than it should have. So many names missing. So many unknowns waiting in silence.

Jeff slid the box onto the table, his smile calm, his voice steady as always. "Alright, Ben. Are you ready to build your tree?" Ben's voice was quiet, but eager. "Yeah… but where do we start? It's all empty." Jeff nodded softly, pulling up a chair beside him. "We start at the beginning — always at the beginning." He pointed gently to the top of the screen. "See this? This is you. We'll build everything outward from there." Ben glanced at the blinking box that held his name. "And here's where I put you, Dad." His voice was tender as he spoke the word, full of affection that only deepened with time.

Jeff's heart swelled, but his voice stayed soft. "That means more than you know, son. But for this part, we have to enter the names where they belong by bloodline. So, for your paternal side, we'll put Alan. That's where your tree's roots begin." Ben's face fell slightly, but he nodded. "Okay… but you'll help me with all the other names?" Jeff ruffled his hair gently. "Every one of them, Ben. We're in this together."

The laptop hummed quietly as Jeff opened the browser, bringing up Ancestry.com. The logo unfurled on the screen like a tree stretching its branches into the future. Ben leaned in close, wide-eyed, watching as Jeff explained each step. "This, Ben, is where people around the world build their trees. It's all done online. No paper, no folders. Everything stays here, on the computer." He pointed to the fields waiting to be filled. "We type in names, dates, locations — and the system helps us find hints and connections."

Ben stared at the blinking cursor as Jeff typed in the first few names: Alan, Annemarie, and then grandparents whose names they had gathered. Annemarie quietly joined them, standing behind with a gentle smile, correcting a date here, offering a birthplace there. "You see how the tree starts to grow?" Jeff asked. "Each box connects to the next one." Ben nodded. "It's like building a puzzle, but backwards." Jeff smiled. "Exactly."

After they had filled in the first few generations, Jeff reached into his bag and brought out the small cardboard box he had carried in. Ben tilted his head, curious. "What's that, Dad?" Jeff opened the box slowly, revealing the AncestryDNA kit. Inside was a sealed plastic tube, a tiny funnel, and a few clear instructions. "This," Jeff said softly, "is your next step."

Ben studied it carefully, eyes narrowing. "But… I already did a DNA test. The blood test, remember? At the clinic." Jeff nodded. "You did. And that one told us some very special things, things about your Y-DNA and your maternal haplogroup — those deep, ancient lines in your blood. But this test is a little different. We do it here at home. You just give a bit of saliva — no needles — and then we mail it off." He tapped the logo on the box. "Ancestry.com has expert geneticists who analyze it. They'll compare your DNA to millions of others. That's how you'll start seeing names of people who share pieces of your DNA. Some of them you might recognize. Some will have different last names. They could be cousins you never even knew existed."

Ben's eyes grew wider. "Like... hidden family?" Jeff smiled. "In a way, yes. People you're connected to, even if you've never met. Your DNA holds pieces of stories that go back hundreds, even thousands of years. And now, we get to uncover some of those stories together."

As the afternoon deepened, they carefully followed the instructions. Ben filled the small vial with quiet determination, giggling briefly when the spit bubbled up inside the tube. "Looks gross, doesn't it?" he joked. Jeff laughed with him. "A little. But it's powerful, too. This little bit holds so much history." They sealed the sample, packed it into the return envelope, and set it by the door, ready for mailing.

The sun dipped low outside the window as the tree on the screen began to take shape. Names. Places. Hints waiting to be explored. Ben glanced up at Jeff, his eyes full of gratitude. "Thanks, Dad," he said softly. Jeff placed a hand on his shoulder. "Always, Ben. And remember — we don't have to rush. We'll take it one name, one clue, one piece at a time. I'm right here beside you."

And so, as the rain continued to fall gently outside, father and son sat side by side, building not only a tree, but a bridge across generations — one step closer to the mystery of who Ben truly was.

The morning sun was gentle, casting long stripes across the kitchen floor where Ben sat swinging his legs under the table. Jeff stood at the counter, stirring honey into two mugs of tea, humming something cheerful under his breath. It was one of those quiet Saturdays when the world didn't seem to be in any rush. They had mailed off the DNA kit a few days earlier. Now, they waited. "Alright, buddy," Jeff said, sliding a mug toward Ben, "today we mix a little old with a little new." Ben grinned, wrapping both hands around his warm mug. "Back to the house?" he asked eagerly. Jeff nodded. "Back to the house. The scrolls aren't going anywhere, and I think it's time we pull back a few more curtains."

Ben sipped his tea and smiled. "And we bring your phone, right? For the pictures?" Jeff chuckled. "Absolutely. We're living in the twenty-first century. If our ancestors had smartphones, imagine how easy this would've been." Ben laughed. "They would've texted each other all the secrets. Maybe even made TikTok's." Jeff made a mock grimace. "Heaven help us — medieval kings doing TikTok dances. That's a horror I don't need in my head."

As they finished breakfast, Annemarie packed them a small bag: sandwiches, bottled water, a notebook, and of course, Jeff's ever-present camera phone. "Careful with the old pages," she reminded them softly. "And no sword fights in the library." Ben giggled. "We promise." Jeff winked at her. "Your knights are honour-bound." The walk through the woods was beginning to feel familiar now. The trees whispered their old song, and the sun winked through the branches like it was keeping an eye on them. "Hey, Dad," Ben said as they walked, "do you think the trees remember?" Jeff smiled at the thought. "Maybe they do, son. Trees live for hundreds of years. Some of these might've watched your ancestors walk by long before us."

Ben looked up at the towering oaks, imagining shadowy figures with old cloaks and crowns drifting silently beneath the branches. "Maybe they saw King Béla." Jeff chuckled gently. "Maybe they did." His hand rested softly on Ben's shoulder. "And now they see you. That's pretty special." They reached the house just as the light shifted, golden beams threading through the ivy that curled like green fingers around the stone. Jeff pulled the old key from his pocket, and Ben stood close, holding his breath as the lock gave its soft sigh once again. The door opened like an old friend welcoming them back.

Inside, the air was still cool and smelled of old parchment and earth. The books, scrolls, and maps waited, exactly where they had left them. Dust danced like tiny fairies in the slanted light beams. The old tapestry still hung on the far wall, its crest glowing faintly in the soft glow. Jeff knelt first, carefully spreading his satchel open on the floor. "Alright, partner," he said, his voice light and easy, "today we're on a scavenger hunt." Ben grinned wide. "Scavenger hunt? Awesome! But... no time limit, right?" Jeff laughed. "Nope. We take our time. Piece by piece. No rushing."

They began slowly, lifting one scroll at a time, gently unrolling each with their fingertips. Jeff took photographs of each document with his phone, making sure to capture every symbol, every faint scratch of ink. Ben watched closely, his eyes bright. "Look, Dad, that one has the three dots again." Jeff leaned closer. "Good eye, Ben. You're already better at this than I was at your age." As they worked, Ben asked question after question. "Why do some names have different spellings?" Jeff smiled. "Because long ago, people didn't always spell things the same way. Sometimes it depended on who was writing it down." Ben scrunched his face. "That would make school tests so confusing." Jeff laughed. "That's why you don't let kings make spelling tests."

They paused often to jot down names into Jeff's notebook: strange names from old families, some with crowns drawn beside them, others with tiny stars or swords. Ben traced one symbol with his finger. "Árpád again," he whispered. Jeff nodded. "He keeps showing up, doesn't he?" After a while, Ben sat back against one of the old beams, resting his head. "Dad?" he asked softly. "Yeah, buddy?" "Will we ever find it all? All the answers?" Jeff set the scroll gently aside and looked his son square in the eyes. "We might never find everything, Ben. But that's okay. Because what we do find — it's like little lights that guide us. Every name, every place, every map is a step closer." Ben's eyes twinkled as he smiled. "Kind of like a treasure map, right?" Jeff smiled warmly. "Exactly like a treasure map."

They worked for hours that day, pausing often to eat their sandwiches and laugh at Jeff's terrible dad-jokes. "Why did the medieval knight always carry a pen, Ben?" Jeff asked with mock seriousness. Ben grinned, playing along. "Why?" "Because he wanted to draw his sword!" Jeff burst out laughing at his own joke while Ben groaned and rolled his eyes. "Dad, that's awful." Jeff held up his hands. "Hey, you're the one who signed up for this partnership." Ben giggled. "Best partnership ever."

As the light began to fade, Jeff closed the notebook and carefully packed the scrolls back into place. "That's enough for today," he said gently. "We don't want to tire your brain out." Ben nodded, standing up and stretching. "I like this, Dad. Even if it takes a long time." Jeff smiled and put an arm around his shoulders. "Me too, Ben. We're walking the path together. One step at a time."

As they locked up and headed home, the stars began blinking to life above them. Ben looked up, his voice full of wonder. "Do you think those stars watched them too?" Jeff smiled. "They've been watching us all for a very, very long time." And under those quiet, ancient stars, a boy and his dad walked home — carrying names, maps, scrolls, and the invisible threads of family that stretched far beyond anything they could yet see.

The house glowed with its evening warmth as Ben and Jeff stepped inside after their long afternoon at the old house. The smells of Annemarie's cooking had already begun to drift into every room — roasted chicken, buttered vegetables, and warm rolls that waited on the kitchen table like quiet little blessings. Jeff ruffled Ben's hair as they set down their satchels. "Looks like your mum's been busy while we were out doing detective work." Ben grinned and kicked off his shoes by the door. "I think the scrolls made me hungrier, Dad."

Annemarie greeted them with a smile that carried both love and a mother's quiet pride. "Washing hands first, gentlemen." She pointed toward the bathroom, pretending to sound strict, though her eyes danced. "Yes, ma'am!" Jeff replied with playful salute, and Ben followed him down the hall. Supper was filled with quiet chatter — not heavy questions about the scrolls or the old kings or the forgotten bloodlines. Just talk about silly things: the squirrel outside that nearly fell off the fence, Jeff's terrible attempt to whistle while unpacking scrolls, and how Ben managed to catch a grasshopper in his palm before letting it hop away.

Afterwards, they cleared the table together, their teamwork as steady as ever, and Annemarie kissed Ben's forehead before Jeff led him into his room to get ready for bed. The evening light had faded into a soft blue, the curtains gently swaying as the breeze crept in from the open window. Ben crawled into bed, tucking the corner of his pillow under his chin. Jeff knelt beside him, pulling the blanket up around his son's shoulders. The soft light of the bedside lamp painted golden edges on the shelves, where old books and a few scrolls rested, waiting for tomorrow's hands.

"I love you, son," Jeff whispered, his voice full and deep. Ben leaned up slightly, wrapping his arms tightly around his dad's neck and squeezing hard. "I love you too, Dad. Always." Kissing his dad on the cheek. Jeff smiled as he returned the hug and kiss, lingering just a moment longer, knowing how much that little heartbeat meant between them. "Goodnight, my boy." "Goodnight, Dad," Ben whispered as his head nestled into the pillow once again. The night slipped by gently, carrying dreams on silent wings.

By morning, the first beams of sunlight crept like soft fingers across the windowsill, waking the house as if it too stretched with them. The smell of toasted bread and fresh eggs filled the air before the clocks had even reached seven. Ben shuffled into the kitchen, still rubbing his eyes, as Jeff poured two cups of tea. "Good morning, sleepyhead," Jeff chuckled, sliding a plate toward him. "We've got more detective work today." Ben smiled and yawned. "I'm ready." They sat together over breakfast, their voices quieter now — the kind of quiet not born from boredom, but from focus. The work ahead wasn't fast, and they both knew it.

Later that morning, after Annemarie waved them off again, Jeff set up the laptop at the kitchen table while Ben brought over the leather notebook they'd been filling by hand. The Ancestry.com account blinked awake on the screen, its green tree growing slowly with every name they added. "Alright, son," Jeff said, smiling as he typed in another name from one of the scrolls, "we're building your living tree, one name at a time." Ben watched as the branches extended with every click, names appearing on the screen like stars twinkling into existence. "Some of these names I never even heard before."

Jeff nodded. "That's the beauty of it. You're discovering your own history while you're still writing it." They worked together, careful and steady. Jeff explained how they connected each grandparent, each great-grandparent, checking spellings, dates, and locations against the old scrolls. "Sometimes you'll see different last names pop up," Jeff explained, "because families change names over generations. Sometimes by marriage, sometimes by spelling changes, sometimes even by accident." Ben's eyes grew wider. "It's like a puzzle that keeps changing." Jeff smiled. "Exactly, buddy."

They filled out the maternal side together too, with Annemarie's help. She sat nearby, gently correcting dates and smiling quietly every time Ben asked for more names. "That was my great-grandfather," she said, pointing at one name. "He was born by the sea. He loved to fish more than anything." Jeff added softly, "And his stories are part of you now too." As the afternoon light dimmed, Jeff checked their Ancestry account again. "Now remember, Ben — the DNA test we mailed in... that part takes time." Ben tilted his head. "How long?"

"Well, sometimes it can take three, maybe even four weeks before all the results come back," Jeff explained. "The lab has to analyze your saliva sample carefully, compare it to thousands of other samples from people all around the world." Ben's face scrunched. "That's a long time." Jeff chuckled. "I know. But trust me — when it comes back, you'll start to see names you've never heard of before. Cousins. Distant cousins. Families with names that don't match ours at all, but are still part of you. People from all kinds of places." He paused. "And even some surprises." Ben leaned forward with a sparkle in his eyes. "Like treasure chests waiting to be opened?" Jeff smiled wide. "Exactly."

They spent the rest of the evening going back through some of the old maps they had photographed from the house. The names of far-off places whispered their presence as Jeff read them aloud: Denmark, Norway, France, Hungary... and beyond. Sometimes, Ben grew quiet as his small fingers traced the winding rivers on the map, his eyes clouding over with thought. Jeff never pushed when those moments came. He simply waited. The night always ended the same way — with stories, hugs, and another whispered goodnight. And as Ben drifted to sleep, his young heart carried both the weight and wonder of who he was, and who he was becoming.

The late morning sun slanted through the living room window as Jeff refreshed the screen. The Ancestry.com dashboard blinked back at them, its green bars slowly inching forward. "The lab says another week or two before the full DNA report uploads," Jeff said, his voice steady as always. "But meanwhile, there's more here we can keep building."

Ben leaned in close, eyes wide with quiet expectation. The little green leaves beside names fluttered on the screen — Ancestry's way of saying, We found something new. He pointed at one. "That leaf wasn't there before, was it?"

Jeff smiled. "Good eyes, Ben. No, it wasn't. The system's starting to connect pieces behind the scenes. It's pulling from historical records and other family trees. When people match with your DNA later, even more will show up."

They clicked the leaf together. A small window popped open, revealing a new hint — a marriage record from the early 1700s. The name was unfamiliar: Johannes Mørch of Denmark. Jeff's eyes narrowed slightly. "Ah. That's interesting."

Ben furrowed his brow. "Mørch? I don't know that name."

"You wouldn't," Jeff replied. "But if this hint's correct, it may trace back through your paternal side. And because we've already seen Denmark on the scrolls, this might not be the only surprise we're in for."
Ben sat back, his head slowly nodding. "It's like the scrolls whispered the names first, and now Ancestry's catching up." "That's exactly what's happening," Jeff chuckled. "Your DNA is like a beacon reaching out. The software is trying to find the pieces that match your blood."

After another hour of adding names, cross-checking dates, and peeking at census records, Jeff closed the laptop lid gently. "Alright, let's give the machine a break." Ben looked slightly disappointed but nodded. "Back to the house?" Jeff grinned. "You read my mind."

The old house stood patiently where they left it — as though it always expected them to return. Jeff unlocked the aged door and held it open for Ben. The air inside smelled of dust and cool stone, but not of decay.

It was like walking into the breath of time itself. Ben's footsteps echoed softly on the wooden floor. He glanced up at the high beams above. "Dad… do you think anyone else has ever found this stuff before us?" Jeff paused before answering. "If they have, they left it untouched. Maybe waiting for you."

They spread their gear carefully across the large round table at the centre of the room. The lantern Jeff brought gave off a steady glow. More scrolls lay bundled in the corner — some brittle, some sturdier, wrapped in linen cloth. Jeff handed Ben a pair of soft cotton gloves. "Alright, partner," Jeff said. "Slow and gentle, like we practised. We're here to learn — not to break history."

Ben smiled and slipped on the gloves, his small hands adjusting to the fabric. "I won't let anything rip." One scroll, more fragile than the others, caught Ben's eye. Jeff helped him unroll it slowly, holding both ends as the parchment stretched open.

The writing was faded but legible. A family tree, though not in English. It branched like the others but bore names they hadn't seen before. There at the top: György Árpád. Ben's breath caught softly. "Dad… that name…" Jeff nodded. "Yes. Árpád. Hungary again." He traced the curling lines with one gloved finger. "We've seen Béla before. But this one's older still. Further back." They spent the next two hours photographing the scrolls with Jeff's phone. Each photo was uploaded into a secure drive on Jeff's laptop for safe keeping, while Ben carefully labelled the files. "One day," Jeff said softly, "this entire room will be inside that little machine. But the real treasure's still in your blood."

As the afternoon light dimmed, Jeff poured them each a glass of cold orange juice from the cooler he always packed for these trips. They sat together in the fading glow, breathing in the quiet. Ben finally broke the silence. "Dad… does this mean I'm part Hungarian? I mean really Hungarian?" Jeff smiled gently. "Yes, Ben. Not just in name, but in blood. Your ancestors walked there long before Canada, long before Kent."

Ben's head tilted as he quietly absorbed the thought. "So I have pieces of them inside me?" "All of them," Jeff answered, his voice soft but sure. "The kings. The farmers. The ones who lived by rivers and the ones who stood in castles. All of them left pieces of themselves behind… right here." He reached out and lightly tapped Ben's chest. "Inside you." Ben placed his small hand over his heart and whispered, "That's a lot of people." "It is," Jeff smiled. "And that's why we take our time. One name at a time. One step at a time."

The sun slipped low behind the trees as they packed up for the evening. Jeff locked the old house carefully before they returned to the car. On the ride home, Ben stared quietly out the window while the countryside passed like a living map. Tomorrow would bring more. New names. New clues. New whispers from the past. But tonight, there would be home. There would be dinner. There would be stories and another warm hug before bed. And above all, there would be patience — because this was not just a mystery. This was his story.

Ben looked up at him. "That's Mum's side, right?" "Exactly," Jeff said gently. "This part tells us where your mother's mother, and her mother before her, came from." Ben leaned closer, his voice softer now. "It's real, isn't it? All of it. The scrolls. The dreams. The names." "It's very real, son." Jeff's voice was quiet, filled with steady pride. "And this is just the beginning." The page refreshed again as they moved into the DNA Matches tab. A long list of names appeared — most unfamiliar, some marked as distant cousins, others as close matches.

Jeff scanned the top name carefully. "Here's your closest match besides your mom." His eyes narrowed slightly. "Alan." Ben froze for a moment, his lips parting. "Alan. That's…" "Yes." Jeff's voice lowered. "That's your biological father's account. He must've done a test too." Ben stared at the screen, feeling something heavy sit in his chest. Not sadness exactly. Just weight. "So even though he's not here… he's still connected."

Jeff placed a calming hand on Ben's shoulder. "DNA doesn't lie, kiddo. It holds everything. Even when people disappear." Ben swallowed and whispered, "But I have you, Dad." Jeff's voice softened. "And I have you, son." They scrolled further, the names spinning like distant stars in the dark. A new name appeared on the lower screen. Not a close relative. But still connected. It read simply: Árpád Connection — Genetic Community: Hungary and Eastern Europe.

Ben leaned forward, his heartbeat quickening. "Dad… that name again. Árpád." Jeff's breath slowed. "Yes." His voice almost whispered. "And now you see how far this reaches." Ben stared, his young face both awed and cautious. "So, it's not just scrolls and dreams. It's in the computer too." "In your DNA, Ben," Jeff nodded. "That's why we started this. To let the pieces meet." For a long moment, neither of them spoke. They just stared at the screen while history quietly breathed through electric light.

The next morning dawned cool and bright, the kind of spring day that made the air taste sharp and clean. Ben woke earlier than usual, stirred not by alarm but by the quiet hum of excitement. His pillow still carried the faint warmth of his sleep as he sat up, rubbing his eyes. The light filtering through the curtains painted golden lines across his small bookshelf. Down the hallway, he could already hear Jeff moving about — brewing coffee, humming softly. Ben slipped into the kitchen, still barefoot, and greeted his dad with a sleepy grin. Jeff ruffled his hair. "Morning, kiddo. Guess what?"

Ben blinked. "What?" he asked, rubbing one eye. "The DNA results from Ancestry finally uploaded." Ben's eyes widened instantly, now fully awake. "Really? They're ready?" Jeff nodded and pointed toward the open laptop on the kitchen table. The green notification box on the screen glowed softly, waiting for them like a sealed letter from the past. "They just came in this morning."

Ben slid into the chair, his small hands gripping the edge of the table. "Can we look together?" "Of course," Jeff smiled. "We're a team, remember?" With a gentle click, Jeff opened the report. The screen filled with bars, percentages, and names—strange, beautiful, overwhelming. Ben's mouth dropped slightly open. "Whoa…" At the top, bold and unmistakable: 46% Scandinavian (Norway and Denmark). 27% France. 8% Ireland. 7% England & Northwestern Europe. 5% Germanic Europe. 2% Wales.

Ben whispered each region softly as Jeff read along. "That's a lot of places, Dad." Jeff nodded, his eyes focused but calm. "This, Ben, is the long trail of where your family's walked through history." Scrolling lower, they reached the maternal side: 46% Norway. 2% Sweden. 2% England & Northwestern Europe. The wind was light that afternoon as Jeff locked the car doors behind them. Ben stood close, his small hand curled around the strap of his backpack. The house loomed ahead, quiet beneath the ivy's heavy green curtain. Shadows leaned long across the grass, but the air felt calm. This time, they weren't nervous. They weren't scared. They were curious.

"Dad?" Ben whispered, his voice steady but thoughtful. "Do you think there's more here? Something that connects to Árpád?" Jeff placed a hand on his son's shoulder. "That's why we came back. Every time we open a scroll or a map, something new speaks." Ben nodded slowly. "I think... the house remembers." The door creaked softly as Jeff pushed it open. The familiar cool air wrapped around them like an old coat. Dust swirled in the thin beams of sunlight slicing through the boarded windows. They stepped lightly across the wooden floor, careful not to disturb anything. The table still held the books and rolled maps where they left them. The air smelled of paper and time.

Jeff set down his bag and pulled out the tablet. "We'll photograph each document today. Piece by piece." Ben opened his own smaller notebook, ready with sharpened pens. "We can match it later with the DNA stuff," Ben said. "Good thinking," Jeff smiled. "Let the paper and the blood speak together." They started with the large scroll from the leather tube. Jeff unrolled it gently across the table, holding the edges flat. The symbols twisted and danced under the dim light. Ben leaned closer, tracing the old ink with his eyes. "That's the triangle again," he whispered. "The same three dots." Jeff nodded. "It's like a signature. A seal passed down."

Ben pulled out his phone and snapped a photo, careful to avoid the glare. "Every part matters," Jeff said softly. "Even tiny marks might tell us something." They worked slowly, their movements careful and methodical. Every curl of script, every faded stamp was captured. An hour passed before they moved to the old ledger in the corner. The spine was cracked, but the pages inside still held strong. Jeff opened it to a page marked with a pressed violet. "Look," he said. "More names." Ben peered over. "Hungarian... I see it again, Dad. Árpád. And Béla." His heart thudded.

Jeff's voice stayed calm but firm. "There's your blood, Ben. Right there." Ben whispered, "It's not just on the website. It's right here too." His eyes gleamed with something close to awe. Jeff smiled faintly. "Yes, son. Both worlds—digital and ancient—are pointing to the same truth." The sun shifted as they worked through each piece. Jeff paused occasionally, letting Ben take the lead when possible. "You're learning fast," he said. "You've got good instincts." Ben grinned. "You're teaching me, Dad." The word still made Jeff's chest tighten with warmth.

As twilight crept in, they packed the documents carefully into folders. Jeff zipped the tablet into his bag, double-checking each photo. "We'll review all this tonight. Compare it with what Ancestry gave us." Ben nodded. "It's like solving a mystery." Jeff smiled. "Exactly. And every clue brings us closer." They stepped back outside, locking the house behind them. The ivy rustled gently as the night breeze swept through. Ben glanced up at the stars blinking awake. "Do you think they're watching us, Dad? The ones who came before?" Jeff glanced skyward too, his voice soft. "Maybe, son. Maybe they've been waiting for us all along."

The kitchen table was covered again. Scrolls rested gently beside Jeff's tablet, while Ben's open notebook waited for more notes. The lamp cast a warm circle of light across the parchment. Dinner plates sat nearby, pushed aside but not forgotten. The night was cool outside, but inside, it was filled with quiet excitement. Jeff adjusted his glasses and tapped the tablet screen. "The Ancestry update arrived earlier today," he said softly.

Ben leaned in, his eyes wide. "It did? Already?" Jeff smiled. "Well, part of it. There's still more to come, but enough to get us started." Ben swallowed, heart thudding. "What did it say?" Jeff scrolled carefully, pulling up the newest family matches. The names came slowly across the screen—some familiar, most not. "Here," Jeff pointed. "See these? These names match clusters from Hungary and Norway. And this one—Denmark. They're connecting back further than your great-grandparents now."

Ben's breath caught as he read the surnames. "But I've never even heard of half of these." Jeff nodded. "That's how this works. Blood travels even when names get lost. Your ancestors carried many names, some of them hidden for centuries." Ben whispered, "It's like finding ghosts that were never scary." Jeff chuckled softly. "Yes, son. And look—there's something else." He tapped a separate chart—"Ancient Connections." A small chart expanded on the screen, showing haplogroups again. "R-S660 and H5a1," Jeff said quietly.

"That's you. Same as the scrolls." Ben whispered the letters to himself. "R-S660… H5a1." His fingers brushed the edge of the scrolls beside him. "It's real. All of it's real." Jeff's voice lowered. "Árpád… Béla… they were not just names in your dreams. They were men who lived, led, and left something behind." Ben's eyes flicked up. "But why me?" Jeff placed a hand on his shoulder. "Because blood remembers, even if people forget.

You didn't choose it. You carry it." Ben blinked, feeling both small and important all at once. "Does that mean… we're royal?" Jeff smiled gently. "You come from a royal line. That's true. But what matters is what you carry forward, not what sits in the past." The tablet screen softly dimmed as Jeff closed the files. "We're going to build the tree piece by piece. Carefully. Patiently. No guessing, no rushing." Ben nodded. "We've got time." Jeff smiled. "Yes, son. We've got time." The house grew quiet as the clock ticked softly above them.

Ben glanced back at the old scrolls one more time. "Do you think they knew I'd find it one day?" Jeff breathed slowly. "Maybe they hoped you would. And maybe, just maybe… they left it for you to finish." The next morning, the house smelled of toast and cinnamon. The scroll tube sat on the table like it always had, quiet and waiting. Ben sat with his cereal, but his eyes never left the leather tube. Jeff noticed and smiled as he poured his coffee. "You're still thinking about it, aren't you?" he asked softly.

Ben nodded. "I keep wondering if there's more in there." Jeff chuckled gently. "We've unrolled the scroll three times. We've read every word." But as he said it, something pulled at him. He set his mug down and reached for the tube. "Let's check once more. Slowly." Carefully, Jeff opened the tube, pulling the scroll out with both hands. The parchment felt thin but strong, breathing as it uncurled. He ran his fingers along the inner leather of the empty tube. "Sometimes, old scroll makers would hide thin inserts behind linings to protect important pieces."

Ben leaned closer, his eyes sharp. "Like secret compartments?" Jeff nodded. "Exactly." His fingertip found a faint crease. "Ah," he whispered. "Feel this, son." Ben reached out, running his small finger along the seam. "It's hollow." His voice rose with excitement. Jeff smiled. "Let's see what's inside." Gently, using a small wooden pick, Jeff worked at the crease until the inner lining loosened. With a soft tug, a thin, folded sheet slid free. It was smaller than the scroll, but thicker, like pressed vellum. The edges were smooth, almost untouched by time.

Ben's breath quickened. "What is it?" Jeff unfolded the sheet carefully on the table. The ink was darker, fresher than the scroll's. At the top, a familiar crest appeared — the lions, the crown, and the three dots in a triangle. Beneath it, delicate script written in a language neither of them had seen before. Ben stared, his eyes wide. "Is that… Hungarian?" he asked. Jeff shook his head slowly. "Older. Much older. Maybe early Magyar, or something that predates it entirely." His fingers traced the edges without touching the ink. "This was hidden for a reason."

Beneath the ancient words was a hand-drawn chart — not a tree exactly, but a chain. Circles connected by lines, stretching backward. Names written in strange symbols, but beneath them, small Romanized names offered rough translations. "Árpád… Zolta… Taksony… Géza… Béla…" Jeff read aloud. Ben's breath caught. "That's the dream name," he whispered. "Béla." Jeff nodded slowly. "Yes, son. And these were kings. Long before even England's kings ruled. Your blood reaches far beyond castles and crowns we read in school."

Ben whispered softly, "It's like walking backward through time." Jeff smiled warmly. "That's exactly what genealogy is, son. Following the river upstream, one bend at a time." Ben's eyes shimmered. "I never thought it would be this real." Jeff placed a hand on Ben's shoulder. "It's real because you're part of it. And we'll follow it together. Slowly. Carefully." The parchment seemed to breathe between them, like the story itself was alive, waiting to be retold. "This is only the beginning."

A few days passed before Jeff and Ben returned to the house again. The air smelled of damp earth as they walked beneath the arching trees, their footsteps cushioned by fallen leaves. Ben carried his backpack tightly against his chest. Inside were the photos they had taken of the scrolls and the hidden chart. Jeff walked beside him, hands in his coat pockets, keeping his pace steady. "You doing alright, Ben?" he asked gently. Ben nodded, but his voice came soft. "It feels like… like we're walking through my own bones, Dad." Jeff smiled, a bit sad but proud. "That's a good way of saying it." The trees seemed to nod with them, swaying softly in the morning breeze. Ahead, the house appeared again, crooked but familiar. The ivy had grown just a little more, curling tighter around the stone chimney like silent fingers.

Inside, the air was cool and still. The room welcomed them like an old friend. Jeff set down his bag and looked around. "We won't touch the scrolls today," he said. "I want us to focus on the maps." Ben pulled out his tablet and camera. "We're photographing everything, right?" Jeff nodded. "Exactly. We'll copy every piece. That way, nothing ever gets lost, even if the house someday fades." They moved carefully through the room. Maps were unrolled one by one, some so fragile Jeff handled them only with gloved fingers. Rivers twisted across faded parchment like veins. Mountains rose in tiny hand-drawn strokes. Small towns were circled in faded red ink. Ben took pictures of each, zooming in on names he couldn't pronounce. "Dad, look. This one says 'Marden.'" Jeff leaned closer. "Kent, England. That's where your surname roots likely began."

Ben's brow furrowed. "But that's only one part." Jeff pointed to another map, this one older. "See this path? It crosses Denmark, Norway, all the way to the north, through Tromsø, then into Hungary." Ben whispered, "Like following threads through time." Jeff's eyes twinkled. "Exactly. Every family is made of threads, son. Woven tighter than most people realize." They continued for hours, photographing every scrap, every mark. Ben's tablet filled quickly. "We'll organize these back home," Jeff said softly. "Piece by piece." Ben's voice came lighter now, filled with quiet excitement. "Dad, can we make our own family book? With the maps and everything?" Jeff smiled. "That's exactly what we're doing."

Back home, the evening was gentle. The air conditioner hummed softly as they spread the printed photographs across the kitchen table. Ben sat cross-legged in his chair, eyes darting between the images. "We've got so many now," he whispered. Jeff placed a hand on his shoulder. "We do. And every single one tells us something new, even if it doesn't feel like it yet."

Ben tapped one image of the Kent map. "This one's my favourite," he said. "Because that's where it started, right? Marden?" Jeff nodded. "That's where your paternal line likely began, centuries ago. Long before surnames even existed the way they do now." Ben's voice softened. "So… they didn't even call themselves Pattenden yet?" Jeff smiled gently. "No. Back then, names shifted like rivers. But the blood was already there."

As the clock ticked, Annemarie brought them warm tea and a plate of oatmeal cookies. "You boys have been at it for hours," she said softly, smiling. Ben reached for a cookie. "We don't even feel the time anymore, Mom." She chuckled, brushing his hair back. "Just don't fall asleep at the table again." Jeff winked. "That's happened twice now." Later that night, Jeff tucked Ben into bed. The boy pulled his blanket to his chin, eyes wide even in the dim light. "Dad… how much longer for the DNA results?" Jeff sat on the edge of the bed. "It could be three more weeks. Sometimes a bit less. They're testing it carefully, son." Ben sighed but nodded. "I hope they find something." Jeff leaned down, giving him a firm hug. "They will, Ben. And when they do, we'll read it together."

The morning came with soft sunlight streaking through the curtains. Ben padded into the kitchen still half-asleep, but Jeff was already there with the laptop open. "Want to update the tree?" he asked with a grin. Ben slid into his chair and nodded eagerly. Jeff guided him through entering the names they had found so far, each one clicking into place like puzzle pieces. "Look at that," Jeff whispered. "It's filling up." Ben paused, reading the growing list of surnames. Some felt familiar. Others looked ancient. "Dad, when we get the DNA match list… will it show us more names?" Jeff smiled warmly. "Yes. And some you'll never have heard before. Cousins you didn't know existed. Families that branched out in ways you never imagined." Ben whispered, "It's like meeting ghosts who are still alive." Jeff chuckled softly. "That's one way of putting it."

The house was quiet except for the soft ticking of the clock in the hallway. Ben lay in bed staring at the ceiling, eyes open wide despite the darkness. The hum of the air conditioner whispered in the background, but his thoughts were louder. The names on the family tree kept swirling in his head like leaves in the wind. Every night brought more questions. More wonder. More waiting. He rolled onto his side, pulling the blanket higher. "Dad?" he whispered into the night. Jeff's footsteps padded softly down the hall. "I'm here, Ben," he said, slipping into the room. Jeff sat beside him on the edge of the bed. "Can't sleep?" Ben shook his head. "I keep thinking… What if there's even more we don't know yet?" Jeff smiled gently. "There always is, son. That's the beauty of it."

Ben's voice softened to a whisper. "I don't want to miss anything." Jeff smoothed the boy's hair back. "You won't. We're taking it piece by piece. That's how real history works. Not all at once, but slowly, like uncovering buried treasure with your hands instead of shovels." Ben gave a small smile. "I like that." Jeff leaned in. "Good. Because that's exactly what we're doing." As the night deepened, the dreams returned.

This time, Ben stood in a great hall lined with torches flickering against old stone walls. Banners hung from the rafters, each marked with the crest he knew so well: the lions, the ribbon, the three dots. Voices echoed in languages he could almost understand. It wasn't frightening. It was peaceful. Like listening to a story being told to him by someone very old.

When morning light spilled through the curtains, Ben woke with the dream still fresh. He sat up slowly, whispering to himself, "Horváth." The name felt heavier now, like it carried weight with every breath. Jeff appeared in the doorway, coffee in hand. "Rough night?" he asked softly. Ben shook his head. "No. Just... full." Jeff nodded. "That means you're learning. That's good." At breakfast, they sat together, reviewing the growing tree on Ancestry.com. "Look," Jeff pointed, "this new branch came in overnight. A fourth cousin in Denmark." Ben squinted at the name. "How do they even find that?" Jeff grinned. "The DNA tells them, Ben. It's like finding little cousins hiding in your blood." Ben giggled. "That sounds weird." Jeff laughed too. "It is weird. But it's true."

Later that afternoon, Jeff and Ben sat at the dining table surrounded by books, maps, and the glow of the laptop screen. "Look here, Ben," Jeff said, tapping the monitor gently. "See how the tree is spreading out now? Some names are unfamiliar, but others might link back to the scrolls." Ben leaned closer. His eyes darted across names like Tromsø, Harstad, and Bodø. "These are in Norway," Ben whispered. Jeff nodded. "Right. And remember? These places showed up on the scroll too."

The scrolls lay nearby, carefully wrapped, waiting for their next examination. "Dad," Ben said softly, "why does it feel like the computer and the scrolls are talking to each other?" Jeff chuckled warmly. "Because, in a way, they are. The DNA helps fill in the blanks, and the scrolls give us the stories." Ben smiled, understanding the rhythm of discovery. "It's like they're building a puzzle together." Jeff patted his shoulder. "Exactly. And we get to be the ones who see the picture forming."

As evening settled in, the house filled with a familiar, calming quiet. Annemarie prepared tea while listening in from the kitchen. Ben traced his finger along one of the Norwegian towns on the screen. "Dad, do you think they lived in castles like the one I dream about?" Jeff smiled but answered carefully. "Maybe some did. But most lived simple lives — fishing, farming, building small villages. The castles were rare. But the bloodlines? They spread everywhere." Ben's eyes widened. "So, I could be connected to both — kings and farmers?" Jeff nodded. "That's what makes it special. Every part matters."

Before bedtime, they returned to one of the old scrolls. Jeff gently unrolled it while Ben watched, wide-eyed. The parchment whispered as it stretched, revealing more names etched in that strange script. "These marks," Ben whispered, pointing to a cluster of symbols, "they keep showing up." Jeff studied the lines. "That's Old Magyar, Ben. It's a language very few people still use. But your blood remembers it." Ben looked up at him. "The voice I heard... it spoke like that." Jeff's expression softened. "And that's why we take our time, son."

Night fell, and Jeff tucked Ben into bed as always. The boy's voice was drowsy but filled with wonder. "Dad," he whispered, "how much further does this go?" Jeff smiled, brushing the hair from Ben's forehead. "Farther than we can see. But we'll follow it together." Ben's eyes closed with a soft smile. "I like that." Jeff kissed his forehead. "Sleep well, my son. Tomorrow is another page."

The next morning arrived with a golden light spilling through the kitchen window. Jeff was already at the table, sipping his coffee, reviewing new updates on the ancestry chart. Ben slid into his chair, rubbing the sleep from his eyes. "Dad... anything new?" he asked with curiosity. Jeff smiled and turned the laptop slightly so Ben could see. "Yes. The lab finished processing part of your DNA match list. Some new connections popped up overnight." Ben's face lit up, his energy instantly rising with the possibilities.

Jeff pointed to one of the names on the screen. "See this match here? This person shares a lot of DNA with you. A distant cousin." Ben studied the list of names carefully. "They live in Denmark?" he asked. "Yes," Jeff answered. "In fact, this one traces back to Sjælland — remember the name from the scroll?" Ben's eyes widened again. "That's one of the places we saw before!" Jeff nodded. "Exactly, Ben. That's one of your ancient homes."

They scrolled further, new surnames appearing that neither of them recognized. "Why are there so many names I don't know, Dad?" Ben asked. Jeff gently explained, "Because families change names over time. People move, languages shift, marriages happen, and sometimes even kings lose their crowns." Ben frowned, trying to imagine it all. "It's like a giant web." Jeff smiled. "That's a perfect way to say it. The family tree isn't just a tree — it's a whole forest."

Ben stared at one particular name for a long time. "Dad, what's this one? Árpád?" The name felt heavy on his tongue, almost familiar. Jeff's eyes grew thoughtful. "That's an ancient name, Ben. A ruler from Hungary many centuries ago. It keeps appearing for a reason." Ben whispered, "The dreams..." Jeff nodded quietly. "Yes. Even your dreams seem to remember."

After breakfast, Jeff pulled out one of the large genealogical charts they had started together. "Let's fill in a few more branches, Ben." With his pen poised, Ben looked at the screen, then back to the paper. "Should I write Alan's name first, since that's where it starts?" Jeff nodded solemnly. "Yes, son. As much as I'm your dad, the tree starts with him." Ben's face showed both sadness and acceptance. "And you'll stay right here with me?" Jeff smiled, placing a hand on his son's shoulder. "Always, Ben. Every step."

As the weeks passed, more results trickled in. Jeff checked the updates daily, always before Ben woke up, so he could have something new ready to explore at breakfast. That morning, Jeff smiled as he saw the message flashing: "New Matches Available." The screen now displayed additional names, stretching beyond Europe and touching parts of Scotland, France, and Hungary once again. When Ben shuffled in, still rubbing his eyes, Jeff was already waiting with the screen lit up.

Ben's face brightened instantly. "More cousins?" he asked eagerly. Jeff nodded. "More cousins. And some interesting surprises." He pointed to a name marked in bold — an unfamiliar surname from Eastern Europe. "This one shares a high percentage of DNA with you. Much closer than the others." Ben leaned in, his eyes tracing the name carefully. "Dad… who's that?" Jeff replied softly, "Someone we'll need to research, Ben. The further we go, the more names we find."

After breakfast, they sat at the big table where the scrolls and old maps still waited. "Let's keep building," Jeff said, unrolling a fresh piece of paper for the growing family chart. Ben carefully added new branches, each name written in neat letters. "It's like a puzzle that never ends," Ben whispered. Jeff smiled. "That's genealogy, son. It's not about finishing. It's about discovering." Ben paused and looked at his dad thoughtfully. "But what if we find something we don't like?" Jeff placed a steady hand on Ben's arm. "Then we face it together."

Later that afternoon, Annemarie joined them at the table. She had pulled out old family photos from her own box of keepsakes. "These were your great-grandparents," she said, handing Ben an old photograph. The black-and-white image showed a serious-looking couple standing outside a tiny stone church. Ben studied the picture carefully. "They look strong," he said softly. His mother smiled. "They were. And their stories flow inside you, just like everyone else we find." Ben held the photo for a long moment, as if memorizing the faces.

As the evening cooled, Jeff sat with Ben on the back porch under a quiet sky. The stars began to appear, one by one, like tiny lights leading them further into the past. "Look up there," Jeff whispered. "Every star is like a name on your tree. Each one a part of your story." Ben leaned against his dad's arm and whispered back, "Then I've got a lot of stars." Jeff chuckled softly. "Yes, you do, Ben. And we've only just begun counting."

The next morning brought an unexpected delivery. Jeff opened the door to find a slim package resting against the step. No sender was listed, but the handwriting was unmistakable — the same old script as the scrolls. He carried it inside with both hands, setting it carefully on the table where Ben was finishing his oatmeal. "Another surprise?" Ben asked with wide eyes. Jeff nodded slowly. "Looks that way. But this one's different."

Ben watched as his dad sliced through the wax seal. Inside was a tightly rolled map, its edges browned by age but still strong. Jeff unrolled it gently, revealing a landscape neither of them recognized. There were mountains, rivers, and coastlines—but no city names, no country borders. Only symbols marked certain spots: spirals, crowns, and those three familiar dots in a triangle. Ben leaned closer, his breath catching. "Dad… look. The dots."

Jeff traced his finger over one of the spirals. "These aren't just places, Ben. These might be migration paths. Routes your ancestors travelled long before maps had names." Ben's voice was soft.

"How can a map have no names?" Jeff smiled faintly. "Because sometimes, places existed before people knew what to call them. This map tells a story older than language." Ben nodded, eyes wide with wonder, as though the paper itself was breathing secrets.

They worked slowly, comparing the map to the scrolls and Ancestry.com results. Some symbols lined up with places they had already discovered—Norway, Hungary, Denmark—but others remained mysteries. Jeff jotted notes in the margins, marking each connection with care. "It's like a trail left for us," Ben whispered. Jeff chuckled. "Or a puzzle only you were meant to solve, my son."

That evening, Annemarie joined them again, studying the map under lamplight. "This one looks different than the others," she said thoughtfully. "It's not just a map. It's a memory." Ben looked up at her. "A memory?" She nodded. "A memory passed down, hidden in drawings and symbols. And now it's waiting for you to finish it." Jeff gently placed a hand on Ben's shoulder. "And we'll finish it together."

Days passed, but the map remained on the table like a sleeping dragon. Ben studied it every morning, tracing his finger over the twisting rivers and the empty spaces. The lack of names no longer frightened him. Instead, it pulled him in, like the map was daring him to listen rather than look. Jeff noticed this quiet obsession but allowed it, watching his son's growing hunger for understanding. "You're hearing the map, aren't you?" Jeff asked one evening. Ben smiled faintly. "I think so, Dad."

They returned to the old house again, taking the careful path they had walked so many times before. The books were still where they had left them, the scrolls wrapped and stacked like patient old friends. Jeff carried a portable scanner this time. "We'll scan the fragile ones," he explained, "so you can study them at home without risk." Ben nodded, excited. "We're building a library, Dad. Our library."

Inside one of the older books, tucked behind a loose binding, Ben found a small slip of paper. It wasn't old like the others—more recent, written in Alan's rough hand. Jeff unfolded it carefully. The note read: The answers aren't all here. Some are in the church records. Start where I couldn't. Marden Parish. Jeff's brow furrowed. "Marden Parish," he repeated softly. Ben tilted his head. "Where's that?" "Kent, England," Jeff answered. "Your ancestral home."

That night at home, the three of them sat around the computer. Jeff pulled up a digital map and zoomed in on Kent. "See? Right there—Marden." Ben leaned in, eyes wide. "That's where it really started?" Jeff nodded. "As far as we can trace on paper, yes. Your blood remembers more, but these records might help us fill in the gaps." Ben whispered, "It feels… close, even though it's far away."

Annemarie placed a gentle hand on Ben's back. "Sometimes your past isn't as distant as it seems. It lives inside you every day." Jeff smiled at her words. "We'll start requesting church records from Marden. Baptisms, marriages, burial registers. Sometimes they hold names never written anywhere else." Ben's heart thudded. "We'll find more names, won't we?" Jeff's voice was steady. "Yes, son. We will."

The days grew busy again. Ben balanced school while Jeff managed the requests. Old scanned documents began to arrive in their email. Faded pages with handwritten entries, dates reaching back hundreds of years. Jeff printed each one, adding them to a growing binder on the dining table. "See this?" Jeff pointed one night. "Here's a Pattenden listed in 1723. A piece of your line." Ben's fingers hovered over the paper like it was made of gold. "That's my family."

Evenings at the dinner table had become quieter but fuller. The binder sat close, always within reach, as though it were part of the family now. Ben often flipped through its pages while eating, his eyes scanning the names like they might whisper their secrets if he looked long enough. Jeff watched this with quiet pride. "The names aren't just names, Ben," he said one evening. "They're pieces of lives. Marriages, births, even heartache." Ben nodded slowly, the weight of it starting to settle. "And they're still part of me."

On weekends, they visited the local archive, pulling up British records that were harder to find online. Jeff showed Ben how to request microfilm copies, how to read old cursive that twisted and looped like vines. Ben learned fast. His small finger followed each entry carefully, sounding out names softly as though afraid to disturb the silence of the room. "This one, Dad—William Pattenden, 1647." Jeff smiled. "Excellent catch, son."

The list of names grew. Pattenden. Baker. Lovelace. And others—some familiar, others foreign. Annemarie helped when she could, filling in maternal lines from her own memory. "Your grandmother was a Jensen," she said one afternoon, pulling out an old shoebox of photos. Ben carefully added the names to the family tree on Ancestry.com, watching the branches expand like the roots of an old oak. "It's getting big," Ben whispered. Jeff placed a steady hand on his shoulder. "And we've only scratched the surface."

At bedtime, Jeff would tuck Ben in, but the conversations didn't stop. They talked about kings and migrations, about people crossing seas long before airplanes or cars. "Did my family ever come from Norway?" Ben asked one night. Jeff nodded. "Yes, from the fjords. And some from Denmark. Some even much further—central Europe, thousands of years ago." Ben blinked. "That long?" "That long," Jeff whispered. "Your story started before even castles were built."

Sometimes, after Jeff turned out the light, Ben would lay awake staring at the ceiling, thinking about those names. He could almost hear them—like voices caught between time and sleep. Árpád. Béla. Names that didn't sound like the others, but stirred something deeper in his chest. He whispered them softly in the dark, like prayers he didn't quite understand. "Árpád," he said. "Béla." The names clung to the air, waiting.

As the weeks passed, an email finally arrived that made Jeff's breath hitch. "Ben!" he called from the living room. Ben came running, barefoot, wide-eyed. "Is it here?" Jeff smiled and turned the laptop toward him. "The DNA results just came in." Ben's heart jumped. The digital wheel spun, revealing pie charts, percentages, and ancient origins. His father's voice lowered with reverence. "It's time to see where you really come from, son."

CHAPTER 3: THE BLOOD THAT REMEMBERS

The morning sun sliced through the kitchen blinds, casting soft gold lines across the small table where Ben sat waiting. His spoon clinked lightly against the bowl of oatmeal, but his eyes weren't on the food. They never were in the mornings now. His thoughts always drifted to the scrolls, to the maps, to the strange names still swirling in his head like half-forgotten dreams. Across from him, Jeff poured coffee slowly, eyes fixed on the steam as it rose like thin smoke toward the ceiling. Neither of them spoke right away. These quiet mornings had become their rhythm.

Finally, Ben broke the silence. "Dad," he said softly, testing the word again on his tongue. It still felt new, but it fit like it was always waiting. Jeff glanced up, smiling gently. "Yes, son?" Ben hesitated a second, then whispered, "Do you think they knew? The people who came before us? That one day we'd be looking for them?" Jeff rested his elbows on the table, folding his hands beneath his chin. "Maybe not us exactly. But they knew someone would have to remember. Blood remembers even when names are lost."

The words hung in the air, both comforting and heavy. Ben pushed the bowl slightly aside and traced invisible shapes across the table's surface with his finger. "It's strange," he whispered, "to feel like I know people I've never met." Jeff nodded. "That's how family works, Ben. You carry their echoes whether you realize it or not." He sipped his coffee, then added, "That's why we keep going, one piece at a time. We're not just building your tree. We're waking it up."

Ben's small smile twitched at the corner of his mouth. "I like that. Waking it up." Jeff reached over, gently ruffling Ben's hair. "And we've got a lot more waking to do." He set his cup down, shifting gears. "After breakfast, we'll scan the next scroll. I brought the portable scanner last night." Ben's eyes lit up. "You mean we get to go back today?" "We sure do," Jeff confirmed. "And after we're done, we'll add anything new into your tree on Ancestry."

The boy bounced slightly in his seat, his earlier nerves washed away by the simple excitement of discovery. Even as the gravity of their task loomed quietly beneath the surface, Jeff kept him grounded. "Step by step, remember?" he said softly. Ben nodded, repeating the words like a promise. "Step by step."

By mid-morning, they stood once again beneath the ivy-wrapped stone archway. The house, though unchanged in its silence, seemed somehow more familiar with each visit — like an old relative growing comfortable with their return. The key, still warm from Ben's pocket, slid into the weathered lock without hesitation. The low sigh of stone welcomed them inside, where the cool air whispered across their faces.

Jeff flicked on his small lantern, careful not to disturb anything. Ben carried the soft-lined case with their scanning equipment tucked inside. They moved together, methodical now, like explorers who had learned how to handle ancient places with respect.

"Same routine," Jeff said softly. "One scroll at a time, nothing forced." Ben nodded, setting the case gently atop the stone table where books and maps already waited like sleeping voices.

Jeff unfolded the first parchment. The edges crackled faintly, but the ink still held firm beneath the years. This scroll was different than the others. Less decorative. More technical. A tree. Not drawn like the electronic charts they'd started building on Ancestry.com. This one was hand-rendered, spiralling outward like branches from an invisible centre. "Look, Dad," Ben whispered. "There's my name again. Benedicere. Near the bottom." Jeff leaned in, eyes narrowing. "And see here—these branches connecting from Hungary... crossing to Denmark... then back through Norway."

Ben's finger hovered over one corner. "That's Tromsø, isn't it?" "It is," Jeff nodded. "That's one of the points your blood carries. You've seen it in the tests." Ben exhaled, his breath fogging slightly in the cool air. "So... they wrote this before there were even DNA tests?" Jeff smiled. "Long before. They couldn't see your genes like we can now, but they understood the line. They recorded what they could feel." The weight of that truth sat heavily between them, but Jeff softened it, as always. "That's why we've got both: their records, and ours."

They scanned carefully, preserving every fragile fold in perfect digital form. As the device hummed quietly, Ben glanced at his father with a question brewing in his chest. "Dad… do you think one day someone will look at my name the way we're looking at theirs?" Jeff's eyes twinkled gently. "Someone already is." Ben's face flushed slightly, unsure if that comforted or overwhelmed him. But the work kept his hands steady. They were waking the tree. And the tree was answering.

The scanning finished just as the afternoon light shifted. Thin beams slipped through the old wooden shutters, making the dust dance like tiny stars caught in some ancient current. Ben carefully folded the scroll back into its protective wrap while Jeff stowed the scanner inside its case. The boy's fingers lingered on the leather tie before fastening it, as if reluctant to let go of the names etched inside. "It feels weird," Ben whispered, "like I'm touching them."

"You are," Jeff answered gently, zipping the case shut. "Every name is a hand reaching back. And now you're reaching forward." They stood still for a moment, letting that thought breathe. The house creaked softly above them, but it was not an unsettling sound — more like a tired building whispering its agreement. Jeff glanced toward the ceiling. "We're not finished here. Not yet. But for today, that's enough." Ben exhaled and nodded. "Step by step."

They stepped back into the cool evening air. The old house behind them seemed to sigh again as the door closed. Jeff locked it carefully, as though tucking an old friend to sleep. "Tomorrow?" Ben asked, hopeful. Jeff smiled. "Tomorrow. But tonight—" He reached over and gave Ben a playful nudge. "Pizza. Extra cheese." Ben grinned wide. "And root beer?" "Deal," Jeff laughed.

As they walked back along the narrow path toward the car, the night crickets began their songs. Ben tilted his head back, studying the first stars punching through the deepening sky. "You know, Dad," he said, "it feels like the stars are part of it too." Jeff looked up beside him, nodding. "The sky's always been the first map, son. Before paper. Before names." They stood quietly a moment longer. The wind curled through the trees like an unseen voice whispering: Remember.

The kitchen table had become their second library. Every evening, after dinner and before bed, Jeff and Ben sat across from each other surrounded by stacks of notes, printed DNA charts, maps, and family names slowly forming their puzzle. The laptop glowed softly, displaying Ancestry.com's branching tree. Each click added a new connection. Each name breathed life into the lines.

Ben squinted at the screen. "So, we put Alan's name here, because... well, that's where the line starts for me on his side, right?" Jeff nodded slowly. "Exactly. Even though he left, he's still part of your genetic path. We don't erase people from the tree. We just understand where they fit." Ben chewed on his lip. "But you're my dad." Jeff smiled gently. "And that's what matters. Blood gives us history. Love gives us family."

They worked slowly, carefully. Annemarie would peek in from time to time with cocoa or slices of apple, offering quiet encouragement. She let Jeff guide Ben through the complicated web of surnames, places, and dates, her presence a steady comfort. When names came up from her side, she would quietly correct spellings or fill in gaps. "That's your great-grandpa from Norway, Ben. He was a fisherman," she'd say softly, smiling as her own memories surfaced.

Jeff explained the charts one step at a time. "You see these percentages here? That's your ethnic breakdown. Like how much of your blood comes from different places." Ben read them aloud slowly: "Forty-six percent Norway… forty percent Denmark and the rest from all these others — Wales, Ireland, France, Hungary…" His voice trailed, thoughtful. "It's like a map made out of numbers."

Jeff chuckled. "Exactly. The numbers tell part of your story. The rest we find together." Ben leaned back in his chair, blinking at the glowing tree on the screen. "Dad, it's so... big." Jeff's voice dropped to a whisper. "That's because you don't just carry one story, son. You carry thousands." A few days later, they made another visit to the old house beneath the ivy. The air was cooler this time, touched with autumn's edge. The leaves whispered overhead as Jeff carried his small digital camera while Ben brought his notebook. They moved through the rooms like quiet explorers, careful not to disturb anything.

Ben knelt beside a stack of ancient scrolls that rested on a side table near the stone fireplace. The scrolls had been carefully rolled and tied with faded ribbon. He glanced up at Jeff. "Should we open them today?" Jeff smiled gently. "One at a time, son. We don't need to race history." Ben nodded. He liked that. The idea of moving slow. Letting the story breathe. Jeff placed the camera gently on the table.

"We'll photograph everything before we unroll them. That way, nothing gets lost if something breaks." The camera clicked softly, capturing the faded wax seals and the elegant, curling script. "This writing feels alive," Ben whispered, watching the screen. "It is," Jeff answered. "Because people wrote it for you, even if they never knew you."

As they continued, Ben spotted a thick leather-bound book tucked behind a carved wooden box. Its spine was cracked, and the leather was darkened with age. Jeff helped him lift it carefully. "Let's see what secrets you're ready for," Jeff said quietly. They opened it on the small stone table beneath the old lantern.

Inside were names — many names — written in narrow columns. The handwriting shifted from page to page, some neat, some rushed, as if several people had written over the years. "Look," Ben whispered, tracing a line with his finger. "There's Denmark again. And Norway." His voice grew softer. "And Hungary." Jeff nodded. "The same lands we saw in your DNA." Ben's brow furrowed as he read another name lower down. "Árpád... Béla." The words tasted strange but familiar in his mouth. "They keep coming back, Dad." Jeff smiled softly, his voice quiet. "Because you carry them, Ben. Not just in your blood. In your memory."

Ben sat for a long time, staring at the open book. His small hands rested on the smooth stone table, but his mind wandered far beyond the room. The names whispered like echoes in his head, soft but persistent. He didn't know how he could feel close to people who had lived hundreds, even thousands of years before him. Jeff watched him quietly, not rushing his son. The boy's silence was thoughtful, not afraid. Finally, Ben looked up. "Dad… do you think they knew about me?" His voice trembled slightly. Jeff leaned forward, resting his arms on the table. "In a way, yes," he said softly. "They knew they were building something bigger than themselves. A family that would stretch beyond their own lives."

Ben's eyes shimmered as he listened. "Like a chain," he whispered, "and I'm another link." Jeff smiled warmly. "Exactly. And you're a strong one." The words comforted Ben more than he expected. He felt important, not because of what he would become, but because of where he came from. The wind outside tapped gently at the old windows as if listening to their conversation. Jeff pulled out his small tablet from his bag and opened their Ancestry.com tree. "Let's enter some of these names while we're here," he said. "If we document it now, we won't forget." Ben nodded eagerly, shifting closer to see the screen.

They worked side by side, filling in names and dates. Each name made the tree on the screen grow larger, its branches stretching wide across generations. "Look at that," Jeff whispered, pointing. "See how the lines connect? Denmark to Norway. Norway to Hungary. Hungary to Wales. It's like the map we saw before — but alive." Ben grinned. "And someday, my kids will see this too?" Jeff's eyes softened. "Yes, son. Someday they will. And when they do, they'll know you were the one who kept the story alive."

The morning light spilled softly through the kitchen window as Ben finished his breakfast. The clink of his spoon against the cereal bowl mixed with the quiet hum of the fridge. Across the table, Jeff sipped his coffee, flipping gently through one of the thin paper notebooks they'd been using for notes.

Ben's eyes darted toward his dad. "Do you think there's more hidden in the house?" he asked. Jeff looked up thoughtfully. "I'd be surprised if there wasn't," he replied. "Old places like that don't give up everything at once. They like to hold their secrets a little longer."

Ben smiled, his curiosity already awake for the day. "Can we go back after lunch?" Jeff nodded. "We'll go back. But remember, Ben, we take our time. The house will wait for us. These stories have been buried for centuries. They're not in a rush." Ben loved that about his dad. Jeff never pushed. He let Ben explore at his own pace, letting the learning settle like soft rain soaking into the ground. As they cleared the table, Annemarie appeared in the doorway. "You two heading back to the old place?" she asked, her voice gentle.

Jeff nodded. "We are. There's still more to sort through." She smiled and placed a hand on Ben's shoulder. "Take your time, sweetheart. Don't forget to breathe it in." Ben grinned. "We will, Mom." By early afternoon, they were walking the familiar path again. The leaves rustled underfoot like old paper as they approached the house. Its crooked frame stood as it always had, weathered but strong. "Same as yesterday," Ben said with a small laugh. Jeff grinned beside him. "Same for a hundred years, maybe more."

Inside the house, the air smelled like old books and dry stone. Sunlight streamed through the small window slits, drawing thin lines across the wooden floor. Jeff carefully set his satchel down near the table where they'd left the scrolls from the previous day. Ben moved first, stepping toward the far wall where the tapestries still hung. "Dad, do you think the symbols mean anything else?" he asked, his voice quiet but full of energy. Jeff joined him, studying the fabric closely. "Symbols always mean something, son. They're like locked doors waiting for the right key."

Ben traced the three dots with his finger. "Like my key?" Jeff nodded. "Exactly like your key. And sometimes, those keys aren't made of metal. Sometimes, they're made of memory." He placed his hand gently on Ben's shoulder. They worked side by side, carefully examining the scrolls again. Jeff opened one of the rolled parchments, pointing to a list of names and places written in the strange curling script. "See here? These are your places. Your people. Every name tells part of the story."

Ben studied the names, recognizing a few from their growing family tree. "Some of these were on Ancestry.com too," he whispered. "But not all of them." Jeff smiled softly. "That's because the internet doesn't know everything. Some of this history lives only here." They took turns gently photographing each scroll with Jeff's camera, saving every detail to study at home. "We'll add these to the tree when we get back," Jeff said. "Piece by piece, Ben. That's how we build your story."

That evening, after returning home, the two sat once again at the kitchen table. The sun dipped low beyond the small window, casting a golden hue across the old wooden surface. Jeff booted up the laptop while Ben sat beside him, watching the loading screen carefully. "Ready to add a few more branches, son?" Jeff asked with a warm grin.

Ben nodded eagerly. "Let's do it, Dad." His fingers hovered above the keyboard, waiting for Jeff's instructions. Together, they navigated through the Ancestry.com tree they had started weeks ago. Each time they added a name or a date, the branches spread wider, stretching like arms reaching for the sky.

Ben paused when they reached a spot where they weren't sure of the next name. "What do we do if we don't know who belongs here yet?" he asked, looking up at Jeff. Jeff leaned in, his voice calm. "That's when we leave space. Think of it like planting seeds. Sometimes it takes time for them to grow." He clicked save, and the screen displayed the expanding tree. "We'll fill it in when we find more scrolls, more records," Jeff continued. "And when the DNA results come in, they might give us new clues." Ben's eyes sparkled with quiet excitement. "It's like a treasure map that keeps growing."

Jeff chuckled. "That's exactly what it is, Ben. A treasure map made of people instead of places." He ruffled Ben's hair and leaned back in his chair, satisfied with the evening's progress. For a few minutes, they simply sat there, both staring at the screen as the family lines webbed outward. Ben whispered, "Someday, Dad, I want to know how far back we can go." Jeff placed his hand on his son's shoulder. "As far as the story lets us, son. As far as the story lets us."

The next morning arrived with gentle rain tapping against Ben's window. He rolled out of bed and rubbed his eyes, already thinking of what he and his dad would uncover today. The house smelled faintly of toast and eggs as he wandered into the kitchen. Jeff stood at the stove, humming a tune that Ben recognized from one of the old vinyl records they played sometimes. "Morning, Ben," Jeff said warmly, flipping the eggs with a practiced hand. "Morning, Dad," Ben replied, sliding into his chair. "Do you think anything new showed up overnight on the family tree?" Jeff smiled as he plated the food. "There's only one way to find out."

As they ate, Jeff handed Ben the tablet that linked to their Ancestry account. The screen glowed softly under Ben's fingers. "Here, you drive this time," Jeff encouraged. Ben scrolled through the pages carefully. New hints blinked like tiny yellow leaves beside certain names. He tapped one. "Look, Dad! A record from Denmark." Jeff leaned in to see. "That's a good one. Let's open it." The record showed an ancestor's name written in old handwriting, with dates from over three hundred years ago. "We're adding him to the tree," Ben declared proudly. Jeff laughed, "Absolutely we are. And see? Every name leads us one step closer to the beginning."

They spent most of the morning like that, adding names, reading documents, and filling in dates. Some records were written in languages Ben didn't fully recognize. "What does that say?" Ben asked when they came across a document in Hungarian. Jeff squinted. "That one... we'll need help with." Ben smiled. "Good. That means it's even older, right?" Jeff nodded. "Older, and even more special. Some names take a little more patience to reveal. And we've got plenty of time, Ben. We're in no rush." The rain outside continued, but inside, the warmth of discovery filled the little kitchen like a soft blanket.

After lunch, Jeff suggested they take another trip back to the old house. "We've added a lot to the tree today, Ben," he said while slipping on his jacket. "But remember, some answers still wait in those old scrolls." Ben grabbed his own light coat and nodded. "Let's bring the camera again. Just in case." The path to the house had grown slightly muddier from the rain. Their boots sank gently into the earth as they walked, but neither minded. "It's like walking through time," Ben said quietly, staring up at the trees. "Exactly," Jeff smiled. "Every step carries us closer to them."

Inside the old house, the familiar cool air greeted them. Dust particles floated like tiny stars in the beams of sunlight breaking through the cracks. The scrolls still rested safely in their storage tubes along the far wall. Jeff carefully unlatched one. "We'll photograph this one today. We won't unroll too many at once." Ben steadied the scroll on the table while Jeff snapped clear photos with his small digital camera. The screen showed sharp images of the curling letters and old seals. "This way, we can study them later without risking damage," Jeff explained. Ben nodded, his eyes scanning the symbols that still felt oddly familiar.

They worked quietly for a few hours, photographing, gently documenting, and returning each piece to its place. The house creaked softly as if whispering encouragement. "Dad," Ben finally said, "do you think anyone else in the world is connected to these scrolls like I am?" Jeff paused before answering. "Maybe, Ben. But no one has your key. This is your journey." Ben smiled, feeling the weight of those words settle in his chest. It wasn't a burden. It was an invitation. An invitation to keep walking further into the mystery, one page at a time, one step at a time. Back at home, the glow of the computer monitor softly lit Ben's face as his fingers traced the growing branches of the family tree. Jeff sat nearby, sipping his tea, quietly watching his son's steady progress. "Look at this, Dad," Ben said, pointing to the screen. "There's another name I didn't know before." Jeff leaned in. "That's your mother's grandmother's brother," he explained gently. "He lived in Norway."

Ben's eyes widened. "That far?" Jeff nodded. "Yes, son. And every name we add helps the puzzle grow a little clearer." Ben entered the new name carefully, spelling each part with care. "I never thought there'd be so many branches," he whispered. "Every person is a branch," Jeff smiled. "And you're one of the newest leaves." The evening grew quieter as the two of them continued adding names. Every so often, Ben would pause and look at a name, tilting his head. "Dad," he asked softly, "how did all these people lead to me?" Jeff placed his mug down, leaning forward. "Through thousands of choices, Ben. Thousands of lives lived long before you were born. And now, you carry all of them inside you."

Ben sat still for a moment, absorbing the weight of that thought. "That's a lot of people trusting me with their story." Jeff smiled. "Yes. But remember, son—it's not pressure. It's a gift. You get to discover them. And tell their stories if you wish." The screen flickered softly as the family tree spread wider. "We're only at the beginning," Ben whispered, his eyes glowing with quiet excitement. "Yes, my son," Jeff replied gently, placing a hand on his shoulder. "And I'll be here for every part of it."

The morning sun peeked through the curtains as Ben rubbed his eyes and sat up in bed. Jeff had already placed a small breakfast tray by the desk—a simple gesture that had become part of their rhythm. "Morning, son," Jeff greeted softly as he entered the room. "I thought we'd start today with something new." Ben blinked the sleep from his eyes, stretching his arms. "What's new today, Dad?" Jeff pulled out a slim, well-worn book from his satchel. "We've been focusing on the tree, but today, I thought we'd look at migrations. How people moved across lands long before they had our names."

Ben slid off the bed and sat at the desk, eager to begin. "Migrations?" he asked, curious. Jeff nodded. "Yes. You see, even your DNA shows pathways—how your ancestors travelled from places like Hungary, Denmark, and Norway, and how they eventually settled in England and Wales." Turning to a map inside the book, Jeff traced slow lines across Europe with his finger. "Look here," he said, "this route likely follows the old trade roads and riverways. Your ancestors may have crossed these paths nearly four thousand years ago." Ben stared at the map, his imagination already painting pictures of old ships and caravans moving through strange, wild lands.

"Did they know where they were going?" Ben asked, wide-eyed. Jeff smiled. "Sometimes, yes. Sometimes, no. But survival, family, and hope pulled them forward." Ben studied the lines again, his voice quiet. "It's strange thinking about how far back it goes." Jeff placed a steady hand on his shoulder. "It is. But it's also beautiful. You carry those journeys inside you." The book closed with a soft thud as Jeff gently laid it aside. "And as we uncover more, we'll fill in these roads with names and stories. Every journey has voices waiting to be heard, Ben." Ben whispered, almost to himself, "And I'm the one who gets to hear them."

After breakfast, Ben followed Jeff into the living room where the computer was already booted up. The Ancestry.com screen glowed softly, displaying a web of names and dates. "Alright, son," Jeff said warmly, "today we're going to start adding some of the places we've been learning about. Let's start plotting the migrations we talked about earlier." Ben pulled the chair closer, eyes scanning the screen. "How do we do that, Dad?" Jeff smiled and pointed to the 'Migration Map' feature on the site. "See this? It lets us mark where your ancestors lived and where they moved. We'll build the path, step by step."

The cursor hovered as Jeff typed in the first location: "Denmark – Hovedstaden." A little dot appeared on the map. Then another for "Norway – Tromsø." As each location lit up, Ben watched the connections slowly form across Europe like constellations in the night sky. "It looks like a giant spider web," Ben whispered, fascinated. Jeff chuckled. "That's exactly how family trees work sometimes. So many branches, so many connections. You've got ancestors stretching all the way into Hungary, Sweden, Ireland, and beyond."

Ben bit his lip, focusing hard as Jeff added more names and places. "What about King Béla? Where would he go on here?" Jeff paused for a moment, his voice gentle. "That will be placed under Hungary. But not yet. We'll add him as we get deeper into the scrolls and the records." As the map expanded, Ben leaned back and whispered, "Dad, is it weird that I feel like I've been to these places even though I haven't?" Jeff placed his hand on Ben's back and nodded. "Not weird at all, son. That's what memory in the blood feels like. You carry their steps inside you."

The afternoon light shifted through the curtains, casting long beams across the wooden floor. Jeff stood from the desk and stretched his arms, the map still glowing softly on the monitor. "Alright, Ben," he said, "let's take a break from the computer. Too much screen time isn't good for our eyes."

Ben nodded but kept glancing at the map. "It feels like the more we add, the more I want to know." Jeff grinned. "That's the right feeling, son. Curiosity is the best tool we've got for this work." They moved into the corner of the room where the scrolls were carefully stacked in plastic sleeves for protection. Jeff handed Ben a pair of thin cotton gloves. "Let's handle these gently, alright? Some of these pages are older than almost anything we own."

Ben slipped on the gloves, his small fingers trembling slightly. "I still don't understand how my name shows up on these old scrolls, Dad." Jeff knelt beside him and spoke softly. "Because your name, Benedicere, wasn't just given to you — it was remembered." Together, they unfolded a scroll that smelled faintly of aged parchment and dust. Strange symbols danced along the borders, some familiar from earlier dreams, others new. Ben traced a spiral with his gloved finger. "Do you think one day I'll be able to read all of this?" Jeff smiled again, patient as ever. "You will. Bit by bit. We'll learn it together."

The next morning arrived with a soft drizzle tapping against the windows. Jeff stood at the kitchen counter, preparing breakfast while Ben sat at the table flipping through one of the ancestry books they had borrowed from the library. The air smelled of toast and rain-soaked earth. "Dad," Ben began quietly, "do you think all of these names, all these people… do they know I exist?" Jeff turned from the stove and looked at him warmly. "They may not have known you by name, son. But in a way, they were waiting for you."

Ben rubbed his finger slowly along one of the family charts. "Because I carry them inside me?" Jeff nodded as he placed a plate in front of his son. "Exactly. Every part of you holds a little piece of them.

That's what family is." The rain picked up for a moment, drumming gently on the roof. Ben glanced at the scroll tube resting by the bookshelf. "Sometimes it feels like I can almost hear them speaking, but I can't understand the words." Jeff sat down across from him. "That's how memory works when it's older than language. It's not always meant to be loud. Sometimes it just hums."

Ben bit into his toast, chewing thoughtfully. "Will the test from Ancestry.com show us more names like this?" Jeff smiled. "It might. But what we're doing here—these books, these scrolls, these maps—it's even older than what the computer can show. Both sides of the story matter." The drizzle outside turned to a steady rain by mid-morning. The house was warm though, with the fire crackling in the little stove as Jeff opened one of the older scrolls on the table. The parchment still gave off that scent of old leather and earth that Ben was starting to recognize as part of their journey.

"Dad," Ben said softly, still tasting the word every time like something precious, "how did these scrolls even survive this long?" Jeff glanced up, adjusting his reading glasses. "Care, Ben. Someone cared enough to hide them. Protect them. And now, you care enough to find them." Ben sat forward, his eyes running over the strange symbols again. "But some of these aren't words I know.
Or even letters." Jeff smiled. "That's because they aren't always letters like we use today. Some are symbols, sigils, marks from different times. Families used them like signatures long before paper records."

Ben's finger hovered above a three-pointed triangle, the same one he'd drawn since he was little. "This one… this is mine, isn't it?" Jeff reached over and gently placed his hand over Ben's. "It's always been yours." The rain tapped on, soft and steady. The old house outside stood as it always did—waiting, patient, part of the story yet to fully unfold. Ben leaned back in his chair, his young mind swirling with both wonder and questions too big for his age, yet too close to ignore. Jeff closed the scroll gently. "We'll get there, Ben. One piece at a time. Just like these scrolls—we'll unwrap your story carefully."

The rain continued through the afternoon, wrapping the little house in a steady hum that made everything inside feel softer. Jeff made a pot of tea while Ben flipped open one of the old books they had found at the house weeks ago. The book's cover was faded green, but inside the ink was still bold. The pages smelled like dust and secrets. Ben traced his finger under the names written carefully in old script.

"These people… were they all real?" he asked. His eyes scanned names that stretched across generations: places like Denmark, Wales, Ireland, and Norway kept repeating. Jeff returned with two mugs, setting one beside Ben. "Every one of them, Ben. They lived, worked, raised families. Each name here led to you." Ben's lips pressed together as he nodded. "I feel like I should know them better." Jeff smiled. "That's why we're here. They left you a story. We're just learning how to read it."

The rain softened into a gentle mist outside, and for a while, they sat quietly, the only sounds being the occasional rustle of paper and the clink of their tea spoons. Jeff glanced at Ben's sketches spread across the table. "Your drawings are part of this too, you know." Ben smiled softly, his fingers tightening on his pen. "They feel like they come from somewhere." Jeff leaned closer. "They do. From memory, from blood, from places your feet haven't touched but your soul still remembers." Ben's eyes brightened at that thought, the weight of his young journey becoming a little easier to carry.

The next morning, the sun finally returned, painting streaks of gold across Ben's bedroom wall. He blinked awake, the familiar sound of birds chirping outside his window mixing with the smell of breakfast drifting from the kitchen. Sliding out of bed, he padded across the cool floor and found Jeff at the stove, flipping pancakes with practiced ease. "Morning, kiddo," Jeff greeted warmly, flipping one perfectly onto a plate. "Today's a big one." Ben rubbed his eyes, still waking up. "Why? Are we going back to the house?" Jeff chuckled, sliding a plate to him. "Not quite. Today, the ancestry results finally arrived."

Ben sat straighter, his sleep fading. "They're in?" he asked, eyes wide. Jeff nodded, pulling a folded paper from the counter. "Came through early this morning. I printed them out so we can go through them together." Ben bit into his pancake, trying to calm the excitement bubbling inside him.

The idea of seeing his bloodline written out made his stomach flip in strange ways. "Is it scary?" he asked quietly. Jeff sat down beside him, placing a steady hand on his shoulder. "No, son. It's beautiful. You're about to meet the people who helped make you who you are."

They finished breakfast slowly, not from delay but from reverence. This wasn't something to rush. When the dishes were cleared, Jeff carefully unfolded the printed report on the table. Names, percentages, and regions appeared like a treasure map waiting to be explored. Jeff pointed to the top of the paper, where bold black letters read: Ethnicity Estimate. Ben's eyes followed eagerly. There it was. Denmark. Norway. Sweden. Wales. France. Germany. Ireland. England. And there, near the middle, Hungary. The words felt like echoes from his dreams.

Ben's finger hovered over Hungary. "That's the one from my dreams, Dad." Jeff smiled softly. "Yes. The Magyar people. Árpád's descendants. You've been carrying them inside you all along." Ben's throat tightened, the reality finally taking shape. This wasn't just old maps or scrolls. It was alive, printed right there. Further down, the paternal Y-chromosome showed the haplogroup: R-S660. Ben whispered it aloud, almost like a prayer. "R-S660." His fingers traced the letters. Jeff added gently, "That line likely goes back over thirty-eight hundred years. That's how far your father's ancestors stretch."

Ben stared at the numbers, the history wrapped in codes and percentages. It was overwhelming but peaceful. His mitochondrial haplogroup, H5a1, traced his mother's side back nearly sixty-five hundred years. "That's older than anything I've ever read about," Ben whispered. Jeff nodded, his voice calm. "It is, son. Before kings, before castles, your family was already walking the forests of Europe." Ben exhaled slowly, trying to absorb the weight of it all. The blood that ran through him was ancient, far older than his mind could grasp.

Jeff tapped the corner of the screen where it read DNA Matches. "Now, this part might surprise you even more." As the list loaded, dozens—then hundreds—of names began to fill the page. Many were unfamiliar, but each one carried a small leaf symbol beside it, signalling a connection. "All these people?" Ben asked softly. "They're all related to you, Ben," Jeff answered with a quiet nod.

Ben scrolled slowly, eyes wide, trying to recognize any names. Some were distant cousins, names he had never heard before. A few bore surnames that made no sense to him. "But I don't know any of them." Jeff smiled, resting a hand on his son's shoulder. "That's the beauty of it. Some are distant, some are close. But they all share pieces of the same beginning." As the names continued, Ben stopped on one that made his breath catch. A surname nearly identical to the one written on one of the scrolls they'd found beneath the old house. "Dad…" he whispered, pointing. "Look. That one." Jeff leaned closer, reading aloud, "Patton... or Pattenden, depending on the older spelling."

Ben's pulse quickened. "That was on one of the scrolls, wasn't it?" Jeff nodded, his voice lower now, as if speaking near something sacred. "It was, son. That surname leads us right back to Kent, England. Specifically, to Marden—where your deeper roots once grew." Ben swallowed, the full circle beginning to form in his mind.

"Does that mean some of my family still live there?" he asked, barely above a whisper. Jeff's eyes softened. "Very likely. The branches of the tree may have spread far, but their roots always remember where they began." The words settled into Ben's chest, not heavy, but firm—like a stone placed exactly where it belonged.

The days following that discovery passed with a strange mixture of excitement and stillness. Every morning, after breakfast, Ben and Jeff would sit together at the kitchen table, the laptop open like a door to another world. They mapped out branches, filled in names, and made notes in a large leather-bound journal that Jeff had brought home for this very purpose. "We'll call this The Book of Us," Jeff had said, his voice warm. Ben loved writing in it. Every name they added felt like adding another heartbeat to a great, old body he was finally beginning to know. Annemarie often helped from the stove, calling out dates, birthdays, or places as she remembered them. "That was your great-grandmother's name," she'd say, or "No, honey, Uncle Leonard lived in Bristol, not Cardiff." Together, they carefully stitched the past into something whole.

As they worked, Jeff continued to explain everything gently. "Every time you add a name, Ben, you're not just recording facts. You're honouring them. Even the ones you've never met." Ben would pause sometimes, staring at the dates. "Some of these people were born hundreds of years ago," he whispered once. "That's right," Jeff answered softly. "And their stories still live inside you." In the evenings, when their eyes grew tired from the glowing screen, they would retreat into the living room. There, by soft lamp light, they returned to the scrolls and maps from the old house. Ben traced lines on ancient parchment while Jeff translated old names and places. "It's like chasing echoes," Jeff mused one night. "But every echo leads us closer."

Ben nodded, feeling it in his chest. "Like following my own voice backward in time." Jeff smiled, leaning back in the chair. "Exactly that." And though neither spoke it aloud, both of them knew they had only just begun. A soft rain began tapping against the windows as they worked through the afternoon. The quiet patter felt almost like company, steady and calming. Jeff glanced over Ben's shoulder as the boy carefully typed in another name on the Ancestry.com chart. "Good," Jeff said gently, his voice steady. "And now add where she was born." Ben nodded, tapping the keys slowly as he read the old handwritten note aloud. "Born in Denmark… Hovedstaden."

Jeff smiled. "That's the capital region. A lot of your father's line stretches back there." Ben paused, his face thoughtful. "Dad… does that mean someone from there was once a king too?" The word slipped from him naturally—Dad—not forced or practiced. Jeff placed his hand on Ben's shoulder. "Maybe. But even if not, every one of them mattered. Royal or not. Every life matters in a bloodline, son." The rain grew heavier, and Annemarie set out cocoa for them both, sitting at the table with her tea. "My mother used to tell me stories about her parents in Norway," she said softly. "Your great-grandfather fished up in Tromsø. It's beautiful there." Ben looked up with wide eyes. "I want to go there someday." Jeff chuckled, ruffling his hair. "One day we will."

They worked through the next hour, filling in names from both sides—Denmark, Norway, France, England, Wales. The tree began to branch out beautifully, curling like living veins across the screen. Jeff reached across, pointing to the top corner. "There," he said. "That's you. Every name leads here." Ben stared at his name in awe. "It's like they were all waiting for me." Jeff leaned back and let out a long breath. "And you're the one carrying them forward. That's what this is all about, Ben. It's not just names. It's a living story." Ben's eyes glowed with understanding. "It's our story, Dad." Jeff's throat tightened at that. "Yes, son. It's ours."

The rain eased into a steady drizzle as evening shadows crawled up the walls. Jeff stood, stretched his back, and glanced at the clock. "Let's stop for tonight, buddy. Your eyes are starting to cross." Ben grinned, rubbing his face. "Yeah… I didn't know names could make your brain tired." Jeff chuckled, reaching for the blanket folded over the couch. "That's because you're learning fast. This isn't just research—it's a journey." Annemarie watched them with a soft smile as she tidied the kitchen.

She noticed how much the two of them moved in rhythm now, like they'd always belonged together. "You've done enough for today, sweetheart," she said gently. Ben nodded, letting Jeff drape the blanket over him on the couch where he often fell asleep after long days like this. "Dad…" Ben whispered, his voice small in the growing dark. "Thank you for doing this with me."

Jeff knelt beside him, brushing Ben's hair softly with his hand. "There's nowhere else I'd rather be, son. This is your story. But I'm here every step." Ben's eyes grew heavier, his breathing slowing as sleep crept in. Jeff whispered, "Tomorrow's another day. And every day we get a little closer." The room fell into peaceful stillness, broken only by the rain's steady hum outside. As Jeff stood, he glanced back at the glowing computer screen, where the family tree stood half-complete but already vast. Dozens of names filled the branches, stretching backward into places few living souls even remembered. He whispered to himself, "We're not just chasing bloodlines… we're unburying forgotten kings." The rain whispered in agreement as Jeff turned out the light.

Morning broke with a soft silver glow sneaking through the curtains. Ben stirred first, blinking at the faint light that filtered across the living room. The house was quiet except for the gentle hum of the fridge in the kitchen. Stretching beneath the warm blanket, Ben sat up slowly, his mind already swirling with the names and stories they had uncovered. The tree they were building wasn't just names—it was becoming real, like a giant puzzle waking up piece by piece.

Jeff entered the room carrying two mugs of cocoa, steam curling gently. "Morning, sleepyhead." He smiled as Ben rubbed his eyes and reached for the warm cup. "You were talking in your sleep again last night," Jeff added softly. Ben blinked. "I was?" Jeff nodded, sitting down beside him. "You kept saying Béla… over and over." The boy frowned, his small hand gripping the mug tighter. "I don't know why. But it feels… close. Like someone I should know."

Jeff nodded, his voice calm but serious. "That's because you're pulling from something deep inside, Ben. Deeper than books or even the tree we're building." He pointed gently to Ben's chest. "From here. From your blood." Ben sat quietly, his mind heavy but curious. "Will the DNA test tell us about him?" Jeff exhaled, his tone patient. "It might. Sometimes it points to where. Sometimes to who. But the most important answers often come when we're not rushing."

Annemarie's voice floated from the kitchen as she prepared breakfast. "You two ready for eggs and toast?" Jeff smiled. "Always." As they moved toward the table, Jeff placed his hand on Ben's shoulder. "Today, we'll dig a little deeper into those maps. I have a feeling they're hiding something important. And maybe… just maybe… we'll finally see where Béla fits into your story." Ben's eyes lit with quiet determination. "I want to know everything, Dad. Everything."

After breakfast, the two of them returned to the table where yesterday's work still lay undisturbed. The scrolls, old documents, maps, and digital printouts sat like old friends waiting for another conversation. Jeff carefully unrolled the map they had studied the night before. His eyes narrowed on the lower portion, where faint markings hinted at a new discovery. "See this curve here, Ben?" he asked, tapping gently with his fingertip. "That ridge connects directly to the shoreline we traced yesterday. It might lead us closer to the source."

Ben leaned over, eyes wide and alert. "It looks like a path," he whispered. "But why would they mark a path on something so old?" Jeff smiled faintly. "Because sometimes paths aren't meant to be walked. Sometimes they're meant to be remembered." His voice softened. "Our ancestors mapped more than land. They mapped journeys. Journeys of families, of bloodlines, of how people moved across the world."

Ben's fingers followed the inked path like tracing a river on a treasure map. "Do you think this could show where my family started?" Jeff nodded slowly. "Possibly. These names—Denmark, Wales, Norway—they're not just places. They're roots. And this map might be showing us how your branches grew." He paused, watching Ben absorb each word like precious drops of knowledge. "That's why we take our time, son."

Ben sat back for a moment, eyes lifting thoughtfully. "I never knew a map could hold so much." Jeff chuckled gently. "Neither did I when I was your age. But you're seeing it sooner than I ever did. That's why this is special. This is your journey. And I get to walk it with you." The boy smiled, his young face glowing with quiet pride. "Thanks, Dad. I don't think I could do this without you." Jeff placed a reassuring hand on Ben's shoulder, giving it a light squeeze. "You'll never have to." The room grew still for a moment, both of them quietly feeling the weight of what they were building—not just a tree, but a legacy.

Later that morning, Jeff carried in a small wooden box he had retrieved from his own home. He set it gently on the table beside the maps, as though handling something fragile and alive. Ben's eyes widened the moment he saw it. The wood was dark, polished by years of handling, with faint carvings along the edges that resembled vines curling around unseen names.

"What's inside?" Ben whispered, voice dropping as though they were standing in a museum. Jeff smiled softly but didn't answer right away. He carefully unlatched the lid and lifted it open. Inside lay several old papers, yellowed photographs, and two small cloth pouches tied with twine. "These belonged to my grandfather," Jeff said quietly. "He was one of the last in my line who tried to trace our family. I thought it was time to share them with you."

Ben leaned in, heart pounding. He had seen old documents before, but these felt different. The photographs showed men and women dressed in dark coats, standing before old stone buildings, their faces both stern and familiar. One photograph caught his attention. A young man, perhaps in his early twenties, stood proudly before an ivy-covered manor that looked eerily similar to the one they had visited.

Jeff followed Ben's gaze. "That's my grandfather," he explained. "The house behind him is long gone, but it stood not far from here. The ivy was always there. That same ivy grew wild and thick. Maybe that's why your dream led us back to that place." Ben's hand hovered over the photo, feeling strangely connected to this stranger from another time. Jeff opened one of the pouches and gently spilled its contents onto the cloth. Out tumbled a few pieces of jewellery— a thin silver ring, an old brass locket, and a small pendant carved with the three-dot triangle they both knew too well. "The symbol again," Ben whispered. "It keeps following us." Jeff nodded slowly. "Because it's never left us."

Ben's fingers traced the pendant, the cool metal humming faintly beneath his touch. "Do you think… they knew? My great-great-grandparents? Did they know where they came from, too?" Jeff exhaled slowly, his voice warm but weighty. "They knew pieces. Fragments. But their story ended too early. Ours… ours is just beginning." Ben looked up, his voice soft but clear. "We're fixing it, aren't we? We're putting the pieces back." Jeff smiled fully this time, pride shimmering behind his steady eyes. "That's exactly what we're doing, son."

Later that afternoon, after a light lunch, Jeff pulled out something Ben hadn't seen before. It was a rolled canvas tube, tied at both ends with faded leather straps. The outside looked almost too worn to trust, but Jeff handled it with the same care as everything else they'd unearthed. He gently loosened the straps and unrolled it across the table. Inside was a map. But this wasn't like the earlier ones filled with rivers and distant place names. This was different. The ink was darker, sharper, almost like it had only been drawn a few years ago, though Jeff confirmed otherwise. "This map," Jeff whispered, "was drawn by your great-great-great grandfather. It was his private record. A tracing of where our line once crossed into other lands."

Ben leaned in closer. The map was filled with markings. Small circles, triangles, even symbols that looked like stars. Along the edges were names—strange ones, many of which didn't match the family names Ben had seen before. "Who are these people?" he asked softly. Jeff placed his hand beside Ben's, his voice calm but focused.

"These are allied families. Other lines that crossed ours—some by marriage, others by blood far back." Ben's eyes landed on one word in particular: Árpád. He recognized it instantly. The name had whispered to him in dreams, pressed itself into his thoughts at night. "That's… him," Ben said. "The name I keep hearing." Jeff nodded slowly. "Árpád. One of the oldest known rulers tied to the Magyar people, your ancestors on your mother's side."

The room grew quieter, heavier for a moment, as if the walls themselves leaned in to listen. Ben swallowed. "And Béla?" Jeff's eyes softened. "Also part of that legacy. A king. His reign was centuries after Árpád, but the bloodline carried forward. Pieces of them are inside you, Ben." Ben sat back, letting the words wash over him like waves. It was a strange kind of knowing—both heavy and comforting. "I don't know why it feels so big," he whispered. "Like my chest can't hold all of it." Jeff smiled gently, resting his hand on Ben's shoulder.

"Because it is big, son. But you don't have to hold it all at once. We'll carry it together." The two of them sat in silence for a moment, eyes resting on the old map, tracing those ancient lines that had traveled through time and now lived inside Ben's small, beating heart.

The evening settled around the small house like a warm shawl. The glow from the desk lamp painted the edges of Jeff's papers with a golden hue. They had spent hours pouring over names and dates, maps and scrolls, but tonight was calmer. Ben leaned back in his chair, staring at the digital chart glowing on the laptop screen. The branches of his family tree sprawled outward like the roots of an old oak, twisting through time. Jeff smiled, setting his pen down gently. "Ben, do you remember when we first did those DNA tests? The bloodwork… the swab… how nervous you were that first time at the clinic?"

Ben chuckled softly, rubbing the back of his neck. "Yeah, I remember, Dad. I thought they were going to drain me like a maple tree." His laughter was light, but beneath it was pride. "But it was worth it, wasn't it? We wouldn't be sitting here if we hadn't done it." Jeff nodded, his gaze drifting over the names that now filled the screen — Denmark, Norway, Ireland, Hungary, Wales, France. "Every time I look at this, I still can't believe how much we've uncovered since then. Just a handful of names in the beginning. And now… this."

Ben leaned closer, tracing his finger gently across the glowing screen. "I didn't think names like Árpád or Béla would ever mean anything to me. But now they do. They're not just old names. They're part of me." Jeff's voice was soft, almost reverent. "And every branch we add, every cousin or great-great-something we find, it brings you closer to who you've always been. The tests just opened the first door. The rest—" he gestured at the scrolls and maps surrounding them, "—this is the journey."

Ben smiled, his eyes bright but thoughtful. "It's strange, isn't it? How one tiny vial of blood and a little tube of spit can tell such a big story." Jeff reached over, placing a firm but gentle hand on Ben's shoulder. "It's not just science, Ben. It's memory. Carried in your blood. Written in your bones. You've always carried them with you. We just finally learned how to read it." Outside, the wind pressed softly against the window, like a distant breath from the past. Inside, father and son sat together, the quiet hum of discovery filling the room like music.

The morning light slid gently across the windowsill, casting long lines across the breakfast table. Ben sat with a bowl of oatmeal, still warm, while Jeff quietly sipped his coffee nearby. The laptop sat open between them, the family tree still glowing faintly. Today, the two weren't in a rush. Some days were about heavy research, but others were about letting it all sink in. Jeff believed that giving Ben space to breathe was just as important as finding new records. He glanced across the table and smiled as Ben absently tapped the spoon against the rim of his bowl.

"You know, Ben," Jeff said softly, "what we're doing here… it's not something most people ever get to do." Ben raised an eyebrow, curious. "You mean building the tree?" Jeff nodded. "Not just building it. Understanding it. Seeing how far it goes back. Most people don't get to meet their ancestors through names and dates like this. But you—you're speaking with them in a way." Ben thought for a moment, stirring his oatmeal slowly. "Sometimes… it feels like they're speaking back. Like the dreams, Dad. Like they're reminding me not to stop."

Jeff's eyes softened. "That's exactly why we take our time. The scrolls, the DNA, the maps—it's all connected. But your heart needs to understand it too. This isn't about rushing. It's about honouring where you came from." Ben smiled, pushing his empty bowl aside. "And sometimes it's about oatmeal," he teased, grinning. Jeff laughed gently. "Yes. Even kings and knights needed breakfast, son." They shared a quiet chuckle, the comfort between them as warm as the morning sun.

As they finished clearing the table, Jeff reached for his satchel. "You up for the old house again today? There are still more scrolls we haven't translated yet." Ben nodded eagerly, his eyes lighting up. "Always. Let's see what secrets are waiting." Jeff tousled his hair gently. "Good. Grab your jacket. The ivy's probably grown a little thicker since we last visited." Together, they stepped into the fresh morning air, ready to walk once more into the past.

CHAPTER 4: THE PUZZLE INSIDE DNA

The afternoon sunlight spilled softly across the oak table, dancing along the edges of the old parchment scrolls and casting elongated shadows that wavered as though alive. I sat quietly beside Benedict, his small hands carefully unfolding another brittle sheet that had been preserved for decades, perhaps even centuries. The faint scent of aged paper mingled with the sweet aroma of the tea Annemarie had just placed beside us.

She offered a quiet smile, her presence always calming, always watchful without being intrusive. Ben furrowed his brow, his lips slightly parted in concentration as his eyes traced the faded ink strokes. He was only eight, yet the weight of this journey pressed upon him as though his little shoulders carried the echoes of generations past. His mind, sharp as a blade honed by unseen hands, absorbed details that many adults would overlook. "Dad," he whispered, almost as if afraid his voice might disturb the ancient script. "What does this part mean?"

I leaned over, adjusting my glasses as my eyes scanned the Hungarian characters, most of which we had become familiar with over the past months. Yet, some portions remained elusive, as though deliberately hiding secrets only time could unlock. The phrase before us read: Árpád öröksége tovább él benned. The translation hovered at the edge of my memory. "It says... 'The legacy of Árpád lives on within you,'" I answered softly.

Ben's eyes widened, reflecting both wonder and an unspoken question. He had heard the name Árpád before, many times now, both from the scrolls and the family tree work we had painstakingly charted. But each appearance of that name seemed to add another layer, another piece to the puzzle we were assembling together. "But why me?" His voice trembled slightly. "I mean, I'm just... me." I reached out and gently placed my hand over his, steadying his trembling fingers. "Because, my boy," I said with warmth, "sometimes history chooses its keepers in ways we don't fully understand. You carry within you not only the blood of your mother and father, but echoes of countless souls before them. This isn't about being someone else. This is about understanding who you already are."

He nodded, though his gaze remained distant, as though chasing a thought too swift to catch. This was not the first time he had asked that question, nor would it be the last. And each time, my answer grew only slightly more complete, as new discoveries filled in the empty spaces of our knowledge. Annmarie quietly settled into the armchair near the fireplace, folding her hands in her lap. Her eyes reflected pride, but also concern. She understood the magnitude of what her son was uncovering. She had lived with the mystery long before the tests had even begun, watching the recurring dreams, the strange language he somehow understood, and the inexplicable sense that something greater pulsed beneath his young skin.

I took a breath, choosing my words carefully, for words have power — especially to a child trying to grasp the immensity of identity. "You see, Ben," I began again, "the Horváth name we keep finding — it's not random.

It's part of your father's family, long before the name became Harvick in England. That name travelled far. Wars, migrations, kingdoms rising and falling — names change, but the blood remembers." Ben's small voice interrupted me, laced with genuine curiosity. "But how did Horváth turn into Harvick? They're not even really close." I chuckled gently. "Ah, but that's where languages trick us.

Imagine someone hundreds of years ago, leaving Hungary, speaking broken English, arriving in a land where no one knew how to pronounce Horváth correctly. Over time, people heard what they thought they heard. 'Hor-vath' might have sounded like 'Har-vick' to their ears. The spelling shifted, the accent faded, but the root stayed buried beneath." Ben's eyes lit up, the corners of his mouth tugging into a small smile. "So it's like a... like a secret code? My last name hides the old one?" "Exactly," I grinned. "A puzzle inside your name. Just like your DNA holds puzzles inside its strands."

At that moment, his gaze shifted back to the scroll. He touched one particular portion, tracing the ornate symbols that framed the family crest drawn there. A crowned stag beneath a rising sun, surrounded by ancient Magyar motifs. "Dad... this symbol keeps showing up. What does it mean?" I studied it carefully. We had seen this stag multiple times now — in the scrolls, in fragments from the Ancestry.com tree when European records linked back to medieval Hungary, and even once, strangely, in one of Benedict's dreams. In that dream, as he had described in astonishing detail, an elderly man seated upon a throne had worn the stag upon his robe.

"The stag," I began slowly, "is very old. Long before Hungary was even called Hungary, the people who lived there — the Magyars — considered the stag sacred. It represented not only nobility, but also guidance. In their legends, a great stag led their ancestors westward into the Carpathian Basin, where Hungary now stands." Ben's voice grew almost reverent. "Like a guide... like in my dream." "Yes," I nodded. "Like in your dream." His face tightened, his eyes moistening just slightly, though he fought the tears valiantly. It was not sorrow that welled up inside him, but an overwhelming sense of connection, of something both intimate and distant, something his young mind struggled to process.

Annemarie's voice joined us then, soft as silk. "You've always carried it, sweetheart. Even when you were just a baby, and you almost left us... three times. Each time, you came back. And each time you whispered things you couldn't have known." Ben turned his head toward her. "The voice, Mom. The one that says, 'You're not finished yet.' I still hear it sometimes." She nodded, her own eyes glassy. "I know. And maybe it's because you're not." The room fell into a tender silence. The fire crackled softly, its glow wrapping us in a cocoon of warmth against the weight of the truths we were navigating. The journey ahead would demand more of us all, but for now, we breathed together in that fragile peace.

I reached across to one of the genealogy binders stacked on the far end of the table, its green cover worn at the edges from constant use. Flipping through the tabs marked Hungary — Royal Lineages, I found the page I had bookmarked days ago but had not yet shown Ben. The name Béla III of Hungary was written in bold, alongside a list of descendants. "Ben," I said gently, "there's more." He leaned closer, eyes wide with anticipation. "You remember the name Béla, from your dreams?" He nodded emphatically. "The man on the throne. The one who looks at me like... like he knows me."

I exhaled slowly. "That man may very well be Béla III. A king who lived nearly a thousand years ago. And through your father's bloodline, there's a very real possibility that you are connected to him. Through Árpád's house, through the Horváth line, your family may trace all the way back to him." Ben's face flushed.

He opened his mouth, closed it again, then whispered, "I... I have kings in my family?" "Not just kings," I smiled. "Stories. Journeys. Battles. Dreams. All woven into your blood. But never forget, my boy, you are not valuable because of kings or crowns. You are valuable because you are you." He nodded slowly, processing my words, then looked down at his hands as though seeing them for the first time. "My crown is a secret," he whispered.

I smiled broadly. "Yes, Ben. And sometimes, the most sacred crowns are the ones the world never sees." The evening had fully set in by the time we carefully gathered the scrolls back into their protective sleeves. The house was quiet now. Outside the tall bay windows, only the whisper of wind among the trees offered company to the steady ticking of the old grandfather clock that stood like a silent sentry in the corner of the room. The tea had long grown cold, but none of us had bothered to notice. The discoveries always held us captive far more than any passing hour could.

Benedict sat cross-legged on the carpet now, his fingers absently toying with the edge of his hoodie sleeve while his mind raced. I knew that look all too well. It was the same look he had worn the day we opened his first DNA results, the day we saw his paternal haplogroup marker — R-S660 — and my heart had to steady itself as I whispered the words Niall of the Nine Hostages. He hadn't fully grasped the magnitude then, but even at eight, he sensed that something profound was being revealed.

"Dad?" His voice finally broke the quiet. "Yes, son?" "Do you think... do you think Béla ever knew his family would one day end up... well, here? In England. In Canada. In me?" Ah, there was the great question again — the one that children often voice better than scholars. The sheer improbable river of history that carries us from ancient courts to modern living rooms, across oceans and centuries. I eased myself down beside him on the floor. My joints cracked in protest — age has little patience for such postures — but the closeness mattered more than comfort.

"Ben, I think kings and commoners alike only see the world they know. They can't see the far banks of the river when they stand at its headwaters. But every step they take sends ripples forward. Maybe Béla could never have imagined you.

But here you are. And every heartbeat in your chest is part of his story now." He was quiet again, though his breathing was deep and steady. His mind was not anxious tonight, just busy. Very busy. And as I watched him, I silently thanked whatever providence had seen fit to place me in this boy's life. Fatherhood is not always written by blood alone. Sometimes, it is carved out by choice, by calling, and by the sacred trust of being invited into another soul's unfolding journey.

Annemarie returned from the hallway where she had been speaking softly with her sister on the phone. She glanced at us, smiled faintly, and gestured toward the bundle of newer scrolls on the side table. "Jeff, there's one we haven't gone through yet," she said. "The one the archivist mailed last week from Budapest." I blinked. In the excitement of today's discoveries, I had forgotten about the new arrival. The parcel had come wrapped tightly in heavy oilcloth, sealed with red wax. We hadn't dared open it while working on the others, not wanting to overwhelm Ben all at once.

"You're right," I nodded. "Shall we?" I glanced at Ben. His face lit up with eager consent. "Yes! Please!" Carefully, I rose and retrieved the scroll. Its casing was newer than some of the others but still carried that unmistakable scent of time — parchment, ink, and the faintest trace of dried herbs, as was sometimes used to preserve documents from mildew during shipment. The seal bore a simple initial: V. I made a mental note to inquire with the archivist as to who might have prepared it. Slowly, I untied the binding cords, my hands steady, while Ben leaned closer to catch the first glimpse of the unfurled document. As the parchment rolled open, my eyes immediately caught something unusual.

"There's no date," I murmured aloud. Ben looked up at me. "Is that bad?" "Not bad," I assured him, "but very unusual. Most of these records include a scribe's notation — the year, sometimes even the day it was copied. But this one..." I ran my finger gently along the upper margin. "Nothing." The handwriting was crisp but markedly different from the other scrolls — more hurried perhaps, or simply unfamiliar in style. The language, however, was once again Hungarian, but older than the forms we had been translating thus far. Some words retained archaic endings, making the sentences twist oddly even after translation.

Annemarie fetched the desk lamp and angled its glow directly over the parchment as I began reading aloud, slow and deliberate for Ben's benefit: "The blood that binds kings will pass like threads unseen through fields of strangers. When the house of Árpád falls silent, yet another branch shall bend westward, carrying names that none will pronounce rightly again. But the covenant remains in the child who bears both stag and sword within his frame." I paused. The air in the room grew noticeably heavier, as though unseen eyes now lingered just beyond the edge of the hearth light. Ben whispered first. "It's talking about me again, isn't it?"

I hesitated only a moment. "It could be, son. It could very well be." The scroll continued for several more lines, each one thick with meaning, though some sections were partially smudged, as if dampness had touched the ink at some point long ago. "One shall carry the western name. One shall carry the eastern memory. And when the two awaken in one body, the ancient bond shall stir again. But the crown shall remain unseen by the world, known only to those who hear the calling voice." Ben's voice was no longer steady. "Dad... that's... that's what I hear."

Annemarie moved closer now, her hand resting on her son's small shoulder. "The calling voice," she repeated softly. I lowered the parchment gently onto the table, swallowing hard against the strange tide of emotions rising in my chest. These were not the fanciful scribblings of a medieval scribe entertaining idle prophecies. Whoever wrote this had understood something deeply rooted in blood — something which, impossibly, was echoing now in this little boy seated before us. "It matches the words from your dreams, doesn't it?" I asked carefully. Ben nodded. "It does. Almost like they were written for me."

We sat there, the three of us, suspended in that moment where time seemed to dissolve. The past was no longer some distant thing behind us, nor was the present simply a passing breath. The layers of history folded inward now, collapsing gently into the space where a child tried to grasp who — and what — he truly was.

The firewood gave a soft pop, and for a fleeting instant, I could almost sense a presence in the room — not something ghostly, but something ancestral, like old watchmen standing quietly, satisfied that their message was at last being received.

Ben's voice came again, this time much softer. "Dad... will we find the rest?" I smiled gently, squeezing his hand. "Yes, son. We will. One piece at a time." And so we sat there, unhurried, while the night wrapped us in its deep, ancient embrace. Morning brought with it that gentle quiet which often follows nights thick with discovery. The household had awakened slowly, almost respectfully, as though none of us wished to disturb whatever ancient spirits had chosen to whisper to us the night before. Even the birds outside seemed to sing more softly, their songs threading through the cool spring air with a certain reverence.

Annemarie prepared breakfast while Benedict and I sat once again at the long oak table. The scroll from Budapest remained unfurled where we had left it, untouched as though afraid to lose the fragile thread that connected it to its own history. The words on its surface no longer appeared simply as ink, but almost as echoes—softly vibrating in the silence between us.

Ben had been uncharacteristically quiet all morning. His usual humming, fidgeting, or random bursts of questions had given way to thoughtfulness. He was studying the scroll not as a child trying to understand, but as someone who knew, somewhere inside, that this belonged to him.

I allowed him the silence, sipping my coffee, waiting for him to speak when he was ready. Finally, his voice broke through, barely above a whisper. "Dad…" "Yes, son?" He swallowed, as though forming the question cost him some hidden strength. "Do you think… the voice… is him?" I set my cup down slowly, considering how best to answer. I already knew which 'him' he meant. "You mean Béla?" I asked gently. He nodded, his eyes still fixed upon the parchment, as if afraid to meet my gaze.

I leaned forward, folding my hands together on the table. "It's possible, Ben. Very possible. The words from this scroll, the words from your dreams—they're too alike to be random. And you've described the man before: seated on a throne, dressed in robes you couldn't have known about. It matches everything we've read about Béla III." Ben finally lifted his gaze to meet mine. His eyes were wet but clear, filled not with fear but with something far more ancient in children—a kind of sacred wonder.

"But why would he talk to me?" he whispered. "Because you carry his line," I said softly, my voice steady. "Through your father's side—through Alan, through the Horváths, and all the way back through Árpád's house. You're part of their story, Ben. And perhaps, just perhaps, some stories don't stop speaking merely because their kings are long gone." He bit his lower lip, thinking deeply. Then, as children often do when the burden grows too heavy, his voice shifted into something simpler—a return to the present. "Mom says I should have some oatmeal." He smiled faintly.

I laughed gently, breaking the heaviness of the moment. "Wise advice. Let's not upset your council of ancestors by letting you go hungry." As Annemarie brought over a bowl, I exchanged a brief glance with her. She nodded in that unspoken way we had developed over these months—a quiet confirmation that we would continue walking this path with him, one careful step at a time. After breakfast, we returned to the research room—the old study I had converted into our sanctuary of scrolls, family trees, and DNA reports. The shelves groaned under the weight of European genealogical records, Hungarian history books, British parish registers, and even the latest printouts from Ancestry.com. Maps of medieval Europe stretched across one wall, red strings tracing the migration of bloodlines like rivers across time.

Today, however, I pulled a different folder from the shelf—a slim, charcoal-coloured binder labelled simply: Transcriptions. "This one might help us make sense of that scroll from Budapest," I explained as Ben followed me into the study. "A professor I know helped me translate some of these old Hungarian dialects. They're not always straightforward. The way people wrote eight hundred years ago doesn't always match how we speak today." Ben climbed onto the high-backed chair, pulling his legs up under him as he often did when settling in for long sessions of listening. His attention was sharp, his young mind seemingly wired for these ancestral puzzles.

I flipped open the binder, reading aloud: "When the branches scatter, the root remains. And though the winds may carry the names far, the seed of Árpád rests within the veins of strangers who do not yet know their names." Ben's face lit up. "That's like me, isn't it?" "It is," I nodded. "Exactly like you." He chewed thoughtfully on his thumbnail. "But what about the 'seed' part? Does that mean I have to do something?" I smiled at his earnest concern. Children had this blessed way of expecting that every great discovery must also come with a great responsibility.

"You're already doing it, Ben," I reassured him. "You're learning. You're carrying their story. And you're honouring it by not running away from it. That alone is enough." His brow furrowed slightly as he asked the question that had no simple answer: "But what happens when I get older? Will it stop? The dreams, the voice?" I took a long breath, choosing my words carefully. "The voice may quiet, Ben. Or it may grow stronger as you grow. Sometimes, it depends on whether we keep listening. But even if the dreams stop, the story never does. Because now you know. And that knowledge lives inside you whether you hear the voice or not."

He nodded slowly, taking comfort in the thought, though I could see the lingering questions still dancing behind his eyes. For all his maturity, he was still only eight, and some answers would need to wait for years yet. Annemarie appeared in the doorway once again, this time holding a padded envelope. "This just arrived, Jeff," she said, handing it to me. I examined the postmark: Hungary again. The same archivist's return address. My heart quickened. Ben's eyes went wide. "More scrolls?" "Let's see," I said, slicing the package open carefully.

Inside were not scrolls this time, but photocopied pages from a recently uncovered church registry. The attached letter explained in neat, careful English: 'Mr. Philips, As per your inquiry, we have located entries from the parish of Székesfehérvár. The surname Horváth appears prominently within the baptisms of the 1600s, including several entries bearing connections to noble households descended from the Árpád line. We trust these will further your research.' I laid the pages flat across the desk. Ben craned his neck to read. "That's the same place we found before!" he exclaimed. "Szé... Szé… I can't say it."

I chuckled. "Székesfehérvár," I pronounced slowly. "It was once one of Hungary's great royal centres. Kings were crowned there. Buried there." Ben blinked. "Maybe Béla was buried there." "Possibly," I said, "though his remains are believed to rest in the cathedral at Székesfehérvár, yes." He leaned closer, his finger tracing the lines of names and dates. "It's like… it's like they're all waiting for us to find them, Dad." I swallowed a lump in my throat, for his words carried more truth than he knew. The ancestors were waiting, indeed. "They are, Ben. And together, we will."

The knock came just after noon. A single, sharp rap on the wooden front door—too polite for a package delivery, too deliberate for a neighbour simply passing by. Annemarie paused at the sink, looking toward the entryway with the same faint curiosity I felt prickling my own skin. The day had been uneventful until that moment. Now, something shifted. I stood from the study table, motioning gently to Ben who was still poring over the Székesfehérvár church records. "Stay here, kiddo," I said softly. "Let's see who's at the door."

Annemarie was already moving toward it, her hand hovering near the knob for just a moment longer than usual, as though even she sensed something unusual. She opened the door. No one stood there. Instead, resting squarely upon the welcome mat, lay a single package—wrapped not in modern cardboard or branded courier tape, but in thick, rough parchment, tied neatly with an aged twine. No shipping label. No postal stamp. No address. Just… there. My skin instantly prickled as if cold air had snuck beneath my shirt collar. Annemarie looked at me, her brow furrowed. "Jeff," she whispered. "There's no delivery truck."

I stepped forward cautiously, my heartbeat slow but heavy. Reaching down, I lifted the parcel carefully. It was surprisingly heavy for its size. The parchment crackled under my fingertips, dry yet firm, as though it had been preserved under conditions long forgotten. Ben peeked his head into the hallway now, sensing something was happening. "Dad? What is it?" "I'm not sure yet, buddy," I said. "Come on. Let's open it together." We returned to the study, laying the package flat on the oak table, the other scrolls and documents making space like silent witnesses. I untied the twine carefully, as though disarming some delicate mechanism that might crumble if rushed. The parchment unwrapped, revealing a thick envelope—deep burgundy in colour, sealed with an enormous wax insignia.

The seal took my breath away. Pressed into the hardened wax was an ancient symbol we had seen before—repeated on scrolls, on family crests, even in Ben's dreams: the crowned stag beneath a rising sun. Ben gasped audibly. "Dad, that's it. That's the stag." My fingers trembled. Slowly, I lifted the envelope, and that's when we saw it.

Written across the front, in broad, looping script—so elegant it seemed painted by a master's hand—were the words:

"To Benedict Adrian Harvick."

I heard Annemarie softly exhale behind us, her hand rising instinctively to her mouth. Ben stood frozen for a moment, then whispered, "It has my full name… Dad, how?" I had no answer. Only a flood of questions. My throat felt tight, my mouth dry. My hand hovered for a moment, then gently broke the seal. Inside, folded into two large sheets of heavy, hand-made vellum, was a letter written entirely by hand. The ink, though faded slightly, was still vibrant—deep black, as though no time had touched it. As I unfolded the letter, an immediate scent of old timber, beeswax, and faint herbs rose up—a scent that should not have survived the centuries. The script was enormous, regal, old-world in every stroke.

And then I saw it. The first line. Székesfehérvár, in the Year of our Lord 1194. The date alone made the room feel smaller. Ben's small voice broke the silence. "Dad… read it. Please." I took a slow, steadying breath and began aloud, though my own voice trembled under the weight of the moment:

To my beloved Benedict Adrian Harvick,

You do not know me, but I have known you all of my life. That is no jest, nor the whisper of a madman. You are mine—born far beyond my years, yet walking now as a son of my house.

I am Béla, the third of my line, King of Hungary and Croatia. Grandson of Géza, son of Euphrosyne of Kiev, sovereign of the kingdom given to my forefathers by the hand of God and the sword of Árpád.

I write this while breath still remains in my chest, though my moons grow few. I will not live to see what you shall see. Yet you have appeared to me in dreams not born of priests or prophets, but visions given by Providence itself.

You, Benedict, are the branch that blooms beyond my sight. You carry the old blood, and with you rests the charge I will not live to complete. The mysteries you now seek have waited for your hands alone to open.

Your surname has changed. Your tongue speaks differently. But your veins carry my breath still. The blood of Árpád, of the Seven Tribes, and of our forefathers before him flows within you. Even now, in my sleep, I see your face: fair-haired, eyes like rivers, hands small yet steady.

When you read these words, my bones shall already lie beneath Székesfehérvár, where kings sleep. Yet know this, truly: you are not alone. The crown rests unseen upon your brow, hidden from the world, but never from the heavens.

I paused for a moment. Ben's hand was gripping my sleeve now, his eyes wide, his face pale. "It… it's really him," he whispered. I nodded silently. Annemarie had come closer now, one hand upon Ben's shoulder, the other upon mine, grounding us all to the present as the ancient words pulled us deeper. I continued reading:

In the sanctuary of Székesfehérvár, where kings are crowned and buried, there are scrolls whose words were sealed by my own hand, containing the names of those who branched from my house. You may seek them in time, though I fear not all survived the fires of war. Yet some still remain where monks have hidden them.

In the halls of Pannonhalma, where the brothers of Saint Benedict labour, copies of the royal genealogies were made under my decree. There the monks may have guarded what was too dangerous to proclaim.

Look for the crowned stag, child. It has never left us. When you find it, you are near to truth.

The name you bear has changed, as I foresaw. The tongues of strangers cannot speak Horváth as we did. They shaped it into new form. Do not fear this change—it, too, was written.

I have seen your world, though I know not its name. I see great towers without stone, light that burns without flame, and carriages that move without horses. I see you standing among them, still carrying our blood.

And so I entrust this task to you, my distant grandson:
Walk boldly where I cannot. Seek that which was hidden, for you carry not only my blood, but my unfinished work.

Do not fear what you uncover. You will unlock puzzles even I could not imagine. Our family's covenant will not be finished in my reign, but in yours. In your hands rests the knowledge of where we came from—of strangers who became kings, and kings who became shadows.

You may question how this letter reached you. That is not your burden. What matters is that you hold it, for it was always meant for you.

And know this: you were chosen not by throne or sword, but by blood and by Providence. My son Emeric shall wear my earthly crown when I am gone—but you, Benedict, you shall wear the invisible one, bound not to rule, but to remember.

One day you will stand before the tombs of your ancestors. You will feel them call to you, as I feel you even now.

There are those who will doubt you.
There are those who will dismiss what cannot be explained.
Pay them no mind. Truth speaks softly to those who listen.
I go now to my rest. My beloved Anna and I shall sleep beneath the stones, but you will walk forward where I cannot.
And as you do, remember this, always:
The blood never forgets.

Ben, my child of the house of Árpád, my grandson across the river of years —
With my eternal love and pride,
Béla, Third of My Name, King of Hungary and Croatia

I paused for a moment. Ben's hand was gripping my sleeve now, his eyes wide, his face pale. "It… it's really him," he whispered. I nodded silently. Annemarie had come closer now, one hand upon Ben's shoulder, the other upon mine, grounding us all to the present as the ancient words pulled us deeper. I continued reading:

When I finished, the room sat in stunned silence. I could hear my own heartbeat. I could feel Ben's hand trembling. My own hands weren't much steadier. Finally, after what felt like ages, Ben spoke—his voice tiny but clear.

"Dad… I understand it. Even the part you didn't read yet." I blinked. "What do you mean?" He reached forward, turning the second page. There, at the bottom, written in a second hand, was a paragraph in old Hungarian. Ben whispered the words, translating as he read: "You have already heard my voice, little one. You heard me when you were but a babe near death. I called you back three times. You are not finished yet." His voice broke. His eyes welled.

Annemarie crouched beside him, pulling him gently into her embrace. "You were never alone, sweetheart," she whispered. I sat back, my own mind spinning. My lips finally formed words I could barely believe: "Holy smokes… Ben… you've got a letter from King Béla III. This is insane." Ben whispered, almost to himself, as though speaking into some ancient corridor of time "The puzzle… is real."

The house had grown so quiet that even the air seemed to hesitate. No one spoke for some time after the last words of Béla III's letter had been read aloud. The wax seal still sat broken on the table, its edges curling slightly as though it, too, knew its ancient duty had finally been fulfilled. Ben hadn't moved much since we finished reading. His little fingers still rested gently on the edge of the parchment, as though afraid that removing his touch might somehow cause it to vanish. His wide blue eyes were locked upon the letter, scanning the looping script over and over again.

Even Annemarie, who had sat quietly throughout, had nothing to say in the face of what we had just witnessed. Some things were too big for words. Some moments demanded reverence. Finally, after what felt like an entire afternoon trapped in that holy stillness, Ben's voice returned — small, fragile, but steady. "Dad…" He didn't even look up. "Yes, son." "It's not just… a letter, is it?" I exhaled slowly, watching him as I answered. "No, Ben. It isn't."

His fingers traced the words once more. "It's like… like he's still here." I nodded. "In a way, he is." Ben finally raised his head then, looking straight at me. His face was pale, but his eyes were burning — alive with something that I could only describe as inheritance. "He knew I'd get this." "Yes," I said quietly. "And somehow, across more than eight hundred years, it found its way to you." He bit his lower lip again, a nervous habit I'd seen countless times, though now it carried more weight. His voice trembled. "But how?" I had no answer. None that made sense, anyway. My voice stayed low, deliberate. "I don't know, son. Some mysteries aren't meant to be solved all at once."

Annemarie finally spoke, her voice gentle as silk. "Sometimes, sweetheart, it's enough to know that something was meant for you—even if you don't understand how." Ben stared at the letter for a few more seconds. "He called me… his grandson." His voice broke slightly on that last word. I swallowed hard. "Because you are." He looked down at his own hands, small and pale against the heavy parchment, as if seeing himself for the first time. Then he whispered something that made every hair on my arms stand: "The invisible crown." I drew a breath. "That's right." "It's real." "Yes." My throat tightened. "It's very real."

The hours that followed felt like walking inside a dream. We laid the letter carefully into a large archival sleeve, sealing it against the elements like a sacred relic. The house seemed different now, as though its very walls carried something older, something watching over us. The shadows outside grew long as evening came. None of us had eaten dinner. Food seemed far too ordinary for a night like this. At last, after the clock struck nine, I knew I had to gently guide us back toward the world of the living. The search would continue tomorrow, but the boy needed rest. "Come on, buddy," I said, gently touching Ben's shoulder. "Let's get you ready for bed."

He resisted slightly, his eyes reluctant to leave the table. "What if something else comes?" I smiled softly. "Then we'll face it together, like we always do." Annemarie kissed his forehead and quietly walked with him toward his room. I stayed behind for a moment, staring at the sealed letter resting in its sleeve. A letter written nearly nine centuries ago. Written directly to him.

The weight of it settled on my chest. What do we do with something like this? How is any of this even possible? I whispered the questions into the quiet, knowing full well no answer would come—not yet. But as I stood there in the silence of that study, I did feel something: A faint stirring beneath my skin. A presence, perhaps. Or simply the living memory of a bloodline not yet finished speaking. The next morning arrived clear and cool, as though the world itself had reset overnight. Sunlight spilled into the study again, catching the edge of the archival sleeve and making the wax seal gleam faintly under its plastic barrier.

Ben came in quietly, still in his pyjamas, rubbing sleep from his eyes. "Morning, Dad." "Morning, buddy." He sat down beside me, his face still serious but calmer now. "Can we… start looking?" he asked. "Looking where?" "Székesfehérvár. Pannonhalma." He said the words carefully, sounding out the strange syllables, trying to make sense of them. I smiled. "You remembered." He nodded. "It's in the letter. He said monks hid things. The scrolls might still be there." I leaned back, impressed by his clarity. "You're absolutely right."

We pulled out the map again. Hungary spread before us like a puzzle waiting to be unlocked. Székesfehérvár stood boldly in the western part of the country—once the very heart of Hungarian kingship. Not far from it sat Pannonhalma Abbey, one of Europe's oldest Benedictine monasteries. "You see this place here?" I said, pointing. "Pannonhalma. That's where the monks copied the genealogies Béla mentioned." Ben whispered, almost to himself. "The monks of Saint Benedict."

"Yes." He furrowed his brow. "But Dad… will the scrolls still be there? After all this time?" I hesitated. "That's what we'll have to find out. But if anyone can uncover them—it's you." His small chest lifted as he breathed in deeply, as though preparing for a journey far larger than his small frame could contain. Then he whispered again, almost reverently: "The puzzle inside the DNA." I smiled. "Exactly." And in that moment, we both understood — the search wasn't over. In truth, it had only just begun.

The following days passed in a strange rhythm. It felt as though time had shifted slightly inside our home—as though history itself had become a quiet guest seated at the kitchen table with us, silently watching, gently urging. Every meal, every moment of rest, even the ordinary tasks of life now carried an undercurrent none of us could ignore. Ben had become consumed by the letter. Not in the way of an obsessed child lost in fantasy, but rather like a small historian already understanding that what he held was something greater than himself.

Every morning, before breakfast, he would stand before the table where we kept the archival sleeve. His fingers never touched it directly—he understood the sacredness of its preservation—but his eyes traced every word, as though absorbing its message deeper into his being each time. He had begun to refer to it quietly as "the summons." I never corrected him. The word felt strangely right. On the fourth day following the letter's arrival, something shifted. Ben stood before the letter again that morning, quietly studying, when his voice broke through the silence.

"Dad?" "Yes, son." "You said Pannonhalma was a real place." "That's right. It's still standing today." "Can we find it? Can we look it up? I want to see what it looks like." I smiled softly. "That's a very good idea." We sat down at the computer together. My fingers hovered over the keyboard for a moment before I typed: Pannonhalma Archabbey, Hungary. Instantly, images of its tall white towers and ancient stone walls filled the screen. Its location marked near the northwest of Hungary, standing like a sentinel overlooking the landscape—a monastery that had survived wars, empires, and centuries. Ben's eyes widened. "That's where they kept the scrolls?"

I nodded. "That's where Béla said copies were made." His small hand pointed at the monitor. "Look… it's so big." "It's one of the oldest Benedictine monasteries in Europe," I explained softly. "Founded more than a thousand years ago. The monks who live there today still carry the name of Saint Benedict." He whispered, "Like me." "Yes." I smiled. "Like you." We read together, scrolling through photos and short articles. The abbey had endured Mongol invasions, Ottoman conquests, Habsburg rule, even both World Wars. And yet it remained—untouched in its deeper secrets, its archives still preserved.

Then, buried inside one academic journal I had pulled up, we stumbled across something that made my skin tighten. I read aloud: "The Pannonhalma archives include thousands of preserved manuscripts, among them royal charters, early genealogical registers, and diplomatic records dating from the 12th century forward. Many items from the Árpád dynasty period are still housed in restricted collections accessible only to authorized scholars." Ben's voice broke into a whisper. "Dad... that could be it. That's where some of his scrolls might be."

I sat back, my mind racing. "Yes, son. It could be." I could feel my own pulse in my neck. Béla's words echoed back to me as if spoken anew: "Some still remain where monks have hidden them." Ben looked at me, his face both frightened and determined. "How do we get there?" I exhaled, steadying him. "One step at a time, buddy." That evening, once Ben had gone to bed, Annemarie and I sat together at the kitchen table, the warm glow of the overhead light cocooning us. She stirred her tea slowly, her brow furrowed as she finally spoke.

"Jeff… do you realize what this means?" I nodded. "I do." Her voice dropped lower. "This is no longer just ancestry, or DNA tests, or family trees. This is… real." "Yes," I whispered. "And far deeper than anything I imagined when we first opened those test results." She paused. "And you believe him? Béla?" I met her gaze. "I do." She nodded again, slowly, her eyes glistening. "So do I." There was a long silence between us as we both stared at the map of Hungary still laid out on the study table across the room.

Finally, she asked the question I had been waiting for. "What do we do now?" I exhaled deeply. "We prepare. And eventually… we go." The next morning, as though the air itself had carried the decision into Ben's dreams, he came into the study before breakfast, eyes wide with conviction. "Dad… we have to go. We have to find Pannonhalma. We have to find the scrolls." I looked at him, this small boy whose life had become entwined with kings and prophecies. His eight-year-old face carried a determination few grown men could match. I placed my hand gently on his shoulder. "Yes, son. We will. But first, we gather everything we know. Every scroll. Every document. Every clue. If we're going to do this, we do it right."

Ben smiled for the first time in days, relief flooding his young features. "We'll find what Béla left for us." "Yes," I whispered. "We will." And somewhere—though neither of us spoke it aloud—we both knew that the invisible crown had already begun to rest heavier upon his head. The days that followed fell into a rhythm unlike anything we had known before. It was as though the air within the house carried an unfamiliar weight, and the walls themselves listened to every conversation, holding their breath alongside us. The presence of Béla's letter lingered heavily, resting quietly upon the oak table as if aware of its own significance. None of us dared move it beyond its protective archival sleeve. It had already crossed more years than any one of us could fathom. To disturb it now seemed almost a violation.

Ben approached the table each morning with an almost sacred reverence. His fingertips hovered near the parchment, never touching but tracing the loops of the script as though absorbing its message one breath at a time. It was not obsession that gripped him, but rather the pull of something ancient now awakened.

This was not a child lost in fantasy; this was a descendant answering a summons. Quietly, almost unconsciously, Ben had begun to refer to the letter as "the summons." I made no attempt to correct him, for I sensed the truth of it as well.

On the fourth day, as the morning sun slipped softly through the curtains, Ben stood once again before the table, studying the letter. His voice finally cut through the stillness, low but certain. "Dad?" he called without turning his gaze away. I moved beside him. "Yes, son." He swallowed and continued, "You said Pannonhalma is real. That it still stands." I nodded. "That's right. It's there today, just as it was in Béla's time." His voice grew stronger, though the awe remained. "Can we find it? Can we see what it looks like?"

Without hesitation, I sat beside him and opened the laptop. My fingers hovered momentarily before typing: Pannonhalma Archabbey, Hungary. Images filled the screen almost instantly. The towering white spires of the abbey rose proudly above the surrounding hills, a fortress of stone and faith that had defied time itself. Its ancient walls, the same ones Béla would have known, stood like silent sentinels guarding the mysteries within.

Ben's breath caught in his throat. "That's where they kept the scrolls?" he whispered, almost as though he feared disturbing the image. "That's where Béla said the monks copied the royal records," I answered. He stared, wide-eyed. "It's so big." I nodded. "One of the oldest Benedictine monasteries in Europe. Founded more than a thousand years ago. And the monks still serve there today."

His small voice barely broke the stillness. "Like me. Saint Benedict." My smile returned, both proud and somber. "Yes, like you."

We read together, combing through historical notes, photographs, and scholarly articles. The abbey had survived countless trials—Mongol invasions, Ottoman sieges, Habsburg rule, the ravages of two world wars—yet its archives remained preserved, as though the hand of Providence had guarded them for this very moment.

Buried within one journal article, my eyes caught a line that made my pulse quicken. I read it aloud for Ben to hear: "The Pannonhalma archives include thousands of preserved manuscripts, among them royal charters, early genealogical registers, and diplomatic records dating from the 12th century forward. Many items from the Árpád dynasty period are still housed in restricted collections accessible only to authorized scholars."

Ben inhaled sharply, his small chest rising with the weight of realization. "Dad… that could be it." I nodded, hearing the echo of Béla's words even as Ben spoke. Some still remain where monks have hidden them. My own voice softened. "Yes, son. It very well could be." The thought of those scrolls, perhaps still resting untouched, sent a chill up my spine. Ben's gaze sharpened, filled with both fear and resolve. "How do we get there?" he asked. The simplicity of his question belied the enormity of the task before us. I placed my hand on his shoulder and spoke gently. "One step at a time, buddy."

Later that night, after Ben had finally drifted to sleep, Annemarie and I sat in the dim glow of the kitchen, the house quiet except for the soft ticking of the wall clock. She stirred her tea slowly, eyes fixed on nothing and everything at once, lost in the enormity of what we faced. "Jeff," she whispered, "do you understand what this means?" I nodded, feeling the gravity pressing down on both of us. "I do." Her voice trembled slightly. "This isn't just genealogy. This is real. This changes everything." I exhaled deeply. "Yes. And far deeper than anything I expected when we first ran those DNA tests."

She paused, her eyes glistening. "You believe him?" The question needed no explanation. She meant Béla. "I do," I answered quietly, without hesitation. Her head lowered slightly, and for a long moment neither of us spoke. The map of Hungary remained spread across the nearby study table, the names of cities and regions now transformed from abstract places into living markers upon Ben's inheritance. Finally, her voice broke the silence once more. "What do we do now?" I breathed slowly before answering. "We prepare. And when the time comes… we go."

By morning, as if drawn by the same invisible thread that tugged at all of us, Ben entered the study before breakfast, his face set with an expression of quiet determination. The weight of the invisible crown sat visibly upon him now, though his eight-year-old frame remained small beneath it. "Dad… we have to go. We have to find Pannonhalma. We have to find the scrolls." I knelt beside him, looking into his bright but serious eyes. "Yes, son. We will. But we must prepare carefully. We need every scroll, every document, every clue that Béla has left for us. If we're going to do this, we do it right."

Relief and resolve washed over him at once. His face relaxed, his eyes shimmering with purpose. "We'll find what Béla left for us." "Yes," I whispered. "We will." Though unspoken between us, I knew in that moment: this was no longer a question of ancestry alone. The search had become a calling.

The days that followed were unlike anything I had ever experienced. Every room in the house had now become part of an unfolding archive. The kitchen table hosted piles of maps and notes; the living room had become a staging ground for genealogy charts; even the hallway shelves were crowded with binders and folders labelled with careful precision. The study, once my quiet retreat, had fully transformed into our research command centre—a place where centuries whispered from paper and parchment.

Ben was at the very centre of it all. He moved through the house with quiet determination, studying each document we unearthed, scanning names with the careful eye of a boy who somehow already understood the weight of his lineage. His small voice would rise periodically, reading aloud strange Hungarian names, testing the shapes of ancient words upon his tongue. At times, it was as if he were remembering rather than learning.

Annemarie worked alongside us, her steady hands keeping order among the growing mountain of documents. She approached the task with a grace and calm that allowed Ben's enthusiasm to flourish while ensuring we did not drown beneath the sheer volume of information.

At the centre of it all remained Béla's letter—a constant anchor amid the swirling sea of papers. Sealed in its archival sleeve, it sat upon the study table like a royal decree, as if silently commanding our every move.

On one of those afternoons, while organizing a stack of old family charts pulled from our Ancestry.com records, I found something I had nearly forgotten—a handwritten tree I had once drawn for Ben when we first began this journey, back when his DNA results had merely been a curiosity. I unfolded it slowly. The branches traced from Alan's side, branching through the Harvick line, then back toward Horváth. I had penned the Árpád dynasty in at the top, half in jest, half in wonder, when we first discovered its possible connection. Now, holding it, the simplicity of that chart struck me differently. What once felt hypothetical now felt prophetic.

Ben stood beside me, watching. His small finger traced the same lines. "That's where I came from," he said softly, eyes locked on the names. "All the way back to Béla." I nodded, my voice quiet. "And beyond him, to Árpád. And even further to the ones who came before." He looked up at me then, his face filled with something deeper than pride. It was responsibility. "And now I have to find what they left behind."

As our research deepened, new clues began to emerge—not only from the royal line, but from scattered records of Hungarian noble families who had branched into Western Europe. Several Horváth entries had appeared in 17th-century British and German registries, their names slowly Anglicized, eventually vanishing into the growing sea of Harvick ancestors in Kent. The migration path was becoming clearer. Béla's prediction had proven eerily precise: the name had transformed through the mouths of strangers, but the blood had travelled, carried through countless generations, landing finally in the hands of an eight-year-old boy standing on the threshold of something few ever experienced.

By the end of that week, the plan had begun to take shape. It was no longer a question of if we would go, but when. Travel arrangements, research permits, and letters of inquiry to Hungarian archives began filling my inbox. I contacted a few colleagues, historians I had once known during my own university studies, seeking guidance on accessing restricted monastic archives. The monks at Pannonhalma were known for their discretion and their ancient loyalty to safeguarding records of the royal house. The abbey was old—older even than Béla's reign—but its archives had endured.

Ben watched each development closely. He was no longer the curious child who once asked simple questions about where he came from. He was becoming a custodian of something sacred, as if Béla himself had passed a torch that burned now in his hands. Late one night, after Annemarie had gone to bed, Ben came quietly into the study where I was reviewing the latest response from a Hungarian archivist. He stood beside me, his voice calm but steady. "Dad… are you scared?" The question surprised me. I paused, then answered honestly. "Yes. A little." He nodded as though expecting it. "Me too." I smiled softly. "That's okay. It means we understand how important this is."

He looked up at me, his voice small. "Do you think Béla sees us now?" I reached out and gently placed my hand on his shoulder. "I think he always has." The plan was no longer a distant idea spoken at the kitchen table. It had become real. The weight of Béla's letter, the scrolls waiting across the ocean, and the whispers of the past had finally pulled us to this moment. And now, for the first time in Ben's young life, he was about to step into the history he carried within his blood.

At night, after Ben had gone to bed, Annemarie and I sat at the kitchen table under the soft light of the old lamp. Maps lay unfolded across the wooden surface. Papers covered in contact information, travel authorizations, and emails to the monastery sat neatly organized into small stacks. The printer had worked overtime printing flight confirmations, hotel bookings, and car rental receipts.

For days, I had corresponded with the monks at Pannonhalma, explaining our purpose and providing the partial translation of Béla's letter. They responded with caution at first, careful in their wording, as monks tend to be. But after several exchanges, something in their tone shifted. They no longer spoke as strangers. Finally, a brief message arrived from the Prior himself: "You are welcome to come. We have been expecting you." The moment those words appeared on the screen, everything changed.

Annemarie read the message several times that evening, quietly tracing the words with her fingertip. Her breath was steady, but her hands trembled ever so slightly. The weight of what we were doing sat heavy on her shoulders. I reached for her hand. "You're sure?" I asked softly. She nodded, though her eyes glistened. "I'm sure you and Ben need to go. But Jeff… you know I can't. I just can't fly."

Her voice was tight, honest, and pained. "I've never been able to get on a plane. Not once. I'd only hold you back." She swallowed and blinked away tears. "I wish I could go with you both. I really do." I squeezed her hand gently. "No one's upset, love. You'll be with us the whole way, even if you're not on the flight." Ben had been listening quietly from the doorway. He approached us slowly, his small voice calm. "It's okay, Mom. I know you'll be with us. You always are." Annemarie wrapped her arms around him tightly, pulling him into her chest. She kissed the top of his head and whispered, "You're my whole world, Ben. You stay close to your father, okay? And when you come home, you tell me everything."

"I promise." We sat together long after that conversation, not speaking much, but sitting hand in hand, surrounded by the soft glow of lamplight and the quiet pulse of history preparing to breathe again. The following morning, we finalized the paperwork. Passports were double-checked, suitcases carefully packed with clothing, travel guides, and the documents I had carefully printed for the monastery visit. Ben insisted on packing a few of his own treasures — a small notepad, several pens, and a little magnifying glass he had used while studying old family trees. "Just in case," he had said with a nervous grin.

The anticipation built slowly in our home. Ben would wander into the study each day to look again at Béla's letter resting inside its archival sleeve, studying its curling script as if it might suddenly reveal a new secret.

The crowned stag stamped upon the seal seemed almost to shimmer under the light, as though watching us prepare. "Dad," Ben asked one evening, "what if the scrolls aren't really there?" "They are," I answered gently. "And if they aren't, we'll still find something. The search itself is part of the story."

He nodded slowly, processing my words. "And the monks?" he whispered. "They're waiting for us." Three days later, we left Kent before dawn under grey skies. Annemarie drove us quietly toward London Heathrow. The motorways were still wrapped in fog as we passed through the English countryside. Ben sat quietly in the back seat, his face pressed against the window, watching the fields roll by. When we pulled up to the terminal, Annemarie parked the car and stepped out with us. She knelt in front of Ben, holding his small face in both hands. "Be safe, sweetheart. Listen to your father. And take lots of notes for me, okay?"

Ben nodded, his voice barely more than a whisper. "I will, Mom." She hugged me tightly as well, her voice cracking. "Jeff… find what you're meant to find." "I will." With one last wave, she watched us Disappear into the airport. The airport itself was loud, crowded, and enormous. We passed through security, waited at our gate, and boarded the plane. For Ben, it was his first flight. He sat wide-eyed at the window, staring out as the aircraft taxied toward the runway. As the engines roared to life and the plane lifted into the sky, Ben gripped my hand tightly. I squeezed his fingers gently, leaning close to his ear. "You're doing great, buddy." "It feels like we're flying into the past," he whispered. I smiled softly. "In a way, we are."

The flight itself stretched nearly two and a half hours across the European sky. Once we cleared the thick English clouds, the world below unfolded in soft blues and greens. The plane hummed steadily as we crossed over Belgium, Germany, and Austria. Ben sat quietly, alternating between peeking out the window and watching the wing slice through the air like a silver blade. Occasionally, small towns sparkled beneath us like scattered lights. He asked gentle questions about what country we were over, and I pointed to the route map glowing softly on the seatback screen. Near the end of the flight, as we began our descent, Ben's eyes grew heavy from the long journey, but his excitement never dimmed.

After several hours in the air, we descended through a blanket of clouds, Budapest unfolding beneath us. The Danube River gleamed below like a silver ribbon. The old rooftops of the Hungarian capital stretched outward in every direction, a city filled with echoes of kings and empires long past. This was Béla's land. The land of Ben's ancestors.

We collected our bags, made our way through customs, and secured the rental car I had arranged ahead of time. The man at the rental desk handed me a map, circling the small town west of the capital. "Pannonhalma," I read aloud. "We're almost there." Ben stared at the map, his voice hushed. "It looks far." "Not too far," I said. "We'll be there before sunset." The drive carried us through open countryside, endless rolling hills painted in green and gold, speckled with small villages and old farmhouses that had stood for centuries.

Ben remained quiet during most of the ride, staring out the window as the distant outline of the monastery finally appeared atop a hill like a great stone sentinel. As we approached, the abbey's towers pierced the sky, rising above the forests like ancient watchmen. The stone walls glowed faintly beneath the late afternoon sun, and for a moment, it felt as though the world itself had held its breath waiting for this arrival. Ben leaned forward in his seat, whispering to himself. "It's really here." "Yes, son," I said quietly. "It's been waiting for you."

The car crept slowly up the winding road as the hill grew steeper, the late afternoon sun casting long shadows across the narrow path. The ancient walls of Pannonhalma Abbey came into view at last, rising like silent witnesses over the centuries. Its towers stood proud and steady, as though untouched by the passing of time. For a moment, neither Ben nor I spoke. The weight of the journey, the long weeks of preparation, and the centuries of history behind us seemed to settle on our shoulders all at once.

Ben leaned forward in his seat, eyes wide with awe. "Dad... it's so much bigger than the pictures." I nodded, my voice low. "Pictures never really capture places like this." We pulled through the outer gates, where a small courtyard opened ahead of us. The car's engine fell silent as I shut it off, and for a moment there was only stillness. Birds sang softly from the trees. A breeze tugged gently at Ben's hair. The abbey itself stood motionless, as though watching us approach.

Ben stepped out of the car slowly, his head tilted back, his eyes following the great stone walls as they stretched into the sky. "It feels... different here," he whispered. "It should," I replied softly. "You've never stood on ground this old before." The heavy oak doors of the abbey creaked open, and from within emerged a man in a long black robe. His steps were measured, his face calm. He was older, his head shaved in the monastic tradition, but his eyes were bright and steady. As he approached, his hands folded neatly before him, I could feel Ben inch closer to my side.

The monk stopped a few feet away, offering a small nod of greeting. "You must be Mr. Philips," he said in accented but clear English. His voice was gentle, smooth, like one who had spent years speaking in quiet places. I nodded. "Yes. And this is my son, Benedict." The monk's eyes rested on Ben for a moment longer than most would. Not rudely. Not even with surprise. But rather with recognition. As though he saw something familiar and long awaited. His mouth curved into the faintest hint of a smile. "Benedict," he repeated softly. "A good name."

Ben's fingers tightened around mine, but he managed to nod respectfully. "Thank you." The monk extended his hand to me. "I am Brother Miklós. I've been asked to receive you on behalf of the Prior." "It's an honour to meet you, Brother," I said, returning the handshake. He turned, gesturing toward the towering wooden doors. "If you are ready, we will take you inside." The moment we stepped through the heavy doors, the world outside seemed to vanish.

The abbey's interior was cool and dim, the air filled with the faint scent of wax and old stone. High arched ceilings soared above us, their ribbed vaults meeting like the branches of ancient trees. Sunlight pierced through narrow stained-glass windows, casting beams of coloured light along the polished floors. Ben walked slowly beside me, his head turning in every direction. His voice broke the silence in a whisper. "Dad... it's like walking into a castle."

"In some ways, it is," I whispered back. "But instead of knights, it holds monks. And instead of treasure, it holds knowledge." Brother Miklós led us along a wide corridor, our footsteps echoing softly with each step. The hall was lined with tall wooden doors, some open, revealing glimpses of quiet reading rooms, libraries, and study chambers. "We preserve many records here," Brother Miklós explained gently as we walked. "But not all are for public study. Some have been held for many generations. Kept safe for a time when they might be needed."

I glanced at Ben. He was listening carefully, absorbing every word. Brother Miklós glanced back at us with a knowing look. "We have long known that someone would come for them. Not by demand. But by providence." I felt my throat tighten. "You mean... for Ben?" The monk did not answer directly. Instead, his soft reply was simple. "For the one who carries the summons." Ben's head snapped upward slightly at the words, his eyes wide. "The summons... like Béla's letter." Brother Miklós nodded once. "Yes."

We continued deeper into the abbey, descending a short stone stairway that led to an older section of the building. The walls here were thicker, darker, the air cooler. It smelled faintly of old parchment and cedar. Heavy wooden shelves lined the passage, filled with ancient books, scrolls, and leather-bound ledgers. At last, we reached a small chamber sealed by an iron-reinforced door. The monk produced a large brass key from within his robe, fitting it carefully into the lock. The heavy mechanism turned with a soft clunk, and the door creaked open.

Inside was a room unlike any I had ever seen. The chamber was modest in size but lined on every wall with shelves stacked with scrolls carefully wrapped in cloth and parchment. A wooden table stood at the center beneath a narrow window, the light falling perfectly across its polished surface. "This," Brother Miklós said softly, "is the archive you have come to see." Ben stepped forward slowly, as though entering a room not meant for ordinary feet. His eyes grew wide as he looked around at the scrolls.

"Dad..." he whispered, "are these...?" "Yes," I whispered back. "These are Béla's." Brother Miklós approached the table where a single bundle of scrolls had already been prepared, bound neatly with an aged ribbon. The seal upon them bore the same crowned stag we had seen before, the very mark Béla had described in his letter. "These were set aside many generations ago," the monk explained. "Not every monk who served here has known why. But some of us have waited." Ben stared at the bundle, his voice trembling. "For me?" The monk lowered his head gently. "For the one called."

The scroll sat quietly before us, resting on the polished wooden table beneath the soft light of the chamber. Brother Miklós, standing beside us, gently untied the aged ribbon, his fingers careful as though unwrapping something sacred. The parchment unfurled slowly, its edges curling with age, revealing beautiful Hungarian script written by hands long gone. Ben leaned in closer, his breath shallow, his eyes wide with wonder. The crowned stag stamped in wax at the corner seemed to watch him, almost as though it too had waited for this moment. Brother Miklós spoke softly, his voice steady, as though teaching a lesson passed down for generations.

"Benedict," he began, "you must understand who your ancestor truly was. This man, whom you have already come to know through his letter, was not simply a king. He was a cornerstone of your family — and of your country's history." Ben swallowed, his small voice barely above a whisper. "Tell me everything." The monk gave a faint smile. "Then listen closely." He paused, collecting his thoughts before continuing. "King Béla, known as Béla the Third, ruled Hungary and Croatia many centuries ago. He was born in the year 1148. His father was King Géza II, who ruled before him, and his mother was Euphrosyne of Kiev. Béla had an older brother, Stephen III, who became king first. But when Stephen passed away, Béla was called to the throne in 1172."

Ben blinked. "That's so long ago..." "Yes," Brother Miklós nodded. "Nearly nine hundred years. Yet his blood still lives in you."

He continued, carefully pointing to the scroll as if guiding Ben through time. "Béla ruled during what many call the golden age of Hungary. He was wise. He encouraged written records, something few kings cared for at the time. In fact, he introduced the two-barred cross—what we call the double cross—which still appears on Hungary's coat of arms to this very day." Ben studied the symbol, his eyes tracing the lines carefully. "Like the one on the letter."

"Exactly," the monk smiled. "That was his mark." As we listened, the chamber seemed to grow smaller, as if folding in time itself, drawing us closer to Béla's world. "Before Béla became king," Brother Miklós continued, "he was almost made a Byzantine emperor. He had been betrothed to the daughter of Emperor Manuel I Komnenos, who ruled Byzantium. Béla lived in Constantinople for a time, preparing for a future that never came. The emperor's own son was born later, and Béla's engagement was cancelled."

Ben frowned slightly, processing the story. "But instead, Béla married Anna of Antioch, the emperor's wife's half-sister. She became his queen, and together they had at least six children. Four of them lived into adulthood. One of his sons, Emeric, would follow him as king after Béla's death." Ben whispered softly, "So Queen Anna is my great-grandmother too?" "Indeed, child," Miklós replied warmly. "Your great-grandmother, many times over." He paused. "Probably about fifteen greats, if I had to count."

Ben grinned at the thought. Brother Miklós's voice softened. "But Béla's time on this earth was not as long as his wisdom deserved. He fell ill in the year 1196. He was only forty-seven, maybe forty-eight, when he passed.

He was first buried at Székesfehérvár Cathedral, where many kings of Hungary lay. His beloved Anna was buried beside him." Ben's eyes lowered respectfully. "They were together." "Yes," the monk nodded, his own voice reverent. "But that is not the end of their story."

I leaned forward. "This is the part I never knew." Brother Miklós continued, "In the year 1848, nearly six hundred and fifty years after his death, Béla's grave was reopened during excavations. His bones, along with Anna's, were carefully removed and later transferred to the Matthias Church in Budapest. There, they rest together still, side by side inside their great stone sarcophagus." Ben's lips parted slightly. "We could visit them?"

"One day," I promised softly. "We will." The monk stepped to another shelf, retrieving a smaller scroll sealed tightly. "In recent years, something remarkable happened. In 2014, scientists were granted permission to study Béla's remains for genetic research." Ben's eyes widened. "DNA?" "Yes," Brother Miklós said, pleased that the boy understood. "They took samples from four of his bones. What they found was extraordinary. His DNA showed the strongest genetic connection to present-day people from Hungary and Croatia."

He lowered his voice slightly. "But the most fascinating discovery was this: Béla's paternal bloodline — his Y-DNA haplogroup — belonged to R1a. This group is traced back to Central Asia, possibly carried by your distant ancestors as they crossed into Europe." Ben whispered softly, almost to himself, "That's where my DNA comes from too." "Yes," Brother Miklós answered. "The same line you now carry. The same line that once belonged to Árpád himself, your ancient grandfather who led the Seven Tribes into the Carpathian Basin long before Béla's time."

Ben sat in silence for a moment, processing the story, his young mind tracing the threads of history that stretched out behind him like endless rivers. The names, the dates, the places—they no longer felt like stories from a distant world. They were his. Brother Miklós rested a hand gently on Ben's shoulder. "You are not here by accident, Benedict. Your ancestor saw you. He knew you would come."

Ben looked up, his voice barely audible. "And now I know him." Two full weeks had passed since we arrived at the great abbey on the hill. The days slipped by gently, like the pages of the scrolls themselves. Each morning, Ben and I would walk down the quiet stone corridors where the monks moved softly, their black robes whispering with every step. The great bells of the abbey rang through the air at regular hours, calling the monks to prayer, but to us, they simply marked the rhythm of our quiet work.

Brother Miklós had become almost like a patient teacher, guiding Ben through the old writings. There were scrolls filled with family trees, others with royal decrees written in bold Hungarian script, some with seals that bore the crowned stag again and again. Ben would trace the old letters with his finger, sounding out names that twisted his young tongue. "István... that's Stephen, right?" "Yes," Brother Miklós would nod, smiling. "Stephen was Béla's brother. Very good."

"And Emeric," Ben added, tapping another name. "That was Béla's son." "You have quite a memory, Benedict," the monk would say, clearly impressed. Ben grinned proudly, his face glowing each time he recognized a name. Sometimes, I caught him pretending to be a small historian, sitting upright, carefully holding a pen in his hand as if taking important notes. The monks had even given him a small desk near the table, calling it his study corner. Of course, not every moment was serious. There were times the monks allowed Ben to join them in simple chores—helping collect fresh honey from the abbey's beehives, watching the old stone bread ovens, and once even helping Brother István feed the abbey's sheep.

Ben giggled when one of the smaller sheep followed him around the courtyard, nudging his leg like a lost puppy. "Dad, I think he thinks I'm his mom!" he laughed. The brothers chuckled, and Brother Miklós said, "Well, you do have the patience of a shepherd." For all its quiet solemnity, the abbey had become a kind of peaceful home for us. But we knew we could not stay forever. As the second week drew to an end, the monks had carefully packed the most important scrolls into a secure archival case—sealed and prepared for our journey home.

"You may study them further when you return to England," Brother Miklós said softly. "But remember, Benedict — these are not simply papers. They are voices." Ben nodded solemnly, repeating almost like a vow: "They are voices." The morning of our departure arrived with a light drizzle falling gently across the abbey grounds. The monks gathered in the courtyard to see us off. Brother Miklós placed his hands gently on Ben's shoulders. "Remember this place, child. You carry something very few have carried."

Ben looked up at him. "I will. And thank you for teaching me." The monk smiled faintly. "It was not I who taught you, Benedict. It was the ones who came before." We drove down the hill one last time, the abbey growing smaller behind us as fog gently rolled across the hills like a great grey blanket folding over the past. At the airport in Budapest, as we waited at the gate, Ben rested his head on my arm, staring at the case of scrolls secured in my lap. "Dad... do you think Béla saw us when we were there?"

I smiled, rubbing his back gently. "I think he's always seen us, son." The flight home seemed longer somehow. Once the plane lifted off and levelled out high above the clouds, Ben pulled out his small notepad, his pens, and one of the copies Brother Miklós had made for him — a simple family tree drawn in careful lines. It showed Béla, Anna, Emeric, Stephen, and so many others. "Look, Dad!" Ben whispered, showing me proudly. "I can remember who's who now!"

I leaned closer, pointing gently at the chart. "Alright, little professor — let's test you." He giggled. "Okay!" "Who was Béla's father?" "Géza the Second!" Ben answered without hesitation. "Excellent. And Béla's wife?" "Queen Anna of Antioch," he grinned. "She was the half-sister of the emperor's wife." "Very good," I said, smiling. Ben wrinkled his brow. "And then... Béla died in 1196, right? He was forty-seven or forty-eight." "That's right." He flipped the page. "And they moved his bones later... to the big church. Matthias Church in Budapest."

"Yes," I nodded. "And Anna's bones too. They rest together even now." Ben paused for a moment, staring out the window at the sky stretching endlessly around us. His voice softened. "It's like... even though he died, he still made sure I would find him." I ruffled his hair gently. "I think that's exactly what happened, Ben." For the rest of the flight, Ben continued tracing names, doodling little crowns next to each king's name. Occasionally, he would giggle and say, "Fifteen greats, Dad. Fifteen!" Then he would count on his fingers just to make sure. The stewardess passed by, smiling at the sight of him. "Doing your homework on the plane?" she asked kindly.

Ben grinned up at her. "Nope! Just learning about my grandpa... a really, really old one." She chuckled, shaking her head. "Well, that's something you don't hear every day." After landing at Heathrow, we collected our bags once more. The long drive home to Kent passed quietly. Ben dozed off in the back seat, the case of scrolls secured beside him, his little notepad resting on his lap, still open to the family tree. As we pulled into our driveway at last, the house stood waiting for us beneath soft evening clouds. I glanced into the rear-view mirror at my sleeping son. The journey had begun with a letter Now, it had only just begun.

CHAPTER 5: DECODING THE TRUTH

The morning after we returned home was unusually quiet. The house in Kent sat still beneath the pale sky, as though even the walls were pausing to listen. After two long weeks at the abbey, surrounded by ancient scrolls, solemn monks, and voices from centuries past, the silence almost felt strange. en had slept deeply through the night, curled into the comfort of his bed, the small leather case containing the scrolls resting on his desk like a silent guardian. But now, as the first rays of sunlight stretched across his room, I found him already awake — sitting cross-legged at his desk, his back straight, a pen in hand.

Without saying a word, he was writing. leaned gently against the doorframe, watching him for a moment. His small face was calm but serious, his tongue peeking out slightly in concentration as his pen scratched softly across the fresh page. His notepad was open to the very first page. Above all else, in bold letters, he had written:

MY CROWN IS A SECRET.

He glanced up briefly and smiled, sensing my presence. "Good morning, Dad," he whispered softly, not wanting to break the peaceful air around him. "Good morning, buddy," I replied, stepping into the room. "You're up early." Ben nodded, tapping the notebook lightly. "I had to start." His voice carried a quiet sense of duty — the kind rarely seen in children his age. "I need to write it down before I forget. Everything I know. Everything Béla showed me." I pulled a chair beside him and sat down, lowering my voice as though we were already sharing a great secret together. "You're writing your own book, are you?"

Ben's eyes shone brightly. "My journal," he said. "Because if the scrolls could survive all that time, maybe my journal will too." He flipped back to the first page, reading aloud what he had written so far: "My name is Benedict Adrian Harvick. I was born in England. But my story is not just English. My story is older than that. My family comes from the Kings of Hungary. My great-great-great-great-great-great-great-great-great-great-great-great-great-great-great-grandfather was King Béla the Third."

He paused and glanced at me, his face suddenly twisting with playful uncertainty. "That's fifteen greats, right?" I chuckled, counting quickly on my fingers. "Yes, Ben. Fifteen. And you've got every single one of them in the right place." He grinned proudly, returning his attention to his writing. His pen moved again. "The crown is a secret because it's not made of gold or jewels. It's in my blood. You cannot wear it on your head, but you can feel it inside your heart." He looked up once more, his young eyes filled with a wisdom far older than his years. "Dad, is that okay? Does that sound right?"

I reached over and gently squeezed his shoulder. "It sounds perfect, son." For several minutes, we sat in silence as his pen danced across the page. He wrote about the abbey, about Brother Miklós and the sealed chamber, about the scrolls wrapped in their linen bindings. But then, his small voice broke through again, his tone more thoughtful now.

"Dad," he whispered, "Béla was part of the Árpád family... but that's not all, right? Brother Miklós said there were others too." I nodded slowly. "That's right. Béla's family was connected to many others. Some lived in France. Some in England. Some were even emperors in Byzantium. It's like one very, very big tree, and every branch touches another."

Ben's eyebrows lifted as though trying to imagine it. "How many families are we talking about?" I smiled. "Quite a few. Do you want to start learning them?" He beamed. "Yes!" Then, like a little scholar ready to begin class, he flipped the next page in his notebook, carefully writing at the top:

OTHER FAMILIES IN MY BLOODLINE.

"Alright," I said. "Let's begin with the Árpáds, since that's where it all started for Hungary. But after them, you also have kings from France, like the Capetians and the House of Anjou. You even have Plantagenet kings from England." Ben's eyes widened. "Plantagenet? That sounds like a plant." I laughed softly. "Kind of, yes. But it was really the name of a very old royal family in England. They ruled for a long time. One of them was King Henry II." Ben's hand scribbled quickly. "Plantagenets... King Henry the Second." He whispered the words under his breath as though they were pieces of treasure.

"And then there were kings from France too," I added. "You're connected to the Capet dynasty. They ruled France for centuries." Ben's pen moved again. "Capet dynasty. France. Got it." "And even before that, there were the Carolingians," I continued, speaking slowly so he could keep up. "That family ruled parts of Europe even before Hungary had kings. One of the most famous was Charlemagne." Ben's jaw dropped slightly. "Charlemagne? I've heard of him!" "That's right," I smiled. "He was sometimes called Charles the Great. And you, Ben, carry his blood too."

Ben sat back in his chair for a moment, his pen resting against his chin. "So... I have kings from Hungary, France, England, and even really old ones from Europe?" "Exactly." His eyes twinkled as he whispered, "I feel like my family tree is bigger than the whole backyard!" I laughed again, ruffling his hair. "Much bigger." He giggled, flipping to yet another page and carefully writing:

MY ROYAL TREE: ÁRPÁD, PLANTAGENET, CAPET, CAROLINGIAN.

"And there's even more," I said, lowering my voice into a playful whisper. "But you'll have to make room for the Habsburgs, the Angevins, and... maybe even some Normans." Ben scribbled the names as fast as he could, pausing every so often to glance up and make sure he had the spelling right. Then he paused, his face thoughtful. "Dad… how can all these people fit inside one person?" I leaned closer, speaking gently. "Because time is like a river, Ben. All the little streams — every king, every queen, every tribe — they flow together. And in the end, they all meet inside you. That's why the crown is a secret. It's not something you wear. It's something you carry.

Ben stared at his page for a long moment, his voice barely audible. "I carry them." "Yes, son," I whispered. "You do." He smiled faintly, gripping his pen again. "Then I need to keep writing." And so he did. For the rest of that morning, I sat beside him as he worked — filling page after page, drawing family trees, writing names, sketching tiny crowns and castles in the margins. Sometimes he'd pause and whisper things like: "Fifteen greats, Dad!" — and we would both laugh softly. The house was still. The world outside went on. But here, inside these pages, Ben was building something precious: A living story. A story only he could write. A story where the crown was secret — but never lost.

The rain had come softly through the night, tapping against the windows like gentle fingertips. By morning, the clouds hung low over Kent, wrapping the house in a pale grey hush that somehow made everything feel even older. There was something about those rainy mornings that seemed to fit perfectly with the work Ben and I were doing. It was as though the weather itself wanted to be quiet so we could listen more closely to the voices of history.

Ben was already at his desk when I stepped into his room. His notepad sat open in front of him again, the pen gliding smoothly as he continued writing, drawing, and connecting lines across the page. The first page still bore his proud title: MY CROWN IS A SECRET. But now, several pages deep, his drawings were filling quickly — family trees, little castles, crowned figures holding sceptres, and even tiny scrolls that looked like rolled-up tubes sketched neatly into the corners. He looked up at me as I entered, smiling like a boy who was guarding treasure.

"Good morning, Dad," he said softly. "Good morning, Professor Benedict," I replied with a grin, pulling up my chair beside him. "Still working on the family puzzle?" He nodded eagerly, his eyes gleaming with excitement. "There's so many pieces, Dad. I didn't know how many people lived before me. And they all connect together. It's like... like a giant tree, but with a million branches." I smiled. "That's exactly what it is. A living tree that's still growing — right through you."

Ben flipped back a page, tracing his finger along one of the long lines of names he had already written: Árpád, Béla III, Emeric, King Géza II, Euphrosyne of Kiev, Anna of Antioch. These were the roots he already knew well — but there was so much more waiting to be discovered. He tapped the pen thoughtfully against his chin. "Dad... you said there were more families. Not just Hungary." "There are many more, buddy," I replied gently. "Do you want to start learning them? I can help you fill in some of the missing branches."

"Yes, please!" he said quickly, sitting up straighter, his little pen poised above the page like a tiny sword ready to carve into time. I paused for a moment, collecting the names in my mind — not to overwhelm him, but to let the story unfold gently, like a winding path through a grand old castle. "Alright. We start even before King Béla. Before Hungary was even a kingdom. There was a man named Álmos, your ancestor. He was one of the first Grand Princes of the Hungarian people, leading them on their great migration toward the Carpathian Basin."

Ben's pen scratched softly. "Álmos... Grand Prince... before Hungary." "Exactly," I nodded. "And Álmos had a son — his name was Árpád. And Árpád, Ben, was the one who led the Seven Tribes into Hungary. He's the founder of the Árpád Dynasty — your first royal house." Ben paused for a moment, the pen hovering above the page as he whispered, "So he's like... the beginning of everything?"

"He is," I smiled. "For Hungary, yes. The bloodline starts with him." He scribbled again: Árpád — First House of Hungary. "Now," I continued, "many generations later came King Béla III — the king you met in the scrolls. And Béla married Queen Anna of Antioch, which brought in another royal house — the House of Antioch, from far away lands." Ben blinked. "That's a long way from Hungary." "It is. But that's how royal families worked, Ben. They married across borders, bringing nations together. Queen Anna's family, the House of Hauteville, ruled over parts of the Crusader states and had deep ties to Byzantium too."

Ben quickly wrote: House of Antioch — Queen Anna. He looked up at me again, wide-eyed. "And what about Béla's mother?" "Ahh, yes," I nodded. "Béla's mother was Euphrosyne of Kiev. That brings the House of Kiev into your story. These were the Kievan Rus — rulers from the great cities in what is now Ukraine and Russia." Ben whispered as he wrote: House of Kiev — Euphrosyne. "And through Euphrosyne," I added softly, "you have even older connections — reaching back to Viking ancestors and Norse princes who settled in those lands many centuries ago."

Ben gasped. "Vikings?!" "Yes, Ben. Even Vikings," I chuckled. "The river of your family flows wide." His little hands scribbled away, as though racing to catch each piece before it vanished into the mist. "What's next, Dad?" I leaned back slightly, letting the next branch unfold. "Next, we travel west to France. Long before Hungary's kings ruled, there was the Carolingian Dynasty. Do you remember Charlemagne?" Ben nodded excitedly. "Charles the Great!" "That's right. He ruled a vast empire across Europe. And you, Ben, carry his blood too. Through many generations of royal marriages, your bloodline touches the Carolingians."

Ben added: Carolingian Dynasty — Charlemagne. "From there," I continued, "came the Capetian Dynasty — kings of France. They ruled for centuries, passing their blood from one generation to the next." Ben's pen never stopped: Capetian Dynasty — France. "After the Capetians," I said softly, "we reach the House of Anjou — also called the Angevin dynasty. They controlled not only parts of France but also parts of England." "England?" Ben asked, looking up again. "Is this where we get to King Henry?"

I smiled. "Yes. The Plantagenets come next. The House of Anjou gave birth to the Plantagenets — rulers of England, starting with King Henry II and Eleanor of Aquitaine." Ben grinned as his pen danced again: House of Anjou — Plantagenet — King Henry II. He sat back, almost breathless. "It's like I'm collecting crowns!" I laughed softly, brushing his hair back. "You are, buddy. But you're not done yet." His eyes widened. "There's more?!"

"Oh yes," I whispered. "After the Plantagenets came the Normans — from William the Conqueror, who came from Normandy in France and ruled England after 1066." Ben added quickly: Normans — William the Conqueror. I continued, lowering my voice to keep the rhythm calm and steady, like telling a great secret by candlelight. "Later came the Tudors, with kings like Henry VIII and his daughter, Elizabeth I." Ben whispered, "Tudor... Henry the Eighth. Elizabeth the First."

"Then came the Stuarts, who ruled both Scotland and England, before the crowns were united. And after them, the Hanoverians arrived, German royals who ruled Britain for many years." Ben scribbled: Stuarts... Hanoverians. "Finally, Ben," I said gently, "after so many centuries, all these streams came together into the House of Windsor — the royal family you know today." He slowly finished writing: House of Windsor — Today.

He stared down at his notepad, the list stretching down the page like a grand staircase of history. His voice trembled as he whispered, "That's all... me." I reached over, resting my hand on his small shoulder. "Yes, Ben. That's your family. Every one of these kings, these queens, these dynasties — they're all part of your story." Ben swallowed, then whispered again: "My crown really is a secret." "Yes, son," I said softly. "It's a secret written in your blood — and now, written in your book." For a long time, we sat together in silence, both gazing at the list of names and houses stretching across the page. The rain continued to tap softly against the window, but inside the little room, the world had grown larger than it had ever been before.

The rain had cleared by afternoon, and the soft grey clouds gave way to a pale sun that lit the study with a gentle golden hue. Ben was seated at the old wooden table beside the window, his notepad spread wide before him. The morning's work still covered the pages — names, dynasties, dates, and houses carefully written in his small, neat hand. But now, a new page awaited him, blank and ready. I stood behind him with my laptop open, scrolling through one of the many royal histories we had begun collecting together. This one, in particular, had caught my attention. As I read, I found myself pausing often, struck not only by the facts but by the quiet sadness woven through its tale. I lowered the laptop slightly and glanced toward my son.

"Ben," I said softly, "there's someone I want to tell you about today. Someone who belongs to your tree." Ben looked up with wide, curious eyes, already reaching for his pen. "Who is it?" "A princess," I answered. "A little girl. Not much older than you are now, actually." I pulled up a chair and sat beside him, speaking gently. "Her name was Princess ÉlIslabeth Charlotte of Lorraine." Ben's pen paused above the page. "Lorraine?" he whispered. "Like the House of Lorraine?"

"That's right," I nodded. "Another branch of your family. She was born in the year 1700, inside the great Ducal Palace of Nancy, in France." Ben carefully wrote at the top of his page: Princess ÉlIslabeth Charlotte of Lorraine — 1700. "She was the daughter of Leopold, Duke of Lorraine, and her mother was ÉlIslabeth Charlotte d'Orléans," I continued. "That makes her part of the French royal family too. But if we follow her line backward, we find something even more familiar. She was the great-great-great-granddaughter of King James I of England."

Ben gasped softly. "James I? The one who ruled after Queen Elizabeth?" "Exactly," I said with a quiet smile. "Through his daughter, Elizabeth Stuart, who married Charles I Louis, Elector Palatine. Their daughter became ÉlIslabeth Charlotte of the Palatinate, who then married into the French House of Orléans. And from there —" I paused, pointing gently at Ben's notebook "— your princess was born." Ben's small fingers moved quickly now, tracing the path: James I → Elizabeth Stuart → Charles I Louis → ÉlIslabeth Charlotte of the Palatinate → ÉlIslabeth Charlotte d'Orléans → Princess ÉlIslabeth Charlotte of Lorraine.

He stared at the names for a long moment, his voice barely a whisper. "She's... my cousin?" "In a way, yes," I said softly. "She was your many-times-great aunt or cousin. The bloodline weaves in many ways, but you share her ancestors." Ben looked up at me, his eyes wide and solemn. "What happened to her?" I paused, speaking with care. "She was meant to become the Abbess of a great Benedictine abbey in Remiremont, where many women from the House of Lorraine served. But something terrible happened. When she was only ten years old — just a little older than you are now — she caught smallpox. It was a horrible illness, and within just one week, she died. And not only her, but her two younger siblings also caught the disease and passed away. All three children were lost in the same week."

Ben's pen slowed as he whispered, "Three... in one week?" "Yes," I said softly. "It was a terrible sadness for the family. She died at the Château de Lunéville, sometimes called the 'Versailles of Lorraine.' And afterward, she was buried in the Ducal Crypt at Saint-François-des-Cordeliers, in Nancy." Ben lowered his head, his pen still against the page. The room grew still for a moment, as though even the walls were listening. "She never got to grow up," he whispered.

"No," I answered gently. "She didn't. But she's still part of your story, Ben. She still belongs to the tree." Ben lifted his head again, his voice steady. "Even though she died, she's still here." "Yes," I whispered. "Because memory carries people forward. And by learning about her, you bring her name back into the light." He carefully added to his growing family list: Princess ÉlIslabeth Charlotte of Lorraine — died 1711, age 10 — Smallpox. After a long pause, he whispered again. "Dad… was her crown a secret too?"

I smiled softly, resting my hand on his shoulder. "Every crown is a secret, Ben. Because it isn't made of gold or silver. It's carried inside — just like yours." Ben stared at his paper for a while, then began sketching a tiny figure beside her name — a little girl wearing a simple gown, her hair curled softly beneath an ornate headdress, with a tiny crown drawn faintly above her head. His voice was low but full of quiet reverence. "She's still part of my book."

"She is," I nodded. "And she always will be." The afternoon light shifted slowly across the room as the hours passed, and Ben continued filling his journal with names, drawings, and quiet reflections. He was not just learning history. He was building a living story — one that connected him to kings, queens, abbesses, warriors, and even a little princess who never lived to see her own crown. And somewhere beyond the rain-washed skies of Kent, I imagined that perhaps Princess ÉlIslabeth Charlotte herself smiled gently, knowing her story had been remembered.

The house stood quiet under the warm afternoon sun, no rainclouds in sight, only the soft golden light seeping through the windows as though history itself wished to sit in silence and listen. The air held that kind of stillness which seemed to hum with unseen voices—voices older than the walls, older than the land beneath Kent, and older still than the nations whose names filled Ben's notebook. I found him once again at his desk, as was becoming our daily rhythm, seated with his small frame tucked forward, the tip of his pen dancing steadily across the open page. But today, his hand moved slower, his expression was different—not simply focused, but almost reflective, as though his mind had wandered somewhere far beyond the paper, reaching for something he had not yet fully grasped.

I sat beside him quietly, not wanting to disturb the gentle current of thought flowing through him. After a moment, without lifting his eyes, Ben spoke softly, almost in a whisper, "Dad… I've been thinking about her." I knew at once whom he meant. "Princess ÉlIslabeth Charlotte?" He nodded slowly. "Yes." His voice trembled ever so slightly as he continued. "The little girl… the one from Lorraine. The one who never got to grow up." His pen paused as he glanced at the name written carefully on his page, her small figure still sketched neatly beside it. His eyes lifted to meet mine, and in them was something far deeper than mere curiosity. It was understanding. Recognition.

"I feel like we have something in common," he whispered, almost afraid to say it aloud. I leaned in closer, lowering my voice to meet his tender tone. "What do you feel, son?" Ben sat back for a moment, his hands resting gently on the edge of the desk. His gaze drifted toward the window, though I knew he wasn't looking at anything outside. He was seeing something within. "She was only ten, Dad. She never had a chance to live long enough to find out who she really was. She was born into the royal family, and even though she never became a queen, her blood carried it. She was part of this huge tree that I'm part of, too." He paused, inhaling softly. "But even though she died so young, it's like… she still stayed part of the story."

I nodded, but I said nothing yet. This was his moment. His thoughts were leading him somewhere, and I wanted him to find the words on his own. "And then I started thinking about me," he continued, his voice steady but filled with quiet wonder. "She died young. But Dad… I almost died too. Three times. Remember?" His small hands pressed flat against the journal as though holding the truth steady. "Three times." I swallowed, the memories pressing gently against my chest. "I remember."

"The doctors said I wasn't supposed to live, right?" he asked, his voice barely above a whisper. "Yes, Ben. That's what they said. But you did." He nodded slowly, his face calm. "And then I thought about Grandpa, your Dad. He died young too. He didn't even get to meet me." My throat tightened, but I let him speak without interruption. "So it's kind of like… all three of us." His voice grew firmer, like a little scholar presenting his discovery. "Princess ÉlIslabeth Charlotte, me, and Grandpa. All of us touched by something. She didn't get to live long. Grandpa's life was cut short. And me… I almost didn't live at all." His eyes flickered upward to meet mine again. "But somehow… I'm still here."

The room grew still, as though even the house itself held its breath to honour the weight of his words. "And I think that's why I'm supposed to write all of this down, Dad." His voice was soft but sure. "Because I was given the chance that they didn't have.

I can still tell their stories. I can carry it. Just like you said — the crown is not something you wear on your head. It's something you carry." His hands lifted slightly from the journal, as if feeling the weight of it. "I carry them. I carry Princess ÉlIslabeth Charlotte. I carry Grandpa. And I carry Béla, and Álmos, and Árpád… and all the others. All of them." I reached out and placed my hand gently on his shoulder, my voice thick with quiet pride. "That's exactly right, Ben. That's why this matters." He nodded once, firmly, as though sealing an unspoken vow. "I don't want them to be forgotten, Dad. That's why I'm writing it all. That's why my journal matters." For several long moments, neither of us spoke.

The house was filled not with words, but with presence. A kind of silent choir of names that stretched across centuries, reaching from Lorraine to Hungary, from Scotland to England, from palaces to battlefields, from abbeys to abbots, from kings to children who never wore crowns but carried the royal breath in their veins. Finally, Ben flipped to a fresh page in his journal, his small fingers pressing carefully against the clean paper as though preparing to begin a new chapter. His pen hovered, and after a brief pause, he wrote slowly and deliberately:

THE ONES I CARRY

Béla III — my fifteen-greats-grandfather.
Queen Anna of Antioch — my great-grandmother through him.
Álmos and Árpád — my first princes of Hungary.
Princess ÉlIslabeth Charlotte of Lorraine — my cousin who died young.
King James I & VI — my many-times-great-grandfather.
Grandpa — my grandfather who never got to meet me.

He paused, looking down at the page with a mixture of pride and solemnity, his voice steady as he read the list aloud. "This is my crown, Dad. These are my people." "And you honour them, Ben," I whispered. "You honour them just by remembering." Ben smiled faintly, setting his pen down. "I think… maybe that's why Béla called me. Why he left those scrolls for me. So someone could finally carry the crown the way it was meant to be carried." "Not on your head," I whispered. "But in your heart." Ben reached forward, gently closing his journal as though tucking the names safely to rest. The sunlight continued to warm the room, and somewhere far beyond the old house in Kent, I imagined that both Béla and Princess ÉlIslabeth Charlotte smiled softly, knowing their stories lived again.

The following morning dawned softer than the ones before, with golden rays breaking through the curtains and stretching like warm arms across the polished wooden floor. The house in Kent, though modern in its walls and windows, hummed with the ancient breath of the ancestors whose names filled Ben's journal. The very air seemed to listen.

Ben was already waiting for me at the kitchen table, his notepad open, his pen standing upright between his small hands like a flag planted firmly into new soil. He had not even touched his bowl of cereal, which sat quietly at his side, forgotten beneath the weight of what was on his mind. There was something different in his eyes today. Something deeper. The boy who once marvelled at discovering kings was now staring into the deeper well that lay beneath the crowns.

"Dad," he said quietly, his voice steady, but his fingers gripping the pen with care, "I want to go back even further." I smiled as I poured my coffee and sat across from him. "How far back, son?" He drew a long breath, as though gathering courage. "Before Béla. Before Lorraine. Before England and France." He paused and whispered, "Back to the beginning of the river." I nodded slowly. "The river of your blood."

"Yes." His voice was soft but determined. "I know the names, but now I want to know what they were like. Why they mattered. Why they're still in me." The way he spoke no longer carried the wide-eyed wonder of a child piecing together a puzzle. Now it carried the solemnity of one who knew he was becoming something larger than himself. It was not play any longer. It was calling. "Well then," I said softly, leaning forward, "let's go back to Álmos." Ben's pen moved at once.

"Álmos," I began, "lived over a thousand years ago. He was not yet called a king, but rather a Grand Prince — a leader of the Magyar tribes. The Magyars had come from far, far east, travelling across the endless grasslands of the Eurasian steppes. They were riders, fierce and free, following the great rivers westward." Ben's pen scratched: Álmos — Grand Prince of the Magyars. "Álmos led his people toward a land that would later become Hungary. But it was his son, Árpád, who crossed the final threshold." Ben whispered softly, "Árpád… like the beginning of the family tree."

"Exactly," I said. "Árpád led the Seven Tribes into the Carpathian Basin. He is called the Father of Hungary. The year was 895, nearly eleven hundred years ago. And that's where your line began to take root." The pen moved again: Árpád — Father of Hungary, 895. "They settled there, Ben. Built cities. Formed the early nation that later your grandfather Béla would rule. But the blood didn't just stay in Hungary. It kept reaching, like roots pushing deep and wide."

Ben looked up, his eyes shining. "That's when the other families started joining, right?" "Exactly." I smiled. "And every time a royal married another royal, the bloodline grew." I rose briefly, retrieved a folder from the shelf nearby, and unfolded the charts we had printed together weeks ago — charts that now looked like forests of names. I spread it gently across the table like an ancient map. "You see here?" I pointed toward one branch near the centre. "This is where Béla marries Anna of Antioch. That pulled in the House of Hauteville." Ben traced the line with his finger. "That's Crusader land, right?"

"Yes," I said, proud of his growing knowledge. "And before her, Béla's mother brought in the House of Kiev. And through Kiev… Norse blood. Vikings who sailed down rivers into what is now Ukraine and Russia." He whispered again, "Vikings." "Now watch," I continued, tracing his finger further west across the page. "From there the Capetians join, the Angevins, and then the Plantagenets in England." My hand moved steadily over the names, guiding his eyes. "Then the Normans, the Tudors, the Stuarts, the Hanoverians — and finally, the House of Windsor."

He sat still, breathing slowly, as though afraid even the smallest noise would break the spell. I lowered my voice, drawing him even deeper into the story. "And then, there's Lorraine." His eyes blinked softly at the word. "Where Princess ÉlIslabeth Charlotte lived." "Yes. The House of Lorraine connects you not only through your royal Hungarian roots but also through France, the Holy Roman Empire, and England itself — back to King James VI of Scotland and I of England."

He carefully turned back a few pages in his journal, finding where he had written her name. His small fingers tapped it gently. "Dad…" he said softly, "do you think maybe that's why I feel her? Like… maybe we were both meant to carry something together." "Yes," I whispered. "Because you both share not only blood, but burden. She died before she could understand her place. But you, Ben, are being given the chance to carry it for both of you." He looked up with wide eyes. "So, I carry her crown too." "Yes, son. Hers, and so many others." Ben drew in a long breath, his shoulders lifting slightly beneath the weight of his invisible inheritance. Then, softly, he spoke again.

"And that's why it tried to take me, too, right? Three times." His voice barely trembled. "The same way it took her, and Grandpa. But I lived." I reached across the table and laid my hand firmly over his. "Yes, you lived, Ben. And because you lived, their stories live too." He stared deeply into my eyes, and then whispered something I knew had been resting in his young heart for some time. "Dad… maybe this is why Béla called me." The words hung in the air like incense, rich and sacred.

"Yes," I whispered. "Maybe it is." For several minutes we sat there, father and son, the map of his bloodlines stretching wide across the table between us — not as a chart of cold history, but as a living testament of survival. The crown was indeed a secret, but one that pulsed quietly inside him, steady as breath. Ben reached again for his pen, flipping to a fresh page. With quiet care, he wrote in neat letters: The Ones I Carry — Their Blood, Their Burden, Their Crown And beneath that, a single sentence: I was not supposed to live. But I did. And because I did, so do they.

The rain had long vanished now, replaced by the kind of quiet only the English countryside knows after a storm — the soft hum of the wind through ancient trees, birds gently reclaiming their morning song, and that distant echo of something timeless in the air. As I pulled the old wooden gate open, the familiar creak made Ben smile. The cottage sat like an old friend waiting for us, its stone walls worn smooth by centuries of wind and rain, ivy curling along the edges like fingers gripping memory itself.

This was Ben's second home. The place where the quiet became his greatest teacher. Inside, the cottage smelled of old parchment, beeswax polish, and the faint trace of peat smoke. Shelves lined every wall, filled with the chronicles of our family's journey: binders, family charts, scroll tubes, maps, letters, DNA reports — a living monument to bloodlines once scattered, now carefully gathered into one space.

Ben sat down at his usual corner of the broad oak table, pulling out his journal. But now, as always, his pen — not pen — glided with authority. No more erasable memories. This was permanence. "Alright, Dad," he said, barely containing his excitement, "today's puzzle pieces." I opened my laptop while he spread out one of the printed family charts we had pulled from the attic last year. The document itself was a condensed labyrinth of surnames, places, and dynasties. The screen glowed softly with open pages from The Royal Burden and The Lords of Marden. This was not just research anymore. This was him. Ben tapped a finger along one particular name — ÉlIslabeth Charlotte of Lorraine.

"Dad, the more I think about her, the more I feel like she's not just a distant person on the tree. There's something... familiar." He paused. "She didn't live long — just ten years — but she was already marked out for a path. Chosen. I was too. Three times I almost didn't make it. She didn't get the chance. But maybe that's why I'm still here. Maybe part of her story had to continue through me." I nodded slowly. "You see it now, don't you? The pattern." He looked down at his ink-filled page where he had written earlier:

- ÉlIslabeth Charlotte of Lorraine — 1700-1711
- Descendant of James I & VI — England & Scotland
- House of Lorraine — House of Orléans — House of Stuart
- Then beside it, he added:
- Ben Harvick — Survived 3 near-deaths
- Descendant of James I & VI
- House of Lorraine — House of Stuart — House of Windsor

He stared at it for a long moment before continuing softly, "It's not just that she died young, Dad. Or that Grandpa died young too. It's that in every generation, someone seems to pay the price for the others to keep going. Maybe I'm one of the ones who gets to carry it forward." "You are, son," I whispered. "You're holding more than names. You're holding the threads of survival." Ben turned his attention back to the scroll table, flipping through one of the old folders. "And look at how deep it runs." He pointed at one of the long dynastic chains from The Royal Burden:

- Álmos → Árpád → House of Kiev → House of Antioch → House of Komnenos → Capetian Dynasty → Carolingian Dynasty → House of Anjou → Plantagenet → Tudor → Stuart → Hanoverian → Habsburg → Lorraine → Windsor.

Ben whispered as he traced them: "It's not just Hungary. It's not just England. It's... everything." "And Lorraine sits right inside it," I added. "Because ÉlIslabeth Charlotte's line is tied to both your Stuart ancestors and to the French royal houses that intermarried through Orléans, Palatinate, and back to James I. The exact same James who ruled both Scotland and England." Ben sat back in his chair for a moment. His little hands carefully capped his pen, his brow furrowed deep in thought.

"You know what I feel, Dad? Sometimes... sometimes I feel like I'm picking up unfinished work. Like they couldn't finish it — like Béla, like ÉlIslabeth Charlotte, like Grandpa — and now it's my turn to finish it for them. That's why the scrolls still exist. That's why the journal matters." I reached out, squeezing his shoulder. "That's exactly why. And that's why you're writing in ink." He smiled faintly. "Because this can't be erased." Then, as if a thought suddenly cracked open inside him, Ben flipped to a fresh page. The tip of his pen touched down with confidence: "The Crown is a Secret — but it speaks in patterns."

He looked up again. "Dad... we have to keep going. This isn't just about who ruled where, or who wore which crown. It's about who stayed. Who survived. And how I fit into all of it." I smiled. "Then let's keep going." And so we did. Page after page, hour after hour, inside that cottage where time stood still. The echoes of Lorraine, Marden, Kent, Scotland, Hungary, and Normandy circled quietly around us. In this quiet place, the bloodlines converged. And Ben was weaving them into permanence — not just for himself, but for all who came before.

The sun shifted through the clouds that afternoon, casting soft beams of light across the long wooden table where Ben sat, his pen moving steadily in hand. Not a pen. Not anymore. He had learned that some things needed to last — that the pages he filled now might be read one day by children who hadn't even been born yet. Ink was permanent. That mattered to him. The journal lay wide open before him, pages full of names, drawings, and carefully written notes. His earlier entries had mapped the royal houses, the dynasties, the kings and queens whose bloodlines had found their way into his own.

But now, his writing had shifted. He wasn't just tracing names anymore — he was tracing something far deeper, something that lived below the surface of the names themselves. "Today I want to write about my blood," Ben said softly, barely lifting his head as his pen glided forward. "Not just the names — but what's inside of me. What my blood carries. How far it's travelled." I sat across from him, watching with quiet pride as he worked. The study felt alive, like the walls themselves were listening.

"See, Dad," Ben continued, tapping the genetic chart we had printed from the computer, "they call it Y-DNA. It's like the father's line — the one that keeps getting handed down, father to son, all the way back." "That's right," I said gently, letting him lead the thought. "My Y-DNA is called R1a," he said carefully, his voice steady. "That's what Béla had too. And Árpád. It goes back even further than them — way back before there were castles or kings. Before there was even a Hungary." He paused for a moment and turned another page.

"And then there's the other part — Mom's side. That's my mitochondrial DNA — my mother's line. That one is called H5a1. That's from way, way back in Europe too. Some of it comes from women who lived thousands of years ago. Even one who lived in Scotland. They called her Ava. She lived before there were even kingdoms." His small fingers traced the lines on the printed map, the one that showed how far these lines had travelled — across Europe, across centuries, from one ancient village to the next. "So when I think about my family tree," he said softly, "it's not really a tree anymore. It's like a river under the ground — always flowing forward. It splits into streams sometimes, and comes back together. But it always moves." His pen moved again across the page, writing:

My Y-DNA: R1a — Father's line
My mtDNA: H5a1 — Mother's line
Both flowing forward — never stopping.

He glanced up at me, his eyes thoughtful. "Dad, I don't just belong to one place, do I?" "No, son," I whispered. "You belong to many places. And to many people."

Ben leaned back, folding his arms for a moment. "It's weird," he said finally. "I used to think a family was just parents, grandparents, maybe great-grandparents. But I've got pieces of people who lived a thousand years ago. And some who lived four thousand years ago. And their stories are still inside me." I smiled. "That's the part most people never get to see, Ben. But you're seeing it." His hand moved again as he added to his journal:

This isn't just a family tree.
This is a journey.
A journey my blood took before I was born.

He paused, thoughtful again. "And that's why it's permanent, Dad. That's why I use the pen. Because I want the words to last. Just like the bloodline lasted." I nodded. "Exactly right, buddy." The room was quiet for a while as he worked, only the soft scratching of his pen filling the air. The old cottage windows rattled slightly as a breeze swept through the trees outside, but inside, the moment felt steady — rooted — like something sacred was being written. And when he finally closed his journal for the day, he whispered one last thought.

"Every name I wrote before...
All those kings and queens...
They were just chapters.
But my blood — my blood is the book."

I didn't speak. I didn't need to. The weight of what he'd said was enough. And somehow, in that still little room, surrounded by the papers, the scrolls, and the hum of the computer screen glowing softly beside us — history sat with us once again. The crown remained a secret. But the secret was safe.

It was another one of those soft, quiet afternoons inside the cottage. The rain had long passed, and the sun peeked gently through the lace curtains, casting strips of warm gold across the wooden floor. The table was covered, as usual, with open books, old letters, and a few of Ben's newest journal pages stacked neatly beside his favourite ink pen. Jeff sat by the old desk, reading through a thick binder filled with research papers while Ben leaned against the window ledge, his head gently resting on his hand as he watched the sunlight dance.

But there was a look in Ben's eyes that Jeff recognized. That little flicker meant his son's mind was spinning again. "Dad," Ben finally spoke, his voice curious and calm. "I know you've told me about my DNA before. You said it's like a library inside of me. But... I still can't quite see it, you know? Like, how do four little letters build me? My hair, my face, my family, even this whole book I'm writing. How does it all fit?"

Jeff closed the binder softly, smiling as he turned to his son. "That," he said, "is a very good question." Ben hopped down from the window and slid into the chair beside his dad. "Can you show me? I mean... explain it in a way I can really see it? Like a picture in my head?" Jeff rubbed his chin, thinking. "Alright, Professor Benedict," he said with a playful grin, "how about we go on a little adventure — inside your own body?" Ben's eyes widened. "Inside me? Really?" Jeff nodded. "Yes. Not with spaceships or magic, but with your imagination. Close your eyes for a second."

Ben shut his eyes tightly, waiting like a child at the start of a wild ride. "Now," Jeff began, lowering his voice like a storyteller, "imagine we are shrinking. Smaller and smaller. We're not just the size of bugs, or grains of sand. We're so small now that we're inside one single cell — one of the trillions that make up your whole body. Can you see it?" Ben whispered, eyes still shut. "I think so."

"Good," Jeff continued. "Now look around. See those tiny spirals twisting like coiled staircases? That's your DNA. It looks like a twisted ladder — we call it a double helix. And inside that spiral are the four heroes who do all the work." Ben grinned. "The superheroes you told me about?" "Exactly!" Jeff laughed. "Let's meet them. First, there's Adenine — A for short. Adenine's job is to always look for its best friend, Thymine — T. They stick together like glue, always holding hands, always loyal. Then you've got Cytosine — C. And Cytosine's best friend is Guanine — G. They always pair up too."

Ben opened one eye and whispered, "So it's like A loves T, and C loves G?" "Perfect!" Jeff beamed. "And these pairs line up one after the other — A with T, C with G — millions and millions of times, like beads on a string, telling your body how to build you." "But what do they say?" Ben asked, his voice filled with wonder. Jeff leaned closer. "Ah, here's where the magic happens. Think of your DNA like the biggest recipe book ever written. Each pair — A-T or C-G — is a tiny instruction. A recipe that tells your body how tall you'll grow, what colour your eyes will be, how your heart beats, how your skin heals, even how your hair curls when it's damp outside."

Ben's hands flinched as if feeling his own curly hair. "So that's why I look like me?" "Exactly," Jeff nodded. "All because your little DNA book has been passed down through your family for thousands of years — written by your ancestors — every one of them adding their own little chapters." Ben giggled. "Even King Béla? And Princess ÉlIslabeth Charlotte? And Charlemagne?" "All of them," Jeff said with a smile. "Each of them passed on little pieces of this code. That's why when you open your journal and write down all their names, you're really writing what's already written inside you."

Ben's mouth hung open for a moment. "It's like... my family wrote a secret book, and my body reads it every day!" "That's right, buddy. And the amazing part is, even though you can't see it with your eyes, the code never sleeps. Right now, as we're talking, your cells are reading those recipes, building proteins, growing your hair, fixing your skin, making your heartbeat stay steady. Your DNA is always working." Ben leaned back in his chair, his little hands behind his head. "I never knew my body was so busy."

"It's the busiest factory in the world," Jeff chuckled. "And every cell has a perfect copy of your entire book — like every room in a castle has a full library." Ben's eyes grew wide again. "Whoa... a library in every room? That's a lot of books!" Jeff nodded slowly. "And each book holds the entire story of you. And because your ancestors wrote pieces of it long ago, you carry them everywhere you go." Ben tapped his chin for a moment, lost in thought. "Dad... that means... even if people don't remember their family, the family is still inside them."

"Exactly," Jeff whispered. "And that's why we write this story. That's why your journal matters. Because one day, someone else will read your pages and see how the library was passed to you — just like you're reading Béla's and ÉlIslabeth Charlotte's stories now." Ben reached for his journal eagerly. This time, he didn't pick up his pen. He chose his dark blue ink pen, just like he always promised himself. He flipped to a fresh page and at the top, carefully printed:

THE CODE INSIDE ME

Then, without needing any help, his small hand moved, writing his thoughts exactly as they came: "Inside me is a library. The library holds my whole family. My hair, my eyes, my hands, my heart. My DNA has little letters: A, T, C, G. They are friends and they hold hands. They build me. They work all day and all night. They are always busy, even while I sleep. That is why my crown is a secret. Because my family wrote it long before I was born."

When he finished, he looked up at his father with glowing pride. "I think I get it now." Jeff leaned in, kissed the top of his son's head, and whispered softly. "You've just written the truest part of your story, Ben." Outside the cottage, the last of the clouds drifted quietly past as the sun continued to shine on the house where history was being written—one secret at a time. The cottage had become our kingdom of learning.

Every time the kettle whistled, every time the clock ticked softly above the mantel, it felt like history was whispering to us. The scrolls rested carefully on the desk, Ben's journal lay open as always, and I sat beside him with a fresh cup of tea. Outside, the garden was quiet, but inside, the world of kings, queens, and family stories continued to grow like vines stretching toward the sun. Ben was scribbling again in his journal, filling another page with drawings of twisting ladders. He had drawn DNA spirals, just like we talked about. At the top of the page, he had written:

THE TWISTY LADDER OF ME

He looked up suddenly, tilting his head with that curious little squint of his. "Dad," he said, "so we know the letters — A, T, C, G — and we know that they're inside every cell, right?" "Exactly," I nodded, sipping my tea. "But..." Ben paused, tapping his pen gently against the paper. "How do all those letters not get mixed up? I mean, it sounds like a really, really, really big book. How does my body even know where to start? How does it know which part does what?"

I smiled. His questions were getting better every day. "That," I said, leaning closer, "is where chromosomes come in." Ben's eyebrows shot up. "Chromosomes?" "Yes, buddy. You can think of chromosomes like shelves in your giant library." I picked up one of the old scrolls lying nearby to use as an example. "Imagine this scroll holds one chapter of your life. But instead of one, you have forty-six of these scrolls in every single cell of your body." Ben's mouth dropped open. "Forty-six scrolls?"

"That's right. Twenty-three from your mom. Twenty-three from me. They're all bundled up into pairs. Each one carefully holds a different part of your instructions. Some scrolls say, 'build these eyes.' Others say, 'make this heart.' Or 'grow this hair.' All of it is kept neat and tidy so your body knows exactly where to look." Ben scribbled quickly: 46 scrolls = 46 chromosomes. "And," I added, lowering my voice like a secret storyteller, "two of those scrolls are very special. They're called your sex chromosomes — and they decide whether you're a boy or a girl." Ben's eyes twinkled. "Like the X and the Y you told me before?"

"Exactly!" I said with a smile. "Mom gave you one X. And I gave you the Y. That little Y-chromosome — well, that's your special royal scroll. It's the one that only fathers pass to sons, all the way back, generation after generation." Ben sat perfectly still, as if balancing that invisible Y-chromosome right there in his hands. "So... that Y-scroll goes back to Béla? And Árpád? And even Álmos?" "Yes, son," I whispered. "That Y has traveled across a thousand years of fathers and sons, kings and princes, right into you."

He shivered slightly. "That's kind of amazing." "It is," I nodded. "And scientists today can even read special codes written on that Y-scroll. That's called your haplogroup. Think of haplogroups like a family name for your Y-chromosome. It tells us where your father's fathers came from, where they traveled, and which ancient groups they belonged to." Ben scribbled again: Haplogroup = my ancient map.

Jeff continued, his voice gentle, pulling Ben into the adventure. "For you, Ben, your Y-chromosome belongs to a group called R1a — the same as Béla's. That tells us that your family long ago came from Central Asia, traveling west, across rivers and mountains, until they reached Hungary and Europe." Ben gasped. "The Y-scroll traveled like I traveled to Hungary." Jeff smiled. "Exactly, buddy. And one day, when you're much older, you might share that Y-scroll with your own son — just like I shared it with you."

Ben looked down at his journal, his little hand resting over his chest. "So… inside me, there's a book of letters, shelves of scrolls, and a secret map that came from my ancient grandfathers." "That's it," I whispered. "Every part of you carries your story." After a long, thoughtful pause, Ben flipped to a fresh page, dipped his pen into the ink, and wrote his newest chapter:

"THE Y-SCROLL IS MY MAP. IT CAME FROM KINGS AND TRIBES. IT IS PASSED FROM FATHERS TO SONS. I AM ONE OF THEM."

He smiled softly, whispering under his breath, "The code is my story." Outside the cottage, the last rays of sunlight painted long golden stripes across the sky as father and son sat together, building a story that stretched back through centuries — one chromosome at a time.

The next morning, the cottage smelled of warm toast and fresh tea. The windows were open just enough to let in the soft sounds of birds outside, while inside, Ben was already at the table, nibbling on a slice of toast as he stared down at his journal. The page before him was full of the Y-chromosome, the "scroll from fathers to sons," as he had written. Tiny drawings filled the edges — a crown, a map, a little scroll tied with ribbon. But now, his pen sat still in his hand, as if waiting for the next great mystery to arrive.

He looked up at me, his eyes wide and full of thought. "Dad," he said softly, "we learned about the Y-scroll yesterday. But… that's only half of me, right?" I smiled, sliding into my chair beside him. "That's a very good question, Ben. You're absolutely right. You see, your Y-chromosome only tells us about one special road — the road from fathers to sons. But there's another road inside you. One that comes from your mother."

Ben leaned forward, his chin resting on his little hand. "Like Mom?" "Exactly," I nodded. "And this part is called your mitochondrial DNA. Or as the scientists say, mtDNA." Ben wrinkled his nose. "Mito… what?" I chuckled. "Mitochondrial. It's a long word, isn't it? But think of it like this: inside every one of your cells, there's a tiny powerhouse, almost like a little battery. That's your mitochondrion. And inside that tiny powerhouse, there's a tiny circle of DNA. That's where your mother's story lives." Ben's mouth opened slightly, his eyes already filling with pictures. "So, it's like a little spark inside me?"

"Yes!" I said excitedly. "A spark passed down from mothers to children. Every mother gives her spark to her children — both boys and girls. But only daughters pass it forward again. So your spark came from Mom, and from her mom, and from her mom's mom — stretching all the way back, just like the Y-scroll did, but through the mothers." Ben quickly grabbed his pen, carefully writing:

Mitochondrial DNA — the spark from mothers.

He paused, then looked up again. "Where did my spark start?" "That, my boy, is one of the oldest stories of all," I whispered. "Scientists say that long, long ago, there was one woman whose spark started the journey for all of us. They call her Mitochondrial Eve." Ben's eyes grew wide. "Eve? Like in the fake story Bible book?" "Yes," I nodded. "They gave her that name because she was the mother of all living people today. But she wasn't the only woman alive back then — just the one whose spark still shines inside everyone on earth. Her daughters carried her spark, and their daughters after them, for thousands and thousands of years."

Ben whispered, "So I have her spark too?" "You do," I said softly. "And along the way, your spark traveled through grandmothers in Norway, in Scotland, in Hungary, in England. All of them carried that tiny circle of DNA, unchanged, passing it safely to the next child, until finally, it reached you." Ben scribbled again: The spark traveled to me. Then, as if struck by a thought, he added: Mom gave me her spark. And her spark came from Ava.

He looked up, his voice low. "Dad... Ava is that woman from long ago, right? The one they found in Scotland?" I smiled. "Yes, son. The scientists called her 'Ava.' She lived thousands of years ago, during the Bronze Age. And your mtDNA, your spark, carries the same code as hers.
That means somewhere, somehow, she was one of your ancient grandmothers too." Ben leaned back in his chair, staring at the ceiling as though looking through time itself. "So... I have Dad's scroll from the fathers. And Mom's spark from the mothers. And they both travel inside me."

"That's right, Ben," I whispered, resting my hand on his shoulder. "Two rivers of stories flowing together in you." He smiled softly, flipping the page and drawing two long rivers merging into one. Above them, he carefully wrote:

THE STORY INSIDE ME.

For a long time, we sat there together, side by side in the cottage, as the morning light painted golden patches across the wooden table. The scrolls, the books, the maps, and the stories — they were all here. But the greatest treasure was sitting right in front of me: a young boy, writing his own book — one spark, one scroll, one story at a time.

The spring morning had rolled in gently over Kent, bringing with it a sky painted soft blue and streaked with the faintest wisps of white. The house sat quiet, as it often did when Ben slipped into one of his thoughtful moods, pen in hand, notebook open across the wooden table.

Jeff watched him from the kitchen doorway, sipping his coffee as the boy's pen traced slow, steady lines across the page. But this time, Ben wasn't writing down names or drawing family trees. This time, he was sketching maps. "I think I know where we should start, Dad," Ben said, glancing up with a small, knowing grin. His young eyes gleamed with excitement, but also with the weight of what he was carrying. "If the scrolls and all the books are right, then we've only seen one piece of it. Béla gave us the beginning — but he never meant for us to stop there."

Jeff stepped closer and set his cup down quietly. "Alright, professor. Where do we begin this quest of yours?" Ben's finger landed on his rough little drawing — a map of England that he'd done entirely by hand. "Here. Right here in Kent. We start at home." The decision felt right. After all, it was here that the family name had twisted from Horváth into Harvick over centuries of change and distance. Kent's fields whispered old secrets beneath every hedgerow and every rolling green hill. This was the soil that had carried the name forward when it crossed from Europe into England long ago.

From Kent, Ben pointed next toward the old city of Canterbury. "We need to go to Canterbury first. Maybe the old churches, maybe even old records. Maybe something about the first family members who came here from across the sea." His voice softened slightly, like a child chasing whispers only he could hear. "It's like following echoes." Jeff smiled, his heart full as he watched the boy find his own rhythm in the search. "And after Canterbury?" he asked.

Ben's pen moved up the map. "Then we drive north a little, still in Kent's countryside. There are manors and little parishes that might still hold records. The name Harvick didn't appear from nowhere. Somewhere there's a first Harvick, Dad." "We'll find him," Jeff promised, resting his hand on Ben's shoulder.

Ben's pen darted again, sliding across the paper like a ship sailing from shore to shore. "Then comes Hampton Court and Windsor Castle. We need to walk where the Kings and Queens walked. The ones that came later, the ones whose blood still ties back into ours." His voice lowered, almost as though speaking sacred words. "The Plantagenets. The Tudors. The Windsors."

Jeff gave a soft nod. "Your branches touch them all, Ben." "And after that," Ben continued, now more animated, "we go north — way up to Scotland! Edinburgh Castle." His eyes sparkled. "The Stuarts, Dad! The kings who ruled both Scotland and England together. My bloodline flows through them too." Jeff chuckled gently, hearing the swirl of history pour out of his son's mouth like the unraveling of a great ball of yarn. "And you're sure you're not forgetting anyone?"

Ben grinned and tapped the paper once more, where new lines stretched across the Channel into mainland Europe. "Germany comes next. Where the Hanoverians once ruled before they crossed into Britain. And where the old Holy Roman Empire left traces of our ancestors too."

He paused only briefly before continuing his line across France, landing squarely on Lorraine. "Then we go to Nancy. And to Lunéville. To visit Princess ÉlIslabeth Charlotte's world. To see the palace where she lived, and the abbey where she was meant to serve." His little hand trembled slightly as he drew a tiny cross near her final resting place. "We honour her, Dad." Jeff nodded, his voice soft. "We will."

"And then France will lead us further south. We visit the places where the Capetians ruled. We walk the old paths where the Carolingians once built their empire." His voice filled with awe. "Charlemagne's empire." The pen slid once more toward Hungary. Ben circled Budapest carefully, then underlined it twice.

"And when we finish, we return to where it all began." His voice became almost reverent. "Matthias Church. The cathedral where Béla and Anna sleep." Jeff let out a long breath as he looked at the map. The journey before them wasn't one trip. It was an odyssey — the living path of his son's bloodline, stretched across kingdoms, centuries, and forgotten corridors of history. "You've planned this like a true historian, Ben."

Ben looked up at him with a mixture of excitement and gravity far beyond his years. "Béla started it, Dad. He sent us to Pannonhalma for the scrolls. But the scrolls only opened the first door. Now we have to walk through the rest." Jeff crouched beside him, gripping his shoulder gently. "We will. Together." For a long moment, they both stared at the hand-drawn map as the golden afternoon sunlight warmed the table. This was no longer a child's hobby. This was Ben's birthright taking form — not through distant DNA charts, but through boots-on-the-ground footsteps retracing the living memory of his ancestors. Outside, the gentle wind stirred the trees of Kent, almost as if the branches themselves whispered their quiet approval. The quest had truly begun.

The evening had settled quietly over the cottage. The air carried that stillness which always seemed to arrive when a heavy day of discovery came to rest. The old desk lamp glowed softly beside us, casting long golden shadows against the wood-panelled walls.

Outside, the Kent countryside whispered beneath a darkening sky, but inside, everything had grown very still. It was just Ben and me now. The books, scrolls, maps, and journals lay scattered around us like the remnants of a thousand-year storm that had passed through these very walls.

Ben sat cross-legged on the armchair opposite me, his small leather-bound journal open in his lap, pen firmly in hand — never pen, not anymore. His notes had grown into something far greater than simple lists or names. They were no longer just words on paper. They were becoming his voice. I leaned back slightly, folding my arms as I studied him for a moment. "Alright, Professor Benedict," I said gently, offering a faint grin. "We've been walking through this story for a long while now. But tonight, I want to hear it from you." Ben looked up, curious. "From me?"

"Yes," I nodded. "Right now. Right here. After everything you've learned — not just about names and places, but about yourself. Who are you, Ben? Tell me." For a brief moment, he stared down at his open journal. The pages fluttered lightly beneath his fingertips as though even the paper itself was breathing with him. His face grew thoughtful. Then slowly, he raised his head. "I'm... not just Ben," he began softly. "Not just a boy who lives in Kent. Not just somebody who likes to draw castles and maps. I think I've always known that — even before I knew how to explain it."

His voice remained calm, almost like he was reading a secret letter aloud. "When I was little, before I could even remember it all, I died. Three times. Not just being sick. But gone. And every time, I heard him — the voice. Not in English. I didn't understand the words back then, but I could feel them. He said, 'You're not done yet.' And I still hear those words now, like they live inside my ears." He paused, glancing briefly at me, but I said nothing. I wanted him to keep going.

"That voice wasn't just anyone," Ben continued. "It was him. My grandfather from long ago. King Béla. He was calling me back. He knew that I was supposed to carry something forward." Ben tapped lightly on his chest. "Something lives inside me that's been passed down. It's not something I can see like a crown, or wear like a cape. It's hidden inside my blood. Like a giant library full of codes. Letters and patterns and pages that belong to all of my family who lived before me. And not just one family, but many."

He glanced down at the scattered scrolls and documents on the table, then returned his gaze to me, his eyes shining brightly. "I have tiny pieces of them all inside me. Some were kings. Some were queens. Some were warriors. Some travelled far across oceans and mountains. And even though I don't remember their faces, my blood remembers them. My DNA keeps their stories." He took a breath, his voice steady.

"And that's why I was born. Not to just live, but to carry their stories forward. To find the ones that were lost. To tell the stories no one else remembers. My journal — this journal — is not just for me. It's like the scrolls. If I write it all down, maybe it will survive a long time like theirs did. So that one day, if another child like me is born, they won't have to search as hard. They'll read this and know who they are." Ben's pen hovered above the page again, but he kept speaking, his words now flowing freely.

"I know I come from so many places. From Hungary and England. From Scotland and France. From Norway and even from the frozen north where the lights dance in the sky. Some of my family were mighty. Some were forgotten. But they all led to me. My family tree isn't just tall. It's wide, like a huge river with hundreds of streams all joining together." His eyes met mine directly now, his voice dropping slightly, but full of quiet wonder. "And that's why I think I died and came back, Dad. Because if I hadn't, none of this would've been found. I was meant to carry it forward. To keep it alive." He closed his journal gently and rested his small hand on its cover.

"This is who I am. I am Benedict Adrian Harvick. But I am also Benedicere of Horváth. I carry kings, queens, princes, farmers, travellers, and warriors inside me. And even though I'm still only a kid, I already know my story is much, much older than I am." The room was silent for a long moment after he finished. His voice no longer carried the nervous tone of a child trying to make sense of something confusing. He had spoken with the quiet certainty of one who had simply remembered what had always been true. I swallowed gently, leaning forward and placing my hand softly on his shoulder. "You've come a very long way, son." Ben smiled faintly. "And I think there's still more to find."

"There always will be," I whispered. "But you're not walking alone." "I know." His smile widened. "Because I've got you." We sat together beneath the old lamp, father and son, as the night wrapped itself around the cottage like a gentle cloak. Outside, the world was quiet. But inside this room, a new chapter of a very old story was being written — not just on paper, but deep inside the boy who carried it forward. The crown remained a secret. But it was no longer hidden.

The morning sun stretched gently across the hills of Kent as Ben and I stood outside the cottage, our breath forming small clouds in the cool spring air. The old house behind us was beginning to feel like a second library, filled with maps and scrolls, but now it was time to step outside its walls. Ben's journal, clutched tightly beneath his arm, had grown heavier — not from pages, but from everything he had poured into it. The story of who he was had become real. And yet, it was not finished.

We stood in front of the car, the old travel bag resting in the trunk, as if waiting for its next assignment. "Dad?" Ben said softly, tilting his head upward. "I think I know who I am... but now I need to see where I came from." I smiled. "Exactly, buddy. That's why we're going." Our first stop wasn't far. Just down the winding roads of Kent, not far from home, lay the ancient city of Canterbury. As we drove along the narrow lanes, past the fields and stone walls that seemed to whisper old stories of their own, Ben stared out the window, watching the countryside roll by like a moving painting.

"You know, Dad," he said after a while, "I used to think history was just... old. Like dusty books and boring stories." "And now?" "Now it feels alive. Like it's been waiting for me." We pulled into Canterbury beneath the towering shadow of its great cathedral. The spires reached up toward the sky like stone fingers, and the bells rang softly in the distance as if welcoming us. We wandered the old cobblestone streets, past timber-framed houses and weathered shops that had stood for centuries.

Inside the cathedral, we walked quietly beneath the vaulted ceilings. Sunlight streamed through stained glass windows, splashing colour across the stone floors. The air was cool and heavy with the scent of old stone, wax, and quiet reverence. Ben ran his fingers along one of the ancient stone columns, as if trying to feel the stories trapped inside. "This place," he whispered, "is older than most people's memories." I nodded. "And yet, places like this help us hold on to the stories that could be forgotten."

As we moved further inside, we stopped at a quiet side chapel, empty except for a few flickering candles. Ben sat on the small wooden bench, his journal resting on his lap once again. For a long moment, he said nothing. His eyes wandered across the carvings, the shields, the names etched into the stone. "This isn't where my kings are buried," he said softly, "but I can still feel them." "They're with you everywhere," I whispered. "Not because of where their bodies rest, but because of what you carry." He glanced at me, smiling faintly. "The secret crown."

I said nothing, but returned the smile, letting him hold that thought quietly. From Canterbury, we followed the old motorways northward toward Hampton Court Palace. The great Tudor palace stood like a fortress of brick and stone, its red towers rising sharply against the grey skies. Ben's eyes grew wide as we walked through the grand archway into the open courtyards. "It's like a castle playground," he whispered in awe. "Kings and queens once walked these very halls," I told him. "Henry VIII ruled from here. Your story touches his too."

Ben ran his fingers along the stone banisters as we climbed the grand staircases, passing portraits of monarchs that stared down at us with painted eyes. He paused at one large portrait, studying it carefully. "He looks serious," Ben said. "He had a heavy crown to carry." Ben lowered his voice thoughtfully. "Crowns are always heavy, aren't they?" "Even the ones no one sees," I said. We continued deeper into the palace, wandering through rooms filled with rich tapestries, golden chandeliers, and polished wooden floors. At every turn, Ben paused, studying, recording small sketches into his journal: a shield here, a royal crest there, even a small drawing of the Great Hall's massive hammer-beam ceiling.

By late afternoon, we made our way west, toward Windsor Castle. As we approached the great round tower, Ben's breath caught in his chest. "It's bigger than I imagined." "It's been here for almost a thousand years," I said. "And yes, part of your story touches these stones too." Inside, we wandered through the State Apartments, past glittering displays of swords, crowns, and royal armour. Ben stood before a glass case holding the Order of the Garter regalia. "Do you think any of our family ever wore one of those?" he asked softly. I smiled gently. "Maybe. But even if they didn't, the weight you carry is heavier than any robe."

He nodded slowly, not speaking, but understanding. The next leg of our journey took us north — far north — into Scotland, where the wind whipped sharply across the walls of Edinburgh Castle. The ancient fortress stood like a stone crown upon its mighty hill, gazing out over the city. We climbed the steep cobblestone path, the grey sky pressing low above us. As we stood at the castle's edge, looking out over the city below, Ben whispered, "The further we go, Dad, the more it feels like all the places are connected." "They are," I answered. "You're walking through the pages of your own book."

From there, our journey would soon take us across the waters. Ahead lay Germany, where old palaces of the Lorraine and Habsburgs waited. Then to France — Nancy, Lunéville, the resting places of the ones whose stories had been stolen by time and sickness.

And finally, the great return to Hungary — to Budapest and the Matthias Church, where the stones still held the bones of Béla and Anna beneath their silent vaults. But that would come later. For now, we stood beneath the old Scottish sky, the wind whipping through Ben's hair. He raised his journal once more, adding a simple line beneath today's entry: The road is long, but my feet are not afraid. I smiled at him, placing my arm gently around his shoulder. The world stretched before us like a giant unwritten page, and Ben — my son — held the pen. The story was far from over. But for the first time, it had truly begun.

The soft hum of the train filled the air as we made our way across the Channel. Ben sat beside me by the window, his small hand pressed to the glass, watching the world blur by as if the tracks were carrying us not only through countries, but through centuries. His journal rested on his lap, opened to a fresh page. The pages before it were already filled with sketches, crests, names, castles, and quiet reflections. And now, new pages waited — just like the places ahead.

He didn't speak for a while, his eyes fixed on the changing countryside. The green fields of England slowly slipped away behind us, replaced by the lands of Europe stretching ahead. "Dad…" he finally whispered. "Every time we go somewhere new, it feels like we're opening another page in my book." "That's exactly what we're doing, buddy," I replied softly. "You're not just reading history anymore. You're walking through it." He turned his head slightly, his voice thoughtful. "But I still don't know what it all means yet. I know the names. I know the places. I even know the people. But sometimes it feels like I'm still missing something."

I smiled gently. "That's because the story isn't finished. Not yet." He tapped his pen gently against his journal. "But I keep thinking about what King Béla told me. The voice that called me back — all three times. It wasn't just about living. It was because I still had something to do." "And you're doing it," I reminded him. "Every step, every place we visit, every name you learn — you're building the map." Ben nodded slowly. "The map inside me." "That's right."

The train slowed as we neared our next stop. We had already passed through Canterbury, Hampton Court, Windsor, and Edinburgh. Now we were headed toward Germany — toward the palaces and towns where more branches of his family once ruled and lived. Ahead lay the lands of the Lorraine, the Palatinate, the Habsburgs — places whose names had filled his journal but whose stones he had not yet touched. Ben stared down at his open page, tapping his pen again as though trying to find the right words to write. "Dad… do you think they know I'm here?" His voice was quiet. "I mean… the people who came before me. Do you think they see me walking through their old castles and churches?"

I paused for a moment, choosing my words carefully. "I think they've always been watching, Ben. Not like ghosts. Not like stories. But like family who were waiting for someone to remember them. You're that someone."

His face grew serious as he stared out the window again, watching as small German villages flickered past under the grey sky. "It's like they handed me a puzzle, but some of the pieces were lost. And now I'm trying to find them again."

"And that's why we're here," I said softly. "To find the missing pieces." He smiled faintly, lifting his pen to the page and writing quietly: The puzzle is big, but I won't stop looking. As the train rolled on, the countryside grew older. The villages looked like paintings — their steep roofs, narrow streets, and tall clock towers standing like quiet sentinels of forgotten stories.

Castles perched on distant hillsides, their grey stones rising out of the forests like ancient kings still standing guard. We arrived in Heidelberg first, the land of the Palatinate — where Ben's ancestors once ruled. The old castle ruins stood high above the Neckar River, watching over the town below. We climbed the worn stone steps, the cool wind whipping through the broken archways as Ben paused to trace the ancient carvings on the walls.

"Do you feel it, Dad?" he whispered. "It's not just ruins. It's waiting." I nodded. "Waiting for you." Ben took his journal out again, sketching the broken towers and the old family crests still faintly carved into the stone. He didn't need to say much. His hands spoke for him as he wrote quietly beneath the drawing: Even the broken stones still remember. From Germany, we travelled further, reaching Nancy and Lunéville in France — where the House of Lorraine once stood in its splendour. The great palace at Lunéville, sometimes called the Versailles of Lorraine, greeted us beneath pale skies. We wandered the long halls, the great gardens stretching out like a green sea behind the grand building.

"This is where she lived, isn't it?" Ben asked softly as we stood in one of the quiet salons. "Yes," I said. "Princess ÉlIslabeth Charlotte. The little girl you wrote about." Ben stood still for a long time, as though listening to something silent in the air. "She was only ten," he whispered. "Like I was, not so long ago." His pen hovered over his journal again. Then he wrote: She never had the chance to finish her story. But I will carry it.

We continued to the church where she was laid to rest — the Ducal Crypt at Saint-François-des-Cordeliers in Nancy. The stone walls were cool and heavy with the weight of generations. As we stood before the crypt, Ben lowered his head slightly, placing his hand gently on the stone wall as if greeting an old friend. "You're part of my story too," he whispered. "And I won't forget you." There was no fear in his voice. Only quiet promise. Our final leg would soon take us east again — to Hungary — where it had all truly begun. But for now, we stood still in that ancient place, father and son, the journal growing heavier with every step, every page, every name.

Ben closed his journal softly and looked up at me, his eyes filled with that strange, beautiful mixture of childhood and something much older. "Dad?" "Yes, buddy?" "I think the crown isn't hidden anymore." I smiled, wrapping my arm around his shoulder as we turned to leave the crypt. "No, son," I whispered. "It's not." And yet, neither of us spoke it aloud — because some truths remain better carried in silence. The journey was still far from over. But Ben was no longer searching for who he was. He was now simply walking toward where he was always meant to be.

CHAPTER 6: THE CROWN BENEATH THE STONES

The wind that carried us home from Scotland had grown tired by the time we returned to Kent. The sky above the cottage hung low, painted with soft greys, as though it too was resting before the next stretch of the journey. The car hummed quietly up the narrow lane, the countryside blurring past us like an old, familiar photograph. Ben sat in the back seat, his journal resting like treasure upon his knees. His head leaned softly against the window, eyes wide open but lost somewhere far beyond the rolling green hills.

I watched him through the mirror — not because I was worried, but because I was listening. Even in his silence, the wheels in his young mind were still turning. The puzzle of who he was had begun long before our first stop in Canterbury. And yet, somehow, every place we visited had whispered to him. The stones, the castles, the halls—they weren't just landmarks anymore. They had become voices. Quiet echoes of old bones, as though the very ground remembered him.

When we finally pulled into the cottage drive, the familiar creak of the wooden gate welcomed us like an old friend. The cottage windows flickered warm behind the lace curtains. For a moment, it felt like time itself paused — like we had stepped out of one chapter and were now standing at the doorstep of the next. Ben quietly unbuckled his seatbelt, slid the journal under his arm, and climbed out. He didn't rush inside. Instead, he stood for a moment beneath the great oak tree by the driveway, staring up into its twisting branches.

"Still thinking, buddy?" I asked softly as I joined him. He nodded without taking his eyes off the canopy above. "The more we see, Dad... the bigger it gets." His voice was quiet but steady. "It's like... like I can feel them watching. Not in a scary way. More like they've been waiting for me to come find them." I placed my hand gently on his shoulder. "You're exactly right, Ben. They have been." We walked into the house together, the door clicking shut behind us. The smell of old books and soft cedar welcomed us back inside, like the arms of the house itself were wrapping around us. The long wooden table was still covered with the maps we'd left behind, the scrolls carefully sealed in their archival cases, and piles of notes that had grown like vines with every passing week.

Ben placed his journal down gently next to the scrolls, running his hand across the leather cover. "You know," he said thoughtfully, "when I first started writing this, I thought it was just for fun. Just to remember things. But it's not just mine anymore, is it?" I smiled. "No, son. It's not. You're writing for everyone who came before you. And maybe even for those who'll come after you." He turned to face me, his eyes filled with that same steady glow that had carried him since the scrolls first appeared. "Dad... what do you think Béla would say if he saw me right now?"

I breathed deeply, choosing my words carefully. "I think he would be proud. Not because of the names or the titles or the blood... but because you're listening." Ben grinned. "And because I'm writing it down." "Exactly," I whispered. For the rest of that evening, the two of us worked side by side beneath the soft light of the old desk lamp. The maps were spread open again — not to review what we had seen, but to mark where we were going next. Germany. France. And then... Hungary.

The names whispered off the paper like old friends calling from across a river. The House of Lorraine. The Habsburgs. The old palaces of Nancy and Lunéville. The resting places where little Princess ÉlIslabeth Charlotte had once lived and where sorrow still lingered like a quiet ghost. We traced the route carefully, connecting the threads like a great tapestry. As I watched him mark the cities, his pen steady in his hand, I saw the boy who was no longer simply following a story — but becoming part of it.

The next chapter waited beyond the water. Ben paused, tapping the page softly. "Dad?" "Yes, buddy?" "Do you think I'll know when I've found everything?" I smiled softly, leaning closer. "No, Ben. You won't ever find everything. But you'll find enough. Enough to carry it forward." He nodded quietly. "Good. Because I don't think it's supposed to end. Not yet." And with that, we closed the books for the night, letting the maps rest beneath the weight of history once more. Outside, the wind had settled. Inside, the story was waiting.

The morning broke with a thin slice of pale sunlight, streaming across the kitchen table where the maps had remained spread open all night. The smell of fresh toast and brewing tea filled the cottage air as I stepped quietly into the room. There, already wide awake, sat Ben. His small frame hunched over the old map, one hand resting flat against the parchment while the other carefully guided his pen. He didn't even look up. "I couldn't sleep much," he said softly, his voice calm. "I kept seeing the map in my head." I smiled as I poured the tea. "That's because it's not just a map anymore, buddy. It's a doorway."

Ben finally glanced up at me, eyes bright and eager. "It feels like the map knows where we're supposed to go." I pulled up my chair beside him and let my eyes drift across the carefully marked lines he had drawn overnight. Thin black ink traced the coast of England across the Channel into France, then curved into Germany, and finally swept down toward Hungary like a long winding ribbon of time. Each city was circled carefully, with faint little notes scribbled in his tidy handwriting. "Look," he said, tapping one of the circles. "Nancy. That's where Princess ÉlIslabeth Charlotte lived, right?"

"That's right," I nodded. "And not far from Lunéville, where she died. You remembered." Ben lowered his voice slightly. "Even though she was only a child, she's part of the story too." He paused, tracing the line eastward toward Austria and Hungary. "And after France, we go to Vienna... then Budapest... and finally, to Matthias Church." His pen hovered over the name for a moment before he whispered, "Where Béla is waiting." There was something gentle and almost sacred about the way he said it — not fearful, but respectful, as though speaking of a friend he hadn't met yet.

I reached for the smaller book beside us — one of the old parchment copies from the abbey, carefully translated and bound for our journey. "Every step we take is part of the trail they left behind," I reminded him. "And you're following it exactly as Béla hoped someone would." Ben sat quietly for a moment, his eyes studying the looping lines and foreign place names, the weight of it all resting gently on his young shoulders. But instead of shrinking beneath it, he seemed to stand taller inside. "You know, Dad," he said suddenly, "it's kind of like playing hide-and-seek. Only this time... I'm finding pieces of me."

I chuckled softly, leaning forward. "That's exactly what it is, Ben. You're searching for your own reflection — not in a mirror, but across time." He grinned. "And all the people who came before me — it's like they left me clues." His fingers traced the rivers drawn across the map like veins on an ancient hand. "The Danube flows through Budapest," he whispered. "That river's like the bloodline." I smiled. "That's a pretty good way to see it, son."

He sat back for a moment, then whispered something that struck deeper than most of his observations. "I wonder if Béla knew my name." I paused, letting the quiet hang for a moment. "Maybe not your exact name, Ben. But he knew you would come. That someone from his family — carrying the same blood — would rise one day and carry the story forward." Ben nodded softly, his face thoughtful. "It's strange to think that people I never met have been waiting for me for so long."

I reached over and rested my hand gently on his shoulder. "And now you're here. You're exactly where you were meant to be." The kettle whistled softly behind us, but neither of us moved. The house was filled with that same gentle quiet — the kind of quiet that comes just before great adventures begin. Not with noise, but with knowing. Finally, Ben stood up, closing his journal and gripping it tightly beneath his arm. His voice was steady but filled with excitement. "Dad, can we pack the books now?"

I smiled. "Yes, buddy. It's time." Outside, the clouds were breaking apart, letting strips of morning sun stretch across the Kent countryside. The journey ahead was long, but the trail was clear. And for the first time, it felt like the map itself was breathing — calling us forward, one heartbeat at a time.

The airport was loud as usual, just what Ben expected. It wasn't the kind of noise you heard at home — no birdsong from the Kent fields, no soft turning of book pages or gentle whisper of parchment. This was the kind of noise that rattled around inside you: the hum of people rushing to gates, the sharp crackle of announcements echoing through wide halls, the whir of luggage wheels spinning over polished floors. Ben gripped my hand tightly as we stood in line, passports in one hand, his journal tucked beneath his other arm like a tiny treasure chest.

"Feels bigger than I thought, Dad," he whispered. I smiled down at him. "That's because it is, buddy. But remember, no matter how big this place feels, you and I — we've got each other. We know where we're going." He nodded, still watching the enormous schedule board blinking with names of cities neither of us could pronounce very well. Frankfurt. Munich. Vienna. Budapest. "That one," he whispered, pointing. "Budapest. Béla's city."

"Yes," I nodded softly. "But first, we stop in France." The voice on the speaker crackled again, calling our flight. We walked down the long tunnel toward the plane, the engines rumbling like distant thunder outside the windows. As we reached our seats, Ben slid into his window seat and stared out at the silver wing stretching into the morning sky. "Dad?" he asked as he buckled his seatbelt. "Do you think when we fly up, we're flying over the old roads they once walked?" I smiled. "Maybe. But they didn't have airplanes back then. They travelled by horseback, wagons, and sometimes by foot. Every step took weeks or months."

He stared out the window as the plane began to taxi. "They would've had to be really brave, huh?" "Very brave," I said. "And very determined. Just like you." The plane lifted into the sky, climbing fast above the rolling green of England. Ben pressed his forehead gently against the cool glass. Far beneath us, rivers twisted like long silver snakes, and fields divided into perfect squares like a giant patchwork quilt. "It looks like a map," he whispered. "Everything does, from up here," I said. "And every map tells a story."

As we crossed the Channel toward France, the clouds broke open, revealing the soft outlines of tiny towns and winding rivers below. Ben reached for his journal, flipping to a fresh page. The pen inked smooth lines as he carefully drew the scene: little houses, winding roads, the airplane wing cutting across the corner like a giant arrow pointing toward tomorrow. "Everywhere we go," he said softly, "feels like turning the pages of the book I was supposed to read." "You're not just reading it, Ben," I whispered. "You're writing it."

The stewardess came by, handing him a small packet of cookies and juice. Ben giggled quietly. "Even ancient explorers didn't have airplane snacks," he whispered to me. I chuckled. "No, they sure didn't." The flight was short compared to the journey that lay ahead. As we began our descent into France, the land below shifted. The lush countryside of England gave way to soft hills and stone villages with orange-tiled roofs, nestled like sleeping cats among the trees. The voice crackled again over the speaker. We were landing near Nancy — the first great stop on Ben's living map.

As the plane touched down and the wheels rumbled against the runway, Ben whispered, "We're really here, aren't we?" I squeezed his shoulder gently. "Yes, son. The quest has just begun." The airport was smaller than Heathrow, but somehow it felt heavier — not with noise, but with something older. History felt closer here. The language of the announcements changed to French, and Ben listened closely, trying to mimic the words under his breath. "Bonjour," he whispered, practicing. "Merci. Au revoir."

"Not bad for your first hour in France," I grinned. Outside the airport, the cool spring air wrapped around us as we stepped into the car rental lot. The trees swayed softly, and for a moment, as the wind shifted, it almost sounded like faint voices — as though the land itself was remembering who had returned. Ben clutched his journal tight again. "Do you think Princess ÉlIslabeth Charlotte would know we're here?"

I knelt beside him, looking directly into his eyes. "Ben, in ways we don't fully understand yet, I think she already does." He smiled faintly. "Then let's find her." And so, we stepped into the car, the doors closing with a soft click behind us, and began the next part of the journey — toward the hidden pieces of the past, waiting for us just ahead.

The drive from the airport toward Nancy felt different than our drives back home in Kent. The countryside here rolled out like green silk, dotted with sleepy villages, quiet rivers, and forests that seemed older than any road we followed. Ben watched everything with wide eyes, his fingers resting gently on the leather cover of his journal. Every so often, he would glance at the little hand-drawn map he'd sketched from the books we studied. The lines were simple, but the places meant something: Nancy, Lunéville, and deeper still, toward Lorraine.

"This place is where her story happened, Dad," Ben said softly. "The princess." I nodded as the road curved gently through the countryside. "Yes. Princess ÉlIslabeth Charlotte lived here. She laughed here. She played here. And..." I hesitated briefly, "she was lost here." Ben's face grew serious, but not sad. "But we found her again. In the stories." "That's right," I whispered. "That's how stories work, Ben. We may not change what happened, but we bring their names back into the light."

The spires of Nancy appeared first on the horizon, like slender fingers rising from the earth. The streets narrowed, curling like ribbons through the heart of the old city. We drove slowly past stone buildings lined with shuttered windows, small shops tucked beneath arches, and little cafés where people sat with warm drinks and gentle conversation. The old palace wasn't far now. The Ducal Palace — where her family ruled, where her life had begun. Its stone walls rose ahead of us, framed by blooming trees, their branches painted in spring colours.

Ben whispered as we pulled to a stop nearby. "This is it, isn't it?" "Yes," I said softly, turning off the engine. "This is where the House of Lorraine once ruled. And where she lived her short, delicate life." We stepped out of the car, our feet pressing softly against ancient cobblestones polished smooth by hundreds of years of footsteps before us. The palace stood tall but quiet, its windows watching us like silent witnesses. Ben reached for my hand as we approached the entrance. "Do you think she walked right here?" I squeezed his small hand gently. "I believe so. Many times."

Inside, the air was cooler, heavier. The halls whispered with the faint echoes of voices long gone. Tapestries still hung on stone walls, and portraits gazed down from high ceilings — noble faces frozen in paint, their eyes following us as we walked slowly. Ben stood before one of the portraits — a young girl, dressed finely, her face solemn but sweet.

"She looks like she was kind," Ben said softly. "She was only ten when she passed," I whispered. "Like a candle snuffed too early." He studied her face for a long time. "She could've been my friend." I swallowed gently. "Yes, Ben. She could have."

We continued walking deeper into the palace, following velvet ropes and creaking floors, until we reached a small gallery that displayed relics of the House of Lorraine. Glass cases held delicate objects — letters, seals, family crests, even a tiny carved cross that once hung around the neck of a child. Ben stopped before one particular display — a faded map showing the old territories of Lorraine. "Look, Dad!" he whispered excitedly. "There's Hungary here too — it connects." He traced the old routes with his finger. "It's like her story and Béla's story meet here. Just like mine." I smiled. "Because your story holds both of them, Ben. Your blood remembers paths even before you walk them."

He grew quiet again, his voice lowering into a thoughtful whisper. "She didn't get to grow up. But maybe that's why I did. Maybe... I was supposed to finish parts of the story she couldn't finish." His words hung heavy in the air — not sad, not boastful, just quietly true. We left the palace quietly as the afternoon sun stretched across the cobbled streets. The bells of Nancy's cathedral rang gently in the distance as we stepped back toward the car. Ben paused one last time, turning to look back at the stone walls. "Thank you, Princess," he whispered softly. "I won't forget you." I placed my hand on his shoulder, and together, we drove onward — the road curving toward Lunéville, where the next whispers of the past still waited.

The drive from Nancy to Lunéville was not long. The road cut gently through the countryside as the afternoon light softened into a golden hue, like warm honey spilling across the horizon. The further we travelled, the quieter the world seemed to become, as though even time itself was slowing down for us. Ben sat beside me, his journal resting on his lap, the pen still tightly held in his fingers, though for now he wasn't writing. His gaze was fixed on the scenery rolling past his window. The little villages faded behind us, and then, rising slowly ahead like a grand memory, stood Château de Lunéville.

"There it is," Ben whispered, almost like he was seeing something out of a dream. The palace stood broad and elegant, its pale stone walls glowing softly in the fading light. Though smaller than Versailles, Lunéville carried a kind of quiet sadness with it — as if it still remembered the children who had once laughed inside its halls and then were lost too soon. We parked just outside the great iron gates, and for a moment, neither of us moved. We simply looked. "This is where she died, isn't it?" Ben asked softly.

"Yes," I replied, my voice calm and gentle. "Here, in these very walls, Princess Éllslabeth Charlotte became sick with smallpox. And not just her — her brother and sister too. All three of them were taken in the same week." Ben's voice lowered. "Three children. Like three candles going out." The palace stood in its quiet dignity as we approached. The gravel crunched beneath our shoes. Though parts of it had been restored, the weight of history hung heavy in the air. Some windows were shuttered; others reflected the setting sun like golden mirrors staring back at us.

Inside, the great halls stretched wide and long, their ceilings painted with faded murals. Ben's steps slowed as he gazed around, his little shoes tapping softly on the polished marble floors. There were no large crowds, no noisy tourists — only us and a few caretakers moving gently about, tending to the quiet corners. Ben stopped in the centre of the grand hall and looked up. "Do you think she played here, Dad? Maybe she ran through here with her brother and sister?" I smiled softly. "Yes, I believe she did. These halls were once filled with music and laughter, not just sadness."

He stood very still, letting the silence wrap around him. Then, gently, he whispered as though speaking directly to her: "I hope you weren't scared." We continued walking through the rooms, each one dressed in rich tapestries and antique furnishings. The chandeliers above caught the fading light like frozen stars, and the mirrors along the walls stretched the room endlessly into itself. In one chamber, we found portraits of the House of Lorraine—familiar faces now, their eyes almost meeting Ben's. Ben whispered again, as though speaking to invisible friends, "You're not forgotten."

In one smaller room, tucked quietly at the back, was a display of small belongings once held by the children of Lunéville: tiny embroidered shoes, delicate silver hairbrushes, and a few fragile toys made of painted wood. Ben's hand hovered over the glass, his voice barely audible. "She never even had time to grow up," he said, his throat catching slightly. "She had a whole life waiting for her." "Yes," I whispered. "And some stories remain unfinished." Ben glanced up at me with quiet certainty. "That's why I'm here. My story is still going." He placed his hand gently over his journal and whispered, "For her."

The sun had fully set when we stepped back outside. The moon had begun to rise above the stone rooflines, and the palace behind us stood bathed in soft silver light, its old windows glowing like watchful eyes under the night sky. As we walked toward the car, Ben looked back one last time. His voice was calm but sure. "I feel like we've closed one part of the book tonight, Dad." I nodded. "And tomorrow we open another." He smiled faintly. "The pages keep turning." "Yes, son," I said softly. "And you're holding the pen." We climbed into the car, the doors closing with a gentle click as the world outside wrapped itself in darkness. But inside, the light of Ben's story burned quietly on — steady, strong, and waiting for what came next.

By morning, the landscape had changed again. The soft hills of France faded behind us as we crossed quietly into Germany, where ancient forests rose like walls of green and winding roads carried us deeper into the lands where some of Ben's forgotten branches had once stretched. The German air felt sharper somehow, cooler, as though the trees themselves carried memories older than the castles they stood beside. Tall spruces and oaks lined the narrow country roads, their limbs arching high above us like the ribs of a great cathedral made not of stone, but of living wood.

As the car hummed steadily forward, Ben sat quietly in the passenger seat, but not idly. His journal was open once more, the pen gliding steadily across the page in his hand. He was not simply writing names today. He was weaving together his map of blood—one that now crossed borders not drawn on any ordinary atlas. This map lived inside him. He paused suddenly, glancing up at me as if a thought had struck like lightning. "Dad... if Hungary was my first root, and France held more branches, is Germany the trunk that connects them?"

I smiled softly at the question. "That's a very good way to see it. Many of your royal branches passed through here. The German states weren't always one country, you know. Back then, they were a patchwork of duchies, principalities, bishoprics, and empires—all tangled together like a forest." Ben's brow furrowed slightly. "Like which ones?" "Well," I began, careful to not overwhelm him, "some of your ancestors came through Lorraine, which sat right at the edge of both France and Germany. But others tied into the Palatinate, the Rhineland, Saxony, even Hesse. Many of your ancestors belonged to what we call the Holy Roman Empire. It ruled over these lands for centuries."

Ben's eyes widened. "The Holy Roman Empire?" "Yes," I nodded. "And even though the name sounds like it came from Rome, it wasn't Italian. It was mostly German-speaking. For nearly a thousand years, kings and emperors ruled over these lands from great cities like Aachen and Frankfurt. Some were crowned right here." Ben scribbled quickly: Holy Roman Empire — Germany. As the forests opened briefly, we passed small stone villages nestled into the valleys, their slate rooftops shining under the weak morning sun. Church steeples pierced the sky like thin fingers, and bells rang softly in the distance.

"Did any of my family live in these villages?" Ben asked. "Some may have ruled nearby, others travelled through. Remember Elizabeth Stuart? She married into the Palatinate—the German royal houses. That's how her descendants reached both France and eventually your own family tree." Ben nodded slowly. "So, my story doesn't just go forward... it also crosses sideways." "That's exactly right, buddy," I smiled. "It's not just a straight line—it's like a giant spider web of kings and queens, marriages and alliances, moving back and forth across all of Europe."

Ben paused again, lowering his pen slightly. "Dad… do you think they knew? I mean... my ancestors. Did they know that one day, I'd be born? That I'd carry all of this?" The question hung in the air like a weight between us. I thought carefully before answering. "I don't think they knew your name, son," I said softly. "But they knew someone would come after them. Every child carries forward the ones who came before. And some of them—like King Béla, and Elizabeth Charlotte, and many more—left pieces behind. Scrolls, letters, seals, and even the blood that flows in you now."

Ben looked down at his arm and whispered, "Inside my veins." "Yes," I whispered back. "That's why we're here. Not to worship these kings or pretend they were perfect. But to honour their stories, so they're not lost." We passed beneath a stone bridge where ivy crawled like green lace across its worn arches. The road narrowed again as we neared our next stop. Ben's voice grew quiet. "Where are we going now, Dad?" I glanced at the map resting beside me. "To Heidelberg." "Heidelberg?" I nodded. "This was where your ancestors once ruled in the Palatinate. Where Elizabeth Stuart—your many-times-great-grandmother—lived after leaving England."

Ben's eyes lit up. "We're following her footsteps." "That's right, buddy." The castle of Heidelberg came into view like something from one of Ben's drawings—a mighty ruin perched high above the Neckar River, its red stone walls broken and worn, yet still holding its head high against the sky. Parts of it had crumbled long ago, but much remained standing. It was neither alive nor fully dead — much like the old stories Ben had uncovered. We parked at the base of the hill, and as we walked the winding path upward, Ben whispered, "It feels like we're walking through my own memories, Dad. Memories I never knew I had."

The air grew cooler as we climbed. The wind danced softly through the ivy-covered walls. The old tower stood like a silent watchman, keeping vigil over the land. Ben gazed up in quiet awe, his small hands clutching his journal tightly. As we stepped through the grand stone gate, I placed a hand gently on his shoulder and whispered, "Welcome back, Ben. You've never been here before—but your blood has." He didn't speak. He simply stood still, taking it all in—the castle, the towers, the echoes. The wind carried the past gently across the stones, and I knew that in his silence, Ben was hearing voices only he could understand.

The cool breeze stirred gently through the old courtyard of Heidelberg Castle, rustling the ivy that clung to the weathered stones like stubborn fingers of history. Ben stood beneath the tall arches, his journal now pressed tightly against his chest. His breathing was slow, his eyes wide, as if listening to something far beyond my own hearing. I let him remain still for a few moments, allowing the castle to speak to him. Sometimes, I had come to learn, silence was the only proper language when you stood among such old bones. "Dad," Ben finally whispered, his voice barely above the wind. "I can feel them." I knelt slightly so I could meet his gaze. "Feel who, buddy?" "The people who were here before me," he answered softly. "It's not like I can hear their voices with my ears… but it's like my chest remembers. Like my blood remembers."

He gently lowered his journal and opened it to a fresh page. In careful strokes, his pen glided across the paper. He was not copying from a book or a tablet; he was writing what he felt. Sketches of towers. A symbol that resembled the Palatinate lion. The faint outlines of a crown, not bold and shining, but faint, almost ghostlike. His hand moved as though guided by something older than his own years. I watched him, and my heart stirred. This was no longer simply a child learning names and dates. This was a boy in communion with his past.

We wandered deeper into the broken halls of the castle. The massive barrel, the famed Heidelberg Tun, still rested in the old cellar—a giant wine barrel large enough to hold thousands of gallons. Ben giggled softly as we stood before it. "Even the barrels were kings here," he joked. I smiled. "Yes. And so much of life here was grand—but also fragile." My hand gestured gently toward the fractured outer walls, where cannon fire from wars long past had left the stones cracked open to the elements. "Even the strongest kingdoms eventually fall." Ben turned serious again. "But the people don't disappear. They live through their children."

"That's exactly it," I said softly. "And you are one of those children." We reached a quiet balcony that overlooked the Neckar River far below, its grey-blue waters snaking gently through the valley like a ribbon of time. Ben leaned against the old stone railing and stared outward. "This is where Elizabeth Stuart lived, right?" he asked. "Yes," I nodded. "After she married Frederick V of the Palatinate. She was a princess of England and the daughter of King James I—your many-times-great-grandfather. When she came here, she became known as the Winter Queen."

Ben furrowed his brow. "Why the Winter Queen?" "Because Frederick's reign as king of Bohemia lasted only one winter before war forced them into exile. But even though her crown was short-lived, her children spread her bloodline all across Europe." Ben whispered, "And that's how she became part of me." "That's how," I smiled. "Her sons and daughters married into many houses—France, Germany, Denmark, Sweden, and eventually… England again. Even today, King Charles carries her blood. And so do you."

Ben gazed into the distance for a long moment, watching the clouds shift over the forested hills. "Dad," he whispered after a pause, "I don't know why… but when I stand here, I don't feel like I'm visiting. I feel like I've returned."

I swallowed softly. "That's because somewhere, deep in your bones, you have." We stood quietly as the breeze played with his hair. The world below us carried on like any ordinary day. Cars rolled through town. Tourists wandered with cameras. But up here on the stone balcony, time had folded itself neatly into Ben's hands.

As the sun dipped lower toward the tree-lined horizon, we made our way back through the archways. Ben carefully sketched a final drawing of the castle as it stood now—broken, yet beautiful. Wounded, but proud. Just like many of the royal houses he carried within him. Before we left the castle grounds, Ben paused and asked, "Dad… do you think Béla ever knew that one of his grandchildren would stand here one day?" I smiled faintly. "I think he always knew someone would carry it forward. And tonight, that someone is you." Ben nodded, holding his journal close. "Then I'll keep writing, Dad. So they'll never be forgotten." The sky dimmed as we walked toward the car, and the stones of Heidelberg whispered softly behind us, like old voices gently thanking a child who had finally returned.

The border crossing into France was quiet, as though the very land itself wished not to disturb our journey. The soft hills rolled gently beneath the overcast sky, and the old villages we passed stood like patient watchers, their windows gazing silently upon the road that carried us ever deeper into Ben's unfolding story. We were not here for grand castles or glittering palaces this time. Our destination was Lunéville, the quiet place where some of Ben's most fragile ancestors had once walked—and where three young lives were lost in a single week, stolen by a cruel disease that neither crown nor bloodline could stop.

As we drove through the narrow streets of the town, Ben sat unusually quiet in the passenger seat, his journal balanced carefully on his lap, his pen resting between his fingers. He gazed out the window, watching the buildings pass like shadows from long ago. At last, we arrived at the Château de Lunéville. It was not like the towering fortresses we had seen before. No towering keeps. No massive stone walls. Instead, it stood with a quiet dignity, its pale stone reflecting the soft light of late afternoon. The fountains stood still beneath grey clouds, and the wide courtyard lay empty but for the breeze that whispered softly across its flagstones.

Ben stepped out of the car slowly, holding his journal close against his chest. His eyes swept across the courtyard, studying every window, every balcony, every step. "This is where they lived?" he asked gently. "Yes," I whispered. "Princess ÉlIslabeth Charlotte of Lorraine. Your cousin many times removed. And her little brother and sister. They called this place home." Ben's voice grew softer. "But not for very long." "No," I replied. "Not long enough." We walked together toward the grand façade of the palace. Though time had worn away some of its grandeur, the echoes of royalty still lingered. Ben paused beneath the central balcony, where once the Duke of Lorraine had stood with his family. He closed his eyes for a moment, breathing slowly, as though reaching into the air to find what could no longer be seen.

"I wonder if she played here," he whispered. "Running across these stones." "I'm sure she did," I nodded. "She was not much older than you are now. Just ten years old." Ben lowered his voice, his eyes growing distant.

"I think I feel her here." He opened his journal and carefully began to draw. First the great front of the palace, then three small figures, holding hands beneath the tall windows. "One for ÉlIslabeth," he said softly. "One for her brother. One for her sister." He paused for a moment, then added gently, "And one empty space."

I watched him carefully. "Why the empty space, son?" He looked up at me, his voice calm but certain. "For all the ones we don't know yet. The ones who didn't get written down. But they still lived. And they're part of us too." I swallowed, feeling the weight of his words settle inside my chest. This was no ordinary child. This was a boy who understood something many adults never fully grasped. We circled quietly through the gardens, where the spring flowers pushed softly from the earth, as though gently reminding the world that life always tries to return.

As the afternoon wore on, we drove the short distance north to Nancy, where the Church of Saint-François-des-Cordeliers stood. The Ducal Crypt below held the resting place of Princess ÉlIslabeth Charlotte, along with her siblings and ancestors from the House of Lorraine. Inside the church, the air was cool and heavy with the smell of stone and candle wax. The faint sound of a choir practicing in the distant chapel added a strange calm to the moment. We stood quietly before the entrance to the crypt, its great iron gate locked but visible through the gaps.

Ben clutched his journal tightly. "They're here," he whispered. "They are," I said softly. "And they know you've come." For a long time, we said nothing. Ben simply stood there, as though his very presence was enough. Finally, after several quiet minutes, he whispered, "Dad… I want to promise them something." I knelt beside him. "What do you want to promise?" "That I'll carry them forward," he said, his voice steady. "I'll keep writing. So they won't be forgotten again." I smiled gently, placing my hand on his shoulder. "Then they'll live on, Ben. As long as you write, they'll live."

He nodded quietly, then opened his journal once more. On a new page, he wrote only one simple line beneath the date: I was here. And I remember you. As we left the church and stepped into the cool evening air, I glanced down at my son—small in frame, but already carrying the weight of centuries with a grace beyond his years. The wind stirred softly through the streets of Nancy, as though whispering its own quiet thanks. The journey was far from over. But tonight, something beautiful had been laid to rest—carried now within the pages of Ben's little journal, inked in permanence, never to be erased.

The plane wheels touched down in Budapest with a gentle sigh, the morning fog rising like soft breath across the tarmac. The city beyond the windows blinked awake under a pale Hungarian sky. This wasn't the first time Ben and I had made this flight. But even as familiar as it felt, there was something different this time. A quiet weight. A deeper pull. Ben clutched his journal tightly against his chest as we walked through the terminal. His face carried a strange mix of excitement and quiet determination. This was no longer the wide-eyed child who had first stood before the monks at Pannonhalma. This was a boy who now knew the weight of the names he carried — and the ones still waiting to be found.

We retrieved our bags quickly and slipped into the familiar rental car, the same drive unfolding before us again — winding roads, low hills, and the old countryside that seemed to breathe its own memories into the air. The farther we drove, the quieter Ben became. He stared out the window, watching the land pass by, as though every tree and field whispered the names of his ancestors. As the monastery hill finally rose in the distance, he spoke softly. "Dad… it feels like the land remembers me." I smiled faintly. "And it does, Ben. It's been waiting for you."

The great towers of Pannonhalma appeared, rising gently against the pale morning light. The Abbey stood like a quiet sentinel, timeless and steady. As we parked near the familiar stone courtyard, Ben took a long breath, his fingers tracing over the edges of his journal. We walked together toward the great doors where we had once stood months before. And just as before, the heavy oak doors creaked open — but this time, they were already waiting for us.

Brother Miklós stood at the entrance, his robe folding gently in the morning breeze. His face broke into a warm smile as we approached. "Welcome back, Benedict," he said softly, bowing his head. Ben returned the smile, his voice clear. "Hello, Brother Miklós." The monk's eyes twinkled faintly as he looked at my son — not as a visitor, not even as a child, but as something more. As one returning to a place that had always been his.

"You've grown since last we met," Miklós said with quiet humour. "In many ways." Ben grinned faintly. "And I've been writing." The monk glanced at the journal under his arm. "Good. That is the true work." We followed him once again through the familiar stone halls, but this time the air felt different. There was no longer the same quiet hesitation of strangers meeting. Instead, it was the comfort of those who already shared a secret.

"We've prepared something for you," Brother Miklós said gently as we walked. "There are scrolls you did not see on your first visit. They were not ready for you then. But now…" — his voice lowered — "they are." Ben's eyes lit softly, but he said nothing, his fingers tightening around his journal. We descended the narrow stone staircase, the cool air wrapping gently around us. The scent of old parchment and cedar wood greeted us like an old friend. But instead of the same archive chamber we visited before, Brother Miklós led us deeper — into a smaller, older vault.

The heavy wooden door creaked open, revealing a modest chamber lit by a single narrow window. At the centre of the room sat a simple wooden table, and upon it — three scrolls, each bound tightly in faded ribbon, marked with familiar wax seals. Ben stepped forward slowly, almost as though afraid to breathe too loudly. "These," Miklós whispered, "were locked away for a time. Not because they were forgotten. But because you had not yet returned." Ben stood before them, his small hand hovering just above the parchment. "May I…?" he whispered. The monk nodded gently. "Yes, Benedict. They have waited long enough."

Carefully, Ben untied the first ribbon, slowly unrolling the scroll. The ink had faded, but the words were still legible. Hungarian script danced across the aged parchment. Names. Places. Dates. And then — a symbol. Ben's breath caught. "Dad… look." At the bottom of the scroll, pressed in deep red wax, was the crowned stag — Béla's mark — but this time, surrounded by three tiny stars in a triangle. "The mark you always draw," I whispered. Ben nodded slowly, his voice trembling. "It was never just something in my head." Miklós spoke softly. "No, child. You were remembering."

The second scroll revealed something different — a list of marriages. Royal unions, carefully recorded. The names were familiar: France, Scotland, England, Byzantium, Lorraine, even German principalities. But at the very bottom of the list, added in slightly newer ink, was something we had never seen before. A note. Simple. Almost like a whisper frozen on paper: "The line continues beyond my sight, but not beyond the river of my blood."

Ben stared at the words for a long moment. "It's his hand," he said quietly. "Béla's." The third scroll was smaller — more fragile. Brother Miklós helped unroll it slowly. This one was not a family record, but something different. A letter. Addressed not to a king or a noble, but simply: "To the child not yet born, but promised." Ben's hand trembled as he read aloud in a whisper, translating the Hungarian carefully with Brother Miklós's help.

"If you find this, you carry what I cannot finish. The blood carries the name. The name carries the truth. The truth carries the burden. But the burden is not sorrow. It is memory. The crown will remain unseen. The world does not yet know you. But you are known to me." The silence in the room grew heavier. Ben turned to me, his eyes shining but unafraid. "He knew, Dad. He knew I would come." I swallowed, my throat tight. "Yes, son. He knew." Brother Miklós placed a gentle hand on Ben's shoulder. "And now you carry the scrolls, not only in your hand, but in your heart. This is why you returned."

Ben nodded slowly, closing his journal and placing it gently beside the scrolls. His voice was soft but certain. "I won't stop writing. I won't stop remembering." As we stood there, surrounded by words written hundreds of years before he was ever born, I realized something simple but profound: This was no longer a search. This was a conversation across time — between a king who once ruled and the boy who now carried his name forward. The true quest was not for the past. It was for continuity.

We returned to the cottage in Kent several days later, the spring winds sweeping softly across the familiar hills. But something was different now. Something had shifted inside Ben — not loudly, not in a way anyone passing by would ever notice. It was quiet. Quiet like roots pushing deeper into the earth. The scroll Brother Miklós had entrusted to him never left his sight during the journey home. He held it like a fragile egg, wrapped carefully in the folds of his jacket, carried through the airports and across the winding motorways of England. And now, back home beneath the slanted beams of the cottage's study, it sat before us on the great wooden table — waiting.

The afternoon sun slanted through the window, casting golden stripes across the floorboards. The house was silent except for the rhythmic tick of the old wall clock. Ben sat cross-legged in his usual chair, his journal beside him, his hand resting protectively atop the sealed scroll. I pulled up my chair across from him, folding my arms. "Are you ready, Ben?" I asked quietly. His eyes stayed fixed on the scroll for a moment longer, as though speaking to it silently before answering. "Yes," he whispered. "I think I'm ready now." Together, we examined the seal once again — the crowned stag pressed deeply into the brittle wax. It was smaller than the great royal seals from the abbey archives, but just as deliberate. A scribe's personal seal, Brother Miklós had called it. A voice from Béla's court.

Ben gently broke the wax with a soft crack. The parchment inside uncoiled like a sleeping serpent stretching after a long slumber. The ink had faded slightly, but the careful strokes of the scribe were still clear and precise — like a message that had waited only for him.

The words were written first in Latin, with smaller notations in Hungarian below, likely added by later monks who had preserved it. And at the top, inscribed in delicate script, was a single phrase: "Ad Memoria Aeternam: For the Eternal Memory of Blood." Ben whispered the words aloud, his voice soft. "For the Eternal Memory of Blood." His eyes turned to me, wide but steady. "Dad... this was written for me."

I smiled faintly. "It was written for whoever was brave enough to open it. And that person is you." We read together slowly, piece by piece, translating as we went. It was not a list of laws or royal decrees. It was not a record of war or treaties. It was a letter. A private letter. Written by one of Béla's scribes — perhaps even at the king's request — addressed not to a person of his own time, but to someone of the future. "We write not for kings, nor for courts, but for the bearer of this blood yet unborn. You are the child of many rivers. Where kingdoms rose, you are the bridge that crosses them still. The languages in your veins are older than your tongue. The winds that carried your ancestors carried burdens you now inherit."

Ben's fingers trembled slightly, but his voice did not waver. "You will know of Álmos and Árpád. You will know of Géza, Stephen, and Béla. But know also that their crowns were but branches of a far greater tree. The rivers from Antioch, Kiev, Francia, Saxony, and Britannia all flow together in you." He paused for a moment, exhaling slowly. "I know those names now, Dad. They're here," he whispered, tapping his chest. I nodded. "Keep reading, son."

"You will face doubt. Some will deny your lineage. Others will fear it. But the weight you carry is not for boasting nor for throne. It is for remembrance. The crown you wear will not sit upon your head, but within your bones." Ben swallowed hard. The words mirrored his very own thoughts — the secret crown that could not be seen, yet never left him. "The one who carries the secret crown carries also the task: to preserve what others have tried to erase. Do not fear your calling. Fear only forgetting." Ben's eyes glistened slightly as he continued.

"The scrolls are few, but the blood remembers all. What kings swore in stone, the blood writes in silence." When at last the scroll ended, Ben sat back, closing his eyes. The golden afternoon light caught his face gently, as though the sun itself bowed before him.

We sat together in the deep stillness of the cottage. The silence wasn't empty. It was full. Full of voices, full of names, full of lives long passed yet somehow still speaking. Ben opened his eyes once more, looking across the table at me. "Dad... this scroll... it's like Béla's voice is still here. Still teaching me."

I smiled softly. "And now you understand why this journey was never just about names or castles or maps." Ben nodded. "It's about memory." "Yes," I whispered. "And about not letting that memory fade." He rested his hand gently upon the unfurled scroll one final time.

"I won't let it fade, Dad," he whispered. "I promise." The sun dipped lower beyond the Kent hills as we sat quietly, father and son, surrounded by parchment, maps, and books — but most of all, surrounded by the weight of story. His story. Their story. The story yet to come. The following morning arrived not with fanfare or drama, but with the soft, familiar quiet of Kent's countryside. A thin mist curled across the fields as though the hills themselves were breathing. The world outside the cottage was calm. But inside, Ben's world was stirring like never before.

He sat at his desk by the small window, his leather journal open, his black ink pen resting between his fingers. The newly unrolled scroll from the abbey was carefully placed beside him, still weighted down by the small brass paperweights he had chosen with care. The words written upon it no longer looked ancient to him — they looked like echoes. I stood by the doorway, watching him as he stared not at the paper, but into it, as though reading between the lines now. After some time, I spoke softly. "You've hardly moved this morning, Ben." He blinked and looked up, not startled, but thoughtful. "I keep hearing it, Dad. The words. Like they're being read to me even when I'm not reading them."

I smiled faintly and stepped inside, pulling up the chair across from him. "That's what real memory feels like. It's not just something you learn — it's something that lives." He nodded slowly, his young face remarkably steady. "It's like the scroll was never lost at all. It was just waiting for me to catch up." I folded my arms gently, lowering my voice as though we were sitting inside a chamber of ancient stone once again. "You're carrying something most grown men wouldn't understand, son. And yet you do." Ben's eyes never wavered. "Because I know now what I was born for."

There was no arrogance in his voice. No pride. Only understanding — the kind of understanding that could only belong to someone who had been called long before he even had words for it. "I know I was born to carry their names forward. All of them." He tapped the journal softly. "Not just Béla. Not just Árpád. All of them." He glanced briefly toward the scroll again before continuing, as though pulling courage from it. "Some people think kings only sit on thrones. Or that crowns are only gold. But that's not true." His voice grew quieter, but stronger. "The real crown is the one you don't see. The one you feel inside your bones. That's why I never really died, Dad. That's why I came back three times." His gaze held mine now, unwavering. "Because if I hadn't, the story would've ended."

I swallowed gently, hearing the weight of those words settle like heavy rain upon old earth. "And it's not going to end." "No," he whispered. "It's only starting." The old clock ticked gently beside us.

The house seemed to hold its breath again, as though even the walls understood the depth of what was unfolding. Ben leaned forward slightly now, lowering his voice, almost as if speaking to the ancestors themselves. "Béla's scroll said it perfectly, Dad. Some will deny it. Some will fear it. But that doesn't change what's written inside me."

He placed his palm flat against his chest. "The blood remembers." I placed my hand on top of his, letting the warmth of the moment bind us. "The blood remembers," I echoed softly. "And you're its keeper." For several moments we sat like that — two hands resting atop a small chest that carried a thousand years of names, titles, vows, and promises. Not because either of us sought a crown, but because the crown had already chosen him. Ben whispered softly, almost reverently now. "And I will carry them. As long as I live." Outside the window, the clouds shifted, revealing a thin break of light that poured across the distant fields — like a silent blessing from kings who could no longer speak aloud, but who still watched.

The cottage stood still, but inside its walls, the boy's crown — invisible though it was — had grown heavier. And yet, in his small shoulders, there was no fear of it. Only quiet courage. The next few days at the cottage fell into a quiet rhythm again, though it was not the same rhythm we once knew. Ben's world had changed. And so had mine. We were no longer simply searching for old names or piecing together family trees; we were slowly unlocking something far more deliberate — something that had been waiting patiently for centuries.

Every morning, as the mist lifted across the Kent hills, Ben would be back at his desk, pen already in hand. The leather-bound journal had grown thick with his notes, drawings, and reflections. But now his writing was changing. It wasn't just lists anymore. It was becoming something like letters—letters to the people who came before him. He called them "The Messages." "Dad," he said one morning as I brought him his tea, "I think they meant for me to find this. All of this. The scrolls, the parchments, even the old books. They weren't just left behind by accident." I set the cup down and pulled my chair close. "What do you mean, son?"

He flipped open his newest pages, pointing to the notes he had carefully written. His finger tapped gently on one particular phrase. "They left it for me on purpose." The words came with an honesty that caught me off guard. I leaned closer, studying his face. He wasn't guessing. He wasn't imagining. He knew. Ben continued, his voice calm but full of something far older than his years. "When Béla wrote the scroll, he talked about how records were hidden. How monks kept things safe. But it wasn't just to protect names. It was because someday, someone like me would need to finish what they started."

I swallowed. His understanding was sharp — sharper than any scholar I had ever studied under. "They knew time would scatter their names, Dad. That rulers would rise and fall. That wars would burn libraries. That palaces would crumble. But they also knew something else." His small hand gently touched his own chest again. "They knew blood remembers." He said it so softly that even the wind outside seemed to stop. I whispered back, "Yes, Ben. The blood always remembers." He sat back in his chair, staring thoughtfully at the pages.

"The more I read, Dad, the more I feel like I'm not really reading something old. I feel like I'm reading something that was always waiting for me. It's like… they were writing to me." A pause, then his eyes lifted. "Do you think they knew my name?" For a moment, I couldn't speak. The question wasn't childish. It was deeply sincere. I took a slow breath. "I think they may not have known your name, Ben—but they knew you would come." He nodded, accepting it like a truth he had already known. "They called me back."

The room sat quietly with those words. Not even the old house creaked. The world outside existed, but inside this little corner of Kent, time folded neatly into one small boy's understanding. Ben leaned forward again, lowering his voice like a secret only the two of us were allowed to share. "Dad… I think that's why I survived." I nodded slowly. "I believe you."

He smiled faintly and turned another page in his journal, where he had carefully written a single line that summed it all perfectly: "Their story is unfinished. But I am not." We sat together for a long while after that, neither of us needing to fill the silence. The message had already been delivered. And Ben, at barely nine years old, carried it with a steadiness most men never find in a lifetime. The quest ahead of us was no longer simply about discovery. It was now about completion. And somewhere across Europe, in the great halls of stone, in the monasteries and palaces still standing, more pieces of that message were waiting.

Waiting for Ben. Waiting for the child they had written to across centuries. The wind carried a soft chill across the Kent countryside as we loaded the car once again. The journey that had started months ago—first with a letter, then with scrolls and hidden chambers—was stretching forward like a great ribbon unrolling itself at our feet. But this time, something was different. Ben wasn't just following the path now.

He was guiding it. The map lay spread out across the small oak table before we left. Not the kind of map you buy in a tourist shop, but one that had grown slowly inside Ben's journal. Handwritten notes, arrows, circled cities, small drawings—castles, abbeys, cathedrals—each place connected by threads drawn in black pen. But it was more than geography. It was a story map. A trail of names, events, and clues leading us forward.

Ben tapped his finger gently on the first stop. "Dad… it has to be Germany first." I looked at him, smiling faintly. "Germany?" He nodded firmly. "Because that's where the Lorraine and Habsburg branches touched before they moved into France and Austria. If I understand this right, that's where part of my family moved before Lunéville." His voice carried the confidence of someone who had rehearsed this in his head many times. "And then after Germany," he continued, "we go to France — to Nancy, where Princess ÉlIslabeth Charlotte lived."

I nodded, listening carefully as he continued piecing it together aloud. "And after France, we return to Hungary—Budapest. But not just for the Matthias Church, Dad. This time, I want to find where the rest of Béla's letters went. If the monks hid some of them, maybe there's more hidden in the other archives."

I sat back, watching him carefully. His fingers danced across the map, connecting dots I had barely even traced yet. The boy who once sat wide-eyed at the discovery of Pannonhalma was now thinking like the historian he was becoming.

"You've thought this through, haven't you?" I asked softly. Ben smiled. "Every night. Before I fall asleep, I see them in my head. The places. The castles. The abbeys. Even the faces sometimes." I leaned forward. "And what do you feel when you see them?" He paused, his voice steady. "I feel like I'm being pulled home." It wasn't just poetic language. I believed him. We folded the map carefully, slid it into the leather case, and gathered our things. As I zipped up the travel bag, Ben walked toward the window. The spring wind pushed gently through the trees, bending the branches into slow, waving motions.

"It's not just about kings and queens anymore, Dad," he said quietly. "No?" He shook his head. "It's about finishing their sentence." I smiled gently at the way his words always carried more weight than his years should allow. "The sentence they never got to finish." He turned to me with wide, serious eyes. "They started writing it, but time stopped them. Wars, sickness, lost scrolls… and now it's like they left me the pen." I stepped beside him, placing my hand softly on his shoulder. "Then let's go help you finish it."

The car hummed gently as we pulled away from the cottage, the narrow roads twisting through the hedgerows like green tunnels carved by centuries of wheels before ours. Ben sat in the backseat with his journal open, carefully copying notes from the family tree he had built. Names that once seemed scattered were now connected like threads in an ancient tapestry. As we drove toward London, where our first flight awaited, he looked up suddenly.

"Dad?" "Yes?" "If this is what they left for me… do you think there's someone else out there who will follow after me one day?" I smiled softly. "Yes, Ben. And one day, your journal might be the map they follow." His smile was small, but full of quiet purpose. "Then I better write it right." The wheels of the car carried us onward, but I knew full well that what truly carried us was not rubber on pavement. It was something far older. Older than roads. Older than even the stones of Canterbury or Windsor. We were following the river that had always run beneath us.

And Ben was slowly learning how to sail it. The plane's engines hummed steadily beneath us as we crossed the thin silver ribbon of the English Channel. Ben sat by the window, his face pressed gently against the cool glass, watching the distant green of England give way to the soft patches of farmland below. His journal sat open on the small tray table, though for the first time in a while, his pen was still. He wasn't writing. He was thinking.

We had left Kent early that morning, boarded the flight from Heathrow, and now, as the first glimmer of the European mainland approached, I could feel the weight shifting inside him. This was no longer research done from the safety of the cottage. This was now the ground itself, the places that his ancestors once stood. The places that still remembered his name even if the people had long forgotten. He whispered, almost to himself, "Dad… this is where they walked."

I glanced over. "Yes, buddy. These fields. These hills. These rivers. Some of their footprints may still rest beneath them." Ben's voice grew quiet. "It feels different. Like I'm stepping into the book I've been writing." The captain's voice crackled through the speaker as we began our descent into Frankfurt, Germany. The skyline unfolded ahead, and Ben watched with wide eyes as the small clusters of old timber-framed villages sat like little toys beneath the broad grey sky. As we stepped off the plane and into the cool German air, the difference struck immediately. The language around us shifted, the signs unfamiliar but inviting. Ben clutched his journal a little tighter as if holding onto a familiar friend in a foreign land.

"First stop, Lorraine's gate," I whispered with a grin. He grinned back, whispering, "Let's find them." The small town of Nancy lay ahead of us after several hours' drive. The roads carried us through stretches of thick forests and sleepy villages, each one holding stories that none of the people in passing cars could hear, but Ben could feel them — like silent echoes trailing behind every tree. We arrived in the soft gold of late afternoon. The old city of Nancy was gentle and quiet, its stone streets smooth beneath our shoes. The grandeur of Place Stanislas spread before us like a painting, its gilded gates gleaming beneath the sun.

Ben stood silently in the centre of the great square. "This is where she walked, isn't it?" he whispered. "Princess ÉlIslabeth Charlotte." "Yes," I nodded softly. "Here. And in Lunéville just a short drive away. This was her world." We continued walking, slowly making our way to the church where generations of the House of Lorraine rested—the Ducal Crypt beneath the Church of Saint-François-des-Cordeliers. The church's tall arched doors creaked softly as we stepped inside. The air was cool and heavy. Ben's small footsteps echoed alongside mine. As we reached the crypt entrance, the world seemed to grow utterly still.

Ben stared down at the stone chamber beneath, his hands resting gently against the railing. For several moments, neither of us spoke. The names engraved upon the walls whispered their long-forgotten prayers into the quiet chamber. "Dad…" Ben whispered. "Even though she died so young… her story still lives. Because I found her." I placed my hand gently on his shoulder. "And now, Ben… because you remembered her, she's not lost." He nodded slowly, tracing his fingers gently across the engraved letters of the Lorraine name. "One day, someone might say that about me too."

I smiled, my voice soft. "They will." The next morning, under a thin blanket of fog, we drove onward — across the German-French border again, cutting east toward Austria, following the trail toward Vienna and the roots of the Habsburg branches. The mountains rose around us like ancient stone guardians, their peaks hidden in the mist. Ben stared at them in quiet awe. "It's like nature is protecting the past," he whispered. I nodded. "In a way, that's exactly what mountains do. They guard the stories until someone is ready to listen."

As we passed old palaces and fields that once hosted royal processions, Ben kept recording. Sketching. Writing. And then quietly, with almost no warning, he whispered: "They were waiting for me." I turned slightly. "Who?" "All of them," he answered softly.

"The ones whose stories were almost lost." His voice didn't carry the weight of arrogance. It was simple. It was true. And I knew he was right. The train carried us next, speeding eastward through Hungary. The closer we moved toward Budapest, the more Ben's energy changed. Not nervous. Not afraid. But something older.

He stared through the window at the rolling countryside, speaking softly as we watched the fields blur past. "It's like coming home." I reached over and gripped his hand gently. "Yes, Ben. It is." And ahead of us, waiting once again beyond the Danube, stood the final gates of the story we had only begun to unlock. The city whispered. The stones remembered. The blood called. The second return to Hungary had begun. The city of Budapest greeted us not with the bright flare of novelty, but with a strange familiarity — like walking into a room you had only ever dreamed of, yet somehow always knew existed.

The Danube shimmered beneath the rising morning mist. Bridges arched like the spines of sleeping giants stretched across its surface, and the great Parliament building stood along the riverside like a silent sentinel watching over the heartbeat of Hungary. Ben pressed his face softly against the car window as we crossed the Chain Bridge. His breath fogged the glass slightly, but he never blinked. "Dad," he whispered without looking at me, "it feels different this time." I nodded. "Because this time, you're not just visiting, son. This time, you've come back."

We drove slowly up the winding roads toward the Buda Castle district, past streets of old stone and quiet courtyards that had seen the march of empires rise and fall across the centuries. And then, as if summoned by an invisible hand, the towering spires of Matthias Church rose before us again. Ben whispered to himself, "The resting place." The last time we came here, Ben was still learning who he was. The scrolls were new. The voices were still distant. But now… the voices had grown louder.

As we approached the steps of Matthias Church, the same familiar figure awaited us at the entrance. Brother Miklós stood in the pale morning light, his black robes still simple, his hands folded with quiet patience. He offered a gentle smile. "Welcome home, Benedict."

Ben stepped forward slowly. There was no awkwardness. No formality. Only recognition. "Thank you for waiting," Ben answered softly. The monk's eyes twinkled. "We never stopped." Inside, the familiar hush of the great sanctuary wrapped around us like a cloak. The vaulted ceilings soared overhead, coloured glass casting jewel-toned patterns across the worn stone floors. Ben moved slowly now, no longer distracted by the beauty, but guided by something unseen.

Brother Miklós led us down the narrow stone stairway once more, into the cool depths of the crypt beneath. This time, Ben didn't hesitate. As we reached the resting place, the twin sarcophagi of Béla III and Anna lay in their silent embrace beneath the carved stone arch. The crests, the dates, the crowns — all sat as they had for centuries. But this time, they weren't just graves to Ben. They were family. He stepped forward carefully, his fingers hovering near the cool marble lid. His voice was quiet but steady. "Grandfather… we're back."

I felt my throat tighten as I watched him stand there — a boy not yet grown, but carrying a lineage older than most nations. And beside him stood Brother Miklós, as patient as time itself. "You have learned much," the monk spoke softly. "The scrolls. The names. The rivers that flow through your blood. But you understand now that these stones hold only a small part of the truth." Ben nodded slowly, eyes still fixed upon the stone. "The rest lives in here," he whispered, tapping his chest. Brother Miklós smiled faintly. "And in there," he gestured gently toward Ben's journal, which he still carried beneath his arm like a sacred relic.

We remained there for a long time — not speaking, but listening. As though the very stones were breathing alongside us. Finally, Ben turned toward me, his eyes shining but calm. "Dad… I don't feel lost anymore." I smiled, placing my hand on his shoulder. "You were never lost, Ben. You were just waiting." He looked down at the sarcophagi one last time, whispering words only the walls could hear.

"Thank you for bringing me here." As we climbed back toward the surface, the morning sun poured through the high stained-glass windows like golden fire, spilling across Ben's face. The boy who had once drawn castles and crests without understanding now stood firmly inside the pages of his own story. The world above had not changed.

But Ben had. And the journey was far from over. Later that afternoon, we sat once more in the quiet room of the monastery's small library, the one that Brother Miklós had quietly unlocked for us the year before. The great wooden table sat beneath the vaulted ceiling like an island surrounded by silent books, old scrolls, and faded parchments breathing gently under the dim golden lights. Ben placed his journal on the table, opening it carefully to a blank page. His pen hovered for a moment. The weight of what to write next sat heavily upon him.

"There's still so much I don't know, Dad," he said quietly. "Even after everything." I pulled my chair closer beside him. "That's what makes the story worth telling, Ben. The best stories are the ones we write while we're still living them." Brother Miklós entered softly, carrying a leather folder in his hands, its edges worn with age. He placed it gently upon the table in front of Ben. "This," he said, "was not ready for you the last time you came. But now… perhaps it is."

Ben's eyes widened slightly. His fingers trembled as he untied the thin cord binding the folder shut. Inside were several old letters — handwritten, fragile, preserved in thin protective sleeves — and a folded map drawn by a careful hand centuries ago. At the top of one of the letters was a symbol Ben recognized instantly. The stag. The crowned stag. His heart quickened. "These letters," Brother Miklós explained softly, "are not royal decrees. They are private writings — personal reflections written by one of Béla's surviving descendants. They were passed quietly through the monastic libraries, too fragile for open display, too important to discard."

Ben gently lifted one of the letters, his eyes tracing the Hungarian script. The words were too advanced for him to fully read, but Brother Miklós guided him through the translation. "It speaks of the carriers," the monk whispered. "Those who come after the kings, born into the line, but not upon the throne. The ones chosen to preserve the memory rather than rule." Ben's eyes met mine. "Like me." "Yes, son," I said gently. "Exactly like you."

He swallowed. "They knew someone like me would come?" Brother Miklós nodded. "Your grandfather, Béla, was wise. He understood that bloodlines do not always carry crowns, but they carry stories. He trusted that one day, a child of his blood would awaken — not to claim power, but to hold memory." Ben sat in stillness for a long while, staring at the elegant writing, as though the hand of his ancestor had only just finished the last sentence. "It's like the pages are waiting for me to finish the story," Ben whispered.

I smiled softly. "Then let's keep writing, together." He carefully copied the heading of the letter into his journal, sketching the crowned stag once more at the top of his page. At the bottom of the old map, he spotted something new — something the scrolls had never shown him before. A small mark drawn near the Carpathian Mountains. The mark was not a castle, nor a city. It was a lone tree, drawn in ink, beneath a tiny curved hill. "What's that?" Ben asked softly, pointing.

Brother Miklós leaned in closer. "That… we do not know. It appears in several of our private maps, always in the same place. The monks have simply called it The Keeper's Tree. But no one in our time has visited it." Ben whispered again. "Is it a clue?" I could see the fire returning to his eyes — that restless pull for the next piece of the puzzle. "Perhaps," Brother Miklós said, his voice calm. "Or perhaps it is simply waiting, like all things do, for the one who understands its purpose."

Ben's hands trembled slightly as he traced the tiny tree on his map, his voice nearly a whisper. "Dad… we have to go." I placed my hand on his shoulder, feeling the ancient pull of his words. "We will." Outside the monastery walls, the late Hungarian sun was already slipping toward the edge of the hills. But here, within these old stone rooms, something far older was awakening once again. The journey wasn't finished. It was only shifting course. The Keeper's Tree waited. And so did the truth.

The next morning arrived quietly, but neither Ben nor I slept much that night. Our minds had been racing ever since Brother Miklós laid the old map before us. The Keeper's Tree — a small mark no bigger than a thumbprint — had become the largest thing in our thoughts. Ben stood by the window of the small guest room, staring out across the distant hills of Hungary as the morning fog lifted. His journal was clutched tightly under his arm. "Dad," he said quietly, "what do you think is there?"

I stepped beside him, looking out at the pale sky. "I don't know, son. That's what makes it worth finding." He nodded, his face calm but determined, as though he were preparing for something much bigger than a simple journey through the countryside. In truth, that was exactly what this was. We met Brother Miklós again in the monastery courtyard before breakfast. The old monk handed me a set of photocopied documents — translations of the letters we had seen the night before — and a more detailed copy of the map.

"There are no roads that lead there directly," he explained softly. "It lies beyond the usual paths. Old hunting trails and shepherd footpaths crisscross the foothills nearby, but much of it is wild forest now." Ben listened closely, already imagining the adventure. "How far is it from here?" "Roughly seventy miles to the east," Miklós answered. "The nearest village is small, called Füzér. From there, you may be able to hire someone familiar with the old woods." Ben scribbled everything quickly into his journal. Füzér — east. Old woods. No roads. Keeper's Tree.

Brother Miklós placed his hand gently on Ben's shoulder before we left. "Be patient, young one. The land carries memory as surely as your blood does." "I'll find it," Ben whispered, gripping his journal tighter. "I know I will." By mid-morning, we had packed the car and left the stone walls of the monastery behind us. The winding Hungarian roads carried us deeper into the countryside, through small villages tucked between emerald hills, and past vast open fields where storks stood quietly in marshy streams.

The land here felt older somehow — untouched in places, as though it remembered what the cities had long forgotten. Ben watched everything carefully from the window, taking notes, sketching hills, rivers, and distant tree lines as though he were already building the next chapter of his journal. "Dad?" he asked softly after a while. "Yes, buddy?" "Do you think the Keeper's Tree is part of Béla's story? Like the scrolls? The letters?"

I smiled gently, watching the road ahead. "I think it's part of your story now. Maybe Béla knew it would be found one day — by someone who carried both the map and the blood." Ben sat quietly with that thought, letting it settle inside him. The countryside rolled on like a quiet companion to our journey. We reached Füzér just before evening. The village was small — no more than a cluster of cottages, a church with a modest stone steeple, and a few scattered barns nestled beneath the hills. The local innkeeper, an older man named István, was kind but curious about our reason for visiting.

"Tourists don't come here often," he said in broken English, setting down our room keys. "Hiking?" "Something like that," I answered politely. "We're looking for an old tree marked on a very old map." His eyes narrowed slightly with interest. "The tree?" he repeated softly. "People here sometimes speak of it. Few go looking. The old forest past the hills... it's quiet, but not empty." Ben's eyes lit up. "You've heard of it?" The innkeeper smiled faintly and tapped the edge of the wooden counter. "Old stories for old people, mostly. They say long ago, kings met there. Secrets buried. But the forest forgets nothing."

Ben scribbled again into his journal: Forest forgets nothing. We settled into our small room for the night, but neither of us truly rested. The excitement — and the mystery — pulled at both of us like a silent voice from the trees ahead. Tomorrow, we would leave the village behind and step into the woods. The Keeper's Tree waited. And Ben was ready. The morning air was cool and sharp, filled with the scent of damp earth and pine. As the sun crept slowly above the distant hills, Ben and I stood at the edge of the old forest beyond Füzér.

Before us stretched a thick wall of towering trees, ancient and watchful, their branches intertwined like outstretched arms protecting forgotten stories beneath their canopy. Ben clutched his journal under one arm, a small pack on his back. His face was calm but filled with quiet determination. This was no longer just a journey for scrolls or maps. This was personal now. "Are you sure, buddy?" I asked softly, glancing down at him. He nodded. "I need to go, Dad. We both do. The tree's waiting."

And somehow, I knew he was right. István had given us directions the night before, marking a crude path on the back of an old receipt from the inn. It was hardly a proper map, but it offered enough to guide us through the narrow trails hidden within the woods. The first steps onto the old footpath felt almost sacred. The world behind us quickly faded, swallowed by dense green walls. The deeper we moved into the forest, the quieter everything became. No birds sang. The wind barely moved. It was as though the trees themselves had paused, listening.

Ben whispered, "It's like we're walking through someone's memory." "That's exactly what we're doing," I answered. "This forest remembers what the world has forgotten." The trail narrowed, winding between mossy stones and thick roots that bulged from the earth like the knuckles of sleeping giants. In places, faint wooden markers — weathered and half-rotted — stood like ancient signposts. Perhaps left by hunters long ago. Perhaps older than that. As we continued, Ben spoke softly, almost as though thinking aloud.

"Do you think Béla ever walked here?" "Maybe not Béla himself," I said, "but others who served him. Or those who kept his secrets after him." Ben paused near one of the markers, running his hand along its rough surface. "Like the monks?" "Yes. Or the ones before the monks. The ones who hid the scrolls, protected the knowledge." He pulled out his journal, jotting another note before we moved on. The path grew steeper as we climbed, the trees thickening around us like tall sentries. Shafts of sunlight pierced the canopy here and there, turning the green shadows into soft golden beams. It was beautiful — but it carried a strange weight.

"This is different than the abbey," Ben whispered. "The abbey was quiet too... but this feels older." "It is older," I said. "The abbey protects history with walls. But this place—this place is history." Ben fell silent, his eyes scanning every branch, every stone, as though he was expecting something to call out to him. And in a way, it did. After nearly two hours of slow climbing, we reached a clearing — small, round, and perfectly still.

In the centre stood the Keeper's Tree. It was unlike any tree I had ever seen. Its thick, wide trunk twisted upward like a giant wooden braid, its branches sprawling outward in a perfect circle above us, forming a high green dome that blocked the sun.

Moss and lichen clung to its roots, which coiled above ground like great stone ropes. At its base, the earth was strangely bare — no undergrowth, no fallen leaves — as though the ground itself refused to disturb the place. Ben stepped forward carefully, his eyes wide. "Dad…" he whispered. "That's it." I said nothing. My throat was tight. The Keeper's Tree stood like a living monument — untouched by time, untouched by man. Ben approached it slowly, his small hand reaching out to touch the bark. He pressed his palm against it gently, as though greeting an old friend.

And then, he whispered something I'll never forget: "I've been here before." The words hung in the air like fog. I stared at him. "What do you mean, buddy?" I asked softly. He didn't turn. His hand remained on the bark. "I don't know how… but I've seen it. In dreams, maybe. In my mind. Like when I was little. Like when I heard the voice." The voice. The one that told him: You're not done yet. For a long moment, we stood in silence beneath the great tree's shadow. The wind gently stirred the leaves above, sending soft beams of light dancing across Ben's face.

And then — as though guided by something deeper — Ben stepped to one side, circling slowly around the trunk. His eyes were searching, scanning every knot and crevice. "Dad… look." He pointed to the base of one of the massive roots. There, almost completely hidden beneath a curtain of moss, was a small carved emblem — three tiny dots arranged in a triangle. Ben traced it with his finger. "It's my mark," he whispered. "The same as the old key." The mark of Constancy. The mark that had followed him since the very beginning.

I knelt beside him, gently brushing away more of the moss. The carving was old — very old — but unmistakable. And beneath it, just barely visible, was a faint line of script, worn nearly smooth by centuries of wind and rain. "Is it Magyar?" Ben asked. I studied the old letters carefully. "It is." "What does it say?" I spoke the words slowly, carefully translating: "For the one who carries what we cannot."

Ben's eyes filled with quiet awe. His voice trembled as he spoke: "That's me." I placed my arm gently around his shoulders as we knelt together beneath the Keeper's Tree. The journey was far from over. In truth, it had only just begun. But here, beneath the oldest witness of all, Ben had found something that few ever do — a piece of himself. The hours that followed beneath the Keeper's Tree moved like a quiet river — steady, patient, almost reluctant to break the stillness. Ben and I sat together beneath its great arms, as though the tree itself was allowing us time to breathe before it released us.

He ran his fingers again and again over the carved mark — the triangle of three dots — like a small ritual, as if making sure it was still there, that it hadn't vanished into mist and imagination. "Dad," Ben finally whispered, "why do I feel like… like I've done what I came here for?" I paused, hearing the truth in his small voice.

"Because maybe you have, son. For now." He nodded slowly, eyes never leaving the tree. "I don't think it's finished though." "No," I agreed gently, "but you've found the next piece. And sometimes... that's enough to carry home."

For a long while we simply sat. And then, almost as though the forest itself exhaled, a breeze stirred the leaves overhead, scattering a soft rain of tiny green specks down upon us — a quiet benediction, as though giving its permission to go. We made the slow walk back through the winding forest path, leaving the Keeper's Tree behind us. Yet neither of us felt as though we were truly leaving it. We carried it now — inside us. Back at the cottage in Hungary that night, as Ben scribbled the newest pages into his journal, I quietly began packing. The scrolls, the books, the copies of the records from Füzér — all carefully sealed and arranged.

Ben looked up from his writing. "Dad... I'm not sad." I smiled softly. "No?" He shook his head. "I thought I would be. But I'm not. Because I know we'll be back." "Yes," I nodded. "And every time we return, the tree will still be waiting." He closed his journal slowly and laid it on the table, resting his hand on the cover. "Home, then?" he asked. "Home." The morning flight lifted gently from Budapest under pale skies. The clouds stretched like white rivers beneath us as we crossed back over Europe. Ben sat beside me at the window, his pen already moving again in his journal, recording every small detail — the sky, the trees, the people in the airport. Even the airport pretzels. His pages were filling fast.

"You know, Dad," he said thoughtfully as we crossed over the Channel, "I don't think I'll ever run out of things to write." "That's because your story's still being written," I replied softly. As the plane dipped lower toward London, the soft green of the English countryside stretched out beneath us like an old familiar blanket. The towers of Kent whispered once more from the distance, calling us home. The drive back from the airport was quiet but comfortable. Ben watched the hedgerows slide past, the little villages we knew by heart, the cottages with their crooked chimneys, the old stone fences.

When we finally pulled into the driveway of our cottage, Ben stared at it for a long moment, smiling softly. "Feels smaller now." "It didn't shrink," I chuckled. "No... I think I just grew." I ruffled his hair. "You've grown in ways that don't measure in inches, buddy." He nodded, stepping out of the car and looking up at the sky. The sun was beginning to lower gently behind the trees, casting warm golden light across the front steps. His journal clutched under his arm again, he turned back to me. "There's more waiting, isn't there?" "Yes," I said. "And it will wait for you until you're ready."

Together, we stepped back inside the house that had once been filled with questions. Now, it was filled with stories. The crown remained secret still — but the boy who carried it now knew just how deeply its roots reached. The cottage in Kent felt both familiar and different when we returned.

The walls still wore the same warm shades of cream and soft oak, the smell of Annemarie's lavender sachets still clung to the hallway corners, but somehow, the house itself seemed smaller compared to the great halls, castles, and stone forests we had walked through these past months. It wasn't smaller because it had shrunk; it was smaller because Ben had grown — in ways that no measuring tape could capture.

The dining room table, which once held evening dinners and quiet tea, had once again transformed into a kind of research headquarters. Scrolls lay unrolled, family charts pinned carefully to corkboards, notebooks stacked with delicate care. Ben stood before it all now, scanning through the assembled pieces like a boy piecing together a giant riddle. But this time, I noticed something different. Before Hungary, Ben had always looked at these records like puzzles waiting to be solved. Now, he handled them as if they were old friends being welcomed back to the conversation.

He turned to me suddenly. "Dad, we've done the names. We've done the kings, the places, the castles." His voice grew more focused, thoughtful, mature. "Now I want to know why." "Why?" I repeated gently. "Why they all connected the way they did. Why they married who they married. Why the lines cross again and again. Why the bloodlines kept weaving together. I don't want just a list. I want to know what they were trying to build." I smiled slowly, feeling the shift within him. "Ah," I said. "Now you're not just building your family tree anymore, Ben. Now you're starting to build your family map."

He raised an eyebrow. "Map?" "Yes," I nodded. "Because kings didn't just have children. They had alliances. Every marriage, every treaty, every cousin who crossed borders — it was all part of something bigger. Not just to make heirs, but to keep kingdoms together. To avoid wars. Or sometimes... to cause them." Ben scribbled a few notes in his journal, his pen gliding smoothly in neat rows. "So I'm not just made up of people who loved each other. I'm made up of people who made choices." "That's exactly right."

He leaned forward on his elbows, his little brow furrowed with concentration. "And some of those choices still live inside me." "Yes," I said quietly. "They do." He closed his journal softly and whispered, "Then we have more work to do." That evening, we pulled out one of the oldest books in our collection — not one of the fragile scrolls from Hungary, but a heavy, hardbound volume full of European marriage alliances. A thick leather cover, faded gold embossing, and parchment-thin pages that whispered as we turned them.

Ben's finger ran down the page, stopping here and there: Lorraine... Anjou... Capet... Plantagenet... Stuart... Hanover... Habsburg. "Every one of them," he whispered. "Their choices are written here." The hours slipped by as the soft tick of the old clock echoed through the house. As I watched him, I saw it clearly now: Ben wasn't just learning names anymore. He was learning motives. Patterns. The invisible threads that had pulled empires together — and sometimes torn them apart.

At one point, as the moon rose high outside, Ben looked up from the book and said quietly, "Dad... it's like a big spider web, isn't it?" I smiled softly. "That's a good way to think about it." He turned his eyes back to the open pages. "Only now I know I'm standing right in the centre of it." The glow of the lamp warmed the table as Ben's pen moved once again across the journal's clean new page. But this time, he didn't write just names. He wrote the words that made the difference: "The reasons why."

CHAPTER 7: THE GUARDIANS OF THE LINE

The sun lingered in the Kent sky like a guest reluctant to leave, its late-summer rays sliding softly across the small flat where Benedict and I had returned only days ago. The house smelled faintly of Annemarie's morning tea, though the kettle had long since cooled, and the echoes of rain from earlier in the week still clung gently to the windowsills, as though even the weather hesitated to shift seasons just yet. Summer, for all its usual brevity in England, was holding on with quiet stubbornness — and perhaps, I thought, so were we.

Benedict sat at the table beneath the living room window, his shoulders slightly hunched as he studied the parchment spread before him. The scroll we had brought back from Hungary rested nearby, still carefully rolled in its protective sleeve, but it was the map that now held his full attention. His small fingers traced the rivers and coastlines inked onto the aged page — not with the idle motion of a child passing time, but with the steady reverence of someone decoding something older than himself.

I watched him from the corner of the room, allowing the silence to breathe between us. There was no need for me to disturb him yet. His mind was already hard at work, piecing together memories, images, and dreams that no textbook could teach. This was the stage of his journey where knowledge no longer arrived simply from what I could explain. It was emerging from within him.

The air conditioner hummed quietly beside the window, its soft current cutting through the heavy heat that had settled like a velvet curtain over Kent these past few weeks. I remembered how suffocating it had been before I installed it. Benedict had sat shirtless one night, sweat clinging to his back, his young frame flushed as he tried to sleep beneath the rotating ceiling fan that did nothing but stir warm air in slow circles. The machine now offered some relief, though neither of us was truly focused on comfort these days.

"Dad," Benedict said suddenly, his voice steady but quiet. I shifted from the chair where I'd been leafing through one of the older genealogy ledgers we'd brought back, setting it gently on the side table. "Yes, Ben?" He didn't look up from the map as he spoke. "How did they know all this before? Before the tests. Before the computers." I smiled faintly. That question had been simmering beneath his ribs for days now, waiting for him to give it shape. "Because they watched. And they listened. And they remembered." "But how?" His fingers paused over a small dot marked Bodø, far up along the Norwegian coast. "These places... they didn't have planes or phones. They didn't even know all the countries like we do now."

I stood and crossed the room, kneeling beside him so our eyes met the same surface of parchment. The lines were intricate, more art than science, drawn by hands that had never touched a keyboard, never uploaded files into databases. Yet, the detail was undeniable. "They knew," I said softly, "because they carried their stories like songs, Ben. Passed down — father to son, mother to daughter. Sometimes written. Sometimes whispered. And sometimes…" I paused, tapping lightly where his finger rested, "sometimes carried in the blood." He nodded faintly but didn't lift his eyes from the paper. "Like me." "Yes," I answered gently. "Like you."

He was quiet for a moment longer, his thumb now slowly circling the curl of the inked river flowing beside Harstad. The names had grown more familiar to him. What once sounded foreign now stirred something deeper — not recognition, exactly, but the same quiet pull one feels when walking into a place they've never visited but instinctively feel they belong. "Dad…" he whispered again, "do you think they—" His voice caught slightly, and his brow furrowed. "Do you think the ones who made this… do you think they knew I would find it?" There it was. The deeper current beneath the surface. The question that had been breathing inside him since the scroll first opened in his hands.

I drew a long breath, feeling the weight of what he had just asked. "I think," I said carefully, "that they hoped someone would. Someone who carried the same echoes they did. Someone who would listen." He swallowed, his voice soft but unwavering. "Someone like me." "Yes." I placed my hand gently on his shoulder. "Someone exactly like you." The late afternoon light shifted slightly as a breeze teased the curtains, sending thin waves of shadow across the table. Outside, children's voices drifted faintly from down the street, where a game of football (Soccer) had spilled onto the warm pavement. The normalcy of it all contrasted sharply with the ancient threads Benedict now held between his fingertips.

"But it's not just stories anymore," he whispered. "It's real. My blood says so." I nodded. "It does. And your dreams do. And your drawings. You've been remembering things before you ever had words for them." He lifted his head then, his dark eyes catching the fading gold of the sun. "I still don't understand how." Neither did I. Not fully. And it would have been easy to lie to him — to offer some polished explanation about genetic memory, or ancestral consciousness, or the poetry of inherited instinct. But this was not a time for polished explanations.

"Because there are some things, Ben," I said, keeping my voice steady, "that live deeper than understanding. Some things you carry not because someone taught you, but because you were meant to carry them." His small hands gripped the edge of the table now, not in tension, but in quiet resolve. "Like a crown." The word landed between us with its usual weight — silent but powerful. I had never once told him he carried one. I never needed to. The crown was not made of gold. It lived somewhere beneath his ribs, coiled into his marrow like a memory waiting for the right heartbeat to awaken it. "Yes," I said. "But not the kind people see." His mouth curled into the faintest smile, almost like he understood more than he could yet say.

We sat in silence for several minutes, letting the weight of the conversation settle. Outside, the wind shifted again, and I could hear the rustle of the great maple tree in the small patch of garden out back, its leaves chattering like old women exchanging secrets. Finally, Benedict drew his hand back from the map and leaned into me slightly, his shoulder pressing gently against mine. It was a small gesture, but one that spoke louder than words ever could.

"Dad?" His voice was soft again, a whisper against the hush of the room. "Can we go back? To the places again?" The question did not surprise me. In truth, I had sensed it was coming, for this was not the first time those lands had called to him. We had stood in some of those places before — walked their stones, breathed their air, listened to the old winds whispering through the ancient streets.

But the journey never truly finishes. Each visit only opens new doors, unearths new voices, and stirs what still sleeps in the marrow of his blood. "We can," I said quietly. "But this time, we'll look deeper. The places don't change, Ben. But sometimes we return with new eyes, and the land gives us what we couldn't hear before." He nodded, his head resting lightly against my shoulder. "I feel like there's more this time. Things I missed."

"There always is," I whispered, wrapping my arm gently around him as the late afternoon light continued its slow descent toward evening. "You've carried these memories your whole life. They're not finished speaking to you yet." And as the room fell into quiet again, I could feel his breath slow, his small chest rising and falling in steady rhythm. He was not asleep, but close. Drifting. The kind of restful quiet that only comes when a child knows they are safe. I turned my eyes back to the map on the table, studying the twisting coastlines, the mountain ranges, the scattered dots of ancient cities whose names still echoed in his blood. We would walk those lands again. Not as strangers, not as tourists — but as those returning to something that had never truly let go of us. And as we did, I would not be leading him. I would simply be walking beside him. For this path was not mine. It was his.

The sun dipped lower still, and I whispered once more, though I was not certain if I spoke aloud or simply inside my own chest: The map beneath your feet, my son, is not drawn in ink. It is drawn in your blood. Morning arrived as softly as the dreams had ended, with pale slivers of sunlight threading gently through the curtains and pooling across the hardwood floor. The summer air still carried its lingering warmth, though now tempered by the hush that often comes with early hours — as though even the birds were reluctant to disturb whatever quiet mysteries the night had left behind.

Benedict stirred first, his feet swinging lightly off the edge of his bed. His eyes, still heavy from sleep, darted momentarily to the corner where the leather scroll tube sat atop the bookshelf — undisturbed, yet somehow always present, like a silent sentinel keeping watch over his unfolding story. The envelope from Alan remained tucked beneath the lower drawer now, its contents already committed to heart, though its physical presence seemed to act as a kind of tether, grounding him whenever his thoughts threatened to drift too far.

I was already in the kitchen by the time his bare feet padded softly down the hallway. The kettle murmured on the stove, sending a ribbon of steam upward in slow spirals. I heard his small voice before I saw him. "Morning, Dad." I glanced over my shoulder with a smile. "Morning, Ben. You sleep all right?" He nodded, rubbing his eyes with the heel of his hand. "Yeah. I was thinking though…" "Of course you were." I chuckled. "You always are."

He smiled faintly but said nothing at first, pulling out the chair at the small wooden table where we'd spent so many evenings lately — pouring over maps, notes, drawings, and dreams. The table itself had almost become a character in our journey — its surface slowly covered with the weight of papers and questions that no school textbook would ever dare to answer. I poured him a cup of tea, light on the sugar, the way he liked it. "So, what were you thinking?" Ben wrapped his small fingers around the warm ceramic, letting the steam rise to his face as though somehow inhaling courage through it. "About where we start." "The field work," I said softly, nodding. "The real walk."

He met my eyes then, his expression steady, older than his years. "If the scroll showed those names — Denmark, Norway, Hungary, all of them — then some part of the path has to start here. Before we go far." I couldn't help but admire how his instincts sharpened. He was no longer asking me where to search — he was beginning to guide the search itself. "That's why I thought we'd take a small trip today," I said. "A bit of local digging before we cross any borders." His brow lifted with interest. "There's an archive in town," I continued. "Old estate maps, land registries, genealogical records — some of it goes back hundreds of years. Property transfers, parish ledgers… even personal journals that never made it into official collections."

Ben sat a little straighter, the excitement subtle but visible in the way his breath quickened. "Like the kind of stuff that wasn't important to governments but was important to families?" "Exactly." I smiled. "Sometimes, the best clues hide in the corners nobody thinks to dust off." He grinned. "Let's go." By mid-morning, we had made our way into the heart of town, tucked behind rows of narrow brick buildings whose chimneys still stood like quiet sentinels against the clear blue sky. The Kent County Archives weren't much to look at from the outside — a simple stone building, two storeys tall, with ivy climbing like slow green flames up its outer walls. But within those unassuming bricks, history breathed.

The moment we stepped inside, the scent of old paper greeted us — that particular mix of time and ink that no modern library ever quite replicates. Ben's eyes widened as they always did in places like this. He was most at home in the spaces where silence hummed and stories waited beneath folded pages. The archivist, an older gentleman named Mr. Carrington, greeted us with a nod. He recognized me from past visits — my quiet obsession with old family charts had earned me both his cooperation and, I suspected, his quiet amusement. "Good morning, Mr. Philips," he said, adjusting his glasses. "Back for more lost relatives, I presume?" "Always," I replied warmly. "But this time, my assistant will be doing most of the work."

Ben smiled politely, lowering his gaze in the modest way he often did when adults addressed him too directly. Carrington chuckled. "Well then, young man — the reading room is yours. And do let me know if you uncover any scandalous family secrets. Those are my favourites." As we settled at one of the long wooden tables near the back, the stacks of old ledgers, scrolls, and brittle maps began to pile quickly. Parish birth ledgers from Sussex. Naval conscription lists from Portsmouth. Nobility registries still written in Latin. Some papers were so fragile they were encased behind glass sleeves.

Ben's small hands moved carefully between the pages, his concentration absolute. He was searching not just for answers, but for patterns — names that danced between countries, between centuries. Every so often, his fingers would hover briefly over a surname that caught his breath, then continue forward. We were looking for lines — and we both knew those lines might not always be straight. It was sometime near noon, as the sun pushed strong light through the tall library windows, that she arrived.

The sound of soft sneakers against stone preceded her — rapid but careful, the way someone moves when they know they're in a place meant for whispers. I glanced up first. She couldn't have been older than nine or ten, her long auburn hair hung loosely at the back of her neck. She carried a thick stack of books in both arms, nearly as tall as her chest, her eyes darting left and right as though already memorizing the entire building on her first approach.

She paused near our table, glancing at the scrolls and maps we'd spread before us. "You're in the genealogical register section," she said, her voice matter-of-fact but not unkind. "Most people don't look at those unless they're trying to prove something really old." Ben blinked at her sudden appearance, caught between surprise and curiosity. "We're... sort of trying to." She shifted her books carefully onto a nearby table, pushing her glasses up with the back of her hand. "What are you looking for? Land titles? Inheritance stuff? Migration patterns?"

Ben looked at me for a moment, silently seeking permission to speak freely. I gave a subtle nod. "Family names," Ben said. "Ones that don't always show up where you expect them." She smiled slightly, pleased. "That's my favourite kind." Her confidence was unusual for her age — not arrogant, but simply comfortable in a place most children might find boring. "I'm Isla" she offered. "Isla Gibb." Ben tilted his head. "I'm Ben." Her eyes flickered across the maps spread before him. "That's old territory stuff. Norway. Denmark. And..." She squinted. "Hungary?"

Ben's breath caught faintly. "How'd you know that so fast?" Isla shrugged. "I read a lot. And I don't forget what I read." Her eyes turned to the scroll tube on our table, her curiosity intensifying. "You're building a migration path, aren't you?" she whispered, her voice lowering like a conspirator. "Following the names." Ben glanced at me again, then nodded. "Kind of." Isla smiled wider. "Good. Because that's the only way you'll ever find what they didn't want written down." The way she said they struck me as particularly sharp — as though she understood something most adults couldn't yet see.

"Do you study genealogy?" I asked gently. "My grandfather's Scottish," she replied. "Obsessed with our family tree. We're Gibb. Old Scottish line. He says we came from somewhere north of Argyll originally — Kilnaish, maybe even Islay before that. But the records are messy." Ben's expression shifted slightly. I saw it — that flicker behind his eyes — the quiet recognition of something familiar nesting unexpectedly inside a stranger's words. "Do you still live in Scotland?" he asked.

Isla shook her head. "No. We're here now. Dad teaches at the university in Canterbury. Mum works with computers. I'm the one who helps grandad with the family tree. Mum says I'm a 'book nerd.'" She said the words with no embarrassment, almost like a badge of honour. Ben smiled shyly. "That's not a bad thing." "Exactly." Isla beamed. "It's a superpower." The three of us stood in quiet accord for a moment — as though the library itself had briefly drawn us into a circle we hadn't realized was forming. A thread had just been tied, though none of us fully knew where it led yet.

"Isla..." Ben said cautiously, "if you ever wanted to... I mean... if you like this kind of stuff... maybe you could help us sometime?" Her face brightened instantly. "You mean... with real research?" Ben nodded. "Yeah. We're sort of looking for stuff that's not easy to find." Isla's answer was immediate. "Deal." And though the full weight of what they were walking toward still rested quietly behind the veil of time, something inside me knew at that moment: she wasn't an accident. This meeting was part of the map too. The map beneath their feet was growing wider.

The air inside the archive room had shifted somehow. It wasn't warmer or colder — just... different. Ben didn't notice it at first. Not in the obvious way. It came like a soft current beneath his skin, unspoken, as he watched Isla Gibb scan one of the old family registers, her fingers dancing lightly along the brittle edge of the page. The overhead light caught the strands of her auburn hair, pulling copper out of the brown as she tilted her head in concentration. Her glasses slid slightly down her nose — again — and with a single habitual gesture, she pushed them back up, never losing her focus.

That's when Ben caught himself staring. Not just looking. Staring. His stomach gave a small flutter — not the sick kind, not nervous in the way he sometimes felt before tests or doctor visits. This was... lighter. Like little wings brushing beneath his ribs. He didn't fully understand it, but it held him in place as surely as gravity did.

Isla turned the page with care, her lips softly mouthing a name as her eyes danced across the faded ink. She hadn't noticed him watching yet. Or maybe she had. She was clever like that. Jeff had stepped away to the front desk to request another parish register. Ben and Isla were alone now at the long oak table, surrounded by maps, ledgers, and scrolls that whispered family stories neither of them fully understood yet. Ben shifted slightly in his chair. His throat tightened. There was no real reason to say anything. But he couldn't stop himself. "Isla?"

She looked up from the book with that easy smile she always wore — that smile that made his chest tighten in the oddest way. "Yeah?" she said. Ben's fingers played nervously with the corner of the parchment. "I... uh..." His voice caught. He swallowed. "I like you." The words spilled out faster than he'd rehearsed in his head. Too fast. But they were out. Floating in the air between them. Unavoidable now. Isla blinked, surprised — but not startled. Slowly, her cheeks flushed a faint shade of pink behind her glasses, and for a moment, neither of them spoke. Then she smiled — wide, warm, and completely genuine. "I like you too, Ben."

The butterflies under his ribs flipped again, stronger this time, but not unpleasant. Ben let out a breath he hadn't realized he was holding. "Really?" Isla nodded, brushing a strand of hair behind her ear. "Yeah. I kinda thought you might say something." She glanced sideways with a teasing grin. "You've been staring a lot, you know." Ben flushed now too. "Sorry." "Don't be," she whispered, lowering her voice, her gaze never leaving his. "I was hoping you would." They sat like that for a moment longer, both oddly comforted by how easy the words had fallen into place. It wasn't dramatic. It wasn't confusing. It just... was.

Isla shifted back to the open ledger, but her hand remained close to his now. She pointed at a section of names carefully scripted along the narrow margin of the old page. "Look here," she said softly, as if still holding onto their shared moment. "This might be where I fit." Ben leaned closer, reading alongside her. The entries were from 1887 — marriages, births, deaths recorded by hand in the neat but fading script of the town clerk. "See the surname?" Isla pointed. "Gibb. That's my line." The names were woven into other families too — Campbell, MacLeod, Stuart — familiar lines that crisscrossed the Highlands and Isles for centuries.

"My grandfather traced us back to Kilnaish," Isla continued. "South of Argyll. That's where a lot of the Gibb lines tangled into other families. Including some that went east, like yours." Ben's eyes widened slightly. "You mean..." Isla nodded. "We're connected." Before either of them could process it fully, Jeff returned, carefully setting down a fresh bundle of records on the table. But his eyes had already caught the exchange. The flushed faces. The soft smiles. The way their hands hovered just a little too close together for two kids doing mere family research. Jeff cleared his throat. "Everything all right over here?" Ben sat up straight. "Yes, Dad." Isla smiled at him politely. "We found something."

Jeff raised a brow, glancing between them. "Oh?" Isla tapped the open page. "The Gibb line connects back into the Harvick bloodline. There's overlap a few generations up." Jeff's smile faded slightly as the genealogist inside him activated. "How far back?" "About four to five cousin levels," Isla replied. "Dropped twice in generational sequence." Jeff's brow furrowed now, protective instincts stirring beneath his calm expression. "So... cousins." Isla nodded. "Technically, yes." Jeff exhaled slowly, rubbing his temple. "That's... a bit close."

Isla tilted her head, watching him with the amused patience of someone who had already done the homework twice. "Actually, not really." Jeff blinked. "Pardon?" Isla smiled, adjusting her glasses. "Let me explain, Mr. Philips." She sat up straighter, as though delivering a well-rehearsed school presentation. "Imagine this," she said. "See that woman over there?" She pointed discreetly to a librarian shelving books across the room. "Let's say you meet her. You talk. You find her interesting. One day, you fall in love. You get married. Everything feels completely normal, right?" Jeff nodded slowly, still cautious. "I suppose so."

Isla continued, her voice calm but matter-of-fact. "Now imagine later — after you've been married awhile — you find out she's your third cousin. Or maybe your first cousin, dropped twice by generation. But you never knew, because you didn't share a surname, never knew the family tree, and the connection was distant enough that no one thought to mention it." She paused for effect. "Does that make the relationship suddenly illegal?" Jeff shifted in his seat, uncomfortable. "Well…" Isla leaned in slightly. "It happens all the time. Names change every generation. Families scatter. Most people marry distant cousins without ever realizing it."

Ben sat silent, watching the exchange unfold like some surreal tennis match. His admiration for Isla's confidence only deepened with every word she spoke. Isla pressed on, her tone never arrogant, simply certain. "At fourth or fifth cousin levels, even with removals, the genetic overlap is microscopic. Legally, it's permitted almost everywhere. Biologically, it's harmless.

Historically, it was normal — especially in royal bloodlines, which, incidentally, is exactly what Ben's line belongs to." Jeff opened his mouth, but Isla raised a hand gently, respectfully cutting him off.

"And before you argue," she smiled, "remember: most of Europe's monarchs were second or third cousins for centuries. The fact that Ben and I might be fourth or fifth cousins? That's practically strangers, genetically speaking." Jeff sat back slowly, processing. "You've… done your research." Isla grinned. "Of course I have. I'm a book nerd." Jeff exhaled again, letting the tension ease slightly, though the protective father still lingered beneath his eyes. "You're remarkably calm about all this, Isla." Isla shrugged. "I read the data. And I trust what's true." Ben finally found his voice again, glancing at Jeff. "Dad… we're not doing anything wrong."

Jeff studied both of them for a long moment — the way Ben looked at her, the way she looked back at him — and in that quiet space, something older than DNA settled softly into the room. Finally, Jeff smiled faintly. "Well…" he said, "I suppose some things aren't as simple as bloodlines." Isla grinned. "Exactly." Ben exhaled slowly, feeling the nervous weight ease slightly from his chest. And yet — as the day carried forward, and they buried themselves again in dusty maps and fragile records — he could still feel the butterflies beneath his ribs, quietly fluttering each time Isla glanced his way.

The afternoon sunlight slanted deeper through the high windows of the archive as the hours rolled forward. The dust particles floated like faint stars in the shafts of light, turning the quiet air into something almost sacred — like the stillness inside a forgotten chapel. The earlier tension that had passed between Jeff and Isla had settled now, like ripples slowly fading across the surface of a pond. They had all quietly returned to their work. But something inside the room had changed — subtly, but unmistakably.

Ben leaned over another stack of brittle parish ledgers, his eyes scanning lists of marriages, births, and land transfers written in looping, fading ink. The family names now began to weave themselves like a complicated braid: Harvick, Gibb, Campbell, Horváth, Stuart — all tangled threads of people who had never met, yet somehow belonged to one another across centuries. Every few minutes, Ben would glance sideways at Isla, as though trying to convince himself she was still really there beside him — and each time he did, the familiar warmth returned beneath his ribs. That gentle pull he still couldn't quite explain.

Isla remained fully immersed in the pages before her, but not oblivious. She was aware of his glances. And every so often, she would respond with a quiet, knowing smile — not teasing him, but letting him know she saw him. And she was not uncomfortable. Not at all. Jeff watched them both from the other side of the table, pretending to focus on a stack of naval registry documents, though his attention drifted often. The father in him was still present — vigilant, cautious — but slowly softening into something else.

They're kids, Jeff told himself And yet... maybe they're something more than that already. It was the strange thing about ancestry. The more you stared into its long corridors, the more you realised how many souls had met just like this — by accident and yet not at all by accident. Perhaps it was simply the way the blood called out from time to time — quietly pairing itself across generations, like old music trying to be played again. Ben suddenly broke the silence.
"Here," he whispered, tapping the fragile page before him. "I think this is another branch." Isla slid her chair closer, her head nearly touching his as they examined the entry together. "See that?" Ben said softly. "Marriage record. 1762. John Gibb married Margaret Horvath — spelled without the accent." Isla's eyes widened slightly. "There it is again." Jeff leaned in now too, studying the entry. "Hungarian blood. Still present in the Scottish branch." Isla sat back slowly, her face thoughtful. "So the Hungarian connection isn't just from your father's line, Ben. It drifted into Scotland too. That explains why my grandfather always said our line was 'half foreign.'"

Ben frowned gently. "I didn't know it reached this far west." "It does," Isla said. "More than people realise. The old bloodlines didn't respect borders the way modern nations do." Jeff chuckled softly. "If only the governments understood that." They continued tracing the names for another hour, following how the lines intertwined, separated, and then knotted together again generations later.

Ben whispered after a long pause, "It's like we were always heading toward each other." Isla smiled, lowering her voice so only he could hear. "Maybe we were." Jeff pretended not to hear that part, though the corner of his mouth twitched involuntarily. At one point, Isla pulled out her small tablet from her backpack — her digital brain always nearby — and began cross-referencing the records with larger online genealogical databases. Her fingers moved with practiced speed, flipping through pages and charts that would have taken grown researchers weeks to build by hand.

Jeff watched her work for several minutes, quietly impressed. "You're very good at this, Isla," he said honestly. "You know that?" She shrugged, eyes still locked on the glowing screen. "I like patterns." Ben smiled beside her. "She's like a walking DNA test with a Wi-Fi signal." Isla laughed softly. "I'll take that as a compliment." A soft chime sounded on her tablet as one of the databases updated with fresh cross-references.

"There." She pointed. "Look at that." The screen now showed the two of them connected on an extended family chart — Gibb and Harvick lines crossing multiple times between the early 1700s and mid-1800s. Fourth cousins. Fifth cousins. Removed once. Removed twice. The branches had drifted wide apart, but the roots had always touched somewhere deep below. Isla tapped her finger lightly on the screen. "There we are. Distant, but linked."

Ben's eyes widened as he stared at the web of names before him. "It's strange," he whispered. "We only just met. But... we were always connected." Isla looked up at him again, her voice quieter now. "I know." Jeff exhaled slowly, running his palm over his mouth. There was nothing inappropriate happening here. He knew that. They were children. But he also knew — perhaps better than they did — that sometimes, even very young souls already sense the shape of something that will matter much later.

It was hard to explain that kind of knowing. Harder still to guard against it. As the afternoon light shifted lower still, Isla finally closed her tablet, setting it carefully beside the stacks of books. She looked directly at Jeff now — as though sensing his lingering unease. "Mr. Philips," she said gently, "I know this feels strange to you." Jeff smiled faintly. "Strange is a polite word for it." Isla's voice remained steady. "But you don't have to be afraid."

She paused for a moment — then spoke the words that rang oddly larger than her years. "Sometimes the blood remembers where it wants to return." Jeff sat back quietly, letting the thought settle. The simplicity of it made his chest tighten for reasons he couldn't fully explain. Maybe, he thought, some things are bigger than my ability to protect. For now, though, there was no need for deeper talk. There would be time for that later. For now, they would keep tracing the lines. Keep unfolding the map beneath their feet — one fragile page at a time.

And as the sun dipped toward the rooftops outside, Ben found himself glancing at Isla again — not nervously this time, but with a quiet peace. Not the giddy flutters of earlier Something deeper Something simple. Something that — even at his young age — somehow already felt like home. The sun outside the archive had begun to tip toward the late afternoon horizon, casting a softer glow through the tall windows. Inside, the three of us remained tucked around the heavy oak table, the stacks of old ledgers, maps, and genealogical charts growing like ancient pillars around our little corner of the world.

Ben and Isla sat shoulder to shoulder now, fully immersed in the deepening tangle of their shared family trees. Names long forgotten by most still lived here: Gibb, Harvick, Campbell, Horváth, Árpád. Threads looping together, drifting apart, only to cross again two or three generations later. Every name was like a tiny echo of something that had been waiting for them to come find it. Jeff sat quietly across from them, observing. He hadn't said much in the last half hour, letting the two of them work, letting their connection — both genealogical and personal — gently expand. He was no longer fighting the weight of it. Something larger was clearly at work here. All he could do now was witness it.

Ben flipped through another brittle page and traced a finger down the list of births from the late 1800s. His voice was soft, almost meditative. "Look here. That's the third Gibb child married into the Horváth line by 1892." Isla leaned in closer, their heads nearly touching. "That explains why the Gibb and Harvick lines crossed more than once." Ben nodded. "Yeah. We've been bumping into each other for over a hundred years." Isla smiled gently, her voice lowering into something warmer. "I guess we finally bumped into each other again."

Ben's breath caught a little, not because he didn't agree, but because hearing her say it out loud made his chest tighten in that way he couldn't fully explain — the way it had been tightening around her ever since they first met. He sat back slightly, staring at the web of names before him. The moment hung there between them, quiet but heavy, as though even the air was waiting. And then, as though the thought simply fell out of him unannounced, Ben blurted it. "When's your birthday?"

Isla blinked, caught off guard, but smiled at his sudden shift. "My birthday?" Ben nodded, his voice a little shaky now, as though even asking it felt oddly serious. "August 1st," Isla said easily. "Next week." Ben froze for a heartbeat. His eyes locked onto hers, widening ever so slightly. Jeff, sensing the shift, straightened slightly in his chair.

Isla tilted her head, catching the strange look on Ben's face. "What?" she asked softly. "When's yours?" Ben's voice stumbled slightly as it escaped him, his throat tightening just enough to make him stutter. "Au... August 2nd." He blinked quickly. "The next day." Isla stared at him now, her smile softening into something deeper. The coincidence wasn't lost on her. Not even slightly.

For a moment, no one spoke. The genealogical charts sat untouched between them, but the discovery was no longer on paper. It was inside both of them now. Jeff finally exhaled, his voice nearly a whisper. "One day apart." Isla didn't blink. She was already piecing it together in her mind. The genealogy, the timing, the strange pull between them from the very start — none of it was random. "It's not an accident," she whispered softly, her voice barely carrying but full of certainty. Ben swallowed hard. "You really think so?"

Isla's voice steadied. "I know so." Jeff sat back in his chair, folding his arms, a strange mix of awe and quiet resignation washing over him. Even as a man who'd spent his life studying the complex layers of bloodlines, he couldn't deny what was happening here. There are patterns you recognize as a scholar — and then there are patterns you recognize because something much older whispers them into your bones. As the silence hung there, Isla slowly closed the old ledger in front of them, her small hands steady and deliberate. She turned toward Ben fully now, her eyes locked on his.

And then, without hesitation — without asking permission or stumbling for words — she made her move. Isla reached forward, closing the small space between them with quiet certainty. Her arms wrapped softly around Ben's neck, and before Ben could fully register it, her lips met his. It wasn't rushed. It wasn't a quick snapshot kiss, as children sometimes awkwardly do. No. It was gentle, slow, but deliberate.

The kind of kiss that doesn't flutter past like a breeze — but lingers, like something meant to stay. Her lips found his like they belonged there, like they had known the shape of that moment long before either of them understood what was happening inside their chests. Ben's hands instinctively found her shoulders, not pulling her closer, but simply holding her there, feeling her breath, her warmth, the softness of her hair brushing against his cheek. His stomach fluttered again, stronger this time — but not from nerves. From certainty. When Isla slowly pulled back, her arms still loosely wrapped around him, her eyes never left his. Neither one spoke. They didn't need to.

Jeff sat quietly, stunned. His mind wanted to speak, to intervene, to somehow protect or explain — but his heart knew better. This wasn't something to interrupt. This wasn't confusion or childhood play. It was real. Quietly, deeply real. Isla whispered, her voice soft, but filled with an old kind of knowing. "See?" she smiled gently. "We were always supposed to find each other." Ben could only nod, unable to form words that could match what his heart already understood.

Across the table, Jeff leaned forward slowly, his voice quieter than it had ever been in their conversations. "I don't know how… I don't know why…" Jeff whispered, "but I believe you." The weight of those simple words filled the room like something sacred.

Outside the tall windows, the sky had shifted into soft amber. The day was quietly ending — but something much older had only just begun. Their birthdays were coming. Their ninth year was arriving. And neither of them would ever be the same. The days that followed unfolded with a strange kind of quiet gravity. Each sunrise brought them closer to the week that neither Ben nor Isla could stop thinking about — their birthdays. August was only days away now. But it wasn't merely the coming of cakes, candles, or presents that stirred the strange undercurrent moving between them. It was something else. Something older.

Ben woke every morning with that same lightness in his chest — a constant flutter that never really went away now. He could eat, yes; he could sleep — mostly. But Isla was always there, living somewhere in his thoughts whether his eyes were open or closed. He couldn't explain it — not fully — even to Jeff. It wasn't obsession. It wasn't fantasy. It was simply there. Like breath itself. And Isla? She seemed to move through each day with the same quiet certainty she'd always carried, but now, when her eyes found Ben across the table, there was a softness behind her gaze that hadn't been there before. A depth. As if she knew what he felt before he could even attempt to explain it aloud.

Jeff observed all of it carefully — never interfering, never correcting, but always watching. At night, after the children had gone home, he sat quietly with his own thoughts, sifting through feelings that no amount of genealogy charts could fully untangle. They're only children, his mind would argue. But they're not just children, his heart would whisper back. There was a gravity forming between them that Jeff had never witnessed before — not even in his own youth. It wasn't puppy love. It wasn't some naïve childhood crush that would flutter away after a few months. No — this was different.

It was as if something ancient inside both of them was waking up — as though the bloodlines that had once crossed hundreds of years ago were calling themselves back together through the only two descendants who were listening. By the following evening, they were back at the archives again. The library's late summer light poured in golden waves through the tall windows, warming the wood beneath their hands as they flipped through more fragile ledgers. The stack of maps beside them had grown even taller now, but neither seemed to mind the clutter. They worked side by side, their bodies almost naturally leaning toward one another without ever needing to think about it.

And yet, for all the pages and all the names they'd uncovered, nothing in the old records could explain what they both felt pulsing quietly between them. It was Isla who broke the silence that night, as they both stared down at a marriage register from the early 1900s. "You feel it too, don't you?" she whispered. Ben didn't hesitate. "Yeah." He glanced up at her, his face soft, honest. "I don't know what it is exactly... but I feel it." Isla smiled faintly, brushing a strand of hair behind her ear. "I think we always have." Ben's heart skipped again, his throat tightening slightly. He wanted to say more, but no words came. Isla didn't need him to. She already knew.

Jeff, sitting just a few feet away, heard every word but remained quiet — as though afraid that speaking might somehow disrupt the invisible thread being spun between them. This isn't just childhood infatuation, Jeff thought again. This is something my ancestors would have understood better than I do. Isla gently reached across the table and placed her hand over Ben's. It was a simple touch, but one that carried more weight than either of them could ever fully name. Their fingers naturally laced together as though they had done it a hundred times before.

Ben swallowed hard, his voice soft. "It's like... we're not starting something. It's like we're continuing something that was already there." Isla nodded, her eyes shining. "Exactly." The days ticked forward. August crept closer. On July 30th, they gathered one final time before the birthdays would arrive. The genealogy charts were complete — at least as much as two determined nine-year-olds could manage with archives and computers. The patterns were undeniable: fourth cousins, fifth cousins, sometimes linked twice through earlier marriages, their lines weaving together again and again across generations.

The same threads — Scottish, Norwegian, Hungarian — all converging into them. Jeff sat with them one last time, quietly reviewing the charts they'd built. He set the papers down gently, letting out a slow breath. "It's extraordinary, you know," he finally said, his voice softer than usual. Ben and Isla both looked up at him. "You two... you're not just family," Jeff whispered. "You're an echo." Isla tilted her head slightly. "An echo?"

Jeff nodded. "An echo of something that started long before you were born. And somehow... it found its way back into both of you." Ben felt the weight of his words settle into his chest. Isla smiled softly. "That's why it feels like I've known him my whole life." Jeff chuckled faintly, though his voice carried the weight of awe. "Maybe you have." They sat like that for several moments, the silence carrying a strange peace none of them dared disturb. Finally, Isla glanced at Ben and grinned. "You ready for next week?" Ben returned her smile, though his throat tightened again. "Yeah. I guess so."

Isla leaned in slightly, lowering her voice into that soft rhythm Ben now recognized so well. "Nine years old," she whispered. "Both of us. One day apart." Ben swallowed again. "August 1st... and August 2nd." Isla's hand found his once more beneath the table. "We share more than just bloodlines, Ben," she whispered. "We share time." Jeff leaned back in his chair, rubbing his chin thoughtfully, staring at the two of them in quiet wonder. Time, he repeated to himself. Yes... they share time itself. And as the clock inside the old library softly ticked toward evening, none of them yet knew how much more that time would reveal.

The first of August arrived beneath a sky so blue it looked almost painted, the kind of summer day that seems to carry its own secret smile. The air was warm, the light soft, and a quiet hum of joy seemed to run like a current beneath everything. The back garden behind Isla's house had been transformed.

Colourful banners swayed gently in the breeze, tables were arranged beneath white canopies, and long picnic tables overflowed with cakes, gifts, and more food than anyone could possibly eat. But what made the scene feel different — almost sacred in its own small way — was the reason they'd all gathered: not one birthday, but two. Isla's parents had been the first to suggest it, after long conversations with Jeff. "If they're one day apart," Isla's mother had said, smiling warmly, "why not celebrate them together? It's always been together, really."

And no one disagreed. Because everyone could see it now — even those who hadn't fully understood before. This wasn't some childhood phase. This wasn't innocent play. This was something rare. And somehow, they all knew it. Isla's parents, Robert Gibb and Claire Margaret Stuart - Gibb, moved easily through the guests, greeting both sides of the family as though they'd always belonged together. Their eyes often found their daughter and Ben, quietly watching them as one might watch a pair of young trees beginning to grow alongside one another — separate but destined to intertwine as their roots deepened.

Jeff stood beside them, watching as well, arms folded lightly across his chest, a faint smile resting behind his eyes. "I'll admit," Jeff said softly to Robert, "it took me a while to see it." Robert chuckled. "It took me even longer. But Claire? She knew from the first moment." Claire, standing nearby, simply smiled. "Some things don't wait for adulthood to begin," she said gently. "Some loves begin before you even know how to name them."

Jeff exhaled quietly, nodding. "You two were young, weren't you?" "Five," Claire said, her eyes bright. "We met when we were five years old." "And never separated since," Robert added. "Through school, university, everything. It wasn't forced. It just... was." Jeff smiled, his chest warming at the honesty of it. "They're the same," Claire continued. "Ben and Isla. We see it because we've lived it." Across the garden, the two children sat at the head of the long table, side by side beneath the banner that read Happy 9th Birthday Ben & Isla!

Friends and relatives mingled around them, but in many ways, the two of them seemed almost in a world of their own — like two tiny stars caught in their own orbit. The gifts had been opened, the games played, but neither seemed particularly interested in any of it. They simply enjoyed being near each other. Even their laughter was softer, as though some unspoken reverence hung in the space between them. At one point, as the sun dipped slightly toward late afternoon, Isla leaned closer, her voice a soft hum meant only for Ben. "You nervous?" she asked. Ben smiled faintly. "A little." "Why?"

He looked down at his fingers for a moment before answering. "Because..." he whispered, "every time I'm near you... I feel like my chest's about to fly away." Isla's smile softened. She reached for his hand beneath the table, their fingers locking together without hesitation. "Me too," she whispered back. "But that's not a bad thing." Ben shook his head. "No. It isn't." They sat quietly for a moment, their hands still joined, letting the warm breeze carry the sounds of their families around them.

Later that evening, after most of the guests had gone and only close family remained, Jeff found himself seated near the garden's edge, nursing a cup of tea while watching the two of them wander near the flower beds. Claire sat beside him, her voice calm. "You worry for him," she said gently. Jeff smiled faintly. "I always will." "That's a father's job," Claire nodded. "But you don't need to worry about this." Jeff turned his gaze back toward the children. Isla was pointing at something in the bushes, Ben laughing as she spoke. The sun had cast their shadows long now, two slender shapes moving side by side like threads being gently woven. "They're still so young," Jeff whispered.

"They are," Claire agreed. "But their hearts are older than their years. Some loves don't wait for adulthood to blossom." Jeff sipped his tea slowly. "I can't pretend to fully understand it." Claire smiled softly. "You don't have to. You only have to trust it." He exhaled, nodding. "I do trust them," Jeff whispered. "That's the strange part. I trust them more than I trust most adults." As dusk fell fully and lanterns were lit across the yard, Isla and Ben returned to the table one last time. The families gathered once more to cut the shared birthday cake — two names etched into the frosting side by side. Ben & Isla — 9 Years

As they blew out the candles together, their wishes unspoken, Jeff felt something stir inside him — not fear, not worry, but something closer to reverence. The bloodlines had called them. The timing had placed them. And now, the hearts had found each other. Perhaps it had always been so. And as the cake was sliced, laughter filled the evening air, and the stars quietly appeared overhead — somewhere, deep inside the old bones of the family trees they had uncovered, the names of their ancestors whispered quietly:

We have returned.

The days after the shared birthday unfolded like soft waves upon a quiet shore — steady, calm, but carrying with them something unseen beneath the surface. Neither Ben nor Isla spoke much about it, but both felt it. It was not discomfort. Not fear. Not even confusion. It was... something else. A kind of hum beneath the chest. A soft current in the bones. As if the very air had shifted slightly around them, and the invisible threads they'd traced through names and records were now vibrating with something older — something neither the scrolls nor the family charts could fully explain.

They returned to the archives a few days later, almost by instinct rather than plan. The library had become something of a second home to them — not because there was anything left to find on paper, but because simply being there felt important. Ben stood beside Isla near one of the tall windows, staring quietly at the afternoon light filtering through the glass. Neither had spoken for several minutes. "Do you feel it too?" Isla finally whispered, her voice barely above a breath.

Ben nodded slowly. "Yeah." She turned toward him, her eyes wide, thoughtful. "I don't know what it is... but it's there. All the time now." Ben swallowed. "Like something's watching." Isla didn't flinch. "But not bad." "No. Not bad." Ben shook his head. "Just... big." Jeff, seated nearby flipping through a few old naval records half-heartedly, heard them but chose not to interrupt. He had felt it too in recent days — not in the same way, but enough to know something larger was quietly unfolding around them.

That evening, as dusk settled once more over Kent, the three of them sat together in Jeff's flat, the small table still cluttered with maps, books, and printouts — though none of them reached for the papers anymore. Instead, they sat in a kind of quiet reverence, as though simply waiting for something none of them could yet name. Finally, Jeff broke the silence. "Sometimes," he said softly, "the old ways didn't need documents to prove who belonged to who." Ben looked up from where his hand was still gently holding Isla's beneath the table.

"What do you mean?" Jeff smiled faintly, his voice thoughtful. "They trusted something deeper. Blood... yes. But not just blood. The... knowing." Isla nodded gently. "Like we do." Jeff exhaled. "Exactly." He looked at them both carefully. "You've both begun to feel it, haven't you? The way things seem... closer now. Heavier. Like something's trying to wake up inside you." Neither child answered immediately. But their silence was answer enough. Ben finally whispered, "It's like... I'm remembering things I don't even know."

Isla added, "Like dreams that don't feel like dreams." Jeff leaned back, rubbing his chin thoughtfully. "You're both connected to something very old," he said softly. "Older than even the records we've found. The blood remembers. The land remembers." He paused, lowering his voice. "And maybe... just maybe... it's beginning to call." The room fell into stillness again. Not fear. Not dread. But that peculiar quiet that sometimes comes before something ancient passes by — like a wind from far older mountains.

That night, as Ben lay in bed, staring at the ceiling while the hum of the air conditioner whispered in the corner, he felt Isla's presence still with him — even though she was three houses away. Not in body. In something deeper. He closed his eyes. And for the first time, without fully understanding why — he saw it.

The stone tower. The foreign banners. The great hall of a place he'd never visited, but somehow knew. And two thrones — one larger, one smaller — standing beneath flickering torchlight. In the corner of the vision stood a figure. Distant. Watching. Not threatening. Not frightening. Waiting. Ben's chest tightened, but not from fear. The dream didn't belong to his mind. It belonged to his blood. And not far away, in her own bed three houses away, Isla stirred in her sleep — her own breath catching slightly — as though seeing something very similar in her own unseen dream. Outside, beneath the Kent moon, the wind shifted softly. The map beneath their feet was no longer only ink and paper. Now, it was beginning to live.

The air had taken on that strange August heaviness now, the kind where even the wind seemed reluctant to move. The weeks following their shared birthday had brought both Ben and Isla into a new kind of stillness — not a lull in feeling, but the quiet hum of something ancient slowly stirring beneath the surface of their young lives. Their genealogical discoveries hadn't simply stopped after the birthday party. If anything, they had become even more precise, more delicate. The work had shifted from broad family trees to the finer, thinner branches — the ones few ever dared trace because of how complex they were.

Ben had been especially focused in recent days. He sat longer at the table, pouring over old records, cross-referencing digital archives, scanning pages Jeff had printed from Ancestry databases and Scottish court registries. Jeff often found him that way — head tilted, eyes narrowed in concentration, papers spread like a miniature kingdom across the tabletop. And though Jeff had been guiding much of the research at first, now it was Ben who seemed to take the lead. One late afternoon, while Jeff was preparing tea in the small kitchen, Ben stood quietly in the doorway holding an envelope in his hand. His fingers nervously fidgeted with the edges as though debating whether to present it.

Jeff glanced over his shoulder, reading his son's face instantly. "Everything all right?" Ben swallowed, stepping forward. "Dad... I need you to read this." Jeff wiped his hands on a towel and accepted the envelope. It wasn't sealed — simply folded and marked neatly in Ben's handwriting: For Dad – Important. He opened it carefully and read the letter in silence.

Dad,
I've been thinking a lot. Not just about me, but about Isla. About what we've found.
You always said that the blood remembers. But maybe it remembers more than we thought.
I know what you see when you look at me. We've talked about the king's blood. But Isla's different.
I think she carries something too. Not just noble blood. Something deeper. I think she carries the blood of a queen.
The records point toward the Scottish royal lines — maybe not directly from a throne, but from those who stood close enough to it for generations. The Gibb family served King James VI, married into houses that once tied to the Stuarts.
If I'm right, she carries it in her blood.
I know it sounds strange. But it feels right.
Could you check? I don't want to say anything to Isla yet until we're sure.
With love,
- Ben

Jeff's eyes lifted slowly as he finished. Ben stood waiting, his small frame tense but steady. "You've been doing this research on your own?" Jeff asked softly. Ben nodded. "Some of it, yeah. After you showed me where to look." Jeff let out a long breath, staring briefly at the paper again. "You're growing up faster than I expected, you know that?" he whispered.

Ben gave a faint smile but said nothing. His eyes held only one question: Well? Jeff nodded. "All right. Let's check." That evening, the two of them sat side-by-side at the desk, Jeff's laptop open as they carefully sifted through the genealogical records together.

Jeff worked slowly and methodically — inputting names, cross-referencing marriage records, and scanning immigration files that connected Scottish nobles with continental houses, even including Hungarian bloodlines that had drifted west. The names began to assemble themselves like old bricks being carefully reset into a wall: William Gibb of Carriber, valet to King James VI. Marriage alliances to MacLeod and Campbell daughters.

Secondary links to minor branches of the Stuart family — cousins to kings, aunts to queens. Jeff sat back after nearly two hours of tracing. "You may have something here," he said softly. Ben's breath quickened slightly. "Really?" Jeff nodded. "Isla's Gibb line served close to the throne for generations. Several marriages pulled their bloodline into the nobility. The recessive markers from these pairings could still be present today. Especially through the maternal lines."

Ben whispered, "So she really might carry it." Jeff exhaled again. "It's very possible. But there's only one way to confirm the genetic side." He looked directly at his son now. "We'll need Isla's DNA."

The next morning, Isla sat at the small garden table behind her house, sipping orange juice as Ben and Jeff carefully explained what they had found. She listened quietly, her expression steady — neither alarmed nor confused. When they finished, she simply smiled. "I kind of figured," she said softly.

Jeff blinked. "You did?" Isla nodded. "I've always felt... connected to something bigger. Not in a silly princess way. Just... like my blood belonged somewhere important. Even before I knew Ben." She reached over and took Ben's hand gently. "I don't love you because of blood, Ben. You know that, right?" Ben nodded quickly. "I know. I feel the same." Jeff smiled faintly at the exchange before regaining his professional tone.

"Well," he said, "if you're willing, we can take two tests." Isla nodded. "Whatever you need." "We'll do a clinical blood test for typing," Jeff explained, "and a saliva test for Ancestry's database. That should give us enough to confirm if the royal markers show up in your maternal line." Isla looked to her parents, seated nearby. Robert and Claire both smiled reassuringly. "It's okay, sweetheart," Claire said gently. "We understand. It's important." Isla smiled back. "Let's do it." By the end of that week, the arrangements were made.

The clinical lab appointment was scheduled for Thursday morning — a simple blood draw that would take only minutes. The saliva test kit from Ancestry had already arrived by courier, neatly packed and waiting on the kitchen counter. As the sun rose that Thursday, Ben stood beside Isla at the clinic, holding her hand tightly as the nurse prepared the needle. "You okay?" he whispered. Isla smiled, squeezing his hand. "I'm fine. Besides... I've got you."

The nurse smiled at the two of them but said nothing, silently observing something she recognized as rare. Within moments, the sample was collected. As they left the clinic, Isla looked up at Ben, her eyes bright with quiet confidence. "Now we wait." Ben nodded, feeling both nervous and excited all at once. And somewhere inside both of them, neither could deny that what they were waiting for wasn't just numbers and charts. It was the beginning of something much bigger.

The waiting had taken on a strange, almost sacred rhythm. Each passing day felt stretched, as though time itself was being deliberately careful not to disturb what was slowly emerging. Though the summer sun still poured its golden warmth across the gardens and rooftops, a quiet heaviness hummed beneath the surface — not the heaviness of dread, but the weight of something old preparing to reveal itself.

Ben felt it constantly now. Every morning, as he opened his eyes and lay staring at the ceiling, his thoughts immediately drifted to Isla and the tests they had submitted. The saliva kit had already been sent off to Ancestry's laboratories, while the blood typing analysis was being processed at the clinical lab in Canterbury. The samples had been collected without incident, but the waiting that followed seemed to pulse in his chest with every heartbeat.

For Isla, the sensation was much the same. She masked it well, of course, with her natural composure and quiet confidence, but beneath her calm exterior lived the same persistent question that whispered to Ben each night: What will we find?

Jeff, too, carried the unspoken anticipation, though his was tempered by years of experience with such research. Yet even he could not deny the sense that this was no ordinary investigation into distant relatives or forgotten names. What they were uncovering was something else entirely — something neither law nor science could fully explain, but which both the blood and the soul recognized before the mind could name it.

It was on a warm Thursday morning, several days after the samples had been processed, that the first answers arrived. The air carried the scent of early summer roses from the back garden, drifting through the open windows of Jeff's small office. He had been reviewing a set of unrelated parish records when the soft chime of his email alert punctuated the quiet. At first, he thought little of it — another subscription notification perhaps, or an update from one of the archival databases he frequented. But as his eyes glanced across the subject line, his breath caught involuntarily in his chest. Ancestry DNA – Your Preliminary Results Are Now Available.

Jeff sat back momentarily, absorbing the weight of the words. He reached instinctively for his cup of tea, lifting it halfway before setting it back down, suddenly finding no need for its comfort. His fingers hovered briefly over the keyboard before calling out into the hallway. "Ben. Isla. Come here, please." The sound of hurried footsteps echoed almost immediately. Ben appeared first, his eyes wide, hopeful, already sensing what the call meant. Isla followed close behind, her expression as calm as ever, though her fingers instinctively found Ben's hand as they entered. "It's here?" Ben asked, his voice tight with quiet excitement.

Jeff offered a faint nod, his expression betraying little of his own tension as he turned the laptop to face them. "Preliminary results only, but yes. We have something." The three of them gathered tightly around the screen, shoulders nearly touching. The monitor glowed softly, casting faint reflections across their faces as Jeff entered the secure portal and watched the page slowly load. The first thing to appear was the ethnicity estimate, as the software parsed the genetic markers into percentages and regions. Jeff read aloud, his voice steady, though every word carried the quiet gravity of ancestral echoes being summoned into the present.

"Scotland — fifty-eight percent." He paused. "Strongly rooted." Isla nodded gently, unsurprised, while Ben's eyes flickered toward her with a subtle smile. Jeff continued, scrolling through the results. "Ireland — twelve percent. Norway — ten percent. Central Europe — eight percent. Hungary — six percent." He exhaled lightly. "And a few smaller regions making up the remainder." Ben swallowed. "Hungary's there," he whispered, unable to hide the weight in his voice. Jeff's eyes softened as he nodded. "It is. The shared thread between you both remains undeniable."

Isla leaned slightly closer to the screen, her eyes scanning the details with the natural curiosity that always animated her research. Yet beneath her scientific focus, there was something else flickering inside her gaze — a quiet knowing that had no name. "It's in me too," she whispered almost to herself. Jeff's attention shifted now as he scrolled deeper into the technical breakdown. The haplogroup assignments appeared next — the ancient genetic lineages that traced maternal descent far beyond the reach of written records. His brow furrowed briefly as his eyes landed upon the data.

Under Maternal Haplogroup, the screen displayed the designation clearly: H5a1. Jeff inhaled sharply, sitting back for a moment as the implications rippled through him. Ben caught the reaction immediately. "Dad? What is it?" Jeff's voice lowered, almost reverent now. "Her maternal lineage carries H5a1, Ben." The boy blinked, trying to process it, though somewhere within him the connection sparked almost instinctively. "That's... that's like Mom's line, isn't it?" Jeff nodded slowly. "Exactly like your mother's. It's the same ancient branch."

Isla tilted her head softly, her voice calm but curious. "So... what does that mean?" Jeff shifted forward again, folding his hands as though addressing both a classroom and a chapel. "It means, Isla, that your maternal DNA descends from one of the oldest European bloodlines, stretching back over six thousand years. Long before any kingdoms were named, before maps were drawn. That ancient blood later found its way into both the Hungarian and Scottish royal houses, through marriages, alliances, and quiet noble unions that most history books barely record."

He paused, glancing at both children with measured seriousness. "You carry those echoes. Not through fiction. Not through story. But through the code inside your very blood." For several moments, none of them spoke. The silence was not one of confusion, but of awe — as though words might cheapen the magnitude of what had just been confirmed. Finally, Isla looked away from the screen and turned fully toward Ben. Her voice was small but firm.

"But that doesn't change anything between us, Ben." Ben's throat tightened slightly as he nodded. "I know. It doesn't for me either." She smiled softly, squeezing his hand. "You're not the king because your blood says so. You're the king because you're you. And for me... well, I don't need a crown to know where I belong." Ben swallowed, his voice catching slightly as he whispered back, "You're my queen, no matter what the test says." The weight of those words settled into Jeff's chest like a stone wrapped in silk — heavy, but beautiful.

He exhaled slowly, leaning back once more as the screen continued to hum quietly before them. "We'll wait for the blood typing results now," he said softly. "But already... the map beneath your feet has become much larger than I ever imagined." As the late morning sunlight streamed through the window, casting long golden beams across the table, none of them fully knew what would come next. But they all understood — in a way far older than words — that this was no longer simply a story of genealogy. This was the awakening of something far more ancient. And it was only just beginning.

The laboratory results had arrived at last. After weeks of waiting, of carefully controlled patience, the second half of the puzzle was now in Jeff's hands. The blood typing was complete. The genetic cross-matching had been finalized. And though Jeff had spent years digging through the bones of ancestral records, what lay now upon his desk was something altogether different. This was no longer genealogy alone. This was biology whispering ancient truths.

The printed report rested beneath his fingertips, its simple courier font unable to mask the weight of what the numbers truly represented. Rows of data, chemical markers, nucleotide sequences, protein flags—all of it reducing thousands of years of human convergence into cold, clinical precision. And yet, as Jeff's eyes traced each line, what he saw was not sterile. What he saw was alive. Ben and Isla sat together across from him at the wide oak table, the same table that had once been cluttered with dusty ledgers and fragile scrolls. Now, no more maps were needed. The map had moved inside them.

Jeff exhaled and finally lifted his gaze. "The tests are complete." Isla's fingers instinctively tightened around Ben's hand beneath the table. The warmth of his palm steadied her, though she already sensed that the coming words would change everything. Jeff spoke gently, his voice measured but reverent. "Isla... I believe you already know much of what I'm about to say. But hearing it aloud may help us all understand the weight of it." She nodded, her expression poised yet brimming with quiet anticipation.

Jeff looked between them both. "Your blood typing came back with several markers that correspond to what we expected—ancestral subtypes associated with Scottish noble lines, as well as recessive markers common to northern and central European dynasties. You share protein signatures that are particularly pronounced in royal Scandinavian and Scottish branches." He paused, letting the air settle around the words. "More importantly, when cross-matching your data against Ben's, we discovered something that even I hadn't fully anticipated."

Ben leaned forward slightly, his heart quickening. "How close?" Jeff's breath was slow. "Very close." He lifted the full genome analysis, turning it toward them. Though the scientific terminology covered the page, Jeff simplified what mattered. "Your shared segments aren't limited to one or two distant matches. They stretch across multiple chromosomes, across both maternal and paternal lines, reflecting a shared ancestral convergence that's staggeringly rare for two living individuals who meet organically."

He tapped the top of the report. "Ben, you and Isla are not simply distant cousins. You are convergent heirs of bloodlines that once ran in parallel but have been reuniting silently for centuries—through different kingdoms, different migrations, and different courts." Ben's eyes widened, his mouth suddenly dry. Isla's chest tightened as her breath shallowed, the words settling heavily into her ribcage.

Jeff continued. "The bloodlines from your father's side, Ben—descending through R-S660, the Uí Néill Dynasty, the Norse incursions, the Viking expansions through Denmark and Norway—intersect astonishingly with Isla's maternal lines. The Gibb lineage, through its entwinement with the Stuart dynasty during the reign of James VI, folds directly into those same northern bloodstreams. The maternal haplogroup H5a1 you both share traces back into the Bronze Age convergence between early continental European farmers and Nordic settlers." He paused again, lowering his voice almost to a whisper. "In simple terms, you are distant reflections of each other. Your bloodlines orbit one another like two stars whose gravity has quietly been pulling them closer for centuries."

Ben whispered, almost breathless, "It's like we're—" Isla finished softly, her voice catching, "—the same." Jeff smiled faintly. "In many ways, yes. You are nearly identical across key genomic markers. Not identical twins, of course, but your inherited ancestries have threaded so closely together that your union would essentially complete a circle that has been fractured across dynasties for a thousand years." Neither child spoke. They simply sat, staring at the paper as though it might begin to glow under the weight of its own revelation.

Jeff leaned forward again, his tone deeply calm. "Do you understand now why you feel as you do? Why your hearts found one another so easily? This is not just chance, or childhood affection. This is the return of what was once split. You are not just young lovers. You are... rejoiners of blood." Isla blinked, her eyes glassing over with the heavy beauty of it. "I... I always knew it felt different. But I didn't know it was this." Ben swallowed hard, his chest rising as his emotions tangled somewhere between awe and quiet terror. "I don't know whether I should cry... or laugh."

Jeff chuckled gently. "Perhaps you should do both." As they sat together, the room fell into an almost sacred hush. It was not the silence of awkwardness, but of deep knowing—a kind of holy quiet reserved for those rare moments when the weight of history becomes personal. Isla finally broke the stillness, her voice softer than any whisper. "Ben... when I first met you, I didn't feel like I was meeting someone new. I felt like I was remembering someone I had always known." Ben's hand squeezed hers instinctively. "That's exactly how I felt."

Their eyes locked, and though no further words were needed, the truth between them stood tall like ancient stones — undeniable, immovable, eternal. Jeff sat back in his chair, his breath steady, as though watching not just his son and Isla, but generations past quietly nodding their approval from the shadows of time. "This," Jeff said quietly, "is why the Crown has always been a secret. Not because of power. Not because of titles. But because its true restoration would never be found in a throne." He gestured toward them both. "It would be found in you." Isla closed her eyes briefly, steadying herself against the emotional tide swelling within her chest. She exhaled and then smiled through the tears that threatened to rise. "This isn't the end of the secret, is it?" she asked softly. Jeff shook his head. "No, my dear. This is only the beginning."

The days following the revelation moved differently now. The air itself seemed heavier, not in a way that choked them, but as though time had thickened around their world, wrapping them in a soft cocoon of something ancient. Every breath Isla took, every glance Ben offered, every gentle squeeze of a hand now carried more weight than either of them could have ever understood only weeks before. They were not the same children who first sat in that archive room, tracing names and wondering at old records. Something profound had shifted beneath their feet. The genealogies they once explored like curious students had now unfolded into a living truth that bound their very souls together.

In the quiet mornings, Isla would sometimes sit at her bedroom window, staring across the garden as the sunlight painted golden threads through the hedgerows. She would trace invisible lines in the air with her fingers, imagining the ancient paths that had led her and Ben to this exact moment. *How many centuries had worked to bring us together?* she wondered. *How many kings, queens, farmers, soldiers, and mothers carried this secret forward in silence?* And then her breath would catch when the weight of it pressed too hard against her chest. She was not afraid. But neither was she untouched by it.

Ben, too, found himself quietly wrestling with the immensity of what they had uncovered. When he lay awake at night, staring at the ceiling above his bed, the same question returned again and again: *What do you do when destiny is written into your very blood?* The feeling was not one of pressure or obligation. No one had handed him a crown, nor laid expectations upon his shoulders. And yet, the deeper understanding settled inside him like something sacred — as if every heartbeat now carried echoes of kings and queens long buried beneath Scottish heather and Norwegian stone.

His mind would sometimes drift to the images that had first haunted his childhood: the stone tower, the flickering torchlight, the tall thrones that waited in that dreamlike hall. Those visions had always stirred something in him. Now they burned with new clarity. He understood now that what he had seen in those dreams was not simply a fantasy or a child's imagination. It was memory. Memory embedded not in the mind, but in the blood itself — reaching back through ancestral memory that neither science nor reason could fully explain.

One evening, as the sun sank low and painted the Kent sky with soft amber streaks, the families gathered once more beneath the same garden canopy where only weeks earlier they had celebrated the children's joint birthday. The tables were smaller this time, the gathering more intimate. It was not a party. It was something closer to a vigil — though not one of mourning. Jeff, Robert, Claire, Ben, and Isla all sat together beneath the glow of the lanterns, the warm breeze carrying the scent of roses through the night. No one had spoken of the test results again since that first revelation, but the silence was never uncomfortable. Each was allowing the truth to settle inside them like sediment slowly finding the bed of a river.

Finally, it was Robert who spoke first, his voice calm, steady, and deeply aware of the magnitude his words carried. "We always knew, didn't we?" he said softly, glancing at Claire. "Even before the papers told us, even before the blood confirmed it... we knew." Claire nodded, her eyes shining gently beneath the lantern light. "I saw it from the first moment they met. The way they looked at each other... it wasn't something that began here. It was something that had already begun long before."

Jeff exhaled, his voice measured and thoughtful. "The tests only gave language to what their hearts already understood." He turned his gaze to Isla and Ben, who sat hand in hand between them, quietly listening as though absorbing wisdom from elders who merely spoke aloud what their young hearts already felt. "What you two carry," Jeff continued, "is not just the memory of titles or names. You carry the reconciliation of something that was once broken. Something fractured by politics, war, migration, and the slow erosion of time." His voice lowered, taking on a reverence that made the night air seem even stiller.

"Yours is not the inheritance of crowns, but of unity. The blood that once splintered across kingdoms has returned. You are living proof that the old lines were never truly lost—they were simply waiting to find each other again." Ben's throat tightened, his breath catching in his chest as he whispered, "But why us?" Isla leaned closer to him, her voice steady as she spoke not just for him but for herself. "Because we listened." Jeff smiled faintly, his eyes glistening with the weight of the truth. "Yes. Because you listened." For a long moment, they all sat together beneath the darkening sky, the stars beginning to pierce through the velvet canopy above them.

The breeze shifted gently, rustling the leaves, as though even the wind itself was offering quiet approval. Isla finally broke the long silence, her voice no longer small, but confident. "I don't care what crown once sat on which head," she said softly. "Ben is my king. Not because of blood, not because of tests or names — but because my soul knows him. It has always known him." Ben's hand tightened around hers as his voice followed. "And she's my queen. She always was." Robert exhaled softly, smiling. "You have something most people never find. Not in a lifetime. And it has nothing to do with the throne."

Claire whispered, "It's the kind of love that belongs to the old world. The kind they wrote ballads about, long before there were books to keep the names." Jeff nodded, staring up at the stars. "And yet somehow, here it is... restored, reborn, right here in this garden." The lantern light flickered gently, casting long shadows across the table, as though ancestors unseen were gathered quietly among them — watching, nodding, approving. As the night deepened, Ben and Isla rose from their seats, hand in hand, and wandered slowly toward the edge of the garden where the tall hedgerows swayed gently in the breeze.

They stood beneath the ancient oak that had been there for generations, its branches wide, its roots deep, as though it too carried some quiet memory of the old bloodlines. Isla leaned into him gently, resting her head against his shoulder. "We were always meant to find each other, Ben." Ben whispered, his voice trembling only slightly, "I know." They stood like that for some time, saying nothing more, letting the old world breathe quietly around them. Above, the stars shimmered — not in celebration, nor in announcement — but in quiet, knowing witness. The map beneath their feet had grown silent now. Silent... but whole.

As the summer days wore on, a strange calm began to settle across both families, but beneath that calm lived a current that none of them could ignore. The facts had been spoken aloud. The blood had been tested. The papers sat filed neatly in Jeff's desk drawer. And yet, no matter how tidy the records appeared on paper, the real story could not be contained by charts or graphs. Ben and Isla lived it with every breath.

Every morning when Ben woke, he could feel her, even before he saw her. It was not a thought, not a craving or a childish longing — it was simply there, like breath itself. Their souls were quietly tethered together now, as though their blood had whispered across centuries and finally tied the knot that history had once tried to sever. Isla experienced the same. Even when separated for only hours, she would catch herself glancing at the clock, wondering what he was doing, what he was thinking, if his thoughts were echoing hers. There was no restlessness in it — no impatience — only that constant, quiet pull that existed just beneath the surface of her heart.

When they were together, the world dimmed around them. The room shrank, the voices of others faded into distant murmurs, and even the passing of time seemed reluctant to pull them apart. Their hands found one another naturally, their shoulders leaned together as though some unseen force pressed them into alignment.

And when their eyes met — even in silence — the dialogue between them continued without need for words. It was as though the very air remembered their ancestors speaking before them, whispering old secrets carried forward through blood and bone.

Jeff noticed it more every day. He had studied bloodlines for most of his adult life, combing through ancient records, tracing forgotten marriages, following trails across kingdoms and empires. Yet never had he encountered anything like this. Not in theory. Not in practice. e watched the two of them carefully, never intruding, but observing with a reverence that bordered on awe. What sat before him was not the product of careful genealogical design. This was not arranged by court nor brokered by powerful men. This had been written into the marrow of their bones long before they ever drew breath.

Jeff often found himself wondering if the secret to royal blood had never really been about thrones or crowns at all. Perhaps the ancient families, for all their politics and ambition, had only been imperfect custodians of something far deeper — a lineage of souls meant to find one another, scattered across ages like seeds waiting for the right moment to bloom. And now, before his very eyes, two of those seeds had found each other at last.

One warm evening, as twilight spread like violet silk across the Kent countryside, Isla and Ben sat together beneath the great oak again. The stars above began to pierce through the fading light, scattered like tiny flames in a vast, endless cathedral. They spoke softly, as they often did now, their voices a private thread between them. "I still don't fully understand how it all works," Ben confessed, his eyes never leaving the horizon. "How two people, separated by so many years, can end up this close... almost identical." Isla smiled gently, her head resting against his shoulder. "Neither do I. But maybe we're not supposed to understand it with our minds."

Ben glanced at her, curious. "Then how?" "With the part of us that remembers," she whispered. "The part that was always waiting." He nodded, swallowing softly. "Do you think... they knew?" Isla didn't hesitate. "Yes. I think they knew." "Their blood carried it," Ben said quietly, almost in awe. "Carried us. Protected the path that led here." Isla reached for his hand again, threading her fingers through his. "And now... it's our turn." "Our turn for what?" he asked softly.

Isla lifted her gaze to meet his fully. In that moment, though neither of them were yet adults, there was nothing childlike in her eyes. There was only the weight of ancient knowing — a gaze that belonged to someone far older than her years. "To finish what they started," she said gently. "To heal what was broken. To return what was lost." Ben exhaled, feeling the truth of her words press warmly against his chest. "But how do we do that?" Isla smiled faintly. "By staying. By loving. That's how."

They fell silent again, letting the stars speak the rest. From the house, Jeff stood watching them through the wide bay window, his arms folded loosely across his chest. Robert and Claire stood beside him, equally silent, equally moved by what they were witnessing. "They've accepted it fully, haven't they?" Robert whispered softly. Jeff nodded. "They have." Claire added quietly, "It's not something they learned. It's something they always carried."

Jeff exhaled, his voice low, thoughtful. "That's the nature of inheritance most people never understand. It isn't always about property or power. Sometimes, it's something deeper. The passing on of knowing... of belonging." Robert whispered, "Of destiny." Jeff nodded once more. "Yes. Of destiny." The three adults stood in reverent silence as they watched the two children beneath the oak, their silhouettes bathed in starlight, their hands still gently clasped as though nothing on earth could pry them apart. And truly, nothing could.

The bloodlines had done their work. The map had unfolded. The echoes had finally found each other again. As the evening deepened, a gentle wind stirred through the ancient branches overhead, and for the briefest of moments, it seemed almost as if unseen voices whispered through the leaves — not in warning, nor in fear, but in quiet approval. We have returned. The words were not spoken aloud, yet they hummed softly through the hearts of those who knew how to listen. And Isla and Ben, sitting beneath the breath of their ancestors, simply held each other close, letting the ancient story unfold around them once again.

The quiet had settled into something much deeper than silence. It was not the absence of conversation, nor the lull that follows great news. Rather, it was the sacred stillness that often arrives when truth has been fully unveiled and there is nothing left to argue or deny. Both families, having digested the enormity of what their children carried, had reached that rare place where understanding required no further proof.

Jeff, however, had been thinking far beyond the laboratory reports and genetic charts. His mind had moved onto something larger — something older. He understood, as few ever do, that ancestry is not confined to names written on paper, nor confined to sterile laboratories. The truest answers were not held within data alone but whispered through the places where their ancestors once walked, where their bones lay buried, and where their voices still lingered if one knew how to listen.

One evening, seated at the long wooden table beneath the soft glow of the garden lanterns, Jeff chose to speak. The others sat with him — Robert, Claire, Isla's parents — while Ben and Isla quietly listened from their seats nearby, their hands naturally intertwined. "I believe we have reached the point," Jeff began softly, "where the records have told us all they can. What remains... cannot be found here." Robert leaned forward slightly, his eyes narrowing with curiosity. "What do you mean?"

Jeff's gaze drifted to the children. "We must go to where their story was first written. Not the printed records, not the computer screens — but the land itself. The old places. The soil that still carries the weight of their ancestors." Claire's voice was calm, but intrigued. "Where would that be?" Jeff exhaled.

"Hungary. Scotland. And several places in between." Jeff spoke with quiet certainty. "Isla's lineage calls from the Scottish Highlands, near the old Gibb estates and Stuart circles. Ben's blood calls again from Hungary — the seat of Béla III himself — and from the northern seas where the Scandinavian tides once carried his Viking ancestors across Europe." There was no hesitation in his voice. No one around the table misunderstood what this was. This was not casual tourism. This was pilgrimage — sacred ground calling them home once more.

"I believe," Jeff continued, "that both Isla and Ben carry echoes within them that can only be fully understood by standing again where their stories were first written. Where their ancestors lived, ruled, suffered... and waited for these two to arrive." Robert looked to Claire, who nodded softly. She needed no convincing. Neither did he. Isla spoke gently, her voice laced with reverence. "I want to go." Jeff shifted his full attention to her now, speaking not as teacher but as guardian. "This journey will not simply satisfy curiosity, Isla. It may awaken parts of you that have been quietly waiting."

She smiled faintly, tightening her fingers around Ben's hand. "I know. That's why I need to go." Ben nodded as well, his voice soft but certain. "Me too. It's time to go back." Jeff smiled, his voice low — as though speaking an ancient vow aloud. "Then it is settled." Preparations began swiftly. Passports were already in hand. This would not be Ben's first crossing — not by far. He had walked the streets of Budapest only months before, during the early summer, when he first stood before the tomb of Béla III and heard the silent pull of memory. But even then, he had sensed there was more waiting for him.

This return would take him deeper, because now Isla would walk beside him. Jeff reached out to trusted colleagues in Hungary and Scotland — historians, archivists, genealogical scholars who knew how to handle delicate truths quietly. This was no tour. These were not stops for cameras or souvenir shops. The places they would visit were far older than tourist maps. They were stitched into Ben's blood and Isla's breath — into the very structure of who they were. Robert and Claire fully embraced what lay ahead. They understood clearly that this was no mere educational trip for their daughter — though homeschooling gave them every freedom to travel — this was her personal crossing into the legacy waiting within her.

When the day finally arrived, their flight carried them east once more. As the plane descended into Hungarian airspace, Ben sat with his forehead pressed lightly against the window. Below him stretched the familiar green valleys and rolling hills. This was no mystery to him now — not a foreign place. He recognized the curve of the Danube like an old friend welcoming him back. Isla studied him quietly. She could feel it — that quiet, charged shift inside him — as though the air itself was different now that he'd returned.

"Ben?" she whispered. He turned toward her, his voice calm, almost reverent. "It's good to be back." Her eyes softened. "You've been here before." He nodded slowly. "Yes. Not just in memory. Earlier this summer. But somehow... it feels different now." She smiled, sensing exactly what he meant. "Because now you're not walking it alone." Ben exhaled softly. "Exactly." And the plane touched down on sacred ground once more.

The next days unfolded like stepping further back through time — though for Ben, some of these steps were already familiar. They visited the Matthias Church in Budapest where the tomb of Béla III rested. The cathedral's vaulted ceilings arched high above them, the air thick with centuries of prayers whispered in languages long dead. Ben stood once more before the stone sarcophagus, his breathing shallow. His eyes flickered across the carved inscriptions, but it wasn't the writing that drew him — it was the presence. The same voice that had once called him back from death still hummed softly in the marrow of his bones.

Isla stepped beside him, her voice gentle as always. "Is he here?" Ben whispered, "He's always been." She reached for his hand, and together they stood, not as tourists, but as children standing again before the silent witness of their own bloodline. That evening, as they walked along the banks of the Danube, Isla asked him the question that had been stirring quietly in her heart for days. "Ben... when you heard him — when you nearly died — what did he say?" Ben exhaled softly, his gaze lingering on the shimmering lights across the water. "He said, This is not over. You are not done yet."

Isla swallowed gently. "And now... do you feel like you're beginning to understand why?" Ben turned to her, his eyes filled with both awe and a strange calm. "Because of you. Because we were meant to find each other. That's why I wasn't done." Isla's eyes filled, but she held her composure, speaking softly through the tightness in her throat. "I feel the same. I've always felt it. Even before I knew why." He smiled faintly. "You're the part I was missing." Isla reached forward, pressing her forehead softly against his, their hands still gently clasped. "And you're the part I was waiting for."

From the distance, their parents watched quietly, speaking little. They did not interrupt. They did not correct. They simply observed, knowing that what they were witnessing was not childhood fantasy but the quiet unfolding of something far older, far deeper. The bloodlines had begun their return. The map beneath their feet had awakened. And together, these two children would walk its path — not as strangers to the past, but as its living heirs.

The journey across Hungary had altered something within them both. Though they were children still, they carried themselves now with a gravity not often seen even in many adults. It was not that they suddenly understood all the mysteries set before them, nor that their questions had been entirely answered. The truth was far more profound: They had come to accept that some things were not meant to be fully explained — only lived.

As the small group boarded the return flight that would carry them back toward Kent, Isla sat nestled quietly beside Ben, her head resting lightly against his shoulder. His hand remained closed around hers, as it had from the very first day of this pilgrimage together, neither one seeking permission nor reassurance. They simply belonged that way, as though their bodies had always known this was how they were meant to sit — bound not by command but by the whisper of ancient threads now tied once again.

Jeff sat across the aisle, his eyes drifting between the two of them and the window beyond. As the airplane climbed higher, slicing through white clouds, he reflected on what they had seen and what had been silently handed down across centuries. He did not need to speak to Robert and Claire, seated just a few rows behind, to know they all carried the same thought in their minds: This was never coincidence. Once home again, the familiar landscape of Kent welcomed them with its rolling hills, stone fences, and quiet villages nestled beneath the warm glow of late summer.

But even as the familiar countryside passed beneath the car's wheels, both Ben and Isla knew that they were not returning as they had left. The world looked the same, but they were not. The evening they returned, Jeff gathered everyone together once more beneath the great oak tree behind Isla's home — the same tree where, weeks earlier, the first whispers of their ancestry had begun unfolding. The tree itself seemed to sense the transformation in its young witnesses. Its broad branches stretched protectively over them like an ancient elder whose long life had already seen many such stories written and rewritten in its shade.

They sat together beneath its arms, the lantern light flickering softly, illuminating their faces against the approaching nightfall. The warm breeze carried with it a quiet, almost reverent peace. Jeff's voice broke the silence first, not commanding, but simply offering the final piece of understanding he had carried since their return. "You've now walked together where your ancestors lived, ruled, and loved. You've stood again before the bones of kings, and for the first time, Isla, you've seen what Ben has carried alone until now. You've felt the echoes stir inside you."

He looked at Ben and Isla directly, his gaze firm but kind. "And you understand now that what draws you together isn't merely love, or fate, or even blood alone. It's something older. Something that was once broken, and has now found its way home again." Isla nodded softly, her eyes moist but steady. "The broken pieces came back together." Jeff smiled. "Yes." Robert spoke gently then, his voice thick with emotion. "We've seen it too, you know. From the very first day. Even when we didn't fully understand, we felt it."

Claire added quietly, "It's in your eyes when you look at each other. You don't look at each other the way most people do. You see each other." Ben whispered, his voice almost trembling, "We're home when we're together." Isla turned to him fully, brushing a loose strand of hair from his face. "No matter where we are in the world, as long as we have each other — we're home." Jeff exhaled deeply, his chest rising with the weight of all they had discovered.

"The Crown has always been a secret because the world was never ready to understand it for what it truly was. It was never meant to sit on a head. It was always meant to bind two hearts. And now... it has." The oak branches swayed above them, the leaves whispering quietly as though the wind itself bore witness. The stars emerged one by one, blinking softly through the canopy, each one a distant spark of ancient light — reminders that time does not forget, nor abandon, the threads it once wove.

For Ben and Isla, the search for their ancestors was no longer simply about discovery. It was now about honouring what had been carried through war, migration, suffering, and exile — all to arrive here, at this moment, in two young souls who carried within themselves not the weight of crowns, but the weight of reunion. As the night deepened, Isla leaned into Ben again, her voice as soft as the wind itself. "There's still more to find, isn't there?" Ben nodded. "Yes." "But we'll find it together," she whispered. He smiled, whispering back, "We always will." And as they sat there beneath the silent oak, the world around them faded gently away. Two children. Two souls. Two ancient bloodlines made whole once more. The map beneath their feet had become more than genealogy. It had become life itself.

For Ben and Isla, the search for their ancestors was no longer simply about discovery. It was now about honouring what had been carried through war, migration, suffering, and exile — all to arrive here, at this moment, in two young souls who carried within themselves not the weight of crowns, but the weight of reunion. For Ben, this was not unfamiliar soil. He had stood on these grounds before, felt its pulse beneath his feet. But now, sharing it with Isla for the first time, everything breathed differently — fuller, more complete.

For a while they sat quietly, neither rushing to fill the silence, as if even their breath was a part of something older now. Then Isla shifted slightly, her eyes rising to meet his. There was a brightness in her gaze — not playful, not fleeting — but full of reverence for where they stood, and what they carried together. "I know what this is, Ben," she whispered, her voice trembling with warmth. "This isn't just a place we visited. This is home."

Ben swallowed softly, his hand closing around hers. "Yes. Our home. The one written long before we ever knew it." Their eyes locked — not with the shyness of children fumbling through affection, but with the stillness of two souls recognizing one another across generations. No one spoke. No one interrupted. Their parents, still seated beneath the oak's protective arms, watched without interfering, sensing that this moment was not for them.

Then Isla leaned forward — slowly, deliberately — and placed her lips upon his. It was not rushed. It was not clumsy. It was sacred. A seal between them, as if to quietly declare that they both knew who they were, and what blood flowed through their veins. King. Queen. But not for thrones. For each other. The kiss lingered, pure and steady, like the silent joining of two rivers that had spent centuries winding toward this meeting place. When at last they parted, neither spoke. They didn't need to. The stars above them said enough. Ben exhaled softly, his voice barely audible. "We're ready now."

CHAPTER 8: THE THREADS WE FOLLOW

Isla smiled, her face glowing beneath the flickering lantern light. "We'll write it all. We'll find everything. The stories, the names, the kings and queens… all of it." "But we won't let the world know too much," Ben added softly, his voice filled with quiet maturity. "Some things… some crowns… are safer kept as secrets." Isla nodded, her small fingers tightening gently around his hand. "Our secret." And so, beneath the ancient oak, with the blood of kings breathing quietly through their veins, two children sat in the stillness of their inheritance — not to rule kingdoms, but to honour them. The journey ahead would be long, but neither was afraid. For now, they had each other.

The wind shifted, low and warm, carrying the scent of summer fields and distant rains. Above them, the branches of the great oak whispered as if approving, as though the ancient tree understood what they had uncovered, and what still waited for them. Its roots, like their own bloodlines, dug deep into unseen soil, older than memory itself. Ben leaned back against the rough bark, his gaze rising toward the sky. The stars were beginning to pierce the dusk, quiet sentinels in the canopy of twilight. He could feel them watching—not as distant cold things, but as familiar beacons that had once watched his ancestors walk under these same heavens.

"Do you think they knew?" Isla asked softly, her voice barely disturbing the hush of the evening. She didn't turn her head as she spoke, her eyes fixed on the fading line of orange where the sun had bowed beneath the hills. "The ones who came before us… did they know how far their blood would reach?" Ben considered the question, his lips pressing gently together as he searched for words. "Maybe not in the way we know it now," he answered. "But I think they felt it. Like… like a river you know is there even when you can't see where it leads."

Isla smiled faintly, her head resting on his shoulder. "I like that." They sat like that for a time, letting the weight of the moment settle into their bones. Neither rushed. Neither felt the need to speak simply to fill the silence. The air carried its own language, one both of them were learning to understand. A soft crunch of footsteps on the nearby path broke the quiet. Jeff emerged from the shadows beneath the trees, carrying a small oil lantern that swayed gently in his hand. The glow cast long shadows across his face, highlighting the gentle lines beneath his eyes—the lines that spoke of years spent walking the edges of forgotten stories.

"You two look like you belong to this place," Jeff said with a small smile, his voice calm as always. "As if the tree was waiting for you." Ben straightened slightly but did not release Isla's hand. "Maybe it was," he replied. Jeff nodded, lowering himself onto the low stone beside them. "Some trees live longer than empires," he mused, his eyes following the twisting branches above. "Their roots drink from history itself. You'd be surprised how many secrets a tree can hold." Isla's voice was quiet, almost reverent. "We're ready to learn, Dad."

Jeff's eyes softened at the sound of her voice. The word still held a quiet warmth in his chest every time she used it, a bond that had grown slowly, naturally, until it fit like breath itself. He placed the lantern on the stone beside him and unfolded a small cloth bundle from his satchel. Inside lay several sheets of parchment, old but preserved, each marked with the careful handwriting that had become so familiar to them both. "These," Jeff began, "were given to me long ago. Passed along like whispers through trusted hands. I never fully understood their purpose until now." He lifted one page, revealing a sketched map—not of cities or borders, but of rivers, forests, and distant hills, marked only by small, almost forgotten names. "This is part of your story. Not just names in a book, but places that still breathe. Places your ancestors once called home."

Isla leaned forward, her eyes tracing the delicate ink lines. "Denmark…" she whispered. "Norway… Hungary…" Her voice grew softer with each name, as if speaking them summoned something ancient from beneath the soil itself. Ben nodded beside her, his voice steady. "They're waiting for us, aren't they?" Jeff's smile deepened, but there was no hint of amusement. Only quiet truth. "Yes, they are. And when the time is right, we'll go to them. Not to claim thrones or titles — but to stand where they once stood. To listen to what still echoes."

The lantern's glow danced across the page as the night deepened around them. Crickets began their chorus in the tall grasses beyond the clearing, a quiet accompaniment to the unfolding of forgotten bloodlines. "You've already walked further than most ever do," Jeff continued, his voice low and rich. "Most people live their lives never knowing who came before them, or what blood carries through their veins. But you… you've listened. You've remembered." Isla's hand tightened slightly around Ben's once more. "Because you taught us how to listen," she whispered.

Jeff's gaze lingered on both of them. "I only showed you where to begin. The rest… you've done yourselves." The parchment shifted gently under Isla's fingers as the wind caught its edge. She looked up, her voice carrying a new weight. "Will it always feel like this?" "Like what?" Jeff asked gently. "Like carrying something heavy… but not bad. Just… important." Jeff's eyes closed for a moment as he nodded. "Yes. That's what it means to hold a crown you don't wear." The words settled over them like the soft drape of nightfall itself. Neither child spoke. Neither needed to.

The morning sun filtered through the lace curtains like a quiet invitation, neither insistent nor shy, but patient. The air in the house carried that unmistakable scent of old wood warmed by light, mingled with the faintest trace of dust from unopened books that waited along the shelves like silent witnesses. Even the floor creaked differently underfoot — not in protest, but in rhythm with the day's unfolding.

Jeff was already at the kitchen table, nursing his second cup of tea. The mug sat between his large hands as though tethered to some private thought. His gaze wandered now and again to the corner of the room, where the map lay partially unrolled on the desk, its edges held down by carefully placed paperweights. The map had become as much a member of the household as any of them, its rivers and mountains silently whispering of paths not yet walked.

Ben entered the room with the kind of stillness that comes from having carried weighty dreams through the night. His small feet moved across the floorboards without hurry, his face calm but distant, as though some part of him still stood in the corridors of his sleep. The boy's eyes flickered once toward the map, then rested on Jeff. For a moment, neither spoke. There was no need. The silence between them had grown into a language of its own.

Annemarie stood by the stove, humming softly to herself as she stirred a pot of oatmeal. Her glance shifted briefly toward her son, reading him the way only a mother can — sensing the fatigue in his posture, the heaviness behind his quiet. Yet she said nothing, letting him arrive on his own terms. She had learned by now that some mornings carried more than others.

Finally, Jeff broke the quiet. "Did they come again last night?" Ben's head tilted slightly, the question landing gently but unavoidably. "Yes," he answered, his voice smooth but distant. "Different this time." Jeff's eyebrows lifted in curiosity, though he did not push. "How so?" The boy moved toward the table, sliding into the chair opposite Jeff, his small hands resting on the edge of the polished oak. "The place was... familiar, but not the same. It was larger. I could see more of it. The halls were lined with banners again, but this time... they had writing. Not just symbols. Words."

Jeff leaned forward, the quiet excitement in his chest restrained behind his steady expression. "Words you could read?" Ben hesitated. "Not exactly. I didn't recognize the language. But I... I felt it. Like I understood the meaning even though I couldn't say it aloud." His voice softened as he added, "It felt like listening to a song I'd known since before I was born." Jeff nodded slowly, letting the boy's words settle into the room. "That's the blood speaking," he said softly. "Memory older than thought. Older than language."

Annemarie placed a bowl of oatmeal gently in front of her son and ruffled his hair with a touch that was more blessing than habit. "Eat, sweetheart. You can talk and eat." Ben offered a faint smile and dipped his spoon into the bowl, the steam curling upward like thin ribbons. But even as he ate, his mind wandered back to the images behind his eyelids — the great stone halls, the flicker of torchlight, the smell of aged parchment and oiled wood.

Jeff watched him closely. "Did you see anyone this time?" Ben nodded between mouthfuls. "Yes. A man. Tall, wearing a robe with the crest again — my crest. The same lions, the same shield. But his robe was darker. And his crown…" The boy paused, his brow furrowing as he searched for the right word.

"It wasn't gold. It was black. Like obsidian." Jeff's breath caught faintly at the detail but said nothing at first. The black crown — a symbol less often spoken of, but known to those who studied certain genealogies. His fingers tapped gently on the table. "And did he speak?"

Ben shook his head. "No. But he looked right at me. As though he was waiting. Or... welcoming me." Annemarie's hand stilled on the counter behind them. She turned, her voice soft but laced with quiet concern. "Jeff, is this safe? All these dreams... these visions..." Jeff answered without turning from Ben. "It's not dangerous, Annemarie. It's not haunting him. It's guiding him." His voice was calm, but his eyes never left the boy's face. "What he's seeing isn't fantasy. It's memory surfacing."

Annemarie sighed, wiping her hands on a cloth. "He's still a child, Jeff." "Yes," Jeff agreed, "but a child who carries the weight of generations inside him. He's not wandering into something unnatural. He's following a path that was laid for him long before we were ever born." Ben's voice broke the adult conversation gently. "Mum, it's all right. I'm not scared. Not anymore." His eyes lifted to Jeff's. "What does the black crown mean?"

Jeff exhaled slowly. The question had waited for its day. "It's a symbol not many speak of anymore, Ben. Most kings wore gold — power, wealth, rule. But the black crown... that was different. It represented something older. A crown of remembrance. Of mourning. Of oaths sworn to protect something too sacred for public eyes." He paused, searching for words the boy could hold. "It was worn by those who kept the secret lines alive. Quiet kings. The ones who ruled not from thrones, but from bloodlines that passed invisibly through history."

Ben's spoon hovered in mid-air. "A hidden king?" Jeff's eyes glimmered faintly. "In a manner of speaking." Annemarie returned to the stove without comment, though her mind reeled with silent questions she dared not yet voice. The conversation drifted into silence once more, punctuated only by the soft clinking of spoon against bowl. The boy's appetite faded, his mind returning again and again to the image of the man in the obsidian crown — not as a stranger, but as something hauntingly familiar, as though staring into an older version of himself.

After a while, Jeff rose from his chair and crossed to the old oak cabinet in the far corner of the room. He opened it carefully, revealing several bound books and a small, worn wooden box. From within the box, he withdrew a folded piece of linen, and unwrapped it with great care to reveal a narrow parchment, no larger than an envelope. "I was waiting for the right time to show you this," Jeff said, his voice lower now, as though speaking to the walls themselves. He returned to the table and laid the parchment before Ben, who studied it intently.

The script was old — not English, not Latin. Curved, elegant letters danced across the faded surface like branches twisting in wind. But at the bottom, beneath the curling text, was the familiar symbol once again: three small dots forming a perfect triangle. Ben's heart raced.

"Where did this come from?" Jeff's eyes narrowed thoughtfully. "From one of the older scrolls we recovered last spring. I didn't fully understand its place until your dreams began shifting." "What does it say?" the boy whispered. Jeff smiled faintly. "That, Ben... is why we're going to Scotland."

Ben blinked, his breath catching. "Scotland?" Jeff nodded, his voice steady. "Your mother and I have spoken. And Isla's parents too. The next part of the map — of your map — isn't here. It waits in places where your blood first rooted itself. You've seen the dreams. You've heard the names: Árpád. Béla. But now it's time for the lines on the other side of the water." Ben's chest swelled. Scotland — the place from the stories Jeff had only hinted at before. The land where his family's threads wove into the Scottish Stuarts and Gibbs, where Isla's path and his converged not merely by coincidence, but by design.

Annemarie approached slowly, her voice softer now, her earlier worry tempered by quiet acceptance. "Ben, we've arranged everything. You'll go with Jeff and Isla. Your studies won't fall behind. They'll grow. Just like we promised." Ben looked between them both, his throat tightening as excitement and reverence twisted together like ivy on stone. "When?" he breathed. Jeff smiled. "Soon." As if on cue, the doorbell rang — two quick chimes that echoed lightly through the house. Ben turned instinctively toward the sound as Jeff rose to answer. On the porch stood Isla and her parents, Robert and Claire, each carrying the gentle smiles of those who understood more than they said aloud.

The children's eyes met instantly, and Isla's face lit with a brightness that seemed to cut through the morning haze like sunlight breaking through fog. Without hesitation, she crossed the room and wrapped her arms around Ben in a hug that spoke of shared anticipation. "We're really going?" she whispered excitedly. Ben nodded, his voice thick but steady. "We're going."

Robert and Claire exchanged a knowing glance with Jeff and Annemarie — a silent pact among the adults that whatever lay ahead, they would walk it together. Jeff's voice brought the moment back to motion. "There's much to prepare," he said, his tone both gentle and firm. "The journey ahead won't be simple. But you two have already done what many grown men never dare — you've remembered." And with that, the threads tightened once more — ancient, invisible, indestructible.

The morning air still carried the faint chill left behind by the retreating fog, as if the earth itself hesitated to fully release the grasp of night. Inside the house, however, the day had already begun its slow orchestration. Books lay open across the table like old confidants called from their long slumber, while maps stretched wide beneath the soft weight of glass paperweights, their yellowed surfaces etched with the delicate veins of age. The house was never truly quiet anymore; even in its silence, it breathed with the hum of purpose, with the pulse of discoveries not yet spoken aloud but already felt in the marrow of its occupants.

Ben sat at the large oak table, his elbows resting against its polished surface, his eyes narrowing as he traced a finger along one of the older family charts Jeff had spread before them. His brow furrowed in concentration, not out of frustration, but from the weight of responsibility that had slowly settled upon him since their return. This was no longer idle curiosity nor simple interest; it was a duty now, one that pressed into his chest like the steady rhythm of an ancient drum calling him forward. Isla's name stood at the centre of the chart, carefully written, her bloodline's path branching upward through her mother, Claire Margaret Stuart, toward a lineage that hummed with centuries of quiet power.

Jeff stood nearby, his hands folded behind his back, observing the boy's intense focus with quiet pride. He had seen Ben's mind sharpen these past weeks, maturing in ways that no classroom could replicate. What had once been a wide-eyed curiosity about crests and scrolls had matured into a focused determination to untangle the invisible threads that wove through Isla's family — threads that reached far beyond mere surnames or distant parish records. This was the search for Isla's crown — not the crown worn atop heads, but the one carried within blood itself.

"The Stuart line," Ben said at last, his voice steady, though shaded by the gravity of what they both knew. "That's where we have to begin. The rest won't matter if we can't prove her maternal house." Jeff stepped forward, nodding. "You're exactly right." His voice was calm but firm, guiding without steering. "The Gibb line carried service and loyalty, but not succession. Her father's name may tell stories of proximity, but it's her mother's blood that holds the line we're after. The House of Stuart doesn't give inheritance by association. It moves by blood. Direct blood."

Ben's fingers paused at Claire Margaret Stuart's name again, his thoughts racing ahead. "We know James VI connects through this branch," he continued, his voice growing more certain with each word. "And we know the Stuarts held their own line intact for centuries, even through exile. But we need to find where Claire's path folds back into the core — not the cadet lines, not the distant branches. The true trunk."

Jeff allowed the quiet to stretch for a moment, giving Ben space to hear the weight of his own conclusions. The boy's mind had always been quick, but now it moved with the tempered pace of one who understood how easily these threads could unravel if pulled too quickly. "We're looking for the queen's line," Jeff affirmed gently. "The core Stuart lineage that would have carried through daughters even when kings failed. That's where Isla stands — not beside the line, but within it." Ben's eyes lifted from the chart, meeting Jeff's gaze with a clarity that had taken root during the long nights of research and whispered dreams. "Her mother carries it," Ben said firmly. "Claire is the key. We follow her."

Jeff allowed the faintest hint of a smile to touch his face, but his voice remained grounded. "Good," he said. "Then we begin here." He reached toward the stack of documents laid out beside the chart, carefully selecting a thin, fragile register bound in cracked leather. "This is one of the few surviving estate records from Perthshire. The Stuart estate's private holdings. Most of these documents were lost, scattered, or quietly sealed by distant cousins after the union of crowns and the later dissolutions. But this one survived because it was never meant for public record."

Ben leaned closer as Jeff opened the register with careful reverence, the pages creaking softly like old bones stretching awake. The names listed on the faded parchment read like echoes from another world: Margaret, Elizabeth, Isabella, Mary — women whose names had often been whispered in quiet halls but rarely etched in the louder tomes of official succession. Yet here they were, anchoring a chain that reached forward across centuries, toward Isla.

"These were not queens by title," Jeff continued, his voice steady, "but queens by birthright. Daughters who carried the seed of the house forward when sons died young or were swallowed by politics. It is through these women the blood survived. And Claire Margaret Stuart is one of them." Ben's breath tightened as the weight of the words sank deeper. "But how do we prove it, Jeff? Without public records, how do we show that Isla belongs to this line? The name alone isn't enough."

"That's where the blood speaks louder than parchment," Jeff answered. He reached once more into the small wooden box that sat like a quiet sentry at the corner of the table. From within, he withdrew a narrow scroll sealed with a simple wax impression — not with the full crest, but with the subtle triangle of three dots that had followed Ben since childhood. "This came to us from Claire's grandmother's estate," Jeff said softly. "Hidden for decades. Not even Isla's parents knew it existed. I've been waiting for the right time."

Ben stared at the scroll, his pulse quickening. "What's inside?" Jeff broke the seal with a slow, deliberate twist of his fingers. The parchment unfurled with a faint sigh, revealing columns of neatly inscribed names, dates, and notations written in a careful hand that had long since passed from living memory. The list traced backward from Claire Margaret Stuart, each mother leading to her mother before her, until at last the chain met with the name that anchored it all: Mary Stuart — a direct line from the royal House itself.

For several heartbeats, Ben could only stare. His lips moved but no sound escaped as his mind wrapped itself around the immensity of what lay before them. "It's real," he whispered at last. "This isn't theory. It's fact." Jeff placed a hand on Ben's shoulder, steadying him as the truth rooted deeper into the boy's consciousness. "This is your answer," he said. "And it's Isla's inheritance. This is the proof that crowns her not by decree, but by birth."

The parchment trembled faintly beneath Ben's fingertips as though it, too, recognized the culmination of generations of quiet waiting. The blood had remembered what men had forgotten, and now, by their hands, the truth stood revealed. Isla was not merely descended from those who served the throne; she was born from the throne itself.

The house had grown quieter as the afternoon wore on, though not from emptiness. Instead, it was the kind of hush that settles when minds are full and hearts are steady, as if even the walls themselves understood that something important was unfolding within their rooms. The golden light of late summer slanted through the windows, casting long beams across the open pages of books, illuminating the gentle dust motes that floated like tiny dancers in slow circles. Outside, the soft chirp of birds filtered through the open screen, but inside, all attention remained anchored around the broad wooden table that had now become their gathering place for truth.

Ben sat once again at his usual place, shoulders square, eyes sharp with quiet determination. To his left sat Isla, her hands folded neatly in her lap, her breath slow but deliberate. On the far side of the table, Claire Margaret Stuart and Robert Gibb exchanged brief glances, their expressions calm, though layered with a kind of silent curiosity that hinted at the questions quietly building behind their eyes. They had come willingly, invited not as bystanders, but as participants in the unfolding discovery. Jeff stood nearby, his steady presence filling the room with a quiet confidence that made the unfamiliar feel safe.

"It's important that we do this carefully," Jeff began, his voice even and warm. "Not because there's anything frightening in what we'll find, but because these answers belong to you as a family. The blood speaks differently for each person, but together, it helps tell a fuller story.

One that's been waiting a long time to be remembered." Robert nodded thoughtfully, his large hands resting firmly on the table. "We've always known the Gibb family served the Stuarts," he said, his voice deep but gentle. "But I never imagined the blood itself might carry more than service." His eyes flicked toward his wife, who sat poised but composed, her gaze steady.

Claire smiled faintly, her voice softer. "I've known our family carried Stuart history, of course. But until now, I hadn't thought of it as something living inside of me. Only as stories passed down." She paused, glancing toward Isla. "If there's more... I want to know." Ben leaned forward slightly, his excitement tempered by the care he had learned to carry through months of research. "That's exactly why we're doing this," he said. "The more pieces we have, the clearer the whole picture becomes. It's not just about names. It's about seeing where all the threads connect."

Jeff stepped forward, placing two small boxes onto the table, each marked clearly with careful labels. Inside were the DNA testing kits — one for blood, one for saliva. The instructions had already been reviewed; everything was ready. "We'll collect both types of samples," Jeff explained.

"The blood sample allows the lab to read the deeper markers — those that travel through many generations, far back into both sides of your ancestry. The saliva test adds a second layer — it allows them to cross-reference and verify what the blood reveals. Together, they create a much more complete map."

Isla shifted slightly in her chair, watching her parents with an expression that blended hope with quiet anticipation. Though she had trusted the path she and Ben had walked, she also knew that this moment held something sacred: the chance to help her parents see what she was only beginning to understand herself.

Claire was the first to extend her arm, her movements graceful yet deliberate. "Let's begin with me," she said softly. "If my line carries these roots forward, I want to honour them properly." The nurse who had accompanied Jeff for the collection worked with practised ease, tying the band, finding the vein, and drawing the small vial of blood that would soon carry Claire's story into the hands of the geneticists. The dark red liquid pooled gently into the tube, sealed with quiet efficiency before being placed into its padded container.

Next came Robert, whose larger frame made the process seem almost effortless, though he winced slightly at the quick pinch of the needle. "Well, there's my contribution to history," he joked quietly, offering a small smile toward Isla as the nurse finished her task. Isla smiled back, though her hands remained folded, her heart beating a little quicker beneath her calm expression.

When both blood samples were safely stored, Jeff opened the second box and withdrew the saliva collection tubes. "These are simple," he explained, his tone light. "A little less dramatic than needles, thankfully. Just a small amount of saliva in the tube, seal it, and we're done." Both Claire and Robert followed the instructions without hesitation, filling their vials carefully before placing them into the sealed kits. The nurse double-checked the labels, ensuring every detail was correct.

As the nurse finished packing the collection kits into their shipping containers, Jeff rested his hands lightly on the back of Ben's chair. "It's a strange thing, isn't it," he said quietly, "how a few drops of blood and a few drops of saliva can carry so many centuries inside them." Robert chuckled softly, nodding in agreement. "It's humbling," he said. "To think we're not just living for ourselves, but carrying the lives of those who came before." Claire's eyes glistened faintly as she looked toward Isla. "And hopefully giving something to those who come after."

Ben absorbed their words, allowing the weight of the moment to settle around them like a familiar blanket. This was not simply science. This was not simply family history. This was legacy — the quiet but unbreakable chain that carried from ancient halls of stone to this small kitchen, beneath beams that had watched them grow. These tests were not the end of their questions. They were keys to doors that had waited long enough to be opened.

Isla's voice rose at last, gentle but full. "When will we know?" Jeff answered softly. "The first results should arrive in a few weeks. And from there... the rest will follow." His words carried the steady patience of one who understood that some truths arrive only when they are ready. "But when they come, Isla, they will not rewrite who you are. They will simply show what you've always carried."

The house grew quiet again, not from hesitation, but from the calm that comes when something meaningful has been set into motion. Outside, the evening light deepened, casting long shadows across the ground, while inside, the family sat together — not in suspense, but in reverence. The blood would speak, and when it did, the story of their house would unfold, one name, one thread, one generation at a time.

The morning air still carried the faint chill left behind by the retreating fog, as if the earth itself hesitated to fully release the grasp of night. Inside the house, however, the day had already begun its slow orchestration. Books lay open across the table like old confidants called from their long slumber, while maps stretched wide beneath the soft weight of glass paperweights, their yellowed surfaces etched with the delicate veins of age. The house was never truly quiet anymore; even in its silence, it breathed with the hum of purpose, with the pulse of discoveries not yet spoken aloud but already felt in the marrow of its occupants.

Ben sat at the large oak table, his elbows resting against its polished surface, his eyes narrowing as he traced a finger along one of the older family charts Jeff had spread before them. His brow furrowed in concentration, not out of frustration, but from the weight of responsibility that had slowly settled upon him since their return. This was no longer idle curiosity nor simple interest; it was a duty now, one that pressed into his chest like the steady rhythm of an ancient drum calling him forward. Isla's name stood at the centre of the chart, carefully written, her bloodline's path branching upward through her mother, Claire Margaret Stuart, toward a lineage that hummed with centuries of quiet power.

Jeff stood nearby, his hands folded behind his back, observing the boy's intense focus with quiet pride. He had seen Ben's mind sharpen these past weeks, maturing in ways that no classroom could replicate. What had once been a wide-eyed curiosity about crests and scrolls had matured into a focused determination to untangle the invisible threads that wove through Isla's family — threads that reached far beyond mere surnames or distant parish records. This was the search for Isla's crown — not the crown worn atop heads, but the one carried within blood itself.

"The Stuart line," Ben said at last, his voice steady, though shaded by the gravity of what they both knew. "That's where we have to begin. The rest won't matter if we can't prove her maternal house." Jeff stepped forward, nodding. "You're exactly right." His voice was calm but firm, guiding without steering. "The Gibb line carried service and loyalty, but not succession. Her father's name may tell stories of proximity, but it's her mother's blood that holds the line we're after. The House of Stuart doesn't give inheritance by association. It moves by blood. Direct blood."

Ben's fingers paused at Claire Margaret Stuart's name again, his thoughts racing ahead. "We know James VI connects through this branch," he continued, his voice growing more certain with each word. "And we know the Stuarts held their own line intact for centuries, even through exile. But we need to find where Claire's path folds back into the core — not the cadet lines, not the distant branches. The true trunk."

Jeff allowed the quiet to stretch for a moment, giving Ben space to hear the weight of his own conclusions. The boy's mind had always been quick, but now it moved with the tempered pace of one who understood how easily these threads could unravel if pulled too quickly. "We're looking for the queen's line," Jeff affirmed gently. "The core Stuart lineage that would have carried through daughters even when kings failed. That's where Isla stands — not beside the line, but within it." Ben's eyes lifted from the chart, meeting Jeff's gaze with a clarity that had taken root during the long nights of research and whispered dreams. "Her mother carries it," Ben said firmly. "Claire is the key. We follow her."

Jeff allowed the faintest hint of a smile to touch his face, but his voice remained grounded. "Good," he said. "Then we begin here." He reached toward the stack of documents laid out beside the chart, carefully selecting a thin, fragile register bound in cracked leather. "This is one of the few surviving estate records from Perthshire. The Stuart estate's private holdings. Most of these documents were lost, scattered, or quietly sealed by distant cousins after the union of crowns and the later dissolutions. But this one survived because it was never meant for public record."

Ben leaned closer as Jeff opened the register with careful reverence, the pages creaking softly like old bones stretching awake. The names listed on the faded parchment read like echoes from another world: Margaret, Elizabeth, Isabella, Mary — women whose names had often been whispered in quiet halls but rarely etched in the louder tomes of official succession. Yet here they were, anchoring a chain that reached forward across centuries, toward Isla.

"These were not queens by title," Jeff continued, his voice steady, "but queens by birthright. Daughters who carried the seed of the house forward when sons died young or were swallowed by politics. It is through these women the blood survived. And Claire Margaret Stuart is one of them." Ben's breath tightened as the weight of the words sank deeper. "But how do we prove it, Jeff? Without public records, how do we show that Isla belongs to this line? The name alone isn't enough."

"That's where the blood speaks louder than parchment," Jeff answered. He reached once more into the small wooden box that sat like a quiet sentry at the corner of the table. From within, he withdrew a narrow scroll sealed with a simple wax impression — not with the full crest, but with the subtle triangle of three dots that had followed Ben since childhood. "This came to us from Claire's grandmother's estate," Jeff said softly. "Hidden for decades. Not even Isla's parents knew it existed. I've been waiting for the right time."

Ben stared at the scroll, his pulse quickening. "What's inside?" Jeff broke the seal with a slow, deliberate twist of his fingers. The parchment unfurled with a faint sigh, revealing columns of neatly inscribed names, dates, and notations written in a careful hand that had long since passed from living memory. The list traced backward from Claire Margaret Stuart, each mother leading to her mother before her, until at last the chain met with the name that anchored it all: Mary Stuart — a direct line from the royal House itself.

For several heartbeats, Ben could only stare. His lips moved but no sound escaped as his mind wrapped itself around the immensity of what lay before them. "It's real," he whispered at last. "This isn't theory. It's fact." Jeff placed a hand on Ben's shoulder, steadying him as the truth rooted deeper into the boy's consciousness. "This is your answer," he said. "And it's Isla's inheritance. This is the proof that crowns her not by decree, but by birth."

The parchment trembled faintly beneath Ben's fingertips as though it, too, recognized the culmination of generations of quiet waiting. The blood had remembered what men had forgotten, and now, by their hands, the truth stood revealed. Isla was not merely descended from those who served the throne; she was born from the throne itself.

The morning arrived with the gentle insistence of sunlight slipping through the gaps in the curtains, painting slender ribbons of light across the polished floorboards. The house stirred softly, as though aware of the importance the day would bring but choosing not to disturb it with unnecessary noise. Even the air seemed different — not heavy with tension, but filled with a quiet anticipation that neither rushed nor hesitated. It was a day that would carry new weight, not because of what might be found, but because of what would finally be revealed.

Ben sat at the dining table, his sketchbook set aside for the moment as he traced his fingers thoughtfully across the corner of one of Jeff's carefully preserved maps. The familiar crests and swirling ink lines had become almost like companions to him now — familiar faces etched into paper rather than skin. Across the table, Isla sat quietly, her hands folded together, her eyes wide with a mixture of curiosity and nervous excitement. She had always known there were stories hidden deep within her family, but today, they would no longer be stories alone. Today, they would begin the work of giving those stories roots.

Claire Margaret Stuart entered the room first, her steps light but measured, her expression calm yet attentive. Behind her came Robert Gibb, carrying a faint smile, though his eyes showed the same steady nerves his daughter carried. Both parents had agreed without hesitation when Ben and Jeff first proposed the next step — not because they had always known what would be uncovered, but because they trusted the hands guiding the search. The weight of ancestry was no longer just Ben's to carry; it was now Isla's whole family stepping forward to meet their history.

Jeff rose from his chair as they entered, offering them both a quiet nod of welcome. His voice was, as always, calm and steady. "Thank you for coming early. The lab scheduled us sooner than expected. The blood tests are booked for this afternoon." He gestured to the sealed envelope on the table containing the appointment details. "Once those samples are taken, we'll have the genetic material needed to confirm the deeper line — including the maternal markers we need for Claire's Stuart ancestry."

Claire approached the table, her gaze falling briefly on the open chart that mapped her family's name across the centuries. She exhaled softly, as though releasing a breath that had waited far longer than her own lifetime. "I've always known the name carried weight," she said gently, her voice warm but contemplative. "But never like this. Not as something living." She reached for Isla's hand, giving it a reassuring squeeze. "Whatever we learn, we'll face it together."

Robert, standing beside them, gave a single nod of agreement. "If this helps Isla know who she is — truly is — then we do it." Jeff smiled faintly, the kind of smile that carried quiet respect. "There's also a second step," he added, reaching beneath the table to retrieve two small cardboard boxes, neatly packaged and still sealed. "We've ordered Ancestry kits as well. Saliva tests. These will give us additional cross-references. Blood will give us the depth, but the saliva profiles will help confirm how distant the branches connect across multiple populations."

Ben's eyes followed Jeff's every word carefully, absorbing the details with the same focused attention he had grown into over these past months. "So we're building two maps at once," he said, more to himself than anyone else. "The blood map tells us the maternal line with precision, while the saliva gives us the whole forest view. Both together help us see where Isla belongs."

"Exactly," Jeff affirmed, handing one of the small boxes to Claire and the other to Robert. "It's a double lens. Blood speaks for the generations carried through the mother's mitochondrial DNA, and the saliva test traces the broader segments — where people moved, who mixed, where the ancient families crossed paths." Isla's fingers tightened gently around her mother's hand as she looked up at Ben. "Will it hurt?" she asked softly. Ben shook his head with a quiet, comforting smile. "Not really. The blood test is just one little pinch — like when I had mine done. And the saliva one is easy. Just a little spit in the tube."

Jeff's voice added calm to the explanation. "The blood test is handled at the clinic, where trained staff will take care of everything carefully and quickly. The saliva kits you'll complete here at home, and then we'll send them out in the pre-labelled envelopes. The lab results will take a few weeks. But the answers will come."

The family gathered their coats as the late morning sun brightened its way through the windows. Outside, the leaves swayed gently, as though echoing the motion of time itself — steady, patient, constant.

There was no rush to what they were doing; these were steps that had waited for generations, and now simply awaited hands willing to carry the work forward. Isla slipped her hand into Ben's as they walked toward the door, the unspoken bond between them drawing closer still. They had begun this journey side by side, and every step ahead would only draw those threads tighter.

At the clinic, the air smelled faintly of antiseptic and clean paper, neither sharp nor offensive — simply neutral, like a place that existed between questions and answers. The receptionist greeted them with polite efficiency, confirming names and birthdates before gently directing them to a waiting room. The chairs were soft, the magazines neatly stacked, but no one in the room needed distractions. The real story was already unfolding in the silence between them.

When Claire was called first, she stood with the quiet grace that always seemed to follow her, as though she carried not only her own name but the weight of every mother who had come before her. Isla watched her mother disappear behind the frosted glass door, gripping Ben's hand a little tighter. Ben squeezed gently in return, offering the kind of strength that didn't need words. Jeff remained beside them, his calm presence anchoring the moment.

The blood draws were simple, quick, and handled with expert care. Claire returned shortly, her arm wrapped with a small strip of cotton and adhesive tape, her expression relaxed but reflective. Robert followed next, returning with the same quiet composure. The family exchanged soft smiles, small nods that carried more weight than words ever could. They were not here for mere tests. They were walking back into the arms of their past.

Later that afternoon, back at the house, they gathered around the kitchen table once more, this time to complete the saliva kits. The steps were easy enough: open the tube, fill it carefully, seal the cap, and place it in the provided mailer. Isla watched intently as her parents followed each instruction. There was a kind of quiet reverence even in these simple motions, as though each small action carried with it the hope of generations finally being seen. As the final tubes were sealed and placed into the outgoing envelope, Isla looked up at Jeff, her eyes full of that same wide innocence that had carried her through the many turns of their search. "When the results come back... will it tell us for sure?"

Jeff lowered himself slightly to meet her eye level, his voice warm and steady. "It will bring us very close, Isla. Close enough to see how your family tree touches the great branches of the Stuarts. And when we match what we find here with what we already hold in your mother's scroll, it will give us what we need to know."

Ben reached across the table, his hand resting atop Isla's. "And no matter what it says," he added softly, "you already carry it. This is just letting the world catch up with what the blood already remembers." The room settled into a hush once again, not out of fear or worry, but out of the sacred patience that true discovery always demands. The past was already whispering. Soon, it would speak.

The days moved forward with the quiet certainty of a river that had long since chosen its path. Though the waiting carried its own kind of weight, it never pressed too heavily on Ben or Isla. Instead, it wrapped itself around them like a patient teacher, allowing the two of them to settle into their routine without fear or urgency. Each weekend became its own small world — a sanctuary where questions could be asked without hesitation, where pieces of long-forgotten puzzles were gently retrieved from the corners of history.

Ben's home sat only three doors away from Isla's, a small stretch of familiar sidewalk that had been walked so many times it no longer felt like distance at all. Each Friday evening, Isla would arrive with her backpack slung across one shoulder, carrying not only her pyjamas and toothbrush, but stacks of notes, printouts, and carefully labelled folders filled with family trees, maps, and historical records. The door was always open for her; there was no need to knock. She would step inside, greeted first by Jeff's warm nod and Annemarie's soft smile, before joining Ben in the living room where their weekend work would begin.

The living room had long since transformed into a kind of study chamber that existed somewhere between a library and a childhood fort. Stacks of books rose like miniature towers on either side of the coffee table, while maps were carefully pinned to corkboards along the walls. The large floor rug had become their command post, where pillows were spread out in a familiar semi-circle that always seemed to reshape itself each time they worked. The soft glow of the floor lamp cast gentle light across their open notebooks and scattered pens, creating an atmosphere that felt both serious and comforting.

Their process was always the same: first, they would review the previous week's findings, cross-referencing notes, adding small corrections, drawing new branches on the charts Jeff had helped them build. Isla would often lean forward with her pen poised, her brow furrowed as she traced delicate lines connecting mothers to daughters, weaving the Stuart bloodline like a thread of spun gold across the paper. Ben would sit beside her, his hand resting on his chin, eyes narrowed as he examined the intersections where records grew faint and names began to fade into obscurity.

They worked tirelessly but never hurried. Each discovery was treated with reverence, each unanswered question met with patient determination rather than frustration. When one of them grew tired, the other would quietly pick up the slack, their silent rhythm never broken. They were, in every sense, a team — not because they divided the work evenly, but because they carried the weight together.

As the hours slipped into the deeper folds of night, the work would gradually slow. Papers would be gently stacked, pens capped, and maps rolled back into their protective tubes. The soft hum of the house settled around them as the world outside grew still. Without ever needing to discuss it, they would pull the shared sleeping bag across the thick rug, each taking their place within its warmth. Two pillows waited at the top, always placed side by side, as though even the cushions understood their belonging.

Isla would nestle into Ben's side, her head resting against his shoulder, while Ben's arm draped naturally around her. The comfort between them was not clumsy nor shy; it had grown into something far more enduring than mere affection. It was belonging. It was recognition — the quiet certainty that they were not simply friends nor passing childhood companions, but two souls braided together long before either had known the names written in their scrolls.

In these quiet moments, as their eyes grew heavy beneath the weight of study and comfort, their voices would soften into whispered exchanges. Sometimes they would review one last question, sometimes they would share a fleeting theory, but most often they simply rested in the silence, letting the warmth between them carry them gently toward sleep. As Isla's breathing slowed, Ben would often press a faint kiss to her temple — not rushed, not perfunctory — but lingering with a reverence that reflected the depth of their bond. And as Isla's eyes fluttered closed, she would whisper softly, "Goodnight, Ben, I Love You" the words falling like a quiet promise into the night.

Morning always arrived in the same gentle way. The first rays of sunlight would break through the window, scattering light across the floorboards where their open notebooks lay. Isla would stir first, blinking softly as she nestled against Ben's shoulder, feeling the warmth of his arm still draped protectively around her. Their mornings held no embarrassment, no awkwardness — only the quiet affirmation of what had always been understood. With a gentle movement, Ben would turn his head slightly, pressing a slow, lingering kiss to Isla's lips, his breath warm against her skin. She would smile faintly, her hand curling gently into his shirt as she whispered, "Good morning."

Jeff would enter quietly not long after, careful not to disturb them too early, but always ready with breakfast waiting in the kitchen. Annemarie would prepare toast and tea, the simple sounds of morning life slowly filling the house like a soft melody. There was no need for questions, no conversations explaining what was already known. Their parents understood. They had seen the bond grow, had watched it settle into something sacred and steady. It was not whimsy. It was not childish infatuation. It was something old — something remembered by both blood and spirit.

When Sunday afternoons came, Isla would gather her things to return home, and as always, before she left, they shared one last embrace at the door. The hug was never rushed. Their arms would wrap around one another, holding for long moments in quiet understanding. And before Isla stepped away, she would lift her face to Ben's, their lips meeting in a lingering kiss that spoke of far more than their years might suggest. Not hurried. Not stolen. Simply present — as if the world itself paused long enough to acknowledge what lived between them.

As Isla walked down the short sidewalk toward her house, Ben would watch her until she disappeared through her front door. He never felt sadness at the distance, for it was only ever temporary.

Each week brought them back together, and each weekend carried them one step closer to the answers that waited patiently in the threads of their shared past. And always, beneath every scroll, beneath every name, beneath every charted bloodline — there lived their unspoken vow: they would find it together.

The rhythm of their days settled into something almost ceremonial, a structure that carried both comfort and purpose. Each morning began in the quiet hum of Jeff's study, where books waited like silent companions along the shelves, and maps were carefully rolled and tucked into their assigned spaces. The house itself had grown into a second classroom, one not built from rows of desks or blackboards, but from the patient guidance of one who understood that education was not a list of facts to memorize, but a journey meant to awaken what already lived inside them.

Jeff stood at the head of the small table where Ben and Isla sat side by side, their notebooks open, pens poised, eyes attentive. His teaching was neither rushed nor distracted; he gave each of them the kind of individual attention that most schools could never offer, adjusting lessons to meet their strengths while gently guiding them through the areas that required deeper focus. Mathematics unfolded like quiet puzzles. History breathed with names and dates that no longer felt distant but personal. Even science lessons bent toward their shared curiosity, often finding their way into discussions about DNA, genetics, and the very research that had filled so many of their evenings.

While Isla's parents worked full-time, trusting Jeff completely, the house became her second home — though in truth, it felt less like second and more like shared. There was never a sense of visiting. She belonged here as much as she belonged in her own house three doors down. Jeff never treated her as a guest; she was one of his students, one of his children. Annemarie's quiet care wove into the background, offering meals and gentle smiles without ever intruding upon their work. It was a home wrapped in understanding — not only of their studies, but of the bond growing steadily between the two young souls who occupied the centre of it.

Every lesson wove itself into the larger tapestry of their search. When they studied history, it was not abstract. It was their history. When they practiced reading, they combed through old manuscripts. Even in their writing assignments, Jeff encouraged them to document what they were discovering — not as distant researchers but as participants within the bloodlines they sought to understand. There was no separation between their education and their quest. Each supported the other, like twin vines wrapping around the same ancient tree.

Between lessons, they would pause for breaks that carried the sweetness of their youth. A cup of cocoa shared by the window, a quiet walk along the garden path, moments of laughter sparked by a sudden thought or theory one of them dared to propose aloud. But beneath the gentle comfort of their daily routines, the gravity of their work remained ever-present. Every name uncovered, every place connected, every missing link filled became another step forward. They weren't simply gathering facts — they were retrieving forgotten inheritances.

As their afternoons drifted into evenings, their closeness grew not out of infatuation or fleeting affection, but from something older, something quieter, something earned. They held hands freely, not as children mimicking adults, but as two hearts naturally seeking the nearness of the one who belonged beside them. In moments of stillness, when the world outside the windows softened into twilight, they would sometimes pause, faces drawn near, allowing their lips to meet in quiet kisses that carried no urgency. The world would fade gently away as their mouths met — not hurried, not stolen — but present, unspoken promises whispered into the space between them.

The words I love you remained sacred between them — never flung carelessly, never reduced to ritual. When they spoke those words, they did so with full hearts and quiet reverence, understanding that love was not simply something they felt, but something they were building. It lived not in grand gestures, but in the countless small moments spent side by side — in the shared pages of family trees, in the patient hours of study, in the quiet of early mornings and the warmth of evening light.

And so, day after day, they moved forward together — seven days a week, never apart. Where one went, the other followed. Their bond was not the fragile spark of childhood curiosity, but the deep, slow burn of something written into their very bloodlines. Even the house itself seemed to know it, carrying their laughter through its rooms and holding their whispered hopes gently in its walls. As the days advanced and the results from the DNA tests loomed ever closer on the horizon, neither Ben nor Isla wavered. They had each other, and that was enough to face whatever truths might soon unfold.

The morning carried a certain pulse to it, though no one had dared say aloud why. The envelope had arrived quietly — as these things always seemed to — resting on the front hallway table like any ordinary letter. But everyone in the house knew it was not ordinary. It was the culmination of long hours, deep searches, and generations of silent waiting. The DNA results had come.

Claire and Robert arrived mid-morning, stepping inside as naturally as if it were their own home. They had long since been granted that silent privilege by Annemarie, who welcomed them both not with formality, but with the comfort of shared trust. The front door had not needed knocking for months; it stood simply as an entrance to another shared part of their lives. As Claire slipped out of her coat and Robert set his keys down on the side table, Annemarie greeted them with a gentle smile. "Coffee's already on," she said softly. "Figured we might need it."

Jeff sat quietly near the far corner, his cup of tea already in hand. He offered them both a nod as they settled into the familiar space, the air carrying the faint aroma of brewing coffee and the gentle hum of the old percolator clicking in rhythm. Though Jeff maintained his own small flat several blocks away, it was here — in this house — where most of his days unfolded.

His friendship with Annemarie had long been one of quiet respect, built not upon any unspoken expectations, but upon simple, enduring friendship. There were no entanglements, no awkward undertones. Simply two people, each carrying their own histories, standing beside one another as life unfolded.

Ben and Isla sat side by side at the dining table, their hands gently laced together beneath the polished wood. They had waited patiently for this moment, but their hearts had carried the weight of what was coming long before the envelope had arrived. Isla leaned slightly against Ben's shoulder, her breath steady but expectant, while Ben kept his gaze focused on Jeff, waiting for him to begin.

Jeff placed his cup carefully on the coaster before unfolding the paperwork. His voice, as always, was calm, steady, and deliberate. "We've received both sets of results," he began, his eyes glancing first toward Claire and Robert. "Both the laboratory DNA and the ancestry cross-references have arrived. And we've confirmed exactly what we had hoped to find." He paused only briefly, not for effect, but to ensure each word was received fully. "Claire, your maternal lineage has aligned precisely with the records we recovered."

Claire inhaled softly, her fingers tightening gently around her coffee mug. "The Stuart line?" she asked, though the answer was already beginning to bloom inside her chest.

Jeff nodded. "Direct. You are descended through the maternal Stuart branch, reaching back to James VI of Scotland — also crowned James I of England. The line remains unbroken through the female descent — your line. It confirms what we first suspected in our earliest research." He turned another page, revealing the charted mapping that now displayed her maternal tree in clear, bold precision. "This is your inheritance."

Claire's eyes misted slightly as she leaned forward to study the chart. The names no longer felt like distant characters from history books, but family — living echoes reaching back through time. She whispered softly, almost to herself, "I always wondered if the name carried something more than just old stories." Her gaze shifted to Isla, whose wide eyes reflected the gravity of the discovery. "Now we know." Robert, seated beside his wife, studied the page with the steady patience he always carried. While the Stuart revelation centred upon Claire and Isla, his attention turned instead to the name that had followed his family for generations. "And the Gibb line?" he asked, curiosity rising more out of intellectual intrigue than personal claim.

Jeff offered a faint smile, adjusting the second document. "The Gibb name traces directly to its known Scottish roots — primarily lowland Scotland near Carriber. The earliest records show the family closely tied to the Stuart courts, primarily in service, particularly to James VI himself. William Gibb served directly within the king's household. While it does not carry royal blood itself, it served within royal proximity for generations." Robert chuckled quietly, nodding to himself. "So, not quite kings, but not far from them either." "No," Jeff agreed, his tone warm. "Not kings. But standing close enough to witness kingship firsthand."

Claire sat back, her hands wrapped firmly around her coffee mug as if grounding herself against the enormity of what had just settled into the room. She exhaled, steadying her thoughts before speaking. "Robert and I have been together since we were children," she said softly, her voice carrying the kind of weight that only comes with shared history. "We met when we were five. And we've never been apart since. Not once. Not a day." She paused, her eyes sweeping gently toward Isla and Ben. "That's what a true soulmate is. Two lives woven so closely that separation doesn't exist. Not even in death, I believe."

Her voice grew even softer as she continued, directing her words toward Ben and Isla now. "You two carry something very rare. This isn't simple childhood affection. I see it every time you're near one another. There's a knowing between you that most people search their whole lives for and never find. Soulmates don't separate. They carry each other — through years, through hardships, even beyond this life. Somehow, someway, they remain." Isla's throat tightened at her mother's words, and she leaned further into Ben's side, her hand tightening within his. Ben, for his part, remained steady, his eyes never leaving Claire's as she spoke. The room held its breath with them, recognizing the sacredness of what had just been spoken aloud.

Jeff lifted his tea cup, gently breaking the quiet tension, though with the same steady reverence. "You two have each other," he said softly. "That will anchor you through all the rest of this journey. Bloodlines may show us where we've come from, but it's these bonds that carry us forward." Annmarie refilled Claire's coffee with a practiced ease, offering her a quiet smile. "Well," she said gently, her voice warm, "I think I'm the only one here who drinks as much coffee as you two. At least we outnumber the tea drinkers today." Robert chuckled softly. "I'd say that's a fair advantage." Jeff lifted his cup slightly. "You can have your coffee. I'll keep my tea."

The gentle laughter drifted through the room like a soft wind clearing the weight of heavy news. But beneath the humour, the truth remained: the map had changed. The names were no longer lost. Isla was not simply connected to history — she was the living continuation of it. And as Ben's hand remained gently wrapped within hers, the two of them knew that whatever came next, they would face it together — side by side, as they always had been, and as they always would be.

The revelations from the DNA results had settled into the house like a warm, heavy quilt — comforting, but impossible to ignore. The knowledge that Claire carried the Stuart bloodline directly from James VI and I had filled each of them with a mixture of wonder, reverence, and quiet responsibility. Yet for all the answers those papers had provided, they had only opened new doors. Doors that whispered there was still more to be found.

Ben sat at the far end of the living room floor, leaning forward on his elbows, carefully studying the fresh set of printouts spread between him and Isla. The room had long since returned to its familiar state — maps pinned to the walls, folders stacked like small towers on the side table, and the soft rustling of papers serving as the background hum to their steady work. Isla sat cross-legged beside him, one hand resting against her chin as she read over another set of notes Jeff had gathered for them. Though her heart still carried the amazement of what they had uncovered, her mind had already leapt forward, hungry for the questions that now demanded answers.

"There's more here," Ben said, his voice soft but certain. "James VI was only the beginning. The Stuart line doesn't stand alone. These houses — these royal houses — they marry, they merge. Lines split and rejoin. One crown sits atop another." His finger traced a set of connected lines branching outward from James's name. "What else is buried inside your family? What other crowns still whisper through the blood?"

Isla's eyes followed his hand as he moved across the chart. She felt it too — that sense of vastness growing before them. The Stuart name had once been a towering discovery. Now, it was a doorway into something far larger, far older. "I want to know, Ben," she said softly. "I want to know everything. Who we are. Where I come from. Who still lives inside my blood." Her words trembled only slightly, not from fear, but from the depth of the search they had committed themselves to.

Jeff sat a short distance away, quietly preparing another set of records. He glanced up at their conversation, his expression calm but attentive. "You're both beginning to ask the right questions now," he said, his voice measured and warm. "Royal blood doesn't stop with one name. The crowns of Europe have always been tangled. Families wove into each other across kingdoms. You may find that what began with James VI will soon reveal ties to other houses — Plantagenet, Capet, Habsburg, even Anjou."

Ben's breath caught faintly at the mention of names he had only seen sketched at the edges of older charts. "So Claire may carry more than just the Stuart line?" Jeff nodded once, setting down his folder. "It's very likely. The higher you climb into the branches of royalty, the more entangled the houses become. Royal blood doesn't flow in narrow rivers. It spreads like the roots of an old tree. You follow one, and it leads you to many others."

Isla reached forward, placing her hand gently over Ben's as she studied the tangled web of names before them. The closeness of their touch had long since become second nature — not possessive, not fleeting, but steady. "And that means," she whispered, "if my mum carries those lines, then... I do too." Ben squeezed her hand gently, his voice filled with quiet reverence. "You carry every name they carried, Isla. Every crown they wore. It's written into you, the same way it's written into me." He paused, his gaze locking fully with hers. "We're more alike than even we first knew."

The thought stirred something deep in both of them — not pride, not vanity — but a solemn weight. They had stepped beyond childhood games of ancestry. They were no longer simply tracing names on paper. They were retrieving lost inheritances, awakening what their blood already knew. This was not about the pursuit of titles, but of truth. Jeff leaned forward, sensing the shift. "The next stage will be deeper," he said, his voice lowering slightly. "We'll pull the next set of genealogical records — estate holdings, old parish registries, royal marriage contracts. But we may also need to examine documents that weren't meant for public record. Quiet agreements between families. Sealed archives that most people never see. That's where the hidden bloodlines are buried."

Ben's mind raced, but his focus never wavered. "We'll find them, Jeff. However far we have to go." "You will," Jeff answered simply. "Because the blood remembers, even when the world forgets." From the kitchen, Annemarie's voice floated gently into the room as she finished preparing another round of coffee and tea. "Everything worth knowing takes time," she said softly, more to herself than anyone, but the words landed all the same. "But it always waits for the right hands to find it."

Robert stepped into the room, having returned from his quiet walk around the block, his usual habit when heavier conversations filled the house. His hand carried his coffee cup, and as he joined them, his face carried a calm curiosity. "It really is remarkable," he said softly. "To think that what we thought were simply old family stories were actually fragments of something far older." He glanced at his wife and daughter, his gaze steady with quiet pride. "Claire, you've always carried it. We just never knew how much."

Claire smiled gently, her hands wrapped around her coffee mug as if anchoring herself against the tide of information swirling around her. "I always felt something," she admitted, her voice calm but weighted. "Even as a child, the name Stuart never felt like just a name. But I never imagined... this." Ben watched her closely, his respect for Claire deepening. She was not overwhelmed. She was steady — like Isla. The same strength moved through them both, and now he saw where Isla's unshakable spirit had come from.

Isla shifted slightly, drawing closer to Ben's side. "Mum," she whispered, her voice full but gentle, "we'll find it. Whatever else is still waiting. We'll find it." Claire's eyes softened, resting on both children with a quiet certainty. "I know you will." And so the work continued — not with fear, but with devotion. The charts remained open. The maps remained pinned. The search had only begun to whisper its deepest secrets. The crown within Claire's blood was no longer a question of if, but of how far.

The hours they kept were not ordinary. Long before the first hint of sunlight crept over the rooftops, the house would already be awake. The soft rustling of papers, the gentle scraping of chairs over hardwood, and the steady tapping of keys upon Jeff's laptop filled the quiet space where most of the world still slept. These early mornings had become their sacred time, where distraction could not intrude, and where every scrap of history was given their full, undivided attention.

Jeff always arrived first, carrying fresh documents in his worn leather satchel, each one carefully selected from archives, both digital and physical, that most researchers never bothered to approach. Ben and Isla followed moments later, slipping quietly into their places at the long table, their faces still carrying the softness of sleep but quickly sharpening into focus. They knew the weight of what they were handling. This was not a game. Each name they uncovered was another piece of a story long buried beneath layers of time and forgetfulness.

The three of them moved with the precision of a team who had long since fallen into a rhythm. Jeff would guide them through the old estate records, foreign registries, and sealed family letters that only surfaced when one knew where to look. Ben would cross-reference every name with modern genealogical software, mapping how marriages folded distant bloodlines into each other across borders and kingdoms. Isla's hands would move swiftly across the family trees, carefully pencilling new branches and noting where certain names reappeared across multiple generations. No detail was overlooked. No assumption was made without evidence.

Claire's bloodline, once a broad path leading only to James VI, now unraveled like a carefully hidden royal quilt. With each record, the web grew clearer. It was not a single royal connection — it was a convergence. The Stuarts, yes — but also distant ties to the Bruce family, Plantagenet threads stretching across England, faint whispers of Scandinavian marriages folded through Norse alliances centuries earlier. The deeper they went, the more undeniable it became. Claire didn't simply descend from royalty. She was a carrier of multiple crowns, each one woven into the next by generations of careful, and sometimes secretive, unions.

Isla sat straighter as she traced one particular branch on the parchment. "Ben... look here," she whispered, sliding the document toward him. "This isn't just James. There's a marriage line that folds into the MacAlpin house two centuries before. That would place us inside the earliest sovereign houses of Scotland." Ben's breath caught as he read the notation. "That's the House of Kenneth MacAlpin," he whispered, his voice thick with awe. "Claire doesn't just carry the Stuart line. She carries the line of the first kings. The very first rulers of Scotland itself."

Jeff nodded as he leaned closer, his finger running along the same line. "You've found it, Isla. This is where it begins. The blood of the earliest Scottish kings — and it now lives directly through Claire, and into you." Isla's eyes shimmered as she stared at the page, her mind reaching backward through the centuries as if the names themselves breathed softly around her. It was no longer theory. It was fact. She carried not just the crown of James, but the ancient crowns of those who had ruled long before Scotland had ever been a united land. It was all within her blood.

Yet as that discovery settled, Ben's attention shifted toward another set of documents Jeff had quietly pulled aside — records focused not on Claire, but on Robert. His surname, Gibb, had originally seemed straightforward — a family of royal servants and trusted aides.

But as Jeff began cross-referencing deeper archives, more complex threads started to emerge. These were not simply household attendants; there was far more beneath the surface of Robert's name. "Jeff..." Ben said slowly, his voice growing curious, "I think we may have overlooked something with Robert."

Jeff turned slightly, his expression already knowing. "We have," he said softly. "And I've been waiting until we had enough to present it properly." Ben studied the records carefully, tracing the lineage backwards, past the better-known Gibb courtiers who served the Stuart monarchs. What emerged were earlier references — to a family whose surname had originally derived from 'Gibb' not as a title of service, but as a shortened version of Gilbert, a name tied to early landholders in Berwickshire. The line itself predated the Stuart courts, stretching into feudal Scotland before James VI ever wore a crown.

"There were landowners named Gibb who held minor estates under the Lords of Douglas," Jeff continued, his voice steady but deliberate. "And before that, possible Norman roots. It seems the Gibb family may have originally arrived with the Norman expansions into Scotland — carrying titles as freeholders, before later generations served as stewards to the Stuart house." Robert, who had quietly entered the room and listened from the edge of the discussion, crossed his arms with a mixture of humility and growing fascination.

"So," he said softly, "we weren't just servants?" "No," Jeff replied, offering him a respectful glance. "Your line served, yes — but it descended first from landholders. Men who once held property granted under Norman charters. While Claire's line sits directly upon royal crowns, your line reflects early feudal nobility, buried beneath the titles of later service." Robert exhaled slowly, his eyes narrowing thoughtfully. "I never imagined any of this. I always assumed my name was tied only to the court. But to think it stretches back further... to Berwickshire, to Norman roots... that's something."

"It is," Jeff affirmed. "It means that both sides of Isla's bloodline carry strength — one from crowns, one from early lords. Together, they make her lineage even more profound." Ben looked toward Isla, his chest swelling with quiet awe. "You really do carry all of it, Isla. The blood of kings, and the roots of those who stood beside them." Isla's eyes never wavered from Ben's. "So do you," she whispered. "That's why we found each other." The morning light slipped gently through the curtains, casting long shadows across the carefully drawn family trees that now filled the table. Their work was not finished. The branches still reached further, whispering of even older roots waiting to be uncovered. But for the first time, they stood upon solid ground — knowing now where the crowns truly began.

The further they traveled into the past, the more the bloodlines began to blur. Borders melted into one another. Kings married queens not for love, but for alliances. And as the weeks of research continued, the work no longer felt like assembling a simple family tree, but rather like unraveling an enormous woven tapestry — one where every thread crossed dozens of others, sometimes looping back upon itself after centuries had passed. Yet still, Ben, Isla, and Jeff pressed forward with the same quiet determination that had carried them since the beginning.

Their mornings remained sacred. Long before the first hint of dawn brushed the sky, the three of them would be gathered at the long oak table, heads bent over maps and ancient registries, their faces illuminated by the warm, steady light of the table lamp. The piles of research grew higher with each passing day, not from disorganization, but because each answer uncovered new corridors to explore. Jeff had begun requesting records from continental archives now — some arriving through digital correspondence, others through trusted colleagues who still held access to closed university vaults scattered across Europe.

Ben leaned in closely over one of the newly delivered French estate rolls, his brow furrowing as his finger traced the elegant but archaic script. "These marriages aren't isolated," he said softly. "The Stuarts didn't just intermarry with local Scottish nobility. They folded into the French houses as early as the twelfth century. Claire's line merges into Capet blood not once, but twice. And those Capet branches stretch outward across France, Burgundy, and into Hungary."

Isla sat beside him, her eyes following the same branching patterns across the large parchment. "That means the crowns don't stop with Scotland," she whispered. "They reach across the continent." Jeff nodded calmly, already cross-referencing another set of documents beside him.

"Precisely," he affirmed. "Royal blood doesn't recognize borders the way modern maps do. The bloodlines of Europe's houses are tied together like an ancient braid. Once you begin pulling on one thread, you often find it wound around others that go far beyond what most people realize."

Ben shifted to the next set of records Jeff had prepared — these from Eastern Europe, marked with elegant Hungarian script. The names of Árpád, Béla, and their royal courts appeared again, echoing names Ben had already seen in other corners of his research. His chest tightened slightly as the weight of the discoveries deepened. "Jeff... Claire's blood isn't just Scottish. This goes into Hungary. The House of Árpád. The very founding kings." Jeff's eyes lifted from his pages, nodding with gravity. "Yes," he replied softly. "The Stuart line folds into the Hungarian Árpáds through Margaret of Scotland — sometimes called Saint Margaret — who married Malcolm III. But her ancestry traces back into Eastern Europe, bringing the Árpád blood into what became the Scottish royal house. Claire carries all of that."

Isla's voice was quiet, nearly reverent as she whispered, "I carry that." Ben turned to face her fully, his hand slipping naturally into hers. "Yes," he said, his voice rich but steady. "You carry all of it. Kings of Scotland, queens of France, lords of Hungary — it all lives inside you." The moment held between them for a long breath, the magnitude of what they were discovering filling the air like a sacred presence. This was no longer simply a search for a single crown. They were walking the halls of history itself, breathing life into names most of the world had long since forgotten.

Robert entered the room quietly, his coffee in hand, his face showing both pride and steady curiosity. Though his own ancestry lacked the direct crowns Claire's held, the depth of his line continued to surprise him. Jeff gestured toward another document recently arrived, this one from Norman archives near Rouen. "And you," Jeff said with a small smile, "carry something unique as well. Your family's Gibb surname, shortened from Gilbert, originally appears in these records as minor Norman knights who crossed into Scotland during the reign of David I. Your ancestors weren't merely commoners who found employment at court — they arrived as part of the Norman migration that shaped early Scottish feudal society."

Robert studied the parchment, nodding thoughtfully. "So my family came north with the Normans?" "Exactly," Jeff confirmed. "Landholders, minor nobles by status, but significant enough to be recorded in the charters of the time. The Gibbs — or Gilberts — received small parcels of land under the Lords of Douglas, which positioned them near the royal courts as the Stuart dynasty grew." Robert exhaled slowly, taking in the fullness of what they were uncovering. "I never imagined any of this," he admitted. "I thought my name was little more than a footnote in royal service — a family lucky enough to serve at the palace doors. But now... there's a whole story I never knew existed."

Ben looked toward both Claire and Robert, his voice carrying that calm reverence that had grown so naturally between them. "You were never servants, Robert. You were part of the foundation that built what came after. Both of you." Jeff leaned back slightly, his voice now carrying the careful weight of experience. "The more you dig into these lines, the more you realize that nearly all European crowns are entwined. The houses of Plantagenet, Capet, Stuart, Árpád, Habsburg — they're not separate stories. They're one great story written across centuries. And your family, Isla, carries threads from every one of them."

The room held a quiet hum of awe, the charts on the table spreading like maps of forgotten kingdoms rediscovered. They had crossed borders of time, languages, and forgotten records — and yet, the work was still not finished. There was more to find. There always was. But they now stood upon ground few had ever dared approach. They had not simply found royalty. They had resurrected it.

The morning sun broke clean across the hedgerows, the sky a rich, endless blue that seemed almost determined to call them outside. Jeff stood in the doorway of the house, watching as Ben and Isla pored over yet another stack of estate ledgers spread across the dining table. Their heads bent in unison, eyes flicking between names, dates, and marriage contracts that had crossed more than seven centuries of royal blood. The room hummed with the same quiet intensity that had filled it every day for weeks.

But this morning, Jeff's patience had reached its limit. He cleared his throat, folding his arms with deliberate finality. "Alright, you two," he said, his voice warm but firm, "that's enough records for one morning."

Ben looked up, furrowing his brow in mild confusion. "But we just found three new marriages into the Anjou house. We're cross-checking them right now." Jeff shook his head, his expression a mixture of authority and humour. "And those marriages will still be there this afternoon. But right now — you need to go outside. Both of you."

Isla's eyes lifted from the scrolls, her face caught somewhere between surprise and reluctance. "But Jeff... we're so close to mapping that French branch." Jeff stepped forward, resting one hand on the back of Ben's chair. "Isla, you and Ben are nine years old. And I haven't seen either of you step foot outside this house for days. You're brilliant researchers, both of you, but even kings and queens went outside once in a while."

Ben exchanged a glance with Isla, both of them clearly torn between the weight of their work and Jeff's insistence. Finally, Ben sighed and stood up, stretching his arms as though his body needed to remember what movement felt like. "Alright, alright," he conceded, his voice lightening, "but if we're going to be forced outside, can we go to the cottage?" Jeff smiled knowingly, his eyes twinkling behind his glasses. "The cottage?" he echoed. "Well now... that's actually not a bad idea."

The cottage sat at the far end of the narrow walking path behind Ben's house — a little stone relic that had stood for generations, its thick thatched roof resting comfortably beneath a crown of ivy, as though nature herself had decided it needed additional decoration. The old building had once belonged to Ben's great-grandparents, its interior still housing boxes of forgotten family papers, dusty books, odd collections of maps, and the occasional peculiar object that no one quite remembered the origin of.

Isla's face brightened at the suggestion. "Do you think we might find something useful there?" Ben grinned. "I don't know. But at least we can pretend we're not working while we're there." Isla giggled as they gathered their jackets and stepped into the crisp morning air. The path to the cottage wound gently past Annemarie's well-kept flower beds, where spring's early blooms were already pushing through the dark earth, reaching for the sun. The air smelled of damp grass and wild honeysuckle, carrying the soft song of distant birds overhead.

As they reached the cottage, Ben fished the old brass key from his pocket. "You know," he said with mock seriousness, "there's probably still at least one family of spiders in here waiting to claim squatters' rights." Isla wrinkled her nose dramatically. "Well, if there's anything with more than eight legs, you're dealing with it." Ben chuckled as he turned the key in the lock, the door groaning slightly as it swung inward. The air inside was cool and faintly musty, but not unpleasant — more like the scent of old pages and quiet stories waiting to be heard. Sunlight streamed through the small diamond-paned windows, catching on floating specks of dust that danced lazily in the beams.

The interior was much as they had left it: two worn armchairs, an old writing desk, several wooden crates stacked in the far corner, and shelves lined with books that looked as though they might crumble if breathed on too heavily. But to Ben and Isla, it was perfect — a treasure trove of forgotten history. They moved instinctively, slipping into their usual rhythm. Isla opened one of the crates, carefully pulling out an old leather-bound journal, its spine cracked and worn. "Look at this," she whispered. "This belonged to your great-grandfather."

Ben peered over her shoulder, reading the careful handwriting. "It's written like travel notes. Look — he documented trips to Paris, Edinburgh, even Prague." "Prague?" Isla repeated, her eyes widening. "That's interesting. That might explain the Bohemian branches Jeff mentioned earlier." Ben nodded, his curiosity sharpening once again. Even as they stepped away from formal research, the discovery pulled them right back in. "Let's keep looking," he said, moving toward the desk.

Within minutes, they had unearthed several rolled maps, two more journals, and what appeared to be an envelope containing yellowed family correspondence. They read aloud old letters written in ornate script, some signed by names they only now recognized as minor nobles and distant cousins. At one point, as Isla brushed a stray cobweb from her arm, she glanced sideways at Ben and grinned. "You do realize, we're the worst rule-breakers ever. Jeff said we should take a break." Ben laughed, unable to hold back the amusement. "We are taking a break. We're outside. That was his condition."

Isla giggled again, her face lighting up. "Alright. Technically, you're right." Their laughter filled the small cottage like warm sunlight, wrapping around the old beams and curling beneath the rafters. Even in their youth, their joy was rooted in the work itself. To anyone else, it might have looked like two children simply playing pretend. But they both knew better. This was their world. This was where they belonged — not running in fields or climbing trees, but tracing the invisible lines of the past, breathing life back into long-forgotten names.

As the morning slipped gently toward afternoon, their small hands carefully turned ancient pages, each discovery drawing them deeper. The search never truly stopped. But within these walls, they could be both children and scholars — laughing, working, and walking their path together.

The morning path to the cottage wound gently beneath the trees, their branches stretching out above Ben and Isla like a long green tunnel of leaves. The birds sang lazily in the canopy, while soft beams of sunlight dappled across the dirt path. It should have been a perfectly calm and peaceful walk. And for a few minutes, it was — until Ben, without warning or ceremony, broke the silence with a loud, unmistakable release of gas that echoed with unexpected force through the still air.

Isla stopped dead in her tracks, her eyes wide, her jaw dropping as she stared at him with exaggerated horror. "Ben!" she exclaimed, her voice rising into half-laughter, half-disbelief. "Are you literally trying to tear the bark off the trees?" She waved her hand wildly in front of her face, as if trying to swat away the invisible toxic cloud that now hung like a curse around them.

Ben burst into laughter, doubling over as he tried to respond between chuckles. "Well—" he gasped, holding his stomach, "at least I know that part of me still works!" He straightened up, grinning mischievously. "I mean, honestly, you could clear the whole forest with that. What did I even eat this morning?" Isla narrowed her eyes, still fanning the air. "You ate the same thing I did!" she snapped, though she couldn't help but giggle. "Is that one of your stomachs doing that weird bubbling thing again?"

Before Ben could answer, Isla suddenly added to the chorus with a loud rip of her own, catching him completely off guard. His eyes widened in horror, his arms flailing in mock desperation as he staggered backwards. "Oh no—oh no!" he cried, gasping for air dramatically. "Isla, what are you trying to do? Kill me?!" The two of them collapsed into laughter, doubling over in the middle of the path, their faces flushed and their sides aching from the fit of giggles that refused to let them go.

It was, perhaps, the first time in weeks that they had allowed themselves to simply be children — ridiculous, laughing, and entirely themselves. And for once, the forest wasn't filled with names and dates, but with nothing more than the purest, silliest joy two nine-year-olds could possibly create.

CHAPTER 9: CHILDHOOD AND RESEARCH

The morning sunlight slipped through the diamond-paned windows of Ben's house, catching the edges of the old parchment that now sat unrolled across the table like a royal decree. For days, they had danced around this moment, edging closer to it with each name uncovered, each document verified. But now, the weight of it lay directly before them. The truth they had always suspected had been stitched together piece by piece, and finally, it stood whole. Isla wasn't simply descended from royalty. She carried a crown — not in ceremony, but in her very blood.

Jeff sat at the head of the table, his glasses resting halfway down his nose as he studied the final certified reports. The DNA analysis had been returned, triple-verified and cross-validated through multiple independent labs. The language was careful but clear, carrying the formal tone of genetic science while delivering a verdict that no parchment scroll had ever spoken with such certainty. Claire Margaret Stuart's line — Isla's maternal bloodline — traced directly through the Stuart dynasty, into the House of Bruce, and further still into the roots of Scotland's earliest sovereigns.

Ben sat directly beside Isla, his hand wrapped gently around hers beneath the table, lending quiet strength without words. Isla's face held the weight of both awe and humility as she listened to Jeff's careful reading of the report. She had known her ancestry carried something rare, but hearing it spoken aloud, seeing the scientific confirmation laid bare before her, filled the moment with a stillness neither of them fully expected. She wasn't simply someone descended from a queen. She was, by DNA, an active continuation of the sovereign blood itself.

Jeff's voice remained steady, reverent but clinical. "The mitochondrial sequencing has fully confirmed what our genealogical tracing had already suggested," he said softly. "You are the direct female-line descendant of multiple crowned lines. The maternal genetic markers place you not only in the Stuart line, but connected to several royal houses that precede and converge into it. In every legal sense of hereditary genealogy, Isla, your bloodline is sovereign." He paused, allowing the words to settle with their full weight. "You are, quite literally, Queen Isla — by DNA, by law, and by legacy."

Isla's breath caught slightly, her chest rising as she took in the truth of it. "Queen Isla," she whispered, more to herself than to anyone else. The title sounded strange on her lips, not because it felt false, but because it felt too ancient to wear casually. She had not earned it through conquest or inheritance of titles on parchment; she had inherited it through every breath of her ancestors who had carried it before her. She was not a queen in the sense of courts and crowns. She was a queen because the blood in her veins demanded no permission to be what it already was.

Ben turned to face her fully, his voice soft but certain. "It was always there, Isla," he said. "We didn't create it. We just found it." His hand tightened gently around hers. "And it belongs to you — not because of who the world says you are, but because of who you've always been."

Claire and Robert stood quietly nearby, their faces filled with the complex mix of parental pride and quiet astonishment. For years, they had raised Isla knowing she carried something unique, though never fully understanding the depth of that uniqueness. Now, standing within arm's reach of the living documents and verified results, there was no longer any doubt. Their daughter was not simply the child of a proud name. She was the living heir of a bloodline whose roots stretched back through centuries of sovereign rulers.

Jeff closed the folder gently, his eyes lifting to meet Isla's. "Titles aren't always worn as crowns, Isla," he said. "But this one belongs to you regardless of whether the world recognizes it. What you carry is older than the nations that came after. This is not about vanity. This is about truth."

The room settled into a still hush, not of awkwardness, but of reverence. The children, still only nine years old, sat within a space very few adults could ever stand — holding in their hands the truth of living history, not imagined, not pretended, but proven. And while Isla would carry the title in name, Ben knew — as did Jeff — that the crown had already made room for both of them long ago.

The afternoon light poured gently through the windows of the cottage, casting warm ribbons of gold across the worn wooden floor. Stacks of books surrounded Ben and Isla like small towers, their fortress of knowledge rising as the research carried on. In front of them lay the latest treasure: the thick, leather-bound volume detailing the Pattenden family name — an ancestral line that Ben's father had once traced back to lands far across the English countryside. For hours now, the two of them had combed through the pages, cross-referencing names, jotting down notes, and building new branches into the web of their expanding family trees.

And yet, no matter how serious the work, the innocence of nine-year-olds refused to stay completely quiet. As Ben leaned over to grab a separate parchment, a faint gurgle echoed from his stomach. Isla paused, raising one eyebrow suspiciously as she glanced sideways at him. "Is that your stomach making that weird noise again, or are you about to destroy the oxygen in this room?" she asked, her voice barely holding back laughter.

Ben grinned mischievously, dramatically placing a hand over his belly. "Oh, it's definitely coming," he warned. "Prepare yourself for the Royal Wind of Scotland." Before Isla could even retaliate, Ben let loose a loud burst of gas that reverberated against the wooden chair beneath him, its echo bouncing off the old stone walls like some ancient trumpet announcing war. Isla burst into laughter, nearly dropping her pencil as she swatted the air in front of her face.

"Ben! You're trying to fumigate the cottage!" she squealed, struggling to catch her breath between the fits of giggles. "At this rate, we're not going to find ancestors — we're going to resurrect them!" Ben doubled over in laughter, barely able to stay upright. "Well," he managed between gasps, "at least if they show up, they'll know who's responsible for clearing out the place."

Not to be outdone, Isla shifted slightly on her cushion, narrowed her eyes with mock determination, and added her own contribution to the growing cloud of mischief. The sound was short but sharp, perfectly timed. Ben's eyes widened dramatically, his mouth dropping open as though she had just committed high treason.

"Oh no—oh no!" he cried, flailing his arms in exaggerated panic. "What are you trying to do to me, Isla? That was worse than mine!" Isla could barely breathe for laughing, falling onto her side and clutching her stomach. "Payback, Ben! Royal payback!" she managed to squeak through the hysterics. "We are the King and Queen of Stink!" Their laughter echoed through the cottage, swirling up into the exposed beams as the old walls absorbed their joy. Even the cottage itself seemed to hum along with their innocent chaos, as though it had waited generations to hear such carefree voices filling its rooms once again.

But as the day stretched lazily forward, their giggles eventually softened. The work called them back once more. They leaned into the Pattenden volume, tracing names that wrapped through Kent and into distant corners of Europe, their fingers carefully following each line as they filled the next pages of their charts. The ancient ink told stories of knights, of merchants, of lost lands, and quiet marriages forgotten by the world but now awakened beneath their hands.

The light outside slowly dimmed as the evening deepened into night, and yet neither of them moved. Their world had grown small and safe within the circle of warm lamp glow, the rest of the house fading quietly into the background. Even Jeff and Annemarie had long since let them be, knowing well enough by now that Ben and Isla's best work often unfolded like this — together, surrounded by old books, in the quiet hum of shared discovery.

At some point, as the clock hands crept toward midnight, the room fell silent. Isla's head gently rested against Ben's shoulder, her breathing soft and steady. Ben, too, had given into the pull of sleep, his arm loosely draped around the large Pattenden book still open across their laps. The faint scent of old paper and warm lamplight filled the room as their small forms curled together, side by side, protected by the ancient names they had resurrected. And there, beneath the silent watch of their ancestors, Ben and Isla slept — not as researchers or royal descendants — but simply as two nine-year-old soulmates wrapped safely in the world they had built together.

The first rays of morning sun slipped through the small cottage windows, casting soft beams of golden light across the old wooden floorboards. Dust motes danced lazily in the still air, floating like tiny stars within the sunlit shafts. The cottage itself seemed to sigh gently, stretching awake along with its young occupants. The light reached their faces as they lay nestled together on the floor, their bodies curled against each other in peaceful, well-earned sleep. Neither stirred with a jolt; instead, they woke slowly, as if rising from the gentlest of dreams.

Ben's eyes opened first, blinking softly as his vision adjusted to the warm glow. Without moving, he turned his head slightly to see Isla lying beside him, her head resting lightly on his shoulder, her breathing steady and calm. The sight made his heart swell with a quiet joy that was both familiar and new. She stirred soon after, her lashes fluttering like tiny wings as her gaze found his. Their eyes locked, neither needing to speak, their smiles forming naturally like the rising of the sun itself.

There was something magnetic in that moment — not forced, not rehearsed, but as if some invisible thread had always tied them together. Ben could feel it deep inside, like two compass needles always pointing towards one another. Isla's small hand reached forward, closing the short space between them as she leaned in slowly, her eyes never leaving his. The kiss that followed was unhurried, tender, a soft brush of lips that carried all the weight of their bond. They didn't need to say the words; they were written in every glance, every breath.

As they parted gently, Isla's arms wrapped around him, pulling him close into a warm embrace that belonged less to children and more to something timeless. It was a hug meant for teddy bears — full, safe, and enduring. Ben returned the squeeze with the same devotion, his chin resting lightly atop her head. The world beyond the cottage was distant, irrelevant for these few sacred moments. Eventually, Ben sat up with a slow stretch, his arms reaching above his head as he yawned. "Bladder chatter," he muttered with a grin, glancing toward Isla, who was now sitting up beside him.

Isla tilted her head, giggling. "Tell me about it," she replied, rubbing her eyes. Ben chuckled, glancing toward the far corner where the small washroom sat behind the closed door. "Well," he began, "you go first, and I'll go after. I don't like rushing these things. And besides, I always sit down when I go." Isla laughed. "You sit down? Always?" He nodded, keeping his tone mock-serious. "Of course. I hate that sprinkled stuff — drives me cuckoo. It's nasty. I refuse to deal with it." Her giggles turned into full laughter. "You're serious? That's why I go into the other room when I'm home. The bathroom gets too busy, and I don't like waiting." Ben raised an eyebrow in playful surprise. "Oh, you've got a separate bathroom?"

"Yup," Isla nodded, still laughing. "That's my little escape." Ben snorted, unable to resist the chance to tease. "Well, if I had to, I'd just go outside and fertilize the garden." They both erupted into laughter again, their playful nonsense echoing softly within the old walls of the cottage. For a brief moment, the gravity of ancestry, crowns, and royal lineage faded away, replaced by the simple joy of their age — two soulmates, wrapped in both love and silliness.

As their laughter settled, Ben stood up and offered Isla his hand. She took it with a grateful smile as they brushed themselves off and began gathering their things. The morning air outside was crisp, cool against their cheeks as they stepped back onto the path leading toward home. The smell of freshly cut grass and distant chimney smoke filled the air, hinting that breakfast was not far away. "You know," Ben said as they walked, his voice light but thoughtful, "I could really use a coffee right about now." Isla giggled and nudged him gently with her shoulder. "Me too. Let's go see if we can grab one. I bet breakfast is waiting."

As they strolled toward the house, the comfort of routine wrapped around them like a familiar blanket. The promise of warm food and the rich smell of coffee greeted them as Annemarie's kitchen came into view. Yet beneath it all, Ben couldn't help but feel it — that strong pull inside his chest. It wasn't just toward Isla, though that was always there. It was toward the rest of the story still waiting for them, buried within the pages of the Pattenden family and beyond. Something inside whispered that there was still so much more to discover.

The morning air had settled warmly around them as Ben and Isla made their way back into the cottage after breakfast. Their bellies now full and their hearts light from the earlier laughter, they returned to the table where the ancestral book The Lords of Marden lay open, waiting. The old volume almost seemed to hum with a silent life of its own, its pages worn but dignified, like an elder inviting them back into the stories it held. As they sat side by side once more, the weight of their task returned—not as a burden, but as a calling neither of them could resist.

Ben gently turned the pages, scanning each name, each recorded birth and marriage, as the family's ancient threads revealed themselves one by one. "There it is again," he whispered, his finger resting firmly on the name Pattenden. "Look here, Isla—Great Pattenden and Little Pattenden. That's where it all began." The dates next to the entries whispered across six centuries, and behind them, thousands of years murmured still deeper in his bones. His heart tightened slightly as the realisation struck him again—these places, once full of life, were now gone. Not simply forgotten, but erased by time, swallowed by shifting lands and changing maps.

Isla leaned closer, her hair brushing softly against Ben's shoulder. She read the entries silently, her eyes widening as the names unfolded like an ancient chant. "It really was Marden," she said softly. "The land itself gave your family its name. And now it's all... just vanished. No more fields. No more hamlets. Just gone." Ben's jaw tightened, not in confusion but in frustration. His breath deepened as he struggled with the thought. "It's not right," he muttered. "Those lands were in my family for hundreds of years. Lords of the Manor. Land stewards. Protectors of the soil. And now, it's like none of it ever existed. As if all that work, all those lives, never mattered."

Isla placed her hand gently over his, her voice steady but filled with a quiet wisdom beyond her years. "But it did matter, Ben. It still matters. The fields may be gone, but their names live in you. In your blood. In this book." She pointed to the passages that traced his ancestors as lords, landowners, and governors, their authority firmly rooted in medieval Kent's complex feudal world. "You're carrying it forward, even if the land doesn't carry their names anymore."

Ben nodded slowly, his chest calming under her words. "The name Pattenden," he whispered, as if speaking directly to the ghosts of his ancestors. "It's older than the villages. It goes back even before the Great and Little Pattendens were first mapped. Thousands of years, Isla. Not just hundreds." Isla's face lit up as she traced another familiar thread through the family branches.

"And here... look at this." She paused, tapping a line that included the Gibb surname interwoven among the Pattenden records. "That's my family, too. The Gibbs connected here through the Pattendens. My ancestors merged into yours long before we were ever born."

Ben looked up, a flicker of shared excitement in his eyes. "So even before we found each other, Isla—our families were already together. Bound by land, by marriage, by blood." He smiled softly, marvelling at how fate had quietly pulled their threads tighter with every discovery. She leaned into him slightly, resting her head against his arm, her eyes still scanning the page. "It's kind of beautiful, you know?" she whispered. "It's like our souls have always known where they belonged."

Ben swallowed softly, his voice steady but filled with reverence. "We were meant to find each other. Not just as kids, not just as friends—but because our blood remembers." His gaze returned to the pages, following the ancient ink as though it were breathing beneath his fingertips. "And now we remember too." The room held a gentle silence, the pages before them glowing beneath the morning light. The names of lords and manors whispered once more, not as forgotten ghosts, but as honoured ancestors whose legacy would now live forward in these two children — bound not just by discovery, but by destiny itself.

The soft creak of the cottage door echoed behind them as Ben and Isla stepped out into the waiting arms of the day. The sky above stretched wide and cloudless, its perfect blue wrapping the world like a giant dome. The morning's discoveries still pulsed inside them, but for once, they both allowed themselves to simply stand beneath the sun, breathing in the fresh air. The warmth touched their cheeks, and the scent of spring grass hung thick and sweet in the air. The land felt alive, as though it too had been listening to their search, now gently nudging them toward a different rhythm for the moment.

Ben glanced sideways at Isla, his voice thoughtful but light. "You know," he said, "Jeff's been right this whole time." Isla looked up at him, her expression curious. "About what?" Ben smiled faintly. "About needing to step away sometimes. We get so pulled into the books, the charts, the names... we forget there's a world outside these pages. We blink, and the whole day's already disappeared."

Isla nodded slowly, her gaze sweeping across the open field before them. "It's true. We sit down in the morning, start digging through one name after another, and before we know it, the sun's already going down." She kicked a small pebble with her shoe, watching it skip along the dirt path. "I didn't even realise yesterday was almost gone until I looked up and saw the stars."

Ben chuckled quietly, his eyes narrowing slightly in reflection. "We've probably lived half our lives inside those books by now. And we're only nine." Isla laughed, her voice soft and melodic. "We really are strange kids, aren't we?" Ben shrugged, his grin widening. "Maybe. But I wouldn't trade it for anything."

They wandered slowly down the familiar path, letting their feet move without agenda. The wind whispered gently through the tall grasses, bending them in slow waves like green ocean tides rolling across the countryside. Small birds darted above them, their chirps adding a playful melody to the afternoon stillness. For the first time in days, neither of them spoke about bloodlines, crowns, or lost estates. Instead, they simply existed — two friends, two soulmates, walking beneath the sky, content to let the world breathe around them.

The minutes slipped by unnoticed. The sun shifted, casting longer shadows across the fields. Afternoon gave its quiet warnings that evening was never far behind. Yet neither Ben nor Isla felt rushed. There was a peace in this pause—a kind of unspoken agreement that they would always return to the work, but today, for this little while, the sun and the earth would have its turn.

Eventually, Ben glanced upward, watching the slow arc of the sun's descent. "You know," he said, his voice warm, "we blink once more and the afternoon will be gone again." Isla sighed softly, leaning gently against him. "And then the night will fold around us like it always does." "And sleep will catch us again," Ben finished, smiling as he slipped his arm around her shoulder.

The two of them stood there for a while longer, wrapped in the stillness, allowing the gentle pull of time to carry them forward. Tomorrow, the books would wait for them again, the names would call, and the lost voices of history would whisper once more. But for now, they were simply Ben and Isla — two children, side by side, learning not just who they were, but how to live within what they carried.

The afternoon softened as the sun dipped gently lower, casting a golden hue across the edges of the trees. A light breeze whispered through the leaves, rustling them like quiet applause for the work Ben and Isla had done. Yet, for once, there were no books in their hands, no charts spread across the table, no scrolls or papers scattered at their feet. Today, they had decided to step back—not from the journey itself, but from the weight of the constant searching. They needed space to breathe, to simply exist, to let everything they had learned settle into their hearts without the pressure of the next discovery waiting just around the corner.

The old wooden swings in the back garden swayed gently as they sat side by side, their legs dangling freely, their toes brushing across the grass below. The chains creaked softly with each sway, but neither of them spoke at first. The silence between them wasn't empty; it was full — full of the names, the places, the histories they now carried within them. For two nine-year-olds, they had uncovered far more than most people did in a lifetime. Yet, as they both knew deep down, this was never only about history. This was about them.

Ben exhaled softly, his eyes scanning the wide sky above them. "You know," he said finally, his voice gentle, "when I think about everything we've found, I still can't believe how deep the Pattenden line runs. Lords of Marden. The old farmlands. Even the old Harvick branch. And then... Horváth. That name's still there too, hiding in the old records. It's like all of it lives inside me, reaching back so far I can't even see the end of it.

Isla smiled, her hand slipping naturally into his as she swung gently beside him. "And for me, it's the Gibbs," she said. "The Stuarts. My mother's side, your father's side. All these names tied together like one giant family long before we ever met." She turned her head toward him, her eyes shimmering in the afternoon light. "But through it all, Ben... no matter how many names we find, the most important thing is still the same." Ben smiled softly, his eyes locking with hers. "Us."

Isla nodded, squeezing his hand. "Us." She breathed in deeply, her voice growing more thoughtful. "And you know, one day... when we're older, when we get married and have kids of our own, I wonder what they'll think of all this. What they'll say about everything we found."

Ben chuckled, glancing down at their joined hands. "Honestly?" he said, his voice filled with a warmth only she could bring out of him. "They'll probably think we're crazy. Spending hours digging through old books, hunting down names most people forgot existed. But at the same time... I think they'll understand why we did it. Because one day, they'll want to know too."

Isla's heart swelled as she listened, the joy inside her overflowing in a way that words could never fully capture. She loved him—not with the fleeting sweetness of childhood crushes, but with a depth that anchored itself in her very soul. It was the kind of love that didn't need grand speeches or dramatic declarations. It lived in every quiet moment, every gentle glance, every small hand squeeze that said without words: I'm yours.

Ben couldn't take his eyes off her. Each time he looked at Isla, he found himself falling in love with her all over again. And though the words I love you often felt too small to contain what he carried inside him, he spoke them anyway. "I love you, Isla," he whispered, his voice thick with affection.

"I love you too, Ben," she answered, her voice soft but certain. She leaned forward slightly, closing the small space between them. Their lips met in a slow, gentle kiss — unhurried, steady, pure. As they pulled back, Ben wrapped his arms around her, pulling her close into a warm embrace that felt like home.

The swing creaked gently beneath them, swaying softly as they sat wrapped together in each other's arms. There was no need for anyone else to understand. Their parents knew. Their families approved. This was simply who they were — soulmates from the start, tethered by blood, history, and something far older that neither science nor words could fully explain.

The day was still theirs, and the studying could wait. The books would call again soon enough, perhaps later this evening when the sun slipped behind the horizon. But for now, the world could wait. The names would still be there tomorrow, and the search would continue. But they had learned one thing that even the thickest books could not teach them: sometimes, even in the greatest of journeys, it was perfectly right to pause, to hold each other, and to simply be.

The evening settled gently around the house, wrapping it in the kind of stillness that made every soft sound seem amplified. The lamps inside the cottage burned with a warm glow, their light flickering against the polished wood of the old study table. The sun had given way to twilight now, casting deep indigo shades across the sky outside. And as planned, Ben and Isla returned to their work — not out of obligation, but because the pull of the mystery was simply too strong to resist for long.

The books lay open where they had left them earlier, as though waiting patiently for their return. The air still carried the faint scent of the old paper and binding glue, a familiar perfume that had become as much a part of their world as the names they chased. This time, though, they approached the table with a different rhythm. The earlier break had eased their minds, allowing them to breathe. Now they returned not with exhaustion, but with renewed curiosity — and that sacred eagerness that had always driven them forward.

Ben leaned in first, carefully turning the next page of The Lords of Marden. His eyes narrowed as he scanned the list of names carefully inscribed in elegant ink. "Alright," he said softly, his voice carrying the quiet weight of focus, "this section deals with the land transfers after the consolidation of Great Pattenden. Look here — you can see how the land started fragmenting once the main house lost its hold."

Isla slid her chair closer, her eyes locking onto the lines as she read alongside him. "Some of these branches didn't vanish completely though," she observed. "Look — there are still some cousins who held onto portions of land well into the sixteenth century. Even after the fields were sold off, parts of the family stayed nearby."

Ben nodded slowly. "And see here — the Harvick branch merges with Pattenden again right around that time. That's the same line I've been following on my father's side." His voice grew softer as his finger traced the looping names across the page. "It's like these families kept circling back into one another. Not just once, but multiple times."

Isla studied the chart carefully, her thoughts moving deeper as she followed his line of thinking. "And with the Gibbs connected to Pattenden as well, that means... Ben, our families weren't just connected once. They've been crossing paths for centuries." She paused, her voice rich with awe. "We weren't some random meeting. We were bound long before we even existed."

Ben looked at her, his eyes carrying that familiar glimmer of knowing. "That's what I've always felt, Isla," he whispered. "Even before we knew the names. Like we were drawn to each other, pulled together by something bigger than us." His voice softened further, as though speaking directly to the ancient blood flowing in both of them. "Like threads finally finding their way back."

The room held the stillness of reverence as the two of them continued to turn pages, each discovery layering on top of the last. Names they once thought were isolated now wove themselves into a vast, intricate web that reached far beyond the borders of Kent. Connections to French estates, brief notations of Scottish alliances, and hints of even older Continental lines emerged with every turn, whispering of stories yet uncovered.

Isla rested her chin lightly against her hand as she stared at the growing chart they had built together. "You know," she said softly, her voice steady but distant, "the names tell us where we've been. But the stories... they're still waiting for us to tell them." Ben nodded, his hand gently brushing across hers. "We'll tell them," he promised. "Every single one."

Outside, the crickets had begun their nightly chorus, their quiet song filling the air like a background melody to the soft rustle of paper inside the glowing room. The evening belonged to them now — as did the generations they carried forward. And though the night would eventually pull them back into sleep, for now, the work continued. The names would not be lost again.

The evening rolled in like an old friend, draping the cottage in its familiar calm. The steady rhythm of flipping pages slowed, not because the work was finished, but because their bodies could feel the day pulling softly at their eyes. The golden lamplight cast a warm glow across the scattered books and open scrolls that lay before them. The names, the charts, the handwritten notes — all stood waiting for further attention. But for now, Ben and Isla both knew that sleep would not wait much longer. They had reached that tender hour where the mind wished to press on, but the body whispered otherwise.

Ben glanced over at Isla, his voice tender, filled with the same gentle reverence he carried every time his eyes found hers. "My Queen," he whispered softly, as if the words themselves deserved to be spoken only under the breath of night.

Isla smiled, her cheeks warming under his gaze. "My King," she replied in kind, her voice sweet and certain. "You're mine, and I am yours — always. For eternity, Ben. I will never give you up." Her words carried no theatrics, no childish playfulness. They were simple, sincere, and rooted in the sacred thread that bound their hearts.

Ben felt his chest swell again with that quiet, familiar fullness — a love too deep for their years, yet too honest to ever deny. He leaned forward slowly, closing the small space between them, feeling the quiet magnetic pull that always seemed to draw them closer. Isla met him halfway, their eyes still locked as their lips finally touched. It was slow, unhurried, gentle — a kiss that needed no urgency, because neither feared losing the other. This was theirs, always had been, always would be.

The kiss lingered for a few peaceful moments before they both pulled back, smiling softly at one another. They knew full well that if they didn't take that moment now, sleep would claim them before they had the chance to share it. These little goodnight kisses had become their quiet tradition — not rushed, not routine, but sacred in their simplicity. It was the kind of closeness that only soulmates understood, a gift they never took for granted.

As they shifted slightly on the floor cushions, preparing to finally close the books for the night, Ben glanced toward Isla with a mischievous grin pulling at the corner of his mouth. Leaning close, he whispered softly into her ear, "You think we should gas Jeff out of the house tonight?"

Isla clamped her hand over her mouth to stifle a giggle, her eyes sparkling with playful wickedness. "Oh, Ben…" she whispered, her stomach already beginning to rumble in anticipation. "You too, huh?" Ben nodded, barely containing his own laughter. "Yep. I feel it coming. What do you think — kaboom?" Isla's grin widened as she bit her lip, nodding. "Oh yes. Kaboom."

With perfect timing — as if rehearsed by some unspoken comedy routine only they could perform — both of them let loose, their synchronised release echoing off the cottage walls. The sound alone sent them both into immediate fits of laughter, their bodies collapsing into one another as their hands grabbed at the waiting pillows, covering their faces while they shook with giggles. The room filled with their laughter, rich and unrestrained, filling every wooden beam with the unmistakable joy of two children being exactly who they were.

Poor Jeff, who had been quietly reviewing a few documents at the kitchen table, froze mid-sentence as the aroma reached him. Gasping dramatically, he bolted to the windows, flinging them open with exaggerated flair. "My god!" he choked, fanning the air desperately with both hands. "What on earth ate what… and what exactly died in the process?"

Ben and Isla were completely lost in hysterics now, their cheeks red from both the laughter and their shared mischief. As Jeff continued his theatrical gasping, both of them snuggled closer under the shared blanket, still chuckling as their breathing slowly returned to normal.

At last, the cottage fell quiet again. The ancient book was gently closed and placed to the side. Isla rested her head on Ben's chest, her small hands curled against his shirt, as his arm wrapped securely around her shoulders. The gentle rise and fall of his breathing lulled her into peace, while Ben gazed up at the wooden beams overhead, feeling her warmth pressed into him. No words were spoken. They didn't need any. The bond between them was stronger than language itself.

As sleep slowly claimed them both, Ben knew the morning would call them back to their books once again. The names, the bloodlines, the histories — all would wait patiently for them to return. But for now, wrapped together under the weight of love and laughter, this moment belonged only to them.

The morning sun crept gently across the horizon, sending soft beams of golden light through the cottage windows. The warmth of dawn slowly chased away the last traces of night, filling the little room with a kind of quiet joy that only Ben and Isla seemed to understand. As always, the world outside stirred long before they did, but the comfort of each other's arms delayed their rise. Wrapped beneath the blanket, their bodies rested against one another in perfect stillness, their breathing synchronized, as if even in sleep their hearts refused to part.

Ben stirred first, blinking softly as his eyes adjusted to the light that now bathed Isla's peaceful face. She remained tucked against his chest, her hair spilling gently across his shoulder. His arm remained draped protectively around her, refusing to let go just yet. After a moment, Isla's eyes fluttered open, her sleepy gaze lifting directly into his. They smiled — not rushed, not forced, but in that warm, silent exchange that spoke far louder than any words could ever manage.

Without hesitation, Ben leaned forward, closing the short distance between them. Their lips met in a slow, tender kiss that lingered softly, as though the entire morning waited patiently for them to finish. The kiss was not ritual — it was belonging. It was how they reminded each other, daily, that nothing in the world was more certain than the love they carried. As they parted, Isla smiled again, her cheeks still warm from the softness of it, and curled closer into his chest for one final embrace.

Only after their morning kiss came the next part of their rhythm. Ben shifted gently, propping himself up and offering Isla his hand. They moved together with quiet coordination, knowing exactly what came next: coffee. It was always coffee after the morning kiss, as though their hearts needed that first before their minds were ready for the weight of research again. They wandered toward the kitchen hand-in-hand, greeted by the familiar, rich aroma already filling the house.

Annemarie, always anticipating their arrival, stood at the counter pouring two perfectly prepared cups. She glanced over her shoulder with a smile, saying nothing, for she had long since accepted their sacred little routine. The mugs were set upon the table, their steam rising lazily into the morning air. Ben and Isla slipped into their seats, their hands still faintly brushing against one another as they sipped from their cups in comfortable silence.

Only after coffee, after those few quiet minutes of warmth, did they rise from the table and return to the waiting books. The volumes lay open as they had left them the night before, the family charts stretching outward like branches still waiting to be explored. The Lords of Marden sat in its place of honour, its worn spine almost humming as if the book itself had grown eager for their return. The day's work could now begin — but only after love, after hugs, after coffee. That was their order. That was their world.

Ben opened the book with care, glancing sideways at Isla. "Alright," he said softly, his voice filled with that familiar mixture of excitement and reverence, "let's see where the blood wants to take us today." Isla nodded, her eyes sparkling. "Let's find what's been waiting for us." And with that, the search resumed — steady, sacred, and always side by side.

The morning research had started just as smoothly as it always did. After their morning kiss, warm hugs, and carefully prepared coffee, Ben and Isla had buried themselves once more into the thick volumes scattered across the table. The old parchment pages of The Lords of Marden rustled softly beneath their fingertips, while fresh printouts and maps sat in organized stacks waiting to be cross-referenced. Their minds buzzed with fresh energy, hungry for names, places, and timelines. But in their eagerness to return to the hunt for their ancestors, they had both neglected one small, but growing, reality.

The first sign came as a slight shifting in Ben's seat — an unconscious fidget as he leaned forward, then back again, pressing his legs tighter together beneath the table. A faint grimace crept across his face, though he tried to keep his focus on the page. Isla, sitting beside him, was already making similar adjustments, shifting her weight from side to side in an almost identical rhythm. Neither wanted to be the first to speak it aloud, but their faces were starting to betray them.

Finally, Ben sighed with quiet frustration, his voice dropping into a half-whispered grumble. "Oh gosh," he muttered under his breath, "bladder shudder." Isla burst into a giggle, though her discomfort was no less real. "Join the club," she said, her voice light but filled with shared sympathy. "This is getting on my nerves too." Ben glanced toward the hallway, then back at her. "Ladies first," he offered with a faint grin.

They both stood, moving quickly but carefully down the hallway, their small footsteps padded softly against the floorboards. Isla slipped into the bathroom first, closing the door gently behind her. Ben waited patiently just outside, arms folded, shifting slightly as he tried to distract himself by counting the knots in the wooden panels on the wall. After a few minutes, Isla emerged, smiling in relief as she passed him with a playful look.

"Your turn," she whispered, brushing his arm as she moved back toward the table. Ben wasted no time, disappearing into the bathroom with a small sigh of relief echoing behind him. By the time he returned, Isla was already seated again, her hands lightly tapping the open pages as though nothing had interrupted their routine. Without missing a beat, they both slipped seamlessly back into their research, their brief detour already forgotten.

The hours passed with their familiar rhythm. Names were traced, dates compared, and family trees expanded. The Pattenden, Harvick, and Gibb lines continued to reveal their deep roots, and each small discovery added yet another layer to the intricate web they were carefully piecing together. Yet, as noon approached, the sunlight pouring through the windows grew stronger, casting long beams of gold across the old wooden floors.

Without needing to discuss it, they both glanced toward the door. Ben closed the book gently and pushed back from the table, while Isla stood and stretched her arms high above her head. The house had grown warm, and the call of fresh air was impossible to resist. Together, they stepped outside into the early afternoon sun, greeted by the soft breeze that carried the sweet scent of grass and distant flowers.

The swings, as always, waited for them. They walked hand-in-hand toward the familiar spot, their steps unhurried. The chains creaked gently as they settled into the seats, swinging lazily beneath the open sky. Neither spoke at first. They didn't need to. The silence between them was full — filled with unspoken understanding, comfort, and the simple joy of being together.

They sat like that for some time, the gentle back-and-forth of the swings rocking them into a peaceful rhythm. The sunlight danced across their faces, warming their skin as the breeze played with Isla's hair, sending soft strands across Ben's shoulder. He reached out without thinking, tucking a loose strand behind her ear, his hand lingering briefly on her cheek. Isla smiled, leaning slightly into his touch, her eyes closing for just a moment as they savoured the quiet. It was not always about the research. It was not always about the names and dates. Sometimes, it was simply about being Ben and Isla — two soulmates who had found each other long before they ever opened the first book.

While Ben and Isla swayed gently on the swings outside, lost in one another's presence beneath the soft embrace of the afternoon sun, inside the house a quiet conversation was unfolding. Jeff sat at the kitchen table across from Robert and Claire, each of them holding warm mugs of coffee. The air was calm, but the weight of what they were discussing was far from casual. They had watched these two children grow into something few ever witnessed — not mere companionship, but the rare, unshakable binding of souls. It was something older than tradition, something far deeper than childhood affection. It was destiny.

Jeff leaned forward slightly, his voice soft but firm. "You know," he began, "I don't just believe it anymore. I know it. Those two were made for each other. You've seen it. You've felt it long before either of them even knew how much they belonged together." Robert nodded slowly, his hand resting gently on Claire's. "We've always known," he agreed. "Long before they understood what they carried inside them. It's not just love—it's something far older, far stronger." Claire's eyes glistened softly as she added, "They are soulmates, Jeff. What they have isn't fleeting. It's permanent. We've seen it growing for years now, and it's only grown stronger. They were never children simply playing house. They carry each other."

Jeff's voice lowered, his eyes steady. "Then let's honour it properly." He paused, drawing a small envelope from his jacket pocket. "I had this prepared. A jeweller I know crafted them — promise rings. Not engagement rings, not yet. But something sacred. A symbol of their bond, a recognition that even at nine years old, they understand something most adults never will." He slid the envelope across the table toward Robert and Claire. "Their names, their birthstones, engraved together. One for Ben. One for Isla."

Robert took the envelope with reverence, carefully opening it to reveal the two small velvet boxes inside. The first was deep blue; the second a soft red. Inside each lay a delicately crafted gold band. At the centre of Isla's ring sat a radiant peridot, her birthstone, surrounded by a halo of small accent stones reflecting soft hues of white and rose. Ben's ring mirrored hers, with his own peridot in the centre, designed with the same precision and care. Inside each band, engraved with precision, were the words: Ben and Isla — For Eternity, A Love Everlasting.

Claire's breath caught softly as she traced her finger along the inscription. "It's perfect," she whispered. "It says exactly what their hearts already know." Robert nodded once more, his voice steady. "Let's give it to them tonight, before evening falls." And so, before the sun dipped fully beneath the horizon, Jeff and Isla's parents visited the jeweller, finalizing the purchase and returning home with the two small boxes in hand. The sacred gift was prepared. The moment had come.

When Ben and Isla returned from their walk, stepping quietly into the house with hands still softly clasped together, they were met with an unexpected sight. Upon the kitchen table sat two boxes — one deep blue, one warm red — each with a small handwritten note resting beside it. Their names were written in careful cursive: For Ben, and For Isla.

Ben's eyes lifted to meet Jeff's, who sat watching them with a knowing smile. Isla glanced toward her parents, seeing the same gentle encouragement reflected in their faces. There was no rush, no ceremony, only the quiet reverence that wrapped the entire moment. Ben reached for his box while Isla opened hers beside him. The sight of the rings pulled their breath into a quiet stillness. Their eyes met once again — no words, only the soft shimmering of shared understanding passing between them. Jeff cleared his throat gently and began to read from the note he had written to Ben.

My son,
There is no greater honour for a father than to witness his child find the one they were always meant to walk beside. You have carried responsibility, wisdom, and love far beyond your years, but none of it was forced upon you — you chose it. Isla is not simply your friend; she is your heart's match, written into your very blood. This ring is not a toy. It is not a symbol of play. It is a mark of devotion, one that recognizes the sacred bond you share. Wear it knowing you have found what many search for and never receive. Protect her. Honour her. And never forget what you carry together.
— **Dad**

As Jeff finished, Isla's hands trembled gently while Claire read softly from her own note to Isla.

Our beloved daughter,
From the first moment you looked at Ben, we saw something in your eyes that we could never explain — a knowing, a deep peace, as though your soul had found its home. You are not too young to understand what you carry, because your hearts already knew before you could even name it. This promise ring is not about your age. It is about your truth. This is your companion. This is your protector. This is the one who sees you fully and loves you without condition. Wear this ring knowing that you belong to each other, not because of any rule, but because of a bond written before you were born. We bless this promise with full hearts and full faith.
— **Mum and Dad**

Isla's eyes filled as she pressed the letter softly to her chest, her tears slipping freely down her cheeks. Ben reached for her hand, his own eyes shimmering as he whispered, "It's alright. We're here. We've always been here." In that sacred moment, the time had come for them to speak the promises they had long carried in their hearts.

Ben took Isla's hand fully in his own, his voice steady, though his throat tightened. "Isla," he said softly, "from the moment we first met, I knew my heart was already yours. I don't need anyone else. I never will. You are my home, my breath, my future. I promise you this — I will stand by your side for all my life. No matter what happens, I belong to you and only you. My love will never leave you, not in this life, nor any life that may follow. This is my vow, not as a boy, but as the one who was born to walk beside you."

Isla sobbed softly, but her voice rose steady and clear as she returned his vow. "Ben, I have loved you since before I even understood what love was. Every time I see you, my heart fills all over again. I am yours. And you are mine. Nothing will take that away. Not distance, not time, not even death itself. If the world allowed it, I would marry you this very day, but until that day comes, this promise is my heart's vow: I will wait for you, stand with you, and love you, now and forever." They slid the rings gently onto each other's fingers, sealing the promises not with grand spectacle, but with a love too real for words. And in the quiet that followed, they leaned into one another once again — a kiss soft, sacred, eternal.

That evening carried a stillness unlike any other. Ben and Isla sat side by side on the floor, their backs gently resting against the edge of the couch, their hands clasped together as though afraid to let go, even for a moment. The promise rings they now wore shimmered faintly beneath the soft lamplight, catching every flicker like tiny beacons of the vows they had spoken only hours earlier. Their hearts still pulsed with the fullness of what had happened, trying to absorb it all. What had once felt like a dream had now become their living truth. This was not some fleeting childhood fantasy, not some temporary moment lost to time. This was real. Permanent. Sacred.

As Ben looked over at Isla, his breath caught briefly in his chest. She was radiant even in the simplicity of the evening — her eyes reflecting both awe and deep peace. He could see the same swirling emotions in her that stirred within himself: amazement, humility, gratitude, and a kind of reverence that words could never fully capture. "Hard to believe, isn't it?" he finally whispered, his voice quiet as though speaking too loudly might disturb the moment.

Isla nodded, her head leaning gently against his shoulder. "It is," she whispered back. "But at the same time, I feel like I've always known. Like we've always belonged here. Not just today — but always." She tightened her fingers around his hand. "It's not just a moment, Ben. It's a lifetime. Our lifetime." Ben closed his eyes for a brief moment, letting her words settle into him like a prayer. "Even as King and Queen by blood," he murmured, "what we have... it's stronger than titles. Stronger than any crown." His voice thickened slightly. "It's forever."

The house was quiet except for the soft ticking of the clock on the far wall. But beyond the house, word was already spreading. Jeff, Annemarie, Robert, and Claire had spoken with the neighbours earlier that evening, sharing not just the news but the video that Annemarie had quietly recorded — not for spectacle, but as living proof that what Ben and Isla shared was real, serious, and blessed. It was not childish make-believe. It was love in its truest form, witnessed and protected.

Back in the living room, Ben glanced at the clock. Midnight was near. They had long since stopped reading for the night, the books temporarily forgotten as they simply sat together, hearts still full. But as the hours pressed onward, the familiar discomfort of biology made itself known. Ben grimaced, shifting slightly in his seat. "Oh gosh," he groaned softly, his tone half-annoyed, half-amused, "bladder chatter."

Isla giggled, her voice light with understanding. "Unfortunately, sweetheart," she said with a small shake of her head, "they don't just go away. No pause button either." Ben chuckled, rubbing his forehead as though defeated by the reality of their little routine. "Yeah, no kidding. Ladies first." They both stood, moving down the hall in their now well-rehearsed ritual. Isla slipped inside first, Ben waiting patiently outside. Once finished, they swapped places, each returning with quiet grins that betrayed the humour of how routine even these moments had become.

With nature's demands behind them, Ben and Isla returned to the living room once more, their bodies relaxing as they slipped beneath the large sleeping blanket spread out across the floor. Their pillows sat side by side, perfectly aligned as always, like anchors holding their small sanctuary in place. The books remained closed for the night, waiting respectfully for morning to come before calling them back into the search.

Ben pulled Isla close, his arm wrapping securely around her as her head nestled against his chest. His breathing slowed into a quiet, steady rhythm as her fingers traced small, soft circles on his shirt. Neither spoke. They didn't need to. The silence between them was sacred, filled with everything that words could never quite hold. Their promises had been made. Their hearts sealed.

Sleep took them gently, not with sudden collapse, but as a slow surrender into peace. And as the moonlight slipped through the windows, casting faint silver beams across their resting forms, they looked more like something ancient — two souls woven together across generations, resting inside the safety of a bond older than even their bloodlines.

Morning would return soon, and with it, their familiar rhythm. Sure enough, as the sun crept back into the sky, its soft glow gradually stirred them awake. Ben opened his eyes first, blinking at the morning light before glancing down to see Isla still tucked quietly against him. She stirred moments later, their eyes meeting in that same quiet smile they had shared every morning since the beginning.

Without fail, their morning hug came first — tight, warm, and full. Then the morning kiss — slow, gentle, as if greeting each other for the very first time. The ritual continued as Isla whispered, "Let's empty bladders first, shall we?" Ben chuckled softly, brushing her hair back. "Agreed."

Their day unfolded in perfect rhythm. Bladders emptied, coffee poured, breakfast served. Only after those sacred rituals did they return once again to the books that waited patiently on the table. The names, the stories, the history — all still there, ready to carry them deeper into the journey that was no longer simply about discovery but about living their legacy side by side. The idea had been building between them for weeks, quietly stirring beneath every name they uncovered, every marriage they charted, every map they studied. It wasn't born from curiosity alone, but from something older — a pull. The kind of pull that doesn't speak loudly, but hums deep within the chest. The pull of land. The pull of origin. The pull of home.

As Ben and Isla sat once again at the research table, surrounded by the familiar comfort of old volumes and worn maps, they knew the moment had finally arrived. The names had been traced. The stories had been pieced together. Now, the land itself was calling them forward. Marden. The old village. The place where the Pattenden family once held their estates, where the fields once stretched out across Kent's rolling countryside, and where time had quietly erased the physical traces — but not the memory.

Ben's fingers gently traced the map's faint outlines, following the soft curve of the road marked Pattenden Lane. His voice was quiet, yet certain. "We need to go there, Isla," he said softly. "We need to stand there. To feel it under our feet. It's not enough to see it in books." Isla nodded, her eyes filled with the same steady pull that had been quietly growing in her heart. "We need to stand where they stood," she whispered. "To breathe the same air. Even if the fields are gone, the land remembers. And so do we."

Ben exhaled deeply, his hand tightening gently around hers. "It's not just about visiting a place," he continued. "It's about honouring them. Those who came before us. The ones whose names we carry. The ones who walked this ground long before our names were ever written down." Isla smiled softly, leaning her head against his shoulder. "We'll remember what others forgot," she whispered. "Because that's who we are."

The thought of Pattenden Lane brought a quiet ache to Ben's chest. The once-rich farmland had long since disappeared beneath modern development, its open fields now swallowed by changing times. Great Pattenden. Little Pattenden. The ancient hamlets that once defined his family's beginning were no longer marked on most maps. Yet the road remained, like a faint thread still connecting him to everything that came before.

Jeff stepped quietly into the room, sensing the depth of their conversation without needing to ask. His eyes fell upon the map before them, recognizing immediately where their thoughts had landed. "It's time, isn't it?" he asked gently. Ben and Isla both looked up, nodding in perfect unison. Jeff smiled softly, folding his arms as he studied the map.

"Then we'll plan it properly. We'll go. You'll stand on your ancestors' land." His voice held the steady warmth of a man who understood fully what this pilgrimage meant to both of them. "And you'll carry them forward, the way you were always meant to."

Outside the window, the afternoon sun began to dip lower, casting soft amber light across the room. The journey that had once begun with names on a page was now preparing to take them back to the very soil where those names had first taken root. This wasn't just a trip. It was a return. And Ben and Isla both understood — this was only the beginning.

The days that followed moved with a strange kind of urgency — not rushed, but filled with a quiet sense of purpose. Jeff, Robert, and Claire worked closely together, coordinating every detail, ensuring that nothing would interfere with what Ben and Isla were about to do. This was not a vacation, not a sightseeing trip for idle curiosity. This was a pilgrimage. And everyone involved treated it with the reverence it deserved.

Jeff sat at the kitchen table late into the evening, cross-checking maps, consulting travel routes, and confirming schedules. He wanted every part of the journey to flow smoothly, to allow Ben and Isla the time and space they would need once they arrived in Marden. Even Annemarie, who usually kept a quiet distance during the research, now stepped forward to offer her help, making phone calls and helping arrange accommodations near the old village. Everyone understood what this meant. This was not simply for history's sake — it was for their hearts, for their very identities.

Ben and Isla hovered nearby as the planning unfolded, both of them full of energy, but also holding back just enough to let the adults handle the more complicated parts. But their excitement was unmistakable. Isla sat on the arm of Ben's chair, her hand resting on his shoulder as they watched Jeff confirm the final hotel bookings. "We'll be staying just outside of town," Jeff said, his voice steady but warm. "Close enough that you can walk directly to Pattenden Lane. The land may have changed, but you'll stand on it nonetheless."

Ben nodded, his eyes glistening slightly as the reality of it settled in his chest. "That's all I've ever wanted, Jeff," he whispered. "To stand there. To feel it under my feet." Isla smiled, leaning closer, her voice gentle. "And we'll stand there together." Claire, sitting across from them, smiled softly as she watched her daughter's hand slip into Ben's. "You two were always meant to walk that ground together," she said. "And you'll carry it forward the way your ancestors could have only dreamed."

The final pieces fell into place quickly. Passports were checked. Flights were booked. Travel documents were secured. Even the smallest details — rental cars, walking routes, and local contacts — were confirmed with care. Jeff left nothing to chance. They would leave within days, crossing the ocean to walk the ancient ground that still whispered the names of those who had come before.

On the final evening before their departure, the house grew unusually quiet. The bags were packed. The documents were ready. The flight itinerary rested neatly on the table. Ben and Isla sat together on the porch, hand in hand, watching the stars blink into existence above them. The silence between them was once again filled with meaning. Ben turned his head slowly toward her, his voice quiet but steady. "Tomorrow," he whispered. "We'll finally see it." Isla smiled, her voice barely above a breath. "Tomorrow, we go home." And beneath the wide, endless sky, they sat in stillness — two soulmates preparing to walk the sacred ground of their own beginning.

The simplicity of the plan almost made it feel more profound. They didn't need to fly across seas or travel through distant lands. The place they sought was already within reach. Marden sat just a quiet drive away, nestled within the green heart of Kent, England — the very soil they had walked since birth, yet had never fully stood upon in this way. This wasn't about distance. It was about arrival. Ben sat at the kitchen table with Isla beside him, a simple road map unfolded between them. His finger traced the short route they would take — familiar names along the way, winding country roads bordered by hedgerows that had likely stood for generations. "It's not far," he said softly. "Just over half an hour, maybe less, depending on traffic."

Isla leaned in closer, her breath warm against his shoulder. "Strange, isn't it?" she whispered. "How something that belongs to us has been so close all along — and yet, today will be the first time we truly stand there." Ben nodded, his voice thoughtful. "It's like the land was waiting. And maybe we weren't supposed to come before now. Maybe it's only now that we're ready to understand what it means." His eyes lifted from the map to meet hers. "To stand there knowing everything we know."

Jeff, standing at the counter pouring coffee, turned with a knowing smile. "You're not just visiting, kids," he said gently. "You're returning." His voice carried a kind of reverence that only deepened the weight of what they were preparing to do. "And the land will recognize you — even if most people have forgotten whose feet once walked it." Claire and Robert joined them at the table, their faces filled with the same quiet anticipation. "We'll drive you out there tomorrow morning," Robert offered. "Nice and early. Let you have the whole day to take it in."

Claire reached out, brushing a hand gently through Isla's hair. "We'll be there, but this is your moment. You and Ben. This isn't sightseeing. This is homecoming." Ben smiled softly, his hand finding Isla's beneath the table. "We want to walk it together," he said quietly. "Just us. No distractions." Jeff nodded his approval. "That's how it should be."

The evening passed with a peaceful quiet as the plans were finalized. There were no suitcases to pack, no grand preparations to be made. This was not a journey of distance, but of heart. And as the night deepened and the stars filled the Kentish sky, Ben and Isla curled together beneath their shared blanket once more, their hearts full with the anticipation of what tomorrow would bring. The land was waiting. And so were they.

The morning sun lifted slowly over Kent's quiet horizon as the small car eased its way down the narrow country roads. With every mile that slipped beneath the tyres, Ben and Isla sat in a reverent silence, hands clasped together tightly, both feeling the invisible gravity pulling them closer to where it all began. Jeff drove steadily, keeping his voice quiet, as though speaking too loudly might disturb something sacred. The countryside opened itself gently before them, a patchwork of green fields, rolling hedgerows, and distant apple orchards still clinging to the same breath that had carried through centuries.

As they approached the village, the wooden sign appeared — simple, yet commanding — MARDEN boldly carved beneath the old tower and the thick apple tree, its branches painted with red fruit that looked ready for harvest even in the etched design. Isla let out a small breath, almost a whisper, as her fingers instinctively tightened around Ben's. "We're here," she said softly. But even as she spoke the words, they felt heavier than sound. They were standing at the edge of time.

The narrow road welcomed them with its familiar quiet, not the bustling echoes of city streets but rather a living silence that seemed to breathe. Jeff slowed the car as they turned gently onto Pattenden Lane. The road, though modest in its appearance, carried within it the full weight of their history. Here was no palace, no towering manor—only brick cottages with ivy gently wrapping their frames, hedgerows neatly trimmed, and the occasional chimney puffing faint wisps into the sky. Yet to Ben and Isla, this was no less grand than any royal court. This was their court. This was where the roots had first found soil.

As the car crept forward, Ben's eyes wandered across the uneven stone walls and ancient fences that lined parts of the lane. His imagination, already well-fed by countless nights of study, now saw the ghosts of children racing barefoot along this same path. He saw them laughing, their baskets swinging as they collected apples from the heavy-laden trees. He could almost hear their calls to one another, the same air now whispering their long-faded voices. "This road has seen us before," he whispered under his breath, as though speaking directly to the very soil beneath them.

Isla's eyes shimmered as she leaned closer to the window, her breath fogging the glass slightly. She saw what Ben saw — the apple trees that still swayed gently as though bowing to welcome them home, the tall hop vines that had once stretched toward the sky like green towers, and the proud hands of ancestors who had made this land sing with life. "I can feel them," she whispered back. "They're still here."

Jeff found a quiet spot to pull over, not far from where the lane bent slightly toward the old village centre. The car engine hushed into silence, and for a long moment, no one moved. The world around them seemed suspended — a stillness that wasn't empty, but full. Full of echoes. Full of memories waiting patiently to be touched again. Finally, Ben opened his door. "Let's walk."

Their feet met the lane softly, but it was enough. The weight of their steps joined the weight of those who had come before them. The dusty road beneath felt warm, familiar, like an old hand welcoming back its children. As they walked, they allowed themselves to drift fully into the living memory of the place. The air was heavy with the scent of apples still growing somewhere nearby, and the quiet rustle of the breeze through the hedgerows sounded like a choir of whispers retelling the old stories.

Ben crouched for a moment and pressed his palm flat to the earth. "This," he said softly, "this is where they stood. This dirt — they turned it from swamp to farmland. This was their kingdom." Isla knelt beside him, her own hand finding his. "It still is," she replied. "Because we are here." Together, they rose, slowly making their way further along Pattenden Lane, following not just the path of the road but the invisible thread that had woven them back into the fabric of their own legacy. Every small cottage, every crooked fence, every patch of earth seemed to nod at them in recognition. They were not strangers here. They were home.

Their footsteps carried them deeper along Pattenden Lane, where every yard of earth whispered fragments of lives once lived. Though modern homes now lined parts of the road, their bricks neat and uniform, neither Ben nor Isla saw modernity. In their eyes, the cottages breathed with the weight of centuries, as though behind each window stood silent witnesses watching them pass. They could almost sense the generations who had once walked these same stones, whose hands had tilled these now-vanished fields, whose hearts had written the chapters of the family they now bore forward.

The lane narrowed slightly, curving through gentle banks of hedgerow where wildflowers grew undisturbed. Bees hummed busily as if unaware of the sacred gravity unfolding on the path. In the distance, the faint shape of the church steeple in Marden Village peeked above the treetops — its bell tower standing as it had for centuries, having marked time for the Pattenden family long before even the oldest books had recorded their names. For Ben, the sight of it brought a tightening in his chest — not sorrow, but awe. "This land watched them live, Isla," he whispered. "It watched them fall in love, watched them raise children. Watched them grow old and return to the earth."

Isla reached out and gently slid her hand into his, her fingers wrapping around his palm. "And now it watches us," she whispered back. "And somehow... they know we're here." Her voice carried both reverence and certainty, as though she could feel invisible eyes watching with approval from every leaf, every blade of grass.

The wind carried a warm, steady breeze that rustled the hedges like soft applause. Further along, an ancient apple tree stood alone at the edge of what had once been open farmland. Its heavy branches reached outward, twisted and gnarled, still strong after hundreds of years. Ben and Isla paused before it, both silently recognizing its significance. It stood like a guardian, a remnant of an orchard that once spread far across these fields under the careful hands of their family.

Ben stepped toward it and placed his palm gently against its rough bark. "You were here when they were here," he whispered. His throat thickened slightly, his voice soft but steady. "You watched them build. You stood while their hands shaped this land. And you waited for us."

Isla stood close beside him, her head resting against his shoulder as she whispered, "We came back." The words were not dramatic, but rather a simple truth spoken into the quiet afternoon. "And we'll carry them forward." They stood beneath the old tree for some time, letting the moment breathe. The wind stirred Isla's hair, casting loose strands across Ben's face. Without thinking, he brushed them gently back behind her ear, his touch light but full of the same tenderness that defined every part of their bond. No grand speeches were needed. Here, the land itself spoke for them.

In the distance, the sound of Jeff's voice broke the silence softly as he called from where the car was parked. "Whenever you're ready, kids. Take your time." Neither of them moved immediately. They stood a while longer beneath the tree, quietly absorbing everything their hearts could hold. Eventually, Ben turned to Isla with a soft smile. "We'll return again," he promised. "This won't be our last visit."

Isla nodded, her eyes shimmering with quiet joy. "No," she whispered. "It's only our first." And as they turned, hand in hand, to walk back toward the waiting car, the wind followed behind them, carrying with it the breath of the ancestors who smiled quietly upon their returning children.

The drive home carried a quiet unlike the ride there. It was not silence born of exhaustion, nor of emptiness—it was the silence of full hearts, of souls heavy not with burden, but with meaning. The car moved smoothly along the winding country roads, the hedgerows passing like green waves upon either side. Jeff glanced at them briefly in the rearview mirror, but said nothing. There was nothing to add. Whatever needed to be spoken now belonged only to Ben and Isla.

Ben rested his head gently against the window, his eyes watching the fields roll by, but his thoughts remained planted firmly upon the soil of Pattenden Lane. His hand never left Isla's, fingers intertwined as though afraid letting go might undo something sacred. He replayed the feel of the earth beneath his shoes, the rough bark of the ancient apple tree beneath his fingertips, and the breath of wind that had danced around them as though welcoming its children home. The lane may have looked quiet to the world, but to him it was alive — whispering stories that only they could hear.

Isla's head rested against Ben's shoulder, her breath steady, her heart still beating to the rhythm of what they had just lived. "I feel different," she whispered softly, her voice barely above a breath. "Like I can finally hear them. Like I belong in a way I didn't fully understand until now."

Ben turned slightly to glance down at her, his voice equally quiet. "I feel it too. We've read their names for months. We've seen their lines written in ink. But today… we stood where they stood. The soil knows us. And we know it." His words came slow, deliberate, heavy with the weight of their shared discovery.

Robert, seated quietly in the front passenger seat, finally spoke, his voice calm and measured. "You'll never see the world quite the same after this. That's the thing about standing where your ancestors once stood — it doesn't leave you." He paused, glancing back toward them with a small smile. "And that's a good thing." Claire added gently, "You don't just carry their blood, Isla. You carry their voices now. You both do."

The countryside slowly yielded back to the familiar edges of town as Jeff navigated through the narrowing roads that led them home. As the house came into view, the spell of the drive seemed to soften, but its weight remained inside them. Ben squeezed Isla's hand once more before they stepped out into the cool afternoon air, as though confirming between them that everything they carried now would remain.

Inside the house, the books still waited patiently upon the table — open charts, marked dates, folded maps — but even the books seemed to feel different now. What was once a hunt for knowledge had now become something more intimate. They no longer studied the past to find their identity; now they carried their identity forward into everything they read.

As they set their coats aside and sat once more at the table, Isla glanced at the open volume of The Lords of Marden, her eyes tracing the old Pattenden entries once more. "I don't feel like I'm reading about strangers anymore," she whispered. "Now I see faces. I see children playing in the fields, women hanging linens, men driving carts through the orchards. I see family." Ben smiled softly, leaning his head closer to hers. "Because that's what they are," he said. "Family." The afternoon faded gently as they resumed their work, but now every name carried colour. Every date breathed. Every old document whispered with voices that no longer felt distant. The journey to Pattenden Lane had not closed the chapter — it had opened it.

Evening settled gently across the house as the sun dipped behind the distant trees. The soft amber glow slipped through the windows one last time before surrendering to dusk, casting long shadows across the familiar research table. The books remained open, the charts still neatly stacked, and the maps spread across the table like a great quilt of their ancestry. Yet as Ben and Isla sat side by side, their hands quietly folded together, their thoughts had shifted somewhere beyond the pages. The discoveries of names, titles, and royal blood had filled their hearts, but tonight — something deeper stirred.

Ben broke the silence first, his voice calm, reflective. "You know, Isla… as much as I love all of this— the books, the names, the history— I've been thinking." He paused for a moment, glancing at her softly. "We're still just kids." Isla smiled as she nodded gently. "I've been thinking the same thing," she whispered. "We've learned so much… but if we keep spending every day buried in these books, one day we'll blink, and our childhood will be gone. Time doesn't wait for anyone."

Ben exhaled slowly, his fingers tightening lightly around hers. "That's what scares me a little. We're living inside all these stories of people who've already lived their lives. But ours… ours is happening right now." His voice steadied as he continued. "If we don't let ourselves be kids — truly be kids — we'll lose something we can never get back." Isla's eyes shimmered beneath the fading light. "But we can have both, can't we? We can know who we are, where we come from, and still live in the present. We can play, run, laugh, and still carry our ancestors with us." Her voice carried both innocence and wisdom. "We don't have to choose one over the other."

Ben smiled, feeling the truth of her words settle into him like a warm embrace. "You're right. We've found the truth. We know what's in our blood. We know who we are." He glanced toward the open book, then back at Isla. "We could make a claim, you know. If we wanted to. If the law allowed it." Isla nodded thoughtfully. "But we don't need to. That's not why we searched. We don't want a throne. We want each other. We want peace. We want life — quiet, simple, and true."

The house grew still again, but the weight in their hearts lightened. They saw it clearly now: the beauty of balance. They were children. Soulmates. Historians. Archivists. Genealogists. And most of all — partners in a bond that no force on earth could ever break. Their love wasn't fragile, nor was it something to outgrow. It was planted deep, stronger than any crown, stronger than any title.

Outside, the early stars began to peek through the indigo sky. Ben and Isla rose from the table hand in hand, their movements slow and peaceful. Tomorrow, the books would still be there. The family trees would still wait. But tonight — they belonged to each other, to the present, to their childhood. "We'll keep learning," Ben whispered softly as they walked toward the living room. "We'll always keep learning. But we'll live too. Every day."

Isla smiled, her heart full. "Because this is our time, Ben. Our time to be kids. To love. To laugh. And to remember who we are." They curled together once more beneath their shared blanket on the living room floor. The world beyond faded, leaving only the warmth of their hearts and the gentle breathing of two souls joined not by chance, but by design. Their crown was real. Their love was real. And though the world might never know the full depth of who they were, that truth belonged to them — and them alone. For now, and for always.

CHAPTER 10: THE SEASONS THAT WHISPER

The months had passed as though the seasons themselves had quietly conspired to steal time from them. One moment, summer had wrapped the world in warmth; the next, autumn's leaves whispered their goodbyes before winter crept silently in. Snow came and went, blanketing the fields in white, and before either of them had truly caught their breath, the world thawed once more beneath the soft hands of spring. And now, as if time had bent again, they stood once more in the breath of June, where everything smelled new, alive, and familiar all at once.

Ben and Isla had lived these passing seasons together as only soulmates could — not simply marking the months, but filling them with meaning. They had studied, researched, and traced their bloodlines with such passion that even the adults around them marvelled at how much had been uncovered in so short a time. Word of their discoveries had somehow escaped the quiet circle of their family, spreading further than any of them intended. Scholars and distant cousins reached out, curious to learn from the two children who, despite their tender age, had assembled genealogical charts that rivalled seasoned historians.

But none of that noise mattered here, not today. For as the sun climbed high once more, ushering in the height of summer, Ben and Isla found themselves craving something simpler. Not ink-stained fingertips nor crinkled parchment beneath their palms. No maps. No scrolls. No charts spread across the dining table. They wanted air. Sky. Grass beneath their feet. The kind of simple freedom that childhood often offers only for a brief, precious while before adulthood arrives too soon.

Their birthdays loomed just ahead — August 1st for Isla, August 2nd for Ben — their tenth year already approaching with quiet but steady steps. And though their hearts still carried the gravity of who they were — King and Queen by blood, by right, by ancient design — neither sought the weight of crowns. Their sovereignty lived quietly within their veins, not displayed upon their heads. The secret of the crown remained safe, nestled inside them where no eyes but their own could ever truly see.

Jeff, too, had recognized their need for balance. With homeschooling still in session for a few more short weeks, he allowed their days to stretch into long outdoor afternoons once lessons were complete. The warm June air called to them like an old friend, inviting them to leave the pages behind for a while, to play, to laugh, to live fully in the youth that was still theirs to claim. And they did — without hesitation.

The backyard became their kingdom. The swings groaned under their weight as they sailed through the air, daring one another to go higher with every kick of their legs. They raced barefoot across the grass, chasing the wind as though it carried ancient whispers only they could hear. They climbed trees that swayed gently beneath their weight, their laughter rising like birdsong into the canopy of green above.

At times, they simply lay side by side upon the cool grass, staring up into the endless blue sky. Fingers intertwined, hearts perfectly synchronized, speaking little but sharing everything.

The weight of history never fully left them, but here, under the open sky, it became light. It lived with them, not upon them. Ben rolled onto his side, propping himself up on one elbow as he gazed down at Isla, her golden hair fanned out across the grass like threads of sunlight. "You know," he said softly, "I'm glad we're doing this."

Isla turned her head, her eyes meeting his with quiet warmth. "Me too," she whispered. "The books will always be there. The names. The charts. But these days… these are ours. And once they're gone, we can't get them back." Ben smiled, brushing a stray blade of grass from her cheek. "Then let's make sure we never miss a single one." The summer stretched before them like an open road, unmarked and full of promise. There would be plenty of time ahead for history, for research, for discovery. But today — today belonged to their laughter, their play, their simple, precious youth.

The peaceful simplicity of summer never prevented Ben and Isla from indulging in their other great talent: mischief. For all their seriousness when it came to history, bloodlines, and ancient names, there was another side of them that flourished just as strongly — the art of laughter, absurdity, and, most especially, fart jokes that could drive even the hardiest adults fleeing for fresh air.

Their thunder-farts had become legendary within their little world. Not just ordinary bursts of wind, but forces of nature that could peel paint from walls and make nearby tree bark quiver under their invisible assault. Ben often joked that if they ever found themselves lost in a forest, all they had to do was let one rip and clear a trail. Isla, always quick to add her own twist, would simply laugh and declare, "Or strip the orchard bare! One blast, and all the apples fall to the ground."

One particular afternoon, the two of them found themselves in the village library. The room was quiet, filled with towering shelves of old volumes, some of which even contained family records they had once combed through together. But today wasn't about research. Today was about fun. They sat side by side at a long oak table, surrounded by rows of perfectly aligned chairs. A handful of visitors sat scattered throughout the room, heads buried in books, oblivious to the mischief building just a few seats away. Ben shifted in his chair, shooting Isla a quick sideways glance, his lips twitching into a mischievous grin. "Are you thinking what I'm thinking?" he whispered under his breath.

Isla's eyes gleamed, her smile stretching wide as she whispered back, "Synchronize?" Ben nodded once. "On three." They counted softly together. "One… two… three." The resulting sound could only be described as catastrophic. A double thunderclap erupted beneath the table, echoing off the stone walls like distant cannon fire. The blast carried such unexpected force that even the old librarian's glasses slid slightly down her nose. Silence fell for a brief second — and then chaos.

The nearest patrons immediately froze, their faces contorting as the invisible fog reached them. One man clutched his nose, bolting upright with a panicked gasp. Another woman quickly gathered her books and all but sprinted toward the door.

Several younger patrons darted for safety as though fleeing a chemical spill, their eyes watering and mouths gaping for fresh air. Within moments, the grand library was emptied — save for Ben and Isla, who now sat alone in triumphant hysterics.

Ben struggled to breathe, his laughter making his chest ache. "Cleared the savannah, Isla!" he wheezed, barely able to finish the sentence. Isla was already doubled over, wiping tears from her eyes. "That... that was legendary!" she managed between fits of giggles. "We've got the library to ourselves now. See? Strategy."

Back at home, Robert and Claire weren't foolish enough to pretend they hadn't heard the latest story spreading through town. Nor were they surprised. They had long since grown wise to their daughter's and Ben's peculiar talents. As Robert often said to Claire with a knowing grin, "It's not just wind — it's bark-stripper, paint-remover, nostril-curler, and evacuation-level wind force. And they know it."

Claire would simply nod, sipping her coffee with amusement. "I've learned to stay upwind," she'd reply softly. "They get that mischievous sparkle, and you know what's coming." But deep down, both parents understood. It wasn't just silliness for its own sake. It was part of how Ben and Isla preserved their childhood — their way of keeping laughter in balance with the heavy knowledge they carried. And truth be told, even Jeff couldn't entirely suppress his grin when the stories reached him. The world outside might marvel at their expertise in genealogy and royal history, but inside their own small world, Ben and Isla remained exactly who they always were — children, best friends, soulmates... and masters of perfectly timed thunder-farts.

If there was one rule that governed Ben and Isla's world, it was this: the good times don't stop unless we say so. And that summer, they had absolutely no intention of letting them stop. The more the world whispered about their genealogical expertise, the more the adults marvelled at their academic brilliance, the more Ben and Isla leaned fully into the joy of simply being children. They weren't naïve. They understood exactly how valuable their knowledge had become. But unlike many who got swallowed by praise, these two had a far more important mission: fun.

Word had spread far beyond their quiet town now. Family members, distant relatives, even professional historians had taken notice. What astonished everyone wasn't merely the depth of their research — it was the precision. Ben and Isla weren't making guesses; they were uncovering lineages with forensic-level accuracy. Documents, timelines, ancestral merges — they could trace marriages, bloodlines, and dynastic ties faster than some seasoned researchers could in an entire fiscal year.

And because of that, Jeff, Robert, and Claire made a careful decision: if anyone wanted to commission their services, it wouldn't come cheap. It wasn't about greed. It was about protection. High fees deterred most of the casual inquiries, allowing the children to maintain control of their own time, while still recognizing the worth of their extraordinary gift. The truly serious researchers — the ones who understood the value — paid accordingly. Meanwhile, Ben and Isla kept their childhood exactly where it belonged: front and centre.

And mischief, of course, remained their favourite side hobby. "Hey Isla," Ben grinned one afternoon while lounging on the swing set, "you ever think we should start a music revolution? Forget 'Girls Just Want to Have Fun.' We need a new anthem." Isla giggled, pumping her legs as she swung higher. "You mean like... 'Kids Just Want to Have Fun'?" Ben nodded, leaning back, his head nearly touching the grass beneath him. "Exactly. Play it loud. All day. Every day. On repeat." She laughed harder. "Oh, imagine it! The historians would lose their minds. Trying to schedule meetings, and we've got our anthem blaring in the background. They'd run screaming."

Ben smirked. "Even better — we charge them double if they make us turn it down." Isla burst into giggles. "Triple if they ask for quiet hours." The thought of it sent them both rolling with laughter. They knew perfectly well how unnerved some of the older historians had become at their abilities. "Two nine-year-olds solving mysteries grown adults have spent decades fumbling over," Isla teased, wiping her eyes. "We've broken their brains."

"And their egos," Ben added with mock solemnity. But behind their playful teasing, there remained an unspoken understanding between them: their talents were real. Their work was serious. Yet they had no desire to let that seriousness steal away what mattered most. They were children. Soulmates. Playmates. And while others were busy fussing over their credentials, Ben and Isla were far too busy plotting their next prank.

The library remained one of their favourite playgrounds for mischief. After the infamous "Savannah Clearance Incident," as Jeff humorously referred to it, the librarians now wore faint expressions of dread whenever they saw the two of them enter. Not that Ben and Isla misbehaved maliciously — no, their pranks were never cruel. They were simply... effective.

One afternoon, they came armed not with thunder-farts but with perfectly timed whoopee cushions disguised beneath the chairs of the unsuspecting elderly patrons who sat at the genealogy desk. The first loud blast came as an elderly gentleman leaned forward to retrieve his notebook. The sudden noise caused him to leap so high that his bifocals nearly launched across the table. Isla whispered through laughter, "Bark stripper, phase two."

Ben nodded, biting his lip. "Operation Bark & Blast is a success." And still, even as they giggled and plotted, they carried in their hearts the full awareness of who they were — heirs to a sovereign bloodline, bound together by something far greater than titles. But for now? For now, the world could wait. Because today — kids just wanted to have fun.

The early morning light filtered through the curtains, casting soft beams across the living room where Ben and Isla lay nestled beneath their familiar blanket. The quiet hum of the waking world stirred outside, but inside, the rhythm of their morning remained as sacred as always. Ben stirred first, blinking slowly as he felt Isla's warmth still curled beside him. She followed moments later, her sleepy eyes meeting his, and without words, they smiled — the kind of smile only soulmates can give after another night spent close.

As always, their first exchange was simple: a soft morning hug, wrapping around each other like a second blanket. Then came their kiss — not rushed, not grand, but tender and full, as though reminding each other, I am still yours, and always will be. It was never routine, but instead their sacred beginning to every day, as natural as breath itself. Even in the quietest hours, their bond pulsed beneath every heartbeat. Ben chuckled softly as he shifted. "Bladder chatter," he murmured. Isla giggled, rolling her eyes playfully. "Tell me about it. Ladies first?" Ben grinned. "As always."

They rose, making their way down the hallway for their usual morning pee break — their private little tradition now so familiar it almost felt ceremonial. Soon after, the rich aroma of coffee filled the house, brewing quietly as Annemarie prepared breakfast. The mugs were already waiting at the table by the time the two of them returned from their bathroom visit, their hands still loosely entwined as they sat. Jeff entered moments later, ruffling Ben's hair with a warm grin before taking his seat. "Another full day ahead, you two?"

Ben smiled, glancing at Isla. "Not so full today, Dad. Just... life." "Good," Jeff nodded. "You both deserve it." After breakfast, with their coffee cups drained and dishes cleared, they slipped outside into the open summer air, where the morning sun painted the grass in brilliant shades of green. The warmth wrapped around them, inviting them to set aside the books for another day and instead chase the wind, the laughter, and the pure mischief that was always waiting just beneath the surface.

Hand in hand, they ran barefoot across the soft grass, their laughter ringing like chimes across the yard. They played their usual games: racing, tree climbing, daring each other to swing higher and higher, almost as if they could touch the sky. And all the while, their hearts beat as one — two children, two souls, one life shared. When the sun grew too high, they flopped onto the cool grass, breathless and grinning, staring up at the endless blue sky above. Ben reached over, his fingers gently brushing Isla's as he spoke softly. "We've got it good, haven't we?" Isla nodded, her eyes never leaving his. "The best."

And when the world felt too full, or the town too noisy, or the library in need of recovery from their most recent prank, they always had their secret escape: the cottage. Quiet, tucked away, far from curious eyes — it was their sanctuary. The place where the only sounds were the whisper of the trees, the rustle of leaves, and their laughter carried on the wind. There, at the cottage, it was just the two of them — no schedules, no historians, no questions. Just Ben and Isla. Just soulmates, living as they always promised they would.

The cottage sat quietly beneath the towering oaks, its wooden frame weathered by time but warm with memory. To anyone passing by, it was nothing more than a simple retreat tucked away from the noise of the world. But to Ben and Isla, it was something far greater — a hidden kingdom where only they reigned. Here, there were no historians knocking at the door, no charts spread across tables, no genealogical puzzles demanding to be solved. Here, there was only them — children, soulmates, and partners in mischief.

The morning air was crisp as they arrived, the soft crunch of gravel beneath their shoes the only sound to accompany their laughter. Jeff had driven them there as usual, but as always, left them to their own privacy once they were settled. "You two behave," he'd chuckled, knowing full well that 'behave' was a relative term when it came to Ben and Isla. With a wink, he added, "And give the trees a chance to keep their bark this time, would you?"

Ben grinned mischievously as he waved. "No promises, Dad." Once Jeff had departed, the true fun began. Inside the cottage, the familiar creaks of the old wooden floor greeted them like an old friend. The air carried the scent of pine and distant rain — clean, pure, and far removed from the world that constantly tried to tug at their attention. It was freedom in its simplest form.

As afternoon slipped forward, Ben and Isla lounged in the reading nook by the large window, a single oversized chair big enough to hold both of them together. Today, the book in Isla's hands wasn't some dusty historical ledger but a simple storybook — one filled with fantasy and adventure, chosen purely for the joy of sharing a tale. They read together, passing the book between them, voices alternating as the story carried them into imagined lands far from royal lines and ancient documents.

Ben closed one chapter with a grin, nudging Isla with his elbow. "See? Even heroes need their mischief." Isla giggled, resting her head against his shoulder. "Sounds familiar, doesn't it?" she whispered. "We're experts at that." As if on cue, the silence of the peaceful cottage was abruptly broken by a loud, unmistakable rumble — not from distant thunder, but from Ben himself. The noise rolled through the small room like a miniature storm, followed quickly by the sharp snap of Isla bursting into laughter.

"Oh my gosh, Ben!" Isla squealed, waving her hand dramatically in front of her face. "That was bark-stripper level." Ben laughed harder, barely able to speak through his chuckles. "Hey, I warned you! The cottage amplifies everything. Acoustics, you know." Isla, wiping the tears from her eyes, responded between giggles. "Well, remind me not to light any matches, or we'll blow the whole place sky-high." They both collapsed into fits of laughter, their bodies shaking, the sound echoing against the wooden beams of the cottage. The world outside faded away as they lost themselves in the purity of the moment — two children wrapped in love, laughter, and complete freedom.

As the sun began to lower behind the trees, painting the walls of the cottage in shades of amber and gold, Ben wrapped his arm around Isla's shoulders, pulling her gently closer. She nestled against him with ease, her head resting softly against his chest, the steady rhythm of his heartbeat whispering beneath her ear. "You know," Ben whispered softly, his voice now calm and filled with warmth, "we could live like this forever." Isla smiled, her eyes closed as she answered just above a whisper. "We already are." The trees outside swayed gently, as though nodding in quiet approval, while the cottage held their laughter like a secret — safe, sacred, and eternal.

The next morning arrived gently, slipping into the cottage like a familiar friend. The golden beams of sunrise poured softly through the thin curtains, illuminating the little room where Ben and Isla lay wrapped together beneath the large blanket. As always, their breathing was calm, synchronized, hearts beating quietly in harmony. It was Isla who stirred first, her eyes fluttering open to find Ben already gazing at her, his smile warm and steady.

Without a word, she shifted closer, wrapping her arms around him in their usual morning embrace. He responded naturally, holding her close, their bodies curling into one another like two pieces that had always belonged together. Then came the kiss, as natural as waking itself — slow, unhurried, a simple reminder that they belonged to one another fully, completely, eternally. After a few more peaceful moments, Ben grinned playfully. "Bladder chatter." Isla giggled softly. "I was just thinking the same thing." She stretched her arms above her head and whispered, "Ladies first, of course."

The morning routine was sacred. Isla slipped off toward the bathroom first while Ben waited, quietly gazing out through the cottage window at the trees swaying gently in the breeze. When Isla returned, Ben took his turn while she set about preparing the simple breakfast they had packed for their little getaway — fresh fruit, toast, and of course, their beloved coffee, already brewing in the small corner pot.

By the time Ben re-emerged, the cottage was filled with the rich aroma of fresh coffee, and two steaming mugs awaited them on the small table by the window. They sat together, side by side, hands brushing as they sipped, their legs swinging freely beneath the table, enjoying the simplicity of a morning shared. "Today's a mischief day," Isla announced playfully, setting her cup down. Ben's eyes twinkled with interest. "Oh? What's the plan, my Queen of Chaos?" Isla grinned, her eyes alight. "We've been too kind to Jeff lately. I say… it's prank time."

Ben rubbed his hands together dramatically. "Excellent suggestion. But we'll need precision. Strategy." They both broke into giggles, already picturing poor Jeff's reaction to whatever scheme they would devise. The cottage wasn't just their escape — it was their planning headquarters, where every mischievous campaign was dreamed up and perfectly executed.

By midday, their plan had taken shape. They gathered small harmless items from their prank kit — a collection of items lovingly curated over time: harmless dye tablets for the shower, a fake plastic spider for the cabin doorway, and their latest invention — a tiny device that released a perfectly timed fart sound the moment someone sat down on the kitchen chair. The brilliance, as always, lay in its simplicity. "It's all about the layers," Ben whispered as they set the final piece. "One surprise after another." "And always harmless," Isla added with a giggle. "We're not mean — just mischievous."

As the afternoon sun hung high above the cottage roof, they sat back on the porch swing, side by side, their fingers laced together, admiring their handiwork while waiting for Jeff's inevitable arrival. The trees swayed around them, the wind carrying the sweet scent of summer, while the birds sang softly in the background. Time seemed to slow whenever they were here — a perfect world, untouched by the noise of the outside.

Ben glanced at Isla, his voice quiet, full of affection. "We've got this figured out, don't we?" Isla smiled, her eyes locking onto his. "Yes," she whispered. "We really do." And there they sat — two soulmates, two children, two masters of both history and harmless mischief, waiting patiently for the next wave of laughter to arrive.

The soft hum of Jeff's car eased up the gravel driveway right on schedule. The low crunch beneath the tyres echoed gently through the cottage clearing, blending with the summer wind swaying through the trees. Inside the cottage, Ben and Isla sat perfectly still on the porch swing, hands folded neatly in their laps, their faces composed with an innocence that would have fooled anyone — anyone except Jeff, who had grown all too familiar with that particular look over the past year.

Jeff stepped out of the car, stretched his arms casually toward the sky, and exhaled as though he'd stepped into paradise. "Alright, you two," he called with a grin, "what have you done?" Ben feigned a look of deep offense, raising his hand to his chest. "Done? Us? dad dearest, how could you accuse such innocent souls of such treachery?"

Isla chimed in sweetly, blinking wide-eyed. "We've been reading quietly. The birds are singing. The squirrels are frolicking. Nothing but peace and harmony here." Jeff narrowed his eyes playfully as he approached the porch steps. "Mhm. And yet somehow, I can feel the mischief hanging in the air like humidity."

He opened the door and stepped inside. The first surprise greeted him immediately: the small, harmless plastic spider suspended by fishing line at eye level. Jeff paused mid-step, blinked once, and then chuckled softly. "Subtle," he muttered, swatting the dangling spider aside.

From outside, Ben and Isla erupted into muffled giggles, struggling to contain themselves as they peeked through the window. "Stage one: success," Isla whispered triumphantly.

Jeff continued through the cottage, setting his bag down by the table. He headed toward the bathroom to freshen up after the drive, where the next surprise awaited him. As he turned on the shower tap, the harmless dye tablet hidden in the spout released a burst of pale green water. Jeff stared for a long moment, watching the stream pour down as though the cottage itself had decided to prank him. He exhaled slowly, rubbing the bridge of his nose. "Well played, children," he said aloud, his voice echoing down the hallway.

By now, Ben and Isla were practically in tears, their laughter stifled behind clasped hands as they silently celebrated from their observation post on the swing. The final piece of their orchestration awaited him in the kitchen. Jeff, ever the optimist, decided a coffee might balance the prank parade. He pulled out the kitchen chair — the one with the small sound device carefully rigged beneath the cushion — and lowered himself down.

The moment his full weight settled, the chair erupted with a resounding PPPPPFFFFFTTTT! — so loud, so sudden, it seemed to vibrate off the wooden walls of the tiny cottage. The birds outside startled into flight as the echo carried. From outside, Ben and Isla exploded into open laughter, tumbling into each other, unable to contain it any longer. "Oh my gosh!" Isla squealed between fits of giggles. "That was the best one yet!"
Ben clutched his stomach, barely able to breathe. "Savannah clearance: cottage edition!" he gasped through his laughter. Inside, Jeff simply shook his head and laughed, raising his voice loud enough for them to hear. "You two do realize I've raised a pair of adorable little terrorists, right?" Ben managed to shout back through his laughter. "Correction: professional mischief artists!"

Jeff chuckled to himself, sipping the coffee he had managed to pour despite the surprises. Truth be told, he wouldn't have changed a thing. In their laughter, their cleverness, and their endless companionship, he saw something far deeper than harmless pranks. He saw two children who understood how to balance the weight of knowledge with the joy of life — children who were not wasting their childhood, but fully living it. And outside, on the swing, as their laughter slowly softened, Ben and Isla leaned against one another once more. Their fingers intertwined, their hearts full, and their laughter still bubbling beneath their smiles. "Perfect day," Isla whispered. Ben nodded. "Always."

The afternoon stretched lazily onward, the sun filtering down through the trees as if unwilling to interrupt the perfect rhythm that had settled over the cottage. Even after the pranks, after the thunderous blasts of laughter, and the echoes of perfectly timed mischief, Jeff sat inside chuckling to himself. He shook his head while sipping his second cup of coffee, marvelling at just how far those two had come — and how much deeper their bond seemed to grow every single day.

But as Jeff sat there, quietly observing from within the small window where the breeze gently stirred the curtains, something deeper tugged at him. Watching Ben and Isla together was no ordinary scene. He could feel it in his bones — the weight of something far older than simple childhood friendship. He had always known, somewhere deep down, that Ben had chosen him — not by blood, but by heart. There was no question in his mind that he was Ben's dad in every way that mattered. Their connection was no accident. It was written.

Ben, for his part, never had to say it aloud for Jeff to understand. But Jeff could see it in the way Ben looked at him, the way he sought his guidance, trusted his words, and leaned into him during both laughter and struggle. And when he looked at Isla — that same bond was mirrored again. Robert and Claire were her parents, and wonderful ones at that. They loved Ben as if he had always belonged to them too. Family, true family, needed no formal declaration. It was simply understood.

Outside, Ben and Isla lay side by side on the thick grass, their hands gently intertwined as they stared up at the lazy clouds rolling across the wide sky. The breeze whispered through the leaves above them, carrying the gentle scent of summer and earth. Neither spoke for some time. They didn't need to. The fullness of the day spoke for them. But Ben's thoughts swirled beneath the quiet. His eyes lifted toward the open sky, his heart heavy with gratitude for more than just the day itself. "You know, Isa…" he finally whispered, his voice gentle but full, "sometimes I think about your mum and dad." Isla turned slightly to look at him, her eyes soft. "What about them?"

Ben smiled, his thumb brushing softly across her knuckles. "I've never really said it to them, but I should. Without them… you wouldn't be here. And if you weren't here… I wouldn't have you." His voice thickened just slightly as he continued. "And you're… you're everything to me."

Isla's chest swelled with quiet emotion, her heart lifting toward her throat. "They know, Ben," she whispered softly. "But someday, you'll tell them. When you're ready. And they'll know how much you love them too."

Ben nodded, his eyes shimmering faintly beneath the sunlight. "You're right. They'll hear it when it's time." The moment wrapped around them like a warm blanket, the weight of their bond drawing them closer. And yet, even within the quiet reverence, their mischievous nature never stayed buried for long.

As the breeze shifted, a familiar rumble built within Ben's stomach, followed quickly by a sharp, unmistakable blast that echoed across the clearing. It was powerful — one of his finest. Birds scattered into the sky. A squirrel shot up the nearby tree as though fleeing for its life. The tall grass even bent slightly under the invisible wave.

Isla, already in a fit of laughter, managed to squeak out between giggles, "You just cleared the nature reserve!" Ben clutched his stomach as he laughed, gasping for breath. "The township of Kent... shall fall!" he announced dramatically. "Squirrels shall seek refuge, raccoons shall flee, trees shall bow, and the winds shall carry my legacy far across the lands!" Isla's laughter grew stronger, her eyes watering. "Oh my gosh! Poor Kent!" she cried. "Even the trees are shaking!"

They laughed until their sides ached, the kind of laughter that carried all the way into the bones, pure and perfect. Even from the cottage, Jeff could hear them and shook his head with an amused smile. "Little bark-strippers," he muttered to himself. "May the forest forgive them." As the sun began its slow descent toward evening, the laughter softened, and Ben and Isla curled together once more in the grass, hearts full, hands entwined, souls wrapped tightly in the kind of love that defied any force — even time itself.

The day stretched on in its easy, familiar way, sunlight dappled across the clearing and the trees humming their endless song. The soft knock at the cottage door was no surprise. Robert and Claire stood on the small porch, smiling, carrying the same peaceful air they always did when they visited. There was no urgency in their manner, no heavy matters to discuss. They came only for the pleasure of company, and for the simple joy of sharing a coffee with Jeff.

Ben and Isla sat up from their nest on the grass, brushing themselves off as Jeff called out, "Come in, come in. Coffee's on, and mischief's only moderately contained today." Robert chuckled warmly as they stepped inside, Claire's smile widening when she saw the familiar glow on Ben's and Isla's faces. These small gatherings had become something sacred in themselves — unplanned, unhurried, woven with quiet laughter and the easy comfort that only true family can know.

As the mugs clinked gently and the rich aroma filled the air, Ben found himself unusually quiet, his hands folded loosely in his lap, his eyes cast downward. He wasn't sure at first what stirred so heavily in his chest, but it grew with each passing moment. He watched Isla sip her coffee, watched Jeff grin and exchange friendly banter with Robert, and he felt it — a kind of pull. A rising wave inside him that refused to be swallowed down. When his gaze lifted again, it found Robert and Claire. They were talking softly with Jeff, but Ben barely heard the words. All he could see was the kindness in their eyes, the quiet patience in the way they sat — two people who, without ever intending it, had changed his life forever.

The shimmer began then, soft at first, a gloss over his eyes that blurred the edges of the room. And before he understood what was happening, tears spilled — not a few, not quietly, but in a steady, overwhelming flood that slid down his cheeks and onto his shirt. The room grew still. Isla turned immediately toward him, her hand finding his instinctively. Jeff paused mid-sentence, his smile fading into something softer, deeper. Robert and Claire straightened, concern etching itself gently across their faces. But Ben shook his head slowly, rising to his feet, his tears unashamed, unhidden.

Without a word, he crossed the small space between them and, before either could react, wrapped his arms around both their necks, pulling them close, holding them in an embrace that shook with the force of all he could not yet say. His voice came thick, tangled with emotion, but clear. "Thank you," he whispered. "Thank you... for her. For Isla. For bringing her into the world. Without you... I wouldn't have her. I wouldn't have my soulmate." Robert's hands lifted first, gently resting against Ben's trembling back. Claire's followed, smoothing lightly across his hair, holding him tighter as he sobbed openly now, the tears pouring from him like a river finally freed from its dam.

Ben pulled back just enough to look at them both, his face wet, his eyes shining with a depth of love that needed no further explanation. "I love you both," he said, his voice cracking. "You're... you're my family, too." Robert swallowed hard, but the tears that welled in his own eyes could not be held back. They slipped free, tracing slow, silent paths down his cheeks. Claire, too, wept quietly, her arms tightening once more around Ben. "We love you too, Ben," Robert managed, his voice rough with emotion. "You've been part of us... from the beginning."

Claire kissed the top of Ben's head softly. "We couldn't have asked for better," she whispered. "You've always been family." Across the room, Jeff stood silently, his arms crossed, but his own eyes glistening. He felt it too — that unseen thread weaving all of them together, a tapestry stitched not by blood alone but by something even greater. Love. Loyalty. Eternity.

Isla rose quietly and moved to Ben's side, slipping her hand into his, grounding him, steadying him. He squeezed back, breathing in deeply as the wave of emotion slowly began to ebb.

For a long while, none of them spoke. They simply stood there, held together by a force stronger than words. The kind of moment that speaks not in sentences, but in heartbeats. Outside, the sun dipped lower, casting the clearing in soft gold.

The trees stood as quiet witnesses, the breeze carrying no laughter now, but something softer, more sacred — the simple, undeniable truth that they were, all of them, a family. And nothing could ever change that.

As the final blush of evening gave way to dusk, Isla looked up at her parents, her voice soft but full of hopeful excitement. "Mum... Dad... Jeff... can Ben and I sleep outside tonight? Just us. Under the stars." Her eyes sparkled beneath the lantern light of the cottage porch, as though the idea itself had already planted a dream within her.

Jeff, who had been quietly sipping his coffee, pulled out his phone and checked the weather app with practiced caution. Normally, the unpredictable moods of Kent's skies would have made such a request difficult — rain, wind, or a damp chill that often snuck in even during summer months. But tonight, something rare smiled down upon them. Jeff's eyebrows lifted as he read. "Clear skies," he announced, a note of pleasant surprise in his voice. "Warm too. No rain, no wind, no clouds. Honestly? Perfect night for it."

Robert smiled, glancing at Claire, whose eyes were already full of motherly warmth. "Of course you can, darling," Claire said softly. "You and Ben have your night." "Yes," Robert added with a nod. "Dream big. Talk about the future. Make plans. Share your hopes. That's what nights like this are for. Don't waste it — life's too short." Ben's face lit up, his heart already swelling with gratitude before a word left his lips. "Thank you," he whispered, his voice soft but full. "Thank you both."

Jeff stood from his chair, stretching his back before offering his playful contribution. "I'll grab the extra sleeping blankets for you. You'll need something under you or you'll wake up sore. And I don't want to hear any complaints about it tomorrow." The preparations were simple but perfect. They spread the thick quilted blanket over a soft patch of grass just behind the cottage, where the clearing opened to the wide night sky. No lanterns. No streetlights. Only the stars above and the quiet hum of crickets in the tall grass nearby. The trees stood silently at the edges, tall and noble, as if standing guard over the sacred moment about to unfold.

Once settled beneath the blanket, Ben and Isla lay shoulder to shoulder, their hands instinctively finding each other. The warm summer air caressed their faces, carrying the faint scent of pine and wildflowers. Overhead, the stars blinked and shimmered, free from the usual cloud cover that often obscured Kent's skies. Isla let out a content sigh, her voice quiet as though speaking too loudly might startle the stars themselves. "Look at them, Ben. It's like the whole sky came out just for us."

Ben turned his head, his gaze landing gently on her. "Maybe it did," he whispered. "Maybe they've always been waiting for us to come out here." For a while, they simply lay there in silence, their hearts synchronized, feeling the ancient pull of the heavens above them. The stars seemed to whisper stories of their own — not of royalty or bloodlines this time, but of dreams yet to be written. The kind of dreams only two soulmates could share in the safety of each other's arms.

Ben broke the silence first, his voice slow, thoughtful. "When we're older... where do you want to live?" Isla smiled, her eyes never leaving the sky. "Somewhere quiet. Like here. Away from cities. With trees, lots of trees. A cottage maybe... and no one bothering us." Ben nodded. "That's what I want too. Just us. And family, someday." Isla squeezed his hand. "And love. Always love." Ben's chest swelled with emotion. "We've already got that," he whispered. "More than anyone could ever understand."

The stars above them blinked as though nodding in agreement. Their crowns might have been secret, but their love was written in every heartbeat — in every glance, in every shared laugh, and in every whispered dream beneath the open sky. As sleep slowly crept toward them, their final words that night were simple. Isla leaned in, pressing a small, unhurried kiss to Ben's lips. "I love you," she whispered. Ben kissed her back, his voice steady but full. "I love you too. Always." And with the stars watching gently above them, they drifted into sleep — soulmates beneath the heavens, children of destiny, dreaming together beneath a sky that had waited lifetimes just to hold them.

The morning unfolded like silk, smooth and slow, as dawn quietly slipped across the clearing. The first warm rays kissed their faces as Ben and Isla stirred beneath their blanket under the open sky. The birds, already wide awake, chirped in their usual morning symphony while a gentle breeze danced softly through the tall grass. Ben opened his eyes first, blinking at the sunlight before turning toward Isla, who was still curled peacefully beside him.

As always, their first exchange came without words — a smile, soft and warm, followed by their shared morning hug. Then came the kiss, slow and sweet, like a whispered promise. The bond between them pulsed steadily, unchanging and eternal.

And soon, as routine dictated, the inevitable arrived. "Bladder chatter," Ben whispered playfully. Isla giggled, already sitting up. "Ladies first, as usual."

With light laughter, they both stood, stretching as the golden beams warmed their skin. The walk to the bathroom was short, their familiar steps unhurried as they relieved themselves in turn — the first task of every new day. And as they returned to the cottage, a familiar, rich aroma met them before they even stepped through the door. Jeff had arrived early. The comforting hum of the coffee machine filled the air, the smell of fresh brew already drifting lazily through the small space. Jeff glanced up from where he stood by the counter, grinning at the pair of sleepy soulmates. "Morning, you two," he greeted. "You two look like you slept right through heaven itself."

Ben smiled as he took a mug from Jeff's waiting hands. "Pretty close." Isla accepted hers, wrapping her fingers around the warm cup as she whispered, "Thank you, Jeff." They settled themselves at the small kitchen table, sipping the coffee slowly, allowing the warmth to fully wake their bodies. And that's when they noticed it. There, sitting neatly on the small shelf by the window, was a small, well-worn leather pouch. Neither of them had noticed it the night before, but now it sat there as though waiting for them.

Ben reached for it first, opening the small brass clasp and unfolding its contents. Inside lay two small travel journals — ones they had both used earlier that year when mapping out distant royal bloodlines, charting family histories that traced their roots across the sea.

Isla leaned closer, her voice hushed as though the journals themselves were speaking. "Denmark," she whispered softly. Ben nodded. "Copenhagen." His fingers ran along the pages, tracing the names they had once scribbled together — kings, queens, marriages that spanned across borders and centuries, the tangled threads that had eventually found their way into both of their veins.

"We wrote this down months ago. But... I don't know. Seeing it now... it feels different." Isla looked up at him, her eyes thoughtful. "I feel it too. Like something's pulling at us." Ben leaned back slightly, taking a sip from his mug. "We've talked about visiting before. But this time... it's not just a history trip. It's something else. Like... we're supposed to go." Jeff watched them both, his eyes narrowing just slightly in thought. "Denmark, huh?"

Isla nodded. "We don't even know exactly why yet. But it's like our hearts are telling us we need to." Jeff gave a small smile, folding his arms as he leaned against the counter. "Well, then, you've got a few weeks to figure it out. But I will say this — when your hearts pull you somewhere, you'd be wise to listen." Ben exhaled slowly, staring back at the open journal on the table. "Three weeks until our birthdays. Maybe that's when."

"Maybe," Isla whispered, her voice soft but certain. "It feels right." Outside, the morning continued to stretch itself across the sky as though giving silent permission for the idea to settle and grow. The thought of Denmark now hovered between them — not as a vacation, not as another research project, but as something... more. Something calling.

The days that followed passed with quiet purpose. Their mornings still began as always — with coffee, breakfast, their gentle morning hug and kiss, and the familiar humour of their daily "Bladder chatter" as Ben playfully called it. But each day, after the laughter and comfort of their routine settled, the books returned to the table. Not for schoolwork. Not for simple research. For something far more personal.

The books now were filled with maps of Denmark, the royal lineage charts of the Danish monarchy, old castle sketches, and photographs of Copenhagen that glimmered beneath the sun like a city carved from old myths. Ben and Isla pored over every image, every name, every story that seemed to hum beneath the printed pages. The facts weren't strangers anymore — they were family.

"It's not just a vacation, Ben," Isla whispered one afternoon as they traced the family trees before them. "It's like the land itself is waiting for us." Ben nodded, his fingers sliding down a page that detailed the line of Danish kings, his breath catching slightly as he whispered back. "I know. It's something more."

As his eyes travelled along the names, a familiar pressure stirred inside him — that pull, gentle but undeniable, as though an invisible hand pressed softly against his chest. It wasn't education pulling him to Denmark. It was Béla — the great-grandfather twelve generations back, whose voice had whispered into Ben's childhood long before books ever taught him who he was. The pull came not from dates or names, but from blood itself. "There's something there," Ben said quietly. "I don't know what, but... he's pulling me there. Béla. I can feel him."

Isla reached over, placing her hand over his. "I feel it too," she admitted softly. "On my side, through my family. It's not about history. It's about standing there. Breathing it in. Feeling it in our bones." They turned their focus to Denmark's castles — each one more magnificent than the last. Amalienborg, standing like a living crown in the centre of Copenhagen; Kronborg Castle, where Hamlet's shadow lingered; and Frederiksborg Castle, with its grand gardens stretching like an emerald sea behind its majestic walls. Each castle told a story, but what fascinated them more wasn't the stones or the towers — it was knowing their ancestors may have once stood beneath those very spires.

They studied the Danish monarchy in greater depth now. They read of HM King Frederik X, born in 1968, and now reigning since January 2024. His family traced back more than a thousand years — kings upon kings, generation upon generation, reaching toward a figure born sometime around the year 900. The sheer age of it all made Isla's breath catch as she softly whispered, "Over a thousand years of kings and queens, Ben." Ben nodded, the weight of it settling like a quiet drumbeat in his chest. "And somehow... we're part of that."

Jeff watched them quietly from the side of the room as they worked. His eyes narrowed, not in doubt, but in respect for the journey they were on. He had long since stopped trying to guide them in this part of their research. This was something different now — something only they could follow.

Robert and Claire too had begun to sense it. Whenever they visited, they saw the same gleam in their daughter's eyes that they saw in Ben's — that shared pull toward something waiting across the sea. And though the adults still spoke carefully, allowing the children space to discover, they too understood something powerful was unfolding. A calling was beginning to form. "We have to go, don't we?" Isla finally said, her voice steady but full of reverence.

Ben answered without hesitation. "Yes. We have to stand where they stood. Not for lessons. Not for books. For us. For who we are." The cottage fell into a quiet stillness as their decision settled like sacred stone beneath their feet. Outside, the wind stirred the leaves gently, as though carrying the faint whisper of ancestors smiling down upon them. Their birthdays were just weeks away. And beyond those birthdays, Denmark waited. The decision was made. There was no more questioning. No more if — only when. And when was fast approaching.

For days, the cottage buzzed with a quiet energy as plans began to form. The air carried a strange mixture of excitement and reverence, as though each suitcase, each document, each travel booking was not simply preparation for a trip, but for something far older — something deeply sacred that was now finally coming to pass. Ben and Isla could feel it in their bones with every passing hour.

Jeff sat with them at the table, scrolling through flight options on his laptop while Robert and Claire reviewed the travel documents and passports carefully laid out before them. Isla leaned against Ben's shoulder, their fingers laced as they watched every detail unfold. The simple act of planning felt strangely ceremonial. "We'll fly directly to Copenhagen," Jeff explained, tapping the screen. "Nonstop. That way you two won't be too exhausted when you arrive."

Ben nodded, studying the screen intently. "We land early morning local time. That gives us the entire first day to breathe it all in." Claire looked over at Isla with a warm, steady gaze. "And you both have your formal clothing ready, yes? You may not be attending any grand ceremonies, but this trip carries weight, my love. You represent your families now — and you represent yourselves." Isla smiled softly, squeezing Ben's hand. "We know, Mum. We're ready."

Robert, ever the quiet strength, added calmly, "You'll be meeting people who live in these stories you've studied. They're not just names on a page anymore. They're breathing, living bloodlines — like yours." Jeff smiled gently, leaning back in his chair. "And you'll walk where your ancestors walked. Feel the stones beneath your feet that they once stood upon. That's something very few people ever get to experience."

Ben's breath caught slightly as a soft chill danced up his spine — not from fear, but from the heavy awareness that had been quietly following him since they first opened the Denmark journals. "I don't even think this is about meeting people anymore," he whispered softly. "It's about... feeling the family. Feeling who we are." Isla nodded, her voice just above a breath. "Reuniting with something bigger than us."

The days ahead filled with small but careful preparations — securing the final documents, printing itineraries, ensuring Isla's travel health paperwork was in order, triple-checking every last detail. Jeff coordinated with the embassy quietly, keeping their arrival low-key as much as possible, though he sensed there would be little secrecy once their feet touched Danish soil. Unbeknownst to Ben and Isla, word of their arrival had already reached the highest ears.

In the royal palace, King Frederik X had been informed days earlier. The message arrived without great fanfare, carried quietly through channels few even knew existed. The moment he read it, a strange calm washed over him. He already knew they were coming. In fact, as he sat alone in his chambers that evening, he smiled faintly to himself and whispered aloud into the empty room, "I was told they would arrive."

It was not by report that he learned of them first — but by dream. As the cottage preparations carried on far away, neither Ben nor Isla yet knew that a door long closed was quietly opening to receive them — not as guests, not as outsiders, but as family returning home. The plane tickets were booked. The clothing neatly packed. The documents carefully secured. In three weeks, just after their birthdays, the royal pilgrimage would begin.

The three weeks slipped past like pages in a book gently turning themselves. And as the calendar brought them forward, it finally arrived: their birthdays. August had come, carrying with it the fullness of summer. The skies stayed clear as though granting one final gift before the journey ahead. The air was warm, the wind gentle, and even Kent — known so often for its temperamental weather — seemed to smile upon the occasion. This year, however, the birthdays held a weight far beyond candles and cake.

Ben turned ten on the second day of the month, Isla just one day before. But their birthdays were never treated as separate affairs — not since the day they had first become soulmates. Every year, it had become their shared tradition: one long birthday celebration wrapped together like their lives. Their parents, as always, respected that deeply.

The cottage buzzed with the warm glow of family as Robert and Claire arrived early that morning. Annemarie had brought the decorations, simple but elegant. Jeff handled breakfast while the children remained outside, breathing in the morning air, their hands clasped as they sat beneath the same oak tree that had so often heard their laughter. Ben glanced up toward the open sky. "This one feels different," he whispered.

Isla nodded, resting her head gently against his shoulder. "It does. Like something's closing, and something else is opening." They sat in that shared silence until Claire called them inside. The kitchen table was neatly dressed with their favourite breakfast — fresh pastries, warm bread, fruit, and the smell of coffee gently weaving through the room. But what stood at the centre wasn't a grand stack of presents. Instead, there sat two simple velvet boxes — one red, one blue — their names embossed in delicate silver.

Ben and Isla exchanged a quiet glance, both understanding that the contents held more than ordinary gifts. Robert spoke softly, his voice full of warmth. "Before you open those, we want you both to know something." Claire continued gently. "We're so proud of who you've become — not for what you've learned, not for the names you've uncovered, but for who you are together. The journey ahead belongs to you, and we believe in it. Completely."

Jeff nodded, his voice steady. "These aren't just gifts. They're reminders. Reminders of where you come from, who you are, and who you're becoming." Ben opened his box first. Inside lay a polished pendant — a simple gold medallion bearing the ancient family crest of Pattenden, carved delicately into its face, the design traced from the very seals they had studied so many nights together. The back carried only two words: Blood Remembers.

Isla's box revealed its twin. But hers carried the Stuart family crest, likewise inscribed in perfect detail. The back bore the same words, etched into the smooth metal: Blood Remembers. Tears gathered in Isla's eyes as she whispered, "It's perfect." Ben reached across the table, taking her hand. "It's us." Their parents smiled quietly as the children carefully fastened the pendants around their necks, each piece falling gently against their hearts.

The rest of the day unfolded in simple, perfect rhythm. There were no grand parties, no long guest lists, no noisy gatherings. Just laughter, quiet joy, a shared cake, and long walks beneath the tall trees that had sheltered them since childhood. As the sun began to lower into its evening arc, Ben and Isla sat once more beneath the stars — as they so often did — knowing that tomorrow would begin the journey they had waited for all their lives.

"This was the best birthday," Isla whispered softly as she lay against Ben's chest. Ben kissed the top of her head, his voice steady. "The best one yet. But next year… we'll celebrate in places we've never seen before."

The stars blinked above them, quiet witnesses to the promise. And as the night softly closed around them, they fell asleep — soulmates, sovereigns, children — on the edge of something far greater than either of them yet fully understood.

The morning broke softly, as though even the rising sun understood the weight of what was to come. There was no rush, no flurry of last-minute panic. Every piece of preparation had already been laid out with careful hands. Their bags stood ready near the door, passports tucked safely inside Jeff's travel satchel. The house, for once, was quiet — not with absence, but with calm. Ben and Isla rose together from their bedroll, sharing their morning hug as they always did. The kiss that followed was tender, unhurried, full of the weight they both carried now. This morning was not like the others. It hummed differently. Beneath the stillness was a pulse neither of them could name, but both of them could feel.

Their usual morning relief was followed by coffee already waiting for them, brewed by Jeff before dawn. He greeted them with his familiar grin as they stepped into the kitchen, their fingers intertwined. "Today's the day," Jeff said softly, as though raising his voice might disturb something sacred. Ben nodded. "It feels like we've waited forever. And somehow, like it was always waiting for us."

Claire and Robert arrived shortly after, their faces glowing with pride. They weren't nervous — not for this. They understood, better than anyone, what this journey meant. The family gathered for one last meal together before departure — simple, quiet, full of shared glances that said everything words could not. And then, it was time.

The drive to London Heathrow was quiet, marked by steady conversation about travel details and light laughter to ease the weight pressing gently on their chests. As the airport neared, Ben's hand remained wrapped tightly around Isla's, both of them drawing comfort from one another in that steady, familiar grasp that had carried them through so many chapters already.

The flight itself was long, but uneventful. They settled into their seats quickly after boarding, wrapped in their blankets, quietly reading, occasionally napping. For much of the flight, they slept, allowing exhaustion and anticipation to blend into restless dreams neither could fully recall by the time they descended.

The soft rumble of the airplane wheels kissing the Copenhagen runway stirred them gently awake. As the engines roared down to a hum, Isla blinked against the cabin light, her head resting briefly against Ben's shoulder before she sat upright, fully alert. Ben stretched his arms and whispered, "We're here."

Even inside the sealed cabin, the Danish air seemed different — cool but not cold, alive but not harsh. It carried something beneath it — a strange familiarity neither of them could quite explain. As though even the wind itself whispered, You've returned. Jeff glanced at them both, his voice barely above a whisper. "This is where your feet meet your blood." They nodded, exchanging quiet glances as the plane rolled to a final stop. The journey was no longer a dream. The ground beneath them was calling.

Passing through customs was smooth — the paperwork prepared, the faces kind but professional. They moved through the terminal like silent observers, soaking in every image: the signs, the language, the architecture, the people. This was no longer just study material. This was real. Outside the terminal waited not a rental car, nor a shuttle, but a sleek black vehicle parked alone near the exit. Standing beside it were two men in formal attire, elegant without flash, bearing no visible insignia yet carrying unmistakable royal presence.

The taller attendant stepped forward, bowing his head with gentle precision. "Welcome to Denmark," he spoke in perfect English. "His Majesty King Frederik X extends his personal welcome. You are to be escorted directly to Amalienborg Palace."

Ben and Isla stood frozen momentarily, exchanging wide, astonished glances. Jeff, ever calm, simply nodded and responded, "We're honoured."

The drive through Copenhagen felt like a surreal dream. The streets moved gracefully beneath them — clean, orderly, filled with the quiet dignity of old Europe. The palaces they had studied for months now stood not as pictures, but as breathing monuments before their eyes. The city hummed, but not with noise — with ancient life. As the car rounded the final bend, the sprawling grandeur of Amalienborg Palace came into full view. Ben and Isla both inhaled sharply, their hearts rising into their throats. This was where their ancestors had walked. And now, where they would walk too.

The car doors opened without command, and they stepped out into the cool Danish air. The great palace doors ahead of them opened as if by unseen hands. Inside, upon gleaming marble floors beneath towering ceilings, stood King Frederik X. Tall, poised, and serene, he carried no excessive ornament, no grand display of opulence. His dark suit was simple but flawless. His eyes, however, held everything. Familiarity. Knowing. Family.

Ben and Isla approached slowly, hand in hand, the weight in their chests almost overwhelming. But as they neared him, his smile warmed, and his arms opened in simple welcome. "Welcome home," King Frederik spoke, his voice like quiet thunder wrapped in velvet. The words struck with gentle force. Isla's eyes brimmed instantly with tears, her breath catching. Ben's throat tightened, words failing him for a moment. He swallowed, whispering only, "You knew?"

The King nodded softly. "Yes. I knew." "But... how?" Isla whispered, barely audible. The King smiled again, eyes warm, lowering his voice. "You may not believe me if I told you." Ben found his voice steady now. "Try us." The King chuckled softly, lowering his hands to gently rest upon their shoulders. "A dream," he said calmly. "I was shown. I don't know how or why. But I was told you were coming. And who you were. King and Queen — not by ambition, but by blood. You are my family. Distant, yes. But blood does not measure distance. Blood remembers."

He paused, letting the words settle in their hearts before softly adding, "Welcome home, my King. My Queen." Neither child could respond. The tears slipped freely down Isla's face as Ben stood frozen, the old hum of his blood vibrating quietly within his bones. This was not a meeting. This was reunion. With a final gentle nod, Frederik spoke once more. "No family of mine stays at a hotel. The palace is your home for as long as you remain here."

And as the royal attendants stepped aside, the great marble doors opened wider — not for visitors, but for family returning to the place they had never truly left. Hand in hand, Ben and Isla crossed the threshold — soulmates, sovereigns, and children of a crown that would forever remain a secret to the world, but not to their hearts.

The great marble doors closed gently behind them as Ben and Isla crossed into the palace halls — but it never once felt like they were closing off the world. Instead, it felt like stepping into something both ancient and alive. The air was cool, but not cold. The marble beneath their feet carried a softness beneath its strength, as though centuries had carefully worn it into familiarity. And everywhere around them, the history they had studied for years now breathed in quiet dignity.

The attendants moved gracefully, not hurried nor stiff, but with the ease of those who had long served a living monarchy that understood its weight. Every movement was purposeful, yet never overwhelming. This was not theatre. This was home — a royal home that carried its age not like a museum, but like a living ancestor who watched kindly over each new generation.

King Frederik X walked alongside them personally, not as a distant sovereign but as kin. There were no guards trailing them, no towering entourage of protocol. It was intimate. Honest. As though he, too, understood how sacred this first step truly was. "Everything you see here," Frederik spoke softly as they moved through the grand corridor, "has stood for centuries. But I want you to understand — these walls are not what make us family." He glanced toward them both, his voice lowering with warmth. "The blood does. The bond does."

Ben listened intently, his hand still resting securely in Isla's. "It's like standing in a story we've read a thousand times," he whispered. "Only now... we're in it." Frederik nodded gently. "You're not in it, my young King — you're part of it." The private guest quarters prepared for them were not the grandest chambers of the palace, but they were no less breathtaking. Large windows overlooked manicured royal gardens stretching far into the distance, while the high ceilings held hand-painted mouldings that traced out scenes of Danish history, their ancestors' faces likely hidden within those intricate details. The rooms smelled faintly of polished wood, old books, and fresh linens — a perfect mixture of age and comfort.

Jeff entered behind them, quietly placing their luggage on the appropriate tables as the attendants discreetly withdrew. Robert and Claire stood near the doorway, quietly allowing the moment to belong to the children. There was a reverence among the adults — an unspoken understanding that what was happening belonged first to Ben and Isla.

The rest of them were witnesses to something older than their own years.

Isla walked slowly toward the tall window, pressing her palm gently against the cool glass as she gazed over the gardens. "It's beautiful," she whispered, her voice soft with awe. Ben followed beside her, standing in silent agreement as he let the sight wash over him.

"It doesn't feel like we're visiting," he finally said. "It feels like... like we never left." Frederik, standing a short distance behind them, smiled at the truth of those words. "That's because you didn't. The blood never forgets where it came from." Isla turned toward the King, her voice small but steady. "We don't know everything yet."

Frederik's eyes softened. "You will. In time. You carry what matters already — the love, the reverence, the understanding that this crown was never meant to be worn, but carried." He paused, letting the words settle gently. "And that, my dear children, is why I've waited for you." Ben's voice trembled faintly. "You've waited for us?" Frederik nodded slowly. "Not by choice. By knowing. I could feel you long before the letters arrived, long before the names reached my table. I knew you would come. And now you are here."

The quiet filled the room again, not with awkwardness, but with a gravity that wrapped gently around all of them — a kind of peace that spoke through silence itself. As the first evening in Denmark drew closer, the King offered one final word before leaving them to settle. "You are home now. This palace stands because of your ancestors, too. Eat, rest, walk the gardens, breathe in your family's history. Tomorrow, we will begin." With a simple nod of farewell, Frederik stepped back into the hall, leaving the doors open behind him — as family always would.

Ben turned toward Isla, their hands instinctively finding each other once more. She smiled, her eyes still shimmering. "We're really here," she whispered. Ben pulled her gently into his arms, his voice warm against her ear. "And we're home." Outside, the Danish sky faded into twilight, its pale blue blending into gold as night approached. The ancient stones of Amalienborg whispered softly beneath their feet — not as cold monuments, but as threads of family — finally restored.

The Danish morning arrived softly, as though careful not to disturb the sacred stillness that lingered inside the palace walls. Pale shafts of early sunlight slipped through the tall windows, casting golden bands across the high ceilings of their guest chambers.

The first gentle breeze from the gardens carried with it the sweet, unfamiliar fragrance of summer blossoms, a scent both calming and strangely familiar.

Ben stirred first, his eyes opening slowly to the grand ceiling above him. He lay still for a moment, his mind catching up to the reality around him. This wasn't home in Kent. This was Denmark. This was family. This was something far older than he could explain. He turned his head and smiled softly at Isla, who was still nestled beside him beneath the light bedding.

As though sensing his gaze, Isla's eyelids fluttered open, and her lips curved gently into a smile that needed no words. She reached out, her hand finding his, their fingers naturally weaving together as though they had never spent a moment apart. Their morning routine unfolded as it always did — sacred in its simplicity. The morning hug came first, their arms wrapping around one another with the quiet steadiness that marked their every sunrise. Then came their kiss — unhurried, deliberate, filled with that same eternal promise they had shared since their earliest days together.

Ben whispered, barely above breath, "Bladder chatter." Isla giggled softly, her voice playful even within the palace. "Ladies first, always." Their morning relief followed, and by the time they returned to their chamber, they found breakfast already prepared on a polished cart beside the window. Warm breads, fresh fruits, and carafes of rich, steaming coffee awaited them — arranged with such care that it spoke of the palace's quiet understanding of their private rhythm.

Jeff entered not long after, his presence as steady as ever, though even he could not fully conceal the awe that remained in his eyes as he glanced around the ornate chamber. "I trust you both slept well?" he asked softly. Ben nodded. "Better than I expected. It doesn't feel heavy here. It feels... right." Isla sipped her coffee and whispered, "It feels like family." As they ate, the morning unfolded in its peaceful cadence until a light knock came at the chamber door. One of the royal attendants stepped inside with a slight bow. "His Majesty would like to receive you after breakfast, when you are ready. Today will be informal. No ceremonies. He simply wishes to begin your time here properly." Jeff smiled reassuringly. "When you're ready, we'll go."

Ben and Isla prepared themselves carefully, wearing simple but elegant clothing — not overdone, but respectful to the dignity of where they stood. Isla brushed her hair softly, securing it with the small pearl clip her mother had given her before the trip. Ben adjusted the pendant around his neck, the golden crest of Pattenden resting just over his heart. They looked at one another quietly, seeing not just themselves but generations standing quietly behind them.

Hand in hand, they followed Jeff through the long corridor toward the royal wing. The palace seemed even grander by morning light — not overwhelming, but alive. The stone whispered as their feet pressed softly against the polished floors. The tall portraits that lined the corridors now spoke to them differently than they had in books. These were no longer distant faces from history. They were family. As they entered one of the smaller private receiving rooms, King Frederik stood waiting near the tall windows, his gaze resting calmly upon the gardens beyond. He turned as they entered, his face instantly warm with that familiar, knowing smile. "Good morning," he greeted gently. "And welcome to your first day... home."

Ben and Isla bowed respectfully, their movements graceful but never rehearsed. There was no stiffness between them — only family meeting family. "Today," Frederik continued, gesturing toward the seats before him, "I simply wish to talk. To sit. To begin." They sat together, the morning light filling the room with a softness that made the grand space feel smaller, more intimate. Frederik studied them both for a moment, not as a king sizing up visitors, but as a man quietly reading the faces of those long expected.

"You do not need to prove yourselves here," he said softly. "You are here because you belong. The blood that runs through you — it was never lost. Only sleeping. Now, you walk among your ancestors once more." Ben swallowed gently, his voice steady as he whispered, "We've read so much. We've traced so many lines. But being here... it's different." Frederik nodded. "Because knowledge fills the mind, but presence fills the soul." Isla, her voice tender but sure, added, "It feels... like we've come full circle." The King smiled. "You have."

They spoke for hours — not in lectures, but in stories. Frederik shared memories of Denmark's deep history, stories of rulers and queens whose names Ben and Isla had once written in neat, careful notes on their bedroom desk at home. Now, those names lived in spoken word, carried in the voice of their cousin-king. There was no distance. No pretence. Only the gentle weaving of a story that was always waiting to be rejoined.

As the morning passed into early afternoon, Frederik finally rose. "Tomorrow, I will show you the private archives. But today... today is for breathing." He led them toward the private gardens beyond the hall — tall hedges, flowering pathways, quiet fountains where no tourists wandered, and where only family was permitted to walk. And as Ben and Isla stepped into the ancient gardens hand in hand, the truth settled fully into their hearts: they were no longer visitors in Denmark. They were home.

The following morning unfolded with the same quiet grace that seemed to settle over every hour inside the palace. There was no rush, no clamour of schedules. Instead, time moved like an old river — steady, patient, dignified.
The staff had already come and gone, leaving a perfectly arranged breakfast for Ben, Isla, Jeff, Robert, and Claire. The smell of fresh coffee blended with the warm notes of pastries and berries gathered from the royal gardens.

As always, Ben and Isla shared their quiet routine before the day truly began. Their morning embrace came first, followed by a long, gentle kiss that neither of them ever rushed. The words I love you passed between them like sacred breath. Then came the soft giggles of their playful Bladder chatter as they took their turns relieving themselves before returning to breakfast, their hands never far from one another's.

Jeff smiled quietly as he watched them. Even here, in the grandest of places, their rhythm remained unshaken. It was one of the many reasons their story was unlike any that had come before them. Shortly after breakfast, a light knock came to the chamber door. One of the palace attendants stepped inside with that familiar blend of grace and discretion. "His Majesty awaits you in the private archives, whenever you are ready." Ben and Isla exchanged glances — wide-eyed, breath steady, hearts quickening.

Jeff offered a gentle nod. "Let's go." They followed the attendant down a long corridor few visitors to Amalienborg ever saw. The stone beneath their feet changed subtly as they moved deeper into the older wings of the palace, where history breathed thickly within the very walls.

The air grew cooler, but not cold — like walking into the soft embrace of a library that had never forgotten its secrets. At the end of the passage, tall wooden doors stood before them, their carved panels worn smooth by generations of royal hands. King Frederik waited there, standing beside the great doors as though guarding a sacred threshold.

"Good morning," he greeted, his voice calm as ever. "Today... you meet the memory." With a subtle turn of his wrist, the heavy doors creaked open, revealing a chamber unlike any they had ever seen before. The private royal archives were not vast in size — not a sprawling hall like the grand libraries shown in books — but what they lacked in scale, they made up for in gravity. Wooden shelves lined the walls from floor to ceiling, each packed with bound volumes, scrolls, sealed cases, and preserved documents wrapped in delicate fabric.

The scent of aged parchment and polished oak filled the air. Soft light poured in through high narrow windows, illuminating dust particles that drifted lazily, as though even the air here moved with reverence. Ben's breath caught in his chest. "It's alive," he whispered. Frederik smiled softly. "Yes. These aren't simply records.

This is blood... written." Isla reached for Ben's hand, her fingers tightening as they stepped further into the chamber. On the far wall, beneath the golden seal of the Danish crown, stood a long oak table where several volumes had already been carefully laid out.

"These," Frederik continued, guiding them toward the table, "were selected because they belong to you. They hold the threads of your families. Denmark. Scotland. England. Hungary. The woven braid that lives inside your veins." Ben and Isla stood in silent awe as they looked down upon the open pages. The first book displayed the Stuart line — carefully handwritten, tracing Isla's blood back through the kings of Scotland, through James VI, across into the House of Rosenshavn through ancient marital ties that spanned centuries of diplomacy, war, and union.

The second book bore the name Pattenden, inscribed in careful, aged script. This one, too, traced lines Ben had already studied at home — but here, the royal archivists had layered the connections far deeper than any public record had shown. The ties into Denmark, through branches long absorbed into European nobility, now lay open before them. "It's all here..." Isla whispered, her voice cracking slightly as tears welled.

Frederik's gaze remained steady. "Yes. Because it was never lost." Jeff stood silently behind them, his own throat tightening as he watched his children stand in front of something far larger than any single man could carry. Robert and Claire stood arm in arm, quietly wiping tears as they beheld their daughter's rightful place revealed before their very eyes.

Ben traced a finger along one of the names. "We didn't just come here," he whispered. "We came back here." Frederik stepped forward, placing his hands gently upon both Ben's and Isla's shoulders. His voice lowered. "And the walls remember you." The weight of the moment settled upon them, heavy but not crushing — like wearing a cloak woven by a thousand hands, each one welcoming them home.

They remained in the archive for hours, studying, asking, learning — not as outsiders, not as researchers — but as heirs being shown what had always quietly waited for them. As they stepped out into the daylight again, the sun felt warmer, brighter, as though even the Danish sky itself had exhaled. The past no longer stood behind them. It stood with them.

The morning after their first descent into the archives felt somehow lighter, though the weight of discovery still pressed gently against Ben and Isla's chests. It was not a burden—it was presence.

The knowledge of their ancestry no longer lived solely in books and family trees; it pulsed in their very skin now. Their feet, their hands, their breath — all carried threads of lives long passed but never lost.

King Frederik met them once more that morning, his presence as steady as it had been since the moment they first stepped foot into his palace. "Today," he said softly, "your history moves from paper to earth. Today, you walk where they once walked." With that, the palace doors opened again, but not for formal ceremony. There were no watching crowds, no cameras, no salutes of trumpets. This was not for show. This was family returning to its soil.

The royal grounds stretched beyond what photographs or maps could ever fully capture. The air itself felt different out here—crisp, clean, as though centuries of sovereign breath still lingered, waiting for new heirs to inhale it. Ben and Isla walked hand in hand along the carefully laid stone pathways, their steps slow, deliberate. Isla glanced up at the towering oaks lining the outer gardens. "They've stood here longer than we've been alive," she whispered.

Ben nodded, his voice low. "And yet... it feels like they've been waiting for us." Frederik walked slightly behind them, allowing the children to lead themselves, but always nearby—a steady pillar of reassurance. "These trees, these grounds, these stones — they have memory," he spoke gently. "Not like ours. Deeper. They carry the weight of every foot that has passed across them. Today, your footprints join theirs." Jeff, Robert, and Claire followed a respectful distance behind, their own hearts full as they watched the children's quiet, unspoken awe unfold. They were not tourists. They were not visitors. They were home.

At one point, near the edge of a quiet reflecting pond, Frederik paused and gestured toward an older section of the garden where a stone bench sat beneath a grand maple. "This was where my great-grandfather would sit and read the family records aloud to me as a boy. Stories of kings. Of queens. Of those who stood where you stand now." Ben sat slowly on the bench, Isla beside him. He glanced out across the water, his voice soft but certain. "Someday... I'll sit like this with our children."

Isla squeezed his hand, resting her head against his shoulder. "And we'll tell them everything." Frederik smiled. "That is how the memory lives." The afternoon unfolded gently, their walk stretching across the vast private grounds that most would never see. Hidden courtyards, secret gardens, aged walls that whispered stories only few were allowed to hear. Every stone held echoes of their blood.

By late afternoon, the royal attendants quietly signalled that preparations for the evening meal had begun. This dinner would not be held in the grand state dining room, but in the private royal dining hall—where only family sat.

As the sun dipped low, painting the Danish sky with streaks of amber and lavender, Ben and Isla were led back into the palace. The quiet grace of the attendants allowed them to change into their formal attire: simple but elegant clothing that carried dignity without spectacle. Ben wore a dark tailored jacket with understated silver buttons, while Isla wore a pale sapphire dress, the soft blue mirroring the northern skies outside. Around both their necks still hung the pendants of Pattenden and Stuart—small, but never unnoticed.

When they entered the private dining hall, King Frederik stood at the head of the long table, his smile warm, his posture relaxed. Two other members of the royal household stood nearby—extended family who had quietly learned of Ben and Isla's arrival and now came to witness the next generation step forward. Frederik gestured toward the table. "Please—sit. Tonight, we dine not as monarch and guests. Tonight, we dine as family."

The table was elegantly set, yet absent of the overwhelming formality many would expect from royal banquets. The meal was intimate: fresh seafood from Danish waters, vegetables grown in the palace gardens, fresh breads, and dishes prepared as they had been for generations.

Throughout the dinner, conversation flowed not as royal business, but as the quiet weaving of lives long separated by geography, now slowly knitting together again. Frederik shared small family stories—anecdotes of old kings, private quirks of queens, humorous tales that never reached public history books. Ben and Isla listened intently, occasionally laughing, sometimes blinking back quiet emotion. Every word was another thread sewing them deeper into the fabric of their blood.

At one point, Frederik looked directly at them both, his voice lowering slightly as though speaking a truth that only they could fully understand. "The world may never fully know your names. Nor should it. But know this—you carry in your hearts the quiet weight of kings and queens who lived so this moment could exist."

Ben swallowed gently, his eyes shining. "We will carry it. Always." Isla added softly, "We won't forget. Not ever." Frederik smiled, his voice calm and sure. "Nor will the blood." As the evening drew to a close, they shared one final toast, raising their crystal glasses beneath the ancient chandeliers that glittered like northern stars. "To family," Frederik said. "To family," they whispered in return. The candles flickered, the room fell into a deep peace, and the quiet truth settled over them once more: They were home.

Their final morning in Denmark arrived far too quickly, as such sacred visits often do. The palace, which had become their second home, breathed softly around them as the quiet hours unfolded. The sunlight filtering through the tall windows carried a kind of golden melancholy, as though even the sky itself recognized that something precious was coming to a close. Ben and Isla sat together in the private parlour just off the royal wing, hands intertwined, hearts full, and eyes still shimmering with the weight of all they had lived in the past days. Though their time was drawing to an end, neither of them carried sadness. What filled their souls instead was something far deeper — completion.

The door opened softly, and King Frederik entered with his usual calm grace. Yet today, there was something different in his bearing — something unspoken resting gently beneath his smile. "My King. My Queen," he greeted, his voice as warm as ever. "There is one final gift." Ben and Isla sat up slightly, exchanging brief glances, sensing something sacred in the air. The King stepped forward, carrying in his hands a long, polished wooden case, its craftsmanship simple but elegant, secured with delicate clasps of gold.

"This," Frederik began, his voice soft but steady, "has been prepared for many years. It was not made for show. It was not made for display. It was made... for truth." He slowly opened the case. Nestled inside, resting against deep blue velvet, were two crowns — one for Ben, one for Isla. These were not heavy, oversized ceremonial pieces designed for grand coronations. These were royal — personal, intimate — crafted to reflect who they truly were.

Ben's crown stood with powerful simplicity, its polished gold band perfectly balanced with elegant fleur-de-lis points. Embedded within the scrollwork were deep sapphire-blue stones — a symbol of his Danish and Pattenden roots, mingled with the Harvick and Horváth bloodlines that travelled through centuries of forgotten sovereignty. The craftsmanship spoke of ancient Europe, refined yet powerful — as though carrying the silent weight of both nobility and humility within its very curves.

Isla's crown was stunning in its delicate majesty. Rising in graceful arcs, the golden frame cradled brilliant blue sapphires set within a pattern of fine filigree. The crown sparkled beneath the morning light, its diamonds and stones reflecting the nobility of her Stuart, Gibb, and Danish heritage. It was both regal and tender — not a crown of war, but of birthright and unity. The central sapphire gleamed like a deep blue eye, as though watching over her every step. Along the inner band, in tiny, perfect inscription, read the simple words: Blood Remembers. Love Endures.

Ben's breath caught. Isla's hands instinctively flew to her mouth, tears welling instantly. "These are not ceremonial," Frederik whispered. "They are not political. They are not public. They are... sacred. A reminder of who you are — not who the world says you are, but who your ancestors know you to be. You are family. You are sovereign. You are whole."

Neither child spoke. Tears gathered and fell freely as they stared upon the crowns that now belonged not to fiction, but to them. "I had these made for you long ago," Frederik continued softly, "for when the day came that your feet finally returned home." The King stepped closer, gently lifting Ben's crown first and placing it upon his head. The gold rested perfectly, as though it had been waiting only for him. He then turned to Isla, lifting her crown and lowering it softly onto her hair, adjusting it with fatherly care. "There," he whispered. "Now the circle is complete."

Ben and Isla turned to one another, eyes locked, souls trembling with emotion, and smiled. They were still children. Still soulmates. But now, they stood as King and Queen in truth — the secret sealed forever within their hearts. Frederik smiled softly. "Come now," he said with quiet pride. "There is one more thing." They were escorted into a sleek royal car that had been waiting at the private entrance. The drive took them to a secluded estate outside Copenhagen — a place few outsiders ever knew existed. It was here that royal portraits were made — not for public galleries, but for the sacred family archives, where bloodlines were preserved in paint and canvas as they had been for generations.

Inside the grand studio, the painter awaited them — a master of the royal house who had already studied their faces with quiet detail throughout their visit. Today was simply the sitting. Ben and Isla stood together before the grand backdrop — crowns resting upon their heads, hands gently joined at the centre. The painter worked swiftly, as though the image itself was simply emerging from the truth already present.

When the painting was finished days later, it would depict not only their features but the weight of their lineage — two children, soulmates, sovereigns, standing before eternity, carrying within them the entire breath of those who had come before. But the first copy was not destined for the palace archives.

As the King promised, a perfect replica would be delivered to Jeff and placed inside their cottage back home — a reminder not only to Ben and Isla, but to everyone who entered their home, that the crown they carried was not lost, not imagined, and never forgotten.

Later that afternoon, as the royal family stood on the private tarmac, Frederik personally escorted them to the waiting aircraft. The royal jet stood tall against the Danish sky, its gleaming white fuselage marked clearly with the personal insignia of the Danish Royal House — the crowned shield, the golden lions of Denmark, and beneath it, an elegant scroll which read in the old tongue: "For blood that lives, and kings that return." This was no ordinary plane. This was family. "No family of mine leaves as strangers," Frederik whispered as he embraced them one final time. "You are home. Always."

The royal jet stood proudly upon the private runway outside Copenhagen, its polished fuselage gleaming beneath the Danish sun. The insignia of the Royal House of Rosenshavn was displayed with unmistakable dignity — the crowned shield, golden lions, and beneath it, the ancient words in royal script: "For blood that lives, and kings that return." There was no mistaking who this aircraft belonged to. This was not simply a flight home. This was a return wrapped in truth.

Jeff, Robert, and Claire stood with Ben and Isla at the base of the boarding stairs as the last of their luggage was carefully loaded. The royal attendants handled every movement with the reverence that such a journey demanded, while King Frederik stood nearby, his presence steady, his smile calm. He embraced them one final time, his arms drawing Ben and Isla tightly against him. "You carry all of us home now," he whispered. "This palace waits for you always."

"My King. My Queen," he added softly, kissing each of their foreheads, one by one. With a final nod to Jeff, Robert, and Claire, King Frederik stepped back as the royal family jet engines purred to life. The flight crew waited with full respect as the entire family boarded — together.

As the jet lifted smoothly into the Danish sky, the city of Copenhagen slowly disappeared beneath them. The royal flight crew operated in silent precision, allowing the passengers to simply rest, reflect, and quietly hold one another. Ben and Isla sat side-by-side as always, their fingers naturally intertwined, Isla leaning into Ben's shoulder as Jeff, Robert, and Claire sat just across the aisle. None of them spoke for some time. Words, for once, were not needed.

The jet crossed the waters, carried steadily beneath a perfect sky, until hours later, the familiar coastlines of England slowly appeared ahead. The green patchwork of the Kent countryside greeted them like an old friend—familiar, yet forever changed. Ben gazed out the window. "Home," he whispered.

"But different now," Isla added, her voice barely breath. The descent was smooth, the royal pilots guiding the aircraft toward the private tarmac already prepared for their arrival. Upon landing, the soft rumble of wheels touching English soil carried a weight that none of them could explain. The world outside continued as usual — unaware of the sacred truth that now travelled inside this small group.

The customs officers stood respectfully at a distance. There were no questions, no forms, no delays. The arrangements had already been cleared at the highest levels. This was no ordinary flight returning from holiday. This was a royal homecoming—one quietly protected by those who understood the magnitude of what now lived within these children. The luggage was unloaded with great care. The special velvet cases housing Ben and Isla's crowns were gently lifted by Jeff himself, as though cradling living bloodlines in his hands. The grand portrait, carefully sealed and cushioned within a protective crate, was transferred to a second vehicle, its journey now nearly complete.

As they departed the airport, the drive home to Kent carried an atmosphere that was peaceful, almost dreamlike. The fields rolled past as they always had, the same narrow country lanes, the same farmhouses, the same hedgerows whispering beneath the summer wind. Yet to Ben and Isla, every tree, every field now carried deeper meaning. They were no longer simply children of Kent. They were children of kings and queens—of blood that reached beyond time.

When they finally reached their quiet cottage, the familiar sight of their home filled their chests with warmth. The small stone walls, the ivy curling along the windows, the flowerbeds blooming gently beneath the English sky — nothing had changed, and yet everything had. Jeff stepped out first, opening the front door wide as though welcoming returning royalty into the palace of their hearts. "Home," he said softly, his voice thick.

Ben and Isla crossed the threshold hand in hand, their eyes absorbing every detail of the familiar room. The scent of aged timber, the comforting aroma of fresh coffee, and the faint creak of the old floors welcomed them as though the cottage itself had been waiting. The delivery team arrived shortly after, carrying the massive portrait through the doorway under Jeff's careful direction. When the protective wrappings were peeled away, all stood silent before it.

There they were: Ben and Isla, crowned in royal truth, their sovereign bloodlines resting visibly upon their brows. The painter had captured something far beyond mere likeness. He had captured who they truly were. Isla pressed her hand to her mouth as tears gathered in her eyes.

"It's us." Ben swallowed, whispering, "The secret is home now." Robert and Claire drew close, embracing both children softly from behind as Jeff stood beside them, one hand on each shoulder. They stood like that for a long moment, allowing the quiet breath of their ancestors to settle inside these small walls.

Later that evening, as twilight settled, Jeff carefully placed the crowns into the glass cabinet he had built for them — a simple but beautiful display in the living room, where they would rest safely, not as museum pieces, but as living heirlooms of truth. The cabinet remained unlocked. The crowns belonged to no one else. They were not to be hidden, nor flaunted — but simply kept.

Ben and Isla curled together beneath their blanket on the couch, hands entwined as always. Isla rested her head upon Ben's chest, feeling his steady heartbeat beneath her cheek. "It's all perfect now," she whispered softly. Ben kissed her forehead, pulling her closer. "It always was. But now... everyone who needs to know, knows." The cottage exhaled softly around them as night gently embraced the land. The world outside continued in ignorance. But within these walls — the crown was no longer a mystery. The secret was safe. The secret was home.

The summer air over Kent remained calm as the days slipped gently into weeks. For Ben and Isla, life seemed to find its rhythm once again, though nothing was as it once had been. The portrait stood quietly above the fireplace, the crowns rested safely in their glass cabinet, and the cottage breathed as though holding its own small kingdom within its walls. Yet for all the sacred truth that now surrounded them, Jeff was careful to protect their childhood first. Lessons continued each morning — their homeschooling uninterrupted — though both children often found their minds drifting to memories of Denmark, of King Frederik's embrace, of the sacred crowns that now lived here with them.

Robert and Claire visited often, sipping coffee with Jeff while Ben and Isla played outside beneath the endless blue sky. The air was full of laughter, mischief, and the kind of pure joy that only soulmates and childhood can weave together. On quiet evenings, the two of them sat beneath the stars on the back lawn, side by side, wrapped beneath their favourite blanket. Ben would tilt his head back, gazing toward the heavens, and whisper, "Do you think they're watching us?" Isla would always smile, leaning her head on his shoulder. "They're always watching. And smiling." The stars, the ancient witnesses to their bloodline, blinked quietly above.

The village of Kent whispered, as villages do. Some neighbours suspected much, others only knew whispers and fragments of truth, and most simply left them be. Jeff, however, remained vigilant — always aware that secrets, no matter how sacred, had ways of slipping beyond their chosen walls. But for now — for this season — peace held. The world outside carried on with its noise, but here inside the cottage, the world was smaller. Quieter. Sacred.

Ben and Isla studied by day, laughed by evening, and fell asleep each night curled beside one another under their open sleeping bag in the living room — soulmates wrapped in soft breathing, the quiet comfort of innocence, and the unspoken weight of ancient crowns that few would ever know. Jeff would often pause in the doorway as he watched them sleep, their small fingers still intertwined even in dreams. His heart would tighten each time, whispering softly in his mind, may no storm ever reach them.

The world remained silent.

The secret remained safe.

For now.

CHAPTER 11: THE SECRET BREACHE

The morning light in Kent held a kind of soft indifference, as if the sky itself had not yet decided whether it would bless the day with sun or grey. But beneath that uncertain sky, the world had already shifted, and none within the house yet fully grasped how permanent that shift would become. Ben sat at the kitchen table, fingers curled tightly around a simple white mug, steam rising in thin threads from his tea. Isla sat across from him, her small hands wrapped around her own cup, her thumb tracing slow circles against the porcelain as if trying to soothe it, or perhaps herself.

The first knock on the door had not come from a visitor or friend. It had not come from Jeff, nor Robert, nor Claire. It had come instead from the low, hollow knock of unease. The phone had rung at dawn, breaking the gentle hush that often lingered in their mornings. Annemarie answered it softly, her voice steady but thin as she listened. A polite, clipped voice on the other end had introduced himself as Inspector Reynolds from the Kent Constabulary. Jeff, standing in the hallway with his arms folded, listened carefully to her end of the conversation, the concern in his eyes growing sharper with every word exchanged.

"They're outside," Annemarie said at last, lowering the receiver, her voice catching ever so slightly as she turned toward Jeff. "Reporters. Photographers. At the gate. Dozens of them." Jeff exhaled through his nose, the breath controlled but weighted. "I was afraid of this," he murmured, stepping into the room as Annemarie glanced toward the children. Isla's wide eyes met his with a silent question, but Ben's face held something different — not panic, but the slow, heavy realisation that the world beyond their door had begun to press its face against the glass.

"They know?" Ben asked quietly. His voice was calm, but it carried the tremor of something ancient beneath it — the same tremor that once guided his hand to draw crowns and crests before he knew why. "They know who we are?" Jeff shook his head. "No, not entirely. But they know enough. Someone saw us disembark in Copenhagen. The royal insignia was visible on the aircraft. And once a single photograph was leaked... well, you know how quickly fires spread." Ben swallowed. Isla's hand slid across the table, her fingers weaving into his, grounding them both.

Robert and Claire entered a moment later, their expressions strained but composed. Robert spoke first, his Scottish accent cutting clean through the tension. "I've already contacted legal. We'll hold the line for as long as we can." His jaw tensed. "But the press don't frighten easily." Claire, ever the voice of steadying warmth, placed a hand gently upon Isla's shoulder. "We'll keep you safe, my love. That's all that matters."

Jeff, however, was already pulling his phone from his coat pocket, his fingers moving with a precision that betrayed how many times he had rehearsed for this moment — though he had hoped it would never come. The name he dialled was not one found in any public directory, nor any phone book available to journalists or curious neighbours. "Majesty," Jeff began when the call connected. His voice dropped into a tone reserved for matters of utmost seriousness. "It has begun."

King Frederik X's voice answered calmly from across the sea, his Danish accent clipped but clear. "Are the children secure?" "For now," Jeff replied, glancing toward Ben and Isla. "The gate is holding. The Kent police have dispatched a local unit, but it's insufficient. We need your agents, Frederik." "They are already en route," Frederik assured. "As of thirty minutes ago, two royal security detachments were dispatched from the embassy. They'll arrive within the hour." Jeff exhaled, his shoulders lowering only slightly. "Thank you. We'll shelter in place until then."

"Good. And Jeff—" Frederik's voice softened, yet carried the weight of sovereign command. "The sanctity of the children's identities remains paramount. The Crown of Denmark stands behind them. This breach will not be tolerated." Jeff's reply was firm. "Understood." As the call ended, Annemarie stepped closer, her voice a fragile thread. "How did it happen, Jeff? We were careful. You were careful." Jeff rubbed the bridge of his nose, the weariness pressing at the corners of his eyes. "There are always eyes. Somewhere along the chain, someone saw something. One photograph at the Copenhagen tarmac showing the King's insignia on the jet was enough to start a whisper. That whisper became a rumour. And rumours, when they reach the international press, turn into storms."

Ben listened in silence. The weight of his lineage — once an invisible thread woven into his dreams and drawings — now tugged sharply at the seams of his life. He had always carried it privately, as a quiet inheritance only he, Isla, and a few trusted adults understood. But the world beyond their small circle did not understand sacred inheritance. It craved spectacle. It devoured whispers. Through the windows, the early morning haze blurred the figures gathered beyond the tall iron gates. Long lenses and flashing bulbs punctuated the fog like tiny weapons. Voices called out faintly from the road — questions shouted into the air, not truly expecting answers but hungering for any response.

"BENEDICT! ARE YOU RELATED TO THE DANISH ROYAL HOUSE?"

"ISLA, ARE YOU A PRINCESS? ARE YOU ENGAGED?"

The words pierced the morning like crude spears. Claire drew the curtains closed with a sharp motion, shielding the children from the worst of it. "We'll move to the interior rooms," Jeff instructed. "They won't leave quickly. But they'll not see the children today." "But what about school?" Isla asked softly, her voice trembling beneath the surface of her usual composure. "What about everything?" Jeff offered a gentle smile, though his eyes remained vigilant. "You're not missing school. Your school is here. That has never changed. And your learning—this—this is part of it. A part none of us wanted for you, but one that finds us anyway."

Ben spoke now, his voice even and firm despite the tightness in his chest. "They don't deserve to know. This isn't their story." "No," Jeff said, placing a hand upon his shoulder, "it isn't. And they will not take it from you." A knock sounded again — this one different. Three sharp, deliberate strikes against the front door. Not the hollow tap of reporters. This knock was calculated, disciplined.

Jeff moved quickly, stepping to the entrance, pausing only briefly before opening the heavy oak door. Two men stood beneath the stone arch of the front stoop, dressed in dark navy suits, their lapels bearing a tiny but unmistakable insignia: the crest of King Frederik X.

"Sir Jeff Philips?" the first man inquired, his voice clipped in Danish-accented English. "Yes," Jeff replied. "We are under direct orders from His Majesty to secure the estate and protect all individuals within. Our jurisdiction supersedes all local press freedoms under sovereign privacy law. May we enter?" "You may," Jeff said, stepping aside. The men moved swiftly, their presence a quiet wall of assurance. One remained near the door, the other swept the interior perimeter before nodding subtly to Jeff. Outside, more vehicles arrived — black sedans, tinted windows, professional agents who blended into the quiet authority of international royal service.

"They'll remain until we're certain the press has been neutralised," Jeff explained to the family. "His Majesty's legal teams have already contacted the Ministry of Justice. Any images taken today will be seized. Publication is forbidden under sovereign privacy protocols." Isla's eyes widened. "They can really do that?" "Yes, darling," Claire answered softly. "When royal bloodlines are involved, and sovereign oaths have been sworn — yes, they can." Ben glanced again toward the curtains. The flashes outside continued, but he felt the subtle shift in the air within their home. The house was no longer vulnerable. It was being defended — not just by law, but by blood, by promise, by nations that understood what sacred inheritance meant.

And yet, even as he exhaled in momentary relief, he felt it. That old familiar stirring behind his ribs, the one that whispered not in words but in knowing: this is only the beginning.

The early hours slipped into late morning, though within the secured halls of the Harvick home, time no longer flowed as it once did. The usual comfort of breakfast dishes in the sink and the soft murmur of tea kettles had given way to the heavy tread of royal agents shifting between assigned posts, their movements quiet but constant. Each footstep served as an unspoken reminder that the house, once simply their sanctuary, had transformed into something more—a royal residence under active protection.

Ben sat once again at the long oak table, its varnished surface now partially covered with legal documents, tablets, and open files spread carefully before Jeff and Robert. Isla sat beside him, her chair slightly pulled back as she traced her fingers along the embroidered edge of the linen runner, lost in thought. Claire stood nearby with Annemarie, speaking softly with one of the agents who provided them intermittent updates.

Jeff exhaled slowly, his eyes narrowed behind his glasses as he reviewed the latest email pulled up on his tablet screen. "The Danish royal legal office has filed a formal privacy breach injunction through the European Court of Human Rights as well as the United Kingdom's own sovereign privacy tribunal." Robert, standing just behind him with arms folded, nodded once. "Good. And the injunction binds the press to a hard silence?"

Jeff tapped the screen, his voice calm but clipped. "Yes. As of this hour, any publication or broadcast of the children's likenesses or any inference to their sovereign affiliations will be met with full legal action. Their status as minor heirs of interwoven European royal houses affords them protections that supersede standard journalistic privilege." Claire's gaze shifted softly toward Ben and Isla, her voice warm but firm. "The world may be loud, but the law is louder."

Ben listened to the words swirl around him, their meanings heavy but distant. He understood what was happening on one level, but his heart sat quietly, lodged somewhere between relief and unease. All his life, the secret had been theirs—his, Isla's, Jeff's, and those who guarded them. But now that secret sat under spotlights, wrapped in the cold machinery of international law. "Dad?" Ben spoke gently, his voice measured as he glanced toward Jeff.

Jeff's eyes lifted immediately, and that single word—Dad—softened his entire face as it always did. "Yes, son." Ben hesitated, gathering the question as if it were too fragile to speak aloud. "What if... what if they don't stop? What if they still try to find us, even with the law?" Jeff's expression didn't harden, but his eyes sharpened with a deeper seriousness. "They may try. There will always be those who chase what does not belong to them. But they won't succeed. They can photograph fences. They can shout questions into the air. But the truth—your truth—belongs to you. Not to their headlines."

Ben swallowed, Isla squeezing his hand gently as the room hummed with the low conversation of adults who spoke the languages of treaties and courts. He looked to Isla, his voice softening as his breath steadied. "It wasn't supposed to be like this." "No," Isla agreed, her voice like a thin reed moving beneath the weight of wind, "but we always knew it could be." Robert's voice rose again, directed toward Jeff. "We've had minor breaches before—whispers, mistaken blog posts, stray genealogy forums—but nothing like this."

"No," Jeff agreed, sliding the tablet aside. "This was deliberate. It's too precise to be coincidence." Annemarie's eyes narrowed at the implication. "You mean someone leaked it intentionally?" Jeff nodded slowly. "Someone saw an opportunity. Perhaps it was a ground crew worker in Copenhagen, perhaps someone closer to our circle who grew careless with a word or a photo. It doesn't matter now. The genie's out of the bottle. Our task is not to shove it back inside—it's to ensure it cannot poison them."

Ben glanced toward the partially drawn curtains, the edge of the street still faintly visible through the sliver left open. Cameras continued to flash in the distance, though the agents had successfully pushed the perimeter farther down the lane. Black sedans blocked the view now, providing the family a fragile buffer of control. Suddenly, one of the agents re-entered from the front hall, his dark suit pristine even after hours of guarding the estate's perimeter. He spoke in flawless, clipped English.

"Sir, Lady Gibb, Lady Stuart-Gibb," the agent addressed them with courteous precision, "the Ministry of Defence has now authorized an additional security team from the Crown Protective Office. They'll take over the external perimeter by mid-afternoon. No press vehicles will remain within one thousand feet of the property line by dusk." Claire exhaled softly. "At least they're acting quickly."

"Your positions," the agent continued, "have been elevated to protected family members under cross-sovereign designation. Any breach going forward will be considered a violation of multiple international treaties on royal minors. The Danish, British, and European councils have all authorized immediate enforcement." Robert raised an eyebrow, glancing briefly at Jeff. "They're invoking the Tri-Sovereign Accords?"

"They are," Jeff confirmed with a quiet nod. Ben furrowed his brow. "The what?" Jeff looked at him gently, folding his hands. "The Tri-Sovereign Accords, Ben, are a long-standing agreement between certain monarchies to preserve the rights and protections of royal minors whose bloodlines cross borders. In simpler terms: multiple nations now recognize your safety as a shared responsibility."

Isla blinked. "But why would they need to make rules for that?" Jeff's gaze deepened. "Because many years ago, children like you weren't always protected. Dynasties often used bloodlines as tools. As bargaining chips. These laws were written to prevent what happened in centuries past—to children who carried crowns they neither asked for nor fully understood."

Ben sat very still, his fingers unconsciously running across the surface of the table. "So we're safe?" "Yes," Jeff answered softly. "Because of who you are. And because of who stands behind you." Robert added quietly, "And because we will not allow anyone to reduce your lives to a headline."

The gravity of the moment settled across the room like a weight gently pressing upon each of them. The weight was not only legal—it was ancestral. They were standing inside the invisible walls of history itself, carried forward by names spoken long before they were born. Árpád. Béla. Stuart. Gibb. Harvick. Pattenden. Names that lived not only on scrolls and certificates but within the marrow of their bones.

And yet, for all the legal maneuvering and sovereign interventions, Ben sensed the greater battle was still one no lawyer or royal decree could fight. It was the battle against the hunger of the world—a world that had begun to catch the scent of something sacred. Jeff reached forward then, his hand warm as it landed over Ben's. "You are not their story, Ben. You are your own." And from across the table, Isla whispered softly, her voice both fragile and unyielding. "And I'll stand with you. Always." Ben's breath steadied once more as he nodded, the room holding its quiet as the storm outside continued to howl, held back for now behind the shield of law—and love.

The afternoon sun began its slow arc toward evening, stretching shadows across the grounds as the Kent estate took on the strange quiet of controlled tension. The reporters had been forced back—physically and legally—but their presence still lingered like smoke after a fire. Beyond the iron gates, the black sedans of the royal protective service stood like silent sentinels, their dark frames reflecting the glimmer of passing light. Helicopters had been ordered from the airspace. Drones were prohibited. Even the neighbours, once kindly distant, had grown cautious beneath the unusual activity surrounding the estate.

But not all eyes outside belonged to the press.
Inside the house, the air remained hushed. Ben sat once more near the large bay window, sketchbook balanced on his lap, pencil in hand. His lines moved with precision, but his mind wandered. He was no longer drawing castles or banners or ancient family crests. His hand now traced something new—a gate. The iron bars, the heavy stone pillars, the ivy curling along their edges. And behind them: shadows. Figures. Not faces, not clear, but present nonetheless. His fingers trembled as the lines formed without his conscious intent.

Jeff sat nearby, speaking quietly with one of the agents reviewing perimeter updates. Though the voices spoke softly, Ben's ears caught the tone—a controlled seriousness that betrayed rising concern. "The vans across the northern approach—have we identified all of them?" Jeff asked, his voice low. "Most belong to registered press credentials," the agent replied. "However, there are two vehicles that arrived late. No clear identification. We've issued soft warnings but they've remained parked along the public road."

Jeff narrowed his eyes. "And the occupants?" The agent hesitated. "Uncooperative. Cameras out, but no questions called. Observing. They've refused to engage with our officers." Jeff exhaled through his nose. "Keep eyes on them. Notify King Kendrick's office if they remain past nightfall." The agent nodded before departing, leaving Jeff to sit back heavily in his chair. His eyes drifted to Ben's drawing, and for a moment he said nothing. Then, gently, he spoke. "You saw them, too." Ben's hand paused over the page, his breath catching. "I didn't mean to draw it," he whispered. "It just… came."

Jeff leaned forward, his voice steady but carrying a new weight. "You're not imagining these things, Ben. You never have. Not when you were little. Not now." His eyes softened. "There are those who observe quietly. And they are not journalists." Ben's lips parted slightly. "Who are they?"

Jeff's fingers steepled, his gaze distant. "Some may simply be curious. But others… they are watchers. They exist in the shadows of every royal family, whether invited or not. They trace bloodlines. They follow names. They study inheritance not for public spectacle, but for ancient reasons." "Are they dangerous?" Isla asked softly, having entered the room unnoticed, her voice no louder than a breath. Jeff looked at her and nodded with painful honesty. "Some are."

Robert entered from the study, having overheard the last exchange. "We suspected as much when we saw the first drone over Denmark last spring," he said gravely. "They've been circling for longer than the tabloids." Claire followed behind him, her voice equally calm. "The more your lineage reveals itself, the more others take notice." Ben swallowed. "But why now? Why after everything?" Jeff answered, his voice slow and deliberate. "Because they recognize something they never expected to find. The bloodlines we confirmed, the DNA results, the recovered scrolls—all of it has awakened a thread long dormant. You are not just a curiosity anymore, Ben. You are verification."

Isla stepped closer to him, placing her hand lightly upon his shoulder. "Verification of what?" Jeff's answer came softly. "Of the unbroken line. A child whose ancestry bridges houses that many believed dissolved generations ago. Árpád. Béla. The Stuart line.

The Danish Crown. And others. Some are watching to learn. Some are watching to protect. But there are always those who watch to control." Ben's voice cracked slightly as he whispered, "I never asked for this." "No," Jeff said gently, his hand resting firmly on Ben's shoulder now. "You didn't. And that is why you will not face it alone."

A heavy silence settled in the room. It was Isla who finally broke it, her voice stronger now. "They won't get to us." "No, they won't," Robert affirmed. "Because the world you belong to now, Ben—both of you—is not ruled by those who chase headlines. It is ruled by the quiet strength of oaths made before cameras ever existed." Claire nodded softly, stepping closer, her eyes glistening. "This house isn't just protected by law. It's protected by love. And by the names written not on paper, but in blood."

From outside the window, a raven landed upon the stone fence, its black feathers gleaming in the fading afternoon light. It watched silently for a moment, then tilted its head and took flight once more, vanishing into the nearby woods. Ben watched it disappear, his chest tightening as something old stirred beneath his ribs again—the familiar pulse of memory that belonged to no age at all. "They're not just watching," Ben whispered, his voice barely audible now, "they're waiting." Jeff's eyes darkened with the truth in those words. "Yes, my son," he answered softly. "Some of them are."

The rain returned by evening—not in heavy torrents, but in fine needles, as though the sky itself whispered warnings only the earth could hear. Every droplet tapping against the windows carried an invisible rhythm, matching the low hum of tension that had settled into the walls of the estate. The house, once lively with the gentle cadence of lessons and books, now breathed like an ancient vault waiting for decisions to be made.

Ben sat in the study alone, lit only by the low amber glow of a single desk lamp. The agents moved quietly through the corridors outside. Their footsteps had become part of the house's new language—measured, constant, watchful. Even the creaks of the old wooden beams above seemed to hesitate, as if unwilling to disturb the storm of silence surrounding the boy.

In front of him lay the scroll again—unfurled just enough to reveal the ancient symbols and names that had begun this path so many months before. Árpád. Béla. The spiral of generations. He traced his fingers lightly along the curling ink, feeling its weight not only upon the parchment but deep within his chest.

Jeff entered softly, closing the door behind him without a word. The air shifted slightly in his presence, but the silence between them remained unbroken for several moments. Finally, Jeff spoke. "They haven't left," he said quietly. Ben's eyes lifted toward him. "The watchers?" Jeff nodded. "The two vehicles remain past the perimeter.

Silent. Cameras down for now, but present." He paused, watching Ben's face closely. "They're waiting for someone else to make the first move." Ben swallowed. "Us." "Yes," Jeff replied. "Or the press. Or the governments. Or even the old families who've long since withdrawn from public eyes but still follow these bloodlines in private circles."

He stepped forward, lowering himself into the leather chair opposite Ben. The lamp cast shadows that danced between them like unseen figures eavesdropping on a conversation carried across centuries. "I don't understand them," Ben whispered. "Why do they care? I'm just… me." Jeff's eyes softened as he spoke. "Because you're more than one person, Ben. You're a collection of stories. Bloodlines. Promises. To them, you are not simply a boy. You are proof. Of something they thought was buried." Ben's hand fell still over the scroll. "But proof of what?"

Jeff exhaled slowly. "That the old line remains unbroken. That somewhere—through the collapses of kingdoms, through marriages, through the rise of nations—there remained a thread they failed to sever." He leaned forward, his voice a steady murmur. "You see, Ben, there are quiet circles who do not want these things fully proven.
They prefer doubt. Mystery allows them to control the narrative, to dismiss claims before they take root. But confirmation? True confirmation threatens to awaken claims of inheritance—claims that could reorder pieces of European royalty none of them want to disturb."

Ben's brow furrowed, the weight of it all pressing deeper. "But I don't want any of that. I don't want palaces or titles or crowns." Jeff smiled softly, sadness resting at the corners of his eyes. "Which is exactly why you were born to carry it." The words hovered between them, neither grand nor sentimental. They were simply true. The lineage had not chosen ambition; it had chosen survival. And survival had chosen him. From the hallway, Isla appeared quietly, slipping into the room without knocking, her eyes searching Ben's face as though sensing the storm swirling beneath his skin.

"They're not leaving, are they?" she asked softly. "No," Ben replied. "They're not." Isla moved beside him, her hand finding his instinctively. Jeff watched them both, studying the fragile strength building between the two children—a strength that no law or bloodline could fabricate. "It won't always be like this," Isla whispered, almost as if comforting herself as much as him. "We'll grow up. One day, we'll decide what to do with it." "Yes," Jeff answered. "But for now, we decide how to carry it." Another knock came from the far door—this one deliberate, rhythmic. Robert stepped inside with one of the agents beside him, his face more serious than earlier in the day.

"We've had a visitor," Robert said carefully. "A letter delivered by private courier—unmarked vehicle, no credentials." The agent handed Jeff the envelope, sealed in thick wax bearing no crest, no signature. Only a simple triangle—three dots arranged in a perfect geometric shape. Ben's chest tightened as he stared at it. The symbol he had drawn since childhood. The one that appeared in his dreams before he ever knew its meaning. Jeff studied the seal closely. "They're introducing themselves," he murmured. "Or at least... reminding us they've been watching longer than the tabloids."

"Who?" Isla asked, her voice thin. Jeff looked at her, his voice measured. "One of the private circles. Likely genealogical observers—families who track royal lines in secret, waiting for opportunities that may never come." Robert nodded gravely. "Many of them descend from the old advisors, Ben. The kingmakers who outlived the kings." Ben whispered, "Are they dangerous?" Jeff answered, "Not like spies. Not like thieves. They operate on patience. Their danger is silence. They rarely move quickly. But when they do... it changes dynasties."

The rain picked up against the window as though answering. Outside, the two vehicles still sat, their silent occupants unmoving beneath the dull glow of the streetlamps. For a moment, none of them spoke. The truth had arrived—not as a headline, but as a presence. Quiet. Waiting. Watching. Finally, Ben spoke again, his voice carrying a maturity far beyond his years. "Then we have to find a way to make them wait longer." Jeff's eyes narrowed thoughtfully, sensing what was beginning to stir inside the boy's mind—a strategy forming not from panic, but from clarity. "Yes," Jeff replied. "And you may already be finding it."

The night had deepened by the time Ben made his decision. The rain no longer whispered—it hammered against the windows as though trying to drown the voices inside. But it could not drown what was rising in him. Not fear. Not anger. Precision.

The house was dim but alive. The agents moved in tighter formations now, maintaining visual lines across each entrance. Robert and Claire had retreated momentarily to speak with the legal counsel assigned to them from Denmark. Jeff sat quietly near the hearth, his hands clasped, reading Ben's face as the boy stood before him.

"I want to speak to them," Ben said finally. Jeff did not feign surprise. He had seen this coming for hours. What he had not expected was the sharpened clarity behind Ben's words. There was no tremor. No hesitation. Only intent. "Speak to whom?" Jeff asked softly, buying a moment, testing his resolve. Ben's voice lowered, steady as iron. "The press. The public. The world."

From across the room, Isla's breath caught. The agent stationed by the far door turned slightly, listening without interruption. Jeff held his gaze firm on Ben. "That is not a small request, son." "I know," Ben replied. "And I'm not asking to confess anything. I'm not going to give them the truth. I want to give them something else." Jeff motioned for him to continue, his brow tense but his voice controlled. "Speak."

Ben drew a breath and stepped closer, lowering his voice so only those in the room could hear. "They want a story. Right now, the silence is feeding them. They're building their own versions while we sit still. But if we give them one — just one — that fits the puzzle they want to believe, it might be enough." Jeff's eyes narrowed. "What story?"

"The simplest one," Ben continued. "We were on holiday. In Denmark. A simple family trip. While we were there, my family was graciously invited as guests of the royal household. Not because of bloodlines. Not because of crowns. Because my father—" he nodded toward Jeff, "—works in private historical research.

He has professional relationships abroad. The King extended hospitality while we were visiting. When our return flight was complicated by logistics, the King offered us safe passage home aboard one of his private diplomatic planes. That is all."

Isla's eyes widened, whispering, "That's brilliant." Ben nodded. "It's clean. It's factual. Every element is defensible. No one can prove otherwise. The press will have nothing left to gnaw on." Jeff leaned forward, his face hardening with the seriousness of what Ben proposed. "You understand what you're suggesting."

"I do," Ben answered. "It buys us time. Time for us to grow. Time for them to get tired. They'll move on once they see nothing left to expose." At that moment, one of the royal agents stepped forward. His posture was respectful, but his face betrayed the weight of the proposal. His name was Sørensen — one of King Kendrick X's most trusted field officers. "It is a bold strategy," Sørensen said, his English crisp, his voice low. "And one that, if done carefully, may succeed in diverting the present storm." He paused. "However, you will require formal consent before you proceed."

"I know," Ben said calmly. "That's why I'm not asking you to authorize it." Jeff's breath slowed, understanding now where this was heading. "You want to speak to Kendrick." Ben nodded. "Yes. This decision belongs to the Crown. If Kendrick grants permission, I will proceed." The room stood still for several beats, the rain crashing harder against the roof, the tension twisting like cables pulled taut.

Jeff stood then, finally rising to meet his son eye to eye. His voice softened, but his face remained stern. "Ben… this is a political move. Not just personal. Once you do this, you'll be playing at a table far older than your years." "I understand that," Ben replied. "But I'm the one they're chasing. I'm the face in the photographs. No one else can make this statement but me."

The weight of those words hovered, heavy as stone. Isla stepped forward, standing at his side. "We believe him," she whispered. "We're strong enough." Sørensen straightened, then turned toward Jeff. "Shall I initiate contact with His Majesty?" Jeff exhaled slowly, his throat tight with the magnitude of the moment. "Yes. Open the secured line."

The agent withdrew quickly. Only a few minutes passed before he returned, this time with a small encrypted tablet clutched tightly in his gloved hands. He placed it carefully upon the table. The screen glowed faintly. A single emblem pulsed across it: the sigil of King Kendrick X. Jeff spoke first, his voice measured. "Sire, forgive the late hour."

The voice of Kendrick X came through with perfect clarity, his Danish-Norwegian accent distinct but fluid, the tone crisp but thoughtful. "There is no late hour for this matter, Jeff. I understand the boy wishes to speak." Ben stepped forward, his shoulders square. "Yes, Your Majesty." "You may speak freely," Kendrick said. "I am listening."

Ben spoke without faltering. "I request permission to address the public. Not to reveal who we are — but to redirect the attention that's building. I will state clearly that we were in Denmark on private holiday. That while there, as guests, we were offered return passage home by your household, in gratitude for my father's professional cooperation in historical research. There will be no mention of crowns. No mention of bloodlines. This will provide the public with a digestible answer — one that cannot be disproven, but also reveals nothing."

The King remained silent for several moments. The stillness pressed across every person in the room. When Kendrick finally spoke, his words were slow, deliberate. "You understand that what you suggest is dangerous, young Harvick." "I do, sire," Ben answered. "But the danger of remaining silent is greater. If we give them no path forward, they will invent one. If we give them a plausible story, one grounded in courtesy and diplomacy, they will lose momentum."

Kendrick's breath was faint but audible. "And if this fails?" Ben stood even straighter. "Then I will answer for it. In full. But I believe it won't fail." Again, the pause stretched, the silence full of ancient weight—weight that only kings fully understand. Finally, Kendrick spoke once more. "You have courage, child. And wisdom beyond your years. But I will not give you my answer tonight. This matter requires thought. I will consult my legal office and my diplomatic council. I will render my decision within twelve hours."

"Yes, sire," Ben answered respectfully. "I will wait for your word." The tablet screen faded to black. The room exhaled collectively, though the storm outside only grew louder. Sørensen stepped closer, breaking the quiet. "If the King grants you this authority, young Harvick... it will be one of the bravest moves any minor heir has made in decades." Ben met his gaze with quiet steel. "I'm not trying to be brave. I'm trying to give us peace." "And sometimes," Sørensen replied, his voice like gravel, "those two are the same thing."

The storm had broken sometime before dawn. The clouds peeled back like a heavy curtain retreating from a dim stage, leaving the morning air thick with mist and the smell of wet earth. The estate stood calm for the first time in days, though the tension beneath its walls remained electric. The waiting had ended.

Jeff, Robert, Claire, Annemarie, Isla, and the royal agents gathered in the large sitting room, where the encrypted tablet sat once again upon the centre table. The emblem of Kendrick X pulsed gently on the screen. Sørensen stood nearby, his hands folded behind his back, silent but alert. Ben entered last, his stride steady, his face composed. The moment the tablet connected, the King's voice filled the room. "Good morning to you all." Jeff bowed his head slightly. "Your Majesty."

Kendrick's tone carried the same calm gravity that had ruled their family for generations. "The decision has been made." No one spoke. Even the creaks in the old wooden beams seemed to hold their breath. "After reviewing the legal landscape across multiple jurisdictions," Kendrick continued, "and having consulted with my private council, I have determined that your plan shall proceed. You have my full consent to make your statement, Benedict Adrian Harvick."

Ben exhaled, though the relief was brief, his mind already shifting to the task at hand. "You will proceed under strict parameters," Kendrick went on. "There will be no deviation from the agreed narrative. The statement will be recorded live. It will serve as the only sanctioned account. All further inquiries will be deflected through sovereign legal channels. This is a tactical operation, Benedict. Not a confession. Do you understand?"

"Yes, Your Majesty," Ben answered firmly. Kendrick's voice softened ever so slightly, though it still carried the weight of command. "And I trust you understand what you are stepping into." "I do." "Good," Kendrick said. "You have courage. Now use wisdom. The world will believe what it wants, but you will give them nothing to sharpen against you. Hold your ground, and you will win." The call ended. The tablet dimmed.

Ben turned slowly, facing those gathered. The agents exchanged brief glances, assessing, recalibrating. Isla's eyes met his with silent encouragement, her hand instinctively finding his. Jeff's hand landed upon Ben's shoulder with quiet pride, though his jaw remained tight. And then Ben spoke. "I have one more request." The room quieted. "Sørensen," Ben said, turning directly to face the lead agent.

Sørensen's head lifted slightly, his posture already prepared. "Yes, young Harvick." "I want you beside me during the broadcast. Standing with me, not behind me." Ben's voice never wavered. "Not as my protection—but as my counsel. If I falter, if I stray, if my words begin to open doors I shouldn't open, I want you there to steady me." Sørensen studied him for several heartbeats. His eyes—those cold, clinical eyes trained by decades of security and diplomatic service—softened just enough to betray his approval.

"That is a very rare thing to ask," Sørensen said quietly. "Most who stand before the world wish to appear alone, unguarded. Untouchable." Ben nodded. "That's why most of them fail. I would rather be correct than proud." A flicker of a smile crossed Sørensen's otherwise stone face. "Spoken like a future sovereign." He stepped forward, placing his gloved hand over his chest. "If His Majesty permits, I will stand at your right. I will not speak unless absolutely necessary. But I will watch every word you give them. And if you falter, I will move."

Jeff spoke softly behind them. "It's a wise choice, Ben." Ben inhaled deeply. "Then let's prepare." Robert and Claire immediately moved to coordinate logistics with the Danish royal press office. Annemarie, pale but steady, retreated briefly to call her own family to inform them of what was coming. Isla never left his side. Hours passed as the agents secured the media protocols. The location would be within the estate, in front of the stone façade beneath the old ivy wall. Cameras would be admitted under strict clearance, limited to one broadcast pool shared globally to avoid manipulation. No questions would be allowed. No journalists permitted to speak. One statement. One time.

The sun had risen higher by the time the agents began setting the stage. Black cables stretched like veins across the cobbled courtyard. Microphones tested, calibrated. International feeds linked into the estate's secure broadcast hub. Royal flags were absent—by order of Kendrick himself. There would be no symbols. No crests. No crowns. Only Ben. And Sørensen.

Jeff adjusted Ben's collar carefully as the final seconds ticked down. "Speak clearly. Breathe between your sentences. And most of all—remember: you owe them nothing." Ben nodded. "I know, Dad." Sørensen approached quietly from the side, standing at his assigned position—exactly one pace behind Ben's right shoulder. The lead producer gave the final cue. The world was watching. Ben stepped forward. The light of the single camera glared into his eyes, but his gaze never flickered. He began.

The cameras flickered live. Thousands watched from around the world—some curious, some hungry for scandal, some poised like vultures circling above what they believed was about to be revealed. And yet, none of them fully understood what they were about to witness. The courtyard held its breath. Ben stood before the microphone. No flags, no symbols. Only the stone wall behind him and the endless sky above. Sørensen stood precisely one pace behind his right shoulder—rigid, calm, and utterly silent.

Ben inhaled once. Then he spoke. "Good afternoon." His voice was steady, his diction clear, each word delivered with deliberate weight. There was no childlike nervousness, no quivering in the throat. Only calm control. A presence far older than his years. "There has been much speculation regarding my recent travels with my family. Many images have circulated. Many questions have been asked. And while I recognize the world's natural curiosity, I wish today to clarify the events that have led to such attention."

He paused, but not out of hesitation. It was controlled pacing—exactly as he had prepared. "Earlier this year, my family traveled to Denmark for a private holiday. During our time abroad, my father—Mr. Jeff Phillips—was conducting private academic research in partnership with institutions overseas. His work, as many of you can verify, pertains to historical records and ancestral research, which has long been a professional focus of his." Ben allowed the words to settle before continuing.

"While in Denmark, and as guests of the country, my family was extended a gracious invitation from His Majesty King Frederik X, whom my father has professionally assisted through his research. This invitation was offered as a gesture of hospitality. Upon our return, and due to a scheduling complication with our regular flight home, we were provided transportation aboard one of His Majesty's private aircraft as guests of the Danish royal household. It was not unusual. It was not ceremonial. It was a matter of hospitality and courtesy."

The camera remained locked on his face, but Ben never blinked. His gaze remained strong, fixed directly ahead. "The assumptions circulating that there is some hidden royal lineage or clandestine title behind these events are untrue. My family was honoured to be received warmly as guests while abroad, but no further conclusions should be drawn from these images or these moments. We ask that our privacy as a family—particularly as minors—be respected." Another pause.

"We are grateful for the kindness extended to us during our travels. My family has no desire to court attention, nor will we engage in speculative conversations that do not reflect reality.

I trust that this statement will bring clarity to what has needlessly become public speculation." And then came his closing. "I thank you for your time." Ben's eyes remained steady for another beat before the director signalled the cut. The broadcast feed dropped immediately. Silence.

The agents held position. The crew froze, as though uncertain what they had just witnessed. Ben did not stumble as he turned. Sørensen, without missing his cue, stepped forward precisely as rehearsed. His presence was like a stone wall rising into the camera's frame. Sørensen stood before the press pool, his voice low but amplified perfectly through the microphone. "On behalf of the Harvick family, I extend our gratitude for your time, and for your willingness to hear Mr. Benedict Harvick's clarification."

He paused only long enough for the weight of his words to fill the courtyard.

"For members of the international press who seek further confirmation, I encourage you to review the professional credentials of Mr. Jeff Phillips, whose academic contributions to genealogical research are well-documented in multiple institutional archives. You will find that the statements provided here today are consistent with his field of study, his work abroad, and the professional engagements that brought this family to Denmark."

His gaze swept briefly across the cameras—a warning delivered without threat. "That is all." Without another word, Sørensen pivoted smoothly, allowing Ben to step back toward the house. The agents closed in with expert choreography, guiding the family back into the estate as the cameras flickered, some attempting to shout last-minute questions that were met only by silence. The media had no new fuel. Only the simple, controlled statement—clean, measured, legally sound. There would be no scandal. There would be no evidence to contradict it. The tabloids would spin their wheels, but they would spin them into the sand.

Inside, once the doors closed behind them, Jeff exhaled deeply for the first time that day. "You did it," Jeff said, his voice soft, almost reverent. Ben shook his head humbly. "No, Dad. We did it." From the far corner, Sørensen allowed himself the smallest breath of approval. "You stood like a prince," he said flatly, though there was something behind his voice—a subtle respect few men like him ever offered. Ben looked toward him. "Thank you for standing with me."

Sørensen dipped his head once. "You gave me nothing to correct, young Harvick. And that is the greatest service you could have asked." The storm was not over. But it had been redirected. And for now—perhaps for many years—they had bought what was most precious of all: time.

The statement aired across every major network within minutes of its live broadcast. By nightfall, it had circled the globe in multiple languages, played and replayed in every corner where curiosity had once grown wild and unrestrained. And yet, as Ben had intended, it gave them nothing.

The press agencies did what they always did: they dissected, analysed, speculated. Journalists filled hour after hour with panel discussions, debating whether his words were carefully scripted or genuinely innocent. The tone varied from network to network—some praising his composure, others attempting to fabricate contradictions where none existed. But no contradictions appeared.

Ben's message was too clean. Too precise. By midnight, several outlets had already begun moving on to other stories. The world's appetite for royal scandal was vast—but it also moved quickly when denied blood. Without fresh leaks or damning revelations, the cameras slowly began to swivel elsewhere. Jeff sat in the study, the television playing softly in the background as another anchor rehashed the coverage for the fiftieth time.

"—while young Benedict Harvick's statement today was unprecedented for a minor, experts in European legal protections confirm that his family's explanation aligns with established protocols for private international academic partnerships…" The anchor continued, but Jeff no longer heard the words. He only watched Ben, who sat on the couch beside Isla, her head resting lightly on his shoulder. Both children had remained awake longer than usual, not out of anxiety, but simply to observe the aftermath. They watched together, knowing the real storm was not what the cameras showed—it was the unseen world beyond the glass.

Sørensen entered the room quietly. As always, his presence was solid, unshaken. His eyes scanned the television briefly before resting on Ben. "The first wave is breaking," he said simply. Jeff nodded. "And the second wave?" Sørensen's voice lowered. "It will be slower. Quieter. The press will move on for now, but the other observers will not." He paused, studying Ben with that sharp gaze that had measured kings and princes before him. "They will wait."

Ben looked up at him. "For what?" "For the proof they could not get today." Sørensen folded his hands behind his back. "Your bloodlines. Your ages. Your maturity. They know that with time, new fragments may surface—pieces no journalist can obtain, but which those in genealogical circles hunt with a patience foreign to the press." Robert entered from the hallway, hearing the exchange. His face was grim, but not defeated. "The private families will mark today's date, Ben. You bought your childhood back—for now. But your name will remain on their ledgers."

Claire followed behind, speaking gently. "You've delayed the public storm, but you've stepped into the private one. They will not interfere directly, not while you're still children. But in the shadows, your names are now permanently entered into circles far older than newspapers." Ben didn't flinch. He had known this before he ever stood before the cameras.

"They'll wait for the day we come of age," he said softly. "Yes," Sørensen replied. "Because only then could claims—should you make them—carry weight within certain courts of Europe. Especially those courts that still hold quiet authority over royal succession laws buried behind constitutional veneers."

Isla's voice was quiet but steady as she asked, "But they can't force anything, can they? Not now?" "No," Sørensen answered. "They cannot force what they cannot prove. You have given them no entry point. And His Majesty Kendrick X has sealed the sovereign files behind layers no court can penetrate without your future consent."

Ben nodded slowly. "Then we hold." Sørensen offered a faint nod in return. "You hold." The night stretched on, but inside the house, the mood had shifted. They had not won a war. They had won time. And time was a currency more valuable than any crown. From the upper floors, another agent entered quietly with a secured report in hand. He handed it to Sørensen, speaking only once.

"The secondary watchers have withdrawn, sir. The unmarked vehicles outside have departed." Sørensen's eyes narrowed as he scanned the brief report. "As expected. They've seen enough. For now." Jeff exhaled. "That buys us some breathing room." "For now," Sørensen agreed. "But there are others who will re-emerge later. You've thrown dust into the eyes of the press. The older circles—those who track ancestral threads—are far more patient." His gaze shifted to Ben one final time that evening. "You've handled yourself with strength few men possess, young Harvick. But understand this: what you carry inside you isn't finished. The blood remembers. And one day, so will the world."

Ben's gaze never faltered. "Then let them wait." And with that, the house returned to its quiet hum. The agents resumed their rounds. The cameras outside were dark. For the first time in weeks, Kent lay still. In the silence of his room later that night, Ben sat at his desk once more, sketching quietly by the soft light of the lamp. His pencil moved across the page not with fear, but with a strange kind of peace. He drew the crest again. The lions. The helm. The triangle of three dots.

But this time, for the first time, he added something new. Above the crest, he drew a single star. And beneath it, in quiet, confident script, he wrote one word: "Not yet."

The morning after the statement passed quietly, but the world beyond their estate had already begun to reshape itself in response. Though the cameras had pulled back, and the international headlines began sliding down the news cycle, something deeper was now breathing beneath the surface — a rhythm the press could not see, but which Jeff and the royal agents understood all too well.

Within the secure operations room set up in the lower study of the estate, the screens glowed softly. Surveillance feeds flickered across multiple monitors, each one showing different locations: public spaces, airport lounges, embassy entries, known hotels—places where those who watched might reappear under different names and credentials.

Sørensen stood near the main desk, hands behind his back as usual, his posture as controlled as the lines of the suit he wore. But his eyes betrayed nothing casual; they were reading patterns far older than simple modern security. Jeff stood beside him, watching the feeds. "Any movement yet?" Sørensen nodded once. "Not from the press. But the private genealogical councils in Brussels and Geneva have been alerted."

Jeff's brow tightened. "As we anticipated." "These are not formal councils in any legal sense," Sørensen continued. "They operate under the cover of 'academic societies' and 'historical research boards.' Their real function is far older. They exist to monitor, catalogue, and, when necessary, control the resurfacing of lost bloodlines." Jeff exhaled, his eyes narrowing as he followed the implications. "The old kingmakers." "Precisely."

Robert entered, a stack of diplomatic briefings tucked beneath his arm. His face carried the same firm exhaustion they all now wore—a mixture of relief from surviving the public ordeal, and preparation for what was coming next. "We've intercepted preliminary chatter from the Lorrainese Lineage Registry," he said, placing the documents onto the desk. "They've begun cross-referencing Ben's surname variants and travel patterns over the past five years."

"They'll find nothing," Jeff said. "They don't expect to," Robert replied. "But they're filling ledgers. Building circumstantial clouds. These groups survive by maintaining possibility—not proof. As long as the possibility remains, they remain relevant." Sørensen turned slightly, his voice calm but absolute. "Our job is to keep the bloodlines protected long enough that possibility fades into apathy." He paused. "For the public, at least."

Ben entered quietly from the far door, Isla following close behind. Though neither spoke at first, both children's eyes scanned the room, understanding now that the battle had shifted into a world far more complex than cameras and microphones. Ben approached the table, his voice calm. "They've started hunting the shadows." Jeff nodded. "Yes. But they'll never stop entirely. This is not about today's headlines, Ben. These people don't chase today. They build webs for tomorrow." "Let them build," Ben answered. "As long as they don't touch my family."

Sørensen regarded him, the barest flicker of respect passing across his face once more. "It is no longer about you alone, young Harvick. The name now carries weight far beyond Kent. Far beyond Denmark. Even far beyond Europe." He tapped one of the screens where several lines of data scrolled beneath an encrypted digital map. The names flickered briefly: Anjou, Árpád, Lorraine, Stuart, Capetian, Habsburg, Béla III, Uí Néill. "This is the real network," Sørensen continued, his voice dropping into the kind of tone one reserves for old ghosts. "Not the governments. Not the courts. Not the kingdoms you see on television. These are private stewards of forgotten power—bloodline observers. Their records go back centuries. They exist to ensure nothing lost ever truly dies."

Isla's voice trembled slightly but remained strong. "They're tracking us." "Yes," Sørensen said, unflinching. "And not just you, Isla. Others like you—across Europe, across North America. Children whose ancestors once sat where crowns now gather dust. They search for them all." Ben narrowed his eyes. "And what happens if they find more?" "They wait," Sørensen answered coldly. "They always wait."

Jeff rubbed his temples. "How many of these private registries are active, Sørensen?" The agent's reply came without hesitation. "We actively monitor fifteen confirmed, though likely over twenty exist globally—spanning Luxembourg, Switzerland, Belgium, Norway, Liechtenstein, and quietly within certain British peerage lines." Robert exhaled. "And all of them are watching the same thing." "Children," Sørensen confirmed. "Heirs the world forgot. Or tried to." Ben remained silent for a moment, his mind processing the enormity of the currents swirling beneath him. Finally, he spoke quietly.

"This isn't about whether we're royals or not," he said softly. "It's about whether they can control which ones are allowed to be known." Jeff looked toward him, hearing in his son's voice not the fear of a boy—but the emerging clarity of a leader. "That's exactly what this is." Sørensen's voice turned almost reverent now, though never sentimental. "What you did yesterday gave them nothing to control. And so... they will wait for time to force your hand." Ben nodded slowly, his voice unwavering. "Then I will wait longer."

The room fell quiet again, the weight of that statement filling the space like the ancient stone beneath their feet. Isla gently slipped her hand into his, her fingers tightening around his with silent support. She spoke in barely a whisper. "And when that day comes?" Ben stared straight ahead, his voice calm, absolute. "Then we decide what world we give them."

The sun had not yet risen when the secured call came through. Jeff, still dressed in his shirt sleeves, was ushered into the private study by Sørensen. The room had been sealed electronically. Only authorized agents remained within earshot. Even Robert and Claire waited outside for this one. The encrypted tablet sat upon the heavy oak desk once again. Its screen pulsed with the symbol of King Kendrick's personal crest—one known to only a handful of men across Europe.

Jeff sat without speaking. The voice of His Majesty came through a moment later. Calm. Controlled. Absolute. "Jeff. We've confirmed it." Jeff exhaled through his nose. "You found the leak." "Yes," Kendrick said, his voice colder now than at any time before. "One of my own. A mid-level staff member assigned to the logistics wing of the royal household. He sold initial flight records to an underground group, which then brokered fragments to various press outlets."

Jeff's face hardened. "How close did they get?" "Close enough to stir international noise," Kendrick replied. "But far from any legally verifiable bloodline disclosures. That part, fortunately, remains locked." He paused briefly before adding, "For now." Sørensen stood silently behind Jeff, his face unmoving. Kendrick's voice lowered, as though now stepping into the world few dared speak of openly.

"The problem, Jeff, is not the press anymore. It's not even the genealogical registries. The problem lies within the old corridors — where certain members of secondary royal houses still operate with their own private councils." Jeff already knew. "The shadow courts." "Precisely," Kendrick said darkly. "They call themselves by many names, depending on which country you're standing in. The Bourbon Collective. The Lorrainese Inquiry. The Strasbourg Bloodlines Office. But beneath the shifting banners, they remain the same."

"They protect the old names," Jeff muttered. "And decide which are allowed to live again," Kendrick answered flatly. A longer silence hung between them now. "But you're not calling to warn me," Jeff said finally. "No," Kendrick replied. "I'm calling to inform you that I'm moving them." Jeff's eyes narrowed. "Extracting?" "Yes." Kendrick's voice left no ambiguity. "Ben. Isla. You. Annemarie. Robert. Claire. All of you."

Jeff exhaled sharply. "How?" "In complete silence." Kendrick's tone was like polished steel. "My sovereign intelligence network maintains dormant extraction protocols for contingencies far more dangerous than this. I will activate one such protocol under my highest personal authority." Kendrick continued without pause. "No formal military. No diplomats. No open flight plans. No press leaks. You will be moved under the cloak of the Prince and Princess Protection Agency."

Jeff's brow furrowed. "The PPA still exists?" "Not by that name," Kendrick replied. "At least not officially. But yes—it exists. Its function has evolved. It no longer simply protects minor heirs—it protects dynastic continuity. Those who may one day be required to step into roles no government publicly acknowledges anymore." Jeff sat back, the weight of what Kendrick was proposing crashing fully into him. "This will be dangerous for you," Jeff said softly.

"It already is," Kendrick replied without blinking. "The leak has compromised too much. If the old genealogical circles continue digging, they will eventually find one of the partial cross-references from Ben's test results. The percentages were masked—but not entirely erased." "And the hidden houses will seize it," Jeff whispered. "They will weaponize it," Kendrick corrected. "Long before Ben reaches legal majority. That is why I must move now."

Kendrick's voice lowered into the deepest register Jeff had yet heard. "I have an asset already embedded inside one of these archival nodes in Denmark. He has been there for years—watching. Quiet. Feeding me partial intelligence." Jeff leaned forward, voice tightening. "One of the genealogical vaults." "Yes," Kendrick confirmed. "The old Jesuit halls. The ones the Vatican never fully dismantled. The true master ledgers that most countries no longer even admit exist. My asset is already in place. But to extract the remaining threads tied to Ben's records will take time. If we move too fast, they'll see the fingerprints."

Jeff rubbed his temples. "So we hide the living while we erase the records." "That is the plan," Kendrick said. "If they can't find him, and can't prove him on paper, the trail collapses into hearsay. The old families will lose interest once they lose leverage." Jeff whispered, "And if they don't?" Kendrick's voice sharpened. "Then I will deal with them directly." There was no boast in those words. Only finality. Jeff exhaled slowly. "How soon do you move us?"

"The extraction is already scheduled," Kendrick replied. "Three nights from now. You'll be moved under deep cover. Private diplomatic routes. Non-commercial, untraceable. By the time the world awakens, you'll be in Denmark.
The children will continue their research. Isla and Ben will remain protected under the sovereign dome. And I will use every lawyer from Geneva to Brussels to silence anyone who raises questions." He paused, then added quietly. "My lawyers, Jeff, are ready to burn entire law firms to ash if anyone crosses that line."

Jeff finally smiled, though the weight never left his face. "You've already been fighting this war for years, haven't you?" Kendrick's voice softened slightly. "Longer than you know." The call ended. Sørensen finally spoke for the first time since the briefing began. His voice was steady, but his eyes carried the faintest edge of grim respect. "He will get you out." Jeff nodded. "Yes. And we will buy these children the only thing they need." Sørensen finished his thought aloud. "Time."

The house was silent. Not the stillness of sleep, but the silence of waiting — the kind known only to those who prepare for movement under the veil of absolute secrecy. Each clock within the Harvick estate had been set precisely to the covert timetable coordinated by His Majesty's private network. Every detail, down to the second, had been calculated. There would be no second attempt.

The agents arrived long before midnight. Not in blacked-out military convoys, not with helicopters or loud engines. They came in unmarked, ordinary estate vehicles—vehicles designed to blend into the night itself. Their drivers wore no insignia, their plates were unregistered to any official body. The only identifying mark was invisible to outsiders: a micro-stitched emblem sewn inside their cuffs, known only to the sovereign extraction unit of the PPA's hidden successor agency. Sørensen stood at the entryway, eyes sharp, giving final commands to his team. His voice, as always, was calm but absolute.

"No outside contact. No device pings. No conversation beyond necessity. We leave no trail—not physical, not digital." Jeff stood nearby with Robert, Claire, and Annemarie—all fully briefed, all carrying only what was authorized. The majority of their belongings would remain behind to avoid suspicion. Everything they required had already been prepared for them in Denmark.

Ben stood beside Isla, his hand wrapped firmly around hers. Their bags were light, their faces calm, though the enormity of the night pressed against them. They were not fleeing. They were not prisoners. But they were, for the first time, fully stepping inside the world that had long whispered their names in secret. Sørensen approached the children directly. "You understand what happens now," he said softly. Ben nodded. "We vanish." "Temporarily," Sørensen corrected. "We are not erasing you. We are protecting you while others forget how to search." Isla whispered, "How long?"

Sørensen's eyes softened briefly. "As long as necessary. But you will live. You will learn. You will continue your studies. Your lives will not end — they will simply change their stage." Outside, the lead vehicle pulled into position. Two agents scanned the perimeter, then gave the silent hand signal. "All clear." Jeff exhaled, his arm wrapping protectively around Annemarie's shoulder. "Let's move."

The entire family exited the estate without a sound. The security grid inside the house reset itself automatically behind them, giving the outward appearance that the home was merely closed for holiday—a tactic used dozens of times before in sovereign relocation operations.

The vehicles moved out under cover of the dense night mist, the winding Kent backroads swallowing them quickly. The chosen route avoided all primary roads, traffic cameras, and common security checkpoints. This was not simply about evading reporters—it was about evading the international tracking grids that major genealogical circles often tapped indirectly through "academic partnerships" and private security contractors.

An hour into the drive, they reached a private airfield—one long decommissioned for commercial use, now maintained solely by quiet private interests linked to European royal corridors. No tower lights burned. Only ground crew, handpicked and sworn to lifetime confidentiality, prepared the small Gulfstream that waited silently under the shroud of night.

The pilot stepped forward, nodding once. "All is secured." Ben looked around the dim field as they approached the plane. Even here, in the darkest pocket of secrecy, the old echoes of power lingered. He could feel them — the weight of ancient corridors pulsing beneath the modern machinery. As the agents loaded their belongings, Sørensen knelt slightly to meet Ben at eye level, lowering his voice into a register meant for his ears alone.

"You must understand something, young Harvick. What you are entering now is older than kings. This is the world beneath the world. There are no public names here. No news stories. Only blood. And memory." Ben nodded, his voice a steady whisper. "I'm ready." Sørensen smiled faintly, rising once more. "Yes. You are." Jeff and the others boarded. Isla remained closely at Ben's side as they stepped into the aircraft cabin. The doors sealed behind them with a soft hydraulic hiss, locking them into the next chapter of their lives.

Outside, Sørensen remained behind, watching the plane taxi into position. A secondary agent stepped forward, speaking softly. "Sir, all tracking diversions have been activated. The digital trail leads to the planned cover route through Switzerland." "Good," Sørensen replied. "By sunrise, the world will believe they are still in Kent under lockdown." As the aircraft lifted into the black sky, vanishing into the shroud of night, Sørensen whispered a final word to himself — a word few men had the right to speak, but which he now offered in silent oath. "Protected." The plane vanished into the clouds, and with it, the Harvick family disappeared entirely from the public world. For now.

The aircraft touched down upon Danish soil long before the first light of morning breached the horizon. The airfield was not one known to the public. It was not marked on commercial aviation maps, nor listed among sovereign government holdings. This was one of the hidden fields — a remnant of older times, preserved under discreet royal management, activated only when necessity demanded it.

The Gulfstream taxied quietly to its secure hangar, where a small convoy of vehicles already waited under the cover of heavy darkness. Every inch of this arrival was orchestrated not for ceremony, but for survival. The men who moved around the plane were not palace guards or servants — they were specialists, trained in the quiet arts of royal security, sworn by oaths that no court could ever compel.

Ben peered out of the small cabin window, seeing only the blur of floodlights moving across the hangar as the aircraft came to a stop. Isla sat beside him, silent but calm, her hand still resting gently on his arm. Neither child trembled. Both understood now that they were no longer passengers in the old world—they were now living inside its deepest sanctum. The cabin door opened, and the cool Danish air swept inside. Sørensen entered first, scanning the immediate area before offering a nod. "It's done. Welcome to Denmark, children."

Jeff stood behind the children, steady as ever. Annemarie remained close, her expression deeply protective as she looked at Ben. Robert and Claire stepped forward, gathering Isla between them, the quiet weight of parental instinct never faltering. Waiting at the bottom of the aircraft stairs was His Majesty King Kendrick himself. He wore no crown, no sash, no ceremonial robes. He stood as a man, tall and dignified in a dark wool coat, his posture exuding the quiet command of sovereign lineage. The security team stood at a respectful distance, creating an invisible perimeter while allowing this moment to belong solely to the family.

As Ben and Isla descended the steps, King Kendrick stepped forward. His arms opened wide before either child reached him. Without hesitation, Ben reached him first. Kendrick's arms enveloped the boy in a powerful, protective embrace—one born not of protocol, but of genuine love. "My boy," Kendrick whispered into Ben's ear, his voice trembling with quiet emotion. "You are home."

Ben's chest tightened as he returned the embrace fully. It was not the stiff formality of political guardianship—it was the embrace of family, of a protector who had already given more than any decree could demand. Isla was next. Kendrick reached for her with equal warmth, pulling her tightly into his other arm, holding both children against him.

"My dearest ones," he whispered, his voice now heavy with the strain he had carried for so long. "You are safe now. No one will reach you here." Behind them, Sørensen stood watch as the family gathered. Jeff, standing back respectfully, watched as Kendrick looked up from the embrace and locked eyes with him. No words passed between them — but the King gave a small nod. Gratitude. Recognition. Jeff returned it with a quiet nod of his own.

As the embrace broke, Kendrick turned toward the small convoy now pulling forward. "We will go to the northern residence," he said gently. "It is sealed. No eyes reach it. No records list your presence. From this moment forward, you live beneath the sovereign dome." Sørensen approached as Kendrick led them toward the waiting vehicles. Lowering his voice, he addressed Jeff as they walked. "There is more." Jeff glanced toward him. "Go on." "The crowns," Sørensen said softly. "And the painting of the children."

Jeff stopped briefly, his breath catching. "You brought them?" Sørensen nodded once. "Under cover of night. They were secured in the aircraft hold before departure. No record of their removal exists. They will be delivered directly to the vault chamber beneath the castle. Only the royal archivists know of its location. The crowns are safe." Jeff exhaled, feeling the full scope of Sørensen's forethought. "Good work."

"They belong to the children," Sørensen continued. "But they must remain hidden until the world is ready — and until they are ready." As the convoy pulled into motion, escorted by vehicles both marked and unmarked, Kendrick spoke softly to the children seated beside him inside the royal limousine. "Here you will have peace," he promised. "You will continue your studies. You will continue your research, Benjamin. Isla, you as well. The library halls are open to you both."

Ben nodded softly. "Thank you, Your Majesty." "No," Kendrick corrected gently. "You call me family. You are no longer guests of the court. You are mine now — as if you were born to me." Isla whispered, her voice catching, "Thank you... uncle." Kendrick's eyes glistened faintly at the word, though he kept his voice steady. "Yes. Uncle. And while you remain under my care, no hand, no council, no forgotten house will touch you."

The northern residence soon came into view. An ancient structure standing atop Danish hills, nestled beneath tall birch trees, its stones carried the memory of centuries. It was neither a palace nor a fortress—it was a sanctuary built precisely for this very function: to shelter young bloodlines that could not yet emerge.

As they entered the private gates, the agents swiftly secured the perimeter while the family disembarked. Staff moved quietly inside, trained to disappear into the background, their loyalty unshakable. Sørensen accompanied Jeff and Robert inside as final security protocols were activated. "No visitors," Sørensen confirmed. "No deliveries without double verification. The only digital activity permitted will be routed through sovereign encryption. If anyone attempts to trace your presence, the system will reflect you are still in Kent." Jeff nodded. "You've buried them."

"As intended," Sørensen said. Kendrick stood in the centre of the great hall, his arms around Ben and Isla once more as they gazed upward at the ancient tapestries and stonework. "This," he said softly, "is your sanctuary. And it will remain so... until you are old enough to decide your own path." Ben's gaze settled upon the great crest etched above the hearth—a blend of ancient houses, including some his own DNA had only recently confirmed. Not yet, he thought to himself. But soon.

The northern residence settled into its rhythm quickly.

Within a few short days, the estate became a quiet living world of its own. The children resumed their studies, protected within ancient stone halls where tutors arrived through concealed entrances. Research materials were delivered through secure channels. No electronic footprints were left behind. Jeff coordinated with international scholars remotely, always routed through sovereign encryption. Annemarie and Claire adapted to the secure routines with steady grace, while Robert liaised quietly with trusted family attorneys on matters of property and future planning.

The house breathed with the pulse of secrecy, but also with a strange calm. It was not imprisonment—it was protection. But even within this peace, Ben carried something else.

It gnawed at the edges of his thoughts. A question that had grown heavier since the moment Kendrick had embraced him on the tarmac. It was not a question for Jeff, nor for Robert or Sørensen. It was not even one Isla could yet fully carry with him — though soon, he would share it with her.

This was a question for Kendrick alone. The opportunity came late in the evening, once the house had grown quiet and the staff had retired to their posts. Kendrick often walked the upper library halls during these hours, reviewing old volumes and studying the genealogical charts that stretched back through the centuries. It was during one such walk that Ben approached him.

Kendrick stood before a large map of Europe, illuminated under a single pool of golden light. His hand traced a faint border drawn centuries ago—one that no longer appeared on modern maps. His expression was thoughtful, but not burdened. Ben approached silently. Kendrick noticed him and turned, his face warming at once. "Come, my boy."

Ben stepped forward, his voice quiet, but certain. "Uncle… may I speak with you? Alone?" Kendrick immediately sensed the gravity of the request. He gestured for Ben to follow him into a smaller chamber connected to the private library—a sovereign reading room rarely entered by anyone other than Kendrick himself. Once inside, Kendrick closed the heavy wooden door behind them, ensuring their privacy. The thick stone walls of the chamber swallowed sound entirely. No ears would hear them here. Kendrick took a seat in one of the two high-backed leather chairs by the low-burning hearth, motioning for Ben to sit opposite him.

"You carry something heavy tonight, nephew," Kendrick said gently. "Speak freely." Ben took a breath, steadying his thoughts. His voice came low, but clear. "Uncle… I need to ask something. And I need you to promise me… that what I ask will remain between us for now." Kendrick did not hesitate. "You have my word." Ben leaned forward slightly, his eyes locked to Kendrick's.

"I've seen the charts. I know what's written in them. Árpád. Béla. Stuart. The bloodlines that run through Isla and me… the ones we've only begun to confirm." Kendrick's expression grew still, but not cold. He allowed Ben to speak.

"I understand why we're hiding," Ben continued. "Why you moved us. Why the press had to be silenced. But… I need to know something else." He paused — this was the part that had been building in him for days. "Is there… is there more?"

Kendrick's brow shifted faintly, his voice lowering. "More?" "Beyond what the genealogies show," Ben pressed softly. "Beyond the crowns and crests. Something deeper. Something that was kept hidden even from the other houses. Something that connects all of it — my blood, Isla's, and even you." Kendrick sat back slightly in his chair, folding his hands, his eyes narrowing as if weighing how much weight this boy could truly carry at his age. His voice came low, deliberate.

"You are not wrong to suspect there is more." Ben's chest tightened, but he kept his breath steady. "Then tell me." Kendrick did not rush. The fire crackled softly between them.

"There are truths, Benjamin, that were buried so deeply even the genealogical councils don't have full access to them. Secrets hidden within sovereign archives that were never shared with the political courts." He paused. "You already know pieces of it. Your blood carries a synthesis — not just of royalty, but of something older. Certain lines that remained unbroken where others fractured. You, and Isla beside you, may one day stand at a point where ancient lines converge again."

Ben's voice softened. "Are we being protected… because of who we are today? Or because of who we could become?" Kendrick's eyes sharpened — but not with cruelty. With truth. "Both." The fire hissed softly behind the words. Ben whispered, "And the others… the hidden families. They know?" Kendrick nodded once. "They suspect. But they do not have your full strand. If they did, they would no longer be whispering — they would already be moving openly." Ben exhaled slowly, his chest rising and falling as his mind processed what had now been confirmed.

"I needed to hear it from you," he said finally. Kendrick's voice gentled again. "You have. And when you are ready for the full truth — not yet, but soon — I will give you everything." Ben sat quietly for another long moment, then stood slowly. "Thank you, Uncle." As he reached the door, Kendrick's voice called softly after him. "Benjamin…"

Ben paused, turning his head slightly. "You were never meant to be ordinary." Ben smiled faintly, answering without pride or fear. "I know." He slipped from the room, leaving Kendrick alone in the heavy silence of the ancient chamber. Hours later, as Isla prepared for bed, Ben sat beside her in the quiet comfort of her chamber. The heavy tapestries muted the night wind against the stone walls.

She looked up at him, curious. "You spoke with Uncle Kendrick." "I did," Ben whispered. "And?" He leaned forward slightly, lowering his voice. "There's more, Isla. A lot more."
Her eyes widened faintly. "How much more?" Ben's answer came in a quiet, steady breath. "Enough to change everything."

The northern residence glowed faintly in the deep hours after midnight. In a heavily secured chamber beneath the western wing, King Kendrick gathered Jeff, Robert, Claire, and Sørensen for a private briefing. No aides were present. No legal teams. Only those who needed to know. The walls of the chamber were six feet thick, reinforced stone originally laid in the reign of Christian IV — designed to hold conversations no nation would ever admit occurred.

Kendrick stood at the head of the long table, the old royal crest embedded into its polished oak. The map of Europe behind him gleamed softly under controlled lighting. On it, the ghost lines of royal genealogical corridors shimmered faintly, updated regularly by the private intelligence staff who operated beyond any court's authority.

Jeff sat quietly beside Annemarie, who listened with growing awareness of just how vast the world surrounding her son had become. Robert sat next to Claire, his hand resting protectively upon hers. Sørensen remained standing, always vigilant. Kendrick began, his voice low but direct.

"You must all understand what we're managing now. The genealogical circles watching Benjamin and Isla are no longer passive observers. While the press may have been silenced, and the international legal protections are holding, the private royal houses — those behind the old councils — have accelerated."

He gestured toward the glowing lines on the map.

"These houses have built private archives. Vast vaults. Some are known publicly as research institutes. Others exist under historical foundations funded by old European wealth. Their agents embed themselves across embassies, universities, even certain clerical offices. Their true purpose is to track lost heirs — to prevent unapproved claims from destabilizing Europe's sovereign balances."

Robert spoke softly, his voice tense. "And now Ben and Isla have landed squarely inside their web." Kendrick nodded once. "Exactly." Claire asked, "How exposed are we, Your Majesty?"

Kendrick's eyes met hers without blinking. "Less exposed than before. But not fully buried. Sørensen's extraction succeeded. Digitally, Benjamin and Isla no longer exist within the international registry systems. The only complete records remain under my sovereign lock, and in select gene-vaults controlled by my personal intelligence cell." He paused. "However... the old councils are growing restless. They know we've moved them. They know we've erased key data threads. But because they lack absolute confirmation, they hesitate to act." Jeff leaned forward. "How long can we hold that hesitation?"

"As long as necessary," Kendrick answered. "But once they sense maturity—once the children reach legal succession age—their tactics may change." Sørensen spoke now, his tone clinical. "They will attempt indirect inquiries. Pressure applied to minor genealogical registries. Leaks disguised as academic studies. Contact with distant relatives to generate unapproved narratives." Robert's jaw tightened. "They'll bait the line and hope someone takes it."

"Precisely," Kendrick confirmed. "Which is why absolute silence remains your greatest protection. Public invisibility grants us legal invisibility." Claire whispered, "What happens if they succeed in building enough suspicion?" Kendrick's voice lowered gravely. "They will approach one of the constitutional monarchies — likely through legal proxies — to demand secret tribunals for bloodline investigation. Once they reach those chambers, the fight changes."

Jeff nodded quietly. "That's why you moved us." "It's why I've moved many over the years," Kendrick replied. The chamber grew still. Only the soft hum of the private servers broke the silence. Finally, Kendrick concluded: "This is not only about Ben and Isla.
This is about controlling which ancient names are allowed to live again in public memory. And there are some in Europe who would rather see entire lines vanish quietly than risk awakening the old claims."

Jeff spoke softly, but with steel beneath his voice. "Then we'll hold. And when they come…" Kendrick finished the thought. "…they'll find no door to knock on." The quiet hours had returned once more to the northern residence. After days of settling into the protective routines established by King Kendrick's private network, Ben moved with a comfort that only few his age could comprehend. Yet, beneath his calm exterior, his mind never stopped working.

There was one more matter that weighed on him. And it required another private conversation—this time, one that was not merely personal, but strategic. He requested audience with Kendrick once more. And as before, Kendrick received him in the private stone chamber behind the library — the sovereign sanctum.
The fire crackled softly as Ben entered. Kendrick, already seated, gestured for him to approach with that quiet warmth that now carried both authority and deep paternal affection. "My boy," Kendrick said gently. "You've carried much these past weeks."

Ben nodded, sitting opposite his uncle, his eyes calm, but intent. "I have one more request, Uncle." Kendrick's face sharpened slightly—not in concern, but in interest. He had learned by now that Ben did not waste words. "Speak." Ben's voice remained steady, though low. "Uncle… is there a way I may reach you, privately? A way that allows me to find you, to speak to you, even without the staff or agents knowing. Not because I distrust them—but because one day, I may need you… without anyone else involved."

Kendrick watched him closely, the firelight flickering against the silver strands at his temples. "You seek a private corridor." Ben nodded. "Yes." Kendrick sat back slowly, considering him. "You are very young to think in such terms." "I know," Ben replied softly. "But if I wait until I'm older to prepare, it may be too late." A small smile crept to the corner of Kendrick's mouth—a mixture of pride and quiet admiration. "There is such a passage."

Ben's eyes lifted slightly. Kendrick continued. "This residence was not built solely for comfort. Its foundations date back centuries. There is a subterranean channel that connects this house directly to the lower east wing of the castle—constructed during the days of my grandfather's grandfather, when sovereign heirs sometimes required absolute discretion." Ben whispered, "No one knows?" "Only the sovereign line," Kendrick said. "And now... you." He paused, then added with absolute solemnity: "But you will never enter it without cause, Benjamin. And only I may give permission for its use, unless the circumstances become... extraordinary."

Ben answered without hesitation. "I understand." Kendrick studied him again, seeing the strange, powerful fusion of youth and old bloodline instinct rising within his nephew. "You were never raised for this, Benjamin," Kendrick whispered. "And yet... you carry it as though you always were." Ben simply said, "Because I know what's inside me."

Kendrick reached forward then, resting his hand briefly upon Ben's shoulder—a silent bond passing between them. "Then let us prepare you for every possibility." The meeting concluded, but Ben had one more piece to put into place. After excusing himself, he sought out Sørensen. He found the agent standing by the west terrace, reviewing perimeter reports under the pale glow of the security monitors. The man turned as Ben approached, offering his usual respectful nod.

"You wished to see me, young Harvick?" Ben spoke now with a precision that almost startled Sørensen—a voice that no longer resembled a child's, but that of a sovereign mind preparing for war. "I require something." Sørensen waited. Ben continued. "If circumstances ever shift suddenly — if I sense something wrong, or if an outside force breaches our walls before it reaches the usual security channels — I need a private signal. A code. One that no one else will know. Only you. And me."

Sørensen's brow lifted slightly — not in disapproval, but in quiet recognition. It was a request no ordinary heir would make at this stage. But Ben was not ordinary. The agent lowered his voice, folding his hands behind his back. "Have you chosen a signal?" Ben nodded. "Yes. Shift and wind." For the first time, Sørensen allowed the faintest ghost of a smile. "Direct."

"It's clear," Ben said simply. "It will sound harmless to anyone listening. But you'll know." Sørensen bowed his head slightly. "Then so it shall be. If you ever speak those words directly to me — no matter the setting — I will know the situation has shifted. I will act accordingly." "Good," Ben replied. "Then we are ready." The agent regarded him with growing respect. "You were born for this, young Harvick." Ben's voice came back low, without arrogance. "No. I was born to survive it." Sørensen nodded once more, then turned back toward the monitors — now aware that the boy standing beside him no longer stood as a child, but as something far more dangerous to those watching from the shadows. A sovereign in the making.

The days at the northern residence began falling into a rhythm, almost deceptively peaceful on the surface. Lessons resumed each morning inside the great east wing study hall. The library's ancient volumes became their companions as Ben and Isla poured themselves into genealogical archives, deciphering lineages that spanned centuries.

Isla worked with the same precision as Jeff, methodically constructing family trees, cross-referencing dates, marriages, and unbroken lines. She rarely asked for linguistic translations — she had little interest in foreign tongues. The patterns of names and bloodlines were her true language, and she spoke them fluently.

Ben, meanwhile, continued working directly alongside her, piecing together not only his family's historical threads, but also growing adept at reading the movements of those who still watched from afar. Even as children, they were becoming royal tacticians beneath Kendrick's watchful eye.

Each morning began as it always had — with their ritual.

As the soft sunlight poured through the high windows, Ben would always be first to rise, brushing Isla's hair gently away from her face as she stirred beside him. They shared the same bed with full parental blessing — not out of impropriety, but out of pure trust and devotion. Their parents understood this truth: soulmates needed no separation.

When Isla's eyes opened, she smiled warmly, and they leaned into one another naturally, sharing their long morning kiss — lips meeting in the way that had become their shared heartbeat. They never rushed it. It was never awkward. Just them. Always them.

Afterward, Isla would whisper softly into his ear, "We're still here." And Ben would reply every morning the same way: "Always." But beyond the quiet sanctuary of their chamber, movement had begun once more in the shadows of Europe.

Downstairs, Kendrick and Sørensen reviewed newly arrived private intelligence reports. The files arrived through encrypted diplomatic channels under the highest sovereign clearance. Though most of Europe's governments remained oblivious to the children's disappearance, there were others — those few who never relied on governments to begin with — who had resumed their quiet inquiries.

Sørensen spoke calmly, but with gravity. "The Lorrainese Inquiry has resumed movement, Your Majesty. Three indirect requests for archived data were made this week through their 'academic affiliates' in Geneva, Strasbourg, and Madrid." Kendrick's eyes narrowed. "What are they seeking this time?" "They're attempting cross-referencing through ancestral marriages from the mid-1700s," Sørensen explained. "They have not directly referenced Benjamin or Isla by name. But they are looking for converging branches that could validate an unknown living claimant."

Kendrick exhaled slowly. "They suspect we moved the heirs. But they cannot prove it." "Correct," Sørensen confirmed. "They are hunting for a cousin branch — one they believe might accidentally lead back to the children through collateral ancestry." Kendrick stood silently, looking toward the northern courtyard through the large window. Outside, Ben and Isla walked together in the gardens, reviewing their research notes, entirely unaware of the growing web still reaching for them from afar.

Robert entered quietly, carrying another sealed folder. "The Bourbon Collective has also initiated a silent review of Danish peerage registries, sire." Kendrick took the file, reading the cover sheet carefully. "They're becoming impatient." Robert nodded. "They want movement. But they dare not risk exposure yet.

Without a confirmed living name, they have no legal traction." Claire soon joined them, speaking softly but firmly. "They know if they're too aggressive, your legal teams will strike first."

"They do," Kendrick agreed. "But they're growing desperate." Sørensen tapped another file gently. "There's one further development, sire." Kendrick looked up. "Go on." "The private council once known as the Herrenhaus Circle has recently reassembled. Quietly. In Luxembourg." Robert's expression darkened. "That group was dissolved decades ago."

"Officially, yes," Sørensen answered. "But unofficially, it seems they have convened again. Their records were never fully destroyed. Some of their elder archivists remain alive." Claire whispered, "They're one of the last royal councils that tracked mixed sovereign bloodlines across multiple kingdoms." Sørensen nodded gravely. "Precisely. And those elder records contain family branches that still intersect directly with Benjamin and Isla's combined ancestry."

Kendrick's voice grew sharp, though controlled. "Do they have anyone inside Denmark?" "Not yet," Sørensen said. "But they're watching." Outside in the garden, Ben paused briefly, glancing back toward the towering residence behind him. His instincts — sharpened far beyond his years — sensed the growing pressure that now pressed against their hidden sanctuary.

Isla noticed immediately. "What is it?" Ben spoke softly. "The air feels different." "Are we in danger?" she asked quietly, drawing closer. "Not yet," Ben answered, his voice calm. "But they're stirring again. We'll be ready." As the wind rustled gently through the tall birch trees, the two of them continued walking — side by side, bound not just by love, but by destiny. For now, the dome held. But beyond the dome, the watchers whispered louder.

The day had been unusually quiet. Even the usual diplomatic reports felt oddly still. Yet Kendrick sensed something — the kind of stillness that precedes a storm. It was then that Sørensen entered the private library with a sealed intelligence packet. His expression told Kendrick all he needed to know: the informant had delivered. "They have found the earliest branching," Sørensen said softly.

Kendrick opened the folder carefully. Inside were ancient scans from one of the oldest surviving Árpád repositories — records that most modern genealogical councils no longer accessed, or perhaps never dared to.

As Kendrick studied the surviving scroll extracts, his eyes narrowed. There it was. A paternal divergence once dismissed as collapsed during the thirteenth century — yet now staring back at him as very much alive, very much present in his own nephew. "Benjamin's line," Kendrick whispered. "Yes, Your Majesty," Sørensen confirmed. "It traces fully from Árpád through Béla III, but uniquely crosses into a preserved collateral branch that merges with certain Danish cadet lines. The genetic analysis confirms full sovereign purity." Kendrick closed the folder slowly, his breath tight with reverence. "They cannot touch him."

"No, sire," Sørensen said. "Not if this truth is publicly secured. The hidden councils cannot override sovereign law." It was later that evening, after this discovery, that Ben requested a private meeting with Kendrick once again. He entered with the same quiet confidence that had grown sharper since their arrival. "Uncle," Ben said softly, as Kendrick closed the study door behind them. "You've reviewed the documents?" Kendrick asked, though already knowing. Ben nodded. "Yes. And I understand exactly what they mean."

Kendrick gestured for him to sit. "Speak your thoughts, my boy." Ben took a breath, measuring his words carefully. This was not something he spoke lightly. "I have an idea. A final safeguard." Kendrick leaned forward, listening closely. "I am not trying to replace anyone. My mother remains my mother. Jeff remains my dad — and always will be. Isla remains my other half. Claire, Robert — our family stays whole." He paused, ensuring that Kendrick heard his intent. "This isn't about taking anything away. It's about protecting what we've built."

Kendrick's eyes grew sharper, sensing what was coming. "If those underground councils ever push too far," Ben continued, "if they ever succeed in assembling enough fragmented records to demand international scrutiny, then we invoke this." Ben laid out the suggestion like a statesman. "You adopt me. And Isla as well. Quietly. Privately. Under sovereign Danish law. No ceremony. No public announcement. Legal only." Kendrick exhaled, his mind immediately racing through the legalities.

"You propose a full sovereign adoption." "Yes," Ben said firmly. "By the time they realize what's happened, it will be untouchable. No council, no underground committee, no rogue genealogical inquisition would dare breach the sovereign rights of the Kingdom of Denmark. The throne becomes my legal protectorate, and Isla's as well, by extension. We would fall under your direct legal guardianship as members of your house." Kendrick nodded slowly, his voice dropping into a tone reserved only for those born into true royal councils. "You would be my legal heirs."

"Not for power," Ben clarified. "For protection. For permanence. For our family's safety." Kendrick studied him long and hard. What he saw sitting before him was no longer a child. This was a sovereign mind, bearing the weight of generations. He finally whispered, "You understand what that would mean." Ben answered softly, "I do. I don't ask this lightly. I ask only because I know what's coming." Kendrick's chest swelled with pride. "And you have earned my respect beyond your years." A long silence passed between them, the kind only two rulers in the making could share. At last, Kendrick spoke with finality.

"Very well. I will initiate the preliminary filings privately. They will exist only under the highest sovereign classification, sealed under my personal authority. If the day comes that we must activate them... we will." Ben smiled faintly. "Thank you, Uncle." Kendrick rose then, stepping forward to embrace him — not as a boy, but as a son of the sovereign house. A king in the making. "My boy," Kendrick whispered. "You carry more than your bloodline. You carry our future."

The summer sun filtered through the tall windows of the northern residence as Ben once again approached Kendrick's private study. These visits had become more frequent, not out of anxiety, but out of purpose. Each one carried new depth as Ben's sovereign instincts sharpened with every passing day. Kendrick sat at his desk reviewing confidential reports, yet as Ben entered, he set them aside at once. His expression warmed immediately. "Come, my boy."

Ben took his seat, folding his hands carefully, his eyes steady. "Uncle, I've one more statement to make. Something I want to make perfectly clear before any papers are signed. Before any adoption is processed. Before this plan becomes permanent."

Kendrick sat forward, listening. "I want you to know where I stand. And where I will always stand." Ben took a soft breath, then spoke with complete conviction. "I am not here to take your crown. I am here to protect it." Kendrick's eyes remained locked on him, measuring every word. "When you adopt me — and Isla too — this is not to place us above you. This is to preserve the sovereign line from being torn apart by those who want to fracture it. You will always remain the King. You, Uncle. Always. Until the day you... well... until you leave the world, and hopefully, that's many decades from now. One hundred years old, even."

Ben allowed the faintest smile to lighten the solemn weight of his words, but the truth within them never faltered. "I'll be eleven soon. Isla too. We are children. You are the sovereign. That never changes." Kendrick's breath slowed as the full magnitude of his nephew's statement settled within the room.

There was no manipulation. No hidden desire. Only loyalty. Ben continued. "What we are doing ensures that no matter who stirs beneath us — no tribunal, no council, no shadow house — no one can break this family. We are here to protect your reign, not to disrupt it."

A silence fell between them. Kendrick slowly rose from his chair, walking to the window overlooking the quiet estate grounds where Isla sat reading beneath the tall birch trees. The leaves swayed gently in the summer breeze. He spoke without turning at first, his voice softer than Ben had ever heard it. "You have given me something many rulers never receive."

Ben listened quietly. "Loyalty freely offered. Without demand. Without bargain." Kendrick turned back, his eyes shining with something deeper than pride — something approaching awe. "Few men wear a crown without fearing who might one day reach for it. And yet you have placed my crown above your own desires, my boy. That is not merely loyalty — that is sovereign love." Ben lowered his gaze slightly, speaking with quiet reverence. "I love you, Uncle. We all do. You are our protector. This is my way of protecting you."

Kendrick crossed the distance between them, placing both hands firmly on Ben's shoulders. His voice carried now the full weight of his station, but also the full warmth of a man who saw his heir as his own blood. "Then it shall be done. And not for power. Not for throne. But for the preservation of this house, and of you both, Benjamin and Isla. The papers will remain sealed, as you've requested, until their need arises. But know this: when the time comes, your shield will be stronger than any sword that moves against us." Ben smiled softly. "Thank you, Uncle."

And with that, the pact was silently sealed — not by ceremony, but by something far older: trust. Yet even as that trust solidified inside the stone walls of the northern residence, far across Europe, in hidden rooms beneath the grand estates of Luxembourg, Vienna, and Brussels, the councils stirred uneasily. The watchers had sensed the shift.

They could feel something had moved, though their sources offered no names, no documents, no declarations. But they felt it. One archivist inside the Bourbon Collective leaned back from his desk and whispered to his colleague. "We've lost our window. Someone has locked the bloodlines." "They moved him earlier than expected," the other replied coldly. "We never found the final convergence points." "Then he is now beyond us."

"Perhaps…" the elder whispered. "Or perhaps we wait. For maturity. For weakness." The junior council member shook his head. "We've waited long enough. The Danish sovereign has buried him beneath protections no council can touch without creating international chaos." The elder stared into the candlelight. "Then we retreat. But we never forget." In Denmark, within the royal dome, Kendrick and Ben stood together in quiet reflection, knowing full well that silence was not the same as surrender — and that the watchers had simply withdrawn into deeper shadows. For now. But the bloodline was protected. The dynasty was sealed. The house stood unbroken.

Summer quietly yielded to autumn in Denmark. The northern residence stood firm beneath the shifting skies, its tall birch trees shedding their leaves like falling pieces of parchment—each one an unspoken reminder of time's passing. But while the seasons changed beyond the stone walls, something deeper was changing within. Kendrick, now fully satisfied that the adoption protocols had been securely filed under sovereign seal, turned his focus to the next chapter—one far more delicate than secrecy or legal protections.

The children must be prepared. Not for rule. Not yet. But for knowledge. For legacy. Ben and Isla had already proven their intellect in matters of genealogy, research, and historical study. Isla continued to grow alongside Jeff as a meticulous family historian, cross-referencing archives with surgical precision. Ben's grasp of political structures, dynastic law, and covert operational strategy had matured far beyond his years. But Kendrick knew full well that intellect was not enough. They would require something rarer: sovereign instinct. It began, as all serious instruction does, with a private conversation.

One morning, Kendrick summoned Ben and Isla into his private study, this time joined only by Sørensen, who stood silently behind him. The King spoke gently, but without any of his usual formality. "My children," he began, "you have both carried the weight of your bloodlines with extraordinary grace. But there is more you must now learn. Quietly. Privately. And only under my direct instruction."

Isla looked up at him with those bright, perceptive eyes of hers, never one to shy away from truth. "Uncle, we're ready." Ben simply nodded, his calm never wavering. Kendrick continued. "You are safe. But that safety does not absolve you from responsibility. What I will begin teaching you in the months ahead is not for today. It is for the distant future. For the day long after I have left this world." Ben spoke softly. "You mean if something ever forces us forward."

"Precisely," Kendrick replied. "If the crown is ever threatened—not by war or scandal, but by bloodline collapse—then it is you two who may be called forward by the sovereign councils of Europe." Isla whispered, "But won't they always block us?" "They will try," Kendrick admitted.

"But history moves in strange currents. Monarchies survive not by strength alone, but by the presence of prepared heirs when all other doors have closed." Ben's eyes narrowed slightly, his sovereign mind already reading several layers deeper. "You're preparing us to protect the line if there's ever a vacuum."

Kendrick nodded. "Exactly. A vacuum invites opportunists. But prepared heirs fill voids before others can exploit them." Sørensen finally spoke, his voice as steady as ever. "Your studies will include sovereign law, emergency governance procedures, dynastic treaty knowledge, succession crisis protocols, and advanced archival classifications. You will also be trained in personal security awareness, intelligence reading, and diplomatic survival."

Isla sat up slightly, wide-eyed. "But we're still only children." "Yes," Kendrick said gently. "And that is why we start now — slowly, quietly, in stages you can absorb. There will be no classrooms. No tests. You will learn the old way: through conversation, observation, and private briefings." Ben leaned forward. "Will anyone else know we're learning these things?" Kendrick shook his head. "No one. This education exists solely between us." Sørensen added, "You will continue your normal studies by day. The sovereign lessons will be held in the evenings, here, in this room. No documentation will be created. Only memory." Isla whispered, "So no one can ever steal it."

"Correct," Kendrick smiled. "It lives only in you." Ben, quiet for a moment, finally asked, "When does it begin?" Kendrick glanced at Sørensen, then back to them. "Tonight." As they left the study to prepare, Kendrick remained seated, staring into the low fire. Sørensen stepped closer, his voice low. "They are extraordinary, sire."

"Yes," Kendrick said softly. "They will carry what we never speak of. And if the world ever demands it—" "They will be ready," Sørensen finished. Outside, the wind swept through the birch trees, carrying with it the faint whisper of dynasties both ancient and unborn. And within the northern residence, two children quietly began their journey toward a destiny carefully hidden — but unbreakable.

Far beyond the safety of Denmark's northern residence, in the chambers where the sovereign councils whispered beneath Europe's oldest houses, frustration thickened like smoke trapped beneath heavy stone. The underground councils had tried everything.

The Bourbon Collective's academic queries had stalled. The Lorrainese Inquiry's data scouts had struck dead ends. The Luxembourg Cell's informants inside minor embassies had failed to produce anything beyond rumours. The sovereign shield Kendrick had built around Ben and Isla was unbreakable. But the councils were not yet ready to surrender.

A meeting convened deep beneath Vienna's private archives—one not recorded in any official ledger. Representatives from multiple houses gathered, their faces half-hidden behind the flickering lights of tall candelabras. The senior archivist spoke first. "The primary lines are sealed. The Danish King has buried them behind sovereign law." "We anticipated this," another said coldly. "If we cannot pierce the house itself, we must destabilize the outer branches."

The archivist gestured toward the thick genealogical scroll laid out on the table before them. "There remain distant collateral lines—ancient marriages, minor cadet branches, cousins twelve and thirteen generations removed. Some of these lines have fractured over centuries, fallen into quiet obscurity." Another council member leaned forward. "Then we pull on those threads. Approach their descendants quietly. Whisper uncertainty into their ears. Suggest that the sovereigns have hidden something from them."

"If even one branch agrees to press a claim," the archivist whispered, "we generate scandal. Not legitimate succession. Scandal. And that may force the Danish sovereign to defend disclosures he would rather leave unspoken." There was silence. Calculated. Dangerous. "Shall we proceed?" the elder asked. The council members nodded one by one. So it began.

Across Europe, subtle messages were delivered—anonymous letters to distant cousins and forgotten branches of various royal and noble houses. Whispers of lost claims. Hints of secret heirs shielded by sovereign authority. An attempt to ignite envy, greed, or opportunism within lines so distant they barely remembered their noble origins. But the architects of these plots failed to understand the one thing that made Ben's family different.

They were already unified. Later that same week, Kendrick received word of these efforts through Sørensen's network. The agent stood once more in Kendrick's study, delivering the newest intelligence packet. "They've shifted their approach, sire.

They've begun contacting distant cadet lines throughout Switzerland, Belgium, northern France, and even remote corners of Scotland." "Any responses?" Kendrick asked. "Some minor interest. A few curious inquiries. But nothing solid. The branches are too distant. The blood too thinned. None possess enough documentation to establish viable challenge. Most have no knowledge of Benjamin or Isla's existence."

Kendrick exhaled slowly, his voice steady. "Desperation breeds foolishness." "It does," Sørensen agreed. "But this shows they are nearing collapse. They have no lever left." Kendrick nodded. "And once their options evaporate entirely?" "They will retreat fully. Or risk revealing themselves." Kendrick's voice dropped to a near whisper. "And if they choose exposure?" Sørensen's eyes sharpened. "Then we strike first." And so, as the watchers fumbled deeper into shadows, unable to penetrate the sovereign protections now fully surrounding Ben and Isla, The Secret Breached came to its close. The war for their lineage had not ended. But the first great battle had been won.

CHAPTER 12: DATA RECORDS BREACH

The autumn wind howled harder across the Danish hills that morning, as if nature itself sensed that something unseen had shifted once again. Inside the northern residence, the children's routine remained disciplined. Ben and Isla sat together as always in the eastern study chamber. The library doors closed gently behind them as their morning instructors quietly withdrew. Today's lessons covered sovereign crisis management: complex historical simulations designed to train them in decision-making under pressure.

Isla, with her typical precision, had neatly arranged her genealogical research charts alongside Ben's. Names of long-forgotten dynasties sprawled across the table. Ben leaned in closer to one particular chart, his voice low. "Do you see that one?" Ben whispered, tapping a 14th-century collateral line off an extinct cadet house of Lorraine. "They'll try these ghost lines next. They're getting desperate."

Isla nodded quietly. "But they don't realize they're too thin to reach us." "They know," Ben said, eyes narrowing. "But they don't care. They only need one tiny spark to light scandal." Just then, Sørensen entered the chamber without his usual subtlety. His face was unreadable, but his pace was deliberate. Ben and Isla instantly sensed the change. Sørensen only walked like this when something had gone sideways. Ben rose before Sørensen even spoke. "It's happened."

Sørensen gave him a single, sharp nod. "We need to move to the secure chamber. Now." The children obeyed without question. Isla gathered their charts instinctively, and the three of them slipped through the private passage toward Kendrick's study, where the sovereign himself was already waiting—standing, pacing, unusually unsettled. Kendrick's expression carried a rare edge of anger, one Ben had seldom seen in his uncle.

"They've breached the archives," Kendrick said flatly as the doors sealed behind them. "This time… from inside." Ben's jaw tightened. "The castle." Sørensen delivered the grim confirmation. "Yes. We have another mole."

Kendrick exhaled sharply, pinching the bridge of his nose before turning toward Sørensen. "Do you have any idea who it is?" "I've narrowed it down to two suspects within the lower sovereign clerical staff." Sørensen's voice was firm, his eyes cold. "But I know where the data landed." Ben's voice came sharp, quicker than Isla had ever heard him. "Which council?"

Sørensen answered without hesitation. "Swiss." Ben closed his eyes briefly, his mind calculating. "Of course. Figures. They never let go of anything." Kendrick, his jaw clenched, muttered bitterly, "Switzerland. Always neutral until the price is right." Sørensen offered a dark half-smile. "The old joke, sire — Made in Switzerland. Doesn't fall apart. Apparently, neither do their vaults." "This breach goes beyond standard leaks," Kendrick growled, his voice heavy with the rare weight of frustration. "We are now exposed at a level that borders on irreparable." Ben remained perfectly still. His sovereign mind shifted from shock to calculation within seconds. "They have the early Árpád entries."

"Yes," Sørensen confirmed. "And if they analyze them properly, they may uncover certain key overlaps that could eventually lead back to you both." Isla's face paled slightly. "Is the family safe?" Kendrick's face softened for a moment as he looked at her. "Yes. For now. But we cannot delay."

"We have to warn everyone," Sørensen added, "especially Ben. The Swiss councils will not act immediately. They will run extensive confirmation models first. But once those models produce convergences, they may attempt to apply pressure—politically or financially." Ben spoke quickly, his voice steady. "Jeff, my mom, Isla, Robert, Claire — they stay under full protection, right?"

"They're not targets yet," Sørensen said. "You are." Ben's voice sharpened. "We invoke the contingency plan if they get too close." Kendrick nodded firmly. "Exactly." "But we're not there yet," Sørensen added. "Not today. This breach gives them data. It does not yet give them legal leverage." Ben whispered softly, "It gives them a trail." Kendrick crossed to him, placing his hand firmly on Ben's shoulder. "And you're prepared to hold that trail closed, aren't you?"

Ben didn't flinch. "Yes. And if we have to invoke the adoption papers, we do it before they move." Isla stood beside him, her small hand sliding into his as always, their fingers interlacing without hesitation. She said softly, "Whatever comes, we face it together." Kendrick looked at them both, pride glowing in his eyes even amid the storm. "And that's why you will survive this. Because no one—no blood council, no underground tribunal—can fracture what you've already built here."

The air in the room grew still again. Sørensen closed the intelligence file on the desk and locked it into the sovereign safe. Kendrick exhaled. "We will monitor the Swiss channels closely. I will deploy additional assets across Zurich and Geneva. The next few weeks may tell us everything we need." "And if they push?" Ben asked.

"Then we pull the final lever," Kendrick answered firmly. The adoption. The sovereign shield. The last resort — still waiting, sealed, untouchable. For now.

The northern residence remained as still as ever, but beneath its stone foundation, the machinery of sovereignty had fully engaged. The breach was real. The danger had moved from theoretical to active. Kendrick wasted no time. His sovereign intelligence network — an entity far older than any single reign — was mobilized within hours of Sørensen's report. New operatives were quietly inserted into Switzerland: Zurich, Geneva, Bern. They did not wear badges, nor carry open orders. They moved in private shadows, trained for precisely this moment. Inside Kendrick's private war room, Sørensen stood over the intelligence board, tracing red string between the clusters of Swiss family councils, financial vaults, and ancient aristocratic archives. Kendrick and Ben entered together as Sørensen laid out the early findings. "The data leak originated not directly from our central files," Sørensen explained, "but from copied fragments hidden inside Switzerland's Zürich Sovereign Archive."

Ben frowned slightly. "How did they get our fragments into Zürich?" "One of our former sovereign aides, likely recruited after being dismissed from service last year. He sold scanned portions of the old Árpád scrolls and secondary cross-marriage logs." Kendrick clenched his jaw. "He sold the cross-marriages?" "Yes, sire."

Ben immediately saw the danger. "Those cross-marriages are where the councils start finding name convergences. That's how they connect us to the outer branches they're already probing." "Exactly," Sørensen replied. "The Swiss council now possesses partial evidence that Árpád, Béla III, and your convergence line still live — here, under my protection." Kendrick's voice grew cold. "Do they suspect Isla as well?" "Not yet," Sørensen said. "But if left unchecked, they eventually will. Which is why we cannot simply monitor anymore."

He turned toward Kendrick fully now. "I recommend active counter-surveillance. Direct penetration of Zürich's archive offices. We must see what data sets they've assembled and intercept their predictive algorithms before they reach the point of legal exploitation." Kendrick exhaled slowly. "Agreed." Ben, standing quietly beside them, suddenly spoke—his voice calm, but loaded with authority neither man had taught him directly.

"I have an additional safeguard." Both Kendrick and Sørensen turned toward him. Ben continued. "We've been playing chess. But we've allowed them to control the rhythm. We keep reacting after they move. I want to set a new trap. Something they won't expect." Sørensen raised an eyebrow. "Go on." Ben took a small data chip from his pocket, placing it on the war table. "While Isla and I have been studying the dynasties, we quietly built a synthetic overlay — an entirely fictional branch of an extinct Árpád collateral line."

Kendrick's eyes widened slightly. "You forged a genealogical ghost branch?" Ben nodded. "Yes. Fully sourced with fabricated citations, dates, and foreign marriages that subtly conflict with their current models. If Sørensen plants this ghost fragment into their Zurich archive through a back channel, it will pollute their algorithm." Isla entered then, joining her soulmate calmly. "They will follow the false trail deeper into dead ends, chasing a branch that never existed."

Sørensen stared at them both for a moment, deeply impressed. "You're proposing active disinformation." "Exactly," Ben answered. "Not to attack — but to confuse." Kendrick finally spoke, the faintest smile creeping onto his face. "Brilliant." Sørensen picked up the data chip, weighing its elegant simplicity. "I can have this inserted into their secondary pipeline within forty-eight hours." "Good," Kendrick said, his voice steady. "Then we force them to drown in their own ambition."

"And by the time they realize it," Ben finished, "we'll be two years further ahead. And their legal window will close permanently." Sørensen bowed his head slightly to both children. "You two will be dangerous monarchs one day." Ben whispered back, calm as ever, "That's not our goal." Isla smiled. "We're not here to rule." Ben finished for them both. "We're here to preserve."

The operation began with absolute precision. Sørensen had activated his Zurich asset — a man whose name existed on no royal ledger, whose service was known only to a handful within Kendrick's sovereign circle. His mission: implant the fabricated genealogical fragment into the Swiss Sovereign Archive's secondary research server. The digital corridor was chosen carefully. Not directly into the primary archive, which would trigger security flags — but into one of the peripheral academic feeds, where ambitious council archivists often scavenged for overlooked leads.

The synthetic Árpád branch, designed by Ben and Isla themselves, had been flawless in its construction. Dates, marriages, distant territorial links — every detail plausible enough to appear authentic, but poisoned just enough to fracture predictive modeling if the councils attempted to process it.

Sørensen monitored the breach in real time from the sovereign command chamber beneath the northern residence. The main data screen displayed multiple server pathways as lines of encrypted code flowed across the monitor.

Kendrick stood behind him, watching silently. Beside him, as always, stood Ben and Isla — fingers lightly entwined, their promise rings catching the soft glow of the chamber's lighting. The pair spoke little, but their presence radiated calm assurance. "Insertion successful," Sørensen announced quietly. "The false branch has been uploaded and indexed within their peripheral archive stream."

Kendrick's voice was low but steady. "Will they detect it immediately?" "No, sire," Sørensen replied. "It was planted during their scheduled system refresh. The file is catalogued as part of a recent inheritance record review. It will appear as an organic archival discovery—an uncatalogued scroll fragment, surfaced through one of their academic exchanges." Ben studied the swirling algorithm models on the screen. "When will they begin running it through their models?" "Within seventy-two hours," Sørensen answered. "They monitor those peripheral channels aggressively. This file was designed to trip their secondary alert system."

Isla leaned slightly into Ben, whispering softly, "They won't be able to resist it." "No," Ben agreed. "That's the point." Kendrick allowed himself the faintest smile, glancing at the two young strategists before him. "You understand what you've done, don't you?" he asked gently.

Ben nodded. "We've weaponized their ambition." Sørensen looked between the King and the pair, adding softly, "When they run this through their algorithm, the system will begin producing false succession branches that conflict with their existing royal tree structures. The more they chase, the more corrupted their model becomes." "Brilliant," Kendrick whispered. "They'll confuse themselves into paralysis." Sørensen's screen pinged gently. "They've accessed the file. Phase two has begun."

In Zurich, deep beneath the surface level of the Swiss Sovereign Archive, the council archivists gathered as the newly discovered Árpád collateral file flashed across their feed. "This is unexpected," one whispered. "A fragment from the Lorraine-Schleswig connection," another muttered, reviewing the false data. "It matches parts of the unresolved French and Eastern crossings."

"Finally." The senior archivist leaned forward, his voice tight with greedy anticipation. "This could be the link we've been waiting for." "And if it is?" his assistant asked. "Then the Danish sovereign will be forced into disclosure. And the Harvick line will finally be exposed to open challenge." Unaware they were chasing a carefully laid illusion, the archivists activated their full data model, feeding the poisoned fragment directly into their succession algorithm. The trap had closed. Back in Denmark, Sørensen monitored the incoming traffic. "They've taken the bait," he reported. "The Swiss data modeling engines are now processing the ghost branch."

Ben exhaled slowly, his hand still wrapped in Isla's. "Now we wait." Kendrick stood tall, his voice filled with quiet pride. "And as they chase the shadow, we continue to protect the light." Isla smiled up at Ben. "We did it." Ben smiled softly, whispering only for her to hear, "We always will."

The tension inside the northern residence had reached its quiet peak. Sørensen stood in the war room beside Kendrick and Ben, reviewing the final breach report. The intelligence feeds were no longer theoretical. The Swiss councils had gone fully active. "They've received the ghost data and folded it into their models," Sørensen began. "But while processing, they've also gathered additional files."

He tapped several windows on the secure monitor. New icons flashed: audio files, video captures, physical scan documents. "Someone inside our perimeter provided them with more than digital records. They physically printed hard copies — full genealogical extracts, Árpád convergence points, along with cross-border marriage records — and couriered them to Switzerland."

Kendrick's face darkened, his anger now heavy beneath his normally steady surface. "The printer logs?" "Wiped," Sørensen answered. "They used secure clearance codes—someone authorized." Ben stood firm, his expression steady but sharpened. "The mole." "Or moles," Sørensen corrected grimly. "At least two. As I previously suspected." Kendrick clenched his fists. "And now they hold physical proof they believe they can leverage."

Sørensen nodded. "It's no longer only theory, sire. The councils believe they have leverage to initiate external sovereign pressure." Ben's voice came now with full sovereign clarity. "Then we no longer delay." He stepped forward, facing his uncle directly. "Invoke the adoption." The room fell silent for half a moment. Even Kendrick took pause, studying his nephew's face — not for uncertainty, but for final confirmation.

Ben continued, his voice calm, deliberate, royal. "Uncle Kendrick, we've played the game. We've misdirected, we've countered, we've buried trails. But they've pushed too far. And you know it. This isn't just about protecting Isla and me anymore. This is about the throne itself. Your kingdom." Kendrick's breathing slowed. Ben continued. "Once the adoption is invoked and legally formalized under sovereign seal, nothing Switzerland or any other council does will matter. The line becomes legally closed. Irrevocable. Your throne will be safe to the end of your reign. Isla and I will serve, one day, only if that day ever arrives."

He paused, locking eyes with his uncle. "This is not to take your crown. You remain sovereign. Always." Kendrick's throat tightened as he absorbed his nephew's full understanding of duty. Then Sørensen — who rarely spoke in matters of personal family — quietly stepped forward. "Sire," Sørensen said softly. "He is correct. We have reached the point where decisive legal sovereignty must override any external speculation."

Ben allowed himself a faint smile as he turned his head toward Sørensen. "Even the Italians would say it, Sørensen..." Sørensen raised an eyebrow, catching the joke before Ben finished. Ben grinned. "It smells like bad fish." Sørensen gave a rare, dry chuckle. "Yes, young sir. Very bad fish indeed."

Even Kendrick's stern face softened for a moment, releasing a low exhale of both stress and amusement. "Then it is settled." Kendrick straightened his posture, fully embracing his role as sovereign protector. "I will sign the adoption documents under full sovereign classification. The seals will be affixed tonight. The Council of Legal Affairs will execute the protocols in silence. By sunrise, you both will be entered officially into the House of Rosenshavn under my blood."

Ben whispered softly, "And the family remains untouchable." "Untouchable," Kendrick confirmed. Isla, who had stood quietly beside Ben throughout, tightened her hand around his. Her eyes glistened with the depth of the moment. Ben whispered to her, "We're safe now." She whispered back, "Because you led us."

Kendrick turned to Sørensen with final instructions. "Double the internal audit. Sweep every clerical, legal, and administrative channel inside the castle. Find the moles. Bring me their names." Sørensen bowed. "Yes, sire. I will begin the forensic trace immediately." "And after that?" Kendrick added coldly. "The Swiss councils will receive silence." Ben and Isla stood now not only as protected children — but as fully legal heirs. The threat from outside no longer mattered. The Swiss had gambled everything. And lost.

The night after the sovereign adoption was finalized, the northern residence slept peacefully. But beneath its vaulted ceilings, a storm was building — silent, precise, unavoidable.

Sørensen had already deployed his internal forensic unit: a small circle of operatives trained in sovereign integrity breaches. These were not ordinary investigators. They were men and women bound by lifetime oaths, trained to expose internal threats before they metastasized into public crises.

Inside the secure chamber, under reinforced lights and ancient stone, Sørensen stood before the full personnel chart of the residence staff. Dozens of names, each tagged with service records, access clearances, security permissions, and daily movement logs. Kendrick joined him at the table, arms folded. "We will find them," Sørensen said flatly. "Do it quietly," Kendrick replied. "I will not have panic spread within these walls."

Sørensen gave a small nod. "Of course." In a side alcove, Ben and Isla sat together, reviewing the data silently. Even in these tense hours, their calm never broke. Ben's mind was already running several layers ahead. Isla, as always, read the genealogical angles while Ben read the operational ones. "The breach wasn't opportunistic," Ben said softly. "They weren't bribed overnight. This was deliberate. Long game." Isla nodded. "Meaning?"

Ben lowered his voice. "Meaning they were placed here years ago. Groomed for this exact moment." Sørensen overheard and glanced back at him approvingly. "Correct." He pointed toward two flagged names on the board. "Both have access patterns consistent with long-term embedded agents." The first: Anton Reiter, junior sovereign archivist. Swiss national. Employed for seven years. Clearance: Level Two.

The second: Gerhard Voss, logistics officer. Austrian descent. Employed for nine years. Clearance: Level Three. Kendrick's brow furrowed. "Both positions close enough to move information... but not high enough to draw attention." "Exactly," Sørensen confirmed. "They both share one other commonality: external contacts tied loosely to Swiss banking circles. Hidden under personal family trusts." Ben leaned forward. "They were paid through private banking conduits?"

"Highly likely," Sørensen replied. "Layered through third-party institutions. But we have the preliminary trails." Kendrick's voice hardened. "How long until you have confirmation?" "Seventy-two hours, sire. The financial teams are already drilling through the shell accounts."

Ben whispered to Isla, "Once their funds are traced, we'll have proof of foreign influence." "Directly linking the councils to internal treason," Isla added. Kendrick glanced at them both, marveling yet again at how quickly they absorbed the depth of royal mechanics.

Sørensen spoke again. "They were clever, sire — but not perfect. We've located security badge activity that places both Reiter and Voss in the restricted genealogy chambers after-hours on multiple occasions. Unscheduled, undocumented." Ben's eyes sharpened. "That's when they printed the hard copies." Sørensen nodded. "Precisely." Kendrick exhaled slowly, his tone darkening. "When you have their financial ties confirmed, I want both detained — quietly, under full sovereign jurisdiction."

"They will never leave this house again," Sørensen promised. Isla whispered softly, "But Uncle... will they talk?" Sørensen answered without hesitation. "They will." Ben and Isla exchanged one last glance, fingers entwined, their rings quietly glinting beneath the chamber lights. The first layer of betrayal was being peeled away. The house would be cleansed. The moles would fall. And the councils watching from across Europe would finally realize: This kingdom was not theirs to break.

Three days later, the operation reached its conclusion. Sørensen's forensic teams delivered the final report with surgical precision. The web had been fully traced: encrypted banking transfers, offshore accounts, discreet deposits layered through Swiss intermediaries, and evidence of foreign correspondence between the moles and the underground councils.

Their work was flawless. Their treason undeniable. Inside Kendrick's private war chamber, the team gathered as Sørensen presented the summary. "Anton Reiter and Gerhard Voss are guilty of high treason," he stated calmly. "We now have full transactional evidence that they accepted financial compensation for transferring sensitive sovereign genealogical data to the Swiss councils."

Kendrick's jaw tightened. "How much did they receive?" "Reiter accepted the equivalent of 7.3 million Swiss francs," Sørensen said. "Voss accepted just under 5.6 million. Both payments were layered across five shell corporations." Ben shook his head quietly. "All of this... for money." "They sold out the blood of a sovereign house for their own comfort," Sørensen replied, his voice dry but sharp.

Isla whispered, "They didn't just betray Uncle. They betrayed the family." Kendrick spoke now, his voice a steel wall. "Have they been detained?" "Yes, sire," Sørensen confirmed. "Both were arrested at separate points in the castle early this morning. The staff never noticed. They were removed through private security corridors. They are being held in full isolation under sovereign jurisdiction."

Kendrick nodded slowly. "Interrogation?" "Already begun," Sørensen said. "They have both confessed. Direct links to Swiss council intermediaries confirmed." Ben stood silent for a moment, processing every detail with that familiar calm that was becoming his sovereign signature. "Good," he finally said. "The councils will learn that even their deepest agents cannot reach us." Kendrick approached the table slowly, exhaling. "Now the question becomes: how do we sentence them?"

Sørensen remained quiet for a moment, waiting for Kendrick to give the order. But before he could, Ben quietly spoke again. "Uncle... may I make a recommendation?" Kendrick looked at him, always willing to listen when Ben spoke. "Go on." "We cannot afford weakness here," Ben said. "If word escapes that these men received even the smallest mercy, it invites future traitors. We must charge them with high treason under sovereign law." Isla tightened her grip on Ben's hand, fully in support.

"No bail, Uncle," Ben continued firmly. "Not even the option. No conditional release. No parole offers. They sit in a sovereign holding facility until trial. And when the trial comes, they face the full weight of sovereign law." Kendrick studied his nephew's face with care. The boy's wisdom continued to astonish him. "You recommend complete sovereign lockdown."

"Yes," Ben replied. "If any external house attempts to fund or petition their release, it must be forbidden under your direct sovereign authority." Sørensen broke his usual reserve and quietly spoke in full agreement. "Sire... I concur. Absolute lockdown sends the only message that matters." Kendrick let out a long breath. "Then so it shall be."

He turned to Sørensen. "I want both men formally charged under Article IV of the Sovereign Treason Act. Immediate court docket placement. No bail. No petitions. And the trial shall be conducted under sealed sovereign protocol. If any external council attempts contact, notify me directly."

"It will be done, sire," Sørensen said. Kendrick turned back to Ben and Isla. His voice softened slightly, though his authority remained absolute. "You both have shown wisdom far beyond your years. You do not merely think as heirs. You think as sovereign protectors."

Ben whispered, "We promised to preserve the crown." Isla smiled softly, "And we keep our promises." As the night closed in, the kingdom stood stronger than ever. The moles were secured. The councils defeated themselves. The House of Rosenshavn had been fortified by its next generation. And Kendrick, though still king, knew that his future now rested in the best hands he could have ever prayed for.

The Royal Sovereign Tribunal had not been convened for treason in over half a century. Its halls were ancient — built of stone quarried during Denmark's earliest dynastic period — and rarely did its great chamber receive matters so grave. But today, under Kendrick's sovereign authority, the court stood assembled once more. Only a handful of authorized witnesses were permitted within the chamber: the royal legal counsel, private sovereign adjudicators, and select members of Kendrick's inner circle. Public record would never see this trial. It was a sovereign matter — one that would live only within the walls of state.

At the head of the chamber sat King Kendrick himself, draped in the formal robes of sovereign judgement. His face was carved from stone — not cold, but unshakable. Beside him sat Ben and Isla, both permitted as heirs-apparent under Kendrick's private adoption act, though their official presence remained unannounced to the world at large. They sat as silent witnesses to the justice that would preserve their family's future. Sørensen stood behind them, ever watchful. The two traitors — Anton Reiter and Gerhard Voss — were escorted in by sovereign guards, their hands shackled, their faces pale, their bravado long since dissolved. They had confessed. They knew there was no plea that could spare them.

The Chief Sovereign Prosecutor stood before the tribunal. His voice rang through the ancient stone chamber with absolute clarity. "Under authority of His Majesty the King, and under full provision of the Sovereign Treason Act, Article IV — let the charges be read."

He lifted the scroll. "Anton Reiter — sovereign treason, espionage, unlawful transmission of genealogical state secrets to foreign councils, conspiracy to disrupt the royal succession, receipt of foreign financial inducements, and violation of sovereign oath." He paused, then turned toward the second man. "Gerhard Voss — sovereign treason, conspiracy to assist foreign agents, unauthorized access to restricted sovereign data chambers, falsification of personnel access records, unlawful transfer of printed classified documents, and receipt of financial compensation from hostile foreign councils."

The chamber stood silent. No defence was offered. None could be. The Chief Prosecutor turned then to the throne. "Your Majesty, the charges stand. The accused have confessed under sovereign inquiry. All evidence has been entered into sealed record. The Crown awaits your final command." Kendrick stood slowly.

His voice was even, yet it filled the hall like rolling thunder. "For the crimes committed against the Crown, against this sovereign house, against the safety of my family and heirs, and against the integrity of this kingdom — I rule as follows." He gestured toward the guards.

"Both men are hereby declared guilty of high sovereign treason. They shall be held in permanent sovereign custody pending lifelong sentence review. No bail shall be granted. No appeal permitted. No foreign council shall interfere. Their names shall be stripped from all sovereign service records and erased from the honour rolls of this house. Their families will receive no benefit, and no further communication shall be permitted."

He lowered his voice, though its power grew sharper still. "Let this be the message to those who would dare think sovereign blood can be purchased: this house will not fall. This kingdom will not break." The gavel struck. "It is finished." As the guards led the prisoners away, Ben whispered softly to Isla. "It's over."

"For now," Isla replied wisely. "But we stay ready." Sørensen leaned forward slightly, whispering so only Ben and Isla could hear. "Your move, young sovereigns, was perfect." Ben allowed himself the smallest smile. "Thank you, Sørensen. You know what the Italians would say." Sørensen smiled faintly. "Yes. It smelled like bad fish." The three exchanged that quiet glance that only trusted allies share — one that said: The house holds. The kingdom breathes. The dynasty endures.

The tribunal chamber now lay silent, its echoes still hanging in the air like faint dust. But inside Kendrick's private study, the tension had finally begun to ease. The family gathered in quiet reflection — no grand ceremony, no public statements, only the intimate shelter of trusted blood and loyal hearts.

Ben and Isla sat across from their uncle, both composed yet carrying that subtle spark of mischief that always danced between them in these rare, softer moments. Sørensen, ever nearby, stood behind Kendrick — hands folded, watchful as always. Ben cleared his throat lightly, catching Kendrick's attention. "Uncle..." Kendrick raised an eyebrow, sensing the tone immediately. "Yes, my boy?"

Ben glanced briefly at Isla, whose eyes sparkled knowingly. Then he leaned forward with that practiced mix of respect and gentle boldness that Kendrick had come to admire deeply. "So... are we still officially under lockdown?" Ben asked carefully. "Or is there room for a little fresh air?" Kendrick tilted his head slightly, curious. "What exactly do you have in mind?"

Isla spoke up now, her voice soft but full of her usual precise logic. "Not public exposure. We're not asking for anything foolish. Just the back gardens, Uncle. The secure grounds. No cameras. No eyes." Ben added quickly, "We've been sitting behind these walls for weeks. We're not asking to parade through the capital." He flashed a quick grin. "Besides, we were thinking maybe Sørensen could join us. After all, even the most loyal guardian could use a little fresh air... and perhaps a good cup of coffee."

Sørensen blinked once, allowing the faintest expression of amusement to pass across his face — that rare flicker of human warmth beneath his eternal professionalism. "I see," Kendrick said, his voice carrying the faintest hint of humour now. "A private parade, is it?" Ben smiled. "Exactly. A royal stroll, but without the royal spectacle."

Kendrick leaned back for a moment, studying them both. These two were far from naïve. They understood the stakes. They understood the risks. But they also understood the balance between vigilance and living. At last, Kendrick exhaled slowly. "Very well. The back gardens remain under full sovereign protection. No surveillance. No press. Only trusted personnel." He turned toward Sørensen. "You will accompany them."

"Of course, sire," Sørensen replied with a light nod. "However," Kendrick continued, shifting back into his role as sovereign mentor, "once your stroll concludes, we will begin the next stage of your education." Ben and Isla straightened their posture slightly, attentive. "This phase will not be simple lessons or historical charts," Kendrick explained. "You are now heirs of state. That means you must be taught sovereign diplomacy, defensive royal strategy, negotiation protocol, and the art of managing hostile alliances."

Ben smiled faintly. "So... the real work begins." "Precisely," Kendrick said. "The work that cannot be taught in books." Isla added softly, "And Sørensen will assist too?" Kendrick looked at Sørensen, who offered a rare, respectful bow. "I would be honoured, young ones. There are many skills I can teach beyond royal protocol." Ben smiled as he rose to his feet, reaching for Isla's hand. Their promise rings glinted softly in the afternoon light as they clasped fingers.

"Well then, Sørensen," Ben said playfully, "how about we start with that coffee and fresh air first?" "And you may consider it... part of the training," Isla added with a wink. Sørensen allowed himself a quiet smile. "Very well. But I'll warn you both — this may be the last easy stroll you take for quite some time." As they made their way toward the secured gardens, the family quietly exhaled for the first time in many weeks. The castle stood unbroken. The bloodline sealed. The house protected. But the training — the true preparation — was only just beginning.

The tribunal chamber now lay silent, its echoes still hanging in the air like faint dust. But inside Kendrick's private study, the tension had finally begun to ease. The family gathered in quiet reflection — no grand ceremony, no public statements, only the intimate shelter of trusted blood and loyal hearts. Ben and Isla sat across from their uncle, both composed yet carrying that subtle spark of mischief that always danced between them in these rare, softer moments. Sørensen, ever nearby, stood behind Kendrick — hands folded, watchful as always.

Ben cleared his throat lightly, catching Kendrick's attention. "Uncle..." Kendrick raised an eyebrow, sensing the tone immediately. "Yes, my boy?" Ben glanced briefly at Isla, whose eyes sparkled knowingly. Then he leaned forward with that practiced mix of respect and gentle boldness that Kendrick had come to admire deeply.

"So... are we still officially under lockdown?" Ben asked carefully. "Or is there room for a little fresh air?" Kendrick tilted his head slightly, curious. "What exactly do you have in mind?" Isla spoke up now, her voice soft but full of her usual precise logic. "Not public exposure. We're not asking for anything foolish. Just the back gardens, Uncle. The secure grounds. No cameras. No eyes."

Ben added quickly, "We've been sitting behind these walls for weeks. We're not asking to parade through the capital." He flashed a quick grin. "Besides, we were thinking maybe Sørensen could join us. After all, even the most loyal guardian could use a little fresh air... and perhaps a good cup of coffee."

Sørensen blinked once, allowing the faintest expression of amusement to pass across his face — that rare flicker of human warmth beneath his eternal professionalism. "I see," Kendrick said, his voice carrying the faintest hint of humour now. "A private parade, is it?"

Ben smiled. "Exactly. A royal stroll, but without the royal spectacle." Kendrick leaned back for a moment, studying them both. These two were far from naïve. They understood the stakes. They understood the risks. But they also understood the balance between vigilance and living. At last, Kendrick exhaled slowly. "Very well. The back gardens remain under full sovereign protection. No surveillance. No press. Only trusted personnel."

He turned toward Sørensen. "You will accompany them." "Of course, sire," Sørensen replied with a light nod. "However," Kendrick continued, shifting back into his role as sovereign mentor, "once your stroll concludes, we will begin the next stage of your education." Ben and Isla straightened their posture slightly, attentive. "This phase will not be simple lessons or historical charts," Kendrick explained. "You are now heirs of state. That means you must be taught sovereign diplomacy, defensive royal strategy, negotiation protocol, and the art of managing hostile alliances."

Ben smiled faintly. "So... the real work begins." "Precisely," Kendrick said. "The work that cannot be taught in books." Isla added softly, "And Sørensen will assist too?" Kendrick looked at Sørensen, who offered a rare, respectful bow.

"I would be honoured, young ones. There are many skills I can teach beyond royal protocol." Ben smiled as he rose to his feet, reaching for Isla's hand. Their promise rings glinted softly in the afternoon light as they clasped fingers. "Well then, Sørensen," Ben said playfully, "how about we start with that coffee and fresh air first?" "And you may consider it... part of the training," Isla added with a wink.

Sørensen allowed himself a quiet smile. "Very well. But I'll warn you both — this may be the last easy stroll you take for quite some time." As they made their way toward the secured gardens, the family quietly exhaled for the first time in many weeks. The castle stood unbroken. The bloodline sealed. The house protected.

But the training — the true preparation — was only just beginning. The afternoon sky stretched wide above them, a soft Danish blue without a single blemish of cloud. The northern residence behind them stood as a quiet guardian, its towers silhouetted against the early autumn sun. For the first time in weeks, there was no storm chasing them — only calm.

Ben, Isla, and Sørensen made their way along the winding garden path, coffee cups in hand, their boots crunching softly upon the stone walkway. The air smelled faintly of birch and fading roses, the last fragrances of the season whispering their goodbyes.

It was Ben and Isla's idea to bring Sørensen out here. The man never asked for reprieve, but today they gently insisted. And now, as they arrived at the quiet alcove — their spot — both smiled with familiar warmth.

"This is where we first sat when we arrived," Isla whispered as they stepped onto the small marble platform nestled beneath two great oak trees. Ben nodded. "Before all of it started." The benches curved slightly inward, creating a small circle. They all took their places — Sørensen at first remaining stiff, until Ben motioned for him to actually sit down properly.

"You might as well enjoy it, Sørensen," Ben said with a grin. "You're here now." Sørensen allowed himself a rare breath of comfort, adjusting his posture. "Very well." For a few quiet minutes, they simply sat, sipping their coffee, listening to the breeze move through the leaves. Then Ben broke the silence. "Sørensen..."

The agent turned his head slightly. "When you were first sent to Kent — to us — what went through your mind?" Isla smiled softly. "And we want the truth. No sugarcoating." Sørensen's eyes narrowed thoughtfully. He paused long enough to weigh his words. He knew the children didn't want politeness. They wanted honesty.

"Truthfully?" he began. "When I was first summoned for the assignment, I assumed it would be simple protective duty. Keep an eye on two royal-linked minors, ensure their safety, report back." He glanced toward them both now. "What I did not expect... was you." Ben raised an eyebrow. "Us?"

"Yes." Sørensen allowed himself the faintest hint of a smile. "I quickly realized you were no ordinary children. The intellectual discipline. The curiosity. The calm under pressure. Most your age wouldn't know how to breathe properly under the weight you carry. But you both…" He shook his head lightly. "You both were already thinking like sovereigns before you even arrived in Denmark." Ben and Isla exchanged a knowing glance. Neither boasted. They simply understood.

Sørensen continued. "When I returned here with you, I recognized what I had not originally anticipated: that you are not simply heirs to a line. You are architects of it." Ben leaned forward slightly, now pushing deeper. "That's exactly why we brought you here today." Isla nodded. "We want to know more. Not just about titles and laws. About everything."

Sørensen studied them both carefully. "What do you mean by everything?" Ben spoke clearly now, with no hesitation. "We understand what Uncle Kendrick is teaching us. Sovereign diplomacy. Defensive royal strategy. The negotiations. The politics. That's crucial." Isla added softly, "But it's not the full picture."

Ben continued. "You've seen it. You've lived it. You trained for it. We don't just need to know how to govern. We need to learn how to protect — if the worst ever comes." The air thickened slightly. This was no childish fantasy.

They were speaking of what most heirs would never dare voice. Ben's voice remained steady. "We want to understand the physical disciplines. Not simply for sport, or vanity, or tradition. But because if danger comes — and one day it might — we don't want others dying for us because we were unprepared."

Sørensen inhaled slowly. He looked not at children now, but at two young sovereigns ready to step into disciplines most royals avoided their entire lives. Ben finished, "I'm not asking for some military training camp. But the basics. The readiness. The mental focus. The self-control. The body discipline. Enough that if all other defences failed, we wouldn't be helpless." Isla's voice joined, firm but soft. "We want to be fully sovereign. Mind, heart, and body."

Sørensen sat in silence for a long moment. The leaves rustled gently overhead. At last, his voice returned — quiet, but resolved. "Then you must understand something first." They both leaned in. "What I was trained for… what I became… it is not easy. It requires patience. Pain. Repetition. Focus. Not for days. For years. What I teach will not feel like royalty. It will feel like struggle. You will sweat. You will fail. And you will learn to master failure."

Ben's eyes never wavered. "We understand." Isla nodded without hesitation. "We're ready." Sørensen looked between them once more — and for the first time since this entire sovereign journey began, he allowed himself a true, small smile. "Very well," he said. "We will begin." He leaned back against the stone bench, taking another sip of his coffee.

"But enjoy your walk for now. Because after this… your real education begins." Ben smiled faintly. "That's exactly why we wanted the coffee first." Sørensen chuckled softly. "Smart." And beneath the late afternoon sun, the three of them sat in quiet unity — the sovereigns and their instructor — knowing full well what the days ahead would require.

The following morning arrived crisp and clear. The northern estate sat quietly as always, but within its private southern wing — an area reserved for sovereign security operations — the next phase of Ben and Isla's training was about to begin.

Kendrick stood in the observation chamber above, overlooking the private training hall. His presence was silent but deliberate. He would not interfere, but he would watch. This was not simply exercise — this was legacy training. Below, Sørensen waited calmly as Ben and Isla entered. Both wore simple training garments — no royal crests, no formal insignia — only the plain attire of students ready to be shaped.

They stood before him without fanfare. Sørensen spoke first, his voice firm but not harsh. "Today begins your first instruction in sovereign discipline. This is not a contest. Not a game. And not a matter of pride. What we begin here is designed for only one purpose: survival."

Ben and Isla nodded together, focused. "You already possess what most sovereign heirs never achieve — mental readiness. But mind without body is incomplete. Sovereign endurance requires that you stand not only at the negotiating table but also, if necessary, in defence of your own person and house." He stepped forward slowly, folding his hands behind his back.

"This is not military training. You will not be soldiers. Your role is far more dangerous than that. You must learn how to survive situations where others may fail — to endure physical stress, to read threats before they form, to control fear when others cannot." Ben whispered, "Situational control."

Sørensen nodded. "Precisely." He gestured toward the open space behind him. "We begin with the fundamentals of balance, movement, and breath. Without them, nothing else will stand. You must first learn how your bodies behave under duress — how to remain calm, even as your muscles fatigue and your breath shortens." Isla asked softly, "And after that?" "Control," Sørensen answered. "Not power. Control. You will not overpower opponents. You will outlast them, outthink them, and outmove them." Ben smiled faintly. "Tactics over strength." "Always," Sørensen replied.

He gestured for them to step forward onto the polished wooden floor. The first day was not to overwhelm them but to begin laying the foundation. "Your posture is your first shield," he instructed. "A sovereign who collapses under pressure gives permission for others to dominate the room. Stand tall — always. Even when you're exhausted." He adjusted Ben's shoulders slightly, straightening his posture. Then Isla's stance — gently correcting her footing for balance.

"Good. Now — breathing." He had them close their eyes and begin controlled breath cycles. In through the nose, out through the mouth — slow, measured, deliberate. "You will learn to command your breathing first," Sørensen continued. "Because when crisis arrives, your breath will be your only friend before your mind catches up."

Minutes passed, but neither child broke focus. Kendrick observed from above, pride swelling quietly within him. He could already see it: not children, but sovereigns in the making. Sørensen gently moved them into their first movement drills — slow, sweeping footwork to train their balance under shifting weight. He watched their stances, adjusting here and there, but allowing them to struggle and correct themselves.

"This will take weeks," he said calmly. "But each step you learn will become instinct. And one day, when you may need it most, that instinct will protect you before thought even arrives." Ben, breathing evenly, spoke softly as he moved, "Not about power. About preservation." "Exactly," Sørensen said. "You are not preparing for show. You are preparing for survival."

Hours passed. The drills continued: balance, breathing, posture, movement — nothing flashy, nothing dramatic. But essential. Foundational. By the time Sørensen finally called an end to the session, both Ben and Isla were sweating lightly but steady. They stood tall, breathing controlled, eyes clear. "You've done well for the first day," Sørensen said. "Tomorrow, we continue."

Ben smiled faintly. "Tomorrow, we improve." Isla added, "One day at a time." As they exited the training hall together, Kendrick descended from the observation gallery. "You have both made me proud," he said quietly. "What you build here will one day protect not only yourselves, but this house."
Ben answered softly, "That's why we're here, Uncle. To protect what matters." "And you will," Kendrick whispered. As they disappeared down the stone hallway, Sørensen remained behind for a moment, quietly watching the empty floor where they had stood. The sovereign house had survived the first storm. Now it was preparing for every storm yet to come.

Two weeks into their private instruction, Ben and Isla had grown more confident in the rhythm of their dual training: balance by morning, resilience drills with Sørensen; diplomacy and sovereign statecraft under Kendrick in the afternoon. Their bodies were strengthening. Their minds were sharpening. But now, their questions were deepening.

This afternoon's session was held in the King's private diplomatic chamber — a circular room adorned with centuries-old maps, intricate royal seals, and carved oaken chairs used only by sovereigns and their personal counsel. Kendrick stood at the head of the chamber as Ben and Isla arrived, seated quietly with their notes in hand, promise rings glinting softly under the chandelier's pale light.

Today's lesson was to focus on negotiation breakdowns — how to recover alliances, manage fragile treaties, and neutralize hostile councils through calculated language. But as Kendrick spoke, Ben's mind travelled beyond the day's curriculum. Finally, Ben lifted his head, interrupting gently but firmly. "Uncle... may I ask something outside the exercise?"

Kendrick's eyes narrowed slightly, intrigued. "Of course." Ben exhaled slowly. His voice was calm, measured — but deadly serious. "We've studied simulations for standard breakdowns. We've role-played hostile debates and diplomatic insults." Isla's voice joined him softly, "But those are recoverable scenarios."

Ben nodded. "What we want to know now... is the worst-case scenario." Kendrick raised an eyebrow. "Worst-case?" "Yes, Uncle," Ben said. "A full sovereign failure. A moment when every safeguard has collapsed — when alliances crumble, rival houses unite, foreign councils move against us, and internal betrayal fractures our court. If everything failed... how would we manage that?"

The room fell heavy. Even Sørensen, standing silently at the far wall, shifted his weight — paying close attention. Kendrick studied them both. The weight of their question was immense, but he did not dismiss it. These were not frightened children; they were heirs asking for truth, not comfort. At last, Kendrick spoke. His voice was steady, but no longer academic.

Now he spoke as a sovereign who had contemplated these possibilities in the silence of long nights. "Very well." He slowly walked around the chamber as he explained. "The worst-case scenario is not simply external war. It is the collapse of internal sovereignty. It begins with division — when royal houses lose unity, when competing claims divide loyalties, when ancient bloodlines turn against each other not in open battle, but through silent legal wars."

He paused, making sure they followed. "In such a collapse, foreign powers move quickly. They do not need armies. They only need to fund the chaos. To divide the remaining houses. To create a succession vacuum so deep that even the sovereign crown becomes paralyzed." Ben whispered, "The throne becomes contested." "Precisely," Kendrick said. "And while the public sees nothing but dignified silence, behind the curtain, the sovereign house burns."

Isla leaned forward slightly. "How would we protect the family?" Kendrick answered without hesitation. "You would disappear." Ben and Isla blinked once, but neither panicked. "Disappear?" Ben asked calmly. "You would be extracted quietly, under sovereign refuge protocols. You would enter what we call dynastic withdrawal — an ancient protocol few outside sovereign circles know exists."

Sørensen spoke now, breaking his silence. "I am one of only seven living officers authorized to execute such extractions." Ben absorbed this carefully. "What happens after extraction?" "You do not emerge until one of two outcomes occurs," Kendrick explained. "Either sovereign unity is restored, and you are summoned back to resume your rightful place… or the sovereign structure collapses permanently, and your only role is to ensure the bloodline survives in secret exile."

Isla's voice softened. "To preserve the line even when the house falls." "Yes," Kendrick said. "And if that moment ever arrives, you must be prepared to sacrifice power for the sake of survival. Sometimes the greatest sovereign act is to protect the bloodline by walking away from the throne entirely." Ben whispered, "The crown isn't the goal. The blood is."

"Exactly," Kendrick nodded. Sørensen added quietly, "And that is why your training blends diplomacy, protection, and survival. Because if you're ever forced to execute dynastic withdrawal, you may have no one left but yourselves." The room went silent for a long moment. Finally, Ben inhaled deeply, his voice firm but calm. "Then we need to be ready for that, too."

Kendrick's voice grew soft now — not weak, but deeply reverent. "That, my children… is why you will succeed where others have failed. Because you are not preparing for the throne. You are preparing for the burden." Isla whispered, "And we will carry it. Together." Ben, smiled faintly, reaching for her hand as always. "Always."

The conversation had grown heavier than the lessons initially intended. But this was where sovereign training lived — not in comfort, but in truth. Ben sat quietly beside Isla, both of them processing every word Kendrick and Sørensen had spoken. Yet there was something still lingering in Ben's mind — a memory that now connected directly to what was being taught.

After a moment, Ben looked up at Sørensen. His voice was calm, curious, but serious. "Sørensen… may I ask you something very direct?" "Always," Sørensen replied without hesitation. Ben sat straighter, hands lightly clasped in front of him. "When we were first brought here to Denmark… that night, when you came for us — was that, in a way, a form of this dynastic withdrawal protocol you're describing?"

Isla nodded softly, adding her voice. "Because you took us in the dark. Quiet. Unseen. No cameras. No media. We vanished. That sounds exactly like what you're teaching us now. Was it the same?" Sørensen allowed himself a brief pause. His eyes narrowed slightly — not in discomfort, but in respect for the depth of their understanding.

"In many ways… yes," he said. Ben and Isla listened intently. "The night I came for you both in Kent," Sørensen continued, "was, in operational terms, what we classify as an emergency extraction. It followed several of the protocols we now discuss — primarily those involving rapid disappearance, controlled transit, disinformation cover, and sovereign secrecy." He paused, choosing his words carefully.

"However, that operation was not full dynastic withdrawal." Ben tilted his head slightly. "Because we still had the sovereign structure behind us." "Correct," Sørensen said. "Your uncle's house was intact. The Kingdom stood. You were being protected, not hidden permanently." Isla whispered, "Whereas full dynastic withdrawal means there is no longer a sovereign house left to support us." Sørensen nodded. "Exactly. Under true dynastic withdrawal, you would not merely vanish for a season — you would vanish indefinitely. There would be no state behind you, no title actively protecting you, no throne anchoring your existence. You would live entirely as private citizens, your blood protected by silence rather than by sovereign law."

Ben's mind remained calm as he processed the gravity of it. "So what you executed that night was a limited withdrawal, built on sovereign discretion, not collapse." "Precisely," Sørensen affirmed. "Your extraction from Kent was preemptive. Your uncle acted to protect you before others could discover you and weaponize your existence. But had the sovereign house itself collapsed — had Kendrick lost his legal authority — I would have taken you into full dynastic withdrawal." Isla's voice was steady. "And we wouldn't have returned."

Sørensen nodded. "Not until a new sovereign structure arose capable of protecting you again." Ben exhaled slowly. "And if one never did?" Sørensen's voice remained calm. "Then your line would survive privately — hidden, protected, waiting for history to correct itself." The weight of that settled deeply into both of them.

Kendrick finally spoke softly now, his voice carrying the personal truth that only a sovereign uncle could express. "That is why we train you for every scenario. Not because I expect the house to fall — but because I will not leave you unprepared should the unthinkable ever occur." Ben smiled faintly, though his eyes carried the full gravity of his understanding. "It's not about fearing collapse."

Isla finished for him. "It's about respecting history enough to never assume it won't happen." Kendrick nodded deeply. "You have learned well." Sørensen added one final quiet thought. "And because you've already experienced the shadows of withdrawal once, you are uniquely prepared to master its lessons should you ever need them again." Ben leaned back slightly, wrapping his fingers gently around Isla's hand. "We hope we never need it, Uncle." Kendrick whispered, "And so do I." The chamber grew silent again, but this time not from fear — from understanding. This was the burden of sovereign blood. To prepare. To endure. And when necessary — to disappear.

The morning sun slanted through the stained-glass windows of Kendrick's private archive chamber. This room was sacred — not open to courtiers, not even to senior staff. It held sovereign secrets dating back centuries, including dynastic withdrawal protocols, succession contracts, and sealed contingency scrolls for every sovereign generation since Denmark's earliest crown.

Today, for the first time, Ben and Isla stood inside its quiet gravity. The ancient shelves were lined with leather-bound volumes, wax-sealed scrolls, and secured cases protected under both royal law and private oaths. Kendrick stood beside them as Sørensen quietly observed from the edge of the chamber.

Kendrick began, speaking gently but firmly. "This is where every sovereign plan lives. In these records are the escape routes, the foreign safeholds, the private accounts that secure the house if disaster ever strikes. You are here now because you are trusted with knowledge that only blood heirs may receive."

Ben and Isla listened quietly, taking in the magnitude of what surrounded them. Kendrick continued explaining certain evacuation routes, coded phrases, and international safeguards — but as he spoke, Ben's mind was already circling the deeper question that had long sat unspoken between them.

Finally, Ben glanced at Isla. She gave a soft nod of encouragement. And then Ben raised his voice gently. "Uncle... may we ask you something now?" Kendrick paused. He recognized the weight in Ben's tone. "Of course." Ben spoke carefully, with great respect but unmistakable seriousness.

"You've brought us under your house. You adopted us fully. You've taught us the sovereign burdens, the threats, the protections. And you've made clear that our place here is real — permanent." He paused, choosing his next words deliberately. "But there's one thing you've never spoken aloud." Isla softly joined him, her voice warm but steady. "You've never told us what we are now. Officially."

Ben finished the thought: "Are we prince and princess under your house? Or something else? We know who we are by blood. But who are we by title — under you?" The room went completely silent. Kendrick lowered his gaze briefly, as if considering words long kept within him.

He approached them slowly, his voice quiet but weighted with profound affection. "My children..." he began. "This question was always coming. And you deserve the truth." He stood directly before them now, no longer speaking as an instructor, but as family — as sovereign guardian.

"You are king and queen by your inherited blood — that truth cannot be altered. The line of Béla flows in you both, as does the weight of the houses before you. But within my house... within Denmark's sovereign line..." He paused, his voice thickening slightly with emotion. "You are my adopted son and daughter — which under sovereign law grants you full rights of lineage succession beneath me." He looked first at Ben.

"You are, formally, Prince Benedict of Denmark." Then to Isla. "And you, my beloved child, are Princess Isla of Denmark." He took both their hands gently into his own. "But titles are nothing beside the truth of who you are to me." Ben's eyes glistened faintly. "And who is that?" Kendrick's voice dropped to a whisper.

"My heirs. My family. My blood. Not by accident. Not by duty. But by choice — by love." Isla's voice wavered slightly, though steady as ever. "You are our family too, Uncle." Kendrick smiled softly. "From the moment you entered my house, you were never anything less." Sørensen stood silently behind them, allowing the sacred moment to unfold. He too had known it all along, but the formal declaration carried weight only Kendrick himself could give.

Ben whispered one final thought, half in jest but fully sincere. "So... does that mean we get new titles printed on our coffee cups?" Kendrick laughed gently — not the laugh of court politics, but of a father who adored them beyond titles. "I suppose we'll have to order new ones," he said.

The tension broke for a moment, but the truth remained. The adoption was no longer only legal — it was sovereign. The titles were sealed. The family, unified. Prince Benedict and Princess Isla of Denmark now stood fully recognised. Not pretenders. Not claimants. Heirs.

The days following Kendrick's declaration passed with quiet intensity. Titles may have been spoken, but now came the greater work: preparing Prince Ben and Princess Isla of Denmark to one day bear them publicly. This would not be announced to the world yet. No press release. No court bulletin. No leaks. For now, it was internal. Inside the royal presentation hall — a chamber rarely used except for state rehearsals and private sovereign briefings — Kendrick waited as Ben and Isla entered together. The tall, arched windows cast angled beams of late morning light across the marble floor, while ancestral portraits looked down in silent witness.

Both children entered calmly, already carrying themselves with increasing confidence. Sørensen stood in his usual position at the edge of the hall, hands behind his back, watching as always. Today, though, even he understood: this was a different stage. The sovereign weight was now being placed upon their shoulders not just in word, but in posture, presence, and bearing. Kendrick motioned for them to stand before him. "Today," he began, "we begin the first lessons in sovereign presence. This is not ceremony. It is not theatre. It is posture, speech, appearance, and command."

He paced slowly in front of them. "Your titles now exist under sovereign law. You are Prince and Princess — heirs within this house. Should circumstances ever require you to step forward in public, you must do so with full command of your presence." Ben spoke calmly. "Presence governs perception." "Exactly," Kendrick said. "Even when your authority is unspoken, your bearing speaks for you." Isla asked softly, "What if the public rejects us? Or questions us?"

Kendrick smiled gently. "Then you give them nothing to tear down. You stand with dignity. You speak only when necessary. You never argue your worth." He raised a single finger, emphasizing the core rule. "A sovereign never explains his right to exist." The words landed heavily. Ben nodded slowly. "Because existence is not argument.

It is fact." Kendrick's eyes gleamed. "Precisely." He stepped back, gesturing now toward two prepared garments laid upon velvet stands. Both were simple — no excessive embroidery, no grand ornaments — but unmistakably sovereign in their design.

"These will be your presentation uniforms. Not for state media. Not for public events. But for your internal training. You must learn how it feels to carry your title physically, to move within the formality of the house." Ben approached his quietly: a deep midnight-blue jacket trimmed in sovereign silver, with a single emblem of Denmark's crowned stag pressed discreetly into the left chest. Isla approached hers: a tailored royal dress in soft pearl, with a matching silver sash crossing diagonally over her shoulder. Her family crest, subtly embroidered into the fabric, shimmered only faintly under the light.

Isla whispered as she touched the fabric, "Simple. But undeniable." Kendrick nodded. "That is precisely the design. Sovereign strength does not shout. It whispers, and the world listens." Ben quietly changed into his garment first, stepping into place once fitted. The difference was immediate. Not in vanity, but in weight. The jacket straightened his posture, called his shoulders back, forced every step into a measured calm. Isla followed, her movements graceful but purposeful. As the sash draped across her chest, she stood taller — not out of pride, but out of respect for what it represented.

Kendrick observed carefully. "You feel it now, don't you?" Ben whispered, "It makes you move differently." Isla added, "It makes you aware." "Good," Kendrick said. "That awareness will one day be your shield." He circled them both now, inspecting not with critical eye, but with pride. "You will practice every motion," he continued. "Your walk. Your greeting. Your stance when entering rooms. You will rehearse posture under pressure, eye contact during diplomatic conversations, and silence when provoked."

Ben smiled faintly. "So the crown sits long before it's placed." Kendrick allowed himself a quiet smile. "Exactly." Sørensen finally spoke from his post. "Presence is a weapon more effective than any army, young sovereigns. Those who carry it correctly never need to raise their voices."

The lesson continued for hours: walking the royal corridors, practicing entrances, standing before imaginary diplomats, learning how to endure prolonged standing without collapse, and how to control the breath even under tension. It was not simply pageantry. It was sovereign conditioning. As the session drew to a close, Kendrick stepped forward one last time. "You are no longer only students of history.

You are now being written into it." Ben whispered softly, "And we are ready to bear it." Isla's eyes glistened slightly, but her voice held firm. "Together." And together they stood — Prince Benedict, Princess Isla — no longer merely heirs in name, but heirs in posture, presence, and sovereign truth.

The royal training chamber had grown quieter with each passing day. Lessons now reached far deeper than ceremonial postures or official protocols. Today was different. Today, Kendrick would expose his heirs to what few outside the sovereign bloodline would ever be permitted to hear. Ben and Isla stood before him, no longer wearing their training garments, but dressed simply — as family, not yet as public heirs. Sørensen remained nearby, present as always, but more silent than usual. Even he understood: these were the most sensitive lessons of all.

Kendrick stood behind the great oak map table — one that had served sovereign kings and queens for centuries. Its surface displayed a detailed map of Europe, but not as the public would recognize it. This version was marked with small brass pins, coloured cords, and sigils—symbols that represented alliances never declared openly. Kendrick rested his hands gently on the edges of the table. "Today," he began softly, "you will learn the truth that stands behind every treaty, every handshake, and every royal photograph." Ben and Isla leaned forward, their minds sharpened by weeks of preparation.

Kendrick gestured to the map. "Sovereign power is not determined by the signatures that appear in public treaties. It is built long before that — in private conversations, quiet favours, whispered debts, and unspoken loyalties." He pointed to a cluster of pins between Scandinavia and Central Europe. "These represent houses whose public alliances are neutral. But beneath that neutrality, sovereign agreements exist — favours exchanged, family marriages arranged, financial support extended quietly." Isla spoke softly, "None of it recorded publicly." "Precisely," Kendrick said. "Because public record invites challenge. But unspoken alliances give flexibility. They allow sovereign houses to protect one another when laws fail to offer protection."

Ben examined the network of coloured cords crisscrossing the map like strands of a spider's web. "And if one thread breaks?" Kendrick nodded slowly. "The entire web shifts. And often, entire houses rise or fall not because of war, but because of one broken private alliance." Sørensen finally spoke, his voice low. "The most dangerous sovereign conflicts rarely involve armies. They involve secrets. Who controls them. Who protects them. And who knows when to reveal them." Kendrick gestured now toward several pins marked with royal insignias.

"These families," he said, "have sustained their survival for centuries not by military might, but by private loyalties. Favour for favour. Rescue for silence. Marriage for influence." He paused, then looked directly at Ben and Isla. "This is the world you are entering." Isla's voice came steady. "And our adoption places us inside this web?" "Yes," Kendrick confirmed. "Your legal adoption into my house secured your positions not only within Denmark, but within this entire structure. There are sovereign houses that now view you as allies — blood-connected — whose interests are now tied to your protection."

Ben whispered thoughtfully, "Even though they don't announce it." "Exactly," Kendrick said. "Because to announce it would invite enemies to disrupt it. The strongest alliances are those no one can publicly attack because they officially do not exist." Sørensen added, "And those alliances are maintained not by law, but by trust — and by knowledge." Ben exhaled slowly. "So sovereign diplomacy isn't just negotiation. It's management of invisible threads." Kendrick smiled faintly, proud of his heir's growing understanding. "You see it clearly." Isla asked softly, "And if these threads are ever exposed?"

Kendrick's voice darkened slightly. "Then sovereign houses collapse. Families are ruined. Kingdoms lose their protection. This is why absolute discretion is non-negotiable." He gestured again to the table. "Your existence now adds two new threads into this web. Some houses will see opportunity in you. Others will fear your place. And some will attempt to pull your threads apart." Ben stood still, his voice strong. "That's why you're teaching us now. Before anyone attempts it." "Yes," Kendrick answered simply. The weight of the moment settled over them all. Isla spoke again, more quietly now. "So if the worst ever happens... the sovereign web may decide whether we survive or fall."

Kendrick nodded deeply. "Which is why you must know every house, every history, every alliance — even those never spoken aloud. The public crown protects only those who understand the private kingdom beneath it." Sørensen added softly, "And because you now understand this world, you are no longer simply heirs. You are sovereign architects in training." Ben whispered, "Architects of preservation." "Precisely," Kendrick said. "And one day, you will know this web as I do — not by fear, but by mastery." They stood in silent understanding, gazing at the ancient map — seeing, for the first time, the true shape of sovereign power. Not armies. Not parliaments. Not public applause. The web.

The chamber had been altered for this lesson. The heavy oak table remained, but the maps were now replaced with multiple leather folders, each sealed in red sovereign wax. Alongside them sat legal parchments, fabricated intelligence reports, mock news releases, and a sealed royal decree — all prepared by Kendrick and Sørensen over several days for this very exercise.

Ben and Isla entered as they always did: composed, steady, eyes already reading the room before a word had been spoken. Their sovereign senses were growing sharper by the week. Sørensen stood at his usual post, but even his stance carried a heightened seriousness today.

Kendrick stood behind the table, his hands resting upon the topmost file. "Today," he said softly, "we begin your first sovereign crisis simulation." Neither Ben nor Isla flinched. They had expected this. But both felt the shift — the weight of this next threshold. Kendrick continued, "This is not a game, though it is a controlled exercise. What you say today, how you react, will teach me where you are strongest — and where we must sharpen you further." Ben gave a slight nod. "We're ready." Isla whispered beside him, "Let it begin." Kendrick lifted the first folder, breaking the wax seal. "Here is your scenario." He began reading, his voice slow, steady:

Sovereign Simulation Crisis: The Hidden Engagement

A private intelligence dispatch arrives late at night. One of Denmark's most critical private alliances — the House of Falkenheim, with whom Denmark holds several secret financial and legal mutual defence treaties — is on the verge of collapse. Unbeknownst to the public, their heir has become engaged to a foreign royal house deeply hostile to Denmark's long-standing interests.

If the marriage proceeds, the hostile house will gain indirect influence over several shared financial entities that underpin the sovereign reserve structure. While this would not trigger open conflict, it would quietly compromise Denmark's financial sovereignty.

The engagement has not yet been announced publicly. You have 48 hours before the engagement becomes official and irreversible under dynastic treaty law.

Several options exist — each carries public, diplomatic, and private consequences.

Kendrick lowered the file and looked at them. "You now sit in the sovereign seat. What is your first move?" Ben and Isla exchanged one quick glance. They didn't panic. They engaged. Ben spoke first, his voice steady. "We request a full intelligence briefing immediately. We must know whether the engagement is one of genuine affection… or arranged leverage." Isla added, "Motive dictates response." Kendrick smiled faintly. "Good. You recognize that the marriage itself is not the threat — it's the intent behind it." Ben continued, "If the foreign house orchestrated this engagement to infiltrate our reserve structures, it represents premeditated encroachment." Isla nodded, "And if so, we must act before it reaches treaty law status." Kendrick placed the next file on the table. "Very well. The intelligence briefing arrives." He opened the folder.

Intelligence Summary: The engagement was initiated through private diplomatic channels. Financial leverage is suspected. The foreign house offered to quietly resolve several of Falkenheim's private debts in exchange for future access to specific sovereign reserve voting rights after marriage. The heir is unaware of the full financial arrangement behind the proposal. Ben narrowed his eyes. "They're using debt as the bait." Isla whispered, "And the heir is being used as the delivery mechanism." Kendrick asked calmly, "What now?" Ben exhaled. "We need to sever the leverage point — the debt. Quietly. If we eliminate the foreign house's financial hold, the engagement loses its purpose."

Isla followed, "We dispatch a private sovereign envoy to Falkenheim. Sovereign house to sovereign house. No intermediaries. No public ministries." Ben added, "We present sovereign settlement of Falkenheim's debts as an offer of internal house protection — sovereign solidarity, not public charity." Kendrick nodded. "And if Falkenheim refuses?" Ben didn't hesitate. "We escalate private pressure. We engage allies bound to us by the quiet web you've shown us. We create alternative risks for Falkenheim should they refuse our sovereign protection." Isla added, "We remind them that sovereign houses rise together or fall divided. Quietly, but firmly."

Sørensen's voice entered now from the side. "And if the foreign house becomes aware of your interference?" Ben answered, "They will. But we control the timeline. Once Falkenheim accepts sovereign settlement, the foreign house loses leverage. They cannot escalate without exposing their original manipulation, which they won't risk publicly." Kendrick finally smiled — deeply, this time. "Excellent." He slowly closed the file. "You've just demonstrated the core of sovereign diplomacy. You recognized that power moves beneath the surface first. You protected your allies without public scandal. You defended the realm without firing a shot."

Isla whispered, "And preserved the web." "Exactly." Kendrick stepped closer, placing a hand gently on each of their shoulders. "You are learning faster than I hoped. But be warned — not all scenarios will allow this level of control. There will be times when you will be forced to choose between risks you cannot fully avoid." Ben whispered, "That's why we train." Isla smiled softly, "To stand when the world shakes." Kendrick's voice lowered to a whisper. "And when it does, you will not tremble." The simulation ended. But the lesson lived. The sovereigns were no longer students. They were in training for the storm.

The chamber was dimmer than usual this morning. Kendrick had ordered the curtains drawn, allowing only slivers of light to cross the marble floor. The atmosphere itself was intentional: the weight of the lesson required stillness, calm, and undivided attention. Ben and Isla stood before the great oak table once again, their breathing steady, their eyes sharp. Sørensen, silent and ever-present, stood watch near the far corner. Kendrick did not open any file this time. There were no mock reports, no sealed decrees waiting to be studied. Only his voice would speak now. He began slowly, each word carrying deliberate weight. "You have both done remarkably well. You've studied the web of alliances. You've learned how to engage. You've learned when to act." He paused. "Now you must learn when not to act."

Ben's eyes narrowed slightly. "The doctrine of restraint." Kendrick smiled faintly. "Yes. But far more than simple restraint. This lesson is known within sovereign houses as The Doctrine of Sovereign Silence." He stepped away from the table, slowly pacing the chamber's centre as he spoke. "In the public eye, sovereigns are often expected to lead with declarations. Statements. Orders. Action. The world sees activity as strength." Isla listened carefully, her head tilting slightly. "But true sovereign power often rests," Kendrick continued, "in precisely the opposite — in silence." He faced them fully now.

"There will be times when provocations will be launched. Rumours will spread. Rival houses will attempt to bait you into conflict — into declarations they hope will expose you, force you into disadvantage, or weaken your alliances." Ben spoke softly, "They try to make us move first." "Exactly," Kendrick said. "Because the first to speak often becomes the first to bleed." He allowed the thought to settle before continuing. "The Doctrine of Sovereign Silence requires two things: unshakable patience, and absolute confidence in your position. You say nothing when provoked. You offer no defence to accusations that do not deserve response. You let your enemies exhaust themselves in speculation while you remain untouchable behind silence."

Isla whispered, "But silence can be misinterpreted as guilt." Kendrick nodded. "Only if you do not control the perception beforehand. That is why your sovereign presence matters so greatly." He gestured toward them both. "When your bearing is unshaken — when your posture conveys unbending confidence — your silence becomes unnerving. It forces your adversaries to question their own positions. They fear what you may know. They fear your unreadable calm."

Sørensen spoke now, his voice low and steady. "And the longer your silence holds, the more their alliances begin to fracture. The ones who challenged you start to turn on one another, suspecting betrayal where none exists." Ben nodded slowly, the understanding fully forming in his mind. "The silence becomes a mirror. It reflects their weaknesses back at them." "Precisely," Kendrick said. He moved back toward the table now, placing both hands firmly upon it. "There will come a time — perhaps many times — when you will be pressured to respond. Reporters will demand comment. Councils will whisper doubts. Rival families will bait you. And your advisors may plead with you to clarify your position." Kendrick's voice hardened now.

"You will answer none of them." The silence that followed his words was itself part of the lesson. Ben whispered after a long pause, "Silence becomes the message." Isla added, "And the longer it holds, the stronger it grows." Kendrick nodded. "You both see it well. Remember this above all: the sovereign who governs his silence governs his enemies." Sørensen added one final thought, his voice nearly a whisper. "And when you finally do choose to speak, after long silence, your words carry the full weight of a thousand unspoken declarations." Ben and Isla stood together, absorbing the depth of the doctrine.

They now understood that true sovereignty was not loud. It was still. It was watchful. It was terrifying in its patience. Kendrick stepped forward one last time, his voice quiet but absolute. "You will carry this doctrine forward. One day, when others attempt to shake you, you will hold your silence. And you will watch as their voices destroy themselves." Ben whispered, "We will not tremble." Isla echoed him softly, "We will endure." Kendrick smiled. "Then you are truly becoming sovereign." The lesson closed. But its echo would remain forever.

The chamber Kendrick chose for this lesson was one neither Ben nor Isla had ever seen before. It lay beneath the deepest part of the castle, through corridors even most staff never accessed. As they walked behind Kendrick and Sørensen, both children sensed the shift in atmosphere. The polished stone gave way to older walls — rough, ancient, bearing the silent witness of generations long forgotten by the world above. Finally, they reached a tall iron door. Two sovereign guards stood watch. Kendrick spoke softly, "Open."

The guards obeyed immediately, and the great door creaked open. Inside stood what could only be called the archive of sovereign failure. Hundreds of sealed files, aged scrolls, and carefully bound volumes rested upon black walnut shelves. At the centre of the room sat a single long table — simple, but heavy, as though it too carried the weight of what these records held. Sørensen spoke softly now. "This chamber is known as The Hall of the Silent Thrones."

Ben whispered, "The ones who lost everything." "Exactly," Kendrick said. "And today, you will learn from them." They approached the table where Kendrick had already placed three files. Each was bound in black leather, each sealed not with red wax, but with black sovereign wax — the mark reserved for the darkest of royal failures. "These are real," Kendrick said softly. "Not simulations. True accounts. And you will see in these where sovereign houses faltered — not through war, but through blindness."

He broke the first seal. File One: The House of Valdenmark — Collapse by Vanity

The House of Valdenmark stood for nearly 400 years, its crown respected across northern courts. But in its fourth century, King Edric IV abandoned the quiet disciplines that had preserved his dynasty. He sought public glory, public adoration — engaging directly in foreign debates, answering every public criticism, defending his honour at every insult.

What began as public confidence soon became public arrogance. The more Edric spoke, the more rivals baited him. Each response drew him further into traps of contradiction. Internal houses lost faith. His constant need to defend every rumour fractured private alliances.

Within twenty years, his house collapsed without a single war being fought.

Kendrick looked directly at Ben and Isla. "You see now why silence is so essential." Ben whispered, "He surrendered his silence. And they dismantled him with his own words." "Precisely." Kendrick opened the second file.

File Two: The Sovereign Line of Astrelia — Collapse by Inaction

The sovereigns of Astrelia faced an external threat from a rising rival house seeking to absorb their commercial alliances. But rather than act decisively, the sovereign council debated endlessly. They feared the optics of any aggressive defensive moves. In waiting too long, they allowed their rivals to embed agents within their own financial institutions

By the time Astrelia attempted to intervene, the rival house had already secured controlling interests. Their dynasty was absorbed, their sovereign name erased, and their former ruling family now exists only as private citizens in foreign lands.

Isla whispered, "They acted too late." "Yes," Kendrick said. "Caution is not always wisdom. Delay can be fatal." Sørensen added quietly, "The art is knowing when silence preserves — and when silence kills." Kendrick opened the final file. This one he handled more solemnly.

File Three: The House of Ormont — Collapse by Internal Betrayal

The House of Ormont ruled securely for generations until division arose within its private council. Secret rivalries grew. One faction — hungry for greater control — leaked internal documents to foreign councils, exposing weaknesses.

The betrayal spread like rot. What began as whispers turned into public scandal. Allies distanced themselves. Legal suits followed. Foreign councils leveraged the fractures to impose crippling trade sanctions. Within five years, the sovereign house was dismantled entirely.

Ben's jaw tightened slightly. "The moles." "Yes," Kendrick said. "Exactly as we faced here. But we acted swiftly. Ormont did not." Isla asked softly, "Did they not see it coming?"

"They saw it," Sørensen answered grimly. "But they underestimated how quickly internal rot destroys a sovereign foundation. Kendrick closed the files slowly, as if sealing the coffins of fallen crowns. "These are the warnings. You will carry their failures with you — not as shame, but as armour." Ben whispered, "Because we must never repeat them." "Never," Kendrick said firmly. "The weight you carry is not simply to protect yourselves. It is to preserve the sovereign bloodline — even against the slow poisons that destroyed these houses."

Sørensen's voice lowered one final time. "And one day, when others seek to bait you — or lull you into comfort — you will remember these black files, and you will remain vigilant." Isla whispered softly, "We will watch the web. Always." Ben added, "And we will act when the time demands." Kendrick looked at them both, his voice full of solemn pride. "Then you are becoming sovereign not by name — but by wisdom." The archive door closed behind them as they left.

The Hall of Silent Thrones would remain sealed, but its lessons now lived within the next generation. The House of Rosenshavn stood. Because its heirs were learning what their ancestors forgot. The afternoon sun had already begun to lower as Kendrick summoned Ben and Isla to the private diplomatic wing — a suite of rooms rarely used even for internal matters. These were not state rooms. These were sovereign rooms — discreet, silent, and protected from the outside world entirely.

Ben and Isla arrived, calm but fully alert. They had learned by now that when Kendrick called them to a place like this, a lesson of weight was always waiting. Sørensen stood waiting at the entry, his expression as unreadable as ever, but even his stillness carried a different tension today. Kendrick greeted them personally at the inner chamber. "Today," he began, "you will meet sovereign envoys — not of Denmark, but of the councils that exist beyond public eyes." He led them into the chamber. Inside stood two individuals. One was a tall man in his sixties, with sharp eyes that missed nothing, dressed in perfectly tailored dark grey, absent of insignias — intentionally neutral.

Beside him stood a woman perhaps in her early fifties, her poise graceful, her expression warm but guarded. She too bore no formal symbols. Kendrick motioned toward them. "These are Council Envoy Markus Halverson and Envoy Lisette Vernau. They represent two external sovereign alliances that have long operated as stabilizers between European royal houses." The envoys bowed respectfully — but not deeply. This was not ceremony. This was recognition of equals in blood. Ben and Isla offered modest bows in return, standing tall.

Markus spoke first, his voice smooth and deliberate. "We have followed your training with great interest." Lisette followed softly, "Few heirs are permitted access to what you have already learned." Ben spoke calmly, without bravado. "We're here to listen. And to understand." Kendrick nodded with approval and stepped back, allowing the envoys to begin. Markus continued, "The councils we represent are not governments. We do not dictate law. We exist to maintain the balance between sovereign houses, to prevent quiet wars from becoming public disasters."

Lisette added, "When one house rises too aggressively, or threatens the stability of others, we intervene through quiet channels. Financially. Politically. Sometimes socially." Ben studied them carefully. "And when houses collapse?" "Then we record their fall, and manage the vacuum to ensure no single faction gains unchecked dominance," Markus answered. Isla's voice was steady, "You prevent sovereign collapse from spreading beyond control." Lisette smiled faintly. "You see it very clearly." Markus stepped closer. "Your recent adoption into His Majesty's house has altered certain balances. Some houses now strengthen. Others… grow uneasy." Ben asked directly, "Are we seen as a threat?"

Markus offered a careful smile. "You are seen as a variable. That is why we observe. We ensure no sovereign shift destabilizes the broader order." Isla asked carefully, "And if we remain stable?" Lisette answered softly, "Then the councils remain allies to your house — unseen, but supportive." Kendrick spoke now, his tone firm but measured. "You see, my children, not every threat comes from rivals seeking your fall. Some come from those seeking too aggressively to control your ascent." Sørensen added, "The councils ensure no one rises too quickly, nor falls too violently." Ben whispered, "You control the wind beneath sovereign wings." Markus's eyes gleamed faintly. "Or calm it, when necessary."

Lisette's voice softened. "You two now join a very rare circle. From this moment forward, your names will be marked within council records as protected sovereign heirs. Your survival is in everyone's interest — so long as you remain steady." The message was both reassuring and chilling. Ben answered calmly, "We intend to remain steady. And prepared." Isla added, "And loyal to the blood we serve." The envoys nodded with quiet approval. Kendrick closed the meeting with one final thought. "This is not a relationship of contracts, but of understandings. Today was not negotiation. Today was recognition." Markus bowed his head once more. "We welcome you to the circle, Prince Ben. Princess Isla."

Lisette followed, her voice gentle but final. "And we pray you never require our hand. But if you do — we will answer." With that, the envoys withdrew, vanishing back into the corridors that most will never see. Ben and Isla stood for a moment in silence, the full gravity settling into their sovereign marrow. Kendrick whispered softly, "You have now seen the invisible keepers. You know how delicate the sovereign world truly is." Ben whispered back, "And how easily the balance can shift." Isla finished, "That's why we prepare." Sørensen smiled faintly, his voice low. "And that is why you will endure."

The moment had arrived. Not for public spectacle, not for global announcement — but for quiet recognition among those who mattered most: the inner sovereign circle.

Kendrick led Ben and Isla through the private eastern hall, the air heavy with unspoken weight. This was not a simulation. This was not practice. This was their first entrance into the chamber where sovereign bloodlines quietly acknowledged one another — where true power whispered its approval.

They wore their presentation attire, previously prepared but never yet used in official form. For Ben: midnight blue trimmed in sovereign silver. For Isla: pearl with the understated silver sash, her family crest woven delicately into the fabric. No excess. No show. Only quiet authority.

Sørensen walked behind them, silent and watchful, as always. Ahead, two great mahogany doors opened slowly under the hands of sovereign guards. Beyond them waited a room unlike any they had seen before — neither court nor council chamber, but something older, something sacred. The Assembly Room. Inside stood representatives of seven sovereign houses, each chosen by their bloodlines to serve as internal witnesses to sovereign transitions and recognitions.

No press.
No cameras.
No spectators.

Only the sovereigns and their blood.

Kendrick motioned for Ben and Isla to pause just inside the threshold. He stepped forward first, speaking clearly into the chamber. "Honoured sovereign representatives. I present before you the newly appointed heirs under sovereign adoption and blood recognition: Prince Ben of Denmark. Princess Isla of Denmark." There was no applause. This chamber did not engage in pageantry. Instead, each representative offered a single, deliberate nod — the silent acknowledgement that carried more weight than any public ceremony.

Ben and Isla stepped forward together, perfectly synchronized, every motion disciplined by weeks of posture, breath, and balance training. They reached the centre of the marble inlay — an ancient crest representing the unbroken chain of sovereign legacy. Kendrick addressed the assembly once more. "These heirs stand recognized not only by the House of Rosenshavn but by the sovereign balance itself. Their presence strengthens our order. Their training prepares them to defend it. May their wisdom preserve what so many before them forgot."

The eldest representative stepped forward now — Lord Etienne of the House of Albrecht, a sovereign house whose bloodlines reached back over six centuries. He studied Ben and Isla with the careful eye of one who had watched sovereign heirs rise and fall for generations. "You have been brought forward," Lord Etienne said, his voice calm and heavy, "not for ambition, but for duty. You will not be worshipped. You will be watched."

Ben met his eyes steadily. "We understand." Isla added softly, "And we accept the burden." Etienne nodded once. "Then you may remain." Kendrick offered a quiet nod of gratitude toward the assembly. No further words were needed. The recognition was sealed. The assembly was dismissed. Quietly, the representatives departed one by one, vanishing back into the corridors of private sovereign governance, taking with them the knowledge that new heirs now stood in place — heirs who had proven worthy not through public display, but through readiness.

As the doors finally closed behind the last envoy, Kendrick turned to Ben and Isla. "You have now crossed the final threshold of sovereign recognition," he said quietly. "What remains ahead will no longer be theoretical. You are now part of the balance. The eyes that watched you today will watch you for years to come." Ben spoke softly. "We will not give them cause to regret it." Isla whispered, "We will stand, Uncle." Kendrick smiled with quiet pride, his voice soft and reverent. "And so the House of Rosenshavn breathes forward." Sørensen, standing slightly behind, allowed himself a rare moment of reflection, watching the two young sovereigns. The storms had not yet come. But when they did — these heirs would be ready.

CHAPTER 13: A STORM IS BREWING

The castle walls seemed quieter that morning, though Ben and Isla both knew better than to believe it was peace. Quiet was rarely peace. It was usually preparation. The kind of stillness that settles before weather turns. And this morning, even the usual sounds of the estate—the birds, the distant clip of guards' boots, the soft creaks of old stone—carried a strange weight to them. The air itself was heavier, as if bracing.

Their private chamber remained their sanctuary, tucked within the southern wing of the royal residence where most dared not intrude. There, their routine carried forward with the same devotion as always. Isla, still in her soft nightgown, sat cross-legged at the small table where their breakfast was laid. The rich aroma of fresh coffee mingled with the light scent of lavender that always drifted through the room after morning mist. Beside her, Ben adjusted his robe, settling opposite her with his familiar quiet smile. Their eyes met, and as always, without speaking, they leaned forward across the small distance and exchanged their ritual morning kiss—soft, steady, and warm, their promise renewed with the simplicity of touch.

Their hands remained entwined as they both sipped from their small cups, the bitterness of the coffee softened by a touch of cream Isla always insisted upon. This was theirs. This was sacred. Regardless of what waited outside the thick stone walls. "Bladder Chatter," Isla whispered, her eyes glinting with mischief. Ben grinned, setting his cup aside. "As tradition demands."

Both rose, their small feet padding across the cool polished stone to the adjoining washroom, where their laughter echoed softly, blending with the splashes of water and quiet giggles as they exchanged their usual morning banter. These little pieces of life remained untouched by sovereign affairs, and they guarded them fiercely.

When they returned, dressed now in their simple day garments, the knock at the chamber door was precise—three short taps, followed by the soft creak as the door eased open. Sørensen entered as he always did—calm, composed, yet alert. His frame carried the quiet tension of a man who lived permanently in a state of readiness. His movements were precise, the product of decades of training, his posture unwavering. More than a protector, more than a soldier— Sørensen was the blade behind the sovereign shield. The one Kendrick trusted without question. And by extension, the one entrusted with Ben and Isla's growing safety.

"Good morning," Sørensen said, bowing his head respectfully. He never called them 'children,' though they were only ten. To him, they were what their station demanded—Prince and Princess. "Good morning, Sørensen," Isla greeted, offering her small but composed smile. Ben mirrored her. "Is Uncle Kendrick ready?"

Sørensen's sharp blue eyes flicked momentarily toward the window before answering. "He is waiting for you both in the inner chamber. There is much to discuss this morning." He paused, allowing the silence to rest just long enough for them to understand the gravity behind his words.

"It would be best not to delay." The children exchanged a glance, fingers instinctively intertwining once more. They didn't need words between them. When one of them felt the pulse of change, so did the other. And today, they both felt it—something was shifting. The storm Kendrick had warned them about in passing now seemed to have found its winds.

They followed Sørensen through the winding inner corridors of the sovereign residence, their small feet echoing softly on the ancient stones. The path led them not toward the grand halls used for state meetings or ceremonial receptions, but into the inner sanctuary of Kendrick's private war room—a place few outside his closest circle ever entered. The heavy oak doors parted smoothly as they approached, and inside, King Kendrick stood by the large window overlooking the southern gardens, his hands folded calmly behind his back. He turned at once as they entered, his face warm but serious, the way only Kendrick could manage—a balance of paternal affection and sovereign authority.

"Good morning, my little storm-watchers," Kendrick greeted softly. Ben and Isla stepped forward, bowing their heads as they had been taught, but with a comfort that bespoke their private bond with the king who had taken them into his house. "Good morning, Uncle Kendrick," they answered in unison. Kendrick gestured for them to sit at the small round table near the centre of the chamber. Maps, documents, and several sealed communiqués lay carefully arranged upon its polished surface. Once they were seated, Sørensen took his position a few steps behind Kendrick, silent but vigilant.

Kendrick's gaze swept over both children for a moment longer before he spoke. "Today, we speak plainly, as we have always agreed," he began, his voice smooth but weighted. "No hedging, no soothing words. You are both capable of truth. And the truth is what I shall give you." Ben sat upright, his hands resting calmly on his knees, while Isla's fingers pressed gently along the edge of the table, steadying herself.

"The storm that we have long sensed is no longer gathering at a distance," Kendrick continued. "It is now shifting closer. Intelligence sources—both those loyal and those foreign—have begun making their moves. Several agencies, including certain Swiss networks you've heard us mention before, are once again probing into matters of your origin." Ben's jaw tightened slightly. "Because of our adoption?" "In part," Kendrick nodded. "But it goes deeper. The bloodlines you carry—yours, Isla's—remain a source of fascination to those who would seek to manipulate sovereign lineage for political advantage. And there are factions who believe that forcing certain truths into the public sphere might fracture alliances before they have properly formed."

Isla leaned forward. "They want to expose us?" "They want to expose what they think you represent," Kendrick corrected gently. "Their error, however, is assuming they know the fullness of your story. They know only fragments, pieces scattered from old archives, whispered names, partial genealogies. Enough to create dangerous speculation, but not enough to land a decisive blow." Sørensen spoke then, his voice cool as steel. "Their greatest weapon is disinformation. Not facts. They spread shadows. Hints. And then wait for the world to fill in the blanks."

Kendrick nodded toward his trusted man. "Precisely. And it is that game of shadows that we now prepare you to face." Ben's eyes narrowed with focus, his voice steady. "Do they know about Mum? About Dad?" Kendrick shook his head once. "Not directly. Jeff and Annemarie remain well-protected under our sovereign veils. Robert and Claire likewise. But whispers exist—there are foreign channels who suspect connections. Swiss agents have attempted to reconstruct your family tree using indirect means. Flights, sightings, old school records from Kent."

Isla spoke then, her voice softer but resolute. "And our DNA?" A brief pause, but Kendrick never flinched. "They do not have your full DNA profiles. They have no legal or scientific basis to obtain them. But some factions have attempted backdoor genetic reconstructions using distant third-party samples. None of these are fully accurate. Their data remains flawed, but their desperation to fill gaps makes them reckless." Ben's fingers curled slightly, his breath steady. "What do we do?"

Kendrick smiled faintly, proud. "We continue exactly as we have trained. You stand calm within the storm. They seek to make you afraid, to force mistakes. But you are not children lost in someone else's game. You are sovereign heirs, positioned carefully under the House of Rosenshavn, shielded not only by legal structures but by the bonds we have built together." Isla's voice lowered, but carried the weight of understanding. "We stay silent."

"The Doctrine of Sovereign Silence remains your greatest strength," Kendrick affirmed. "When you are questioned publicly, you give them nothing they can twist. You hold your ground. And privately, we prepare you for the day you may one day face these matters openly, but only when you are ready." Sørensen stepped forward now, laying a folded dossier on the table before them. "These," he said softly, "are profiles of the individuals who have surfaced in recent days. You will study them. Not to fear them, but to understand how such men operate."

Ben opened the dossier carefully, his sharp young eyes scanning faces and names—some foreign, some familiar from prior briefings. Isla leaned in, absorbing every detail as though each line of text was a thread she was weaving into their defence. As they read, Kendrick allowed them the space. No sugar-coating. No half-truths. Only the steady presence of trust between them. That, more than any army, was their fortress.

When they had finished the first pages, Kendrick reached across the table, his voice quieter but no less resolute. "You both are stronger than they realize. Stronger than most adults. And I will not hide these realities from you. For you are not like other ten-year-olds. You never have been." Ben and Isla both nodded, their hands once more finding each other beneath the table. Their bond, forged long before Denmark ever knew their names, remained their compass. And far beyond the castle, in distant boardrooms, encrypted networks, and shadowed meetings, the storm gathered. But within these walls, they stood ready.

The storm outside had grown thicker as the morning unfolded. The winds whistled faintly against the stone windows of the inner chamber where Kendrick, Ben, Isla, and Sørensen now sat in quiet council. The air inside remained steady, warm, but the world beyond these walls had begun to stir. What had once been whispers from foreign circles had now grown into deliberate attempts to breach the shields that protected Ben and Isla's identities.

Yet, within the sanctuary of these stone walls, none of them flinched. They gathered not in fear, but in preparation.

Kendrick stood by the long map table, fingers resting lightly on the edge as he reviewed the sealed intelligence reports that Sørensen had placed before him earlier. Isla sat close beside Ben, both of them watching the adults with an attentiveness far beyond their years. This was no ordinary meeting. This was family. Ben's hands were folded before him, steady. His eyes moved with calm precision from Kendrick to Sørensen, and then finally to Isla. She gave him a small, knowing nod—the kind they often exchanged before one of Ben's ideas surfaced. And this morning, he was ready.
Ben drew a slow breath, and as always, Kendrick's attention shifted immediately, reading his posture. Kendrick knew his adopted son well enough to recognize when something deeper was stirring. "Speak, my son," Kendrick invited softly, his voice firm but warm. "You've been thinking."

Ben's voice remained level, though a quiet current of energy hummed beneath his words. "Uncle Kendrick, do you remember... when a designer deployed a false DNA record system? The disinformation shield? The program that generated alternate family trees, falsified haplogroups, ghost ancestries, and more?" He paused briefly, ensuring he had the full attention of both Kendrick and Sørensen. "The one I designed."

A faint smile crept across Kendrick's lips, but it was not patronizing. It was pride. "Of course I remember," Kendrick answered, voice even. "It was brilliant then. And it remains one of the primary reasons these foreign agencies still stumble when they attempt to build your lineage." Sørensen's head tilted slightly, his eyes narrowing as he, too, leaned forward, recognizing that Ben was about to extend the chessboard.

Ben continued, his confidence growing with each word. "I've been thinking about the next step. About closing any remaining gaps. I believe I can block them even further. But this time... by going after my real DNA profile." Kendrick's brow lifted, intrigued. "Explain." Ben sat upright now, his voice steady and methodical. "I know where my original samples are stored. The unaltered profiles—the pure data—from the earliest tests before my records entered sovereign protection. During one of the private tours through Denmark's archives, you allowed Sørensen to show me how the secured vaults operate. I paid attention. I memorized locations, security patterns, and redundancies."

Sørensen glanced briefly toward Kendrick, his eyes narrowing in impressed recognition. "You retained all that detail?" Ben nodded. "I did." "And your plan?" Kendrick asked, gesturing for him to continue. Ben inhaled deeply. "I can't access the vault directly myself.

That would raise questions, trigger logs. But I know how to make the data inaccessible to outside parties without raising internal flags. I have a secure channel—an independent route that can bypass public traces. One of Dad's trusted friends—someone in the genetic data field who owes Dad more than one favour—can be reached through sovereign-grade private lines. No network leaks. No digital breadcrumbs."

Kendrick's eyes narrowed, studying him. "You're proposing to retrieve your original DNA profile... and then destroy it?" "Exactly," Ben replied. "Shred it. Not just deletion, but data-level eradication. I can have it permanently removed from any vulnerable system before outside factions can ever trace it. I can eliminate every last fragment of authentic data that could be used against us." Sørensen folded his arms, eyes sharp. "You're talking about tampering with state-protected archives. This isn't a children's prank, Your Highness."

Ben met Sørensen's gaze without hesitation. "I understand the weight of what I'm saying. But these records are a liability, even within friendly walls. Once they exist, anyone with enough reach—and enough ambition—can eventually find cracks. The safest data... is no data." The room stilled for a long breath. Even Isla leaned forward now, her hand resting gently on Ben's arm, lending him silent support. Her eyes reflected her complete trust in him. He was not speaking out of recklessness. He was speaking out of sovereign clarity.

Finally, Kendrick broke the silence. "You're proposing pre-emptive data sterilization. A surgical strike on your own genetic records to ensure total disinformation control." "Yes, Uncle Kendrick," Ben affirmed. "And you believe you can execute this without detection?" "With Dad's friend's help, yes. He has the skill, and more importantly, he has the proper clearances that allow such actions to be quietly authorized under archival maintenance protocols." Sørensen exhaled slowly, the weight of the plan settling over him. "This would make the underground factions lose their remaining footing entirely. Without any pure data source, their speculative trees collapse."

"Exactly," Ben said again, now with firm resolve. "All they'll have left are the false genealogies I've already seeded. The fake haplogroups. The ghost ancestries. Nothing concrete. And nothing usable." Kendrick slowly circled the table, hands clasped behind his back.

He studied his adopted son with a long, steady gaze that carried no judgement—only calculation. And admiration. "You are not merely protecting yourself, Ben," Kendrick said finally. "You are designing a sovereign countermeasure." Ben nodded. "I'm building a firewall they cannot breach."

Kendrick's lips curled slightly, the pride unmistakable in his voice. "At ten years old, you're already thinking like a sovereign architect." His gaze softened, becoming that of a father rather than a king. "And you intend to act on this soon?" "Yes," Ben said firmly.

"With your permission." Kendrick looked briefly toward Sørensen. The man inclined his head, giving his silent approval, though his protective instincts would ensure he personally oversaw every layer of this operation.

"You have my permission, my son," Kendrick said at last. "But this will be carried out under my authority. Sørensen will manage all external parameters to ensure your safety." Ben's breath eased. "Thank you, Uncle Kendrick." Kendrick stepped forward then, placing both hands gently on Ben's shoulders, drawing him into his embrace—the fatherly embrace they both shared each time. Ben rested against Kendrick's chest, feeling the strong arms of his sovereign father encircle him.

"You continue to make your House proud," Kendrick whispered. "Not because of your bloodline. But because of your wisdom." Isla smiled softly, her own pride shining through as she stood and gently joined their embrace, leaning into Kendrick's side. The family bond stood stronger than any data trail. Outside, the storm winds rattled once more against the windows. But inside, the storm no longer mattered. The House of Rosenshavn was already one step ahead.

The storm winds continued their low, distant howling as though nature itself sensed the games unfolding behind these stone walls. But inside the royal chamber, the air was thick not with fear—but with revelation. Kendrick sat once more at the briefing table, his hands folded beneath his chin, while Sørensen stood behind him like a coiled spring, every muscle alert, though his face betrayed the growing surprise already building inside. Ben sat opposite, calm as always, Isla at his side. She offered him a brief, quiet nod—the kind of nod that said: It's time.

Kendrick had just finished granting his permission for the disinformation expansion Ben proposed, but something in Ben's eyes suggested there was more. Far more. Kendrick spoke first, sensing it. "You're not finished, are you?" Ben smiled faintly. "No, Uncle Kendrick. I'm not." His voice remained steady, but beneath the words was a force even Sørensen could feel tightening like an unseen rope.

Kendrick gestured softly. "Continue." Ben drew a breath. "The shield I created—the false genealogies, the ghosted haplogroups, the misdirection programs—they're already doing what we designed them to do. But you've always said a sovereign's greatest defence is not simply the systems others can see." He paused. "It's what remains unseen." Sørensen's eyes narrowed slightly, tracking every syllable now. He could feel something building beneath the boy's calm surface.

Ben continued. "That's why, even before we finalized the false records, I quietly prepared... insurance." Isla's hand slid into his, as steady as his own voice. She already knew every layer of this. She had carried his secrets since the beginning, her loyalty as impenetrable as the walls around them. "I made full backups of the original DNA profiles," Ben said. "My haplogroups. Isla's. Her parents. The full mitochondrial chains. The deeper extended families. Everything."

Kendrick's brow lifted slightly, but he said nothing. He was listening now—not as a king, but as a sovereign father watching his son exceed every expectation. Ben pressed on. "But I never allowed those backups to exist within any system that could be accessed—even by sovereign state protocols.

No digital servers. No encrypted archives. Nothing." "Then where—" Sørensen began, but Ben raised his hand gently. "They exist," Ben said, his tone precise, "only on a single, air-gapped, offline drive. Encoded, layered with my own security sequences, and physically secured inside the castle."

Sørensen leaned forward sharply now, unable to hide the growing astonishment in his voice. "Inside this castle?" "Yes," Ben confirmed. "Hidden in a chamber where even moles or compromised agents would never think to look. Even if someone managed to bypass multiple levels of security—which they won't—they wouldn't recognize the device for what it is." Kendrick's eyes sharpened as the full picture came into focus. "You're telling me... you created a private sovereign vault. Unauthorised. At ten."

Ben nodded calmly. "I did." Sørensen exhaled sharply through his nose, shaking his head. "My God." Kendrick remained silent for a long moment. His eyes did not waver from Ben's. And then, his voice dropped lower—both awed and fatherly. "How long has this been in place?" Ben's answer came without hesitation. "Since my tenth birthday."

Sørensen stepped closer, studying him almost as if seeing the boy for the first time. "Nine years old," he whispered. "A fully sovereign-level security partition... built by a child." "Not a child, Sørensen," Kendrick corrected softly, never looking away from his son. "A prodigy." Ben continued, calmly. "Even if everything else failed—if the disinformation shield was breached, if a mole embedded inside the council, even if an enemy somehow compromised sovereign channels—my lineage, Isla's lineage, remains protected. Uncorrupted. Untouchable."

"And Jeff?" Kendrick asked softly. "Annemarie? Robert and Claire? Do they know?" "No," Ben replied firmly. "No one. Not even Dad." His voice softened, but never wavered. "Because the fewer who know, the stronger the defence." Kendrick let out a long, deliberate breath, his mind rapidly absorbing every calculated measure. "And Isla?" he asked, though he already suspected the answer. "She knows everything," Ben said simply. "I've never kept anything from her."

Isla squeezed his hand gently, adding with quiet pride, "And I will never speak a word to anyone. This is ours." Sørensen shook his head slowly. "You've never worked with a 10-year-old like this before," Ben remarked gently, sensing the man's astonishment.

The operative laughed under his breath, but the humour was genuine, filled with reluctant awe. "No, Your Highness. I most certainly have not." He looked toward Kendrick and added with full sincerity, "In all my years, I've trained and protected men who run some of the most secure intelligence services in Europe. But not one of them could have designed something this effective, this early, with this much foresight."

Ben spoke again, lowering his voice, as if offering one final card. "Even if the worst happened tomorrow... even if I were ever taken... there is nothing they could find. Because I've placed misdirection inside the misdirection."

For the first time, Kendrick allowed the faintest smile to break across his face—not because he was amused, but because he was proud beyond words. His voice was soft now, almost reverent. "You are not simply a prince, Ben," Kendrick whispered. "You are already building your kingdom."

Isla's eyes glimmered beside him, proud of the boy she loved, proud of the man he was becoming. Ben sat back slightly, letting the moment rest. "I just think ahead, Uncle Kendrick. That's all." Sørensen exhaled once more, stepping back, but his head continued to shake as if trying to realign his own understanding of what now stood before him. "No, young prince," he said softly, almost as if speaking to himself, "you think like no one I've ever met." Outside the thick walls, the wind struck once again, stronger than before—beating against the glass like the fingers of those desperate to break through. But inside, the storm had found no breach. They were ready.

The storm had not lessened. If anything, its rhythm had grown more erratic, the wind slapping sharply against the tower stones. But within the inner chamber, the world remained stable, anchored beneath the weight of something far more powerful than mere wind — the unspoken coordination of sovereign minds.

Ben sat now before a secure console tucked into a smaller adjoining room, one used only for the most confidential transmissions. Kendrick stood nearby, hands loosely folded behind his back, while Sørensen stood at attention a few paces behind, his eyes fixed on every movement the young prince made. Isla, as always, sat quietly nearby — her presence steady, her silence sovereign.

The castle's sovereign-secure channels were built for moments such as this: communication beyond even Denmark's state protocols. Lines that even global intelligence circles barely knew existed. And Ben was about to employ one of them — not for diplomacy, not for negotiation — but for the quiet execution of an erasure. "Connection established," the system whispered in its cold digital voice, flickering softly in green across the dark screen. The channel had linked — routed not through public servers, but through deeply buried sovereign infrastructure known to only a few.

Ben adjusted his headset and spoke in a low, steady voice, coded, precise. "Primary key authentication: Harvick Protocol Three-Seven-Sigma." The voice on the other end responded after a slight pause — calm, measured, and unmistakably familiar. "Confirmed. Secure. Encryption full spectrum. Good evening, Ben." The man's voice belonged to one of Jeff's closest associates — a specialist who had once worked for private forensic labs before entering sovereign consulting under Jeff's network. His name never appeared in public files. Not even Sørensen knew his full identity.

"Evening, Carter," Ben said simply. "I trust you're still watching the mirrors?" "As always, young prince," Carter replied with a faint smile in his tone. "I see you're calling for the... deeper protocols." "Yes." Ben's voice remained level. "It's time to sterilize." A brief pause followed. Carter's voice lowered even further, acknowledging the weight of the request. "You're certain?" "Completely," Ben answered. "Shred everything. Full-spectrum deletion—both physical and electronic. I want every existing strand of my original blood samples eliminated. Isla's, mine, and any attached familial record fragments that were archived at collection."
"Understood." The man never questioned further. He knew who he was speaking to. "Electronic fragments first. Physical destruction by dawn. Retention logs will show nothing but standard archival maintenance sweeps." "Good." Ben exhaled slowly. "All access queries flagged over the past six months?" "Already isolated and tagged for disinformation propagation. All foreign pings have been routed into the falsified branches you originally created." Carter paused again. "Frankly, Ben, your shield has become... masterful. The agencies still believe they're chasing real lines."

"Let them," Ben answered calmly. "The more certain they become, the more blind they grow." Carter gave a faint chuckle. "Very well. You'll have full confirmation packages on your private drive in forty-eight hours." "Thank you, Carter. And as always — purge this call." "It's already gone." The screen dimmed to black. The entire exchange had lasted no more than five minutes. But within that narrow window, an entire branch of the world's most dangerous data was quietly buried. Forever.

Ben pulled off the headset and sat back, eyes steady. Kendrick was the first to break the silence, his voice filled with something between admiration and awe. "Executed flawlessly," he murmured. Sørensen, for his part, took a small step forward, his voice lower now, not as a specialist addressing a child — but as a man addressing someone whose skills far exceeded even his own. "Ben," he said softly, "I want to learn." Ben turned slightly, raising an eyebrow. "Learn?"

"Yes." Sørensen's eyes sharpened with quiet humility. "I've served in counter-intelligence my entire life. I've built defensive grids for sovereign houses. But I've never seen someone construct a network this intricate, this adaptive, this... anticipatory." Ben regarded him for a long moment, his ten-year-old frame sitting within the chair like it belonged to a man decades older. And then, with a faint smile, he nodded. "I'll teach you, Sørensen." Kendrick smiled faintly behind them. "You've found your apprentice, my son."

Sørensen straightened. "I will observe. I will listen. And I will learn. Every layer you are willing to share." Ben's voice remained quiet, but there was no arrogance in it — only the cool steadiness of a sovereign mind beginning to understand the full breadth of his power. "Good. Because this chessboard, Sørensen... has only just begun to move." Isla squeezed his hand gently at that, her smile steady, proud. She had always known. From the beginning. She never needed explanations. She carried every secret alongside him, a partner not in mere affection, but in strategy.

Kendrick spoke then, his voice fatherly but filled with the unmistakable gravity of sovereign foresight. "The world will not understand who you are for many years, Ben. And when they finally begin to realize it... it will already be too late for them to stop you." The storm continued beyond the walls — but within this chamber, the winds were under control. The sovereign game was no longer defensive. Now, it was offensive. And the young prince was holding the board.

The council room was unusually silent that evening. The rain had paused, though the low winds still scraped lightly against the high stone windows, as if the storm were holding its breath, sensing that the true tempest now lived inside the minds gathered here.
Ben sat at the central table once again, Isla at his side, her hand resting quietly on his forearm as his thoughts began to unravel themselves aloud. Kendrick stood nearby, watching his young sovereign with a gaze both deeply paternal and acutely aware that something unexpected was forming. Sørensen stood quietly behind them, arms crossed, no longer as the superior officer, but as the student studying the sovereign in front of him.

Ben exhaled softly, gathering his words. His voice was calm, even playful in its delivery, but beneath it ran an undercurrent of pure sovereign calculus. "Uncle Kendrick," Ben began softly, "I have a proposal." Kendrick's lips twitched with amusement. "You usually do."

"This one is a little… unusual." "I've come to expect that from you." Kendrick folded his arms, his eyes narrowing slightly with interest. "Speak." Ben drew in a slow breath. "It's temporary. It's not entirely… legal, by most definitions. But it's useful. Tactical." He paused, ensuring his words landed properly. "How about — for the time being — you put me in charge?" Kendrick blinked, not from shock, but from the sheer audacity of what he knew was not a joke. "You mean…" Kendrick's voice trailed for a moment, weighing the gravity of what his nephew had just offered, "…declare you king?"

Ben shook his head gently. "Not permanently. Symbolically. Strategically. Think of it as hyperbole — nothing binding, nothing that threatens your sovereignty. This is still your House. Your bloodline. Your castle." He gestured lightly around them. "You remain sovereign. Your hand remains steady on the wheel. But we let the world think you've… stepped aside." Sørensen's eyes narrowed now. He said nothing, but his breathing slowed. He was listening to something far deeper than the words themselves.

Ben continued. "To our adversaries, this will trigger uncertainty. If they believe there's been a shift — a young sovereign taking temporary control — they won't know where to aim. They'll question whether you've abdicated, whether you're preparing a succession, whether you've abandoned your station, or whether they've entirely miscalculated the House of Rosenshavn's internal structure." He leaned forward slightly, his voice dropping lower now, the true weight of his plan pressing into the room. "The moment they start questioning which of us holds the crown, they fracture. Because sovereign enemies thrive on predictable targets. But this? This muddies the water."

Kendrick exhaled, his brows drawing together, staring at his nephew with a mixture of fatherly love and pure strategic awe. "You're proposing to weaponize confusion." "Exactly." Ben smiled faintly. "They won't know which hand holds the blade. They'll waste months trying to decipher whether you've disappeared or merely repositioned.

Meanwhile, you remain in full control behind the curtain. Guiding my hand, yes — but never holding it. Because frankly, if you were holding my hand the whole time…" Ben chuckled softly, glancing at Isla, "…well, that might look a bit odd for two people who are family."

Even Kendrick couldn't suppress the small laugh that slipped through. "That it would." Isla squeezed Ben's arm, her face glowing with pride. She had known about this plan for days already, holding it quietly as always.

She never needed to be reminded to guard his secrets; she carried them as her own. Sørensen finally spoke now, his voice low, respectful, and utterly serious. "And the press?" he asked. "The foreign networks? The private intelligence circles? They'll run wild."

"Precisely," Ben replied without hesitation. "Let them. Every headline, every whisper, every diplomatic dispatch will become noise. The more desperate they grow to confirm the facts, the more erratic their moves will become. And the moment their aggression turns sloppy…" He paused with a faint glint in his eye, "…we counterstrike. Quietly. Without mercy." Sørensen lowered his gaze slightly, taking in the entirety of the boy before him. "You're using yourself as bait."

Ben simply nodded. "Calculated bait. I control what they see. I control how far they pursue the illusion. And if I need to pivot, I have the sovereign shield of your House behind me. Uncle Kendrick remains untouched. The true sovereign remains hidden in plain sight." Kendrick studied him, and for a moment, there was nothing but silence. The kind of silence that few sovereigns ever shared — one of deep, unspoken recognition. Kendrick saw it fully now: the child who no longer stood as a student, but as a sovereign architect in his own right. Finally, Kendrick spoke, his voice softer but filled with both pride and weight. "Ben... you may very well be the most dangerous ten-year-old alive."

Ben smiled, but his eyes stayed calm. "That's the idea." Kendrick exhaled again, then nodded. "Very well. But hear me on this: you carry my authority in name — not in substance. Should this move grow too bold, too fast, I remain sovereign. My hands remain ready to intervene." "I would expect nothing less, Uncle Kendrick." Sørensen let out a small, quiet chuckle now, shaking his head as though marvelling at some rare instrument being built before his eyes. "If I may say, Your Highness..." he said, looking directly at Ben now, "...you have just given me another chapter of lessons to learn."

"You're still observing?" Ben asked lightly. "More than observing," Sørensen answered. "I am studying. And I intend to study until I understand how you think — because you are reshaping the way I see this entire game." Ben leaned back, allowing the conversation to settle like embers glowing beneath the surface. "Good. Because we're not playing games anymore, Sørensen." The storm struck the tower again. Harder this time. The world outside was growing desperate. And Ben — calm, calculating, sovereign — was still three moves ahead.

The atmosphere inside the royal war room had shifted again. It was no longer the tense space of mere defence—it had become something else entirely. The centre of a calculated storm, where sovereign hands moved pieces across invisible lines. Every breath now carried weight. Every word was measured.

Sørensen stood near the tall windows, the soft tapping of rain once again returning as evening descended. Isla sat quietly, her fingers laced gently with Ben's as always, reading him better than anyone alive. Kendrick leaned forward on the table, watching his nephew closely, for he sensed Ben was about to throw the board into a spin no one outside this room could predict.

Ben's smile came slowly—too controlled to be innocent, too sharp to be mischievous. It was sovereign. "Uncle Kendrick," Ben began, glancing between his uncle and Sørensen, "I believe it's time we hand them something." Kendrick raised a brow. "Something?" Ben leaned forward, his voice lowering slightly, as though even the stone walls themselves were eavesdropping. "We give them a hyperbole. A stink bomb." Sørensen's eyes lit up instantly, the humour already reaching him before Ben could even explain. He gave a small chuckle. "A stink bomb, Your Highness?"

Ben nodded, his tone now dancing between irony and brilliance. "Yes. Not a literal one, of course. A sovereign-grade information stink bomb. We give them a piece of information so absurd, so confusing, so dramatic — that they won't know which end of their own head is pointing north. And if they manage to pull it out far enough, they might just get a whiff of oxygen long enough to realize they've been played." Sørensen broke into open laughter then, shaking his head. "Now that," he said, still chuckling, "is exactly why you scare them so much. You don't simply block your enemies — you make them question their own sanity."

Uncle Kendrick chuckled too, rubbing his chin thoughtfully. "And what, precisely, do you have in mind for this... stink bomb, my son?" Ben gestured lightly to Sørensen, his voice perfectly calm, but with an unmistakable sovereign edge beneath.

"Actually... I want Sørensen to craft it." Sørensen blinked. "Me?" "Yes." Ben smiled. "Consider it your first sovereign assignment in misinformation architecture." The security specialist's face turned thoughtful, the wheels already turning inside his head. "And you want me to build something they'll believe?"

"Something too believable," Ben corrected softly. "Something juicy enough that the intelligence circles won't be able to resist. A piece of false genealogical bait—perhaps suggesting that I am secretly being groomed as a shadow heir to a now-defunct European house. Or maybe link me to multiple disputed claims across Hungary, Denmark, and Norway all at once." He paused, allowing the absurdity to rise. "Maybe even suggest that there's an internal royal fracture—that you, Uncle Kendrick, have stepped aside because of growing... 'private tensions' inside the House of Rosenshavn. Play with the fiction that I am being positioned by international sovereign networks to reclaim ancestral territories long thought dissolved."

Kendrick's eyes narrowed in sharp amusement. "My, my. That would certainly get them spinning." Sørensen nodded slowly, the grin growing on his face. "The media would implode. Private intelligence groups would be in full scramble mode. Diplomatic chatter would light up every encrypted network on the continent." "And that," Ben said, with sovereign calm, "is precisely the point. While they chase false fractures, we reinforce our actual shields. They'll exhaust themselves trying to verify details that don't exist."

Isla finally spoke now, her voice quiet but strong. "And because they won't trust each other, they'll second-guess every source." "Exactly," Ben smiled proudly at her. "They won't know whether their intelligence is solid or planted. Because it is planted." Kendrick exhaled slowly, deeply impressed. "It's disinformation layered on top of disinformation." "And wrapped in sovereign misdirection," Sørensen added, unable to hide his genuine admiration. "Brilliant."

Ben leaned back slightly, allowing the momentum to build. "Sørensen," he said softly, "I want you to build the release. You know the channels. You know the agencies. Leak it subtly. An anonymous insider. Let the media believe they've tripped across something forbidden." Sørensen nodded firmly. "I'll begin constructing the operation immediately." "And Sørensen?" Ben added with a small grin.

"Yes, Your Highness?" "Make it your best. Let them chase ghosts they'll never catch." Sørensen smiled wide now. "It will be done." Kendrick rose from his chair, crossing to Ben and placing his hand firmly on his adopted son's shoulder, his voice heavy with admiration and pride. "Ben, you are not simply playing this game. You are redefining it." Ben looked up at him, his voice steady as stone. "I protect my family, Uncle Kendrick. All of them. I will give our enemies nothing to hold — and plenty to fear."

Isla's hand squeezed his, and the two exchanged the same unbreakable glance they always did—a glance that said: We stand together. Outside, the winds screamed once more — not as nature's fury, but as a warning carried through the night air. For the enemies who watched from their distant towers and hollowed halls — they had no idea how badly outmatched they now were. His Majesty Prince Benedict (Ben) Adrian Harvick was not simply playing. He was hunting.

The storm that had hovered in the distance for days finally made landfall in the early hours of the morning. The first rolls of thunder cracked through the skies above the castle, shaking the heavy glass panes in their casings as rain lashed furiously against the old stones. But inside the heart of Denmark's sovereign stronghold, the true thunder was not in the sky — it was in the war rooms, where the newest phase of Ben's operation had already detonated across the global chessboard.

Sørensen stood before the main projection wall, where encrypted feeds streamed live data from across multiple intelligence channels. The swirling ocean of misinformation was already spreading faster than any one agency could contain. Reports came flashing across the board:

Source: Swiss Private Channels — CONFIDENTIAL:
Reports suggest internal fractures in the House of Rosenshavn; Prince Benedict Harvick positioned as emergent claimant to multiple European royal titles. Alleged strategic withdrawal by King Kendrick to preserve sovereign stability.

Source: French Royalist Circles — ALERT:
Speculation mounting around Benedict Harvick's ancestral linkages to disbanded Hungarian dynasties. Possibility of secret negotiations underway.

Source: Russian Observers — HIGH PRIORITY:
Benedict Harvick rising as central figure in sovereign realignment; potential collapse of existing diplomatic arrangements; all channels ordered to monitor shifts.

Source: Private European Banking Interests — URGENT:
Noble estates quietly reassessing sovereignty investments tied to Denmark. Advisors instructed to prepare for radical shifts in inheritance control.

The feeds continued to flood the board as Sørensen read each one with growing satisfaction, his expression somewhere between awe and dark amusement. Kendrick stepped forward, scanning the reports with his hands clasped behind his back, his face composed but quietly burning with pride. "You see it, don't you?" he said, turning slightly toward Sørensen.

"I do," Sørensen answered. "They've taken the bait." He allowed himself a brief exhale. "Every agency, every private network, every royalist remnant—they're scrambling like rats in a sinking ship." Ben sat calmly at the side table, Isla leaning against his shoulder, both of them watching the thunderstorm of misinformation they had unleashed upon the world. His hands rested casually on his lap, as if they had simply invited friends for tea, not launched one of the most sophisticated disinformation campaigns the modern sovereign world had ever witnessed.

"They're not thinking clearly anymore," Ben said quietly, his voice barely rising above the rumble of distant thunder. "They're panicking. Their own greed has made them stupid." Kendrick nodded, still watching the data roll across the screens. "The best part is that none of them can trust each other now. Every private agency thinks the others know something they don't."

"And none of them know anything at all," Isla added with a small, victorious smile. Sørensen, still absorbing the scale of it all, shook his head slowly. "This... this is absolute genius. They're cannibalizing themselves." He looked toward Ben, eyes narrowing in wonder. "And we haven't even triggered the second wave yet." Ben's smile deepened ever so slightly. "Exactly."

Kendrick's voice dropped lower, contemplative now. "What you've done, Ben, is not simply misinformation. This is psychological warfare at a sovereign level. You've weaponized their ambition, their greed, their need to know." "They wanted to find me," Ben said calmly, his voice as steady as steel. "Now they can't even find themselves."

The next report came flashing across the screen:
Source: Vatican Correspondence — Internal Eyes Only:
Speculative meetings called regarding possible Harvick Line restoration. Papal advisors requested background files on Benedict Adrian Harvick.

Sørensen let out a slow whistle. "Even the Holy See is starting to react." "They're all dancing now," Ben said softly. "Every faction scrambling for a piece of a throne that doesn't exist — at least not the way they think it does." The thunder outside cracked again, louder this time, almost as if the heavens themselves had applauded the move. Kendrick stepped closer to his nephew, lowering his voice so that only those inside the chamber could hear. "You understand what you've done, don't you?"

Ben looked up into his uncle's eyes, his voice never faltering. "Yes, Uncle Kendrick. I've made sure they cannot hurt us. Not now. Not later. Every move they make now is reactionary. They no longer control the tempo.

We do." "And what of the real bloodlines?" Kendrick asked softly. Ben's voice was like sharpened glass. "They remain right where they belong. Hidden. Untouchable. Only we know the truth. And the world can spin itself senseless chasing illusions."

Sørensen crossed his arms, still grinning. "This is... historic." "It's sovereign warfare," Kendrick said, smiling faintly. "Pure. Surgical. Elegant." Isla rested her head gently on Ben's shoulder, whispering softly so that only he could hear, "You've already won." Ben looked down at her, his expression softening only for her. "Not yet," he whispered back. "But very soon." The next wave of reports would come soon — false confirmations, rival agencies accusing each other of holding secret files, sovereign watchers leaking "insider" details planted by Sørensen's operatives. The storm had only begun to rage.

The enemies outside were drowning in shadows. The sovereign house within the castle stood calm, untouched, commanding the thunder itself. The game was his. And King Benedict Adrian Harvick — sovereign prodigy, master strategist, protector of his family — sat firmly at the helm.

The dawn broke like a muted blade against the storm-soaked horizon. Grey skies hung heavy above the castle, but the rain had finally surrendered. The land below remained drenched, as though the heavens themselves were exhausted from watching what had unfolded within these walls over the past two days. Inside the secured wing, Sørensen stood silently at the northern gate — his breath rising faintly in the cool air — as the sovereign courier approached. No markings. No identifiable uniform. No insignias. Just a simple, private operative of the House, known only by those within the inner sanctum.

The courier gave a brief nod, handing over the small titanium case. It was cold to the touch, sealed with multiple physical and biometric locks. Sørensen studied it carefully, eyes narrowing as the scanner embedded in his wristwatch flashed green — confirming the package's encryption authorization. "Secure delivery completed," the courier whispered. "Internal protocols fully observed. No external scans detected." "Good." Sørensen nodded. "You're dismissed."

With the package in hand, Sørensen returned swiftly through the winding halls, navigating the private corridors that only those at Kendrick's level ever walked. He moved like a man carrying not a case, but a sovereign secret that could tilt the global balance. And indeed, he was. When he entered the chamber, Ben was already waiting — Isla at his side, as always. Kendrick stood nearby, observing the storm within his adopted son's eyes. The sovereign war was moving again.

"It's arrived," Sørensen announced, setting the titanium case gently on the table before Ben. Ben wasted no time. His small hands danced across the biometric pad, scanning his thumbprint and retinal pattern in rapid sequence. The locks disengaged with a soft hiss. Inside, perfectly organized, sat the evidence he had been awaiting:

- Complete forensic destruction records.
- Full certified deletion certificates, both digital and physical.
- Lab reports confirming total annihilation of the original DNA storage.
- And beneath it all — one final encrypted drive: **the backup.**

The drive contained the only surviving full sequence of his real DNA, Isla's, and their families — the sovereign truth that only he controlled. Ben exhaled calmly, nodding. "Perfect." Kendrick folded his arms. "The slate is now yours alone." "Exactly," Ben replied, his voice carrying a sharpened calm. "And now, Uncle Kendrick... now we make it stink." Sørensen raised a brow. "The next stink bomb, Your Highness?" Ben's eyes gleamed as he gently slid the encrypted drive across the table. "We're going to rewrite the narrative entirely."

Kendrick watched carefully as Ben began to explain. "You see, they thought they were chasing one sovereign bloodline. Me. Denmark. Maybe a few ancestral branches they suspect. That's why they've been so aggressive — they believed if they compromised one tree, they compromised the entire house." "But they've failed," Kendrick said softly.

Ben nodded. "They've failed because their thinking is small. Linear. Predictable. What if, Sørensen..." Ben paused dramatically, "...we show them something far more terrifying?" Sørensen's eyes narrowed, absorbing every word. "Go on." Ben's voice dropped lower, each word deliberate. "We leak a controlled sample — verified, fabricated, but built off my real haplogroup structures. But this time, we alter key markers... subtly. Enough to appear scientifically irrefutable."

He gestured to the drive. "We adjust the Y-chromosome markers. The mitochondrial sequences. The autosomal chain indicators. We give them a bloodline web that links me — not just to Denmark — but to six fully sovereign global houses." Isla smiled faintly, proud, already knowing where this was going. Kendrick's eyes sharpened. "You want them to believe you are the hereditary descendant of multiple royal houses simultaneously."

Ben nodded. "Denmark. Hungary. Norway. England. France. The Holy Roman remnants. All cross-pollinated. All leading... to me." Sørensen blinked, letting the scope of it wash over him. "They'll lose their minds." "Exactly," Ben whispered. "Imagine it, Sørensen: the global media, the intelligence agencies, even friendly sovereign allies... suddenly faced with the possibility that I am not simply heir to one disputed house, but potentially the unifying sovereign claimant to half of Europe's most fractured royal legacies."

Kendrick exhaled, half-laughing under his breath, though his admiration was impossible to hide. "You're about to light a sovereign powder keg." Ben smiled. "No. I'm about to set their entire map on fire." Sørensen stepped forward, his voice steady but filled with awe. "Your

Highness... this will trigger diplomatic seizures everywhere. Bank holdings. Estate claims. Political leverage. Entire governments will start speculating whether you're being positioned as a global consolidation figure."

Ben's voice dropped to a razor whisper. "Let them speculate. Let them choke on their own ambition." He turned to Kendrick now, locking eyes with his sovereign father. "Uncle Kendrick, you will remain precisely where you are. Sovereign. Safe. Above the storm. But while you remain, I will create enough disarray to make every adversary second-guess every move they've made since this began."

Kendrick finally allowed the full smile to break across his face, stepping forward and gripping Ben's shoulder firmly. "Ben... you're not defending the family anymore. You are conquering the battlefield." Ben looked up at him, his voice still calm. "Because if you control their fear, Uncle Kendrick... you control their moves." Isla leaned closer, whispering into Ben's ear, her eyes gleaming. "You've made them blind." Ben whispered back, "That was always the point." The thunder cracked again outside — louder than before. The global chessboard had been flipped upside down. And now, the true sovereign war — the real war — had begun.

By the time the morning sun breached the castle towers, the sovereign world was already in free fall. The diplomatic cables were burning. The intelligence networks were eating themselves alive. The Houses — royal, financial, political — were all thrashing beneath the weight of their own paranoia. And inside Denmark's most secure chamber, Ben sat like a composer at the centre of his sovereign symphony. Before him stood Sørensen, now fully engaged in his role as the architect of disinformation, no longer simply a protector — but an active weapon.

The projection wall flickered again with panicked reports:

United Nations Analysts — CONFIDENTIAL:
"Urgent reassessment of Harvick Line implications underway. Potentially connected to long-buried royal successions across six historic sovereign dynasties. Stability risk assessments elevated."

US Intelligence Leak:
"Harvick bloodline linked to disputed claims across European, Nordic, and Eastern royal houses. Potential consolidation risk flagged. Presidential advisors alerted."

Vatican Internal Memo:
"Multiple Papal envoys requesting urgent clarification on Harvick lineage. Secret talks proposed with House of Rosenshavn to avert possible theological crisis."

Ben watched each one scroll with a calm smile as Sørensen leaned forward, reading the latest files aloud. His voice was filled with a combination of professional detachment — and unrestrained delight. "They are absolutely losing it," Sørensen said with a smirk. "Of course they are," Ben answered, almost casually. "They can't map the board anymore."

Kendrick stepped in then, rubbing his temples, eyes darting between his nephew and his chief operative. "And now you want to make it worse?" "Oh yes," Ben said with a bright grin. "Much worse." He glanced over at Sørensen and, with a small mischievous chuckle, simply said: "Sørensen... let's go have a field day." The room hung silent for a moment before Sørensen's face broke into a wide grin — a grin so large it nearly consumed his usual controlled demeanour. "Oh," Sørensen said, chuckling now, "I've been waiting for that... for a very long time." Kendrick looked at the two of them like a father who just realized his sons had stolen the keys to the sovereign war machine. "A field day?" he repeated, his voice half incredulous, half amused. "You're calling this a field day?"

Ben turned his grin toward his uncle, eyes sparkling. "Yes, Uncle Kendrick. You see, the beauty of a sovereign field day... is that no one knows it's begun until it's already over." Kendrick's eyes narrowed, but the pride in his voice was undeniable. "God help the rest of the world." Sørensen was already pacing toward the data console, hands moving swiftly as he prepared the next operation. "We'll seed three sources," he announced. "One into private Vatican channels — hinting at secret Papal endorsements. One into Eastern European monarchist circles — suggesting clandestine alliances seeking Benedict's leadership. And one... into Swiss financial boards — suggesting undisclosed estate transfers are being quietly positioned into Benedict's control."

He paused, looking back at Ben with a gleam in his eye. "That should trigger absolute diplomatic hysteria." Ben nodded approvingly. "Perfect. The more they scramble, the more desperate their intelligence pings become.

And every single one will lead right back into the illusions we planted." Kendrick crossed his arms, shaking his head with both caution and awe. "You're orchestrating a sovereign mirage, Ben. They think they're mapping truth — but they're drawing shadows." Ben leaned back, voice quiet but charged. "That's how sovereign wars are won."

As Sørensen finalized the data packet injections, the screens flashed:

OPERATION STINK BOMB — PHASE II ACTIVATED.

Isla, watching quietly as always, smiled and whispered into Ben's ear. "You've made yourself untouchable." Ben whispered back, eyes still focused on the screens: "No. I've made us untouchable." The next wave of misinformation detonated across the world within hours. Royalist factions began issuing internal memos. Monarchists demanded emergency sessions. Secret financial institutions panicked at the thought of hidden estate shifts. Several European governments initiated crisis meetings, desperately attempting to verify conflicting genealogical webs that couldn't possibly coexist — but now appeared to.

Sørensen sat back as the data flooded the room. "I'll say this, Your Highness…" he chuckled, "…for a ten-year-old, you're the most terrifying adversary any of these Houses will ever encounter." Ben smiled. "That was always the plan." The castle remained silent. The sovereign war was no longer brewing. It was roaring. And Benedict Adrian Harvick — sovereign architect, sovereign predator — sat firmly in control of the storm.

The sovereign war chamber hummed like the engine of an ancient machine now fully awakened. Reports flooded the monitors — every screen filled with the latest panicked moves of the world's most powerful Houses. Diplomatic cables were flying. Emergency royal summits were being called. Financial markets were freezing. And inside the stone walls of Denmark's sovereign stronghold, Ben sat as the architect of it all — calm, precise, and now ready for the final phase.

Sørensen stood at the central console, his eyes dancing as he monitored the streams of chaos they had successfully unleashed. The grin across his face had grown wider with every passing hour.

Kendrick approached the table slowly, arms folded, watching his nephew like a man watching a storm he no longer commanded — because the storm now belonged entirely to Ben. Ben turned his gaze to Sørensen, his tone sharp but playful. "Sørensen."

"Yes, Your Highness?" Sørensen answered, never taking his eyes off the screens. Ben leaned forward, the faintest glint of mischief burning in his eyes. "How would you like to create the biggest stink bomb of all?" Sørensen finally turned, blinking once — and then laughed, low and dangerous. "The biggest, sire?" Ben nodded. "Yes. A complete and total sovereign lockdown."

Kendrick's eyes widened slightly, his brows lifting. "Say again?" Ben stood now, walking toward both men. His voice dropped into the kind of controlled power that no ten-year-old should ever carry — and yet, in him, it felt entirely natural. "A total sovereign lockdown," Ben repeated calmly. "We freeze everything."

He gestured to the swirling data feeds. "Their money. Their trusts. Their offshore accounts. The royal claim registries. The diplomatic back channels. The genealogical councils. The advisory networks." He smiled faintly. "We suffocate them with paperwork. Legal freezes. Emergency sovereign filings. Conflicting claims filed through multiple state proxies — all simultaneously." He turned to Sørensen. "Would you like to explain it?"

Sørensen chuckled, almost bowing. "Sire, it would be a total honour." Turning to Kendrick, Sørensen adopted the voice of a man delivering a sovereign masterclass. "Your Majesty, what His Highness proposes is, quite simply, global paralysis. We file so many conflicting sovereign claims and freeze so many legal channels simultaneously that none of the royal houses can move a single piece on the board without risking catastrophic violation of international treaties, property seizures, or diplomatic collapse."

Sørensen allowed himself a small breath. "It will create a perfect storm of hesitation and panic." Ben added, "And while they're frozen, any attempt to act rashly exposes their alliances — and leaves them legally vulnerable." Kendrick stared at both of them for a long moment. "And you can execute this?" Sørensen nodded. "The triggers are ready. Multiple sovereign registries. The legal teams His Highness pre-positioned under aliases have all been standing by. All I need is the signal." Ben's smile widened now — not out of arrogance — but out of sovereign purpose. "Let's make them feel what it's like to be played with." Sørensen's fingers danced across the console, activating the next operation.

The screen flashed:

OPERATION TOTAL SOVEREIGN LOCKDOWN — INITIATED

The effects were nearly immediate. The private monitors flickered with live updates as royal banks flagged massive asset freezes across multiple states. Inheritance courts were forced to halt proceedings as contradictory bloodline claims arrived through legitimate sovereign channels. Embassies across Europe began ringing with conflicting orders and frantic diplomatic calls.

Vatican State: "Papal claims suspended pending further genealogical review."

Swiss Banking Consortium: "Multiple Harvick-linked estate trusts now frozen due to legal irregularities."

Eastern Royal Courts: "Emergency conferences called; Harvick bloodline consolidation claims in dispute."

Nordic Union Response: "House of Rosenshavn remains sovereign — all external claims suspended."

Sørensen laughed openly now, reading the data aloud. "They're eating themselves alive." Kendrick simply shook his head in amazement, whispering softly. "My son... you've created sovereign chaos." Ben smiled softly. "Chaos is only dangerous when you're not the one controlling it." And then — the final twist. Ben reached forward, activating the last channel: the one they had prepared for Kendrick. A private encrypted message flashed across the room. The connection stabilized. Kendrick's familiar face appeared on the screen — calm, poised, already briefed. Ben spoke first. "Uncle Kendrick... the final stage is yours."

Kendrick smiled, nodding. "Understood." With a small sip of his tea, Kendrick's voice rang through the chamber with quiet amusement — and deadly sovereign finality. "Checkmate." The word echoed through the secure chamber like a hammer blow to the entire world stage. Outside the castle, the winds of Denmark howled louder than ever before. The sovereign war had ended — not with a battle — but with a single word. The Harvick Dynasty was now untouchable. Denmark was safe. The royal family stood above it all.

The sovereign lockdown had been executed with precision so sharp that even the oldest dynasties had not seen the blade until it was buried into the heart of their networks. But now — as the waves of panic settled into place — the aftershock truly began. And it was here that Benedict Adrian Harvick — sovereign architect at ten years old — delivered the lesson they would never forget.

The news agencies across Europe had become nothing more than glorified rumour mills. Headlines ran wild across digital and paper formats alike:

"Harvick Bloodline Revealed: Global Sovereign Crisis Escalates!"
"Multiple Dynasties Linked to Danish Prince — Royal Powers Shaken"
"Genealogical Sovereignty: The Child King or The Global Monarch?"

And beneath the headlines, the whispers swirled: private intelligence forums, hidden underground networks, black market sovereign brokers — all frantically trying to extract one clear truth from the firestorm of sovereign chaos.

But there was none.

Because Ben had removed the truth entirely.

Inside the war chamber, Sørensen stood at the helm once more, his fingers gliding across the secured data panels, watching as their enemies desperately clawed for a foothold that no longer existed.

"They've lost control," Sørensen reported, his grin still wide. "All private royal archives are frozen. Global intelligence agencies are conflicting with each other. Half their internal sources no longer trust the other half."

Ben stood before the central monitor now, eyes cold — not with rage, but with absolute, calculating clarity. "They wanted to unearth my family. My DNA. My secrets. They were warned."

Kendrick, standing beside him, watched his adopted son with equal parts awe and solemn recognition. "They believed they were dealing with a child."

Ben's voice was razor-sharp. "They made a mistake."

The monitor flashed again, new reports flooding the screen:

Swiss Consortium Confidential:

"Asset freezes have triggered sovereign lawsuits totaling over $8.2 billion. No verification of Harvick DNA disputes located. Financial institutions exposed."

Vatican Archives — INTERNAL:
"Unable to disprove Harvick lineage claims. Religious diplomacy in paralysis."

US Federal Report — CLASSIFIED:

"Advise full non-engagement with House of Rosenshavn and Harvick Line. Potential diplomatic liability. Recommend sovereign recognition be maintained."

Ben allowed himself a small exhale. "Good. Now... let's make them feel it."

Sørensen turned sharply. "Orders, Your Highness?"
Ben stepped forward. "Release phase three."
Sørensen blinked. "The **Sovereign Burn**?"
Ben nodded once. "Exactly."

Kendrick raised an eyebrow, glancing between the two. "The Sovereign Burn?" Ben explained calmly. "They sought to expose me. Threaten my family. Now, we expose them."

His eyes locked onto the display. "We release targeted financial data dumps into controlled leak channels — the off-shore holdings they've tried to bury. The secret estates, the trust funds, the sovereign assets hidden from public view. Let their own nations see the depth of their corruption."

Sørensen activated the sequence, hands dancing rapidly across the encrypted console. "The files are primed for controlled release. Multiple diplomatic channels will receive anonymous leaks within twenty minutes."

The screens pulsed again:

OPERATION SOVEREIGN BURN — ENGAGED

Across the world, the ripple was instantaneous. Royal courts in France, Switzerland, Hungary, and Norway ignited into scandal as exposed wealth files triggered government investigations. Private holdings were frozen. Diplomatic alliances ruptured overnight.

Media outlets, once hungry for scandal against Ben, suddenly found themselves drowning in the blood of their own sovereign sponsors.

And in the chaos — Benedict Adrian Harvick stood above them all. "They sought dirt," Ben whispered, almost amused. "Now they choke on it." Kendrick exhaled slowly, staring at his nephew with something deeper than pride. This was no longer just brilliant strategy. This was *dominion*.

"You've made them beg for mercy," Kendrick said softly. "I'm not finished," Ben answered. His voice dropped to a chilling calm, a tone that would haunt every enemy who dared whisper his name again. "Sørensen — send them the final message." Sørensen smiled grimly. "Yes, sire."

The final message flashed across every diplomatic and intelligence channel that had tried to target Ben:

TO ALL WHO WOULD THREATEN THIS HOUSE:
You sought the Harvick bloodline. You played your hand. Now feel the weight of what you disturbed.
We hold the crown. You hold nothing.
This game is finished.
*— **The House of Rosenshavn***

And as the message distributed across the world's sovereign networks, Ben stood perfectly still, eyes never blinking, as he whispered with a faint, dangerous smile: "They'll never come for us again." The storm had passed. The sovereign war had been won. The aftershock would leave scars across global royal networks for decades. And at ten years old — Benedict Adrian Harvick had become the most feared sovereign strategist the modern world had ever known.

The war room stood still. The glow from the data screens softly illuminated the stone walls as the final streams of chaos rolled across the world. The once-vocal enemies had fallen into paralysis. No more accusations. No more leaks. No more games. The world had gone silent. In that silence, sovereignty was reborn. Uncle Kendrick, His Majesty King Kendrick X, stood at the head of the chamber, watching his adopted son — no, his sovereign son — with a pride so deep it could not be measured. He stepped forward, placing his hand gently on Ben's shoulder, his voice low, strong, but filled with warmth.

"Son," Kendrick said softly, "you just sank their battleship." Ben allowed himself a small chuckle, his eyes never leaving the fading intelligence feeds still scrolling the final panicked signals across the global channels. "Good for you, son," Kendrick continued, his voice growing even steadier. "Because now — you are His Majesty King Benedict Adrian Harvick of the House of Rosenshavn.

This, son... is your war." Ben turned, his face lit by both humility and fierce resolve. For a brief moment, the sovereign mask slipped into something softer — and for the very first time, he said it:

"We'll do a lot more than that, Dad." The word hung in the air, powerful and raw — not just because it was the first time Ben had called Kendrick "Dad", but because in that one word, two sovereigns — father and son — had become one house. One crown. One unbreakable shield. Kendrick's eyes gleamed as he winked. "Understood, son." And then, in the voice of sovereign certainty, Kendrick added: "Let's do this." The circle was complete.

At Ben's right stood Isla — his partner, his promised queen — her hand never leaving his. She had stood beside him through every move, every secret, every danger, carrying the weight of his crown before it ever formally rested upon his head. At his left stood Sørensen — the man who had once sworn to defend the House — now reborn as the apprentice of the sovereign prodigy. The man who had watched, studied, and learned what sovereign warfare truly meant. And in his eyes, there was no fear — only fierce loyalty to the boy-king who now sat above the world.

The four stood together — and beyond the castle walls, the world waited in terrified silence. The House of Rosenshavn was no longer simply safe. It was absolute. Unassailable. Ben raised his eyes to the massive strategic map now glowing before them — red dots blinking across every continent, showing where the ripples of his moves had reached.

"You see it now?" Ben whispered to his inner circle. Sørensen answered first. "Yes, sire. They've stopped moving." "Because they finally understand," Kendrick added. Isla spoke softly, her voice steady, almost reverent. "They're afraid." Ben smiled faintly. "As they should be." The sovereign war was never about battles. It was about perception.

And perception was now fully his. Outside, the sovereign courts sat paralyzed. The financial markets remained in frozen stasis. The royal families whispered behind shuttered doors, afraid to move. The intelligence agencies pulled back, unwilling to trigger what none could control. For the first time in modern sovereign history — one House stood above them all.

Untouchable. The world had learned its lesson. They had poked the sovereign storm — and paid the price. And now, in their terrified silence, they watched. Ben turned to his father, his voice quiet but steel-forged. "This... is the Silence of Power." Kendrick smiled, nodding. "And it belongs to you, my king."

Ben stood taller now, not simply as a boy — but as a sovereign force. "I will protect our house. Our family. And any who dare challenge us again..." he paused, letting the weight settle into the stone walls, "...will feel the storm return." The chamber remained still, silent, sacred. The House of Rosenshavn had risen. And the sovereign world would never be the same.

It was no longer called a storm. It was now called a reckoning. The dust from Ben's sovereign lockdown had barely settled when the world's deepest underground networks — the parasites who had hunted royal families for centuries — found themselves standing naked before the law.

Their crimes had festered for decades. Selling forged genealogies. Running black-market DNA testing rings. Manipulating bloodlines to serve political agendas. Attempting to destroy sovereign houses from behind closed vaults. And for all that time, no one had ever truly stopped them. Until now. Thanks to Ben.

His operation — the master disinformation network, the sovereign lockdown, the global sting — had drawn these underground organizations into full exposure. And while they scrambled to destroy what remained of their corrupted archives, it was already too late.

Because **Interpol was watching.**

Under private coordination with the House of Rosenshavn — through sovereign channels few even knew existed — Ben's operation had quietly fed Interpol the names. The banking trails. The genetic forgeries. The money laundering routes. The hidden laboratories.

And Interpol moved swiftly.

In a single coordinated strike spanning multiple nations, hundreds of agents stormed secret facilities across Europe, the Middle East, South America, and Southeast Asia.

The arrests were staggering. By the end of the sweep:

- Seventeen sovereign-forgery networks were dismantled.
- Dozens of false genealogists and DNA manipulators were captured.
- Hundreds of terabytes of falsified data were seized.
- Entire criminal dynasties crumbled.

The world gasped. The sovereign courts fell silent. And in the centre of it all, Benedict Adrian Harvick — at just ten years old — had delivered them all into judgment. Inside the castle, Kendrick stood beside his son as the latest report arrived from Interpol's central command.

Sørensen read aloud, voice steady with pride:

INTERPOL — INTERNAL COMMUNICATION
Operation Final Extraction: COMPLETED

"The House of Rosenshavn's cooperation and strategic brilliance enabled the most comprehensive eradication of genealogical corruption ever achieved. The House's sovereign intelligence operation exceeded anything our agency could have executed alone."

The message continued: "His Majesty King Benedict Adrian Harvick's foresight, discipline, and sovereign mastery have saved millions of international investigative dollars, dismantled multiple organized crime factions, and preserved the dignity of sovereign bloodlines worldwide. We extend our deepest gratitude." A second message followed:

"We have framed your sovereign commendation letter and placed it on permanent display within Interpol Headquarters. It will remain as an eternal reminder: 'True Sovereigns protect not only their houses — but the world itself.'" As Sørensen finished reading, Kendrick exhaled slowly, his voice soft but heavy with pride. "You've done what no agency, no government, no monarch has ever done, son." Ben remained quiet for a moment, letting the weight of what they had accomplished settle.

"I didn't do it for the power," Ben said softly. "I did it because they crossed a line. They thought they could play with bloodlines — with my family. With all sovereign families. They forgot that sovereignty is not a game."

Isla squeezed his hand, her eyes glowing with admiration. "You made them remember."

Sørensen smiled. "You didn't simply stop them, sire. You *educated* them." Ben chuckled quietly. "Sometimes... you have to teach your enemies how to think." Kendrick placed his hand once again on his son's shoulder. "And now they know, son. The world knows."

The chamber settled into a sacred silence — not of fear, but of sovereign peace. The royal family stood united: Ben, Kendrick, Isla, and Sørensen — the four who had rewritten the rules of sovereign defence forever.

Beyond these walls, the enemies who once plotted in darkness now sat in prison cells — sentenced to life without parole, never to emerge again. Interpol's plaque hung proudly on their wall — not as a symbol of political favour — but as eternal recognition that when true sovereignty is threatened, there still exist those who defend it.

Benedict Adrian Harvick had shown the world that **sovereign nations do not play dirty — they play smart.**

He had saved them all. The reckoning was complete. And Denmark stood invincible.

The great hall of Denmark had not been filled like this in generations. Not for war. Not for treaties. But for a moment that would define the soul of the kingdom. Ben stood upon the elevated platform, not out of arrogance, but by tradition. The banners of the House of Rosenshavn hung silently above him. Isla stood just behind him, her hand resting softly upon his arm, never separate, never apart. Kendrick stood off to the side, his eyes steady, his heart filled with both pride and sovereign restraint. Sørensen stood behind the royal line, observant, watchful — but today, not as a guardian. Today, as family.

The hall was filled with nobles, sovereign envoys, and, most importantly — the common people. Farmers, workers, tradesmen, teachers — the lifeblood of Denmark. They had come not to hear a king dictate, but to witness what their sovereign would become. Ben looked out over the crowd, his heart calm but pounding with purpose. He was ready. Not because he was forced — but because this moment was earned.

He raised his hand gently and the hall quieted. He began, not with declarations, but with honesty. "My people of Denmark... and my family of this kingdom I love." His voice was steady, filled with warmth that no speechwriter could ever script. "I stand here before you, not because I have chased a crown — but because you have chosen to stand with me. Together, we faced enemies that sought to divide us. Together, we defended what mattered. Our families. Our bloodlines. Our very sovereignty. And I did not do this alone." He paused, turning slightly toward Isla.

"This young woman beside me — Isla — has stood with me through every battle, every sleepless night, every choice I made. She has held my hand not as a duty — but as a partner. As my queen — not because of ceremony, but because of what we share here."

Ben lightly touched his chest.

"Before I accept the full crown, I ask you — my people — to accept her. To recognize her not because of titles, but because of who she already is. She will one day become my wife — by our own promise — not by decree. But she already carries my heart, and my soul, and always has."

The hall remained silent, not in hesitation, but in awe. Ben smiled gently.

"You see, my friends — a true sovereign doesn't hide behind a throne.
We don't sit in golden chairs, staring down at you.
We walk among you.
We hear you.
We laugh with you.
We even let out thunder farts at times—"

The crowd burst into laughter — real, warm, honest.

Ben chuckled with them.

"Yes, we're human too. We eat, we work, we raise our children. Sovereignty is not a mask to wear. It is a responsibility to bear. And I promise you now — I will not rule as a distant king locked behind marble walls. I will stand among you. Listen to you. Understand your lives. Because a king who forgets his people forgets himself."

The hall now thundered with applause, some wiping their eyes, others beaming with pride. Kendrick stepped forward, smiling as he spoke to the assembly. "You have heard your king. Not only a sovereign by birth, but a sovereign by heart." He turned to Ben. "Son, by the will of Denmark, by the love of your people, by the strength of your house — you ascend today not just as King Benedict Adrian Harvick, but as our king."

The hall erupted. The thunder roared inside the walls, but it was not fear. It was love. Ben stood tall, his hand gripping Isla's, their eyes locked — as equals. As soulmates. He whispered to her alone. "We did it." She smiled back. "No, my king — you did it." But Ben knew better. "We did it." The House of Rosenshavn had risen. And now, the world no longer questioned who led it.

The celebration had roared across the castle grounds for hours after Ben's ascension, but now the night had grown calm once more. The great hall, once filled with thunderous applause and laughter, had grown quiet, lit only by the flicker of torches and the soft glow of the moonlight pouring through the tall windows.

Ben sat with Isla, Kendrick, and Sørensen at the private council table — no ministers, no advisors, no titles in play — only family. It was Isla who spoke first, as always, understanding the unspoken weight within him. "You've carried this for so long, Ben. Now it's done." Ben shook his head slightly, his voice calm. "No, love. Now it's begun." Sørensen leaned forward, sensing the shift in his king's tone. He had watched Ben win battles, dismantle enemies, and confound sovereign networks across the world. But tonight, what he heard was something purer — the philosophy that had guided every move.

Kendrick said nothing, only watching his son with quiet reverence. Ben looked at them all, speaking slowly, as if laying bare the sovereign code etched in his heart. "We were never meant to rule with fear. Fear is simple. Any tyrant can rule by fear. You don't need wisdom for that. You only need power. But power without heart is an empty throne."

His hand tightened gently around Isla's, grounding him as always. "A true sovereign must first master himself. You cannot lead if you cannot govern your own heart. And when you govern your heart, you govern your house." He paused, breathing deeply. "Sovereignty is not shouting orders across gilded halls. It's not hiding behind guards and titles. It's walking among your people. Hearing them. Laughing with them. Knowing their joys, their struggles, their stories."

Sørensen spoke quietly, his voice steady. "And when the enemies come, as they always do...?" Ben's eyes sharpened, but his voice never raised. "Then you defend what is yours with absolute clarity — but you never strike first unless forced. We don't start wars, Sørensen. We end them." He smiled faintly, his tone gaining warmth again. "And sometimes, when the people least expect it... you remind them that even kings can laugh. That even sovereigns can still joke about thunder farts."

Isla giggled softly, squeezing his hand. Sørensen chuckled, shaking his head. Even Kendrick allowed himself to laugh. "My king," Kendrick said warmly, "the world has never seen a sovereign like you." Ben's eyes softened. "And they never will again, Dad. Because our people don't need perfect kings. They need honest ones. Sovereigns who see them not as subjects, but as family."

Kendrick exhaled slowly, as if releasing years of silent hope he had carried for this very moment. "You are that king, son." Sørensen raised his glass. "And you've taught even me, sire." "You've all taught me," Ben replied. "Every one of you." For a while, they simply sat in that stillness, breathing in the peace they had fought so fiercely to secure. No more enemies knocking on their gates. No more threats hiding in shadows. The world was silent — not because it was conquered — but because it had been tamed by wisdom.

After some time, Ben leaned back, glancing playfully at Kendrick. "Now, Dad... I believe a certain vacation has been long overdue." Kendrick smiled, raising an eyebrow. "You're actually going to allow yourself to step away from all of this, son?" Ben grinned. "That's the plan." He turned to Sørensen with a grin growing across his face. "And Sørensen... this time, remember: it's vacation." Sørensen gave a mock salute. "Understood, sire. Vacation. Not work." Ben's eyes sparkled. "Good. I meant it. Twice." The four of them laughed — not as royals, not as guards, not as rulers. But as family.

The morning broke early in the castle, as the first light painted soft golden streaks across the high windows. Sørensen was already awake, as always, seated quietly in the corner of the grand kitchen, sipping his first cup of black coffee. The stillness of the early hours suited him — the calm before duties called. From the upper floors, quiet stirring began. The rhythm of a familiar routine. Ben was the first to rise, his eyes blinking open gently. Beside him, Isla stirred as well, yawning softly, their bodies naturally synchronizing as they always did.

As they sat up, Ben chuckled lightly. "Bladder chatter." Isla giggled in agreement. The two slipped out of bed and padded toward their oversized sovereign bathroom — a design unique to them: two toilets, side by side, deliberately installed with a quiet humour that only they truly appreciated.

Side by side they sat, taking care of morning business without the slightest hesitation. Privacy, for them, was never a barrier. With the 'bladder chatter' officially resolved, they made their way downstairs to the kitchen where Sørensen was quietly waiting.

"Morning," Ben said softly, grabbing his own cup of coffee. "Morning, Your Majesty," Sørensen nodded, smiling faintly. "Though I'm starting to think you two invented mornings solely to torment me." Isla grinned, taking her coffee as well. They sat together, enjoying their breakfast as the light poured in. As they finished, faint sounds filtered through the tall windows — the echo of children's laughter. Soccer balls being kicked. Voices rising with excitement. Ben listened for a moment and then smiled.

"You hear that?" he asked. "Children outside. I think it's time we go be kids for once." Isla chuckled. "You're always a kid at heart." "Not always," Ben grinned. "But I do miss the simplicity sometimes." Sørensen snorted softly, a rare unfiltered sound from the usually composed man. "Kids for once? You've been locked inside a sovereign war for how long now? Go on, Your Majesty. I think you've earned a bit of childhood." Ben beamed, finished his coffee, and stood. "Permission granted, sweetheart?" he asked Isla with a wink. "Granted, my king," she laughed.

Ben made his way outside, where a group of boys and girls had already gathered on the wide castle lawn, playing soccer in the crisp morning air. As soon as they saw him, the children froze in awe. "Hey!" Ben waved. "Mind if I join?" The children stammered for a moment before one of the older boys grinned nervously. "Of course, Your Majesty!" "Ben," he corrected them with a smile. "Just Ben, while we're playing." Within moments, Ben was running alongside them, dribbling the ball, passing, laughing — a king fully at home among his people. The children couldn't contain themselves. They had never imagined their king would come outside to play alongside them like any other boy.

Word spread like wildfire throughout the village and beyond. News ran through every corner of the city: The King is playing soccer with the children. As the game ended, Ben gathered the group together, breathing lightly from the exercise. "That was fun," he said, grinning. "Next time you're playing, don't be shy — come knock on my door. I'll join anytime." The children laughed, nodding eagerly. "By the way," Ben added, his voice lowering slightly, "I'm heading home to Kent, England for a few weeks — just a little vacation, that's all. Keep it quiet, though, alright? But if anyone asks, you may let them know we'll be gone for two weeks." "Yes, Your Majesty!" they answered in unison.

"Thank you," Ben said. "And great game. Boys and girls — you're all champions." Isla soon joined him outside, but her attention was drawn toward a small girl standing quietly on the side — no more than seven or eight years old. Isla walked gently toward her, kneeling down. "Hello there," Isla smiled warmly. "What's your name?" "Clara," the girl answered shyly. "C-l-a-r-a." Isla's eyes softened. "That's my mother's name too. It's a beautiful name." "Thank you, Your Majesty." "Just Isla," she smiled, gently brushing Clara's hair back. "May I meet your parents?" Clara nodded, leading Isla back to her family.

Soon Kendrick joined them as well, and as introductions were made, the quiet truth emerged. Clara's father had recently lost his job. The family was struggling. Not from failure, but from cruel circumstance. Kendrick reviewed the documents presented by the employer. It was clear: bankruptcy was imminent for the company.

Kendrick's eyes darkened slightly. "No man willing to work should ever be cast aside because of someone else's collapse," Kendrick said firmly. Turning to Clara's father, Mr. Nielsen, Kendrick extended his hand. "I have an offer for you." "Sir?" Nielsen asked, nearly breathless.

"We have an opening at the castle for a groundskeeper. Full-time. No games. No traps. A real position. And you'll have time to spend with Clara. She may visit the castle anytime." The man stood in stunned silence, overwhelmed. "I... I don't know what to say," he stammered. "Then say yes," Kendrick smiled. "Yes, Your Majesty. Yes. Thank you." Kendrick nodded. "We'll finalize everything when I return. For now, enjoy these next weeks. When I return from Kent, I'll come to your home. We'll share coffee. We'll talk. You and I — kitchen table. Man to man." Tears welled in Nielsen's eyes as he tried to compose himself. "I... I would be honoured, sir."

Kendrick's voice lowered, taking a softer, more personal tone as he reached into his coat and drew forth a small sealed envelope — bearing not the royal crest, but his own private seal. No ministers. No bureaucracy. Just one man speaking to another. "Mr. Nielsen," Kendrick said gently, placing the envelope into his hand, "while we are away for these next weeks, I do not want you or your family to worry for even a single moment. This is not part of your salary. This is not charity. This is my personal gift — from one father to another. To ensure your home remains warm, your table remains full, and your dignity remains untouched. You have nothing to prove to me except your willingness to accept this small measure of peace until we return."

Mr. Nielsen looked down, his hands trembling slightly, unable to speak as his throat tightened. For a long moment, he said nothing — but the tears in his eyes carried more than words ever could. "Thank you, Your Majesty... I..." He paused, forcing himself to steady. "Thank you for seeing me — not just my need — but me." Kendrick placed a firm hand on his shoulder. "Always. That is what a sovereign is meant to do." Ben smiled softly. "We'll see you soon, Mr. Nielsen. And Clara, you'll always have a place here."

As the sun continued to rise, the family returned inside to prepare for their departure. Bags were packed. Final calls made. Plans secured. And at last, standing upon the royal tarmac, their sovereign aircraft waited. Kendrick glanced at his son, Isla, and Sørensen. "Well, my family... let's go home for a little while." Ben smiled, gripping Isla's hand gently. "Time for vacation." The engines roared to life as the aircraft ascended into the morning sky, cutting clean through the clouds, headed for Kent. The world below grew smaller. But the House of Rosenshavn remained sovereign — above all.

The sovereign jet sliced smoothly through the high cloud cover, its engines humming softly as the coastline of England emerged beneath them. Even after countless political trips across Europe, this one felt entirely different.

There were no press vans parked by the terminal. No security barricades. No paparazzi lenses chasing the royal motorcade. No frantic officials running up with documents in hand. Just quiet. The silence was, at first, strange. Foreign, even. But everyone aboard knew exactly why it was happening. Sørensen glanced out the window, noting the lack of escorts along the airfield as the plane gently descended toward Heathrow. No crowds. No disturbances. "It's eerie, isn't it?" he finally said, speaking to Kendrick quietly as the jet's wheels touched down.

"Eerie?" Kendrick repeated, smiling faintly. "No. It's refreshing." Ben chuckled from his seat behind them, sipping his tea. "They finally learned." Isla leaned gently into him. "You mean they finally fear you." Ben shook his head softly. "They finally respect boundaries." The aircraft taxied to its private hangar, where a simple convoy of discreet vehicles waited. No state escorts. No security caravans. No flashing cameras. The driver, a trusted family steward from Kent, greeted them with nothing more than a respectful nod. "Welcome home, Your... well..." The man paused, smiling nervously.

Ben raised his hand, already anticipating the hesitation. "No titles, Joseph. Not here. Not for the next few weeks. Just Ben." "Yes, sir," Joseph smiled. "Ben it is." The convoy pulled away from Heathrow, slipping quietly onto the motorway. As they crossed into Kent's rolling countryside, the air shifted — a softness filling their lungs, a kind of calm that no throne room ever offered.

The familiar roads curled around ancient hedgerows and farmlands. The homes here didn't boast of sovereign wealth. They whispered of history, of simplicity, of life. They soon reached the hidden turnoff — the narrow country road that led toward the private family cottages. Tucked beyond the woods, unseen from the public lanes, these cottages stood as they always had: private sanctuaries where the Harvick family became simply themselves.

As the cars came to a stop, Ben stepped out and stretched his arms wide, inhaling deeply. "Now this is vacation." Isla joined him, smiling as she admired the familiar cottage roofs peeking through the trees. The world's storms, battles, and sovereign wars faded into distant echoes. Sørensen climbed out behind them, scanning the perimeter as his instincts flared — though he quickly reminded himself: this is vacation. Ben caught the slight furrow in Sørensen's brow.

"Hey," Ben called out playfully. "Remember what we agreed." "Vacation," Sørensen repeated, breathing deeply. "I know. Vacation. Not work." Ben grinned. "Say it twice. For insurance." Sørensen chuckled softly, exhaling. "Vacation. Vacation." Kendrick joined them, placing a hand on his son's shoulder. "Well, my family... enjoy it. No titles. No crowns. No threats. Just time." For the first time in months — perhaps years — there were no decisions to make, no enemies to track, no alliances to manage. Just quiet mornings, soft sunsets, and the gentle rhythm of life.

As they walked up toward the cottages, the birds sang above them, the trees swayed gently, and for once, the king, the queen-to-be, the sovereign father, and the watchful guardian — were simply people. Not rulers. Not strategists. Just family.

The world could wait. The cottage sat in its familiar silence, but inside its private study — tucked behind a concealed panel — lay one of the family's most precious sanctuaries: the Harvick Archives. It wasn't grand like the state libraries of Europe, nor glittering like royal museums. It was simple. Humble in appearance. But to those who knew what rested within these walls, it was one of the most sacred genealogical vaults on earth.

Bound leather volumes filled every shelf — thick, worn, lovingly handled. Parchment scrolls, delicate maps, handwritten journals, family chronicles, correspondence stretching across generations. This was where kings studied. Where sovereign knowledge lived. Sørensen followed Ben and Isla into the room, his eyes immediately widening. Though his life had been spent guarding sovereign secrets, even he was unprepared for the sight before him. "My God," Sørensen whispered. "I've never seen a library like this before."

Ben smiled, hearing the awe in his voice. "Yeah. I get that a lot." He ran his hand gently along the binding of one of the older tomes. "Some of these books are older than most kingdoms still standing," Ben added. "Though… not literally a thousand years old. I know that's what you're thinking." Sørensen chuckled. "You caught me." "But they've been here long enough to feel ancient," Ben continued. "Isla and I have gone through most of these three… sometimes four times. Each."

Sørensen blinked, turning toward him in surprise. "Each?" "Oh yes," Isla chimed in with a soft smile. "Sometimes we'd spend entire weekends here. Reading. Studying. Cross-referencing maps, journals, bloodlines. The kind of stuff historians would fight over." Ben laughed, recalling their long days. "We'd start after breakfast and sometimes not even notice when it got dark outside. Hours would pass. Then we'd both fall asleep right here with books still open in our laps."

Sørensen glanced around slowly, taking in the weight of their private sanctuary. "No wonder you two know so much," he said quietly. "No wonder you were able to outthink them all. You didn't just study to prepare for war — you studied because you loved it." Ben smiled at him, eyes gleaming with sincerity. "That's exactly right, buddy. Sovereignty isn't just birthright. It's what you choose to understand. What you choose to carry. These aren't just stories. They're our bloodlines. Our mistakes. Our victories. Our history."

Sørensen stood there, silently respecting the immense discipline these two had poured into their lives long before titles ever entered the picture. "You know," he said finally, "historians would do anything to get their hands on this." Ben nodded. "Which is exactly why they never will." "Sacred ground," Sørensen added. "Exactly," Isla said softly. "This isn't for public curiosity. This is our family's soul." Sørensen smiled, turning to both of them with deep respect. "I've guarded sovereigns for decades. Protected bloodlines, defended secrets, risked my life for Houses that barely know my name." He paused. "But I can tell you something with absolute certainty: there is no House on this planet like yours."

Ben looked at him, his voice warm. "Thanks, buddy." Sørensen chuckled, patting him gently on the shoulder. "Anytime, my friend." The three stood there for a moment, not as sovereigns and guards, but as kindred spirits — sharing in the quiet legacy of generations.

For Ben, this was peace. For Sørensen, this was revelation. For Isla, this was home. And beyond these cottage walls, the world remained still — not because it had forgotten them, but because it finally understood not to disturb them.

The days in Kent flowed like a quiet river, gentle and uninterrupted. The cottage stood nestled beneath tall trees, the early morning sun slicing its rays through the gaps in the leaves. Birds sang softly as a breeze carried the sweet smell of earth and grass. For the first time in months, there were no political whispers, no intelligence reports, no coded transmissions flashing across secret screens. Just the simple rhythm of life.

In the cool of one such morning, as the family gathered after breakfast, Ben leaned forward across the oak dining table where Sørensen sat finishing his coffee. Isla was beside him, her arm gently linked with Ben's as always, her smile as soft as the morning itself. The casual conversation paused as Ben's eyes met Sørensen's with an unexpected glint of purpose. "Sørensen," Ben began, his voice calm but carrying a hint of quiet invitation, "there's something Isla and I have discussed." Sørensen lifted his brow slightly, curious, waiting.

"If you ever want to," Ben continued, "we'd like to offer you something. We can do your chart. Your full genealogy." He paused for a moment, as if measuring the weight of what he offered. "We can trace your family, your name, your roots. No questions. No strings. If you ever choose to know where you came from, we'll do it for you. Thoroughly. Honestly."

The words settled gently into the space between them, but their meaning was far heavier than the air itself. Sørensen sat perfectly still for a moment, his cup resting halfway between his hand and his mouth. His eyes blinked softly, the offer sinking into him fully.

He exhaled slowly, not from hesitation, but from the unexpected weight of being seen. Truly seen.

"I… I don't know what to say," he finally managed, his voice steady but touched with a quiet awe. "That's an offer I never expected."

"You're family," Isla said gently, as though stating something obvious. "You've always been family to us."

Sørensen swallowed hard. He had spent most of his life in service to sovereign houses, protecting bloodlines, defending heirs, standing silently in the background of powerful people. But in all his years, no one had ever turned toward him like this — not as a protector, but as one of their own.

He glanced around the table as Kendrick—known simply as Ken during these peaceful family retreats—sat back with a warm, knowing smile. Ben's chosen father Jeff, his mother Annemarie, Isla's father Robert, and her mother Claire—all were gathered here now, not as royal extensions, but as one seamless family. The lines between blood and bond no longer mattered. Here, in this cottage tucked into the Kent countryside, titles held no power. Love did.

"You're protecting more than royals, Sørensen," Ben added softly. "You've always protected family."

The old operative finally smiled, eyes moist with quiet gratitude. "Then I accept."

Ben nodded, his face lighting with an ease few had seen on him in the months of war and strategy. "When we get back home, we'll start. I promise you—we'll find every branch."

"Thank you," Sørensen whispered. "Truly."

From there, the days unfolded into simple, beautiful routines that none of them took for granted. Morning coffees were followed by long walks through the sprawling estate grounds, where the air was cool and sweet beneath the tall oaks. Sometimes, the entire family would walk the distance into the nearby town, dressed casually—just jeans, T-shirts, and sneakers. To the passing townsfolk, they were merely another family enjoying the warmth of late summer, and no one looked twice.

Kendrick himself was especially amused by how easily anonymity settled on him when the heavy layers of royalty were peeled away. Even strolling into the local library, he passed unnoticed, running his fingers along shelves of old English literature, blending in among university students and retirees browsing dusty volumes. There was something freeing in it. Something rare. For once, he was not King Kendrick X. He was simply Ken.

For Isla, anonymity was a little harder. More than once, she was recognized by villagers who had seen her face before. But even then, people treated her with respect rather than intrusion. No crowds formed, no photos were requested, and no one whispered behind her back. It was as though Kent itself understood the weight she carried and chose to honour it through quiet dignity.

Ben, for his part, suspected the news of what had unfolded in Denmark had traveled far enough. The media may not have printed it, but word-of-mouth traveled quickly in sovereign circles. And perhaps that was why they were left in peace. Perhaps the world finally understood that even kings need rest.

Evenings brought laughter. The family would gather around the oversized dining table for warm meals, sharing stories of childhood, playing light-hearted games, debating over ancient maps and family records, and, always, plenty of coffee. Jeff and Annemarie would sit side-by-side, their laughter blending effortlessly with Robert and Claire's, while Kendrick leaned back in his chair, proud to watch the world he had fought so hard to protect finally breathe.

For Sørensen, these nights were especially profound. He found himself drawn not just to the comfort of security, but to the intimacy of family dinners, where no one spoke of titles, duties, or wars. They spoke instead of books, of recipes, of silly childhood memories, of Isla's garden ideas and Ben's latest historical curiosities.

It was peace—not temporary, but deliberate. Chosen.

As the evening stars crept over the Kent sky and the cottage windows glowed softly from within, it was clear to them all: the war had ended long ago, but now the healing had truly begun.

They were no longer simply sovereigns.

They were home.

The morning broke early in the castle, as the first light painted soft golden streaks across the high windows. Sørensen was already awake, as always, seated quietly in the corner of the grand kitchen, sipping his first cup of black coffee. The stillness of the early hours suited him — the calm before duties called. From the upper floors, quiet stirring began. The rhythm of a familiar routine. Ben was the first to rise, his eyes blinking open gently. Beside him, Isla stirred as well, yawning softly, their bodies naturally synchronizing as they always did.

As they sat up, Ben chuckled lightly. "Bladder chatter." Isla giggled in agreement. The two slipped out of bed and padded toward their oversized sovereign bathroom — a design unique to them: two toilets, side by side, deliberately installed with a quiet humour that only they truly appreciated. Side by side they sat, taking care of morning business without the slightest hesitation. Privacy, for them, was never a barrier. With the 'bladder chatter' officially resolved, they made their way downstairs to the kitchen where Sørensen was quietly waiting.

"Morning," Ben said softly, grabbing his own cup of coffee. "Morning, Your Majesty," Sørensen nodded, smiling faintly. "Though I'm starting to think you two invented mornings solely to torment me." Isla grinned, taking her coffee as well. They sat together, enjoying their breakfast as the light poured in. As they finished, faint sounds filtered through the tall windows — the echo of children's laughter. Soccer balls being kicked. Voices rising with excitement. Ben listened for a moment and then smiled.

"You hear that?" he asked. "Children outside. I think it's time we go be kids for once." Isla chuckled. "You're always a kid at heart." "Not always," Ben grinned. "But I do miss the simplicity sometimes." Sørensen snorted softly, a rare unfiltered sound from the usually composed man. "Kids for once? You've been locked inside a sovereign war for how long now? Go on, Your Majesty. I think you've earned a bit of childhood." Ben beamed, finished his coffee, and stood. "Permission granted, sweetheart?" he asked Isla with a wink. "Granted, my king," she laughed.

Ben made his way outside, where a group of boys and girls had already gathered on the wide castle lawn, playing soccer in the crisp morning air. As soon as they saw him, the children froze in awe. "Hey!" Ben waved. "Mind if I join?" The children stammered for a moment before one of the older boys grinned nervously. "Of course, Your Majesty!" "Ben," he corrected them with a smile. "Just Ben, while we're playing." Within moments, Ben was running alongside them, dribbling the ball, passing, laughing — a king fully at home among his people. The children couldn't contain themselves. They had never imagined their king would come outside to play alongside them like any other boy.

Word spread like wildfire throughout the village and beyond. News ran through every corner of the city: The King is playing soccer with the children. As the game ended, Ben gathered the group together, breathing lightly from the exercise. "That was fun," he said, grinning. "Next time you're playing, don't be shy — come knock on my door. I'll join anytime." The children laughed, nodding eagerly. "By the way," Ben added, his voice lowering slightly, "I'm heading home to Kent, England for a few weeks — just a little vacation, that's all. Keep it quiet, though, alright? But if anyone asks, you may let them know we'll be gone for two weeks." "Yes, Your Majesty!" they answered in unison.

"Thank you," Ben said. "And great game. Boys and girls — you're all champions." Isla soon joined him outside, but her attention was drawn toward a small girl standing quietly on the side — no more than seven or eight years old. Isla walked gently toward her, kneeling down. "Hello there," Isla smiled warmly. "What's your name?" "Clara," the girl answered shyly. "C-l-a-r-a." Isla's eyes softened. "That's my mother's name too. It's a beautiful name." "Thank you, Your Majesty." "Just Isla," she smiled, gently brushing Clara's hair back. "May I meet your parents?" Clara nodded, leading Isla back to her family.

Soon Kendrick joined them as well, and as introductions were made, the quiet truth emerged. Clara's father had recently lost his job. The family was struggling. Not from failure, but from cruel circumstance. Kendrick reviewed the documents presented by the employer. It was clear: bankruptcy was imminent for the company. Kendrick's eyes darkened slightly. "No man willing to work should ever be cast aside because of someone else's collapse," Kendrick said firmly. Turning to Clara's father, Mr. Nielsen, Kendrick extended his hand. "I have an offer for you." "Sir?" Nielsen asked, nearly breathless.

"We have an opening at the castle for a groundskeeper. Full-time. No games. No traps. A real position. And you'll have time to spend with Clara. She may visit the castle anytime." The man stood in stunned silence, overwhelmed. "I... I don't know what to say," he stammered. "Then say yes," Kendrick smiled.

"Yes, Your Majesty. Yes. Thank you." Kendrick nodded. "We'll finalize everything when I return. For now, enjoy these next weeks. When I return from Kent, I'll come to your home. We'll share coffee. We'll talk. You and I — kitchen table. Man to man." Tears welled in Nielsen's eyes as he tried to compose himself. "I... I would be honoured, sir."

Kendrick's voice lowered, taking a softer, more personal tone as he reached into his coat and drew forth a small sealed envelope — bearing not the royal crest, but his own private seal. No ministers. No bureaucracy. Just one man speaking to another. "Mr. Nielsen," Kendrick said gently, placing the envelope into his hand, "while we are away for these next weeks, I do not want you or your family to worry for even a single moment. This is not part of your salary. This is not charity. This is my personal gift — from one father to another. To ensure your home remains warm, your table remains full, and your dignity remains untouched. You have nothing to prove to me except your willingness to accept this small measure of peace until we return."

Mr. Nielsen looked down, his hands trembling slightly, unable to speak as his throat tightened. For a long moment, he said nothing — but the tears in his eyes carried more than words ever could. "Thank you, Your Majesty... I..." He paused, forcing himself to steady. "Thank you for seeing me — not just my need — but me." Kendrick placed a firm hand on his shoulder. "Always. That is what a sovereign is meant to do." Ben smiled softly. "We'll see you soon, Mr. Nielsen. And Clara, you'll always have a place here."

As the sun continued to rise, the family returned inside to prepare for their departure. Bags were packed. Final calls made. Plans secured. And at last, standing upon the royal tarmac, their sovereign aircraft waited. Kendrick glanced at his son, Isla, and Sørensen. "Well, my family... let's go home for a little while." Ben smiled, gripping Isla's hand gently. "Time for vacation." The engines roared to life as the aircraft ascended into the morning sky, cutting clean through the clouds, headed for Kent. The world below grew smaller. But the House of Rosenshavn remained sovereign — above all.

The sovereign jet sliced smoothly through the high cloud cover, its engines humming softly as the coastline of England emerged beneath them. Even after countless political trips across Europe, this one felt entirely different.

There were no press vans parked by the terminal. No security barricades. No paparazzi lenses chasing the royal motorcade. No frantic officials running up with documents in hand. Just quiet. The silence was, at first, strange. Foreign, even. But everyone aboard knew exactly why it was happening.

Sørensen glanced out the window, noting the lack of escorts along the airfield as the plane gently descended toward Heathrow. No crowds. No disturbances. "It's eerie, isn't it?" he finally said, speaking to Kendrick quietly as the jet's wheels touched down.

"Eerie?" Kendrick repeated, smiling faintly. "No. It's refreshing." Ben chuckled from his seat behind them, sipping his tea. "They finally learned." Isla leaned gently into him. "You mean they finally fear you." Ben shook his head softly. "They finally respect boundaries." The aircraft taxied to its private hangar, where a simple convoy of discreet vehicles waited. No state escorts. No security caravans. No flashing cameras. The driver, a trusted family steward from Kent, greeted them with nothing more than a respectful nod. "Welcome home, Your... well..." The man paused, smiling nervously.

Ben raised his hand, already anticipating the hesitation. "No titles, Joseph. Not here. Not for the next few weeks. Just Ben." "Yes, sir," Joseph smiled. "Ben it is." The convoy pulled away from Heathrow, slipping quietly onto the motorway. As they crossed into Kent's rolling countryside, the air shifted — a softness filling their lungs, a kind of calm that no throne room ever offered.

The familiar roads curled around ancient hedgerows and farmlands. The homes here didn't boast of sovereign wealth. They whispered of history, of simplicity, of life. They soon reached the hidden turnoff — the narrow country road that led toward the private family cottages. Tucked beyond the woods, unseen from the public lanes, these cottages stood as they always had: private sanctuaries where the Harvick family became simply themselves.

As the cars came to a stop, Ben stepped out and stretched his arms wide, inhaling deeply. "Now this is vacation." Isla joined him, smiling as she admired the familiar cottage roofs peeking through the trees. The world's storms, battles, and sovereign wars faded into distant echoes. Sørensen climbed out behind them, scanning the perimeter as his instincts flared — though he quickly reminded himself: this is vacation. Ben caught the slight furrow in Sørensen's brow.

"Hey," Ben called out playfully. "Remember what we agreed." "Vacation," Sørensen repeated, breathing deeply. "I know. Vacation. Not work." Ben grinned. "Say it twice. For insurance." Sørensen chuckled softly, exhaling. "Vacation. Vacation." Kendrick joined them, placing a hand on his son's shoulder. "Well, my family... enjoy it. No titles. No crowns. No threats. Just time." For the first time in months — perhaps years — there were no decisions to make, no enemies to track, no alliances to manage. Just quiet mornings, soft sunsets, and the gentle rhythm of life.

As they walked up toward the cottages, the birds sang above them, the trees swayed gently, and for once, the king, the queen-to-be, the sovereign father, and the watchful guardian — were simply people. Not rulers. Not strategists. Just family. The world could wait. The cottage sat in its familiar silence, but inside its private study — tucked behind a concealed panel — lay one of the family's most precious sanctuaries: the Harvick Archives. It wasn't grand like the state libraries of Europe, nor glittering like royal museums. It was simple. Humble in appearance. But to those who knew what rested within these walls, it was one of the most sacred genealogical vaults on earth.

Bound leather volumes filled every shelf — thick, worn, lovingly handled. Parchment scrolls, delicate maps, handwritten journals, family chronicles, correspondence stretching across generations. This was where kings studied. Where sovereign knowledge lived. Sørensen followed Ben and Isla into the room, his eyes immediately widening. Though his life had been spent guarding sovereign secrets, even he was unprepared for the sight before him. "My God," Sørensen whispered. "I've never seen a library like this before."

Ben smiled, hearing the awe in his voice. "Yeah. I get that a lot." He ran his hand gently along the binding of one of the older tomes. "Some of these books are older than most kingdoms still standing," Ben added. "Though... not literally a thousand years old. I know that's what you're thinking." Sørensen chuckled. "You caught me." "But they've been here long enough to feel ancient," Ben continued. "Isla and I have gone through most of these three... sometimes four times. Each."

Sørensen blinked, turning toward him in surprise. "Each?" "Oh yes," Isla chimed in with a soft smile. "Sometimes we'd spend entire weekends here. Reading. Studying. Cross-referencing maps, journals, bloodlines. The kind of stuff historians would fight over." Ben laughed, recalling their long days. "We'd start after breakfast and sometimes not even notice when it got dark outside. Hours would pass. Then we'd both fall asleep right here with books still open in our laps."

Sørensen glanced around slowly, taking in the weight of their private sanctuary. "No wonder you two know so much," he said quietly. "No wonder you were able to outthink them all. You didn't just study to prepare for war — you studied because you loved it." Ben smiled at him, eyes gleaming with sincerity.

"That's exactly right, buddy. Sovereignty isn't just birthright. It's what you choose to understand. What you choose to carry. These aren't just stories. They're our bloodlines. Our mistakes. Our victories. Our history."

Sørensen stood there, silently respecting the immense discipline these two had poured into their lives long before titles ever entered the picture. "You know," he said finally, "historians would do anything to get their hands on this." Ben nodded. "Which is exactly why they never will." "Sacred ground," Sørensen added. "Exactly," Isla said softly. "This isn't for public curiosity. This is our family's soul." Sørensen smiled, turning to both of them with deep respect. "I've guarded sovereigns for decades. Protected bloodlines, defended secrets, risked my life for Houses that barely know my name." He paused. "But I can tell you something with absolute certainty: there is no House on this planet like yours."

Ben looked at him, his voice warm. "Thanks, buddy." Sørensen chuckled, patting him gently on the shoulder. "Anytime, my friend." The three stood there for a moment, not as sovereigns and guards, but as kindred spirits — sharing in the quiet legacy of generations. For Ben, this was peace. For Sørensen, this was revelation. For Isla, this was home. And beyond these cottage walls, the world remained still — not because it had forgotten them, but because it finally understood not to disturb them.

The days in Kent flowed like a quiet river, gentle and uninterrupted. The cottage stood nestled beneath tall trees, the early morning sun slicing its rays through the gaps in the leaves. Birds sang softly as a breeze carried the sweet smell of earth and grass. For the first time in months, there were no political whispers, no intelligence reports, no coded transmissions flashing across secret screens. Just the simple rhythm of life.

In the cool of one such morning, as the family gathered after breakfast, Ben leaned forward across the oak dining table where Sørensen sat finishing his coffee. Isla was beside him, her arm gently linked with Ben's as always, her smile as soft as the morning itself. The casual conversation paused as Ben's eyes met Sørensen's with an unexpected glint of purpose. "Sørensen," Ben began, his voice calm but carrying a hint of quiet invitation, "there's something Isla and I have discussed." Sørensen lifted his brow slightly, curious, waiting.

"If you ever want to," Ben continued, "we'd like to offer you something. We can do your chart. Your full genealogy." He paused for a moment, as if measuring the weight of what he offered. "We can trace your family, your name, your roots. No questions. No strings. If you ever choose to know where you came from, we'll do it for you. Thoroughly. Honestly." The words settled gently into the space between them, but their meaning was far heavier than the air itself. Sørensen sat perfectly still for a moment, his cup resting halfway between his hand and his mouth. His eyes blinked softly, the offer sinking into him fully.

He exhaled slowly, not from hesitation, but from the unexpected weight of being seen. Truly seen.

"I… I don't know what to say," he finally managed, his voice steady but touched with a quiet awe. "That's an offer I never expected."

"You're family," Isla said gently, as though stating something obvious. "You've always been family to us."

Sørensen swallowed hard. He had spent most of his life in service to sovereign houses, protecting bloodlines, defending heirs, standing silently in the background of powerful people. But in all his years, no one had ever turned toward him like this — not as a protector, but as one of their own.

He glanced around the table as Kendrick—known simply as Ken during these peaceful family retreats—sat back with a warm, knowing smile. Ben's chosen father Jeff, his mother Annemarie, Isla's father Robert, and her mother Claire—all were gathered here now, not as royal extensions, but as one seamless family. The lines between blood and bond no longer mattered. Here, in this cottage tucked into the Kent countryside, titles held no power. Love did.

"You're protecting more than royals, Sørensen," Ben added softly. "You've always protected family."

The old operative finally smiled, eyes moist with quiet gratitude. "Then I accept."

Ben nodded, his face lighting with an ease few had seen on him in the months of war and strategy. "When we get back home, we'll start. I promise you—we'll find every branch."

"Thank you," Sørensen whispered. "Truly."

From there, the days unfolded into simple, beautiful routines that none of them took for granted. Morning coffees were followed by long walks through the sprawling estate grounds, where the air was cool and sweet beneath the tall oaks.

Sometimes, the entire family would walk the distance into the nearby town, dressed casually—just jeans, T-shirts, and sneakers. To the passing townsfolk, they were merely another family enjoying the warmth of late summer, and no one looked twice.

Kendrick himself was especially amused by how easily anonymity settled on him when the heavy layers of royalty were peeled away. Even strolling into the local library, he passed unnoticed, running his fingers along shelves of old English literature, blending in among university students and retirees browsing dusty volumes. There was something freeing in it. Something rare. For once, he was not King Kendrick X. He was simply Ken.

For Isla, anonymity was a little harder. More than once, she was recognized by villagers who had seen her face before. But even then, people treated her with respect rather than intrusion. No crowds formed, no photos were requested, and no one whispered behind her back. It was as though Kent itself understood the weight she carried and chose to honour it through quiet dignity.

Ben, for his part, suspected the news of what had unfolded in Denmark had traveled far enough. The media may not have printed it, but word-of-mouth traveled quickly in sovereign circles. And perhaps that was why they were left in peace. Perhaps the world finally understood that even kings need rest.

Evenings brought laughter. The family would gather around the oversized dining table for warm meals, sharing stories of childhood, playing light-hearted games, debating over ancient maps and family records, and, always, plenty of coffee. Jeff and Annemarie would sit side-by-side, their laughter blending effortlessly with Robert and Claire's, while Kendrick leaned back in his chair, proud to watch the world he had fought so hard to protect finally breathe.

For Sørensen, these nights were especially profound. He found himself drawn not just to the comfort of security, but to the intimacy of family dinners, where no one spoke of titles, duties, or wars. They spoke instead of books, of recipes, of silly childhood memories, of Isla's garden ideas and Ben's latest historical curiosities.

It was peace—not temporary, but deliberate. Chosen.

As the evening stars crept over the Kent sky and the cottage windows glowed softly from within, it was clear to them all: the war had ended long ago, but now the healing had truly begun.

They were no longer simply sovereigns.
They were home.

The last few days of their stay in Kent had unfolded gently, as though even time itself understood the delicacy of what was approaching. The family dinners continued, full of laughter and quiet conversations that stretched late into the evening. They walked the gardens in the soft afternoons, sipping coffee beneath the great oak trees that lined the estate's edge.

But beneath the calm, something heavier hung in the air—unspoken but deeply felt.

Ben sensed it most of all. He had seen it in Jeff's eyes for days now: a certain distance that wasn't cold, but quietly reflective. Jeff was thinking. Debating. Wrestling with something that his son could feel but not fully grasp yet. And though the others around them remained content in the serenity of these days, Ben could not rest. Not entirely. Not until he understood what was weighing on his father's mind.

The morning was quiet when Ben finally spoke. The sun filtered lazily through the curtains as father and son sat alone in the small reading room off the library. The others were out for their walk; Sørensen had taken Isla and Annemarie into town, while Kendrick remained quietly reading beneath the trees. Ben had asked for this moment, just the two of them, knowing it could not wait any longer.

Jeff sat opposite him, coffee in hand, eyes tracing the swirling patterns of steam, avoiding his son's gaze for as long as he could manage. "Dad," Ben said softly, using the word he always had — not because of titles, but because of truth. "We need to talk." Jeff finally looked up, offering a tired smile that could not hide the weight behind it. "I know, son." There was no anger in Ben's voice, but there was ache. "You've been thinking about staying here."

Jeff exhaled slowly, nodding. "Yes." For a moment, the room held nothing but silence. The kind of silence where hearts speak louder than words. "You're my dad," Ben continued quietly. "You've always been my dad. Long before all of this. Before Kendrick. Before crowns. Before wars. You were there. When I was five... you were my world." His voice trembled, but he steadied it. "You still are." Jeff placed his cup gently on the small table between them. His voice, too, was unsteady. "And you will always be my son, Ben. That will never change."

"Then why?" Ben whispered, blinking back the tears he refused to let fall. "Why are you thinking about staying here? Why not come back with us? With me?" Jeff leaned forward, resting his elbows on his knees, his hands clasped tightly together.
"Ben... you know where my life has always been rooted. My work... my archives... my research... it's here. This is my place. My calling has always been to preserve history, to study it, to document it. Not to live it in the centre of power."

"You wouldn't be living in power," Ben said. "You'd be living with your family."

Jeff shook his head gently. "But you are power now, son. Whether you like it or not. You sit on a throne that commands more than any of us ever imagined. And while I will always be your father, I am not built for that world. You have Kendrick. You have Annemarie. You have Isla. You have a family in Denmark. I... I don't want to be the man who lives in your shadow."

Ben's heart cracked as he listened, fighting the sting behind his eyes. "But, Dad," he said softly, "you're not in my shadow. You're my foundation. Without you… none of this would exist." Jeff's voice softened further, his own eyes moistening. "And I will always be here. This cottage is still part of your world. My door will always be open. But son… I need to stay where I belong. Among my books. My scrolls. My records. This is where I can still serve. Quietly. In my own way."

The weight in Ben's chest pressed tighter. "I just don't want to lose you." "You won't," Jeff whispered. "You never could." Their conversation paused again as emotion choked the air between them. After several long breaths, Ben lifted his eyes, his voice quiet but steady. "Then promise me something." "Anything."

"That if you ever change your mind, you'll come." Jeff smiled fully for the first time that morning, reaching across the table to squeeze his son's hand. "I promise." At that moment, Isla entered the room softly, reading the weight in Ben's expression instantly. She said nothing, only coming to sit beside him, wrapping her arm through his, offering silent comfort. Jeff looked at her, gratitude in his eyes. "You'll take care of him." Isla smiled gently. "Always."

Kendrick entered a few minutes later, having allowed them privacy but sensing the weight of the conversation had lifted just enough to rejoin them. He stood quietly by the doorway, saying nothing, but offering Ben a look only a father could give—a look of understanding and of support, no matter the outcome.

The rest of that day unfolded with an extra tenderness between them all. Every shared meal carried unspoken meaning. Every cup of coffee was savoured a little longer. Every laugh was a little softer, as though none of them wanted to shatter the fragile peace of those closing hours.

That evening, as the stars came out above Kent, the family gathered one last time beneath the great oak trees. Sørensen lit a small fire in the pit, the smoke curling gently into the cool night air. The flames flickered between them, dancing shadows across their faces as they sat shoulder to shoulder—father, mother, son, daughter, and those who had become something more than bloodlines could ever explain.

For Sørensen, this moment was more profound than anything he had experienced as a protector. He saw now that he was no longer simply a security detail. He was family. Adopted not by decree, but by love. For Robert and Claire, it was the reassurance that their daughter had found not just a king, but a man whose heart was forged in loyalty, tenderness, and wisdom far beyond his years. They trusted him—fully.

The sun was setting behind the cottage when Ben asked his mother to join him privately, pulling her aside near the garden wall. The air was cool, but the weight in his voice was unmistakable. "Mom," he began softly, eyes never leaving hers. "Before we leave tomorrow, I need to ask you something." Annemarie smiled gently, sensing the seriousness in his tone. "Of course, sweetheart. Anything." Ben exhaled deeply. "Stay here." Her brow lifted, surprised. "Stay here? Ben, you know I—"

He raised his hand gently to stop her words. "Mom, please. I know where your heart is. I see the way you look at Jeff. I see the way he looks at you. Don't tell me you don't feel it. Don't tell me you don't know. Because I know." His voice never wavered. "I'm not blind, Mom. I may be ten years old, but I know what love looks like. And I know you've loved him for years, even if neither of you have had the courage to say it." Annemarie's eyes misted instantly, her breath catching. She opened her mouth to speak but found no words.

"I have Robert and Claire. I have Isla. I have Uncle Kendrick. I am not alone," Ben continued, his voice softer now, but stronger still. "But Dad—Jeff—he's been alone for a long time. Too long. And you… you could fix that." Her hand trembled slightly as she reached for his cheek, her thumb brushing beneath his eye. "You've always seen more than any child should, Ben." "I'm not a child anymore, Mom," he whispered. "Not for a long time." Behind them, Jeff had quietly stepped closer, hearing enough of the conversation to know what was unfolding. His own eyes moistened as he finally spoke. "Ben's right," Jeff said softly, his voice breaking. "I won't pretend anymore."

Annemarie turned, seeing in his eyes the same truth Ben had carried. The years of missed chances, quiet dinners, unsaid words — all of it now standing in the open between them. Ben smiled faintly. "Then stay here. Take care of him. Take care of each other." She nodded through tears that finally fell freely. "I will." Robert and Claire approached from the patio, having sensed the family moment unfolding. Robert placed his hand gently on Ben's shoulder. "We'll take care of your son, Annemarie," Robert said softly. "As if he were our own." "He already is," Claire added, her voice warm, steady, and full of love.

Isla stepped beside Ben, her hand finding his instinctively, her smile proud but gentle. "And you know I'll always be at his side." Annemarie looked at them all, her heart both breaking and swelling at once. "Thank you," she whispered, her voice nearly shaking. "All of you." Jeff stepped closer, reaching for Annemarie's hand. Their fingers interlaced naturally, as though they'd always belonged there. Ben smiled quietly, watching the two who had never needed permission — only courage. "This is how it's supposed to be," Ben whispered to Isla. "Yes, it is," she answered softly.

That night, as the stars returned once again to the Kent sky, peace finally settled completely over them. For Annemarie, it was the peace of knowing her son was not alone. For Kendrick, it was watching both his son and his sovereign become what few rulers ever become: fully human. And for Ben—it was both everything and not enough. But it was enough for now. As the fire crackled, Ben looked around the circle, his heart full, his voice soft.

"We built this. Together. And we'll always have it." The stars blinked silently above them, as though nodding in agreement. By morning, the bags were packed, the cars loaded, and the family gathered at the airstrip. The sovereign jet hummed quietly in preparation for departure. As the engines whirred, Ben turned to his father one last time before boarding. "I'll be back," Ben whispered. Jeff nodded, holding his son tightly. "And I'll be right here."

The embrace lingered longer than either wanted to admit, but eventually, they pulled apart. Isla slipped her hand into Ben's as they ascended the steps into the plane, Sørensen following closely behind. Kendrick gave Jeff one final nod of quiet respect before boarding himself. The hatch closed. The engines roared. And soon, the jet lifted skyward, disappearing into the clouds. Kent faded behind them. Denmark awaited. But the bond remained unbroken.

Always.

CHAPTER 14: HOMEWARD SOVEREIGNS

The engines rumbled beneath the sovereign jet as it sliced through the blue heavens, the white trails behind them slowly fading into nothing but memory. Kent was no longer visible. The green fields, the rolling hills, the narrow roads winding through the countryside—all of it now resting far beneath the clouds. And yet, within the pressurized cabin, the weight of what had been left behind lingered palpably.

Ben sat quietly, his hand laced with Isla's as they stared through the wide windows. The sky seemed endless ahead, yet it could not hide the small pit resting inside Ben's chest. It was not grief, nor regret. It was that strange ache one feels when leaving a part of their own soul behind. He had seen the strength in his father's eyes that morning, but also the softness—the acceptance that life had guided them onto two separate, yet eternally connected, paths.

Kendrick sat across from them, reviewing a small leather-bound notebook—a habit he kept on all flights. But even he looked up from his pages periodically, his eyes gently scanning his son, seeing not just the young king before him, but the boy who had grown so profoundly within the span of mere years. Sørensen sat several rows behind, one eye closed as if resting, but his other eye discreetly watched the cabin, his instinct to protect still humming in the background even now, in these moments of peace.

The cabin remained quiet, filled only with the soft hum of the engines and the occasional gentle clink of coffee cups being carefully handled by the onboard steward. The royal jet, for all its luxury, had adopted the atmosphere of a family's living room rather than a floating palace. That, after all, was Ben's doing. He never cared for excessive ceremony.

Ben's gaze remained fixed outside for a long stretch of time, his thoughts swirling far beyond the clouds. Isla squeezed his hand softly, drawing him gently back into the present. "You're thinking about him again," she said with her warm, knowing voice. Ben allowed himself a faint smile. "Of course I am." He turned to her, his eyes soft but steady. "I know he's exactly where he needs to be. But it still feels... empty. Like a chair at the table will always be missing."

Isla nodded, her hand running gently along his arm. "I know, my love. But you gave him something far more valuable than your company. You gave him his place—his peace. And you gave your mother hers." Ben exhaled, closing his eyes briefly as her words anchored him. "I see them together in my mind. It helps." "It should," Kendrick spoke then, his voice calm but firm, folding his notebook closed and placing it on his lap.

"You've acted as any sovereign should. You've seen beyond your own desires to what was best for them. That is no small thing, son. You honoured them."

Ben nodded quietly, hearing the truth but feeling the ache nonetheless. "Sometimes, doing the right thing still hurts." Kendrick smiled faintly. "Only because you carry their love with you. That is not weakness, Ben. That is why you sit where you sit now." The words carried more weight than any ceremonial speech could have.

For all his titles, Kendrick remained first and foremost a father—able to see the complexities within his son's eyes, even when others could not. The sovereign was rising in Ben, but so too was the man. And with every decision he made, that man was becoming stronger.

As the aircraft continued its steady flight eastward toward Denmark, the conversation gradually shifted, the heaviness giving way to lighter moments. They spoke of what awaited them upon arrival—the familiar grounds of the royal estate, the trusted staff who had kept watch during their absence, and of course, the ever-curious eyes of the world who would inevitably try to interpret their every move. But for now, none of that weighed heavily. The flight was their final sanctuary before re-entering the orchestration of sovereign life.

Sørensen eventually made his way forward, coffee in hand, settling into the open seat beside Kendrick. His eyes glanced toward Ben and Isla with a faint glimmer of warmth that had become his silent way of speaking. "Everything's in place for our arrival," he said quietly, addressing Kendrick but glancing toward Ben. "The estate has been secured since we left. No disturbances. No surveillance. The media hasn't stirred either—not a single photographer or helicopter. I believe they've finally learned to respect the boundaries His Majesty has set."

Ben smiled lightly. "I suppose fear can be an effective teacher." Sørensen chuckled. "Or perhaps they simply realize there are far easier targets than crossing swords with a ten-year-old who outplays intelligence networks in his sleep." Isla laughed softly. "You say it like it's a compliment." "It is," Sørensen replied with sincerity. "Not many sovereigns your age—or any age—would have managed what you have, Your Majesty." Ben shook his head, dismissing the title gently. "Not right now, Sørensen. We're still in the air. For the next hour or two, just Ben."

Sørensen offered a respectful nod. "Very well, Ben." Kendrick leaned back in his chair, his gaze thoughtful as he stared out toward the clouds. "The question that awaits us now is no longer about protecting the sovereignty of the house.
That war has been fought and won. What we face now is maintaining it—quietly, daily, patiently." "That's the harder part," Isla added softly. "The world forgets that peace isn't passive. It requires constant work."

Ben nodded. "I'm ready for it." "And you won't be alone," Kendrick added. "Not one step of the way." The words carried tremendous comfort as the family settled once more into silence. The hum of the engines remained their only company for long stretches, broken occasionally by simple touches, exchanged glances, and the comfort that only deep, unbreakable bonds could provide.

As they approached the Danish airspace, the captain's voice eventually broke across the cabin's intercom, calm and steady. "Your Majesty, Your Highnesses, we are now beginning our descent into Denmark. Estimated arrival at the private terminal will be within twenty-five minutes. Weather is clear and conditions remain ideal for landing." The soft chime of the cabin lights followed as the steward returned to secure the cabin for their descent. Ben exhaled slowly, almost as though preparing to lower his own emotional landing gear as well. "Back to it," he said softly. "Back home," Isla corrected gently, squeezing his hand.

He turned to her, his lips forming a quiet smile. "Yes. Home." Outside the cabin windows, the vast sea gave way to the outline of the Danish coast—familiar, strong, welcoming. The city of Copenhagen sparkled faintly beneath the sunlight as the aircraft banked gently in preparation for its approach. The sovereigns were returning. The storm had passed. The sovereign war was won. The world had been warned. But now—now the real work of ruling would begin. And Ben was ready.

The sovereign jet touched down smoothly on Danish soil, the familiar bump of wheels against the private royal runway barely jostling its passengers. The engines reversed, slowing the aircraft's glide as the terminal grew larger through the cabin windows. Ben sat upright, his hand still tightly held in Isla's, his eyes forward, unblinking. They were home. Or at least, that's what everyone would say. The motorcade was already waiting as the jet taxied gently into position. Black state vehicles stood in a perfect row, polished and prepared, flanked by discreet security personnel who knew better than to act like bodyguards in front of their king. This was Denmark, after all. And Denmark had learned the very hard way to never invade Ben's peace unless invited.

The hatch opened with its usual smooth hiss, releasing the cabin's recycled air into the cool Danish breeze. Kendrick stepped out first, greeting the attending steward with a silent nod, followed by Sørensen, always scanning, always protective, but with a softer edge today. Isla stood from her seat, tugging gently on Ben's hand. "Come on," she whispered, her voice gentle, encouraging. Ben inhaled, slow and deep, before standing to his full height. He was ten years old, yes, but he walked down those stairs with the grace of a king twice his age. The cameras would capture no weakness today. Not yet.

As they entered the waiting vehicles, the motorcade pulled away from the airfield with perfect orchestration. The roads were cleared, traffic respectfully rerouted, and soon they were rolling through the familiar streets that led toward the royal estate. The fields and trees blurred by as Ben sat silent in the back seat, his eyes fixed on nothing in particular. The closer they came to the castle, the tighter the invisible rope inside him wound. He said nothing, but Isla could feel it—like a growing storm trapped beneath his ribcage, gathering strength. Kendrick watched his nephew closely from the opposite seat, seeing the lines of quiet strain forming behind Ben's eyes. Kendrick had seen it before—in soldiers, in sovereigns, in grieving fathers. But never in one so young.

The castle gates opened smoothly as they approached. The towering stone walls stood tall against the sky, both fortress and home. As the motorcade curved up the familiar driveway, staff had already gathered quietly along the entry stairway to greet their returning sovereigns. The castle was spotless, the gardens freshly tended, the banners of the House of Rosenshavn fluttering proudly in the breeze. Ben stepped from the car, his posture flawless, his head high. He nodded graciously to the staff, offering small smiles where appropriate, but his eyes remained distant, fixed somewhere far beyond the physical realm of this return.

Isla stayed close at his side, never releasing his hand. She knew this wasn't finished. Not yet. The first few hours back at the castle unfolded like any other homecoming: staff reporting in, formal briefings postponed, meals offered and respectfully declined.

The sovereign household allowed its returning family space, understanding the unspoken exhaustion that came with not just travel, but the emotional weight still lingering in the air. By mid-afternoon, Kendrick prepared to fulfill one of the promises left waiting from before their departure. Mr. Nielsen and young Clara had arrived, quietly escorted to the estate's outer guest quarters where final employment arrangements would be discussed.

Kendrick had instructed the meeting to be informal — no chambers, no sovereign theatrics. Just a man speaking to another man. As it should be. Mr. Nielsen, humble but steady, sat across the small kitchen table as Kendrick accepted the coffee offered graciously by Clara. The little girl beamed with joy at seeing the king again but was equally comforted by the calmness in his manner.

Kendrick took a long sip, savoring the simple warmth of the mug in his hands. "Well, Mr. Nielsen," he began with a small smile, "it seems your journey with us officially begins today." The man nodded, his voice trembling with gratitude but not weakness. "Thank you, Your Majesty. I never dreamed... well... you know."

Kendrick reached across the table, placing a firm hand on his arm. "I know. And you've earned your place here. This estate isn't built on titles. It's built on people. Loyal, honest, hard-working people. You'll fit in just fine." Clara watched her father proudly, her eyes wide with joy. Kendrick smiled warmly at her. "And Clara, you'll be welcome here anytime you like. The castle isn't only for sovereigns. Sometimes it needs laughter too." "Thank you, sir!" she beamed. For a time, it was nothing but gentle conversation, two fathers talking about life, about work, about family. Kendrick enjoyed these moments more than most royal councils. Here, there was no manipulation. No politics. Just truth. But elsewhere in the castle, the storm inside Ben had reached its peak.

For hours, he had held it together. The return, the greetings, the formalities—it all sat heavy on his chest like stones piling higher and higher. Isla had stayed at his side through every breath, her fingers never releasing his hand, but even she could feel the tremors starting to surface. Finally, the dam shattered. It came without warning.

As Kendrick remained at the guest house, Isla had brought Ben back up to their private quarters, hoping the quiet might ease his mind. But as she closed the door behind them, Ben stopped mid-step. His breath caught sharply. His chest heaved. And then it came—the release neither of them could stop.

The sob tore from his throat like a roar—a raw, primal, guttural cry that erupted so violently it shook the very air in the room. His knees buckled beneath him, and Isla was there instantly, wrapping her arms around him, holding him against her chest as his small body collapsed into her embrace. The sound echoed through the thick stone walls of the castle. Staff froze in place. The guards paused at their posts. Even outside in the garden courtyards, heads turned toward the high windows as the echoes reached their ears. No one had heard such a cry before.

It wasn't just grief—it was the heartbreak of a sovereign boy forced to carry the impossible balance between duty and longing. A boy who had held entire kingdoms steady while his own heart had quietly cracked beneath the weight of missing his mother and father. The cost of being who he was—who the world required him to be.

Isla whispered softly into his ear as he sobbed uncontrollably against her, tears soaking her blouse as his entire frame shook violently. "It's okay, my love... let it go. I've got you. I'm here." Ben gasped through the sobs, clutching at her tightly, his voice breaking into fragments. "I... I miss them... Isla... I miss them... so much... I can't—"

"Shhh," she whispered, rocking him softly as though cradling a baby. "I know. I know you do. And you're allowed to." The cry did not last minutes—it lasted nearly an hour. An hour of broken sobs, gasping breaths, trembling shoulders, and unfiltered agony. The weight of sovereign duty cracked open, and for once, the boy was allowed to simply be a child again. Kendrick eventually returned from the guest house, his face sobering as he approached their quarters. From outside the closed door, he heard the cry and paused, his hand resting on the frame. He whispered quietly to himself, "Let him break. He needs this." And Kendrick, the sovereign father, turned silently away, ensuring no one disturbed the storm within.

The echoes of Ben's sobs still lingered faintly in the air like a passing storm, the castle walls absorbing the weight of his heartbreak as though the ancient stone itself grieved with him. The staff remained respectfully distant, standing silently in the corridors, exchanging quiet glances as the magnitude of what they had heard settled upon them. The castle had faced many storms before—but none quite like this.

Outside the private quarters, Kendrick remained near, standing as a quiet sentinel just beyond the door. He did not enter. He would not intrude. He knew, with a father's wisdom, that Ben needed space to crumble where he was most safe. Isla was inside, still holding him, anchoring him with her steady presence, her small hands gently rubbing circles along his back as his sobs slowed into tired gasps.

But they were not alone. From behind Kendrick, a small hand gently tugged at his sleeve. He looked down to find little Clara standing beside him, her wide, observant eyes searching his face with a quiet maturity far beyond her years. She had heard the cry from the lower quarters where she and her father had settled. That sound had reached every corner of the estate, piercing not only walls but hearts. "Is it him?" she whispered. Kendrick knelt slightly to meet her gaze, lowering his voice into a soft, fatherly tone. "Yes, little one. It's Ben."

Clara nodded gently, her small brow furrowing. She did not hesitate. "I want to go to him." Kendrick inhaled, his eyes reading her pure intent—there was no hesitation, no fear, no confusion. Only the simple heart of a child who recognized another soul in pain. He placed his hand softly on her shoulder. "Then go, Clara. He'll know you're there for him."

Without waiting for formal permission, Clara stepped toward the door and gently pushed it open. The heavy wood creaked softly as she slipped inside the quiet chamber. The room was dim, lit only by the filtered afternoon light that streaked through the tall windows. Isla sat on the bed, still cradling Ben against her chest as his sobs faded into exhausted breaths, his face buried in her shoulder.

Clara climbed onto the bed without a word. She crawled across the wide mattress, her small frame slipping into the space beside them like she had always belonged there. Gently, she wrapped her arms around both Ben and Isla, forming a small, warm cocoon of comfort.

Ben felt her presence instantly. And instinctively, his arms extended without thought, pulling Clara into the embrace, holding her tight alongside Isla. The three of them remained like that for long moments—no words, no explanations—only the silent ministry of presence.

After a time, Clara whispered softly into Ben's ear, her voice like a gentle melody. "It's okay, Ben. Let it go. I'm here." Her simple words reached further into Ben's heart than any royal counsel could have. A child comforting a king. A friend holding another friend's breaking heart together. They stayed like that for nearly half an hour. The room remained still, as if time itself had stepped back, allowing them the privacy to heal. Ben's breathing slowly steadied, his trembling lessened, and the tight knot in his chest began to loosen. The tears eventually subsided, replaced by long, slow exhales as the heavy waves finally receded.

Only when Ben finally pulled back slightly did Clara shift, looking up into his eyes with an innocent smile full of both warmth and wisdom. "You're family," she said simply, her voice unwavering, her small hand resting on his cheek. "Always." Ben's throat tightened again, but this time no tears followed. Instead, a smile formed—gentle, raw, grateful. He leaned forward and placed a soft kiss on Clara's cheek. "Thank you." Clara grinned mischievously, breaking the heavy moment with the innocence only children can carry. "So… are we going to play soccer or what?"

A small chuckle burst out of Ben, the first true sound of joy since their return. Isla smiled too, watching as the sovereign weight in Ben's chest lightened at last. "Maybe after we both get some breakfast tomorrow," Ben said, his voice stronger now. Clara nodded enthusiastically. "Deal." Meanwhile, in the lower estate, Mr. Nielsen had begun his first official day as groundskeeper. Though formally hired, he was still adjusting to the surreal reality of working for the House of Rosenshavn.

Kendrick had walked him through the initial grounds that morning, guiding him personally along the gardens, the outer walls, and the service tunnels that ran beneath the estate. The king treated him not as a subordinate, but as an equal, discussing landscaping decisions, equipment upgrades, and long-term care of the estate with sincere interest. "You'll have full authority over your staff," Kendrick assured him as they walked beside the royal greenhouse. "But I expect you to run things with honesty and respect. The same way you've carried your family through these past years."

"I will, Your Majesty," Mr. Nielsen replied, still adjusting to the reality of standing shoulder-to-shoulder with a king as if it were casual. "And one more thing," Kendrick added as they paused under an ancient oak. "You don't call me 'Your Majesty' when we sit for coffee. I'm Ken, remember?" Nielsen smiled, a warm, humbled grin spreading across his face. "Yes… Ken." "Good," Kendrick chuckled, clapping him gently on the back. "Tomorrow morning, I expect you at your kitchen table. I'll bring the pastries." They both laughed softly as they continued their walk.

Back inside the castle, after the storm of Ben's breakdown had passed, Isla gently guided him to sit by the wide balcony that overlooked the estate's western gardens. Clara stayed close, still seated beside him on the cushioned bench, her head lightly resting against his shoulder. For once, the world had grown quiet—not because of isolation, but because healing had finally begun. Isla spoke softly, breaking the silence with a whisper only meant for his ears. "You did it, Ben."

He turned slightly toward her, his voice softer now, but steady. "I didn't do it alone." "No," Isla smiled. "You never do." From the doorway, Kendrick stood, watching his adopted son carefully from a respectful distance, ensuring he remained invisible to the boy's fragile peace. He saw the healing slowly working its way through Ben's heart—not completed, but begun. And for the first time since returning home, Kendrick allowed himself to exhale fully. The sovereign storm had passed. The boy was still standing.

The castle had grown quieter in the days that followed Ben's emotional collapse. Not silent — but peaceful. The kind of peace that feels earned, as though the stones themselves exhaled after long years of carrying burdens too heavy for most sovereign homes. Life resumed its gentle rhythm inside the vast halls, but this rhythm was different now. Softer. More intimate.

Ben wandered the corridors that afternoon, his hands in his pockets, quietly taking in the life unfolding around him. Staff members moved respectfully, nodding politely as they passed. The gardens were trimmed, the kitchens bustling, the small orchestras rehearsing softly in the music chambers. His kingdom lived—but it no longer pressed against his chest like armor. It simply existed around him, and for once, he allowed himself to breathe within it.

Yet even with this comfort, Ben's feet soon carried him—almost instinctively—toward the study where Kendrick often retreated in the late hours of the afternoon. He found the heavy door slightly ajar, the warm amber glow of desk lamps illuminating the richly polished wood inside. Without knocking, Ben simply pushed the door open further. His uncle—his father in so many ways—was seated behind his desk, spectacles perched low on his nose as he scribbled careful notes into one of his personal journals. Hearing the creak of the door, Kendrick looked up instantly. His eyes softened as they landed on Ben.

"Come in, my boy," he said warmly, setting his pen aside and opening his arms without hesitation. Without a word, Ben crossed the room and stepped directly into the embrace. No tears. No breaking this time. Only a deep, longing need to be held — the kind only a father can satisfy for a son. Kendrick tightened his arms around him, resting his chin lightly atop Ben's head. "You're doing well, son," he whispered. "Very well."

Ben breathed deeply into his chest. "I didn't come to disturb you." Kendrick chuckled softly. "You could never disturb me. And besides, I knew Isla was there for you when you needed her most. That's her role — your anchor. And you had Clara, too." Ben giggled slightly against his chest, pulling back just enough to look up at him. "Yeah. I did, didn't I?" "Oh yes." Kendrick smiled. "You're not just a king, Ben.

You're still a young man. A child, in the purest sense of the word." "I know. I'm still ten," Ben admitted with a faint grin. "Then be one," Kendrick said gently. "Be a child, son. Don't let the crown steal that from you. You want to go play soccer? Go play. Have fun. Laugh. Fall down. Skin your knees. There's time enough to rule. But childhood… childhood is fleeting."

Ben smiled fully now. "I'd like that." Kendrick reached over to his desk drawer and pulled out a small package, offering it forward. "And to make sure you don't get interrupted by business while you're out there…" Ben opened the box carefully to reveal a sleek, modern cell phone. "Texting only when you're playing," Kendrick explained, his voice light. "No ringing in your pocket while you're kicking a ball. If something's urgent, I'll text you. If I need you immediately, I'll call—but only then." Ben's eyes lit up. "Thank you, Dad."

The word slipped out naturally—once in a while, it still surprised them both—but it was always received with warmth. "You're very welcome, my son," Kendrick whispered, pulling him into another firm embrace. The door creaked gently again. This time, Sørensen entered quietly, nodding his head respectfully to both of them. "Majesties," he said with his usual steady calm, "all is secure. The castle is peaceful today." Kendrick grinned. "Finally, some quiet." Sørensen chuckled faintly. "Indeed. No crises. No threats. No leaks. It's… almost unsettling."

Ben turned to him with a playful grin. "That's how it's supposed to be, Uncle Sørensen." The agent's eyes warmed as he heard the title again. Uncle. Not chief of security. Not agent. But family. "Thank you, Ben," Sørensen said softly. "I appreciate that more than you know." Without hesitation, Ben walked across the room and opened his arms. Sørensen hesitated for only a heartbeat before opening his own, accepting the embrace. The hug was firm, steady. Sørensen's heart swelled unexpectedly at the gesture—accepted not just as protector, but truly as kin.

As they stood together, the moment was softly interrupted by a quiet knock at the door—a distinctive little rap that Kendrick instantly recognized. "Clara," he called warmly, "come in, little one." The door opened and Clara peeked her head through, smiling brightly. "Thank you... um... Your Honor." Kendrick chuckled. "Ken. Just Ken, remember?" "Ken. Yes, of course." She beamed. She turned to Ben, her eyes sparkling. "So... tomorrow morning, soccer?" Ben grinned. "After breakfast." She nodded eagerly. "Good. I'll see you at breakfast then."

"Oh, you'll see me at breakfast, will you?" Ben teased, his grin widening. Clara giggled. "Oh yes. Absolutely." The playful exchange was light, but beneath it sat something far deeper—something neither child needed to say aloud. Clara had stood beside him during his most vulnerable moment. And in that silent act of friendship, something unspoken had permanently bonded them.

Ben opened his arms gently. Without a second thought, Clara ran forward and leapt into his embrace, wrapping her arms tightly around him as though she belonged there. And she did. "Thank you, Clara," Ben whispered into her hair. She pulled back slightly, reaching up to gently hold his cheeks between her small hands. Her voice was soft, but unwavering. "You're my family now." Without hesitation, she leaned forward and gave him a small, innocent kiss upon his lips—a gesture full of pure, childlike affection rather than ceremony or awkwardness. Just love, as simple as it should be.

Ben chuckled softly, wiping a single tear from the corner of his eye. "Thank you." From his place near the window, Mr. Nielsen watched the entire scene unfold, his chest swelling with pride—not for his daughter's place beside royalty—but for the kindness and purity that radiated from all of them. Sørensen caught his gaze and nodded respectfully toward him, as if acknowledging the man's quiet role in bringing such light into this house. Mr. Nielsen nodded back, smiling with deep gratitude. And for that moment—for that room, for that family—the world outside disappeared completely. There were no kings or queens. No security teams. No crowns. Just a family. A sovereign circle of love.

The late afternoon sun drifted lower behind the castle's high towers, bathing the estate in that golden hour warmth that seemed to soften even the hardest stone. The gardens glistened under the amber light as the day slowly surrendered to evening. Inside the castle walls, a quiet comfort had settled among them — the kind of comfort that only comes when hearts are beginning to heal, when grief has had its say, and love gently fills the spaces where pain once lived.

Dinner preparations were well underway as the long table in the family dining hall was carefully set. The kitchen staff moved with polished precision but wore relaxed smiles. This was not a formal state dinner. This was family. Ben and Isla entered the hall first, hand in hand as always, their steps light and easy. Sørensen followed behind, casually observing as he always did — guardian of both body and heart, though no threat loomed tonight. Kendrick arrived moments later, pausing briefly to survey the scene, as if mentally cataloguing the rare serenity that had finally been restored within these ancient walls.

Mr. Nielsen appeared shortly after, his uniform crisp, but his manner unchanged—still the quiet, humble man he had always been. And finally, little Clara slipped in behind him, her face lighting up the moment she spotted Ben and Isla already seated. "Ah, good evening, Miss Clara," Kendrick greeted warmly, waving her over. "You're right on time." Clara smiled brightly. "Of course. I didn't want to miss dinner." "You never do," Sørensen chuckled softly, pulling out her chair next to Ben, exactly where she always sat — to his left, with Isla to his right. Her spot. Her place.

The family sat together as the first of the meal arrived—steaming plates of waffles, pancakes, thick-cut bacon, sausage links, bowls of fresh fruit, and of course, pots of freshly brewed coffee set neatly at the centre. Evening dinners at the castle often mirrored their breakfasts, a familiar comfort that suited their simple pleasures.

As the plates were being filled, Ben reached for the coffee carafe and poured two cups — one for himself, one for Isla. Then, glancing mischievously toward Clara, he raised an eyebrow. "You sure you want to keep drinking that tea of yours?" he teased. "Here, try mine. This is how real coffee tastes."

Clara giggled, curious, leaning in. Isla grinned and added her encouragement. "I drink mine the same as Ben, Clara. No difference." Ben carefully handed the cup toward Clara, allowing her to take a small sip. She cautiously tasted it — her little nose wrinkling for only a moment before her eyes widened slightly with surprise. "Oooh…" she gasped, almost whispering. "Yes… now that's coffee." Ben chuckled, clearly pleased. "Good. Then tomorrow morning, I'll fix it properly for you." "Deal," Clara beamed. "Coffee it is."

Kendrick laughed softly, shaking his head. "She's seven going on thirty." Sørensen added with a grin, "Next thing you know, she'll be asking for diplomatic briefings." They all shared a gentle laugh, and the meal continued with its usual warmth. Conversations flowed easily—nothing heavy, nothing political. Talk of soccer matches, garden plans, books they were reading, small castle projects Kendrick wanted to finish—normal life, beautifully unremarkable, and deeply cherished. As the meal drew to a close, the plates cleared and cups refilled one last time, Clara leaned into Ben's shoulder with a small, familiar yawn.

"Long day, little one?" Ben asked softly. She nodded, her voice sleepy but content. "Yes... but a good one." Mr. Nielsen rose from his seat. "Alright, Clara. Time for us to head to your room." But as was now part of their unspoken ritual, Clara didn't move right away. Instead, she looked at Ben with wide eyes, silently asking for her nightly moment. Ben smiled and opened his arms. Without hesitation, Clara slid off her chair, crossed the small distance, and climbed into his embrace. He held her tightly, allowing her head to rest against his chest as Isla gently rubbed Clara's back, the three of them forming their nightly circle of love. "You're safe, Clara," Ben whispered softly, as he always did. "Always safe."

"I know," she murmured into his shirt. "Because I have you." A few more moments passed like this before Clara finally lifted her head and gave him a small kiss on the cheek, then another quick one to Isla. Ben returned a gentle kiss to her forehead, whispering once more, "Goodnight, my girl." "Goodnight," she smiled. Mr. Nielsen stood by patiently, quietly moved as he always was by the sovereign kindness shown to his daughter. As Clara returned to her father's side, she took his hand, and together they made their way out of the hall toward their rooms.

The remaining family sat for a moment in the quiet after her departure, each lost in their own peaceful reflections. Kendrick leaned back slightly, his voice gentle. "These small moments, Ben… they are worth more than all the crowns in the world." Ben nodded quietly. "I know, Dad." Sørensen smiled from across the table. "The House of Rosenshavn is more than stone and banners. This is what makes it strong."

"Yes," Kendrick added. "This is what keeps it sovereign." The candles flickered softly as the conversation faded into comfortable silence, the warmth of the evening wrapping itself around them like a protective cloak. Soon, each would retreat to their rooms, to their showers, their fresh pyjamas, their nightly routines that had grown into sacred rhythms. Ben and Isla returned to their private quarters hand-in-hand, as always. Once inside, the doors quietly closed behind them.

They shared their shower in unspoken harmony, only their familiar, private comfort between them. Dried, dressed, and quietly refreshed, they slipped into bed as the soft moonlight spilled across their sheets. As always, they lay face to face. As always, their first instinct was to lean forward, their lips meeting for their gentle, unrushed evening kiss—never hurried, never awkward, always natural.

When they finally pulled back, Isla whispered with a sleepy smile, "Bladder chatter?" Ben grinned, replying, "Absolutely." Hand-in-hand, they padded toward their side-by-side toilets, chuckling as they always did at the routine they never once found silly. Life was simple here. Honest. Pure. Once they returned to bed, Ben pulled Isla gently against him, and with her head resting safely on his chest, their breathing softened together. The castle, and the kingdom beyond, fell into peaceful sleep once more.

The castle was still wrapped in soft silence as dawn broke gently over Denmark. The first golden rays of morning light slid through the tall windows, slipping past heavy drapes and gilded stone to find the small, familiar figures curled beneath the sheets. Ben stirred first, blinking as the early light touched his face. Within seconds, Isla's eyes fluttered open, meeting his as they did every morning — their own unspoken ritual. Without a word, without hesitation, they leaned toward each other. Their lips met, slow and tender, that soft morning kiss they never rushed nor skipped.

Pulling back with matching smiles, Ben chuckled softly. "Bladder chatter?" "Absolutely," Isla whispered back, her voice playful. Together they slipped out from beneath the covers, hand-in-hand as always, padding barefoot toward the adjoining bathroom where their side-by-side toilets waited like two old friends sharing another secret morning together. The routine never grew old, never lost its humour, and neither had they ever felt shame about it.

Life was life, and between soulmates, it was simply natural. As they finished, a soft knock came to the outer door. Both of them smiled, recognizing the familiar pattern.

"Coffee on your table," called the gentle voice of one of the senior castle attendants. In unison, Ben and Isla called back warmly, "Thank you very much!" The tray was brought in quietly and placed upon the low table near the windows — two steaming cups prepared exactly to their liking, alongside the soft aroma of breakfast rolls, butter, and fresh preserves to gently start their morning. But before they could sit down, another knock came — lighter, quicker, full of youth.

"May I come in?" Clara's cheerful voice chirped from behind the door. Ben grinned and called out, "Of course, Clara! Always." The door creaked open, and Clara padded in wearing her simple but tidy morning dress, hair lightly tousled from sleep but her face already lit with excitement. "Coffee time, I see," she said with a mischievous glimmer. "I already had my tea, you know — but they still won't let me have coffee." Ben grinned. "Well, not today."

He walked over to the coffee tray, expertly preparing a small cup — carefully balanced between strong and gentle, sweetened just enough for her young palate, the way she'd liked it after her little taste test the night before.

"Here you go," he said, handing her the cup with all the ceremonial flair of a master barista. "Your first official coffee." Clara accepted the cup with both hands as though receiving a priceless treasure. She blew on it gently, took her first real sip, and then her eyes widened, followed by a little delighted gasp. "Oooh, yes," she sighed. "That's so much better than tea."

Isla laughed softly beside her. "See? Told you." Ben nodded, pleased. "I told you I'd fix it." Clara beamed at both of them, feeling just a little older, just a little more grown up. And perhaps she was. Though still seven — almost eight, as she frequently reminded everyone — her heart and mind often danced well beyond her years.

Even Ben had quietly noticed how quickly her instincts matured. Sometimes, watching her, he saw shades of a girl wise far beyond her age — not merely eight years old, but carrying the depth of someone well into her twenties. Perhaps life had gifted her that maturity too soon. Perhaps she would need it.

But for now — she was just Clara. Their friend. Their family. Breakfast followed soon after, as it always did. The three of them sat together in their private nook while the staff delivered waffles, pancakes, bacon, sausage, and fresh fruits. As always, no eggs—Clara's firm stance on that had never wavered.
"Eggs are disgusting," she reminded them, wrinkling her nose dramatically. "It's like eating a chicken that's not even born yet." Ben laughed heartily. "No kidding. They are disgusting."

Isla grinned. "Guilty as charged for eating cooked chicken, though." Clara shook her head. "That's different." Ben chuckled. "We'll stick to our pancakes and waffles, thank you." Their laughter filled the air as they ate, the morning light dancing across their table like an invisible guest. After breakfast, as promised, the trio made their way outside toward the royal fields behind the castle — their soccer field, trimmed and perfectly maintained by Mr. Nielsen and his small grounds crew. The air was cool but bright, the perfect morning for running barefoot through grass still damp with dew.

Ben, Isla, and Clara wasted no time. The ball was rolling before the staff had even fully retreated from tidying breakfast. Shoes were quickly abandoned. Ben called out playful instructions as Isla darted around him, her light frame agile and quick. Clara chased the ball with fierce determination, holding her own impressively against two sovereign children who might easily forget her younger age. Ben couldn't help but marvel at how natural it all felt. No guards hovering nearby. No nobles watching from balconies. Just children, being children, as Kendrick had always encouraged.

When Clara finally tumbled into the grass after missing a kick, she burst into peals of laughter, raising both arms above her head in playful surrender. "Okay!" she gasped through giggles. "Maybe I need more coffee after all." Ben laughed as he helped her to her feet. "You'll get there, champ." The game continued for nearly an hour, their laughter rolling across the castle grounds like music. The House of Rosenshavn was alive, thriving—not because of courts or council chambers, but because love and laughter echoed through its walls. Later that afternoon, when they returned inside to wash up, Ben found a small folded note waiting for him on the breakfast table. Neatly written, placed carefully under a small glass to keep it from blowing away, was Sørensen's familiar handwriting.

Ben unfolded it slowly, Isla and Clara leaning close to read over his shoulder.

To my beloved family,
My niece, my nephew — Ben and Isla —

I would be greatly honoured to take you up on your offer.
You once said you would help me explore my family's past. My ancestry. My bloodlines. To finally see where I came from. I accept your offer, with both humility and gratitude.

Always, and forever yours —
Uncle Sørensen.

Ben smiled deeply, folding the letter gently and holding it to his chest. "We'll do this for him," Isla whispered. "We will," Ben agreed. "And we'll do it together." Clara grinned up at them both. "Maybe we'll even find out that he's royalty, too." Ben chuckled softly, reaching to ruffle her hair. "Wouldn't that be something."

The early afternoon sun hung high in the Danish sky, its rays falling softly through the tall arched windows of the castle, spilling patterns of golden light across the stone corridors. The day had been gentle so far — morning routines carried out, coffee shared, soccer played — but beneath the serenity, an unseen weight had begun pressing quietly into the edges of the House.

Ben first noticed it when he passed one of the upper gallery windows, his eyes instinctively glancing down into the rear courtyard below. There, on one of the stone benches tucked beneath the old elms, sat Clara — alone, motionless, her small frame curled forward as though trying to fold into itself. Her face was buried in her hands. Even at this distance, Ben recognized the posture immediately.

She was breaking. He didn't need to ask what had happened. He already knew. The divorce proceedings her parents had entered into were no longer theoretical — they were now very real. And Clara — sweet, innocent Clara — was sitting alone with that pain. Without a word, Ben turned away from the window and made his way swiftly down the corridor, his feet carrying him quietly through the castle halls, past staff who wisely stepped aside without inquiry. His pace was steady but unhurried. He knew that this moment required not words, but presence.

Stepping out into the courtyard, the fresh breeze greeted him gently, carrying the faint scent of the gardens nearby. The birds chirped softly in the distance, but Clara heard none of it. She sat in silent agony, her sobs muffled into her palms, her shoulders rising and falling with every quiet gasp. Ben approached slowly, stopping directly in front of her, lowering himself gently to one knee. He said nothing at first. There was no need for ceremony here.

No throne, no titles, no sovereigns — only a boy and a girl, one hurting, one ready to catch her fall. Reaching forward, Ben softly placed his right hand upon her cheek, guiding her face upward. As her hands lowered, tear-streaked eyes met his, filled with unspeakable hurt.

"Clara," he whispered tenderly, "you're not alone." Her lip quivered as the tears threatened again, her throat tightening as she tried to speak but failed. He saw it in her — the flood pressing behind her chest, waiting to burst. Ben leaned forward, opening his arms wide, never needing to say more. Without hesitation, Clara collapsed into him, her small arms wrapping fiercely around his neck as her sobs finally erupted with full force. Ben pulled her close, holding her tightly against his chest, his hand cradling the back of her head gently. "Let it go, sweetheart," he whispered into her hair, his voice steady, unwavering. "Let it all out. I'm here. I always will be."

Her cries echoed softly through the courtyard, growing louder with each passing second. Her pain was raw, her heart breaking open in a way no child should have to endure — but Ben never let go, never loosened his hold. She clung to him as if the world might fall apart if she loosened her grip. From the distant archway, Mr. Nielsen stood silently, his eyes misting as he watched his daughter collapse into Ben's arms. He made no move to interrupt. His role in this moment was not to intervene, but to witness the miracle of someone giving his daughter the safe place to grieve she so desperately needed.

Minutes turned into tens of minutes. Thirty. Forty-five. The time was irrelevant. Ben never shifted, never flinched, even as his own arms grew tired from holding her. He simply held her tighter, whispering quiet reassurances as her cries gradually softened into exhausted hiccups. When at last her breathing slowed and her tears thinned, Clara pulled back slightly, wiping at her damp cheeks with trembling hands. Ben reached forward and gently used his thumbs to clear the remnants from under her eyes. "You're safe, Clara," he said softly. "You'll always be safe. You are not alone. Not ever."

Her lower lip quivered again, but this time she smiled through the remnants of her pain. She reached up and cupped his cheeks with her small hands, mirroring the same comforting gesture he often used. "You're my brother," she whispered. "That's who you are." Ben smiled, his own voice thick with restrained emotion. "And you're my sister." With that, Clara leaned forward once more, pressing a gentle kiss to each of his cheeks, then a final, small, innocent kiss upon his lips — not out of romance, but the simple, pure love of family. She hugged him again, fiercely, the way she had when he himself had broken upon returning home.

Ben chuckled softly into her ear. "Let's go have some lunch, honey." She nodded but didn't release him fully. Instead, she let him scoop her gently into his arms, resting her head on his shoulder as her arms wrapped tightly around his neck. She wasn't heavy — at least not for Ben — and carrying her was no effort. If anything, it was a privilege. As they re-entered the castle, staff respectfully stepped aside, heads bowed not out of protocol, but out of quiet reverence for the bond unfolding before them. They passed through the kitchen corridor and down toward the dining hall where the others had begun gathering for lunch.

Upon entering, Isla immediately understood without a word. She stood from her chair as they approached, reaching out to brush Clara's hair tenderly as Ben gently lowered her to the ground beside Isla's seat. Clara slid naturally into place next to her, still holding Ben's hand as he sat beside her. Across the table, Kendrick's eyes met Ben's. No words were exchanged.

Only a solemn nod — a silent father's acknowledgment of what his son had just carried. Lunch was soon served — roasted lamb, baked potatoes with thick butter, fresh vegetables from the castle's own gardens. The aroma filled the room, but the warmth wasn't just from the food. It was from the family gathered here, stronger now than ever.

As coffee was poured, Ben made sure Clara's cup was filled, prepared just the way she liked it now. He set it before her gently. "For me?" she asked, her voice small but bright. "For you, sweetheart," Ben answered with a smile. "Always." Clara lifted the cup with both hands, sipping carefully, her eyes brightening once again. As she settled in between Ben and Isla, and as the first bites of lunch passed quietly between them all, Clara looked around the table — at Kendrick, Sørensen, her father Mr. Nielsen — and something within her finally settled. She was home. Truly home. Her heart, though cracked, was full.

The dining hall had long since grown quiet, the remains of lunch cleared away, replaced now by soft candlelight glowing gently across the table. The afternoon sunlight had shifted, casting long beams through the high windows as the castle prepared to settle into its evening rhythm once more. But for those seated at the family table, this moment was not about meals or duties. It was about hearts. Clara sat nestled between Ben and Isla, still holding Ben's hand, her little fingers lightly wrapped around his. Her eyes, though no longer flooded with tears, still glistened with their recent memory. She glanced up toward him, sensing something different now — not heavy, but profound.

Ben had been waiting for this moment all day. The words had sat quietly in his chest for too long. He'd held them for days — perhaps for weeks — but today, it had to be said. No more hinting. No more leaving things unspoken.

He gently squeezed her hand, drawing her attention fully toward him. Her gaze rose to meet his, full of trust. He took a breath, steady but full, and then spoke — not as a king, not even as her brother by bond, but as the boy who loved her fiercely. "Clara," Ben said softly, his voice smooth but carrying weight, "my sweetheart... my sister... my baby girl." His voice caught slightly, emotion thickening as the words finally began pouring from the place they had lived inside him.

"I love you, Clara," he continued, his eyes never leaving hers. "I love you more than words could ever say. You're my family. And nothing — nothing — will ever change that. Not distance. Not time. Not sorrow. Not anyone else's decisions." Clara's lower lip quivered as the words found their mark, sinking deep into her heart. "You've been through so much already," Ben continued, his voice softening as it deepened. "And I know that pain — I know it because I've felt it, too. And when you cried into my chest yesterday… I understood everything you couldn't even say."

He opened his arms wide again, inviting her close without demand — only love. Without hesitation, Clara leaned in, sliding into his embrace with the full trust that only family can know. Ben wrapped his arms around her once again, pulling her tightly against him, her small head resting beneath his chin. "You're not just some guest here, Clara," he whispered into her hair. "You're my sister. My family. And you always will be." Tears slipped quietly from her closed eyes, but these were not the uncontrollable sobs of before. This was release. Healing. Safety. "You don't ever need to ask for a hug," Ben whispered. "If you need it, take it. You don't even need permission."

He paused, then smiled softly into her hair. "And if you need to plant one on my cheek — or even my lips — you have that right, too. Anytime. That's what family does." Clara pulled back slightly, her face lifting toward his. Her tears remained, but her smile grew. She cupped his cheeks gently between her small hands — the same way he often comforted her — and leaned forward, placing two small kisses on each cheek. Then, without pause, she pressed a sweet, soft kiss upon his lips. Pure. Innocent. Family. Ben smiled wide, resting his forehead gently against hers as they breathed together.

"You're worth more than any crown," Ben whispered, his voice trembling slightly. "And I wear a crown." Clara giggled softly at that, her smile widening. Isla, who had sat quietly all this time, reached across and gently stroked Clara's hair. "And I love you, too, Clara," she said sweetly. "My little sister. Always." Ben glanced over and chuckled. "Here we go again... she says 'always,' and I say 'forever.' We've been arguing over that for years now." Isla grinned playfully. "Forever. Eternity. Infinity. What's the difference?"

Kendrick, seated across the table, let out a quiet chuckle, shaking his head in affectionate disbelief. "You two never cease to amaze me." Sørensen watched silently, arms crossed lightly over his chest, but his eyes full of warmth as he nodded softly. "They remind us why family is stronger than any sovereign seal." Mr. Nielsen, standing a short distance away by the wall, felt his chest tighten as he observed the scene. His daughter — not a guest, not merely a servant's child — but a sister to royalty, loved as family by sovereigns who carried far more than crowns. And in that moment, he felt it: he, too, was no longer standing as an outsider in the House of Rosenshavn.

He was part of it. Even if he hadn't fully realized it until now. As the candlelight flickered around them, Clara snuggled closer to Ben again, resting her head against his chest once more. The steady beat of his heart beneath her ear was all the reassurance she needed. She had found her place — not because someone gave it to her, but because love made it inevitable. Ben kissed the top of her head softly. "We're forever, Clara. That's a promise." "Forever," she whispered back, eyes closed, fully safe at last.

The long table had grown still once more. Evening light pooled softly along the polished surface as the sun dipped lower, brushing faint orange streaks across the castle walls. The candles glowed in steady rhythm, their warm light surrounding the small family gathered at its centre — no longer sovereigns and subjects, but simply: family.

Clara sat nestled between Ben and Isla again, her hands now resting in her lap, fidgeting slightly. But this time, her breathing was steady. She was ready. The weight that had pressed against her chest for days had found its breaking point, and Ben saw it even before she spoke.

He didn't speak first. Instead, he only reached over and gently touched her hand, lacing his fingers into hers, grounding her. "It's your turn, sweetheart," Ben whispered softly. "Take your time. We're here." Clara took a deep breath, her small chest rising slowly, her throat tightening slightly as she searched for the first words. And then it came. Quiet. But steady. "It hurts." Her voice trembled slightly, but she didn't falter. "It hurts so much more than I thought it would." She glanced up, her eyes meeting Ben's for just a second before lowering again, as though confessing something she'd carried far too long.

"I thought that maybe... maybe it would get easier when they first started arguing. I told myself it wasn't my fault, that grownups have problems sometimes. I tried to believe that." Her voice cracked briefly, but Isla reached out and gently brushed her back, steadying her. "But it didn't get easier. It just got... heavier." She swallowed hard. "I would listen to them late at night, you know.

Through the walls. Through the doors. When they thought I was asleep. But I heard them. I heard every fight. Every word. And every time, I kept wishing... please stop. Please stop fighting."

Her lip quivered, but she steadied herself. "But they didn't stop." Ben's hand tightened slightly, silently giving her strength. "And then one day..." Clara paused, her breath catching. "My mom packed a bag. She left." Tears welled in her eyes, but she pushed forward. "She said she needed 'space.' That she needed 'time.' But she never came back. And I kept thinking: did I do something? Did I say something? Was it my fault?" Ben opened his mouth, but she held up a hand quickly — not to silence him harshly, but to ask for space. She needed to finish this. "You know what's the worst part?" Clara whispered, her voice cracking again. "Not knowing who to cry for. My mom? My dad? Me?"

Her shoulders trembled as the next words tumbled out. "Sometimes... sometimes I wonder if my mom even wanted me at all. Because she barely calls. She doesn't visit. She doesn't even ask Dad how I am. It's like she... like she left both of us behind." The tears began sliding freely now. "But then I look at Dad... and I see how hard he tries. He works so much, and he smiles when he sees me, but I can tell it hurts him too. He's tired, Ben. But he still shows up for me." Ben's throat tightened, but he remained silent, his eyes fixed on her, absorbing every word.

"I feel torn in two," Clara continued. "Like half of me lives here, and half of me is still stuck waiting by the door, hoping my mom will walk back through it." Her tears grew heavier now. "But... but I know she won't." Her small hands trembled as she wiped her eyes roughly. "And that's the part I hate most... knowing she won't. Because that means I have to stop waiting.

And I don't know how." At that moment, one of the staff nearby instinctively began stepping forward with tissues — but before they even reached halfway, Ben quietly lifted his hand without looking. His palm rose, steady and firm: Shush. Do not interrupt. The staff froze, understanding immediately.

This was not their moment to enter. Kendrick, watching from the head of the table, gently rose, crossed over to the staff, and whispered something softly, ushering them quietly away before returning to his chair without making a sound. The room belonged to Clara's voice. She swallowed again, finding her breath once more. "But then... you're here. Isla's here. Dad's here. Sørensen's here. And now you're my brother." Her eyes locked fully into Ben's now. "And you let me cry. You let me scream. You let me fall apart and didn't try to fix me. You just held me."

Her voice wavered deeply now, but she refused to stop. "When you held me... I felt safe again. Like I wasn't broken. Like I didn't need to be perfect to be loved. You made me feel like family. Real family." Ben could no longer stop the tears that filled his own eyes, though he kept his breathing calm, letting her continue. "I love you, Ben," she whispered. "I love you, Isla. And you, too, Uncle Kendrick. And Uncle Sørensen. You're my family. And no matter what happens with my mom... I know I still belong here." She reached forward then, grasping Ben's cheeks gently, just as she had done before, but this time with a kind of fierce certainty. She leaned forward and pressed her small lips against his forehead in a soft, steady kiss.

"You're my home now." Ben's voice, heavy with emotion but steady, finally answered. "And you, my sweetheart, are my sister. My baby girl. My family." There was no applause. No ceremony. Just silence — rich, deep, full. Sørensen's chest swelled as he watched from across the table, his own eyes misting. He remained quiet, not out of distance, but respect. This was not the moment for him to speak — but to witness. Mr. Nielsen, standing farther back, covered his mouth briefly with his hand as tears filled his own eyes.

Ben, still holding Clara's hand, then gently turned his gaze toward Kendrick. "Dad," Ben said softly but firmly. Kendrick met his eyes fully, giving him his full attention. "There's something I need to ask you. As much as I love Clara as my sister... I want to make this clear." Kendrick nodded. "I'm listening, son." Ben drew a steady breath. "She is my sister by choice. My princess by choice. And I wish to have her titled as Princess Clara — with your blessing."

Kendrick inhaled slowly, studying the weight of his son's words. The sovereign heart behind the crown was speaking now, not for titles, but for love. After a moment, Kendrick's face softened into a proud, fatherly smile. "You are King, Ben. You hold that right by sovereignty. But I am still head of this House... and as head, I grant your request." He paused, turning toward Clara now. "With full blessing — from this moment forward — you are Princess Clara of the House of Rosenshavn. Not by accident. But by family." Clara gasped quietly, tears springing fresh as Ben pulled her close again. "You see, sweetheart?" Ben whispered gently in her ear. "You are family. You always were. Now the world knows it, too." She hugged him fiercely, never wanting to let go.

The candles flickered softly around them as the evening light faded beyond the tall castle windows, allowing the warm amber glow of the room to deepen into something sacred. This wasn't dinner anymore. This wasn't court or counsel.

This was family—breathing, holding, healing. Ben shifted slightly in his chair, never breaking eye contact with Clara, his hand still cradling her smaller one. She had already poured so much from her heart, but he knew — and she knew — that there was more. More that needed to rise. More that needed to leave her chest so it would no longer sit like a stone pressing against her every breath.

He spoke softly, gently — but with unwavering love. "Sweetheart... my Princess Clara..." His voice dipped tenderly on the title, giving it the weight it deserved. "I want you to hear me clearly now." Clara's tear-streaked eyes stayed locked on his. "What happened between your mom and dad—none of it was your fault." Her lip quivered again, but she didn't speak yet. Ben continued slowly, not rushing, careful with every syllable as though carrying precious glass. "Yes... sometimes parents fight. Sometimes words get loud. And yes... sometimes those arguments feel like the whole house is splitting apart."

He swallowed softly. "I know what that feels like." Isla, sitting quietly at Clara's side, gently rubbed her back, her touch constant and steady. "But, Clara..." Ben continued, "did you ever hear your name? Did they ever say that you were the reason?" Clara shook her head slowly, her lower lip trembling again. Ben smiled gently. "Exactly. You see, sweetheart? It wasn't about you. Even when grownups break apart... children are never the fault." He paused, letting that sink in. "And you know about your dad's job," Ben added, glancing briefly at Mr. Nielsen. "That wasn't his fault either."

Mr. Nielsen sat nearby, his eyes brimming. He tried to speak, but no words came. His throat locked. Ben noticed instantly and turned his eyes toward Sørensen, who quietly stepped forward from the background. Without words, Sørensen handed Mr. Nielsen a notepad and pen, along with a soft white tissue. He whispered something softly in Mr. Nielsen's ear—an invitation to write what he could not speak. Mr. Nielsen nodded, his hand gently trembling as he scribbled a short note, tears sliding silently down his face. "Ben is right. Clara... you were never the reason. Not for one second."

He slid the paper toward her across the polished table. Clara's eyes landed on the words, her breath catching slightly. She reached out, tracing her tiny fingertips along the edge of the page. Ben spoke again, gently but firmly. "The company didn't close because of anything your dad did. He worked hard — he always worked hard. But when the owner had to shut the doors... that was the owner's burden, not your father's failure. You understand that, sweetheart?" Clara nodded softly, but her tears came again, streaming now in silent rivers.

Ben gently reached forward and cupped her cheeks, guiding her face upward so their eyes locked. "Say it," Ben whispered. Clara swallowed hard. "It wasn't my fault." "Again, honey." "It wasn't my fault." "Louder." "It wasn't my fault," she whispered shakily.

"One more time, for you. Not for me." Clara took a deep breath, closing her eyes as her voice finally rose: "It wasn't my fault!" The moment settled heavily into the room like a stone being gently placed down after years of being carried. Ben pulled her back into his arms immediately, holding her tightly against his chest as she sobbed again — but this time, not with despair, but release. Minutes passed — long, healing minutes.

When her tears finally slowed once more, Ben leaned back, wiping her face with his thumb. "Good girl. That's my Princess Clara." Clara managed a small, trembling smile as she rested her forehead against his. At that moment, Kendrick, who had sat silent and reverent through it all, cleared his throat softly. "May I say something, son?" Ben nodded gently. "Of course, Dad." Kendrick turned his gaze toward Clara, his voice steady but full of warmth.

"Clara, my dear... you have shown more courage in these last few days than many adults show in a lifetime. And while titles are often given to people because of their birth, tonight... your title has been sealed by your heart." He smiled softly. "Princess Clara is not a formality. It's who you already are." Clara's eyes shimmered again, but this time, her smile broke wider, genuine.

Ben kissed her forehead once more. "See? You belong here. You always have." "I know," she whispered. Sørensen, still standing near the edge of the room, quietly rubbed his jaw, observing the entire scene with quiet pride. He was not needed here to speak — only to protect this circle from the world that often intruded far too easily. He smiled faintly to himself. This was real sovereignty. Mr. Nielsen, seated nearby, wiped his eyes again, looking at his daughter now not as a broken child — but as something far stronger: whole.

Ben looked once more at Clara, his voice calm but steady. "Sweetheart, I want you to keep talking whenever you need to. You don't ever have to hide how you feel here. This castle isn't just your home now. It's your sanctuary. We listen. Always." Isla nodded beside her. "We're always here, Clara. Forever." Clara chuckled faintly through her sniffles, leaning against Isla now, resting comfortably between her two siblings. "You're both crazy sometimes," she whispered with a grin. Ben raised his eyebrows playfully. "That's not a denial." They all laughed gently together, the tension dissolving at last into something lighter.

The next morning broke with a subtle dignity that seemed to permeate every stone of the great castle. Today was not like the others. Though the sky outside was calm, a different kind of anticipation hung inside the sovereign walls of the House of Rosenshavn.

The halls bustled with quiet preparation as the staff moved efficiently through their duties, knowing the significance of the day ahead. Word had already begun to trickle throughout the country — something was coming. The king was preparing to speak. But this time, it would not be about foreign dignitaries or sovereign alliances. Today's declaration belonged solely to the family itself.

Ben stood in front of the full-length mirror inside his private chamber, Isla gently adjusting the collar of his ceremonial jacket with tender precision. Clara stood nearby, dressed in a simple but elegant pale blue dress, her hair lightly curled for the occasion. She fidgeted slightly, not out of nervousness, but from the sheer reality of what was about to unfold.

"You're certain about this?" she whispered softly. Ben smiled warmly and knelt before her, adjusting the slight gold pin upon her shoulder — a tiny emblem of the House of Rosenshavn newly crafted for her alone. "I've never been more certain about anything, sweetheart," he said gently. "Today, we're simply making public what's always been true." Isla stepped forward, kneeling alongside him, placing a calming hand over Clara's. "You are family, Clara," Isla said softly. "You've been family since the moment you walked into our lives. Today, the world simply gets to see what we've always known."

Clara took a small breath, nodded, and whispered, "Okay." Ben rose and extended his hand, which Clara immediately took, her tiny fingers slipping into his palm with full trust. The grand chamber had been prepared for the announcement — not a full ceremony, but something formal enough to carry weight. The press stood gathered at respectful distance, the royal flags of Denmark hanging tall behind the speaking platform.

Royal council members, noble dignitaries, and castle staff lined the edges of the great hall. The people watched eagerly, many present physically, others tuning in by broadcast throughout the kingdom. At the front, two sovereigns stood together — King Kendrick of the House of Rosenshavn, and beside him, his son: His Majesty King Benedict Adrian Harvick. Though both kings stood as equals in royal authority, their presence carried different roles this morning. Kendrick stood as head of the sovereign house; Ben stood as the heart of the next generation, the one building his kingdom not through politics, but through love.

And on Ben's right stood Isla, regal and graceful as ever. On his left — her hand still in his — stood Clara. Small, brave, with steady nerves held by the anchor of her siblings' love. Kendrick was the first to speak. His voice, steady as ever, filled the chamber with calm dignity. "Today, the House of Rosenshavn acknowledges not the arrival of foreign powers, nor the conclusion of treaties, nor the exercise of rule. Today we acknowledge family." He glanced down to Clara for a brief moment, his eyes warm, before returning to the chamber.

"For the bonds of blood, while sacred, do not solely define what it means to be sovereign kin. The truest measure of family is found in love, in trust, and in sacrifice. It is in this spirit that I, Kendrick of Denmark, declare before all sovereign houses, all people of this realm, and before history itself... that Clara Ann Nielsen is hereby, with full blessing of the sovereign house, recognized as a daughter under this family." He paused slightly, allowing the words to land with weight before gently turning to Ben. "By sovereign right, my son, it is now your voice that completes this declaration."

Ben stepped forward with perfect poise, his voice steady, though rich with emotion that all could feel. He spoke not as a ruler speaking to subjects, but as a brother speaking to the nation who loved him. "My people," Ben began gently, his voice clear. "Today is not simply an announcement — it is a recognition of truth. This young girl beside me has already earned her place in our hearts and in this house. She carries no royal blood, but she carries something even greater: loyalty, courage, and the soul of this family."

He squeezed Clara's hand gently. "I declare, before my people, before the sovereigns, and before our House... that Clara Ann Nielsen, from this day forward, shall bear the title of Princess Clara Ann Nielsen of the House of Rosenshavn. Not by politics. Not by alliances. But by choice." He looked down at her with full warmth, his voice softening. "My sister. My Princess." A long breath seemed to release across the hall. The crowd, though respectfully silent, could not hold back the waves of emotional admiration that rippled through them. There was no applause — that would come later. For now, it was reverence.

Clara's eyes shimmered, her throat tightening as Ben leaned closer, whispering softly so only she could hear. "You belong here. You always have." Clara nodded quickly, barely able to whisper, "Thank you, Ben." Isla gently slipped her hand over Clara's shoulder, leaning in as well. "You're safe, sweetheart. Always." As the declaration ended, Kendrick stepped forward once again, speaking for both sovereigns as his voice wrapped the chamber in its final word:

"The House of Rosenshavn stands strengthened, not because of its crowns — but because of its love." He bowed his head slightly in respect. "Let it be written. Let it be known. Let it be remembered." As the chamber's doors opened, the family turned and slowly exited the grand hall together, stepping into the sunlight that now bathed the courtyard beyond. Ben walked forward, Isla on his right, Clara on his left — exactly where they belonged. For now, the nation rejoiced quietly. But tomorrow? Tomorrow would belong to Princess Clara's birthday.

The sun crested gently over the towers of the House of Rosenshavn, painting the sky with soft amber hues that carried a promise of something extraordinary. The entire castle estate glowed beneath the morning light, alive with anticipation. This was no ordinary day — not for the kingdom, not for the family, and certainly not for one very special young girl.

Today, Princess Clara Ann Nielsen turned eight years old. Preparations had begun before dawn. The grand courtyards of the castle, which had seen many royal occasions before, had been transformed overnight into something far more magical than any diplomatic banquet or state event. This was not about politics, nor about sovereign duty. This was a birthday — and not just any birthday. It was the birthday of a child who had recently found her forever home within these sovereign walls.

Ben had overseen every detail personally, alongside Isla, both of them working hand-in-hand with Kendrick and Sørensen to ensure this would be a day Clara would never forget. The entire courtyard had been dressed for joy: long flowing banners of soft blue and white — Clara's favourite colours — danced lightly in the summer breeze, fastened from the castle balconies. Rows of round tables had been carefully arranged under pristine white canopies, trimmed in golden ribbons that caught the sunlight like little sparks of celebration.

A grand stage sat toward the north end of the courtyard, draped in royal fabrics but softened with garlands of wildflowers carefully woven by hand — many by Isla herself — who had insisted on personally adding her own touch of love to the decorations.

Large archways of intertwined flowers and greenery lined the pathways, creating an enchanted maze of colour for the arriving guests to walk through. The castle staff had worked tirelessly to prepare tables stacked with food, sweet treats, and pastries, while a towering cake stood proudly at the centre of its own display — six layers high, each adorned with delicate sugar flowers, elegant piping, and a glittering number "8" perched at the top.

This was an open-door birthday, as Ben had declared boldly. No rigid guest list. No formality. The people of Denmark — noble and common alike — were welcome. Friends from the villages, playmates from the castle grounds, local children who had once played soccer with Ben and Isla — all were invited. As the morning unfolded, guests began to stream in, their faces beaming with joy. Children squealed with excitement as they explored the courtyard, running freely through the decorated paths. Parents chatted softly at the tables, sipping coffee and smiling as the air filled with laughter.

Clara stood at the upper balcony for a moment, gazing out over the scene below with wide, sparkling eyes. Her small hands clutched gently at the fabric of her soft white-and-blue birthday dress, carefully chosen for her by Isla — elegant, but still playful enough for a girl who wanted to run outside and play. Ben stood beside her, dressed handsomely in his light royal attire, not the heavy regalia of sovereigns, but the more relaxed dignity of a brother hosting his sister's greatest day.

"Breathtaking, isn't it?" Ben whispered, looking out over the crowd. Clara nodded, her voice catching slightly as she whispered back. "I never thought… I never imagined anything like this." Ben smiled, leaning down to kiss her forehead softly. "You deserve every bit of it." Isla joined them from behind, wrapping one arm around Clara's small shoulders and giving her a gentle squeeze. "And just wait — we haven't even started yet." By midday, the courtyard was alive with the music of laughter. A group of musicians played gentle, festive melodies beneath a shaded pavilion. The smells of freshly baked breads, roasted meats, and warm pastries filled the air. Large tables lined with fruit displays and delicate confections offered something for everyone.

Clara's friends — children from both the castle grounds and the nearby village — gathered around her in playful excitement. Soccer balls were soon rolling across the grassy lawn, and Ben, true to his nature, was among them, running, laughing, and playing with his usual boyish energy, sovereign title momentarily forgotten. Isla joined the game as well, effortlessly slipping between childlike joy and graceful dignity, her laughter blending naturally with the children as she dribbled the ball between Ben and Clara.

Sørensen, standing quietly near the edges of the celebration, smiled to himself as he observed the unfolding happiness. His role today was simple: observe, guard from a distance, but more importantly — witness. For today, even Sørensen allowed himself a rare ease. The threat of politics and the burdens of sovereignty were absent. His sharp eyes remained alert as always, but his shoulders rested lighter. Ben had remarked earlier that morning with a grin, "You know, Sørensen, I think today will stay quiet. No trouble. No nonsense." Sørensen had chuckled at that, shaking his head. "I'm not one to make predictions, sire… but today feels… peaceful."

Ben smiled. "Then let's enjoy it." As the sun dipped lower into the afternoon sky, the festivities shifted toward their centrepiece. A gentle chime rang through the courtyard as Kendrick stepped forward with microphone in hand, his voice steady but warm, carrying across the sea of guests. "May I have your attention, my dear friends, family, and honoured guests." The laughter and conversations quieted as every eye turned toward the platform. "Today," Kendrick began, "we do not gather for politics, nor for power, but for love. Today, we celebrate one who reminds us all why this House stands strong — because family makes it so."

He turned and extended his hand, inviting Clara forward. With gentle encouragement from Isla and Ben, Clara walked forward, her tiny feet careful at first, but her confidence steady. Her smile beamed as she reached Kendrick's side.

"My dear Clara Ann Nielsen," Kendrick continued, "Princess of Denmark, beloved daughter of this House — today we celebrate not only your eighth birthday, but the life you have brought into this family." He paused, looking across the gathered guests.

"To the people of Denmark, I say this: behold your princess — not born into title, but chosen by love." The crowd erupted into warm applause — not the polite clapping of state ceremonies, but genuine, heartfelt cheers of joy. Children cheered louder than anyone, calling Clara's name as she blushed brightly under the praise. Ben stepped forward now, joining Kendrick beside her, his voice rising with proud conviction.

"Clara, my sister — my princess — today belongs to you. This is your moment. This is your family. This is your home. And I will stand beside you forever." Clara looked up at him, her lips trembling with joy. "Thank you, Ben." "And now…" Ben grinned playfully, "…it's time for cake." The towering cake was brought forward to centre stage as guests gathered tightly around. Eight candles flickered brightly, their flames dancing in rhythm with the late afternoon breeze. Ben knelt beside Clara one last time before the candles.

"Make your wish, sweetheart," he whispered. "Only you will know what it is." Clara closed her eyes tightly, holding her breath for a long moment, her small hands clasped in front of her chest. Then she blew. The flames extinguished in a single breath, and the crowd cheered once again as the cake was carefully sliced and shared. The evening continued with music, laughter, games, and joyful chatter. As twilight began to settle gently over the castle, Clara found herself once more between Isla and Ben, safe within their protective circle.

Her voice was soft as she whispered, almost to herself: "This is the happiest day of my life." Ben smiled, wrapping his arm gently around her shoulder. "And there are many more to come, my princess." The sun had long since dipped behind the castle spires, leaving the courtyards bathed in the soft golden hue of torchlight and lanterns strung like stars across the sky. The festivities of Clara's eighth birthday continued to hum with life as the evening embraced the sovereign grounds.

Children still laughed as they chased one another in the grassy corners of the courtyard, their shoes long since abandoned. The air smelled richly of roasted meats and warm bread as preparations for the grand dinner carried on. Laughter and quiet conversations filled every corner, but amidst it all, Clara stood quietly near the edge of the central platform, her small hands gently clasped together at her waist. She had something to say.

And she knew it had to be now. Sørensen approached her with his usual quiet attentiveness. He bent slightly, speaking softly so only she could hear. "Are you ready, my princess?" Clara nodded, her eyes sparkling under the torchlight. "Yes, Uncle Sørensen. I'm ready." With a small smile, Sørensen stepped back and signalled discreetly to the castle staff. At his quiet direction, the soft background music gently faded. Conversations around the courtyard began to hush as people sensed something meaningful was about to happen.

The news crew, who had respectfully observed from a distance throughout the day, readied themselves without being intrusive. Their cameras rolled quietly, capturing history — not as paparazzi, but as honoured chroniclers of the House of Rosenshavn. Ben, Isla, Kendrick, Alex, and the entire extended family turned their full attention toward Clara as she stepped confidently up to the small speaking platform. A simple wooden stand had been prepared for her, her height carefully accommodated with a small step beneath her feet.

The entire courtyard fell silent. Even the youngest children paused, sensing the weight of this moment. Clara paused, taking one deep breath, and began. Her voice was small at first, but steady. "Everyone... may I say something?" The soft murmur of affirmations rippled through the courtyard. She glanced toward Ben and Isla, drawing her strength from their steady smiles. "I know today has been so special. And... I can't even find enough words to say how thankful I am for everything you've done for me."

Her voice cracked slightly, but she pushed through. "I've had friends here for years — many of you, since I was just three years old. You played with me. You laughed with me. You made me feel like I belonged." She smiled shyly at her young friends scattered among the tables. "And today... I want you to know that you are part of my family too. All of you." The children beamed with pride. Clara took another breath, steadying herself as her voice grew stronger. "But now... there are some people I need to speak to directly. Because without them... I wouldn't be standing here."

Her eyes shifted first to her father, Alex Nielsen, seated near Kendrick. "Daddy... you never gave up on me. Even when you were tired. Even when you were hurting... you still smiled for me. You worked hard, even when it was scary. And you always, always made me feel loved." Alex wiped his eyes openly, his hand clutching a tissue Sørensen had once again quietly passed to him. Clara smiled tenderly at him. "You'll always be my daddy. And I love you." She turned now toward Sørensen.

"Uncle Sørensen... I know you're usually standing in the background, watching everything. But I see you. I always have. You keep us safe. You don't always say much, but I can feel your love." Her voice trembled. "You don't just protect me like a guard. You protect me like family. And you are family." Sørensen's face softened with rare vulnerability. His chest swelled as he quietly dipped his head in a respectful bow toward her, unable to find words, but fully receiving hers.

Clara now turned toward Kendrick. "Uncle Kendrick... my king." The courtyard grew even quieter. "You didn't have to make me your daughter. You didn't have to welcome me into your house. But you did. You gave me something I never dreamed I'd have... a home. A real home. And I promise... I'll never forget it. I love you." Kendrick's voice broke slightly as he nodded. "And I love you, my daughter." Finally, Clara turned back toward Ben and Isla, her eyes now shimmering with tears — but tears of full joy.

Her voice was tender, but strong. "Ben... Isla... you are my brother and sister. You're the ones who held me when I cried. Who let me fall apart and never made me feel ashamed. You never told me to 'be brave' when I couldn't. You let me feel. And then you carried me." She paused, her voice catching again. "You don't love me because I'm a princess. You love me because I'm Clara. And that's all I've ever wanted."

Ben swallowed hard, holding Isla's hand tightly as she stood at his side, her own eyes glistening. "I don't want to ever be anything different," Clara finished. "I just want to always be your sister. And always be loved." She paused a final moment before whispering her closing words to the entire courtyard: "This is my forever home. And I will always be grateful." The courtyard held its breath for a moment — a beautiful, fragile silence where no applause came too soon. And then — the applause began. First soft. Then louder. Then full.

Children, parents, nobles, citizens — all standing now, clapping not for royalty, but for love itself. Ben stepped forward to the platform, kneeling once again to her level. "You will always be my sister, Clara," he whispered softly. "Always." He opened his arms wide, and she flew into them, burying her face into his chest as he lifted her easily from the stand, carrying her back toward Isla. Isla gently took Clara into her own arms for a moment, hugging her tight before wrapping her arm around both of them as they stood together before the gathered crowd.

Kendrick raised his voice one final time for the evening: "Tonight, my people, we dine together — not as sovereigns and subjects, but as one family." And with that, the feast began.

Tables overflowed with every delicacy one could imagine:
Roasted lamb, golden brown and tender.
Thick cuts of roast beef, carved fresh at long tables.
Succulent roasted chickens and pork, glistening with herbs and spices.
Boiled, baked, and mashed potatoes in every form — the best potatoes on earth, as Ben had jokingly declared.
Fresh vegetables, glistening with butter and seasoned to perfection.
Endless platters of fruits, breads, and desserts, all prepared for Clara's perfect day. As the stars emerged fully above them, the House of Rosenshavn rejoiced together — not for crowns, not for power — but for love that had chosen them all.

The evening wore on in a gentle, glowing hum, the sky deepening into a rich navy as twilight surrendered to night. The courtyards of the House of Rosenshavn, still bathed in golden torchlight, seemed to wait, almost holding their breath for something unseen. Children still chased one another in quieter games now, their laughter softer, the adults leaning back in their chairs with the heavy satisfaction of a feast well enjoyed. Conversations faded into the kind of easy murmurs that only come when the heart is full and the body is content.

Ben, standing quietly at the edge of the main table, watched the horizon darken. His fingers brushed the inside cuff of his jacket, feeling the tiny, almost imperceptible device nestled there. A subtle gesture, a barely-there motion of his wrist, sent a signal — and across the far side of the castle grounds, a pyrotechnician saw the cue.
The air shifted. The music playing softly through the courtyard speakers, a selection chosen carefully from Ben's private collection, mellowed and slowed, drifting into a gentle, melodic pause.

Then— BANG. BANG. BANG. BANG.
The first round of fireworks exploded into the sky with a ferocity that stole the breath from every gathered guest. Bright, cascading streams of crimson, gold, sapphire, and emerald blossomed high above the castle towers, lighting up the night with thunderous brilliance. There was a collective gasp from the crowd — adults and children alike — as the sky came alive. Fireworks in shapes of hearts, of diamonds, of twining wreaths of light — each more intricate and dazzling than the last — burst one after another in perfect, choreographed succession.

Ben stole a glance at his father. Kendrick nodded slightly, an unspoken signal of approval. This display, this symphony of light and sound, had been no accident of fortune — it had been chosen. Planned. For Clara. And as Ben turned his gaze to her, standing just ahead of him near the platform, he saw it: Clara's face, tipped skyward, her mouth slightly agape in pure, unfiltered wonder. The light of the fireworks reflected in her wide eyes, making her seem to glow from within.

For forty-five full minutes, the sky rained colour and sound. Massive blooms of brilliant gold gave way to shimmering tendrils of silver that fell like meteor showers. Spirals of green and blue raced each other across the darkness, colliding and erupting into new constellations of fire. But it was not just the splendour that made it unforgettable. It was what it meant. This was not fireworks for a nation's independence, nor for a sovereign's coronation. This was not for treaties, alliances, or wealth. This was for Clara. For her eighth birthday. For her life, her joy, her belonging.

As the final crescendo of light burst above them — a massive, golden heart that shattered into a cascade of silver stars — the courtyard erupted into cheers and applause once more, not for the fireworks, but for the girl at the centre of it all. Clara turned toward Ben, her cheeks flushed with pure happiness, her eyes shining. Ben leaned close and whispered, "This day — this sky — it's yours, sweetheart." Clara threw her arms around his waist, and Ben chuckled as he hugged her close.

"I love you, Ben," she whispered into his jacket. "And I love you, Princess Clara," he whispered back, ruffling her hair. The night slowly wound down, the stars reclaiming the sky from the fading smoke of fireworks. The torches burned lower. The guests, full from food and filled to the brim with joy, began to quietly drift away, many offering quiet goodnights and soft words of blessing for the young princess as they left.

Inside the castle, the warmth of the hearths replaced the torchlight. Ben and Isla, walking hand-in-hand with Clara between them, made their way back toward the family chambers. Alex followed quietly, smiling softly as he watched his daughter practically float between her brother and sister, her little hand clasped tightly in Ben's.

They reached the family quarters, and as they passed through the great wooden doors, Ben crouched to Clara's level. "Come here, sweetheart."

She turned, curious, and Ben glanced to Isla, who smiled knowingly. "We have one more gift for you tonight," Ben said. He took her small hand in his and led her gently down the corridor toward their shared room. Isla followed, quietly closing the door behind them. Inside, the room was softly lit, the great bed freshly made, the cool night breeze lifting the sheer curtains at the windows. Ben sat down on the edge of the bed, pulling Clara gently forward.

"Tonight," he said, "you're staying with us." Clara blinked, surprised, and her small mouth broke into a wide smile. "Really?" "Really, Isla said, sitting on the other side and patting the spot between them. "Right in the middle, sweetheart," Ben confirmed. "Right where you belong."

Clara climbed up without hesitation, nestling herself comfortably between them, her heart full to bursting. But before the final descent into sleep, Ben grinned, lifting an eyebrow in mischief. "Now, before we settle in for the night... you know the rule." Clara groaned playfully. "Bladder chatter," she said, rolling her eyes with a giggle.

Ben chuckled. "Exactly. Go on — do yourself a favour." Clara hopped off the bed with a grin and disappeared into the adjoining bathroom. Moments later, she returned, hands on her hips. "Your turn," she said, smirking. Ben laughed as he rose, ruffling her hair on his way past. "Bossy already," he teased. When he returned a few minutes later, the room was filled with soft giggles.

"You know," Clara said, mock-stern, "if your royal bottom had a gold seat, I think I'd have to call you King Potty." Ben burst out laughing, Isla covering her face with a pillow as she dissolved into giggles. "That," Ben said, wiping tears from his eyes, "would be a royal throne, and no — thankfully, I'm still common enough to avoid that."

Clara beamed, proud of herself, as Ben slid back into bed. With their nightly "bladder chatter" duties behind them, they snuggled close. Clara nestled herself tightly between Ben and Isla, her small arms tucked under the heavy comforter, her breath slowing into the easy rhythm of a child at peace. Ben kissed the top of her head. "Goodnight, sweetheart."

Isla leaned over and whispered, "Goodnight, Clara." Clara's voice was a sleepy murmur. "Goodnight, Ben... goodnight, Isla... I love you." Within minutes, all three were asleep, the castle settling into its midnight silence.

Outside, the stars blinked gently over the House of Rosenshavn — and within, so did the dreams of a little girl who now knew, with every beat of her heart, that she was exactly where she belonged. Home. Forever.

The first soft hints of dawn filtered gently through the tall windows, wrapping the royal chambers in a muted golden glow. The castle stirred faintly, though much of the estate still slumbered in the comfort of the deep morning hour. The air was calm, the mood unhurried, and inside the family quarters, all was as peaceful as any sovereign house could ever wish to be. In the centre of the great bed, nestled between her brother and sister, Clara stirred first. Her small eyes fluttered open, taking a few seconds to register her surroundings, and then a gentle smile stretched across her face.

She was home. Still here. Still safe. Still with them. For a few moments, she lay perfectly still, not wanting to disturb the gentle rhythm of Ben's and Isla's breathing on either side of her. She could feel the warmth of Isla's arm draped protectively across her waist and the steady comfort of Ben's shoulder beneath her head. The even rise and fall of their breathing was like music, wrapping around her like the softest lullaby.

And then came the voice she half-expected. Ben, barely opening his eyes but already sensing her movement, spoke softly. "Good morning, sweetheart." His voice was low and calm, still heavy with sleep but rich with warmth. "Morning, Ben," Clara whispered back, her voice no louder than the breeze dancing through the slightly open window. On her other side, Isla stirred, her hand tightening momentarily around Clara's waist before she opened her eyes.

"Morning already?" Isla yawned, rubbing her eyes with her free hand. Clara giggled softly. "It is." Ben stretched lazily, glancing at the clock on the far wall. "Just past six. That's not bad," he said, voice still half-drowsy. "You made it longer than I thought you would." Clara smiled shyly. "I didn't want to wake you." Ben chuckled. "You could've woken us anytime. That's part of being family." Isla propped herself up slightly, planting a soft kiss on Clara's forehead. "Happy first full day as an eight-year-old, Princess Clara."

Clara's cheeks flushed at the title but glowed with the happiness that came with it. Then, as if on cue, Ben grinned. "Well… before we start this perfect day, you know the rule." Clara groaned playfully and threw her hands over her face. "Bladder chatter." Ben nodded. "Exactly. Bladders first, breakfast later." Isla laughed. "Go on, sweetheart. You first." Clara hopped off the bed, padding barefoot across the soft carpet toward the bathroom. A moment later, her voice called out playfully from behind the door.

"Ben, you're next!" Ben chuckled. "Why am I always next?" he grumbled in mock protest as he rolled out of bed. Isla giggled. "Because you always insist on making the rule." Soon enough, all three returned to the bed, refreshed, laughing softly as they settled into the morning rhythm that was quickly becoming familiar. A gentle knock came at the chamber door. It was followed by the familiar voice of one of the castle's trusted staff.

"Coffee's on your table, Your Majesties." Ben and Isla answered together, still smiling: "Thank you very much." Clara wrinkled her nose. "And my tea?" The staff chuckled from behind the door. "Your tea as well, Princess." Clara giggled. "Thank you!" Breakfast arrived soon after — trays of fluffy pancakes, waffles drizzled with syrup, sizzling strips of bacon, golden breakfast sausages, fresh fruits and berries glistening in the morning light.

As they gathered around their private breakfast table, Ben raised his coffee mug. "To you, Clara. May every morning be as happy as this one." Clara blushed, lifting her own cup of tea. "And to my brother and sister — who make it perfect." Isla raised her cup as well. "To family." They clinked cups gently, a quiet, perfect start to the day.

By mid-morning, the three of them had ventured outside into the castle gardens, where the air smelled sweet from last night's celebration.

The staff had already cleared much of the decorations, but a few remnants remained: bits of ribbon, the faint scent of fireworks still lingering faintly in the breeze, the echoes of laughter still present like warm ghosts of the night before.

Clara twirled once in the open lawn, letting the morning sun kiss her face. "I still can't believe it really happened," she whispered softly to no one in particular. Ben, watching her with quiet pride, replied gently, "It did, sweetheart. And it always will." By late morning, they had found their usual rhythm. Soccer balls rolled across the grass once more as their friends joined them for a casual game, laughter echoing across the grounds as Clara raced after Isla in playful competition. Ben played goalkeeper, grinning broadly as he blocked shots and dove across the grass, his royal jacket long since tossed aside, replaced by a simple t-shirt and rolled sleeves.

Kendrick stood at a respectful distance, chatting quietly with Alex Nielsen, both fathers watching their children with the same quiet, satisfied pride. Sørensen, ever watchful, kept his station farther back — still sharp, but today at ease. His expression carried a rare softness, watching the children with a certain kind of reverence.

The sovereign house was at peace. When lunchtime arrived, Clara was still glowing with energy, bounding between her brother and sister, linking arms with them both as they walked inside for the midday meal.

Her face lit with a grin as she leaned toward Ben. "This is my first full day as an eight-year-old." Ben laughed. "And you're already making it perfect." "Isn't it always like this now?" she asked, eyes wide with innocent joy. Ben paused thoughtfully before answering. "Yes, sweetheart. It is." Isla nodded, smiling. "This is your life now. Family. Forever." As they entered the dining hall, the family gathered once more — Kendrick, Alex, Sørensen, and the entire circle seated comfortably, the table already laid out for another simple but rich family meal. No ceremony. No fanfare. Just home.

As the meal began, Ben sat back for a moment, watching Clara as she laughed, talked, and enjoyed every bite. The light shone through the windows behind her, making her hair glow softly as she smiled at her father, leaned against Isla, and beamed up at him. And in that moment, Ben knew that everything they had built was exactly as it was meant to be. Not perfect because of crowns or sovereign duties. Perfect because of love. And because Princess Clara Ann Nielsen had found her place. At last. The early afternoon sun cast its soft golden rays over the sprawling grounds of the House of Rosenshavn.

The gentle hum of castle life continued, but at a peaceful rhythm — no ceremonies, no formal gatherings, no dignitaries to entertain. It was the kind of afternoon that Ben cherished most: quiet, meaningful, yet filled with the richness that sovereign life rarely allowed. At precisely two o'clock, Ben, Isla, and Clara settled themselves inside one of the castle's private study rooms—a place that carried far less of the stiff formality of the royal libraries, and far more of the atmosphere Ben and Isla had always sought: a place for family learning.

Books lined the shelves, not by the thousands as in the royal archives, but carefully selected volumes, scrolls, and records that told the story of families — not just kings and queens, but ordinary men and women whose names whispered through the bloodlines of history. Today, Clara would begin to understand the deeper art behind it all. Ben gently unrolled one of the large genealogy charts across the polished oak table. The parchment's carefully drawn branches spread like an ancient tree, names scripted in fine calligraphy, dates and places anchoring each branch like roots pressing into soil.

Clara leaned forward, her eyes widening with curiosity. "This... this is how it starts?" she whispered, tracing a tiny fingertip along the curling lines. Ben smiled, nodding. "This is how it always starts, sweetheart. Every family has a beginning.

Every name tells a story." Isla added softly, "You see, Clara — it's not just about kings or thrones. Every person matters in a genealogy. Every branch matters. Without even one name, the tree is incomplete." Clara's eyes moved carefully over the lines of names: fathers, mothers, children, marriages, dates of birth and passing, migrations across countries. She could see how lives had moved like rivers across the world.

"It's like a puzzle," she whispered. Ben chuckled. "Exactly. A puzzle made of names and years — and sometimes, thorns." "Thorns?" Clara blinked. Isla nodded. "The hard parts. The secrets. The broken places in families. The parts that hurt." "But we still write them down?" Clara asked. Ben's voice grew gentle. "Yes, sweetheart. Because even the broken parts are part of the truth. And the truth always belongs to the family."

They continued for over an hour, moving through charts, explaining the codes, the notations, the reasons behind migrations, adoptions, marriages, and even lost branches. Ben pulled out DNA charts next, explaining the complicated but fascinating world of genetics. "See these little codes here?" Ben pointed to the haplogroup charts. "That's what helps us trace ancient lines, back thousands of years sometimes." Clara's eyes grew even wider. "Thousands?" "Sometimes longer than recorded history itself," Isla added with a small grin. "It's like speaking to people we never met, but who made us possible."

After some silence, Clara finally asked the question sitting in her heart. "Ben... do you ever miss Kent? Like, really miss it?" The question carried a weight she hadn't spoken before. Ben paused. His gaze softened, looking toward the distant windows, as if Kent lived just outside the castle walls. "All the time, sweetheart," he said quietly. "Every single day." Isla gently rubbed his arm. Ben smiled faintly, though his voice quivered slightly. "My mom and dad are still there. Jeff, my dad — I think about him constantly. And Annemarie... she'll always be my mom, no matter how far we are apart."

Clara, thoughtful, spoke with surprising maturity. "I know you talk to Isla about it... but would you always tell me if you ever feel that way? If you ever feel sad or lonely?" Ben's throat caught for a moment. She had spoken not as a child, but as a sister. He reached across and cupped her cheek gently. "Clara... thank you, my princess. That means more to me than you know. Yes — I promise. If ever my heart is heavy, I will share it with you too." Tears welled briefly in both of their eyes, and Isla smiled quietly, watching the two siblings draw closer still.

After a pause, Ben reached for a small sealed envelope sitting beside him — Sørensen's note. "You remember when we promised Uncle Sørensen we would build his family tree?" Ben asked gently. Clara nodded quickly. "Back in Kent. When he was on vacation with us." Isla laughed. "Well, trying to be on vacation. We had to keep reminding him not to work." Ben smiled, holding up the note. "Today, we're starting." Clara's eyes lit up. "Finally!"

Ben nodded. "I left this on his nightstand this morning. Hand delivered by me. Only me. No staff entered his room." He chuckled "Uncle Sørensen likes his privacy." The note was short but clear:

Uncle Sørensen,
Your genealogy project officially starts today.
You will be scheduled for a blood test this week, and your Ancestry DNA kit will arrive shortly.
No further work required — just show up and let the science do its job.
With love,
Ben (and Isla, and Princess Clara — your family)

Across the grounds, Sørensen had received the note earlier that morning. True to form, he read it quietly, smiled faintly to himself, and tucked it neatly into his private desk drawer — as always, a man of few words, but much heart. Meanwhile, outside beneath the gentle shade of the great oaks, Kendrick and Alex sat together at one of the garden tables, each holding their afternoon coffee. The lawns, trimmed to perfection, rolled outward like a painting, every blade of grass appearing as if it had been hand-placed.

Kendrick leaned back in his chair, surveying the grounds with quiet satisfaction. "Alex," he said with genuine warmth, "you are the best groundskeeper I've ever had. You've made this place something out of a fairy tale." Alex chuckled, his broad smile reaching ear to ear. "Some days I think it feels that way too." Kendrick shook his head with admiration. "No exaggeration — this is art. Not just a job. You've made it a living portrait." Alex's grin only widened. "Thank you, Your Majesty. Though I must admit... even I sometimes walk out here and think, 'How on earth did I do that?'" Both men laughed softly, sipping their coffee while the light breeze danced between them.

And so the afternoon rolled on — genealogy lessons inside, conversations under the trees outside, gentle laughter throughout the castle halls. No court sessions. No political duties. No press conferences. Just family. A kingdom at peace, breathing. The afternoon sun had begun its gradual descent, casting long, golden rays across the stone terraces of the castle. The grounds glimmered softly, every hedge, every walkway, every tree standing tall beneath the care of Alex Nielsen's impeccable work. The castle felt alive, but not in the frantic way that sovereign halls so often did.

Today, life moved as it should — steady, unhurried, and deliberate. Inside the family wing, the quiet hum of progress continued. The genealogy table remained spread with parchments, charts, and folders — some old, others freshly prepared. In the midst of it all sat Ben, Isla, and Clara, still very much absorbed in the process, but with a new name now written across the top of their working chart:

SØRENSEN FAMILY LINE — INITIAL ENTRY

Ben tapped his pencil gently against the chart as Clara leaned over his shoulder, watching intently. "Now," Ben said softly, "we begin." Clara tilted her head. "But we don't know anything yet, do we?" Isla smiled. "That's exactly why we start here.
You build from nothing — one branch, one date, one name at a time." Ben added, "Think of it like planting a seed, sweetheart. We don't see the tree yet, but it's growing. Piece by piece." As if on cue, a quiet knock sounded at the chamber door. Ben glanced up. "Enter."

Sørensen stepped inside, his tall, composed frame casting a familiar presence over the room. But today, his usual crisp professional demeanour carried a softness around the edges. "You summoned me, Your Majesties?" Sørensen asked with a faint smile, his voice respectful but tinged with something warmer: family ease. Ben motioned him inside. "Uncle Sørensen, right on time." Clara beamed. "Come see what we started!"

Sørensen stepped forward, peering over the edge of the parchment. His eyes scanned the heading, taking it in with a quiet breath. "So... it has begun." Ben nodded. "Indeed it has. This is your family, Uncle. Or rather... it will be." Sørensen's voice lowered, touched with something he rarely showed aloud. "I never expected... I never imagined I would have anyone trace me." Ben reached across the table and rested his hand gently on Sørensen's forearm. "You're not just security. You're not staff. You're not a distant observer. You're family. This... is what family does."

Clara, eager as always, leaned forward excitedly. "And you'll need to get your DNA test this week! Ben already scheduled your blood draw — that's step one. And Isla and I will help you do your ancestry kit when it arrives." Sørensen chuckled softly, his rare laughter echoing in the chamber. "You're not wasting any time, I see." Ben smirked. "We're thorough. Besides, you've waited long enough." Sørensen looked at each of them in turn, his eyes pausing briefly on Clara. "I am grateful."

Clara smiled sweetly, her voice soft but full of affection. "We're just happy you said yes." There was a long, warm pause — one of those silences that fill a room not with emptiness, but with understanding. Finally, Sørensen spoke again.

"Your Highness—" he caught himself, correcting with gentle familiarity, "—Ben... I never knew what it meant to belong like this." Ben's voice came steady. "You do now, Uncle. And you always will." Isla nodded softly. "Family is not always who you're born to. Sometimes, it's who finds you."

Sørensen's eyes misted faintly as he gave a small nod of his head. The moment was tender but grounded — and true to form, Sørensen instinctively shifted the conversation toward something lighter. Ever watchful for the balance of emotion. "Your father — His Majesty — sent me with a message," Sørensen said. Ben arched an eyebrow. "Oh?"

"He and Alex are calling for you three. Coffee's being served outside. And I believe there's apple pie involved." Clara gasped dramatically. "Pie?!" Ben laughed, standing from his chair. "Well now, we can't say no to that." Isla rose, linking arms with Clara. "Come on, sweetheart.

Let's take a break." Together, they made their way out to the gardens once more, where Kendrick and Alex sat under the shade of the great oaks. The coffee table was already set with fresh cups, saucers, and indeed, two large pies — one apple, one cherry.

"About time you arrived," Kendrick teased as they approached. "The pie was beginning to worry it would spoil." Clara immediately scurried forward, taking her seat beside Alex and looking up at him with a smile that could've melted stone. "Daddy, Ben says you're the best groundskeeper ever." Alex chuckled, reaching over to ruffle her hair. "Well, that's very kind of him." "He's not wrong," Kendrick added. "This place looks like it belongs in a storybook."

Alex's grin stretched wide again, that ear-to-ear gratitude still shining just as bright as the day before. As the coffee was poured and the pie sliced, the family settled into the kind of conversation that only sovereigns who have finally learned how to breathe get to enjoy. No politics. No press. No threats. No pressures. Just voices. Laughter. And simple belonging. The genealogy papers remained spread inside, the research only beginning. Sørensen's family tree would take time, care, and patience.

But as Ben glanced across the garden table, watching Isla and Clara giggle over whose slice of pie was larger, and seeing Alex sip his coffee while Kendrick admired the handiwork of the immaculate grounds, Ben felt it settle deeper into his chest. They weren't building only family trees. They were building family itself.

The afternoon light had begun its slow stretch across the western sky, softening the castle's grand stone walls in a warm, amber hue. The peaceful hum of life inside the House of Rosenshavn continued, as though the castle itself was breathing—calm, steady, and full.

Ben, Isla, and Clara had returned to the study after their coffee and pie, their stomachs full, their hearts light, but their minds ready to resume the work they had begun earlier. The genealogy table remained spread, but now, several fresh documents sat beside it — the first forms needed to initiate Sørensen's full genealogical review. The time for theory was over. The real work had begun. Ben stood before the table, reviewing the paperwork carefully while Clara sat cross-legged on one of the oversized armchairs nearby, watching attentively.

"So, Uncle Sørensen's medical appointment is scheduled for Thursday morning," Ben explained. "Bloodwork will be taken, then the labs will begin processing his DNA for the full sequencing." Isla added, "And his Ancestry DNA kit should arrive tomorrow morning by secure courier. The saliva kit will give us parallel data for cross-matching." Clara blinked in wonder. "So you're really going to find out where he comes from?" Ben smiled. "We are, sweetheart. And if we're lucky, we'll uncover family branches he never knew existed. "Like… cousins?" Clara asked softly.

"Exactly," Isla replied. "Sometimes distant cousins. Sometimes very close ones. You never know what the past will give you." Sørensen, entered the study quietly, as he so often did, like a respectful shadow stepping gently into a room. His eyes fell immediately upon the neat rows of paperwork now prepared for him. "You've been busy," he said, a faint note of dry amusement in his voice. Ben gestured toward the chair across from him. "Come. Sit. This is your journey now."

Sørensen hesitated only for a moment, then crossed the room with a silent grace, lowering himself into the chair opposite Ben. For a long moment, they sat in quiet reflection, the weight of the moment pressing softly between them. "This feels… strange," Sørensen finally admitted. "After all these years of protecting everyone else's secrets… now my own story opens." Ben nodded gently. "Yes. But it's a story you deserve to know." Isla added softly, "And one we will walk with you. Every page."

Clara, sitting wide-eyed nearby, finally asked, "Uncle Sørensen… do you ever wonder what you'll find?" Sørensen turned his gaze toward her, his expression softening further. "Many times, my little princess. I have always wondered. I was adopted when I was very young. I've known no other parents but those who raised me… and even they shared little of my beginning." Ben leaned forward. "And now we'll give you those answers." Sørensen's voice lowered. "If any exist." Ben's voice carried a quiet conviction. "They exist. You simply haven't seen them yet." The forms were reviewed carefully. Sørensen signed each document with deliberate precision, his pen strokes as steady as his nature. The genetic consent forms. The privacy agreements. The permissions for data analysis. Each page brought him closer to truths long hidden by time.

When the last signature dried, Ben gently gathered the papers, sliding them into a folder embossed with the royal seal. "It's official," Ben said softly. "Your search is no longer theoretical, Uncle. It's underway." Sørensen exhaled slowly, as though releasing years of quiet anticipation. "Then I entrust it entirely to you." They sat quietly for several minutes afterward, letting the moment breathe as it deserved. Finally, Clara broke the silence with the innocent simplicity only a child could offer. "Uncle Sørensen... when we find your family... can they come visit?"

Sørensen's smile broke softly across his face. "If they exist, sweetheart... I would very much like that." Ben smiled warmly. "And when the time comes, we'll welcome them as family. Just as you were welcomed." Sørensen dipped his head. "You honour me." Outside the tall windows, the soft winds of late afternoon rustled through the castle gardens. Far across the grounds, Alex Nielsen continued his meticulous work, pruning and inspecting the gardens with the same careful attention he always offered — his quiet devotion to beauty never wavering.

At one point, Kendrick stepped outside to join him once more. The two men stood side by side beneath the great oaks, their coffee cups freshly poured, watching the work as the breeze carried the sweet scent of the earth. "You're an artist, Alex," Kendrick said, admiring the view. "You don't just care for the grounds. You sculpt them." Alex grinned humbly. "Thank you, Your Majesty. It feels... right. Like this is what I was always meant to do."

Kendrick nodded slowly, his eyes scanning the perfection before him. "Every one of us has our calling, Alex. Some on thrones, some at tables, some with shears and soil... but all equally sovereign in what they do." Alex's eyes misted faintly at the unexpected weight of the compliment. "I don't serve a king, sir," he whispered. "I serve my family." Kendrick placed a firm hand on his shoulder. "Exactly."

Inside, the sun had lowered just enough for the study to darken into a warm, amber glow. Ben closed the genealogy books softly, glancing at Isla and Clara. "That's enough for today." Clara yawned slightly, stretching her arms as Isla pulled her into a soft hug.

Sørensen rose smoothly from his chair and quietly took his leave, his heart lighter now than it had been when he entered. The family followed behind slowly, their footsteps echoing softly in the quiet halls. And so the day deepened — not into complexity, but into meaning. The work had only begun, but the family itself stood stronger than ever. Sørensen's history was beginning to speak. And they would be there to hear every word.

Evening had settled over the House of Rosenshavn like a soft wool blanket, wrapping the castle in peaceful shadows and muted light. The golden rays of the afternoon had long since faded into the violet hues of dusk. Throughout the halls, the staff moved quietly, drawing heavy drapes closed, lighting the wall sconces one by one, and preparing the estate for the quiet hours that now approached. The echo of children's laughter from the day's earlier games had softened into stillness. Inside the private family wing, the rhythm of royal life had shifted once again — not into business or ceremony, but into something far more valuable: rest.

The family gathered as they so often did at day's end, in the grand sitting room that overlooked the western gardens. The wide windows offered a full view of the night sky as stars began to blink into place, one by one. Ben, Isla, and Clara sat together on the long, velvet sofa, with Clara nestled comfortably between them, her head resting against Ben's shoulder, while Isla gently ran her fingers through Clara's soft hair.

Across from them, Kendrick sat with his coffee, while Alex occupied the seat beside him, nursing a cup of tea. Sørensen remained nearby, as always, quietly stationed with them, though not out of duty. His presence had long since shifted from protection into shared belonging. "I think we made excellent progress today," Ben said softly, breaking the gentle silence. Isla nodded, offering a small smile. "The start of Uncle Sørensen's tree is officially planted." Clara, still half-sleepy but listening intently, mumbled, "And I can't wait to see who he comes from…"

Sørensen smiled faintly, his voice calm. "Neither can I, little one." Kendrick, sipping his coffee, added thoughtfully, "Patience is the greatest tool in genealogical work. You never know when the past will finally speak… but when it does, it often says more than we expect." The conversation drifted for a while into lighter matters — into simple memories of their time together in Kent, into the smaller joys of daily life that few sovereign families were privileged to savour. Ben, after a quiet pause, looked over at Alex.

"How's the grounds looking for tomorrow?" Alex grinned humbly. "Perfect as always, Your Majesty." Ben chuckled. "I never doubt you, Alex." Alex's voice softened. "It's a labour of love, Ben. That's all it's ever been."

Kendrick, setting his coffee aside, nodded in agreement. "And your love for it shows in every corner of these grounds." Alex's eyes glistened faintly at the sincerity in their voices. "I just want it to always feel like home for Clara… for all of you." Clara stirred slightly at hearing her name, lifting her head from Ben's shoulder.

"And it does," she said softly. "It's the most beautiful place in the world." Ben smiled, pulling her gently closer. "That's because you make it beautiful too, sweetheart." She giggled quietly, snuggling back into him, her eyes growing heavier with each passing moment. Isla glanced to Ben and whispered, "We may have tired her out today." Ben chuckled softly, brushing Clara's hair back. "That's what a proper first day as an eight-year-old should feel like." Isla grinned. "We should declare it official."

Ben smiled. "Consider it done." The room grew quieter as the hour moved closer to bedtime. Kendrick finally rose from his chair, stretching slightly as he glanced toward Sørensen. "Let the staff know we'll be closing the wing for the night." "Yes, Your Majesty," Sørensen replied, moving with his usual calm precision to relay the order. As he stepped out, Alex also rose, gently smoothing his shirt as he turned to Clara. "Come, little one. Let's get you ready for bed."

But Clara hesitated. She turned to Ben and Isla, her voice barely above a whisper. "May I stay with you again tonight?" Ben smiled warmly. "Of course, sweetheart." Isla nodded. "Always." Alex chuckled softly. "She's already spoiled." Ben stood, gently lifting Clara into his arms. "And I intend to keep it that way." They all laughed softly at the tenderness in his words, and Alex stepped forward to place a light kiss on his daughter's forehead. "Goodnight, my princess." "Goodnight, Daddy."

As Ben carried Clara toward their chambers, Isla walking quietly beside him, Kendrick stood for a moment, watching them with a peaceful pride. His heart swelled not from crowns or power, but from the rare satisfaction of seeing a sovereign house built not by force — but by love. The castle settled into deep silence. Guards took their stations. The staff retreated for the night. The winds outside whispered gently against the stone walls.

Inside, beneath the safety of its ancient roof, a young princess fell asleep between her brother and sister, wrapped not in ceremony — but in arms that promised her belonging forever. And in another wing of the castle, inside his private quarters, Sørensen sat at his desk. The genealogy folder sat before him, the sealed forms prepared earlier that day. He placed his hand gently upon the cover, exhaling slowly. For years, he had protected the bloodlines of others. Now, at last, his own was beginning to speak.

Three weeks had passed since the blood test. Three silent, waiting weeks. The castle's rhythms had carried on as they always did — breakfasts shared, gardens tended, soccer played, lessons taught, walks taken, and dinners enjoyed under quiet candlelight — but beneath it all, a growing anticipation pulsed quietly beneath the surface. Especially for Sørensen. He carried the wait with the same dignified calm that had defined him for years, but those closest to him could sense it.

They saw it in the way his gaze lingered a little longer on the distant horizon, or how his hands clasped just a little tighter when in thought. This was a man who had lived his life protecting others — and now he was standing quietly on the brink of discovering where he had come from. It was late morning when the call came. Ben had personally arranged for the genealogical specialist, Dr. Petra Holm, to oversee Sørensen's file. Only she was authorized to deliver the results — directly, securely, and without delay.

As the secured royal line lit up in Ben's study, he answered at once. "Dr. Holm?" "Yes, Your Majesty," came the calm voice on the other end. "We have the full sequencing results. The match is confirmed. Adoption records successfully unsealed." Ben sat forward, heart quickening. "How certain?" "98.9% certainty," she said. "We have identified both of his biological parents." Ben exhaled deeply, almost reverently. "You've done it."

"It's an honour, Your Majesty," she replied. "The full genealogical package will be delivered within the hour by sovereign courier. I'm already transmitting the digital files directly to your private system." Ben smiled, his voice full of quiet gratitude. "Thank you, Dr. Holm. Truly." By noon, the entire family had gathered. The documents arrived precisely as scheduled — hand-delivered by the sovereign courier into Ben's own hands. No staff. No intermediaries. Only family.

Inside the family study, the table was cleared. The sealed folder, thick with the carefully prepared records, sat at the centre. Sørensen stood still, his face calm but his breath slightly uneven. Ben placed a reassuring hand on his shoulder. "Uncle," he said softly, "today... we finish your tree." Clara sat quietly beside Isla on the sofa, holding Isla's hand tightly as she watched her uncle closely, sensing how important this moment was.

Kendrick and Alex stood nearby, both respectfully silent, giving the moment its full weight. Ben broke the seal and carefully lifted the cover sheet. "Confirmed birth parents," Ben read aloud. "Both traced. Both verified." He carefully laid out each document as he spoke — birth certificates, adoption transfer papers, lineage charts, DNA sequencing graphs — each one a piece of the puzzle that had eluded Sørensen for a lifetime.

Ben's voice softened as he continued. "Your father... Henrik Sørensen. Born 1962. Danish lineage, native to the Jutland Peninsula. His ancestral line runs back twelve generations here in Denmark."

Sørensen's eyes blinked softly, his breath held tight. "Your mother... Astrid Henriksen. Born 1964. Norwegian lineage. Trondheim region. Nordic bloodline extending back to early recorded Viking settlements." Isla added softly, "That explains your height, Uncle." A faint, rare chuckle escaped Sørensen's chest, but his eyes never left the papers. Ben continued. "They were both very young when you were born. Records show financial instability. No criminal records. No scandal. Just... life. They placed you for adoption voluntarily when you were six months old. You were adopted here, in Denmark, by the family you've always known."

He paused, his voice lowering even further. "There was no abandonment, Uncle. No rejection. Only a hope that you would have a better chance than they believed they could give." The room sat heavy with silence for a long moment. Sørensen lowered his head slightly, his breath catching quietly. Ben and Isla both stepped closer, each placing a hand gently upon his shoulders. Clara's voice broke the quiet with soft, innocent warmth. "You've always been family to us, Uncle Sørensen. But now... you know where you come from."

Sørensen lifted his head slowly, his eyes moist but controlled. "Yes, sweetheart," he whispered. "Now I do." Kendrick finally stepped forward, his voice carrying both the solemn weight of a king and the tenderness of a father. "You have walked through life for many years without knowing your beginning, Sørensen.

But now, that chapter is written. Your identity is fully yours." Alex nodded in quiet agreement. "You belong. Always." Ben stepped to the centre of the table once more, carefully arranging the full genealogical chart now fully constructed — dozens of names, dates, regions, and connections filling the branches, reaching deeply into both Danish and Norwegian history.

With the final name carefully entered, Ben smiled. "Your tree is complete," he said softly. Sørensen exhaled slowly, as if releasing decades of weight from his chest. "It is... beautiful," he whispered. And then Clara, true to her tender heart, stood from her place, walked gently over, and reached her small hand up to him. "Uncle Sørensen... I'm really proud of you." Sørensen knelt instantly to her level, opening his arms. She stepped in without hesitation, wrapping her small arms around his broad shoulders. "I love you, Uncle Sørensen," she whispered. "I love you too, little one," he whispered back. The family stood in complete unity — no titles, no thrones, no court — only the truth of what they had built together. A family now complete.

As night settled softly over Rosenshavn, the castle lights dimmed, but the hearts within burned brighter than ever before. The branches of one family tree had finally found their roots; yet, even as one search closed, countless others were only just beginning.

For Ben, Isla, Clara, and all those bound by love rather than blood, the true legacy was no longer merely found in the past—it waited in the unfolding pages of the future.

There were still lessons to learn. Promises to keep. Vows to be fulfilled.

And far beyond the peaceful stone walls, destiny quietly stirred, preparing to call them forward once again.

— End of Volume I — The journey continues in *My Crown Is a Secret: Volume II.*

www.ingramcontent.com/pod-product-compliance
Lightning Source LLC
Chambersburg PA
CBHW060453300426
44113CB00016B/2573